Praise for *The Power of Beauty*

'this book...is the product of a clever, compassionate woman who feels that today's feminists denigrate men at their peril, and that far too many children grow up without fathers and all the good that a male figure can bring to their lives. So she is pro-men and positive about being middle-aged. Women need people like Friday to write the script for them.'
Janet Street Porter - *Sunday Times*

'*The Power of Beauty* is an idiosyncratic sparkling tome of statistics, fairy tales and personal anecdotes...in fact, there are so many personal anecdotes that *The Power of Beauty* might well be renamed The Power of Nancy Friday. But then again, that power is indisputable'
Evening Standard

'keeps you away from the mirror long enough to set you thinking about what you actually see in it.'
The Times

'We might have gained freedom, independence and sexual equality, but in the process we feel that we may have lost our female identity...in the long-awaited book by Nancy Friday, guru to a generation of feminists...a startling new philosophy will emerge. One that acknowledges a woman's need and desire to be feminine.'
Jane Gordon - *Daily Mail*

'Catherine Hakim of the London School of Economics claimed in the British Journal of Sociology this year that only a third of women wanted careers, the rest wishing to devote their lives to husband and family. Then...Betty Friedan...accused feminists of ignoring the central role of the family. Now Nancy Friday...in her forthcoming book, *The Power of Beauty*, turns on "the anti-men, anti-sex matriarchal feminists". '
Natasha Narayan - *Observer*

'Friday's political sin is that she despises
man-bashers, claiming women blame men, rather
than confront their own sexual power, their desires, or
the anger and competitiveness Nice Girls feel towards
each other. Provocative, thoughtful and enjoyable to
read...particularly if you're a man.'
David Thomas - *Mail on Sunday*

'Friday...fills 600 pages with her analysis of women's
attitudes to their looks in terms of self-esteem, image
and sexuality...One theme in her book is that many
women deny their looks or feel uncomfortable about their
sexuality because they don't want to create envy among
other women...Friday also feels that women should
confront the femininity that the first wave of women's
libbers were so keen to reject...Surely few women
would argue otherwise in the nineties.'
Emma Cook - *Guardian*

'Her seventh book is on a similarly sexy subject, what
with Friday's apologia for the codpiece and hymns to the
genitalia. *The Power of Beauty* explores the effect of looks
on our lives. But it's also a paean to the adorableness of
men, and the nastiness of domineering women. Having
made her name as a feminist, Nancy Friday has become
the ultimate masculinist.'
Syrie Johnson - *Evening Standard*

'Germaine Greer's *The Female Eunuch* celebrated the
gorgeous reality of women's bodies and erotic
life...Camille Paglia's appeal has centred from the
beginning on her ability to revel in heterosexual erotic
culture...Nancy Friday is working on the same lines. She
remembers how important beauty was for her in the
sixties and seventies, and the way that physical display
added to her sense of independence rather than detracting
from it. So she reminds us of the upfront, mischievous
female power that often got lost in more strait-laced
feminist ideals.'
Natasha Walter - *Guardian*

Nancy Friday is the author of six books, including *My Secret Garden*, *Forbidden Flowers*, *Jealousy* and the internationally bestselling *My Mother My Self*, *Women on Top* and *Men in Love*. She lives in Key West and Washington, Connecticut with her husband.

NANCY FRIDAY

The Power of Beauty

HUTCHINSON
LONDON

© Nancy Friday 1996

The right of Nancy Friday to be identified as the Author
of this work has been asserted by Nancy Friday in accordance
with the Copyright, Designs and Patents Act 1988

1 3 5 7 9 10 8 6 4 2

This edition first published in 1997 by Hutchinson.
First published in the UK in 1996 by Hutchinson.

First published in the USA in 1996 by
HarperCollins Publishers, Inc.

Random House (UK) Limited
20 Vauxhall Bridge Road,London SW1V 2SA

Random House Australia (Pty) Limited
20 Alfred Street, Milsons Point, Sydney,
New South Wales 2061, Australia

Random House New Zealand Limited
18 Poland Road, Glenfield, Auckland 10, New Zealand

Random House South Africa (Pty) Limited
Endulini, 5A Jubilee Road, Parktown 2193, South Africa

A CiP record for this book is available from the British Library

Papers used by Random House UK Limited are natural,
recyclable products made from wood grown in sustainable forests.
The manufacturing processes conform to the environmental
regulations of the country of origin.

ISBN 0 09 177800 X

Printed and bound in Great Britain by
Mackays of Chatham PLC

Grateful acknowledgment is made for permission to reprint
excerpts from the following material:

In Full Flower by Lois Banner. Copyright © 1993 by Lois Banner.
Reprinted by permission of Alfred A. Knopf Inc.
The Uses of Enchantment by Bruno Bettelheim. Copyright © 1975, 1976 by
Bruno Bettelheim. Reprinted by permission of Thames and Hudson.
Anatomy of Love: The Natural History of Monogamy, Adultery and Divorce by
Helen E. Fisher. Copyright © 1992 by Helen E. Fisher. Reprinted by per-
mission of W. W. Norton & Company, Inc.
Sex and Suits by Anne Hollander. Copyright © 1994 by Anne Hollander.
Reprinted by permission of Alfred A. Knopf Inc.
Diary of a Baby by Daniel N. Stern. Copyright © 1990 by Daniel N. Stern,
M.D. Reprinted by permission of BasicBooks, a division of HarperCollins
Publishers, Inc.

For Patricia Colbert Robinson

It is, in the final analysis, loves which transforms even ugly things into something beautiful.

–BRUNO BETTELHEIM
The Uses of Enchantment, 1976

Contents

Acknowledgments

A book is a journey, or as Bruno Bettelheim might put it, a quest filled with trials and tests. Five very special people helped me past the many obstacles along the way:

Dick Duane was the muse to whom I spoke each morning. His gift is knowing how to talk to writers. His words gave me courage when I needed it most.

Diane Reverand, my editor, always "saw" this book in that way I use this most significant verb, freeing me to find myself.

Julie Roth, my splendid researcher, was the finest gatherer of clues, solver of riddles, and best companion a writer could ask for.

Caroline Fireside was the Wise Woman who, if you are lucky, you meet on the road. She saw many of the dragons before I did and knew the paths around them.

As for my prince, my husband, Norman Pearlstine, I reserve all the love and gratitude I never realized I possessed until I completed this journey.

1

The Gaze

My Mother's Eyes

I am a woman who needs to be seen. I need it in a basic way, as in to breathe, to eat. Or not to be seen, that is the other increasingly attractive option, to give up the lifelong preoccupation of finding myself in others' eyes, the need to be taken in so that my existence is noted.

Ambivalence explains so much of life. As in, I love you, I hate you. As in, how much to show, how much to let another see of one's needs, one's naked self. What bliss to show all and be adored; what agony to be judged, then abandoned after having revealed so much of one's fragile self. Better to show nothing. But then, who would have seen us?

Do we begin life all open? Is ambivalence born of little rejected bits of the exposed self? Once, long ago, we were naked. We loved—no, love is learned—we needed the first eyes, the arms that took us in. Did they love what they saw? We can't remember and so we stand at the mirror, unbuttoning the top button, inviting the eye, and then buttoning back up, playing it safe. But love is not safe; when we fall in love every button is undone, the risk of rejection taken. These eyes that look at us promise adoration. Of course we save our hottest rages for the people we love the most. How dare they take their eyes off us after all we've shown them? We love them, we hate them. High ambivalence. Aren't the first suspects in a murder always those who are the nearest and dearest?

Ambivalence certainly explains my frame of mind regarding the influence I am willing to give external mirrors. I take it very seriously indeed, what it would mean to shed the baggage that has weighed me down all my life, others' opinions, the way they see me. And, quite literally, to travel with one small suitcase, my promise to my husband.

You are already thinking that this is not about you, who are not a clotheshorse or a starer into mirrors. Perhaps you have already begun to disdain my vanity. But your life has been as fashioned by mirrors as mine; none of us escapes the influence that our looks have had on our lives. Later we may choose to live without mirrors, but we begin life very much in need of reflection. Did you begin rich or poor, seen as the Christ Child or left, invisible, to make yourself up?

Perhaps you ducked out of the competition over looks so many years ago that you can't remember. But once you did want to be seen, taken in, and loved. If you don't today, consider that it might be because you tried and lost. Lost to your brother or sister; maybe got lost in the abyss of invisibility, a parent demanding that all eyes be on her or him. Who wants to remember such pain? Perhaps, instead, you won and were hated for it. Envy can be a killer.

The universal power of looks is free-floating, an electrical charge between hungry eyes and the objects of their desire: "Let me feast my eyes on you. Let me take you in." It is an open market, traded on more exhibitionistically today than at any time in my life. Near-naked bodies demand our attention on the streets, undressed fashions fill the restaurants, the television screens in our living rooms: "Look at me!"

Those of us who are old enough remember a world that prized invisible virtues such as kindness, generosity, empathy, which are out of fashion today. Now we wear our identities on our backs. Who cares about invisible values? "See me or I won't even know I exist." Ours is the age of The Empty Package. Vanity is all. You are part of this story, believe me.

In the beginning, loveliness is all. The more drawn a mother is to her child, the greater the likelihood that the child will survive. The more consistently the infant's needs are met, the more beautiful and good the mother. To each, the other is perfect. When that face is present, life is sustained; absent, there is no warmth, no love. What does the infant know of standards of beauty, or the good mother care? The child may be too fat or too thin, the mother plain, but when I remember the early Renaissance artists' golden beam painted between their eyes, joining their gazes, they were flawless. When you and I take in that ancient idealization, painted in countless variations by as many artists, we recognize what we once had and lost, or longed for all our lives.

We never outgrow our affinity for what is conveyed in the luscious paintings of mother and child, the most compelling of which I feel to be circular and cinematic in composition, belly round, affording a keyhole through which one spies and feeds on the intimacy of others. And there is that equally heartbreaking icon of the *Pietà*, Mary holding the dead Christ, her Child, in her arms, His head once again on her breast. There was a man who was jailed several years ago for desecrating that particular sculpture, hacking it with his rock hammer because, he is said to have told the authorities, "Mary isn't looking at Him!" Indeed, Christ's mother stares downward, her gaze not on His face.

Those Madonna and Child images were, in fact, my least favorite when I was a young art historian; I preferred the cool asymmetry of the post-Renaissance mannerists to Raphael's passionate equilibrium. Not for me someone else's blissful infancy; anyone who had what I had missed, even the divine Mother and Child, aroused envy. The irony is that the simple golden beam linking their gazes has stayed with me far longer than anything I can recall from the mannerists. Twenty years ago, when I was writing *My Mother/My Self*, it swam up from my unconscious as the perfect picture of earliest mother love, The Gaze captured in a beam of light remembered from a college art class when I was still too young and vulnerable even to let myself know how deeply moved by it I was. Here, within the context of looks and the need to be seen, it is even more apt.

The Gaze is where it all begins. "Soon after we can see, we are aware that we can also be seen," writes art critic John Berger. "The eye of the other combines with our own eye to make it fully credible that we are part of the visible world." You and I required that loving focus early on. Our infantile selves cried out for the nonjudgmental mirror of adoring eyes in which we saw ourselves reflected, warmed, taken in, and rolled lovingly around, then returned via The Golden Beam to be stored inside, the self at rest within the self. This is the beginning of self-esteem.

What is even more confusing, indeed is a tribute to the unconscious, is that I was certain that this golden beam motif was everywhere, in countless paintings before and during the early Renaissance; after all, it had meant so much to me. But I cannot find even one today, though I have called various art historians, curators at the Metropolitan Museum, art history teachers at universities. I know it is there, this painting I have magnified into an entire school. Consider memory holding on to an image, refusing to let it go, not because it was what I had actually seen, but was what I missed and grieved for. The Gaze.

Nowadays I say to my husband, "Let's run away, buy a farm, be with animals, get one of those Vietnamese pigs." I grow tired of caring about how I look. I want to be loved the way my dog Bongo loves me, uncritically, faithfully. The faithful bit is important in any discussion of the power of looks. The faithful don't give a damn about how you look. They love you for the inner you, believe more in your worth than you do. Never mind that Bongo's unconditional love is confused with dependency—without me he'll die—at root I know that even if I didn't fill his bowl, he'd adore me regardless of what I was wearing.

Could I actually turn my back on external reflections and live on what is inside? Is there enough? This morning I spoke with Dick, my dear friend who phones each day before I sit down to write. He knows how to talk to writers, having once loved a man whose career as a writer he helped build. He told me that this man committed suicide last night. I remembered a remarkable photo of the two of them, both beautiful men, in which my friend's eyes stare fixedly at his lover, who himself has turned full into the camera lens. Dick had given this man his own power, not just his worshipful gaze, but had abandoned his own career to focus on his lover's work. The more successful the writer became, the more he hated his dependency on Dick. He loved Dick, he envied him. Eventually, he bit the hand that fed him. When they parted, the writer's career spiraled down. Recently he'd had a masterful face-lift, but it hadn't accomplished its goal. "He killed himself because he was no longer seen," said my friend. There was nothing inside.

I think of the side of me that wants to abandon looks as the Good Nancy, the sweet child who for many years buried her rage at not catching her mother's eye, in the way the Christ Child is adored by the Madonna, the gold beam of light like some adorable feeding tube between mother and babe. One day I saw an aerial photo of a big mother jet fueling a small plane in midair, nursing like some big mother cow, and this is what came to mind: a celestial feeding of mother/child regard, replenishment, refueling. Could Jesus have completed his selfless mission without that reflection in his mother's eyes? I don't think so.

"Someday," I say to my husband, "I will recant all my books and ask God's forgiveness for writing about sex, the ambivalence of mother love, jealousy, and envy." My husband doesn't think this is funny. He loves my books. He knows that who I call the Bad Nancy, who writes about forbidden subjects, is at war with the Good Nancy, who never missed a day of Sunday school, and that out of this constant war comes whatever creative fire I have. My husband sees me as Doris Lessing, in a passage from *The Golden Notebook*, described a man who loved her: "he saw me." I knew the power of what she was saying years ago, long before I'd become a writer myself. Oh, yes, I certainly understand the magnetic power of a man who sees you.

I have sought out men's eyes, required their gazes as far back as I can remember. There is nothing like the mystery of an absent father to addict you to the loving gaze of men. I have missed my father all my life, a void that would have remained behind the barriers of denial if I hadn't become a writer. My mother wanted to protect me, and herself, and so told me nothing, showed me nothing. I wanted to be a good daughter, and so I asked nothing, needing her more than the information: Where was he, who was he? I grew up without his eyes reflecting me, giving back to me his impression of my form and face, my intellect, my sexuality, everything. Perhaps he was a cold man, the kind of person who didn't like children, wouldn't have liked what he saw in me. Ah, but you see, I'll never know. Having nothing, knowing nothing, I have idealized him all my life. I would have been different if there had been a man present, this other half of me.

When exactly did he leave, on what day of what year? No one ever said, or spoke his name, or cautioned, "Don't ask about him." As far back as memory goes, I knew that these were the words that could not be said: "Where is he?" Fact or fiction, what remains to this day is a love affair of what he and I might have had, a search for my self in the faces of all the members of my mother's family, her beautiful mother who died of sleeping sickness before I was born and, of course, her father, her sisters, and brother, the gods and goddesses of the Pantheon of my childhood. They beamed on me from on high, imbued with all the power I so desperately wanted them to possess. To me they were as glamorous as the great stars of the movies of the forties and fifties to which I was addicted, people bigger than life.

Today my home is filled with photos of my mother's family, my favorites dating from the years when I was very young, most vulnerable, and unformed. In all their beauty, they speak to me with the reassurance that I am part of them, that there is a physical link between us, and maybe a hint of character too, a touch of my own exhibitionism in the way my grandfather sits his horse, their group glamour at a table at El Morocco. I was never a beauty, but even in my pigtails and steel-rimmed glasses, I told myself I was one of them. Because they let me in, I believed it.

Neither my grandfather nor my uncle ever presented himself as a father substitute; it was I who chose each in that way that children of either sex go looking for the male and female parts of themselves, their genetic missing halves. They look unless, of course, they take in their mother's anger at men, the fear of betraying her should they desire the enemy. One of the greatest gifts my mother gave me was an unconditional, unspoken permission to turn to others for love. It may sound like a nongift but I can assure you that doctors' offices are crowded with people whose parent or parents didn't love them but didn't want them finding love, closeness, elsewhere.

My mother has always said that when she brought me home from the hospital, she put me in my nurse Anna's arms. It is a black-and-white movie in my head, the car pulling up, Anna waiting at the curb, bending over to take this bundle, me, from my mother, who is tired, sad, probably relieved and grateful to have someone take responsibility for this second child. She is young, on her own, her husband, my father, dead, or so I will be told, though I've never been able to remember anyone actually saying it to me.

Anna takes me in her big German-Irish arms and that is where I stay. Her lap will be my safety, the vantage point from which I will soon see all those movies, the addiction I learned from her. Her kitchen will be my domain, her vision of me will be what I become until others begin to take me in, recognize traits that escaped Anna, perhaps didn't interest her, didn't catch her eye.

I doubt that looks mattered much to Anna, who set more store by bravery and adventure—oh, the rides in the front seat of the roller coaster!—than by a pretty face. Neither of us looked in the mirror when she braided my hair in the mornings. Who needed mirrors when I had her all-accepting gaze, never questioning that I had none of my mother's pretty looks?

"Anna hated me," my sister insists to this day, which wasn't true, I'm sure, but that I was Anna's favorite had something to do with the obvious closeness between my mother and sister, who together had known a life with my father, a bond between them. My father the mystery.

My mother had her own share of mysteries, not the least of which was her father's vision of her, his eldest child, the firstborn of the great love of his life, who died when my mother was a young girl. "Mama, Mama!" she would call out at the foot of the stairs when she came home from school, knowing her mother was dead but not knowing, unable to accept. Her father never saw her as the lovely young woman she became. Therefore, neither did she.

He had his own idea of how women, among them his daughters, should look. When his beautiful wife died, he was still a "great catch," according to my first step-grandmother, and the women he chose were petite beauties, who, either by nature or by design, responded to his godlike persona with subservience. Tall, willful women abound in my family. My poor mother, she is no more at peace with how she looks than I. To this day she hides the hands he critiqued as "too large!" when at twelve she was ordered to play the piano for guests. How do you play the piano with unacceptable hands?

My mother, more than any of the other of his five children, stayed the closest to him. When I went to college, she left Charleston and moved up north, less than a mile away from him, making herself available for bridge parties, spontaneous evening sails on Lake Ontario, and criticism. To the end, he never really saw her, but I never doubted that he loved her and needed her near, just as she never stopped trying to please him. Or not to displease him. "Oh, Daddy . . . ," her sigh of resignation, anger. Ambivalence.

Each of us treats our grief at invisibility in a parent's eyes with characteristic survival behavior or, of course, we go under. I have a memory of coming home from kindergarten with a painting, something I have made for my mother; in this image, one of my earliest, I stand at the foot of the stairs and call up to her as she hurries across the upstairs landing. I want her to look at me and see what I have done, but she is in a hurry and goes instead, unseeing, into her bedroom. That memory remains in my mind as the moment in time when I decided never again to try to catch her eye, to punish her by taking my achievements, my trophies, my perfect grades and accomplishments not to her but to others, to her father especially.

My five-year-old self convinces me that I don't mind her taking little pleasure in my success; it was I, after all, who "left her out." But I mind sorely, still. Ambivalence.

By the time I was ten I had created a brave, charming girl who had invented ways of getting herself seen, picked up, and loved. If I couldn't catch my mother's eye, very well, I would sing a song, do a dance, tell a story until I had won visibility, affection. This became who I was, steel-rimmed glasses, braces on my teeth, standing in my old jeans and flannel shirt atop one of the walls that surrounded our house. I was at my best, only ten, survivor and benefactress of all that had gone before. It was a trusted image I would abruptly abandon in a few years in order to fit the rigid stereotype of adolescence. The girl I then tried to become in order to belong put far more faith in mirrors than in what she had inside. No mirror was more necessary than a man's eyes. It is men's judgment I seek because of that first man's absence. All my life I have never doubted that I would have been a different person if I had known my father.

So many children today grow up without a father that my own childhood no longer sounds exotic. The number of children living with a single parent who never married soared to 6.3 million in 1993, or 27 percent of all children under age eighteen, up 70 percent from a decade earlier. Increased numbers, however, don't make a father's absence felt less acutely. It can be lived with, obviously must be lived with in some cases, but as with every painful loss within the family that adults would rather not discuss, it can more gainfully be lived with if his absence is understood by the child. Family mysteries grow in the dark. Little girls and boys, we miss his gaze always. All of our lives are spent in reaction to the void, the mirror that might have been, if only— if only what?

Along the way we find father substitutes. One of my first was the loving eye of God. I didn't so much become religious in my faith as in my attendance. An omnipotent father figure smiled down on us children at Sunday school, loving us equally and without favoritism. Bible stories were almost as good as the movies, and the hymns, well, they were meant to be sung full throttle; to this day I can render all the verses of "Follow the Gleam." What a family! What joy! What love! For perfect attendance at Sunday school I won the complete collection of Nancy Drew books, a superfluous prize given that nothing could have kept me away. After confirmation I was equally faithful in my favorite pew at St. Phillips Episcopal Church, whose lovely graveyard backed onto the high walls that surrounded our house.

Sunday morning I became part of a congregation, whose members I felt to be kind, good, and generous. Surely, many were flawed, but in that day and age, most probably thought of themselves as good people, and when they were not, they knew guilt, and shame too, feelings that had not yet become vestigial. The mothers and fathers among that congregation saw me as being as complete as any other child, or at least in their gazes made me feel that way. No one asked about my father, though many of them must have known, mine being the only family I knew that had no father, and our world below Broad Street being something of a closed community. Don't sigh for me, for these were some of the happiest days of my life; nonetheless, I will tell you that I've never gotten over the child's ability to make something fine out of a missing part. Optimism, says anthropologist Lionel Tiger, is in great part genetic; if he is right, I am grateful to my ancestors, for I got a healthy dose of it.

It was sex that ultimately separated me from the church and its loving eye. The enormous charge of adolescent sexual energy, which might have fed me intellectually and socially and made me more articulate and able to structure a life of conscious choices, was instead made to feel in opposition to God and goodness. There were no sermons against sex, nothing preached at church, school, or home; perhaps that was it, the silence, the absence of both spoken celebration and caution, as in being given the keys to a new car: Yours to enjoy, but be responsible.

Until adolescence I don't remember looking in mirrors. Now, with the promise of identity in the eyes of boys, I focused all the longing of my twelve years on them. How to get them to see me, love what they saw so that I might know I existed? It wasn't sexual intercourse that I so desperately wanted; I could live with the Nice Girl Rules and indeed remained a virgin, albeit by centimeters, until I was twenty-one. It was my need to be recognized, wanted, loved that made me feel I had to choose to see my salvation, my self, my future in the eyes of men or in those of God. It was not a conscious decision, but it marked the birth of the Good Nancy/Bad Nancy split, an overly harsh con-

science, a divided self that turned a bright, responsible girl into a cripple who learned to bite her tongue, shorten her steps, suppress intellectual curiosity, and wait too long to get a diaphragm. I accepted that
a woman's worth lay in men's eyes, and that all the skills I'd mastered
were without value.

In fairness to the boys of my youth, let me say that they never
asked it of me. They too abandoned preadolescent dreams to inherit a
system which taught a man that his worth lay in the role of The Good
Provider, the problem solver, the first of which was to master their fear
of beautiful young girls.

Imagining the Beautiful Baby

How to convince you that the way you look has changed your
life? That it requires persuasion is a better question, but I know it
exists, a built-in Calvinist refusal to place too much importance on
looks, especially within the family, where equal love is sworn, even
though there were nine months of expectations before the birth—
longer, a lifetime if you include the years that parents dream of a picture of the baby.

We are born with a look as unique as the print of our thumb. The
look comes from within and is a part of our growing into our special
identity. It is why the penetrating, parental gaze of love is so reassuring. To be seen instead as someone else's projection of what *they* would
like us to be is deeply unsettling because it is not us. To be ignored is to
feel invisible: Where will the next meal come from if she doesn't take
me in? How will I be safe if she sees me as the child she dreamed of
and planned for, but not as the person I am, good and bad, *me*?

We spend our lives going from one pair of eyes to another, one set
of expectations to the next, looking for our selves until one day, if we
are lucky, we stop and decide to look inside, where, indeed, beauty is
in the eye of the beholder.

When an infant is not seen and loved whole and instead only sees
a blank screen that takes in nothing no matter how loudly the wailing
grows, the baby is filled with rage. To survive, an emotional network
of iron denial is built around the rage. "Who, me, angry?" We can't
remember infancy, but the notion of how we fall in love today can give
us an inkling of how the dependent child feels. Think of the emotional
paralysis we endure after having handed over our tender adult selves

to another and having them not appear, or telephone, or feed us with promises of love eternal. Our terror is followed by infantile rage.

The psychiatrist Melanie Klein says that when we are born we do not so much love mother and her bountiful breast that feeds us as *envy* her power. When we bite the breast, it is our fury that she should have so much and we so little. How dare she! Klein does not spare us in her description of the titanic fury of an infant's envy; when I first read Klein I threw her book across the room. What softens the envy is the repeated awareness that mother is meeting our demands, perhaps not perfectly, but well enough; the blanket comes, the food arrives, the loving arms reach out for us again and again. There can be no love, says Klein, until gratitude is learned. It is gratitude that opens the door to love. Is it really so different today when we "envy" the power of the beloved to raise us to heaven or make a hell of life on earth? The bad news, says Klein, is that if we don't learn to love at the age-appropriate time, in that first relationship, it is much, much harder later on.

Each of us treats our grief at invisibility in a parent's eyes with survival behavior. When eventually I accepted that I would never be able to catch my mother's eye, in my omnipotence I decided to punish her. What did I have in my arsenal? I told myself I didn't mind. Others would love me. I would make it so. But I minded sorely that my comings and goings, my many accomplishments, weren't even noticed. I still mind. Ambivalence.

We love our mothers, we hate our mothers, with that infantile omnipotent rage we refuse to abandon. Until we do, the rage/hate at her often remains buried, denied, and is spewed out on anyone else whom we choose to love. If we don't come to accept mother as a person who did her best but was not perfect, we go through life trying to create an idealized version of what we had with her. Of course, others never live up to our grandiose expectations of love.

The feeling of dependency that is a part of love is only sweet when we have the ability to walk away and return to a state of self after our needs have been met, as in deeply satisfying sex. If there is no sense of self and the beloved is felt to have all the power, to keep us in heaven or abandon us, then when we fall in love we live in jeopardy; at any moment of any given day our loved one could take it all away and we would die. We love this powerful person, but we also hate him. There is no middle ground. It is why divorces are so bloody, all that pent-up rage vented now unto death.

Poor little infantile us. How to convince you to accept rage, let it go, and be grateful for whatever of the good mother is left? Maybe then we can find adult love, imperfect, yes, but that is how love is. But there is an alternative that more and more women are choosing. If mother didn't focus her gaze on us in that way that makes us feel substantial today, then damn it, we will never love anyone. That will show her. We will live alone. "There are no good men out there," women say. They would never admit that their solution has anything to do with unresolved nursery issues. It is far easier and more popular these days to blame problems of intimacy on men, who are not the necessary meal tickets they used to be. Men are today's preferred dumping ground on to whom women can hurl all the bitterness and fury that cannot comfortably find the appropriate target. Problems of economic parity in the workplace, sexual harassment, the return of beauty tyranny—everything is blamed on the untrustworthiness of shiftless men who, unlike we morally superior women, think only of themselves.

Women's preference for other women, the ever expanding lesbian world, is in flower, another woman being a perfect mirror in which to see ourselves as we would have liked to be seen at the beginning, the essential partner with whom to re-create what we once had, or never had, with mother. Another woman's body is reminiscent of Eden, having none of that unfamiliar terrain of hairy chest, perturbing penis with its strange texture, smell, its fluids that men expect a woman to swallow. But a woman's body, ah, it is rich in memories, softness of skin, breasts on which to pillow the head, nipples from which to nurse, the belly in which we once curled and slept, and a cunt's cleft which promises that our own might also be acceptable. This is like coming home, a reunion. Precisely because it is a homecoming, when she doesn't deliver, and paradise is lost, when the other woman fails us— as she inevitably must, being no more able to deliver perfect love than a man—then the source of our titanic rage is even more accessible, all parties being female. According to an article in Ms. magazine, "Battering has long been one of the lesbian community's nastiest secrets."

In a book of old rhymes, collected from schoolchildren who had learned them from other children, I find this ditty:

I one my mother.
I two my mother.
I three my mother.

I four my mother.
I five my mother.
  I six my mother.
I seven my mother.
  I *ate* my mother.
(emphasis added)

The couple who collected the rhymes from the children point out that these "were clearly not rhymes that a grandmother might sing to a grandchild on her knee. They have more oomph and zoom; they pack a punch . . . pass from one child to another without adult interference." I would say so; I "ate" my mother, indeed! Wouldn't Melanie Klein have loved this little jingle with its attendant drawing of a plump mother suckling her child, a giant cartoon baby who wails until the breast is offered and then, while feeding, systematically devours the dozing mother until there is only a huge, smiling infant.

Klein began as a disciple of Freud but broke with the master to establish her own school of psychoanalysis in London in 1927. While Freud emphasized the Oedipal years, roughly ages three to seven, Klein placed more importance on the struggle between parent and child in the first year of life. She was among the first to experiment with child play therapy in the 1920s. I would imagine that a troubled child would take some comfort in chanting this rhyme with other children. It is a relief to have things named, to know that we are not "the only ones" to hate people we also love. It is why I have remained a writer, with each book moving out from under one level of denial in my life to the next. It didn't begin that way. Writing page one of *My Mother/My Self*, for instance, I had no idea what I was getting into. My relationship with my mother was totally idealized, all anger with her repressed, boxed, wrapped, and tied with strings of denial. Ours, I told everyone, was the best mother/daughter relationship I knew. When the anger began to surface, I lost most of my hair and the partial use of my right leg in a last-ditch effort to keep the bad feelings from hurting her, to keep her from hurting me. Nursery terror.

The picture that comes to mind had I not become a writer is not a pretty one. Had I been born beautiful, would my anxious mother have smiled and beamed on me, filled me with a sureness of self as lovable? If that had been the scenario, I wouldn't have this life today, which I love. Nor would most of the people I admire who, almost without exception, out of a need to be seen seem to have invented themselves, developed alternative powers to beauty.

Literature is rich with tales of anger at not being seen and loved for who we are, how we look, rage buried until "something happens," the author's creation mined from the bowels of his or her own life, resurrected so deftly that the reader of the book, the viewer of the play recognizes himself or herself and weeps. No one worked that vein more profitably and painfully than Tennessee Williams, whose own family history drew him back again and again into what he once described to me as "the curse of beauty," or in his own case, a failure at beauty. *Cat on a Hot Tin Roof, Sweet Bird of Youth, The Glass Menagerie*, now that I think of it—is there anything Tennessee wrote that didn't deal with beauty and rage? He had what is called a "lazy eye," a muscular problem worse than my own, which was operated on once he'd made enough money to afford it. Years later he would say with that funny cackle of his, "Don't you think it made me more handsome?" But he still wrote about what he knew best—beauty, fury, and lost love.

There was a period of years, beginning in the late 1960s with the flowering of feminism, when marriages and motherhood were dead subjects. You could walk for miles and not see a pregnant woman. Men themselves were suspect, and a tight relationship with a man jeopardized membership in a consciousness-raising group, where women caught up in the frenzy of sisterhood often divulged the most intimate secrets of their marriages. The New Woman was identified by her job and her success at it. My friend Jane remembers being pregnant in New York in 1971, walking to her job and feeling as if her tummy bore the scarlet letter.

Now babies are back, and pregnancy is absolutely in vogue. Pregnant models proudly walk the runways, expectant movie stars pose, nearly naked, on the covers of international magazines, and when a woman breast-feeds in public, you can hear the envious sighs of other women. Some older feminists now write bitterly of The Sisterhood not encouraging motherhood from the beginning, for now they have waited too long and are unable to conceive.

Even before the child is born there are expectations, fantasies that parents have for nine months, no, longer, for some people dream of a child, a specific kind of child, for years. There is a shape, a size, a certain sex, a color of hair created from the parents' own lives, what they had, or wish they'd had. "All parents, when they're pregnant, have some picture of their baby, conscious or not," says Dr. Nancy Poland, who works with expectant parents at the Brazelton Institute. "We think there are three babies that they think about during the last trimester of pregnancy. One is the perfect baby, the Gerber baby, the baby of their dreams. The other is the damaged baby, an image that might be the result of an emotional crisis they have had, or a congenital problem in the family, or even a fight they had. And then there is the baby that is inside them, the real baby. We try through talk, delicate questioning, to close the gap between the baby that exists and either the damaged or the perfect baby."

"And if the child is born who doesn't look or act in a manner that the parents have expected, dreamed about?" I ask.

"Then the parents must begin to adjust, genuinely come to say, 'This is my baby.' Only then can there be a relationship embedded in trust and safety. If this acceptance doesn't happen, then the baby feels unimportant, unnoticed, invisible, and grows into a child who doesn't feel accepted for who he or she is."

The truth is that parents feel different emotions for each of their children, and looks have something to do with it. How could it be otherwise? Each arrived at a different point in the parents' lives when, separately and together, they were different people. There is no God-given maternal/paternal instinct that magically wipes clean parents' visions of how they view themselves and others. Major battles have been won and lost, hostages taken, concessions made over the influence of looks.

Was beauty important in the parent's own family, or were kindness, an open heart, achievements stressed? The list is endless, but looks are always on it, somewhere, top or bottom. So how did they fare, these grown people who are now going to beam down upon this infant with eyes that are at best loving, but also skewed, programmed to see what they want to see and to be blind to what they do not want to see?

There will be a day when couples will be able to choose not just the sex of their unborn child, but also its attributes, according to Sherman Elias, director of reproductive genetics at the University of Tennessee at Memphis. "Today it's the preference for gender," he says. "Tomorrow we're making designer kids." Will the Power Couple sit at a machine similar to that on which a person designs his new face prior to surgery and "design" the look of their Power Baby? When the beautiful baby can be ordered on demand, adequate finances notwithstanding, will we then be willing to discuss the power of beauty as we discuss the power of money?

To this day, the birth preference is that the first child be a boy, the second a girl. How many of us have tripped up our parents expectations, not just in our looks but in our sex too? A couple we are close to had hoped for a daughter after their firstborn son. The whole family is gorgeous, and the mother still jokes about how her secondborn issued forth not only another male, but "tinted slightly green. . . ."

"And I looked like a frog when I was born, all pop-eyed," he contributes, smiling, for they have told this story many times.

"And look at him now!" his smiling mother says, for he is the handsomest of the family.

Almost ten years ago, when I was beginning this research, he took a day off from college to drive four hours for a videotaped interview. I had the feeling then that he had nowhere to put this seemingly irrelevant business of being born not just the wrong sex, but unattractive too. The pop eyes and the odd hue of skin were gone by the middle of his second year, but the nickname, Frog, still occasionally comes up. He never criticizes his family; they are tight, loving. I tell him of my own family, the old rages that sometimes have me grinding my teeth at night while I sleep.

"In my dreams, all my teeth have fallen out. They're loose in my mouth," he says. "I've always had that dream."

Ah, the old universal rage dream wherein we destroy the teeth that would bite the "bad mother"; to protect her we turn the instruments of destruction against ourselves, gouging out our own teeth. We don't want to think of her as bad; we love her. Ambivalence. Half the world is grinding its teeth at night, many of us because we were the wrong sex, the wrong look, wrong. Dentists fit their patients with plastic mouth guards as routinely as they clean their teeth.

He likes the rage dream, something being given a name, an explanation. He is a grown man and can deal with anger, which fits in with his adult picture of himself as a rebel on his college campus, where he has no patience with "political correctness." Women as victims? Oh, no, that isn't how he views women's power. Today he is in no hurry to marry; he reminds me of myself at his age, restless and less interested in making money than in finding out, What does it all mean? In a few days he will leave for Croatia to work with the refugees. I send him a note in which I include one of my favorite movie lines, which John Garfield delivers to a woman he's just met: "You're beautiful, you're level, and you're different." The beautiful part he won't believe, but he certainly knows he's different.

A generation apart, he and I take comfort in talking about the "unspeakable," the anger with people we love, an ancient rage we seem destined always to carry around.

Referring to the disappointment parents feel when babies don't turn out to be what was hoped for, dreamed of, psychologist Aviva Weisbord says, "Although it may be unconscious, there is a discontent that remains that the child will pick up as nonacceptance."

As for women pregnant with an unwanted infant, a study at the University of South Carolina indicated that they "had a greater than twofold increased risk of delivering a child who died within the first 28 days of life." The study was not comprehensive, but one of the epidemiologists concluded, "Being unwanted puts children at increased risk of a range of adverse health outcomes, including child abuse and delayed cognitive and social-emotional development."

What a responsibility these Power Babies carry: how to live up to the expectations of a Power Couple, especially today when looks, at the expense of less visible attributes, are so loaded with significance. We seem to be at a crossroads where the current overexposure of fashion and beauty maintenance has collided with our well-scrubbed Calvinist-Protestant ethic. Don't judge a book by its cover, indeed. Why, it is exactly what we are doing, all the while preaching the same homilies our parents preached to us.

Children must be yearning for straight talk. At school, on television, on the billboards that paper the highways, children see absolutely what beauty buys, the power of it. But nobody, no adult discusses it out loud, explaining the natural attraction we feel to beauty: "You're a sight for sore eyes!" Nor do most parents explain how envy works, precisely why we want to scratch out the eyes of the adorable one, our baby sister, or that girl at school. Yes, we know that envy and jealousy are sins, that we aren't supposed to feel them, but then we do, and it makes us sick, this gnawing at our guts, the desire to destroy. "Be good, be kind, be generous," the teacher says, but none of these much talked about virtues gets a child anywhere near the amount of attention that the latest pair of Reeboks instantly buys. Meanwhile, children are born into families who pretend that appearance isn't what really matters. The child grows up maneuvering to fit the lie.

During pregnancy, parents "transfer many different emotional investments to the child-to-be," says psychiatrist Ethel Person. She continues, "As Freud suggested, a predominant kind of fantasy investment endows the child with potential to realize our unfulfilled fantasies. . . . Feelings develop for an imaginary child in a process similar to the choice of a potential lover. Both involve a preexisting fantasy, with both conscious and unconscious components, about who one wants the other—lover or child—to be." A mother may see the child as the hated self or the idealized self, a replacement child for one who previously died, a copy of a hated sibling, or even "a substitute for the mother's mother. This fantasy text is often enacted when mother comes to lean on the child. . . . Examples are mothers who cultivate their daughters as their best friend and confide in them—even when they are in their preteens or early teens—material as inappropriate as their own adulterous affairs. . . . However the unborn child is imagined, the fantasies affect the mother's perceptions of and responses to the child. . . . If [the mother] cannot align the fantasy and the reality, at least to some degree, she may deinvest in the real child or actually come to hate it, viewing it as the clone of a hated husband, parent, or sibling, or as a disappointment, inferior to the imaginary child."

We each have our story of how we were seen within the family and can imagine, if we haven't actually been told, how our parents anticipated our arrival and pictured us in the nine months of our becoming. Other things happen that will determine how our lives turn out, but looks, defined as the image of ourselves in our parents' eyes, have something to do with it. The promise we saw in their eyes is what we will remember.

There are mirrors in the offices of plastic surgeons, one side of which shows a face we recognize, which is how we are used to seeing ourselves; the flip side of the mirror shows the face that others see when they look at us. "Oh, how ugly!" I exclaim when shown this latter image. "We don't know how others see us, though we think we do," explains plastic surgeon Sherrel Aston. Which face is real? If our parents loved what they saw from the day we were born, would we see the same face in both sides of the mirror, carrying as we did inside us their loving image as "good enough"? Maybe we would not even look in mirrors, having such healthy self-esteem, which is at its core a good opinion of oneself.

"Even children with defects, who are deformed, can turn out okay," says Nancy Poland. "It's the love and the nurturing that they get from parents. They've been made to feel beautiful. Someone has talked to them about human worth so that they are able to transcend their appearance."

But to make the invisible qualities of kindness, generosity, and goodness believable—qualities that last longer than a pretty face—don't we first have to acknowledge beauty's power, especially today? I think we are getting there, growing more and more impatient with the prissy disclaimers that have kept beauty in the closet, guarded by such Pollyannaish sentiments as "beauty is as beauty does." Nothing announces our readiness more than today's emphasis on beauty, models being the icons of the age. Several seasons ago, smocked baby dresses, pinafores, and patent-leather Mary Jane shoes stole the fashion limelight. These were baby clothes for adult women who indeed wore them with unabashed enthusiasm. After my initial reaction of horror, the look struck me as absolutely appropriate for a society in desperate need of understanding its beginnings.

Simultaneously with baby clothes comes fashion's fascination with enormous breasts—nudity, not just cleavage and transparency, but photos of male models nibbling on, kissing women's bare breasts, shots of models with a child suckling, the expensive garment opened wide so that the baby, and we voyeurs too, can witness . . . what? An exercise in discovering through fashion and looks where and who we are? With the millennium at hand, as our society unravels, we have perhaps intuitively returned to view our selves naked, in baby clothes, not yet fully formed, our self-image just beginning. Maybe in bare breasts and baby clothes we will find a look with which we can live.

The infantilism of our culture is broadcast by our refusal to look and act like grown-ups; motherhood may be in vogue again, but no one wants to look like a mother, meaning old. Women's and men's eagerness to steal their children's fashions, to wear anything the mad tailors have whipped up in the night while we slept, lampoons adulthood. There are no adults, therefore no respected parenthood. The luxury of childhood is also at an end. The very concept of childhood is based on secrets from which the child is excluded, and there are no secrets anymore. Television has seen to that. It is fitting that the riddle of looks and beauty should carry us out of this century and into the next.

Pretty Babies Get Picked Up First

Did you know that pretty babies get picked up first, are held more, and get their needs attended to before the other babies? We don't need scientific studies to confirm our own life's lessons, that all eyes go to the Gerber baby, the adorable one whose dimpled cheeks and puckered lips send irresistible wavelengths to our hungry eyes: See me! Kiss me! Love me!

The judges in the studies on infant attractiveness aren't civilians like you and me, but are professional caregivers in day care centers and pediatric wards. They are people trained to respond automatically to a wailing baby who needs feeding, holding, and clean underwear.

Mothers too respond to this irresistible attraction to their own pretty babies, cooing and smiling at their children, kissing and holding them more often than do mothers of plain babies. What an auspicious beginning to have this power of beauty that grabs the attention of those who can save our lives.

And lest we think that this motivation is felt only by women, a study finds that fathers' expected degree of responsibility for infant caregiving was significantly related to infant attractiveness: "The greater the infants' attractiveness, the higher were fathers' expectations for involvement."

Writing of her study on mothers still in hospitals with their newborns, psychologist Judith Langlois concludes, "The less attractive the baby, the more the mother directed her attention to and interacted with people other than the baby. . . . By three months . . . mothers of more attractive girls, relative to those with less attractive girls . . . more often kissed, cooed and smiled at their daughters while holding them close and cuddling them."

There seems to be no getting away from the universality of beauty's power, for we also seem to agree on the facial features most likely to get an infant labeled "cute." In a study done by psychologist Katherine Hildebrandt, line drawings of infant faces, ages three, five, seven, nine, eleven, and thirteen months, were altered millimeter by millimeter, each picture varying in the measurement of forehead, eye height and width, iris size, pupil size, nose length and width, mouth height and width, and cheek size. When the adult subjects were asked to judge the drawings for cuteness, they tended to agree: Cute babies were the ones with short and narrow features and large eyes and pupils and large foreheads.

As for the babies themselves, they too prefer to look at pretty faces. According to another study by Langlois, babies look longer at attractive faces than at unattractive ones, regardless of their own mother's appearance; twelve-month-olds prefer to play with strangers (women other than their mothers) and dolls that have attractive faces. Nor does it matter whether the babies are white, black, or Hispanic.

These studies on infant attractiveness began to multiply in the 1980s, when appearance in people of all ages began once again to take center stage. Fashion designers were being elevated to the rank of celebrities; the birth of the model as idol had begun. But there is something timeless and fascinating when the beauty study findings are focused on such tiny people, barely alive and already loaded with expectations. Here are the results of two more studies by Hildebrandt, in which photos of newborn infants were rated by three groups of adults: male college students, female college students, and pregnant women. All three subject groups perceived the more physically attractive newborn boys and girls as "more sociable, less active, more competent, more attractive, and physically smaller and more feminine" than they did less attractive newborns. Three years later, in 1990, she did a study that confirmed the stereotype that "what is beautiful is good," but also suggested that "for infants . . . what is beautiful, happy, and male is especially good."

Yet, luckily, life is not a series of quantifiable studies in which we act reflexively. We are pulled momentarily toward a pretty face until something alters our decision before we are even consciously aware of it. So we turn instead to the other face, the one that reminds us of something or someone. There is a study, for instance, in which nurses in a day care center who were more experienced chose to give more attention to the *less* attractive babies, "presumably to compensate for the lack of attention these children received from the new [less experienced] caregivers."

The new scientific findings, weighted with objectivity, resonate because they separate us from emotion, telling us truth, wisdom, in a different voice. Both emotion and cold fact play a part in our understanding of the role of beauty in our lives, a subject so loaded with admonition we would only recently approach an understanding. "What is there to say about beauty? It exists, right?" friends quizzed me when I began this research in the mid-eighties. I wasn't yet sure, but I knew beauty was once again out of the closet, stalking the streets in high heels, red lacquered nails. The studies quoted above were done in the past fifteen years. Today, nobody questions why I or anyone else is looking anxiously at the effect of appearance on our lives.

"Let me take you in," we say. "You're so adorable, I could eat you up!" How oral these grown-up desires sound, as likely to be spoken to a lover as a child. How hungry the words, reverential at the sight of a face, a form that replenishes a vacuum in a life. We cannot live without beauty, need to satisfy our hunger, to see and be seen.

"Let me look!" pleads the voyeur. "Look at me!" demands the exhibitionist. Opposite sides of the same coin. But we were speaking of parents and infants, and I am getting ahead of myself, or am I? Isn't what goes on in the nursery a pattern of seeing and looking, of getting oneself noticed, that is repeated or reacted against throughout life? Isn't it being laid down here, the expectation of success or failure? We should look closely at the adult-infant interplay of eyes and learn about the rest of life. We adults tell our stories to analysts who lead us back to the nursery. Might we not advantageously look at infants to understand ourselves today, why beauty brings us so little happiness and why we crave it nonetheless, to own it, to see it?

"He's only a pretty face," we say.

"Only?"

We cannot remember the first years of life; studies suggest we can only remember back to somewhere between our third and fourth birthdays. If we do not remember, perhaps we "know" things on some other level than conscious memory. For instance, I cannot remember my father, ever, but I know something happened at which I was present and he too was there and it was not a happy scene. My handsome father, or so I'm told.

One of the most impenetrable barriers against memory is fear of being back in the nursery, being powerless opposite the Giantess whom we loved, or wanted to love, who loved us back or didn't. Thirty, forty, fifty years old today, we shrink at remembering her disinterest or her overprotection. My dearest friends are drawn inexorably into this book; sitting under the fans on the porch in Key West during the drinks hour, I'll read a few pages to them after a day alone in the writing room. Stories swim up that they had forgotten, dreams that night interrupt their sleep. Yesterday, for instance, Jack drew me aside as we walked to the waterfront grocery store.

"I've always felt different from my brothers and sisters," he said.

"I thought the reason they got more affection from our parents was because they were handsomer than I. Listening to you last night, I remembered that my mother told me that when I was a baby I looked like 'a little Jap.' That was right after World War Two. I grew up thinking that is why she dotes on the others and not on me. She's a very beautiful woman. Looks mattered a lot in our lives."

"But you are handsome," I say. "And you're more successful than any of your siblings." All this is true, for Jack, like many of us, compensated for his inability to catch his parents' eyes by developing other talents and skills that last far longer than surface beauty. Late last night he telephoned his mother, who today thinks the sun rises and sets on him.

"I had to know what that 'little Jap' business was all about, if it had really happened. Know what she said? 'The reason I didn't hold you as much as the others was because I loved you too much.'"

He smiles ruefully at me, shaking his head. He is not a whiner, but he knows he'll never be able to leave the house without first checking the mirror to be sure "the little Jap" has his tie on right, trousers pressed, shoes shined.

Mother blaming is a terrible waste. The victim mentality only assures that we will never see mother as a whole person, good and bad. Instead, we idealize her or denigrate ourselves or make a cocktail of denials that keep us as tied to her as children.

The more books I write, the more I clean out the nursery and discard old angers and baby fears of mother's reprisals, the less need I have of beauty maintenance. So much of what goes into my closets is there to make up for what I didn't get back then, to disguise the ugly child who wasn't really all that bad. It was the feeling of being left out among a houseful of beautiful women; of course I grew up thinking, ". . . had there only been a man." By and large, what I wear has as its objective the approval of men.

The weight of the clothes in my closets, the very sight of them, grows increasingly onerous. On impulse, I'll go to the attic or down to the basement to the cedar closet where an eight-foot rack of out-of-season clothes recently collapsed. "You're supposed to allow two inches between hangers," the carpenter grumbled, adding extra supports, his comment seeming to blame my greed and not his workmanship. Now when I open closet doors, any closet doors, I look for the requisite two inches as an indication of my goodness.

Not that I have stopped buying clothes, but I am onto them, the eye-grabbing traitors that originally promised a look, an image arresting enough to make people change focus, abandon whatever, whomever they were taking in, leave them. Take *me* in.

Lately my unfaithful clothes seem to multiply while I sleep, reminding me of fairy tales in which foolish maidens spin countless yards of flax into gold by night, only to find in the morning that it has returned to its original worthless state.

The Mutual Gaze and the Crying Storm

Here is the heart of it, what I was searching for earlier, calling it The Golden Beam between the eye of the Madonna and Child, the "feeding tube," that elusive symbol in my first art history class in college that, I am sure, more than anything else, led me to major in that subject. What better reason to become an art historian? My "beam of love," it seems, has an official name; the Baby Watchers, those psychologists and psychiatrists whose work is to study the mother/infant relationship, call it The Gaze.

And because it is all a miracle and life's coincidences crazier than anything we can make up, who should be the maestro of The Gaze? He who has described it in clinical observation more poetically than any doctor should be able to—my analyst, Daniel Stern, to whom I talked for five years when my old world was falling apart and this new life I lead was struggling to be born. We never discussed The Gaze in so many words back in the early eighties when I visited his office next to the room where he observed, videotaped, and wrote about mothers and their infants. But I saw the irony of it, his little babies in one room, and in the adjoining room, me, his big baby, long legs seductively crossed, her Geoffrey Beene jumpsuit unzipped a little too low, laughingly trying to seduce him and only occasionally falling into the deepest, saddest reveries about My Father The Mystery.

Now, ten years later in the middle of this research I find his book, *Diary of a Baby*, published in 1990. There is his dear picture on the back, my unseducible friend, who now reenters my life when I need him most. I tell you this because miracles should be recorded and this subject of looks and mirrors is about miracles, about how in infancy The Gaze sets a pattern of being able to love, to see our selves, and to see others too, both separate from us, and in those rare moments, as our beloved.

Love songs are all about The Gaze. Listen to what could easily be a love song, a page from Stern's book describing how the infant feels about his mother, though I would steal his verse for my beloved tonight, or wish to have him make me feel these words with his eyes:

I enter the world of her face. Her face and its features are the sky, the clouds, and the water. Her vitality and spirit are the air and the light. It is usually a riot of light and air at play. But this time when I enter, the world is still and dull. Neither the curving lines of her face nor its rounded volumes are moving. Where is she? Where has she gone? I am scared. I feel that dullness creeping into me. I search around for a point of life to escape to.

I find it. All her life is concentrated into the softest and hardest points in the world—her eyes.

They draw me in, deep and deeper. They draw me into a distant world. Adrift in this world, I am rocked side to side by the passing thoughts that ripple the surface of her eyes. I stare down into their depths. And there I feel running strong the invisible currents of her excitement. They churn up from those depths and tug at me. I call after them. I want to see her face again, alive.

Gradually life flows back into her face. The sea and sky are transformed. The surface now shimmers with light. New spaces open out. Arcs rise and float. Volumes and planes begin their slower dance. Her face becomes a light breeze that reaches across to touch me. It caresses me. I quicken. My sails fill with her. The dance within me is set free.

Until recently behaviorists assumed that the breast was the most important object that the infant sees, but today the Baby Watchers agree that the breast is too close for the feeding baby to focus on. It is the face that is the perfect distance away. And the most fascinating feature of that face, just about ten inches from the feeding infant's eyes, are the mother's eyes.

"Babies act as if the eyes were indeed windows to the soul," says Stern. "After seven weeks of age, they treat the eyes as the geographic center of the face and the psychological center of the person."

In time, the child becomes like his vision of mother and thinks of his own eyes as his psychological center too. From now on, throughout life, he will feel that others have not really seen him if they do not see his eyes. When, for instance, famous people do not want to *feel* that they are recognized, but instead have maintained their privacy, they learn to pass through crowded rooms staring just above the eyes of others. People may look at them, but to themselves, they have not been seen. The expression is "blindsighted," which almost implies that they are invisible.

Stern gives a more charming example of a six-year-old covering her eyes with her hands while playing a game. And if "you ask her, 'Can I see you?' she will answer, 'No!' Although we used to think that the child could not imagine you could see her if she couldn't see you, that is not the problem. She knows perfectly well that you can see not only her but even her hands covering her eyes. What she really means by 'No!' is, 'If you can't see my eyes, you don't see *me*.' Seeing her means looking into her eyes."

When a Zulu greets another Zulu in South Africa, he says, "Sawubona," meaning "Hello," but literally translated, "I see you."

More than anything, it is the sharp angles of the corners of the eyes, the light/dark contrast of pupil and white of eye and of eyebrows against skin, that are especially fascinating to the infant. Stern says that the baby is, in fact, "pulled to her eyes. . . . Locked into mutual gaze with her, he passes into the 'distant world' of her eyes alone."

We grow to ages three and four and still what we prefer in the human face are the eyes. When, in a psychoanalytic study, children of this age did figure drawings to test a theory that it was the mouth that they preferred as the focal point of body image, the great majority of the children drew eyes; again and again, the eyes had it.

Mutual Gaze. It has a lovely ring to it. Eyes, no matter what our age, are central to all of us, but this business of Mutual Gaze, "looking into eyes that are looking back into yours," says Stern, "is like no other experience with another person." When we shift our gaze back and forth from the other person's left eye to the right, and that person does the same with us, the shifts and focus "seem to each gazer like a reflection of the other person's thinking." When the other person doesn't follow our gaze, when our eyes aren't dancing together, well, to quote Stern, "Someone who doesn't do it is not all there for you." As if we needed the good doctor to tell us, as if we didn't know the excitement, the arousal when someone attractive, loved, holds our gaze. In the earliest cycle of "satisfaction-pleasure-reanimation" with his mother is the model the baby builds that will be the prototype for what he will expect to happen with other loved persons whom he encounters in life.

People who are neither lovers nor babies cannot hold a stare into one another's eyes for more than a few seconds; a mutual gaze without speech arouses too much emotion, becomes awkward, even hostile. When two animals lock in mutual gaze, either the submissive one looks away or the more powerful may attack. But lovers and babies, ah, they are born to look, gazes locked, their intimacy visible to the outsider who envies their voluntary entrapment.

"Perhaps it is the eye—not the heart, the genitals, or the brain—that is the initial organ of romance," says Helen Fisher, "for the gaze (or stare) often triggers the human smile." We have been reading faces since we were born. In the first twelve weeks of life, when the social smile emerged, along with extended eye-to-eye contact, we began a pattern that has lasted all our lives of seeing others and feeling ourselves taken in. Those early mirroring eyes, or their absence, have determined how we see ourselves, read ourselves in other people's eyes. "After all, it is mainly in the face that we feel we can read one another's feelings and intentions," says Stern. "And we start becoming experts at the very beginning of our lives."

When we fall in love, we lie together so closely that it seems we breathe life into one another, so closely our eyes see, as if into deep liquid, little patterns of light, colors, shards of minuscule browns and blues, down, down into the bottom of the sea, his essence, a private screening room between lovers. Nothing that we see in his face, no scar, no wrinkle is unadorable; in some magical way our unconditional love has opened us to an awareness of our own perfect love, our ability to love perfectly. In loving him, in allowing ourselves to free-fall into those eyes in total trust, we come to love ourselves too. There is nothing about our so recently imperfect body that hasn't been transformed by this intense intimacy, the *face-en-face*, the vision of a new self born in the intense scrutiny of our look of love, our Mutual Gaze.

When our friends see us, they whisper, "I wouldn't have recognized her, she must be in love!" When we enter a room, his face "lights up," an amazing expression when you think of it and its opposite, when it no longer comes to life when he looks up and sees us, when love is over. "How can I tell her that I no longer love her?" he puzzles, but he doesn't need words; his face, the empty eyes have told us all.

Some of us cannot find ourselves in a beloved's eyes today. We didn't get the early prototype of satisfaction-pleasure-reanimation with mother. We experience the momentary high of love, but it is like a drop of rain that remains on the water's surface because there is no deep reservoir which adult love replenishes. It is all surface. We can neither give love—believing others are like us—nor take deep comfort from anyone who professes to love us. If we didn't get this visual one-ness, the locking in via The Gaze at the age-appropriate time, the inevitable casualties of life leave us vulnerable to disintegration, or so it feels. When someone who professes to love us tries to comfort us, the reassuring reflection of ourselves as lovable is not there in his eyes. We don't know what to look for. We never learned how. We blame his inability to make us feel lovable, beautiful, on his lack of love when the lack is within us.

Oh, we say we love and we mate, but know in our souls that we are alone in the world. Even when the image we see in our mirror is successful and lovely, we know it is the chance combination of the right clothes, makeup, and hair, not that of a substantial person. Rage, especially our own, is always there, threatening to turn the attractive person others see into a monster, Jekyll to Hyde.

Days, months go by when we are content, but then he talks too long to another woman, or we are passed over for a promotion, and our anger rages out of proportion to what has happened because we have experienced a bewildering loss of center. We are not unlike the infant who has neither a picture of himself nor of the world around him, nor even a focus on exactly what it is that is so infuriating him. The infant has what Stern calls a "crying storm."

"The world is howling. Everything explodes and is blown out and then collapses and rushes back toward a knot of agony that cannot last—but does." This is Stern explaining how the hungry baby feels in the throes of his crying storm. "This 'global' interference must feel to [the baby] like a sudden disharmony in his world, a 'something gone wrong.'" It con-sumes him—it is everything to him.

The tiny baby's features twist into a swollen, red mask of fury, not unlike an expressionist painting of a grotesque baby from hell. Not unlike the equally contorted, unnatural image of ourselves betrayed, eyes swollen with rage in our own crying storms. The image in our mirror is frightening but not altogether unrecognizable. It is, in fact, more credible than the image of our beauty in a brilliant new dress. We stare back at the misbegotten face and recognize a self-portrait that is ageless.

Now, here is what happens to the six-week-old baby in his crying storm when the good mother enters the room. Suddenly arms reach out to raise him out of his misery and soften his rage. He is held to the warm breast, fed, and miracle of miracles, he sees her face, gazes into her eyes. "And his new animation in response to her brings her face even more to life . . ." and there is harmony in the world. Describing the infant's reaction to the return of his mother's full, loving attention, how like the return of a lover's gaze Stern makes it sound: "[The baby] experiences the entire transformation as a demonstration of the return of her life force, a return that affects him directly and immediately. . . . In reaching across to touch him, her smile . . . triggers a smile in him and breathes a vitality into him. It makes him resonate with the animation she feels and shows. His joy rises. Her smile pulls it out of him. . . . He is both responding and identifying now."

Mother isn't always there; she doesn't have to be. It is more a matter of the focus of her attention when she is present, the smile and, always, of course, the look. The beloved eyes with their fascinating contours and contrasts, the infant's own beloved likeness reflected in them, which is what builds trust, the sureness of self and the image of oneself as beautiful enough. Why else would she return, or twenty years later, the beloved return, no matter how the face ages, for it is the soul beyond the windows of the eyes, what Stern calls the "psychological center of the person," that has brought the mother/beloved back again and again.

Seeing how her smile brings forth his, how her love creates love, the good mother's reward is that her baby gives back to her an awareness of her own goodness and beauty. In time the infant imitates her smile, is the initiator, and now she responds. Back and forth they go, with each smile and look soldering the attachment between them. The Baby Watchers have found that the more "visual regard" there is, the more smiling. Smiles, looks, these "are the stuff of being-with-another-person that constitute the ties of attachment."

It is easy to see how some mothers cannot bear to let go of the child, ever. Someone, her own flesh and blood, is seeing her in a way that perhaps no one else ever has. Around the sixth week of life, when the baby is capable of visually fixating on mother's eyes and holding her gaze, she feels for the first time that the infant is really looking at *her*. It is a different kind of gaze than that in which she indulges with her husband. This divine creature, this baby, is totally dependent on her, which can be read to mean, "This baby is my very own." She may begin to feel Madonna-esque, totally good, generous, and, yes, for the first time in her life, even beautiful.

Until now, she has never been able to elicit from men the feeling that they have seen and loved her for who she is. Many times she has wanted to take hold of a man's chin with her fingers and gently turn his eyes to her. "You are looking at me, but you don't really see me. You don't understand what I am like, and it is driving me crazy." She has wanted so badly to say it, but couldn't. And it was not just her lovely hair and sensual mouth she wanted recorded, but the total acceptance that she is finally getting, not from a man but from an infant.

Then something happens. For the first time, the infant can choose *not* to see mother. By the end of the third month, his focal distance has a range almost as extensive as that of an adult. The infant can track the mother as she leaves, approaches, and moves around the room. Toward the end of the sixth month, his visual focus turns from exclusive interest in the human face to a consuming curiosity about objects. Mother has lost her sovereignty as the focal point of her child's universe. Does her hand reach out when she holds her baby, to turn the little head back to her, or does she delight in his interest in others as, one hopes, she will delight in his later crawling, walking away from her to find himself? His chances at finding love and a good enough image of himself all rest in this delicate balance of togetherness and separation.

Obviously, there are countless variations on the theme of this first love, the primal gaze. When a mother, for instance, is disappointed in her baby's appearance because he reminds her of someone in the family she doesn't like, or because he isn't beautiful enough, her own narcissism is injured. She doesn't meet his gaze as often as she might, and the quality of her attachment to the child may be affected.

Perfection isn't required of the mother. The word I would choose is generosity, the good mother giving enough of her self so that the child is filled, so nourished by her vision of him that he must exercise his new self, experiment, try out his beauty and lovable qualities on others. It is the best gift in life; it *is* life. Only a year old, less, and she has packed his bags with an internalized picture of her unwavering love. Why would questions of being beautiful enough, lovable enough, enter his mind? Why should he later feel unable to return love when this was how life began?

It is the bedrock of oneness and separation in the first years of life that subsequently make us capable as adults of loving without possessing and of being loved without losing our identity. Embedded in this process of falling in love, patterned on our earliest years in the nursery, will be our ability to retain our loved one's image of us, to have it locked inside so that when he is away, or looks at someone else, we don't fall apart.

After twenty-five years of writing about the mother/child relationship, jealousy, envy, and sex, I've not a doubt in the world that the misery expended over beauty is, like everything else, wound up in that first relationship. It doesn't mean we cannot change it, but it is much, much harder after the first years of life. When women describe what makes them jealous, at the top of the list is "when he looks at another woman." He is just looking; nothing has been said or done. Why do we interpret that look to mean that she is lovelier than we, that he prefers her to us, that he will now leave us? Until he looked at her, we felt beautiful. We say men are cads, that they only want one thing, that they can't control their sexual appetites, that having "looked," they will now pounce on the other beautiful woman, leave us. We are projecting. We give men too much power.

We would not concentrate so much today on looks/beauty, pay so much, die so much, seeing our "beauty power" coming and going, never owned, never ours, if our look, our sense of self were owned. The sureness of our beauty comes with the package of unconditional love internalized in the first years of life. "Fine, yes, look at the beautiful face across the room," we would say to our beloved, allowing him to admire whomever he finds attractive because we know *why* he loves us, and *what* he loves in us. He sees what mother saw, what father saw when we were held and came to know our image reflected in their eyes, again and again. We never question it. It is there, planted deeply inside, a given, a known. That woman at whom our lover is looking is indeed beautiful but doesn't affect what he feels for us. Here come his eyes now, back to us, as we knew they would. We know we are not easily replaceable, a promise given to us long ago when our parents saw us as the sun and the moon and the stars. "Basic trust" is what psychoanalyst Erik Erikson called this gift.

Now, today, because we women can afford to pay our own rents and don't need a man to play mirror-mirror as our own mothers did with men, we turn our backs on faithless men who were never good at making us feel lovely, which, salary or no salary, is still a woman's birthright. Women today look for mirrors everywhere, changing our clothes, our style, the color of our hair more frequently than the seasons, desperate for an inner picture of ourselves that we can live with.

Here we are, more women in the workplace and fewer in the nursery than ever before. The great upheaval of the past twenty-five years has made Baby Watching more intense than ever. The revolutionary changes in women's lives—which have in turn triggered changes in men's lives—have left the door to the nursery wide open. Please, someone enter! There is no Madonna in the nursery. There never was, of course, but so long as women had no other role, and no economic power, this one had to be idealized to keep women satisfactorily in their place.

I would never have written *My Mother/My Self*, nor would so many women have read it, if the need hadn't been there to look honestly at this relationship that forms our lives and sets up how we will love men and, in turn, raise our own children. It was my fascination with women's guilt about our sexuality that prodded me into the mother/daughter research; I had just finished *My Secret Garden*, a book on women's sexual fantasies that in its turn had been born out of The Sexual Revolution, a time in the late sixties and early seventies when women were taking off our clothes, lying down with men, and opening our minds to thoughts that would have been unthinkable for Nice Girls just a few years earlier.

There we were, openly breaking mother's rules, having sex, but when women tried to tell me their erotic fantasies, the doors in their minds slammed shut. The guilt was overwhelming. It was a time of enormous contradiction, those years, nowhere as dramatic as in all matters sexual. We were going against generations of sexual repression; how ironic that it was easier to "do it" than to accept the forbidden scenarios in our imaginations, most of which had plot lines that unconsciously had the mother of the nursery as the adversary of sexual freedom. Of course women were guilty. We still are.

Timing. It all comes down to timing, the ideas that come to writers and scientists that begin perhaps unconsciously, moving us toward a theme that resonates, then takes root in the conscious intellect, eventually producing the wealth of books and scientific research we've had access to in recent years. In order to see the plight of the baby, we've had to come to this, to women's moving out of the nursery. The infant's needs that influence his life had always been there, but the idealization of mother obscured our vision. We gave women too much power of one sort and not enough of another; we did the same with men, forking over to them all the economic power but cutting them off from their humanity.

Now we have the opportunity to outfit a finer nursery than we've ever enjoyed, one in which, finally, there could be a full genetic team representing both male and female sides of the infant, two people to gaze on him and infuse him with a picture of himself that will shine back at him throughout life whenever he passes a reflecting surface.

No one has taught me more about all of the prickly subjects to which I am drawn than the man I call my mentor, psychiatrist Richard Robertiello, whose moody office with its African masks and sculptures of one-legged women was my haunt during the writing of *My Mother/My Self*. No one is wiser than he on the subject that is the darling topic of our times, self-esteem. The Gaze, as interpreted by Robertiello, is crucial to the development of self-esteem, which in simplest terms means a good opinion of oneself. Why should something as obvious as a good opinion of ourselves today be so mysteriously unattainable?

Without that good opinion, we either soar to the heights of grandiosity, wearing our outlandish, exhibitionistic clothes, or we plummet to the depths of self-denigration, slogging about in running shoes and a long face. There is no middle ground, no self-esteem, no inner beauty. Visibility becomes everything: I am seen, therefore I exist. We diet, we buy clothes, we work out, spend more on beauty than ever before and believe in it less. That this happened at a moment in history when we have less time than ever to stare adoringly into the eyes of an infant is not without meaning.

The Beauty of Separation: A Second Birth

If there were a gift I could give to every child at birth, one of those certificates not to a day but to a life of beauty, I would wish them a mother and father who accepted Margaret Mahler's theory of separation and individuation. I would pray that they had been held close, in a state of symbiotic bliss if you like, and then—and here is the hard part—the good parents would release the child and encourage his moving out into the world with all of their best wishes and love internalized. This child would be a secure and independent little person with an ability to love himself and others too, a child whose ease in self and openness to love would be so appealing that others would see him as he sees himself. The truth is, the world is starved for people who are at ease in their skins.

When I fell into writing about the mother/daughter relationship—and the verb couldn't be more appropriate—I had never heard of Margaret Mahler's theories. The words "symbiosis" and "separation" weren't in the outline I'd submitted to my publishers, but once discovered, Mahler's thinking became exactly what my book was about. For three years we swam underwater together while I fought the denials that protected me from the relationship I honestly had with my mother. Up until then I had convinced myself that our relationship was perfect. Wasn't I independent, successful, my life totally different from hers? When I came up for air, the book completed, I felt safe in my life for the first time. The last draft was finished, lying on the floor, my back in spasm, but the lie was gone, and lo and behold, there were two people, my mother and myself, and some real love. Yes, some anger too, but that is the inevitable other side of love.

Mahler's theories apply to sons as well as daughters. We are all born of woman, most of us raised by a woman who dominates our lives when we are dependent and she the only source of everything, including the mirroring eyes that will determine how we see ourselves. Oh, yes, men are very much a part of Mahler's theories, and now that they are entering the nursery, God bless them, their involvement will enrich their children's lives. If I use the "she" to cover the caretakers, it is because women still predominate, though I would urge you to read in "father" as well.

There are endless variations on the theme of attachment and separation, but being held too close for too long or not being held at all can lead to a particular face that all of us recognize: the woman who grows up to hate what she sees in the mirror. We love our mothers; why then do we hate this face, these expressions of ours/hers? When we cannot face our anger at her (inevitable in the best of relationships, no one being perfect), we build a fortress around the rage that still feels at age thirty that it will destroy Mommy as it did when we were three. "Who, me, angry? See, Mommy, I don't hate you, I have become you. I love you. I look just like you!"

The grim monument of our denial is that we imitate not the qualities of hers that we loved—which would be obvious and easy—but instead those looks and mannerisms that we hated most: her anxiety, rigidity, fastidiousness, asexuality, her wounded look. We keep these despised parts alive in ourselves because, like the two-year-old who can't afford to see Mommy whole, good and bad, we think she will kill us, or we her, if she knew that we didn't love her perfectly. Whether they are physical, emotional, or temperamental characteristics, the person who never emotionally separated from mother ends up with them in the manner in which she carries herself, round-shouldered, rigid, lines of tension in the forehead, lips as thin as a pencil. This is our *look*, the glimpsed reflection in the store window as we pass and the one we want to be rid of more than anything, to paint out with makeup or alter with surgery. All this because—at least in my book—we could never let go of mother.

Need I add what father, another face to mirror, another model of bravery to encourage our moving out into our own separate identities, what he would bring to this legacy of confused love and rage?

If we don't become our *selves*, we miss us all our lives. Like the amputee who has lost his leg, we will itch for the person we should have been. What happened? We look in the mirror and neither recognize nor like what we see. It isn't how we think of ourselves, isn't really who we are.

We are each designed uniquely. All we require—actually, it is quite a lot—is an initial period of love in a warm climate, where we feel as one with the person who is dear to us, who is us and we she, so close it is impossible to know where we begin and she leaves off. Totally dependent, this symbiosis is heaven. Nourished by the body which so recently contained us, precious egg, and fueled by the image of our selves in mother's eyes, we thrive. And yet, and yet, perfect as this heaven is—in part because it has been so perfect—before the first year of life is over, we are sated. Enough oneness! Time to push off. Why else would we leave symbiotic bliss if life's plot wasn't to discover ourselves, including the unique look of who we are? Safety only lies in knowing one's perimeters; if we do not feel our boundaries, we will go through life secure only in tight relationships, terrified at the thought of being left, alone.

Separation. I often think it is the word itself that is the problem, what I call the Semantic Jungle, wherein one word is so overloaded that we get entangled in the meanings. Just the sound of separation conjures up a cruel and cutting division, like that grim period before "the divorce," which marks the end of love. But when Mahler speaks of separation she means it as the beginning of a new life, wherein a new individual who is capable of love emerges. Until we have a self separate from Mommy, we are more dependent than loving. A tiny child doesn't so much love mother as need her. Love, Melanie Klein tells us, is born out of gratitude and can only be felt when we are no longer dependent on the good mother with all the power. We want some power of our very own, which is our due, our birthright; if she doesn't let us go, with all her love on board, our voyage is aborted. I think of separation as a second birth.

The first year of life is not yet over before symbiotic closeness with mother has served its purpose. Mother's arms now feel as restrictive as life within the womb at nine months. There is an energetic pull to discover what is in the next room. Off the baby goes on all fours—No, no, don't hold me back!—and there it is, a space that is new because we have found and claimed it as our own, by ourselves. Suddenly panic grips the baby—Whoa, where's Mom? I am alone!—and back the baby goes to her, home base, where loving arms, kisses that say "I'm still here" await. The next journey is a few yards farther, and then back to her again for what Mahler calls "refueling," a word I love. And so it goes, each voyage out into the sea of life a practicing step into independent security. Practice, practice, practice.

Eventually the move is out into the yard, then down the street, farther and farther as we extend our trusted self. Every fear conquered is a new territory of the self. Anxiety at beginning school, the new job in the new town will also be lessened with practice, making it exciting, an accomplishment, another stage in belief in our separate identity, the picture of an admirable person whom we will one day see in our passport, permitting us entry and exit throughout a manageable world. What a generous gift from parents to child. What is more noble than a mother filling a child with courage, belief in self to the point when the child says, "Yes, you are right, I am this beloved person whose quest is to establish my own life where I will know how to love others as you have loved me. But I will never be far, for I carry you inside, and your gift to me will grow into the unique life you gave me. It will be your legacy that I will pass on to my child."

If, however, leaving mother in our earliest efforts was fraught with fear—her fear, which we learned from her—we will not separate emotionally. Oh, we will go physically, but we will simply be stretching an invisible umbilical cord that keeps us dependent on her approval, an anxiety we couldn't specifically name but which is a baby's fear of the loss of Mommy's love.

Women who were not encouraged to win emotional separation go from mother to the arms of other little girls and then to men, merely changing partners, each of whom stands in for mother. When we are attracted to a certain man who makes us feel excruciatingly alive, we look for ourselves in his eyes but do not trust what we see. She would not approve. Not that we think of the disapproval as hers, for it is ours now. She is us and we are she. We marry, have children, but we need her approval still, if only by phone, even more than we need our husband's. One disapproving word from her and we are shattered. She can be dead, but when we act in a way of which she wouldn't approve, or wear an exhibitionistic dress, our disapproval and rejection of the "New Us" is hers.

Perhaps a clearing can be made in the Semantic Jungle by taking the overly loaded word "separation" and putting it in a less threatening context than that of mother/child. Instead of the nursery, think of a heated sexual relationship between a man and a woman. Initially, when they meet, there is an excitement between two people who have their own lives and identities. The distance between them is what allows the spark to ignite. Then they have sex. Like a litmus test, the woman who never went through a healthy separation with her mommy will now lose herself by falling into this man like a pool and drowning her frail identity in his. Sex with him felt like a giving over of her self, arousing in her all her yearning for what she once had or wished she had, the symbiotic union with Mommy.

Women don't consciously decide this, but it happens. The man will feel it less, his mother having felt pressured by the rigorous demands of society to let him practice again and again his ability to stand alone. Not all men will accomplish healthy separation, but they must put a good face on it. The man's problem will be letting down his iron defenses enough to sink into the momentary oneness of love and great sex in full knowledge that he will rise again, renewed, into his known self. "Where is my exciting, sexual woman?" he wonders. "Why doesn't he reconnect?" grieves the woman who was an independent siren minutes ago but now feels little, lost, and frightened by fears of abandonment without her mommy/man.

It grows ever more awkward these days: The deeper into the workplace we move, the thornier the issues of separation become. The money, the seeming independence, says one thing, but when we have sex, the siren song of symbiosis is awakened. How to work properly with one ear cocked for his telephone call, his promise of love eternal? It is infuriating to a woman of independent means! Damn men for not being good at mothering grown-up babies! Men are only out for themselves. Only women know what another woman needs. And so women lie down with one another.

Meanwhile, the beauty industry thrives, women having more money to spend on looks than ever before. Needing no one's permission, we buy one new "look" after another and wonder, when we stand before our crowded closet in the morning, why we don't recognize anything as particularly "us." Closets are filled and emptied every season, so unsatisfying is fashion's futile effort to dress women who don't know whose judgment to trust when we look in the mirror. Our anger grows ever more monumental, keeping us locked in the past, having us spin our wheels deeper and deeper into the sand. How humiliating to be in the adult workplace and still stuck in nursery anger. We deny it, proving independence with sexual display, higher heels, lower necklines, until we see the anxious little face through our cigarette smoke in the mirror over the bar. Whose awful face is that?

Separation, beauty, competition—would any of these thorny subjects have been questioned, dissected, and argued about had our entry into the workplace not necessitated understanding ourselves? So long as we lived in a strictly patriarchal society, wherein women were confined to the home and were defined by our maternal role, there was no burning need for theories on separation and individuation. It was expected that a daughter would automatically repeat her mother's life. A mother who watched her daughter like a hawk, monitored her every move, even read her diary, was a good mother. A daughter who had freedom, too much individuality, who looked and acted different from all the other girls was thought to be unlucky.

In society's eyes, mothers who gave up their lives for their children were the best mothers. Sacrifice defined a good mother, even if that sacrifice included a woman having only her children in her life, nothing and no one else that made her feel alive. If she clung to the child, teaching the child to cling to her, what did it matter? The child wasn't going anywhere except to another pair of arms, another protector, a husband. "A son will leave you and get himself a wife, but a daughter's a daughter for all of her [or is it "your"?] life" wasn't just an amusing sampler over the bureau. It was reality.

The Women's Movement may have marked women's exit from the home into the workplace and demanded a reassessment of how women are raised, but the necessity for a sharp image of ourselves as individuals had always existed. Such photos are rare in old family albums—a faded snapshot of a singular presence, a woman standing alone with neither husband nor children to define her. In fact, we had been at risk for generations without an image in our heads of who we were alone; husbands, after all, were known to wander, and children do grow up and leave.

The anxiety and anger at having no self outside a relationship were swallowed, the depression went undiagnosed, the envy of men's economic power unnamed, for how could one bite the hand that fed us? Even to try to voice anger at men's power would ultimately lead to another source of anger, which no nice woman acknowledged, to mother, whom we loved and who loved us. In the old days, prior to modern feminism, women gagged, choked, got migraines, fell into depressions, and died rather than admit to the ambivalence of mother love.

Anger at mother denied, women tried to find with a man the only replica of love known, a symbiotic oneness in which we gave ourselves totally to him—regardless of whether he'd asked. Women's expectations of men were enormous; after all, hadn't we given up everything for him? Hadn't mother promised that if we rejected all the possibilities of a life—especially sex—that we would get a prince as our reward? It was now surrendered to him, our sexuality, handed over for him to reconstitute and bring back to life. Virginity is one thing, and when consciously selected, a fine choice. But the woman who expected a man to bring her to sexual life by "giving" her an orgasm usually had a long and unhappy wait.

Eventually, women gave up on sex, on even trying. The sexual urge disappeared because it never had fit the internal self-image the woman had as a Nice Girl. In that short gap of time between mother and husband, whatever sexual spark had been ignited by boys was charged with the forbidden thrill of breaking mother's rules. Those nights in boys' arms, parked in dark cars with romantic music feeding the illicit loss of control, had been a thrilling but scary sampling of independence. Marriage, a husband, now this felt like going home. Without conscious decision, the daughter began to dress like her mother, talk and walk and decorate her house like mother's. Soon there was a child, another daughter to replay the generational image.

I choose to write about sex because it is the missing piece in most women's lives, the booster that could fire us out of dependency if only we would take sexual responsibility. The Nice Girls wear a "look" that identifies them as belonging to a women's world that defines itself as hating sex. You can choose not to have sex, but to hate it is to hate any woman who drinks from its spring, for the women's world is only bearable when all the girls refrain from sex.

Before I became a writer I told myself that I was "different" from my mother in that I was sexual and she was not. It was in this self-congratulatory mood that I sat down to write about women's sexuality. Didn't my mirror reflect a very sexual presentation—the see-through clothes, the no-bra nipples, the swagger of the seventies? Most women, my research showed, traced their sexual shame as far back as they could recall; very well, the nursery was the place to begin. The original title of *My Mother/My Self* was *The First Lie*, which should have warned me of the difficulties ahead.

Three years later, when I stood up after writing the words "The End," I was a veteran of a war. My prize for my work was that I'd stripped the idealized trappings from my relationship with my mother. I saw her as a woman, good and bad, a woman in whom I also saw my self. We weren't all that different; she was brave, sexual, competitive, and, yes, a bit of an exhibitionist too. It was a gift.

Certain Matriarchal Feminists now attack Mahler for encouraging mothers to separate from their children. These are the women who have become mothers themselves during these past ten, fifteen years. Maybe they once marched for freedom, fought for feminist rights, but they are still loath to practice independence with their babies. "Mother blamers!" they yell at those of us who say and write that women's true freedom begins in the sureness of who we are, separate unto ourselves.

As usual, the antiseparation people aim their heaviest artillery at men, a false target. "Patriarchy thrives by keeping women divided," they write, "setting them up to compete with each other. . . . Scientific experts tell mothers that each child should separate to achieve autonomy. This is a lie. This distorted view of good mothering places a mother's feelings at odds with cultural perceptions of what is necessary for her child's growth and well-being. Moreover, this lie of separation leads mothers into an unintentional betrayal of daughters."

This is absurd. To accuse men of creating the idea of separation allows misguided women to sidestep the problems with their own mothers and find with their daughters the oneness no man could ever give them. Patriarchy? Mahler was the *mother* of the theory of separation and one of her closest students was another woman, psychiatrist Louise Kaplan, who has written brilliantly of her teacher's philosophy.

Many feminists who marched twenty years ago gave up men because to love them drained a woman of her newfound sense of identity. Love with a man rearoused the old overwhelming desire to mesh, an alien feeling to those fighting for women's rights. But what was worse, humiliating when you think of it, was that men were/are reluctant to mesh, to lie down and mold their bodies to women, fearing that the lady of the lake would pull them down. How easy, and useful, to turn rejecting, unyielding men into the beasts, the ogres, the source of all of women's problems. Men were already the enemy that didn't want to yield to women an equal wage in the workplace; very well, dump this thorny issue of separation on men too. Make men the brutes, the origin of all of women's worries, including the pursuit of beauty.

Mahler's teachings have only been popularized in the past twenty years. Moving into the workplace in the mid-seventies meant that women were turning the world upside down, changing the most venerated tenets of society. We needed road maps, diagrams, explanations of who we were, how we had become this way if we were to create this new identity of woman the provider. To become the New Woman, we had to understand traditional woman, ourselves. Mahler was key.

It should be remembered that motherhood wasn't a popular role for much of the sixties and seventies. We were competing with men, and other women, for jobs and assignments and we had to be assertive, tough, feelings that were at odds with motherhood. Mahler fit this time perfectly; the idea of emotional separation was palatable because it promised selfhood, independence, the identity we needed in our Dress for Success suits.

So long as this first generation of feminists in the workplace were on their own and single, Mahler was a champion. It was when these same women decided to become mothers that the theory of separation no longer worked for them. Holding their babies in their arms, they didn't want to hear about separation; they felt reunited with their own mothers. "Ah, so this is why she didn't want to let me go!" (Let me emphasize that Mahler never teaches us to abandon our own mothers; emotional separation doesn't require divorcing mother, or even confronting her.) This oneness, this symbiotic bliss they felt with their own babies, this was what mothering, womanliness, was all about, not competition or sexuality.

"As soon as I saw my daughter . . . and felt how much I wanted for her," one of these anti-Mahler women writes, "I knew that whatever my mother had done in her relationship with me, she did it out of love." Impossible. Nobody loves perfectly. To expect it of a mother, or to attempt to give it, is doomed. Love is imperfect. Most mothers do their best, but none is perfect, nor should they ask it of themselves. Immortalizing our mothers as perfect is a false monument, an impossible model to emulate. In this idealized image are buried mother's inevitable imperfections, little burials that we will resurrect and internalize as a way of forgiving her for her "imperfections": See, Mommy, I'm just like you, nagging, overly critical, possessive.

Women who blame everything that is wrong in women's world on men would set up a frightening new world in which we have projected all that is bad in women on to men; we are good, they are evil. Even as women compete with men and with one another in the workplace—which is inevitable—these women deny that they, the holy ones, are at all competitive. Only Bad Men compete. And only women can love. And on and on it goes, a battle plan that attempts to wrest from men as much economic and political power as possible while at the same time keeping daughters intimately tied to women, content to live in blissful oneness because to acknowledge anger at and competition with Mommy/women is as terrifying as death.

Women today don't need or require men, even in a family situation, as we once did. So, again, women write books against the idea of separating from their daughters, in which they blame men for inflicting the idea on women. "The relationship most essential to disrupt in order for Patriarchy to work is the relationship between mother and daughter," writes Shere Hite. "Mothers and daughters are not 'natural enemies' (competing for the father as Freud egotistically imagined), but 'natural' friends, as they have many things in common. If this relationship were unbroken, however, patriarchy could not continue, since all power would not be in the hands of men."

It is the ultimate power of control of a women's world, a matriarchy, that these women want; and they use the hated word *separation* as a battering ram against evil outsiders who would force women to face anger at one another and thus break up the world of women in which there are no fathers and no men. Statements like "Whatever my mother [did] with me, she did it out of love" now give the new mother who wrote these words permission to repeat with her daughter the same relationship she had with her own mother, in which everything she does, good and bad, can be said to be out of love.

Thus she betrays her daughter. By not letting her go, allowing her a private space in which to create her own boundaries, she will never know her self, never know the "someone" who can love and not just need another. Because healthy separation is so difficult to argue away, some women try to have it both ways; they write books about "separated attachments" and "connected autonomy," thus making the Semantic Jungle more impenetrable than ever.

In a world as disruptive as ours is today, where there is no constancy and nothing lasts or holds together, it feels more painful than ever to let go of someone. We fear for them and for ourselves too, alone. All the more reason for Mahler's theory of oneness and separation to be in place; a child can only be protected for a short period of time. Before the first year is over, safety must begin to be felt from the inside, a learned process of individuation best taught by the people who love the child most dearly. Without this gift, the child, the adult, is in jeopardy. Beware the Hallmark greeting cards that once again promote the idealization of motherhood.

Lest you think I am writing as the omniscient observer, let me say that in my first marriage I exemplified a woman raised without Mahler's internalized sureness of identity, who tried to find with men the symbiotic bliss I had never had with my mother. Had this thorny word *separation* been thrown at me, I would have laughed contemptuously. Did I not enter marriage as the most self-supporting, independent single girl in town? Had I ever let a man pay a penny for my rent? More than anything, my sexuality promoted me as Miss Autonomy.

He may not have been the first man to whom I surrendered myself, but my former husband was the first with whom I played house, making him the home base I'd never had as a child. Because he was the mother I'd never had, who adored only me, I remained in that marriage far longer than I should have. Having created Eden, I could not easily leave.

No sooner was I married than my look changed. It wasn't simply the more conservative dress and carefully coifed hair, both of which became more matronly without my consciously thinking it through. I carried myself less assertively too, shoulders not quite so thrown back, the chin down, rather like a nice lady cow. Let me add that my husband was not averse to the scenario; men may strut and posture, but many are surreptitiously looking for another mother too.

And in my way I was the good mother a man like him could live with. I bought his clothes, packed his suitcases, and, as my success as a writer grew, deflected praise, deferring to him as the "real" writer in the family. "Why don't you get into your success on a bigger scale?" an old friend once asked. But if I had let myself get bigger than my husband, who would have taken care of me?

So I handed him whatever money I made, at first refusing even to have my name on the checks. It was important that he take note of my smallness and dependence. That I eventually became the breadwinner in the family never altered my emotional picture of myself as the child and him as the mother, though I would never have consciously allowed myself such a description. "He never takes his eyes off you!" women friends would say enviously. I was getting what I always wanted, a mommy.

And he didn't ever look at another woman while we were together: Now I can see that more than anything, it was the prime characteristic that persuaded me to marry him. Oh, he was attractive, amusing, and an intellectual, but other men had these qualities; no, what he alone offered was something I'd first noticed when we were still dating other people. I had observed how closely he kept to his woman, never really "looking" at me or any other woman. Until I presented myself to him.

"He will never satisfy you," warned the man whom I was leaving him for.

How could that ex-lover understand that sex wasn't what I was looking for in marriage? Even I hadn't yet understood. Yes, I could overpower a man by seducing him, but he could then turn around and respond to another woman's sexuality. What I required was a man not driven by Eros, one who would see me as a prize and never, never look at another woman.

"How did I win you?" my husband would ask again and again.

He didn't. I chose him. I chose him knowing that once his gaze had taken me in, he would never leave. Ours was a marriage of togetherness wherein we were mother and child, attached, wary of being apart; like the one hand caressing the other, comforting but not exciting.

I remember being in a restaurant one night shortly after we were married. Two men sat at a table nearby, talking, smiling, looking at me. I was used to this, but then I heard one say, "Is she twenty or forty?"

Not until I became a writer did I understand how much my looks had changed once I was married; certainly, it had to do with an unconscious reunion with my mother. Equally frightening was the awareness that in marriage I had abandoned the spirited girl I'd invented for myself to make up for my invisibility in my mother's eyes; as a small child I found ways to get myself seen, picked up, and loved. As deftly as I had buried anxiety within my family behind the smiling mask of a charming kid, I was now burying that person I'd been all my life behind the guise of Sadie Sadie Married Lady, a very tense-looking woman indeed.

Some women don't require marriage to become their mothers; we look in the mirror, see little lines and a narrowing of our once full lips; we see aging that others don't yet see, the sagging skin, the ripples in our thighs. We are only twenty-five, still young, forever Mommy's girl and forever Mommy.

Giving Up the Idealization of Mother/Women

I write to free myself from nursery anger, to escape from the past so that I have more energy for love today, but when I get up from this table I will walk into the next room and before long lose myself again in one of the bewitching photos of my mother's family romance. Not my own, for there are no photos of us as children; as I've mentioned, there are no pictures of my father, so I've adopted my mother's family. I've been in love with pictures of them all my life; in these framed moments they are all very young, my beautiful grandmother whom I never knew and all of her children, my mother and her three sisters and brother. They hang on their mother's neck like puppies, they lean against her knee in their soft white clothes tied with wide sashes, droopy bows in their hair, a nimbus of absolute tranquility around them.

Even the tall, stern patriarch, my grandfather, sits in these idealized domestic scenes with his handsome head inclined toward the little boy in the sailor suit who sits on his knee.

An entire day, I've been told, went into Bachrach's immortalization of my family's romance, more than thirty beautifully matted sepia-toned photographs bound in a rich caramel leather album the size of a coffee table. As a child I would turn these pages with reverence, imagining myself in each of the rooms of the large house in which they lived until my grandmother died and my grandfather lost his fortune in the Depression. While it lasted, it must have been perfect.

But I knew it was not perfect at all. My grandmother was a resolute individual with a mind of her own. On my desk is a faded newspaper photo of her standing in an artist's smock beside her easel, on which rests a portrait of my aunt, one of her paintings then on exhibit at a gallery in town. My aunts tell tales of spaghetti dinners in her studio with her "bohemian" friends, while downstairs my grandfather entertained the steel barons of Pittsburgh. How much they idealized her after her death I will never know, but they have never spoken a critical word of her. In a way I wish they had, just to bring her down to human scale. As for my grandfather, well, he was a womanizer, loved beautiful women, and from the sound of it, pursued and bedded them. When my grandmother died, he subsequently married only compliant women, or at least they pretended meekness.

We are loath to abandon our family romances, and why not? Who wouldn't prefer to believe in perfect love, familial devotion passed from generation to generation, especially now, today, when the entire world seems so fractured and untrustworthy? Intellectually we may know that there is no such thing as the "maternal instinct"; we were well into the seventies when the tough message came down that mothers do not automatically love their babies at birth; a mother's feelings for her child hopefully grow into love over time. Nevertheless, we cling to the promise of "natural" mother love as tenaciously as we hold to the belief that a child is born loving its mother.

Is it a contradiction, this work I do to demystify the family romance even as I wax nostalgic for an easier, sweeter time, if only in Bachrach's lens? I don't think so. I've only come to appreciate what is in the silver frames since I became a writer. It is as if in coming to terms with what really exists between my mother and myself, I have sequentially found with each book that a layer of idealization gets stripped away; I am invariably rewarded with a reality I can live with far more gratefully than the illusion.

Now I choose to imitate only those parts of my mother that I admire, to look in the mirror and see something of her that gives me pleasure, to hear my voice on a tape recorder and recognize her laugh. I don't want her anxious look, her all-suffering tone on the telephone. Writing has taught me that I will only be able to imitate what I love if I first give up the fantasy of perfect love and the infantile rage at her for not being perfect.

It is all part of this business of separation, which in theory is accomplished in the first years of life, but which in fact continues all our lives long. Letting go of Mommy, abandoning the idea that we can change her, that she really loves us ideally is harder later on, but never without reward. It is why I write.

We become our mother, we say, because we love her. Then why do we take on the characteristics of hers that we liked the least? Real love, genuine love, requires two individuals consciously choosing to care, not out of need and fear but from a sense that this "other" expands our universe rather than simply making it safe.

Does the old adage still apply, that a man should take a good look at his future mother-in-law, for that is how his pretty young wife is going to turn out? Because women's lives today look different, because we go to an office and our own mothers stayed at home, which implies that we dress differently, behave differently than they did, because these relatively simple things have changed, we think we will not become them. Do not underestimate the power of that first relationship. Only a daughter raised with a sense of her own identity, lovingly encouraged to find it and wear it, will grow into a woman who can look uncritically into a piece of reflecting glass. Such a woman can say to her adult beloved, "I cannot live without you," and mean not that she would die without him but that life would be less without his dear presence.

My grandmother, standing at her easel, was no "domestic nun," but she wore, like all the women of the day, the stylish look of soft compliance demanded of a wife and mother; nevertheless, it must have grated. Hers is the look of attractive resignation my mother wore until recently. Did she give it up, or is it my vision of her that has changed? It is becoming a writer that has allowed me to see her as a woman and not as just my mother. Only when I learned to stop wanting the child's idealized relationship with her could I give up the halo that protected her from my rage. She's never looked better.

The idealization of women no longer even remotely defines how we women live, what we do, or how we look. Women's work today has become in large part how we look. It isn't as though we've had the family romance, wherein mother alone raised the children, for a long time. We've only been able, literally, to afford the modern family in the past few hundred years. In this morning's paper is a story of an infant cemetery recently unearthed in Rome. According to the archeologist at the dig, it was common practice in ancient Rome to discard unceremoniously the bodies of dead infants, who were not considered by the ancient Romans to be "worthwhile family members and should not be lamented much if they died."

Three, four hundred years ago, a maternal instinct was a luxury few could afford. A family was a working unit, bent on survival, children only useful if they lived long enough to till the soil or weave the cloth. Until the seventeenth century there was literally no childhood, no concept of it, no such person as a child; the word was simply used to express kinship. "Of all the characteristics in which the medieval age differs from the modern," wrote Barbara Tuchman, "none is so striking as the comparative absence of interest in children."

Children in medieval artworks were depicted as small adults, dwarfs, whose expressions and musculature were just like those of the taller, older people within the picture frame. In the real world of the Middle Ages, as soon as children were able to do without their mothers, they went immediately into the adult community.

Because life was tenuous and death among infants and children so ordinary, adults couldn't afford to invest them with emotion. The practice was to have as many children as possible in the hope that at least a few would survive to help support the family. The turning point was the moralization of society, beginning in the fifteenth century and conducted by churchmen, lawyers, and scholars, who taught that parents were "responsible before God for the souls, and indeed the bodies too, of their children. . . . The care expended on children inspired new feelings, a new emotional attitude, to which the iconography of the seventeenth century gave brilliant and insistent expression: the modern concept of the family." Our ancestors began to look like the morally responsible people we are used to seeing in portraits of subsequent years, taking their virtuous "look" from the respected role that gave them an identity.

Interestingly, it was the printing press, literacy, says Neil Postman, that "gave us our selves, as unique individuals, to think and talk about. And this intensified sense of self was the seed that led eventually to the flowering of childhood." It did not happen overnight. As late as the eighteenth century, mothers still routinely abandoned their children to orphanages and farmed out their infants to wet nurses, where their chances of survival were halved. It would require the economic surge of the Industrial Revolution to pay for the modern family as we know it. Until man's work moved from home and field into the factory and public sphere, there was no such concept as a separate domestic sphere. Only then was the idea born that a woman's primary job was to raise children alone at home, provided for by a man whose goal it was to earn as much money as possible for housing, food, and clothing for the family. Thus was born The Good Provider, which, before long, became the widely accepted definition of "masculinity." And you could recognize him from the appearance of his family, who "wore" his success.

The family romance was an economic luxury. The better provider a man was, the greater the security and stature in the community his family enjoyed. A nineteenth-century man expected his "household nun," his wife, to possess a saintliness that appeared to absolve him of the filth and corruption increasingly encountered in "big business." The vacuity in the portraits of the women's faces attested to their asexuality, and a certain complacency at having arrived at the only position to which a woman aspired. In some ways, the young adults in these centuries-old portraits resemble in set of chin and self-satisfaction the look of young parents in the fifties, when getting married on graduation day was a popular goal. Gone was the girlish, eager sexuality from high school photos just a year earlier, and in its place was a pretty young matron. It was what one did, how one looked, and it still is in many communities. Nor do I mean to trivialize it; in a world where women had no wealth, staying single too long was a gamble; looking "different" from all the nice young married women made a twenty-five-year-old female look in the mirror for the reassurance that she still had the looks to find a man before it was too late.

The idealization of mother and child gave women a sense of power and community opposite men, who controlled economic power. But putting women on a pedestal performed another, not insignificant, piece of work: The Madonna was desexualized, meaning that for the simple price of forfeiting a sexual mate, a man could rest, at peace in his office, miles from home, where he was unable to keep an eye on his woman, that untrustworthy sex known to be wantonly driven by insatiable lust unless neutered. It may have meant a dreary sex partner at home, but it guaranteed free child care, a housekeeper, and, besides, there were always lustful bad women, whores to be had for exciting sex. The Bad Women of the 1950s movies—Gloria Grahame, Marilyn Monroe, Jane Russell come to mind—could be separated on sight from the Goody Two-shoes like June Allyson. Blood-red lipstick, pointy bras (as my mother called them), ass-tight skirts, and eyes that looked at a man as if to undress him, these were the signature looks of women who didn't hold babies. And of course the men these women ran with, like Robert Mitchum, didn't look like patriarchs.

The economics of a paternalistic society dictated the structure of the family romance. The sharp division of labor separated a man from his child; after all, there was no need for a man in the nursery. Until now. Now the movement of women out of the home and into the workplace has created The New Economics, leaving a vacuum in the nursery. Women's roles have evolved to include anything a man can do, suggesting that men's roles might also evolve to enrich their lives and their children's. Many women don't have the luxury of being a Madonna, and some don't have the inclination, though many would die rather than abandon their post to a man; somehow it signifies forfeiting the most trusted definition of what a woman is.

And don't assume it is just women who want to keep men out of the nursery. Unlike the dramatic entry of women into the tough, grown-up world of business, the idea of men moving into women's traditional turf looks like abdication to many men; an army of sissy men surrendering their roles as real men, thus further weakening the trusted image of "a real man." In a speech before fellow Republicans, the candidate for governor of Minnesota proclaimed that men have a "genetic predisposition" to be heads of the household, obviously implying that women's "genetic predisposition" is where it has always been, caretaker of the hearth.

In a lighter vein, but still touching a nerve, a man ponders in a magazine article titled "Samurai Father," "Be it subtly, ostentatiously, debonairly, raucously, or downright obstreperously—a man's gotta swagger. But I submit to you, gentlemen, that it is not physically possible to swagger with a sleeping pink papoose slung across your chest. You just can't swagger in a Snugli."

The idealization of our modern family romance came to its fullest flower in the 1950s. Mother/daughter look-alike dresses captured the essence: We are as one, into which pretty portrait could be read that mother had devoted her life to her little girl who, in turn, would grow up and replay mother's life with her little girl. It never was a healthy idea, especially for the child, who was reminded externally of what she felt inside, that she was not a unique creature but was Mommy's double. There was a period of about twenty-five years, beginning in the seventies, when women were aggressively fixated on seeing themselves in the workplace and these symbiotic Siamese twins clothes were mothballed. They are back. Women's magazines abound with pictures of little girls dressed to look like Mommy, or is it the woman who has tired of the demanding workplace and wants to return to looking adorable, dependent, and innocent?

Many women have found the workplace less rewarding than they had hoped; those who are able to economically may opt to return home, but it is a new woman who enters the nursery after a stint in the workplace. She brings with her a cellular phone and a competitive muscle that obviously affects how she functions as a caretaker; the *Wall Street Journal* recently ran an article on returning moms who were running their car pools, PTAs, and cookie bake-offs with the same combative zeal they had shown at the office sales conference. Women are experts at competing even as we say we hate the word. Whatever the look of the new nursery, it isn't the 1950s.

The answer to the once amusing question bandied about at exclusive all-male clubs, "What do women want?" is, clearly, "Everything." Why then are men so silent, so seemingly unmoved by women's growing accusations that they are responsible for all of women's ills? Men's best tactic seems to be to hunker down and refuse to take women on, not unlike Dagwood and Desi Arnaz opposite Blondie and Lucille Ball; in their silence men are banking on the tradition of male stoicism. The War Between The Men and The Women rages on, and no one suffers more than the children.

I have been accused by angry Matriarchal Feminists of being too soft on men, too much in love with them and, by extension, unsympathetic to women's hard times. I will not defend my own feminist credentials; my books speak for themselves. I do not light up for all men, but if there is a light in my window, it has been there all my life. When you grow up without a father, you never stop being hungry for a man.

And some men never stop being hungry for a part of themselves, their feminine side that they jettisoned years ago, when the narrow definition of manhood called. Just as I learned to stifle my aggressive, outspoken side, these men smothered their "softness" with bullying tactics or silence. Fatherhood could be the opportunity for men to regain their compassionate selves. Not all men are born with the heart of a caretaker, but neither are all women. Nevertheless, we expect women automatically to become maternal once they give birth, just as we expect men to be good providers. Well, the workplace is over-crowded, and the nursery too empty. It's time to shuffle the deck and re-deal assignments, each given to what he or she does best with the child, the first priority.

Overworked as women may be, they will not easily relinquish the nursery role. And though many deny it vehemently, on some level they know that she who bears and raises the human race plays the most powerful role in all of human life. The prospect of giving men parity in the nursery, of seeing some men doing "women's work" as well as they, is intolerable.

Without thinking it through—and I do not believe there has been a conscious secret strategy—the oldest, most infallible tactic is employed to ensure women's monopoly of what has always been ours: Idealize women. Keep woman on that pedestal with a baby in her arms, deny ill feeling and competition between women, and blame men for all that is awry in the world.

The nursery may still stand as women's turf, but I see hope for the fatherless child from an unlikely quarter: the emergence of the female fullback, a.k.a. the corporate killer. Take the story in this morning's paper, the profile of an obnoxiously loud and aggressive, highly suc-cessful woman in publishing. If a woman can do the nasty business of the most cutthroat and mercenary men, surely we must accept the corollary that a father can be as good a caretaker as any woman. As more of this type of female hell-raiser gain political office, they throw their weight around, bully, destroy, even call armies to war. In sum, they act like men.

I embraced Christina Hoff Sommers's book, *Who Stole Feminism?*, for its rogues gallery of self-aggrandizing women nefariously hacking their way into profitable areas where they can control as omnipotently as any male dictator. This is life as it is today. "Covert operations," "dirty tricks," "plumbers," and "misinformation," all familiar terms from the world of Bad Men, today appropriately belong in modern feminism. It is a relief to have some female villains exposed by other women. Sommers's book opened a window, clearing the air briefly with a gust of fine research on the holy sisterhood; in retaliation, they campaigned to cancel her scheduled appearances to promote her book on television talk shows.

No less telling, a spate of "Mommy horror movies" has appeared, which I doubt would have found their audience ten years ago. In *Serial Mom* Kathleen Turner got big laughs for killing people who didn't recycle their garbage, and Roseanne, who is quoted in the *New Yorker* saying, "I think women should be more violent, kill more of their husbands," well, from the millions she earns it is clear that half of America sees themselves or their wives/mothers in an angry/loud, aggressive mom. Caught in the throes of her own dark scandal, Whitewater, Hillary Rodham Clinton might as well be starring in a made-for-television movie.

What is fascinating is that all these seismic energies coexist today, and without much public comment. Few men criticize the wildly contradictory forces within feminism. Perhaps men think women will self-destruct. Perhaps they are afraid of these giantesses; I often am. But I grow impatient with men; their children are on the line. "Damn it," I want to yell at them, "do something!"

No role cries out for men's involvement more than that of a father involved in his child's life, from conception on. Unsure that they are qualified, reluctant to interfere without the heartfelt invitation from the "natural" caretaker, men hover at the door of the nursery.

Life changes nowadays at the rate of geometric progression. Who, for instance, would have imagined twenty years ago that so many "deadbeat dads" would run out on their families, or that so many women would consciously decide, before conception, to leave men out of their child's life? One does affect the other. My point is this: We must agree on what is best for the child, for we adults are in flux, seemingly out of control in our relationships with one another.

Psychologist Penelope Leach—England's answer to Spock and Berry Brazelton—lays it on the line: "Babies and young children have to be cared for by committed adults in suitable environments for twenty-four hours of every day. Society expects all able-bodied citizens of working age to earn the money they need and the satisfaction they crave at specialized all-day jobs in special, distant and unsuitable places. People cannot be in two places at once; ergo one person cannot be simultaneously a solvent, self-respecting citizen and an actively caring parent."

Nothing has changed my own life more than the absence of my father. I sometimes think of myself as the first "sperm bank" baby. It was the most constant deprivation I have known, a void that has alternately pushed me forward and held me back, always off balance. Because he was "the great secret," I obediently did what children who want to please Mommy do: I protected my mother and her secret. It would be years, decades, before I dared to allow myself to think about him. Writing books allowed me to do it, to think about "the secret," about how much I have missed him, about what it would have been like to have had a father. A child wants the feel of the man and the woman who make up his genetic bank, a mother and father to send him on his journey, no, not send, for the baby will go and go better and farther with the unconditional love of two parents. An ideal? Well, women in the workplace was an ideal. Things change. Evolution.

Men in the Nursery

The final decision on beauty, the judgment of Paris, belongs to women, not to men who cannot see us as critically as another woman. Her eyes will look for flaws we know are there, something we never have been able to get quite right. Men don't know how to look, really look. Weren't the judgments most critical to our lives the appraisals of another woman? Wasn't it her eye that never said, "Go, my darling, you are perfect just as you are!"

At the beginning of life, had there been a father whose eyes reflected us, we would believe men today. Had his arms held us, his eyes looking into ours as he fed us, his hands bathed us, his voice sung to us and scolded us too so that we saw him as both good and bad, men's eyes would genuinely be the trusted mirrors.

For whom do women dress? Did you ever doubt the answer?

Without a father in the nursery, mothers'/women's eyes are omnipotent. If she didn't see in us something she loved, some feature, curl of hair, length of torso, we felt inadequate, worse, invisible in her world, which was *the* world. It was her total control of us in her nursery that was monitored by her omnipresent eye—not unlike the electronic, sensory eye that watches a house, seeing everything—her power to come and go at will, to feed us, warm us, or not. Eventually, in our symbiotic oneness with her we internalize her eye, meaning that we carry her judgments with us. Her sense of right and wrong becomes our conscience. When we eventually join the world of "other girls," their eyes will own women's decisions on beauty and all else too, for other women take mother's place in the mirror. Their eyes follow, control, and judge us. When "the girls" leave us out, when they whisper and look at us critically, their looks cut: Something is terribly wrong, and it goes beyond how we look, to the very core of our being. We are terrified by exclusion from the Group Gaze, as disoriented as when mother didn't see us.

"It has often been said that woman dresses to inspire jealousy in other women," remarked Simone de Beauvoir, "and such jealousy is in fact a clear sign of success." In the absence of men's eyes in the nursery, we learn our sureness of the tyranny of beauty from other women, a disadvantage we can no longer afford. Women's move into the workplace is the greatest "image change" for women in history and, by extension, for men too. Obviously, our self-image, like our self-esteem, goes beyond surface appearance to what we do, how we act, think about, and see ourselves, consciously and unconsciously. Having moved outside the home into a more complex relationship with men, how much more in focus our picture of ourselves would be if a man had raised us, along with mother, from the beginning. Need I add how helpful it would also be for men to have another man around from the beginning, a man's eyes as well as a woman's mirroring them, loving them? The single-sex nursery was never perfect, but stood inviolate opposite the single-sex workplace.

As if on cue, "The New Fatherhood"—as it was titled in a *Time* magazine cover story—has grown into a powerful voice. Unfortunately, this is not like feminism's cross-cultural, cross-sexual revolution. Who could argue that women had a right to an equal wage? This "fatherhood" army remains mostly on paper, a body of research by psychologists, psychiatrists, child care professionals, writers, fathers, and, yes, thank God, some women too. Rightness is on their side, but mass public opinion/sentiment is against them. Why doesn't it feel as "right" having men in the nursery as it does having women in the workplace?

There is an impressive library on what we *know* fathers bring to their children's lives, and it grows steadily. Let us begin with Grandfather Spock, who abridged his original 1933 advice, ". . . fathers . . . get gooseflesh at the very idea of helping to take care of a baby," to read in 1993, "The father—any father—should be sharing with the mother the day-to-day care of their child from birth onward. . . . This is the natural way for the father to start the relationship, just as it is for the mother."

We *know* from scientific studies that fathers, just like mothers, have prebirth fantasies of their children, that they get morning sickness, that today 90 percent of them are present in the delivery room when their children are born, that they are elated at the presentation of their newborns, that fathers are able to bottle-feed their babies as efficiently and effectively as mothers, regardless of how much experience the fathers have with infants; we also know that fathers find their babies more beautiful than any other, that they see them as perfect, feel drawn to "their" baby like a magnet, that men automatically speak to their infants in a falsetto voice without being told that babies respond more to higher voices than the lower-pitched.

"Contrary to the notion of a maternal instinct," says psychologist Michael Lamb, "parenting skills are usually acquired 'on the job' by both mothers and fathers." As for the fathers, "They feel different, swept away, overwhelmed by their feelings, their self-esteem enormously increased," says psychiatrist Martin Greenberg. Obviously, there are some fathers who cannot or will not form a tight relationship with their infants, but there have always been mothers unable or unwilling to do the same. We simply didn't want to abandon our dream of a maternal instinct, one inherent in the idealized mother.

Given what we now know fathers can bring to their children's lives, why do we not turn the world upside down to make it a given that the father is expected to be as involved in his child's life as the mother? Why doesn't society rush to materialize what has been proven: that babies and fathers bring to each other a missing piece of the puzzle?

I remember the first time I heard of women deciding to have children on their own, intentionally, without a man involved in the child's life. It was early spring, close to fifteen years ago, and I was sitting in the kitchen, drinking coffee, reading the paper, when I saw a full-page article with the photos of women holding their babies. I thought it was a love story and dove in.

I can't remember if I was more shocked or confused. Why would a woman do this to a child and why would the *New York Times* print such an article as if it were just another family story? The impression that article left with me has never diminished. As early as it was that morning, I telephoned a woman friend, a therapist, so fair in her judgments that I was staggered by her easy reply: "Oh, sure, I've several women patients who have decided to do the same thing." And then, when there was no response from me, "Nancy, women are entitled to have babies."

"But aren't children entitled to have fathers?" I blurted out, something I would repeat again and again until I learned to hold my peace as some of my dearest women friends decided to make the same, increasingly popular choice.

Even when fathers are a part of the family, something more granite than our resistance to women entering the workplace keeps us from wanting men in the nursery: It is much more revolutionary to couple a man with his baby. In a world that loses constancy daily, we can accept a woman at the head of a conference table in an office with far more comfort than we can imagine her husband at home, holding the baby in his arms, their eyes locked in Mutual Gaze. Why, we can look at a transvestite with more equilibrium than we can at a man changing diapers in the men's room, or leaving his job for a year to be with his infant son. Men know this.

"Society sends men two messages," says psychologist Jerrold Lee Shapiro, father of two and author of three books on fatherhood. "The first is, We want you to be involved, but you'll be an inadequate mother. The second is, You're invited into the birthing room and into the nurturing process—but we don't want all of you. We only want your support. We're not really ready as a culture to accept men's fears, their anger or their sadness. This is the stuff that makes men crazy. We want men to be the protectors and providers, but we are scared they won't be if they become soft."

Even if the mother isn't there half the time, or doesn't enjoy mothering as much as work outside the home, and/or she isn't good at it, the nursery remains women's inviolate territory. If the baby responds to the father as lovingly and automatically as to her, then who is she, given the definition of womanliness in almost all cultures as "caretaker"?

Change on the deepest, unconscious level involving feelings that we got from our parents, which they got from theirs, these gut feelings change over generations, if they change at all. First, attitude and behavior have to change, words spoken, acts repeated again and again before the unconscious shifts. Can you think of anything more deeply ingrained than the nursery belonging to women who have the womb, breasts, all the equipment? Even if the image of men raising children doesn't feel right intellectually, doesn't look right in the balloon over our heads, we have to stick with it; eventually a new image will evolve, an image in which he looks as appropriate and comfortable feeding and holding a baby as a woman does in an office.

Close to fifteen years ago in an interview with Berry Brazelton, I remember asking, "How are we going to get more men into the nursery given women's reluctance to make them anything more than lieutenants rather than equal caretakers?"

"You must say it again and again in a strong voice," he replied.

Very well, we must hammer away at it until that deep, not-so-unconscious image of man is altered to include empathic caretaker. If it still sticks in our craw, consider that studies indicate that men involved in the early care of their children are far less likely to become abusive.

As it is, 27 percent of all children now live without a father—up from 12 percent in 1970. "In the most perfect of single-parent households," says American Association of Sex Educators, Counselors and Therapists (ASECT) president Judith Seifer, "there is no way that a child will be as well-equipped to go out into the world and function as an adult, as he is in a two-parent household. It is an extraordinarily selfish decision on the part of the person—male or female—who chooses to be a single parent."

In a report released in 1994, it was noted that "nearly one-fourth of all American infants and toddlers live in poverty . . . [that] children in single-parent households . . . are more likely to experience behavioral and emotional problems"; even though mounting scientific evidence indicates that children's environments, from birth to age three, help determine their brain structure and ability to learn.

The most powerful force working against men getting equal emotional responsibility in the nursery is the invisible but impenetrable refusal we all feel in giving up our image of father/man as unyielding. No one says to a woman, "Prove you're a woman." Born female, we are complete in our gender. But for men, proving their manliness is a lifetime job, meaning that it can be forfeited if the beach isn't taken, if they don't bite the bullet or bring home the bacon. Men are fully aware of how society sees the man who takes advantage of his company's parental leave program. His fellow workers may slap him on the back and tell him he's doing a fine thing, but there is the unspoken belief that a man who leaves his post, even for his child, is less of a man. His associates will not be thrilled that they must now shoulder the responsibility for his work, and his vacated desk will be fought over by everyone beneath him on the corporate ladder.

Because it wasn't how you and I were raised, the image of a man feeding an infant from a bottle the same distance from dad's eyes as the breast would be (if the breast were there instead of mother sitting in an office, bringing home the bacon), well, we can accept the woman in the office much, much more readily than we can live with this soft-focus man. We must acknowledge how loath we are to relinquish our image of "man the conqueror" before anything of any consequence changes in the understaffed nursery. The not-so-unconscious pressures to keep men distanced from "women's work" are winning a contest that disenfranchises children and, by extension, society.

The competitive corporate world, as it exists, has no tolerance for parental leave programs, especially for men. "What [fathers] are hearing, from their bosses, from institutions, from the culture around them, even from their own wives," says the *Time* article on fatherhood, "very often comes down to a devastating message: We don't really trust men to be parents, and we don't really need them to be."

Does it come as any great surprise that the corporate culture clashes with the notion of family leave, especially for men? In 1992, *Child* magazine tracked father-friendly companies, but so few qualified, or even cared, that the magazine dropped the survey the next year. And when Yale psychiatrist Kyle Pruett addresses women's groups and fundamentalist Christian groups, he is roundly criticized for attempting to usurp the "natural" place of women in the nursery.

Most women want what is best for their children. They do not belong to the political women's world, but they are nonetheless reluctant to see men taking from them a role that they and their mothers shared. They would never cheat their own child, but in the same study that showed a majority of men wanting to be more involved in child-rearing, between 60 and 80 percent of the women surveyed said they did not want their husbands more involved in child-rearing than they already were.

Ambivalence. When women work outside the home and it becomes essential for the husband to be the caretaker, even though they have agreed on their roles, many women remain conflicted. "[My husband] and I have a balance so far because I've been breast-feeding," one mother confides. "But it's going to be harder when I stop."

It is difficult to give up or even share a role as powerful as raising members of the human race. Until now, we have always chosen to read the mother's role as one more of sacrifice than power. Well, men want some of that power too, and they are willing to make the sacrifice.

The argument isn't whether men have or don't have nurturing qualifications, whether they can care for a baby as well as women. That has been proven. The issue is that we can afford to abandon the traditional womanly-looking mothers/women to the competitive workplace far more easily than we can part with our fantasy of Big Daddy. I sometimes think that his not having been emotionally present in our early lives has allowed us to cling to our exaggerated vision of fathers/men. And father is nowhere more opposite mother than in his genital erection.

Dependent as we were on mother for everything, we could not afford to show her or to admit to ourselves the other side of our love, which was rage. But father can take it; father is big, tough; his granite-hard look is impervious to our anger. Tough-looking men keep us sane, and mother—whom we can't afford to lose—safe from us. A man can take all that fury that our first enemy, who had all the power in the world, couldn't. What would we do if men lost their hard selves, their erections? We would have to deal with the rage at its original source.

We would send our men to fight and die in a foreign country, and they would go, more readily than we would see them enter the nursery. On some level we know that the current disintegration of society has something to do with women's movement into the workplace and the subsequent lack of child care in the home. Our queasiness with the image of men doing women's work isn't all that far from consciousness. How interesting that the look of a man with a papoose is more upsetting than that of the corporate female captain, she who orders men around, makes big money, and is as tough as nails. But this is precisely what I mean: The big, bossy woman in the workplace is intimately familiar. In her tyranny she reminds us of the Giantess of The Nursery. To keep ourselves safe from her, and her from us, we need a monolith, a Schwarzenegger; lately he has also become the dumping ground for all of feminism's complaints: Bad men! Where would women put their bile if men's look mellowed?

Today it seems inevitable when another *New York Times* article announces, "Pregnant Teenagers Are Outcasts No Longer." And there is the photo of an adolescent girl feeding another child, her baby, and in the text, "Today, pregnant teenagers are even beginning to be viewed by some of their peers as role models." Have we gone mad? Certainly no pregnant girl should be ostracized, but glorified, a "role model"?

As with the story fifteen years earlier—which I couldn't help feeling had contributed to this one—I wondered, Where is the public outcry? Shouldn't a child have a chance for a father as well as a mother? The irony is that even as this adolescent girl's place in society worsens, we continue to present this image in the press and on television of the single mother as part of life as usual, while a father is extraneous.

"The women who try it alone come eventually to the realization of the need for a man," Berry Brazelton told me years ago. "If you can help them see that nurturing had better be a shared proposition, they often come to it in time to save the child, which is my goal. It's one thing for a woman to want a child all her own, but I get worried about the kids. 'What do I tell my little girl about her father?' a mother with a three-year-old asked me. 'What?' I said in amazement. 'I know a little girl needs a fantasy of a father,' she said. 'She certainly does!' I replied. 'Do I make one up?' she asked. And I replied, 'I think you ought to find out about the father, let her know enough about him and at least give her some idea of why she's different from everybody else.' And the woman said, 'You know, I never wanted a man at all, so when I went to get inseminated I told them not to tell me anything about the father.'"

When I was growing up, I never knew another child without a father. I told myself that it didn't matter. I had to.

The mysterious absence of my father, I am sure, also has much to do with why I choose to write about forbidden subjects. My husband jokes that my epitaph will read, "What does it all mean?" Well, what does it mean, this idealization of mothers without husbands, women who choose to leave men out of the act of procreation? Do we think this has nothing to do with men's anger today, or with the move to center stage of looks/fashion/the model as an icon, men's decision to get their share of beauty power? It is all of a piece.

On their own, most men will not enter the nursery to help raise their children without their wives' approval. If ever there was a feminist issue, this should be it: to give a child a chance at having two involved parents, two adults who work out the warring issues between themselves instead of idealizing themselves and their individual adult rights over those of the child. Instead of drawing up ever longer lists of crimes committed by men against women, we should be asking, Why? Why do men commit these crimes of which they are accused? Why are men so angry, and what is the origin of a rage that makes them abuse women and children? These men are our fathers, husbands, lovers, friends, the seed of our children. Men can't/won't ask these questions of themselves (nor do we women ask how many of the same crimes we ourselves commit, and how much we contribute to the fury that drives a man to crime).

Perhaps stoic silence is the last shred of what being a man means in this day of "women who hate men." Perhaps men's reluctance to defend themselves against women's accusations is what my husband called his own "Jell-O defense," opposite the angry women who entered his office to harangue—they would scream, shout, then cry; he would sit, nod, and then they left.

Men don't write much about their pain and anger at competing with and losing to women in the workplace. This is the area in which men traditionally prove themselves. Their fathers never had to compete with and lose to a woman, not here. Nor were their fathers consistently accused of the litany of crimes women today say men commit against them. If men were accusing women of harassment, child abuse, and rape—and some rightfully could—there would be a furious chorus of women defending themselves in emotional, articulate voices. The few male voices who have spoken up against anti-male feminists sound as lonely as moose calls; a "real man" just doesn't join in.

My feeling is that as more men realize what they are losing, this is changing. The pioneers in the men's rights movement require steely backbones, for they are on tenuous ground and nowhere so much as in the issue of child care. Even when the woman cries, "I need you!" to her husband, when he enters and holds the baby, she criticizes. He wants to demand that she treat him as an equal, but in the nursery, her critical voice reminds him of another woman, the mother who dominated him. So he leaves.

How good it would be for the man as well to hold his child, to be reunited with the tender part of himself most men have forgotten how to express. Just as women in the workplace have reacquired skills and talents lost in adolescence, men can find the missing part of themselves in caring for a child. Given the man's independence and resilience, already practiced for a lifetime, he will be a fine teacher of loving separation for his child. Studies have already found that fathers do not hover over their small child's eager desire to explore the world as closely as mothers do; father watches, encourages, but does not transmit a mother's anxiety.

By the nature of their lives, men are already equipped to encourage the process of maneuvering out of and away from the loving arms that hold a baby; they do not see danger where it doesn't exist. Father's own mother may have tried to keep him close forever, but because he was male, she was reluctant to discourage his tentative moves away from her. Which is precisely how separation, The Second Birth, begins: an exploratory crawl into the next room, powered by a baby's curiosity about his or her life. The more bountiful the blissfully symbiotic union, the more eager the baby is to move on.

"Fathers bring a different kind of nurturing to a child, which complements the mother's," says Shirley Hanson, professor of family nursing at Oregon Health Scientists University. "Where women tend to cuddle and hold the child close, fathers play more psycho-motor kinds of activities, toss the kids up in the air, then put them on the ground and step them, help them walk, use their legs, move out and into the next room. They broaden the child's horizon in this way. They enhance a child's physical, social, and mental growth and development. This playfulness adds a different dimension than women bring. A mother is actually more able to fulfill her potential with a father present."

I doubt that most women would call their decision to control procreation and caretaking "competitive," for we have been raised to deny the emotion even as we feel it. Oh, yes, I would definitely call it competition, this angry denunciation of men, the desire to create a matriarchy in which women will continue their competition with one another, calling it, you can be sure, by some other name.

Competition begins early in a child's life. Not all men carry it to deadly limits, but they do know the rules of how to win and lose, which many women haven't yet learned. What takes the fear out of life and opens the heart to the larger adventure is practicing, until the sureness is internalized, separation with the two most loved and important people in our lives. "I can have my own life and the unconditional love of my parents too. It is not either/or. I know this because from the very beginning I have practiced these moves away from them and into my own identity again and again. Creating my self has never felt like the loss of them. This knowledge is money in the bank for my life's journey."

I see my relationship with my mother nowhere as clearly as when I write about sex, where I am faced with what she taught me silently, without saying the words: Sex is dirty, bad, my genitals ugly and unacceptable. Her mother taught it to her just as mothers and daughters today continue the legacy of The Cloaca, which is Latin for sewer. This lesson of The Cloaca begins in the earliest communication between mother and child and is the hardest image for women to unlearn. Mothers don't have to speak to communicate. But the unmentionable Cloaca is part of the emotional glue that keeps us from separating into our own safe selves; every time we part our legs, no, every time we even think of sex, the image of our own unappetizing parts comes alive as a negative, uneasy feeling. Imagine. After all my writing about sex, the inherited taint of The Cloaca remains.

Oh, Dad, poor Dad, would that you had been there! Would that a loving man in that first precious year of life, which never gets a rewrite, had communicated to me men's far more liberal and healthy attitude toward genitals. Isn't this dirty place that will never be prettified at the root of women's conviction that our faces and the rest of our bodies too are never lovely enough?

If my fears of being abandoned turn up at night in my dreams, this repugnance for what lies between my legs is fodder for my daytime fantasies, those erotic plots that get their energy from defying my mother/woman's rules against that forbidden, foul little area between my legs. In my sexual fantasies, men overwhelm women's legacy by adoring what they see.

Knowing men, loving them, how can I not wish one of them had bathed me, kept me clean, toilet trained me, and passed on his opinion of genitals from day one? If a man's eyes and loving hands had given me my first preverbal sense of self, if as an infant there had been no disruption in the harmony between us because there was a part of my body whose emissions offended, surely I would have grown to be a woman who had a good enough opinion of her genitals. For this reason as much as any other, and because I wholeheartedly believe that women's lifelong unhappiness about appearance lodges here, between our legs, I would wish for every child a father as intimately involved as a mother. We know that babies' tiny hands finger their genitals, that area that responds so pleasantly to touch. Why do I think that fathers would be less likely to take the little hand away; not all men, not all the time, but *less likely* to make disapproving noises and wrinkle their noses, thus turning the loving, open face into an anxious, less symmetrically pleasant one?

There is no scientific study, not yet, that I can locate that indicates that a man would be more open than a woman to a baby learning that it is all right to touch himself or herself. When that study is done, it will be a fine argument for bringing men into the earliest caretaking. When we love our genitals, we are more likely to love ourselves, to respect and take care of our sexual parts. In an age when sex and death are spoken of in a single breath, how can we not see father as a lifesaver?

We may not consciously remember infancy, but on some level we "know" certain things. We have been collecting pictures and sensations since we were born. Even before toilet training has taught us what others think of our success or failure at controlling emissions, we have been reading the eyes of those who take us in, felt in their hands and heard in their voices precisely how they feel about that area between our legs; they, being our whole universe, will decide what we in time will also think.

Who can argue with the opportunity to give children a healthier picture of their genitals? If we love our bodies, we will take care of them, be responsible. If we grow up feeling that there is something wrong with what lies between our legs, we will not just see that place as repugnant, a sewer, The Cloaca that we can never make beautiful, but we will assume that like the ugly birthmark on a leg or arm, this is what people see when they look at us. The original ugliness is, of course, displaced; one day it is our hair, the next our weight or fat arms—but the scar, the disfigurement, the memory of it never goes away. No matter what we do with makeup or surgery, we imagine the eye of the beholder seeing and rejecting the lifelong source of our own happiness about beauty.

We adults like to think that we have carte blanche in the nursery; what does a tiny baby know/remember about our feelings regarding genitals and their functions and excretions? According to UCLA psychiatrist Daniel Siegel, an infant's brain is not physically able to form *explicit* memories until the age of three years, mostly because the hippocampus, where such memories are stored, is not fully developed until that time. Explicit memories are those you can tell someone about; you're aware that you are remembering when you think of them. But *implicit* memories begin forming at day one of life, and remain with us our whole lives because they are stored all over the brain. Implicit memories are those you don't remember learning and are not conscious of remembering, as with using a spoon. Emotions, how our parents reacted to us, whether they enjoyed us, the model of who we are with others are all implicit memories.

"Our implicit memories are based on our experiences with our earliest attachment figures and are fundamental to the way we continue to experience ourselves as we grow," says Siegel. "We may not have the capacity to be aware of what these internal representations are, but they are always, always, always affecting how we experience life and how we are judging the world. These earliest memories are the filter through which we perceive the whole world, the human experience of reality. They are that fundamental."

Lessons in body love, or loathing, begin at the beginning. Woman born of woman is not a good teacher, especially in that area where she has been taught to deodorize, to treat as an offensive necessity. As erotically aggressive as the New Woman may appear in her leather bikini, paratrooper boots, and little else, she still carries the passport photo imprinted in the first years of life: the implicit memory of her sexual self in her mother's eyes. Did her mother love her own genitals as well as her lovely hair, face, hands? When she looked at her tiny daughter's body, did she smile at the dear sight of the tiny cleft between her legs; or did the look and smell of it shift her gaze away, make her shoulders rigid and elicit a clicking of tongue against teeth? And if some men grow up to be overly penis proud, is it in part a reaction to the disapproval of the first and most important person in their lives? "Very well, if this part of me that distinguishes me as different from you offends you, then I shall flaunt it as my flag, my weapon!"

The average father may not love the soaking diapers, the vomit, a little body smeared in its own excrement, but he is less likely to make a terrible face and take in his breath in disapproving tsk-tsks, thus giving baby a bedrock impression of the value of the natural function of genitals. We are not born hating the smell of shit, sweat, the look of penis and vagina; it is all learned.

Men bring to the nursery a respite from absolute cleanliness, the every hair in place obsessions more characteristic of women; father is less likely to be constantly straightening the little garment, cleaning hands and knees dirtied in the effort to stretch, walk, move. Even if I am only partly correct in this, isn't it worth solving the existing problems of getting men into the nursery to have a generation of women grow up who aren't besotted with cleanliness, odors, feminine humiliation, all of which boil down to an obsession with looks?

The entire world is raised on women's attitudes regarding genitals. By the time we lie down together, our feelings about sex, our image of our partner's genitals and our own will have grown from the seed a woman planted. Oh, these pictures will in time be modified by our rebellion, influenced hopefully by healthy education, but it will all be in reaction to the first years of life. Wouldn't it be a terrible disservice to raise another generation of women as uncharitable about the poor vagina as we?

So long as "it" is dirty, we will never believe in whatever beauty we possess. We will always find fault with the shape of our nose, the breasts, the thighs. Things will never be right so long as that one thing is "wrong." The ugliness between our legs is a lifelong reminder of our failure at beauty, a defeat that sets us in competition with all other women whom we suspect have mastered the art of beauty better than we, a rivalrous loss that goes back to the beginning of time and which we refuse, according to Women's Rules, ever to acknowledge.

A father who does not see women's bodies as dirty is the ideal candidate to break this generational curse among women.

"One of the most dramatic findings in the research into father infant care is its relationships to subsequent sexual abuse of children," writes Kyle Pruett. "Whether the child is the father's or someone else's, if a man is involved in the physical care of his child before the age of three, there is a dramatic reduction in the probability that that man will be involved later in life in sexual abuse of children in general as well as his own. The humanization of both father and child inherent in such activity erects a strong barrier against later exploitation of that intimacy."

From the moment we are born, finding home in father's arms, seeing ourselves in his eyes, the first impression of "beauty" will be learned in part as his touch, his smell, his voice, musculature, as well as a woman's. With this beginning, a female child might grow up to believe in men's words of praise, men's vision of their beauty, and not rely totally on the opinion of other women. As for a son, a boy would take in from his father an essence of maleness as beautiful, having seen himself thus in that first man's eyes. He would not have to run from woman/mother in order to prove his maleness, to get away from the Giantess; and when he grew to be a man, he would not have to acquire beauty through a woman he wore on his arm, in turn disparaging her for having such power over him, for as far back as he could remember, power was shared.

Today men move steadily into beauty, reclaiming a share of it in reaction to women's movement onto their traditional turf, the workplace. How much more agreeable men's reentry into the mirror will be, how much less anxiety and rivalry women will feel opposite men if, from the beginning, both sexes found an estimable self-image in the eyes of both a man and a woman.

2

Envy

═══

The Dark Side of Beauty

Mother basks in the admiration lavished on her newborn baby.
The tiny person is a miracle, still feels a part of her, therefore praise of
the baby's beauty spills over onto her, drawing her even closer, which
is good, given the child's total dependency.

"What a beautiful baby!" strangers on the street cry, and still
mother smiles, understanding their awe of her baby's beauty. Until one
day—a day like any other—she stops smiling and verbally puts herself
between the admirer and her baby. "Oh, but he cries a great deal," she
says, her words deflecting the praise away from her child. Why? If
beauty is baby's ticket to survival, why interfere with its acknowledgment? Because admiration, especially admiration of beauty, can
quickly turn to envy.

Envy is pernicious; it seeks to destroy the object of admiration.
How then to protect the baby? "Kenehore," the Jewish mother murmurs, the ancient mantra against envy when too many compliments
fly in her vulnerable baby's direction. This is a modern mother, someone who runs an office as well as her home. She didn't learn to say this
at Lamaze, hadn't consciously planned to say it. Perhaps it came spon-

taneously, out of an unconscious memory of her own mother, a feeling as primal as throwing her body over her child to protect him from an oncoming truck.

"Instinctively you know that too much admiration will bring bad things," says my friend Catherine, whose young son is exceptionally beautiful. "You feel threatened." She warms when heads turn to admire her boy on the street, for she is accustomed to being praised for her own beauty. A career woman of great ambition before she decided to become a single mother, it is as if she intentionally decided to keep the weight she has put on during pregnancy, as if, I suggest to her, "it would be excessive, too much beauty, if both of you were eye-stopping." Without a blush, she concurs. Recently she allowed a lover to sleep over; it was the first time a man had shared her bed since her son's birth. The next morning the boy broke his arm and replaced the intruder in his mother's bed. "We don't need him," he told her.

Malocchio is the Italian expression for "the evil eye," which cannot stand another's good fortune and projects misadventure onto the envied object. For centuries, cultures have had their respective rituals and potions to keep the admiring eye from souring, from going from praise to poison. So much rests on the need to be seen and nourished by an appreciative eye, but even in the process of visual regard, the admired one senses danger, a delicate line between desire and destruction; as for the hungry eye, at what point does the pleasure of regarding beauty turn to resentment that the power is not within ourselves, but is without? In the very process of absorbing beauty, we despair that we can only borrow and not own. The eye seeks to destroy what it loves most.

Nothing defines our badness more precisely than envy; the loss of innocence is in us all. Eve "saw that the tree was good for food, and that it was a delight to the eyes." When she and Adam had eaten the fruit, "the eyes of both were opened, and they knew that they were naked."

Nothing good can be said of envy, that meanness of spirit which describes the convoluted influence of beauty on our lives, especially women's, for whom beauty has been our traditional source of power. Life around us changes at the rate of geometric progression, but the deeply entrenched rituals surrounding beauty's uses and abuses do not disappear in a mere thirty years of social and economic upheaval. The laws surrounding beauty's power and the envy of it are as timeless as the stones on Easter Island.

Bringing envy into this discussion stiffens my spine in apprehension, and my resolve too, for nasty envy is the most spoiling emotion in life and is at the very heart of this book. If I can persuade you how beauty inspires envy and then how resentment sucks all the joy out of beauty, I will have accomplished something that is not easy for me, for I have envied nothing more in life than beauty, envied it in others and never believed in a bit of what I might have owned; to have enjoyed my own would have invited the spiteful envy of others, or so I feared. It is not a pretty statement to make about oneself, not ladylike or feminist, but it does describe my territorial claim to this subject, for which my earlier books prepared me.

I may not be as evil as the villainous Claggart in Melville's *Billy Budd*, but I nod my head when I read of him: "did ever anybody seriously confess to envy? Something there is in it universally felt to be more shameful than even felonious crime. And not only does everybody disown it, but the better sort are inclined to incredulity when it is in earnest imputed to an intelligent man. But since its lodgment is in the heart, not the brain, no degree of intellect supplies a guarantee against it."

Some say that envy is in our genes, meaning that some of us are born more temperamentally inclined to be envious, just as some of us are born lovelier. Do not expect, however, to sight the haves and the have-nots easily; beauty and envy are not mutually exclusive. They often come in the same pretty package. Fearing that the killer envy will be directed against them, to deflect it, the beauties quickly spoil their own good looks by pretending to take no pleasure in their power: "Who, me, pretty? Have you seen my ugly thighs, my big nose?" Nor do the envious want to be recognized as vile and so deny, "Who, me, envy her? I could care less!" It is all a game of mirrors; nothing is what it seems. No wonder the character Beauty is often called Poor Beauty in fairy tales.

The sorrow is that envy begins with admiration. For a moment, there is the Ahhhh! of seeing someone, something that catches our critical eye, mellowing it, warming us until reality bites, awakening us to, "Why that person and not me?" Instead of the world being a sweeter place for beauty's presence, and our feeling some gratitude for having spied this oasis of loveliness in a cold world, we grind our teeth and smile when the six-foot-tall runway beauty trips in her stiletto heels.

We call this period in which we live The Age of Envy; do we realize that we are labeling ourselves as mean-spirited possessors of that emotion of which nothing good can be said? Characteristically, we are determined to let no one have more than we do, meaning power over us, even if it is the power to love us and make us happy. Love, family, community, even the air and water we have polluted in our greed, which is envy's close relation. It is as though we cannot bear the good feeling of gratitude for what we have been given; for the envious, to be grateful feels like impotence. Of course beauty is the icon of our Age of Envy, deeply rooted in our dysfunctional society. "Envy is the sin that festers in hierarchies and families, in structured societies of all kinds," writes novelist A. S. Byatt.

Do not confuse envy with jealousy, which is an appropriate emotion to feel when we are in danger of losing our loved one to a rival. Jealousy is always a triangle involving the loved one, ourselves, and the rival who would take away our beloved. I would not want a lover who did not feel jealous at the prospect of losing me; would you? It is how we deal with our jealousy that shows us to be either base or noble. Within the jealous triangle we may envy what our rival possesses—greater beauty or wealth—or we may envy our loved one's power to raise us to heaven or dash us to hell. In the instance of a Cyrano de Bergerac, who loved truly and withdrew from the triangle to ensure his beloved's happiness, we would say that his jealousy inspired nobility. In contrast, envy, as *The Oxford English Dictionary* puts it, is "the feeling of mortification and ill-will occasioned by the contemplation of superior advantages possessed by another."

In societies all over the world, a person who stands out above others is regarded with ambivalence. Anthropologists cite a phrase that is universal: "He will be brought down." Especially in the traditional women's world of limited resources, isn't this how women regarded the beautiful woman, the feeling being that there is only so much beauty out there, therefore, when one woman gets more than her share, it feels as though she has deprived the others. Envy feeds on deprivation: Why you and not me? We love the beauty/we hate the beauty. We want to bask in her glow, share her power/we wish her ill. Ambivalence.

Writing about envy in a primitive tribe of Indians in Mexico, anthropologist George Foster might easily be describing women and beauty in what he calls the Image of Limited Good. These Indians seem to feel that the world bestows only so many rewards. Your gain must be my loss. To assuage your resentment I would be wise to devalue my good fortune. Writes Foster, "If good exists in limited amounts which cannot be expanded, *logically an individual or family can improve its position with respect to any good only at the expense of others."* Hence, if you do or get something much admired, you are a threat to the entire community, despoiling the rest of us. Economists, sociologists, anthropologists, psychologists—practically every social scientist has made note of this all too human phenomenon, calling it "The Zero-Sum Game."

Hence, the fashion models of today who earn a million dollars for a television commercial quickly remind us, "Oh, I hate my ears, my hair, my feet, the way I looked when I was twelve!" Conversely and similarly, when I approach a group of women sitting by a pool, gossiping snidely about the gorgeous woman on the diving board, they quickly deny the evil intent of their whispers, "Oh, we don't dislike her! She's our best friend, we love her!" It is said without embarrassment or hesitation; they hate her/they love her, and feel both simultaneously.

Ambivalence. The baby loves the breast/the baby hates the breast because it has all the power. The baby bites the breast. Some of us, however, feel envy more than others and I go along with Melanie Klein, who believed envy to be both learned and constitutional. Let me quickly add that Klein emphasized that any predisposition toward envy will be heightened by bad mothering and ameliorated by good mothering.

Do you remember the ditty chanted by little children that I quoted in the first chapter that begins, "I one my mother, I two my mother," and ends, "I ate my mother"? The rhyme was accompanied by an assuming illustration depicting the tiny baby actually consuming the nursing mother. Well, that is pure Klein. The baby loves the mother/the breast, the baby *envies* the mother/the breast because she/it has all the power. And so the baby bites the breast. Only with constancy, with the mother being "good enough," is the baby's envy lessened, until a feeling of guilt juxtaposed with the mother's goodness is born. Guilt, says Klein, is the paradoxical beginning of the turning of the infant's envy/hatred into gratitude and love. Following guilt, the infant makes "reparations," meaning that he smiles, sensing that mother does her best, for here she comes again to hold and feed him; he touches the good mother to make up for his earlier envy of her total power. Gratitude has entered his life. And gratitude, says Klein, opens the door to love.

I can think of no emotion other than dark envy that better explains our convoluted attitude and behavior regarding lovely beauty; let me therefore quote Klein's definition of envy, she being the grandmother of our understanding of that emotion: "Envy is the angry feeling that another person possesses and enjoys something desirable—the envious impulse being to take it away or to spoil it. Moreover, envy implies the subject's relation to one person only and goes back to the earliest exclusive relation with the mother."

What she is saying is that how you react to beauty today—your own and others'—has everything to do with what went on between you and the first most important person in your life. Can you take pleasure in the good things that others possess? Can you enjoy your own accomplishments without diminishing their value? Families are always the stuff of analysis because, like fairy tales, the outcome depends on the beginning.

For instance, a man marries a beautiful woman but after a while grows anxious about the envious stares of other men who admire his wife and resent his having her; he loves his wife's beauty, he hates it, and he soon turns to other women to assuage his resentment of her power over him: He bites the hand that feeds him, just as the envious baby bites the breast. Turn the story around to the wife's point of view: Her wealthy husband is giving her all she desires; but at any moment of any given day, he could take it all away. He has all the power. She loves him/she hates him. She envies his authority to ruin everything; she turns to another man or denies her husband sex; she bites the hand that feeds her.

While Freud placed great emphasis on the constitutional differences in people's sex drives, Klein lays it on the line with even more emphasis in her seminal tome *Envy and Gratitude:* "I consider that envy is an oral-sadistic and anal-sadistic expression of destructive impulses, operative from the beginning of life, and that it has a constitutional basis. . . ."

For ten years—and the clock is still ticking—we have been living in the belly of beauty, focusing on it as never before in my lifetime, and deriving little pleasure from it, I might add. Nothing satisfies, nothing endures; we go through fashion statements as we go through love affairs and marriages. Beauty is the allegory by which we will remember these years, a metaphor we will later ponder, asking, Why was no one happy then? Whatever we may buy to please ourselves—cars, houses, vacations—we buy beauty with more desperation, investing in its power because of the gnawing envy we feel when we see beauty in others.

When Klein explains that some of us *are born* with the potential to be more or less envious of beauty's power in another, we should listen. It means that we will be especially aware of other people's envy of our own beauty as well as more disposed to resent good looks in others. And the advertisements, the billboards, the beauty magazines, and the television commercials fan these flames of resentment: Why them and not me? Look at your friends; not all of us react with the same emotional heat when a good-looking person joins the group, or drives up in a Jaguar. Some people rest easy, while others become anxious when beauty's power skews the status quo.

Better still, look at your family, parents and siblings, your genetic inheritance back through the generations; were they envious of what the neighbors owned, always comparing wealth, power, handsome features within the immediate family to what cousins and other relatives had, never allowing themselves to enjoy what was already possessed out of anxiety over other people's envy? Or did they take pleasure in the success and possessions of others, giving easily and genuinely of praise?

Children, raised by parents to succeed, find it confusing when the parents envy them for achieving the very things they know their parents admire. Having worked and sacrificed to produce a successful son, a beautiful daughter, how could father and mother now resent their children's happiness? Do not look for logic in envy. When parents ruin their children's happiness by constantly comparing them to someone more beautiful, more successful, unhappiness reigns. "In a house where envy is in the air, however, the child need but look, listen, and breathe to be instructed in consolation and counterattack," says psychoanalyst Leslie Farber. "*If* he accepts the conditions offered him and agrees to be instructed by the example of his elders, thus will their envy breed his own."

When I look at my own extended family, I'd say we were an envious lot. The adults were very clear as to just who the beauties were, and comparisons were made among us children. Having envied beauty so acutely in others as a child, I am quick today to inform an admirer that my Geoffrey Beene dress is ten years old.

Nowadays, any constitutional inclination toward envy is exacerbated by advertising that pummels away at us, devaluing everything we already own in the effort to make us go out and buy whatever new model of television, car, computer, or clothing that was designed last night while we slept. Gratitude is not encouraged, for appreciation of what is already owned is antithetical to commerce, which survives on greed. In The Age of Envy, children are particularly susceptible to the messages of a society that puts no value on invisible virtues such as kindness, honor, generosity.

And it isn't just commercials and advertisements that nudge our envy; in the content of newspaper articles and popular books, brand names specify exactly what it is that we don't own; beautiful people who lead beautiful lives stare out at us from the tabloids, ruining what had up till now been a fine day, their clothes and houses making our own look shabby and inadequate by comparison.

How ironic that our first reaction to the beauty was admiration, an emotion based on respect. In an envious society, admiration quickly sours and twists in on itself. We do not wish them well, those people in the photographs who live in such a magnificent house, drive such an elegant car, and go to parties with movie stars.

"Bring me her heart!" cried the envious, evil queen when the mirror informed her of the more beautiful Snow White, and she proceeded to devour the heart and liver of what she thought was her slaughtered rival. Now there's envy!

When the subject of admiration is human beauty, perniciousness escalates, for envy of beauty goes back to the earliest years of life; it has been cooking for a long time. On some level, we all know that if we were beautiful, our lives would be different. It is ludicrous to deny that beauty is a resource that gets the best table, the best breast. Pretty babies do get picked up first. Other things happen to alter this auspicious beginning, and they will happen quickly. When we meet a beautiful person, how can we know that envious siblings, envious parents, envious friends have soured beauty's life? We don't care about their hard-luck stories, we wish we'd had a chance to have that face, that body. We are envious and they know it, especially today when polite disclaimers are out of fashion.

In Ovid's *Metamorphoses*, Envy is described as living in a cavern, wrapped in thick black fog, a creature that eats snakes' flesh: "Envy's face was sickly pale, her whole body lean and wasted, and she squinted horribly; her teeth were discoloured and decayed, her poisonous breast of a greenish hue, and her tongue dripped venom. Only the sight of suffering could bring a smile to her lips. She never knew the comfort of sleep, but was kept constantly awake by care and anxiety, looked with dismay on men's good fortune, and grew thin at the sight. Gnawing at others, and being gnawed, she was herself her own torment." Our refusal to understand the power of beauty is in part based on a reluctance to recognize our own moldy, poisonous envy.

I have come to feel that writing this book is my protection, my Wonder Woman's "golden girdle." As Graham Greene said, "Writing is a form of therapy," a remark with which few writers would argue; sitting alone in a room for years isn't always the choice of a happy, complacent mind. As personal as this odyssey may be, I am not alone in my preoccupation with beauty, which is hot and papered all over town; the covetous looks on the street are alive with hisses, "Why him, her, and not me?" Today is the stuff of Klein, Bettelheim, the Brothers Grimm, tales of people with envious stepsisters covered in warts. Listen to the old tales, the older the better, which means that they were handed down orally, so full of wisdom were they.

Writes A. S. Byatt in "The Sin of Families and Nations," her essay on envy, "Allegory and fairy tales are solidified morals and psychology, and in the case of envy they work particularly well, because envy works by paralysis and self-consumption—the envious do indeed *become* Envy."

Throughout the world, societies different in all other respects have evolved their unique defenses against envy's desire to destroy. "Welcome to my humble abode," intones the Chinese mandarin, bowing low at the door of his palace.

We thoroughly expect wealthy, powerful people to enjoy their privilege; even if a part of us wishes them ill for having so much more than we do, we grudgingly understand why they receive preferential treatment. Having made his obligatory bow to the gods so that we will not kill him for his "good luck," the mandarin or the mogul now proceeds to accumulate even more power—as we would were we in his place.

We do not, however, surround physical beauty with such protective mantras, thus allowing the beauty to comfortably accumulate even greater power. Instead, we invoke the caveat "Beauty is only skin deep." Such a prissy admonition wags its finger at those who would wield beauty's power; better play it down, even be blind to it, or best of all, deny it: "Who, me, beautiful?" The worst thing the beauty can do is to try for more than is already possessed. Dumb blondes don't just happen, they evolve.

In the late eighties, when I was producing a short documentary on the power of beauty, a print advertisement turned up for Pantene hair spray in which a gorgeous, drop-dead model intoned, "Don't hate me because I'm beautiful." She then goes on, in small print, to explain that she was really just as plain as you and I until she used this product. What a clever copywriter, I thought; this was the perfect ad for our envious era, which has gone berserk over physical beauty. Suddenly the ad disappeared and I was told, sotto voce, that Feminist Headquarters had objected to the inference that we Nice Girls felt envy.

Every society has its arrangement, a deal between the sexes regarding resources and roles. This is how beauty came to serve material wealth. In our society, economic power has traditionally belonged to men, the power of the caretaker to women, who for several hundred years have also enjoyed the monopoly on beauty. It is, however, a monopoly with strings attached. For Paternalistic Society to function, beauty's ability to divert the eye from the wheel of progress had to be contained. The job was given to women. By relegating beauty to women, men freed themselves from their envy of beauty's power and made women one another's jailers.

A mother scanned her baby daughter's face and saw her future. If she was pretty, mother rested assured that one day a prince would come and take care of her lovely child, buy her a house and give her a place in the community. This was the societal arrangement: To the most powerful man went the prettiest girl. Such a simple formula. So weighty in its implications. A boy, born poor, could go out and seek his fortune, but a girl was born with hers, apparent to all who looked at her.

Rules therefore had to be set up to protect the beauty from other women's envy, rules that also provided for the women who were less endowed. Most important, in a world where men had all the economic power, women couldn't afford to let beauty's advantage pit them against one another. In the women's world of limited resources, beauty was so critical, it could not be honestly discussed; therefore, codes, screens, euphemisms, the language of the fan were practiced to protect the beauties as well as the have-nots.

Beauty was given her due but kept "in her place" too. Above all, open competition had to be avoided. It would not be tolerable for women *to be seen* competing over beauty. When competition did happen, it was denied: "Competing? Oh, no, we love one another!"

Today, nothing cuts the newly won economic ground out from under women like our inherited denial of competition, which began as a defense against the envy of beauty in a time of women's limited resources. We compete nonetheless, calling it by other names rather than learn the rules that would allow for healthy competition.

I've never met a woman who actually remembers a cluster of girls sitting down and agreeing, "Now, here they are, The Nice Girl Rules, and anybody who doesn't abide by them is out." To be ostracized from women's world when we were young was to be totally abandoned, for "little women's world" replaced the attachment to Mommy. I remember a heart-wrenching Jules Feiffer cartoon, the theme of which was "Three Little Girls Can't Play Together," because two always leave one out, who runs crying to mother, "Mommy, Mommy, yesterday she was my best friend!" Well, it is a refrain in this book; big girls also leave one another out. I've seen it all my life, at work, socially, even (especially) among close friends, where little/big girls still can't resist "punishing" one girl, thus drawing the others tighter. Until we give up the no-compete clause and allow ourselves to recognize that beauty is no longer our one resource, we will enviously continue to police one another.

Beautiful women tell tales of a childhood in which they learned to know their places. They didn't try to shine too brightly (didn't compete) in other areas, such as intellect, sports, leadership; their cup was perceived as already too full. "Who, me, pretty?" the lovely little girl said, denial being the first and most effective defense against envy. If mother didn't communicate the lesson, a sibling did. Sooner rather than later, other girls let the beauty know the wisdom of being "beautiful but dumb." It is one of those "implicit" early memories, an anxious feeling rather than an "explicit" memory of being told not to shine brightly in class or on the playing field. It is a memory kept alive whenever an opportunity is offered to excel at anything aside from beauty.

Twelve years of Women's Rules have been learned by the time adolescence rolls around, and the beauty becomes the most powerful boy's obvious partner. In time, when youth and beauty fade, or when the powerful man leaves her for a younger woman, the once beautiful woman has little to fall back on. The homily of her youth has come true: Beauty is only skin deep; there is nothing inside—no wit, no speed, no intellect.

Today a mother has no way of knowing whether her beautiful baby girl will grow up using her looks to win a wealthy man or to build her own empire and leave men out of her life. What hasn't changed is beauty's purchasing power: what it buys a woman, and increasingly today, what it buys a man. As beauty's role evolves, by which I mean how we are going to use our looks to get what we want, you can be sure that ever present will be beauty's evil companion, envy, that venomous emotion of which nothing good can be said. Now that men and women share the power of material wealth and beauty, we would be wise to study envy, become more conscious of its feel so that we recognize it before we injure people whom we admire and love, for this is precisely what envy seeks: to bite the hand that feeds us.

"How remarkable it is that one can admit to feelings of guilt, shame, pride, greed and even anger without loss of self-esteem," says anthropologist George Foster, "but that it is almost impossible, at least in American society, to admit to feelings of envy. . . . In recognizing envy in himself, a person is acknowledging inferiority *with respect to another*; he measures himself against someone else and finds himself wanting. It is, I think, this implied admission of inferiority, rather than the admission of envy, that is so difficult for us to accept."

Women's entry into the workplace is an economic upheaval that alters the oldest societal contracts between the sexes. The rules surrounding the uses of beauty, by which we have lived for hundreds of years in Patriarchal Society, are fast becoming obsolete in this oncoming society, which, alas, I would call Pre-Matriarchal. The formidable defenses that once protected the sexes from envy of one another's power aren't holding up too well.

As for women's own world, we no longer have to rely solely on our looks as our meal ticket. Women today have economic muscle. Having spent good money—not Daddy's or our husband's but our own—on clothes, makeup, the beauty parlor, we're no longer so agreeable about playing down our looks. We want to take it in. "Who, me, pretty?" just doesn't go down the way it used to.

Also, we've noticed that men in our office don't devalue praise or hang their heads boyishly and turn away from a compliment for work well done. Now they too are getting into looking good, and when someone compliments them on the new Armani suit, they don't say, "Oh, this old thing?" Men take the compliment and put it to work for themselves. It isn't that men are less envious, it is simply that they envy assets other than beauty and usually react to the feeling of "Why him and not me?" more competitively than do women. Men have been raised to act, to perform, rather than to fade, demur. As men continue to move deeper and deeper into women's oldest power base—and they will—women will be hard-pressed to employ the little girl denials of envy in opposition to beautiful men who step eagerly forward to snatch beauty's rewards.

Now, at the turn of the century, men's and women's roles are up for redefinition and, appropriately, our looks are changing inside and out. Thinking of ourselves differently, women look into mirrors and expect to see some new reflection of what we are becoming. We can't afford the skewed vision our mothers saw staring back at them, wherein all the joy was sucked out of beauty power for fear of arousing envy. Certain feminists chant that competition is the evil legacy of Big Bad Patriarchal Society, men the brutes; they would like to extend the "no compete" rule of women's world into the workplace, meaning that they would control the marketplace with the same denials that for centuries regulated beauty's power. Oh, they would compete and heads would roll, but on their faces would be those painted smiles that contradict ill feeling, hostility, and murder; Nicole Kidman had it down pat in the film *To Die For*, where she maims and destroys, deflecting suspicion with her Nice Girl smile.

But what of men's feelings regarding the Women's Movement having brought beauty's power to the workplace? So long as they had all the economic power, the diffidence men felt toward women's beauty was lessened. The sting was removed. The arrangement was codified: To the conqueror went the spoils. No matter how old and ugly the man, the deal was never questioned. It still isn't. Seeing the exquisite freshness of the young woman opposite the swollen, blotched face of the old patriarch, we shrug. After all, exchanges as deeply entrenched as those surrounding beauty and wealth don't go away quickly, and twenty-five years is a speck in time.

The irony is that women feel easier about entering the workplace, providing for ourselves, challenging and acting like men than we do in confronting one another over the uses of beauty. We still practice the denial of beauty's power out of fear of reprisals from other women. At times it is as if men don't even exist.

For instance, when a woman walks into the office in her expensive Chanel suit or high heels and miniskirt, whose eyes is she testing as she walks between her colleagues' desks? The other women are evaluating what she spent on that suit, deciding whether or not her legs are good enough for a mini; other women's eyes are stripping her naked and imagining themselves in such an outfit; comparing, evaluating, judging. It is fine to wear the Chanel suit; after all, this is what we work for, to spend our money as we wish. What is irresponsible is not to appreciate what beauty sets in motion, how quickly admiration becomes envy. If we can't live with or diffuse the whispers, the barely veiled resentment in the critical eyes, we have invested our money unwisely.

Envy isn't going away any more than women are going to leave the workplace and return to total economic dependence on men. What is required is that women see themselves as men always have: as powerfully beautiful as the first woman who held them. Born of woman, raised by woman, a man has the truest understanding of the uses of female beauty. Before women can enjoy the rewards that come with the beauty we now work so hard to purchase, we must learn to see our beauty as power.

Some feminists argue that an army of powerful women is one that absolutely denies nursery angers, meaning anger at other women. The enemy is "out there," this line of reasoning goes, not here in us Nice Women. "Take Back the Night" marches feel good, but only lead to more rage because the target is often inappropriate. Yes, some evil men hurt women, but men are not the original origin of our deepest rages. Not even men want to admit to the real source because it is so belittling for men to prod an old wound inflicted by the first most important woman in all of our lives.

The unexamined life is one of denial. Denial eats up energy, and, as we know, an army marches on its stomach. The furnace requires constant stoking to turn out sufficient smoke screens to obscure what we don't want to see. Maybe twenty-five years ago when the army was assembling, we women needed to spend our energy hoisting ourselves out of the iron tenets of women's traditional world. Not surprisingly, the first thing to go was the wardrobe, the pretty costumes slipped over our heads as children to show off our worth. We marched in jeans.

But neither nursery anger nor the importance of beauty has gone away. We have new options, thank God, but they are less available and enjoyable than they should be; buried battles won and lost with parents and siblings over issues of beauty hold us back. Women's new alternatives aren't going to make the power of beauty go away. We may find more lasting identities in the work of our choice, but whether we decide to eschew appearance or pursue its prizes is going to be influenced by what happened in the first years of life.

We bow down to material wealth at beauty's expense not because we outgrow the primitive power of beauty but because our unrequited hunger for it has fired our destinies from the time we were born. When unattractive little men use the fuel of primitive rage to create an empire, nothing, as Melanie Klein tells us, breeds rage like a dried-up mother tit, or, even worse an absent one—the first thing these men buy themselves is a beautiful face and a great pair of tits. But the revenge is never complete; the beauty, the tits are hers, not his. The anger never goes away. Respect for economic clout was learned late, too late if you believe in the formative power of the first years of life.

Our blind eye to beauty omnipotence has been passed down through generations. Given that Patriarchal Society was based on material wealth as the ultimate goal, beauty's potency had to be denigrated in every way possible. Of course we have no mantra to ward off the envy of beauty.

We need to lighten the load of polite denials. I wrote *My Mother/My Self* out of a fear that I would never feel whole and independent if I had to live with the homilies of denial that kept that Nice Girl smile on my face. Actually, I began that book in a state of innocence; the anger would only surface as I got further into the writing, which pulled it out of me, terrifying me and sapping my vitality, making me sick. For way back in the first years of life I'd built emotional conduits to channel rage away from Mommy and on to safer targets. All the while, other energy had to constantly rebuild and prettify my relationship with mother/women: "Angry at my dear old mom? You must be joking! Don't we have great times together? Why, I have a better relationship with my mother than anyone I know."

Women who had read the book used to write to me saying that they initially wanted to kill me, that the rage I had awakened had them hurling it across the room. I sympathized. I'd locked Klein's *Envy and Gratitude* in a closet for months to forestall facing the reality of my relationship with my mother. But the subject of this book is richer still, for how we see ourselves in others' eyes, how they take us in and what we see reflected in store windows when we pass, well, beauty's roots are mother, father, siblings, the lot.

The richness of this subject is only surpassed by its timeliness. Beauty has become what our lives are about, not the clothes and seasonal fashions, but the rage, grief, a terrible sense of isolation that we get when we don't get back any good feeling from the money and time we invest in appearance. Appearance is everything, appearance is empty. It's a miserable cheat, this mirror today in which we look nice and feel hollow. Why aren't people more generous and kind, as they used to be? Where are the nice grandmothers who once smiled at young, pretty girls? They are at the gym, getting beautiful, getting in shape, getting rid of the soft, sagging underarms that remind them of their envy of pretty young girls.

Feminism has split into so many theoretical camps, it is difficult to keep track. This is good. Feminists are individuals with varying ideas on how we want to live. But even as we grow into our highly differentiated beliefs, there is no respect for diversity. Each group acts as if those with differing opinions from their own were traitors, as if there were only "one feminism," theirs. Women still speak of a sisterhood, when in fact it is more akin to a highly diverse same-sex community. We can't even agree to disagree in what could be a healthy argument precisely because we are so different. Only when we can fight it out verbally, will we reach a declaration of independence that we can live with and then shake hands.

But to argue without fearing that our anger will destroy the opponent, or vice versa, requires healthy, individuated people. Acquiring a trusted voice for anger demands practice so that we know, again and again, that it is not a killer but simply one of life's emotions. The young boy gets better practice at this, which is why men's groups can argue and either stay together or splinter. Feminism cannot tolerate dissent because we women never felt safe differing with the first woman in our lives, who would not tolerate our anger. Emotionally, we are still unseparated, and our original anger boils up whenever another woman takes us on. How dare she! Total conformity is the only way these feminists can live in the narrow world they inhabit and intend to control. They will "kill" with accusations and threats any of us who try for a larger life than their own; witness the current girlish name-calling where dissenters are labeled "pod feminists," "faux feminists" . . . I'm embarrassed to go on.

I cannot imagine a better battleground on which to examine our independence than the subject of this book—looks, beauty, dress, the way we present our selves to others' eyes and see our selves in all reflecting surfaces. Fashion appropriately spins like a top today, throwing away one look after another, bringing to mind the obsessed heroine of *The Red Shoes*, destined to dance her life away whenever she dons the slippers, which to me symbolize denial.

Women, men, none of us will ever understand or change our attitude about the way we look without going back to the source, she whose eye was our most critical mirror. She, along with father and siblings, created the primal stage on which we were cast in a role we continue to play or to deny. How were we seen by them? Were we so much the apple of mother's eye that our sister or brother hated us? Did father love to gaze at us and thus arouse mother's envy so that she came between us, literally to divide and conquer? Or were we the plain one opposite mother, or father, or the more lovely sister, and thus forced to invent other ways of getting ourselves seen and loved? Or did we just go under, hide?

The combinations and permutations of roles within the family are not finite; they shade into ever more complex solutions of rivalry and competition. Early family is where the bedrock of our self-image is laid down. If thinking about the early injustices of childhood fills us with rage today, *don't blame mother!* Don't set her up as the scapegoat. Blame is a trickster, the devil. When we blame mother for all our problems, we think we're not part of the problem: "All her fault!" when indeed, what we've done is to embed ourselves in childhood, guaranteeing that we'll never grow up. We are the ones who want to get past the rage; she won't even remember. We must do our homework, think it through honestly, keeping what is good and loved with her so that we can be grateful. Gratitude is important. So she wasn't perfect. Who is?

"Bring Me Her Heart!"

Everything around me seems redolent of the first years of life these days, perhaps nothing more so than the New Baby Boom, the proliferation of pregnant tummies, breasts, the engorged bosoms of beautiful women thrust in our faces on television, in advertisements on the sides of the passing bus, blotting out the sky in the billboards above. In this morning's newspaper, naked men and women sell products that don't require their taking off their clothes, but they do. It is as if they can't help themselves. Often they hold babies, who are also naked. Naked supermodels smile as if to assume that we love them for their beauty, when indeed we don't so much love as envy them, craving to *be* them and wield their power.

Our culture promotes envy, stirs it up and applauds what is, by definition, that emotion of which nothing good can be said. Envy sells; the advertising agencies have learned that making people unhappy with what they own is an excellent means of getting them to replace what is barely worn, barely used. "You thought you were happy with that car you bought six months ago?" the commercial intones. "Well, you idiot, look at what your neighbors just bought, look at what the really important people are wearing, eating, drinking. Better still, outdo your neighbor, get a car that's even flashier than his and watch him squirm!" Envy, that slimy, ooze-infested emotion, has become so familiar that children pick up guns and kill other children to steal the gold chain, the running shoes, or just to dissipate the rankling inferiority that envy produces: Why him and not me?

Why, we even envy the power we have given to our beloved to make us happy or sad, the power that he or she has to take their beauty and bestow it on another. Hating the power they have over us, we leave them for another. Adultery is a popular TV talk-show subject, and the divorce rate soars. There is no constancy. There is no gratitude, and without gratitude, says Melanie Klein, there is no love.

There is nothing evil in competition per se, but when it is employed without practice and safe rules, as with a loaded gun, it is only a matter of time before something bad happens. "The fact that in our paranoid society we need no spur for competition to develop does not belie the original useful purpose of the emotion," says psychiatrist Willard Gaylin. "It is likely that the exclusive possession of the mother is the primary goal of all children, that competition is normal, and that sharing must be learned." But learned from whom? Feminism has for twenty years preached to women that all competition is evil. What are children to do when mother doesn't name or explain the "useful purpose of the emotion"? Oh, yes, it is a wonderful time for fairy tales, the grimmer the better to reflect real life honestly to a child.

The child, about to go to sleep, is listening to the dearest voice in the world; dreams and nightmares are going to occupy him. It isn't the gory plot of "Hansel and Gretel" that structures the dream, but instead the child's own destructive emotions felt that day toward a sibling, a parent, a friend. When a parent's loved voice reads the story and ends it with a kiss before sleep, the child is less harsh on himself because the fairy tale has told him that he is not the only one to feel nasty emotions, and the parent's kiss before sleep assures him that he will not be abandoned. Small wonder that family members are stock characters in fairy tales; for a child, his family is his entire world, upon whom he is totally dependent for everything. When it works, the family is a trusting network, but it becomes a frightening microcosm when the child feels threatened from within.

What to do? Prettify the unconscious? Read to children only what grown-ups want them to hear? Take away from them the recognition of their own inherent nastiness, destructiveness, as part of the full spectrum of human emotion? If our dark side isn't recognized early, how then consciously to decide whether or not to act on malice or to temper the nasty emotion? Fairy tales abound with heroes and heroines who must choose. So must the child.

In recent years some Matriarchal Feminists have criticized exposing children to the old fairy tales, which they say endorse stereotypical sex roles. Most "storybook" heroines, they complain, are portrayed as passive and submissive, functioning primarily as a prize for a daring prince and thus dependent on the prince for identity. As the nihilist Andrea Dworkin puts it, fairy tales exhort girls to "become that object of every necrophiliac's lust—the innocent, *victimized* Sleeping Beauty, beauteous lump of ultimate, sleeping good."

In her own books, Dworkin gives us an alternative to fairy tale wisdom by writing fiction in which her heroine systematically castrates all the males. Not a pretty picture, but a gruesome depiction of Dworkin's own particular brand of feminist rage at men. Though she may not be writing bedtime stories for children, the venom she spurts and the rabble-rousing "Take no prisoners!" tactics her followers favor toward anyone who doesn't agree with them are every inch the nihilism bubbling up in a child's unconscious. Dworkin admits in her various writings to a very unhappy youth, the horror of which is laid at the boots of men who have raped her, not once, but many times. As Freud once remarked to a patient—and I paraphrase—"I can understand this misadventure happening once, even twice, but at some point your own involvement in your unhappiness must be questioned."

In my opinion it is thrilling that women are creating new fairy tales in which heroines are no longer depicted as woebegone and helpless but take courage in hand and accomplish the gallant end of freeing themselves and others from evil oppressors. In the story "Petronella," the princess eventually marries, but only at the conclusion of her own personal quest, which is dangerous and demands both cleverness and valor. In "The Forest Prince," the "Rapunzel" tale is reversed, and the princess rescues the prince.

Too often zeal overwhelms the storyteller of some of these new fairy tales, and the result is narratives no less stereotypical than the crudest patriarchal stories. When women create fairy tales to celebrate women's world, we should remember that to the listening child, male or female, women do have the total power to give or withhold love, to punish, to dominate, to settle all quarrels and differences, in short, the power of the nursery. If new feminist fairy tales present male characters as one-dimensional and weak, opposite all-powerful females, we do a disservice to our sons and our daughters too, who look to fairy tales not so much for the promise of a rosy future as for communication with their own destructive unconscious.

"While some literal-minded parents do not realize it, children know that, whatever the sex of the hero, the story pertains to their own problems," writes Bruno Bettelheim, disputing the idea that the ancient tales result in sexual stereotyping.

We are foolish to throw out the old tales because they do not subscribe to our militant agenda. Long before these tales were written down, hundreds of years ago, the important plot line of beauty and its powerful influence over our lives is what parents spoke to children *and what those children chose to remember and to tell in time to their own children*. Almost twenty-five years into modern feminism, have you noticed a lessening of beauty's importance in men's and women's lives? Quite the contrary. Can you honestly suggest that this reassertion of beauty's power is a dastardly act thought up by evil men to divert women from the workplace and back to the dressing tables? It is we women who want beauty back in our lives, but the structuring of its practical uses is being hampered by those women who do not want to see it used at all. Beauty's power is eternal, not something we can turn on and off. Because it was once our only power is no reason not to employ it still; better to understand it, learn to use it effectively by facing its luminous power straight on, from the cradle up.

"Let me feast my eyes on you" will be in style until we all go blind; even then we would use our fingertips to delicately trace the beloved outline of our dear one's lips and eyes. The power of beauty has nothing to do with changing political machines and should be included in feminist handbooks to enlighten women and make us more aware of its many uses and responsibilities.

To leave beauty out of contemporary fairy tales when women are pursuing appearance more ravenously than at any other time in my own life is to twist reality for the purpose of one's own dream of how life *should be*. Because boys too will grow up to use their looks to achieve their ends, not just with women but also in the workplace, well, all the more reason to write tales that mirror the feelings of the boy child sleeping alongside his sister, whom he hates for getting all the hugs and oohs and ahs, and who would feel far better for knowing/hearing that rivalry doesn't make him evil.

Whatever is said to a child, it must have the virtue of truth, represent what the parents genuinely feel, for children know their parents like the insides of their pockets. Parents should explain what looks engender, both the good and the bad. Yes, beauty will open doors, but it will close others. Beauty is such a free-floating form of power, walking in when we least expect it, in the form of the stranger, the new girl in class, at the party, that a child should be prepared to deal with beauty and with envy of beauty too, in others and in himself or herself. The power of money makes no visceral sense to a child and will only come later. First comes beauty, the earliest currency. Spoken about honestly by people a child loves most, beauty's power and problems become a given, so that in time, when superficial beauty fades, when the child ages, the old adage bears fruit: Beauty *is* in the eye of the beholder.

It wouldn't hurt a bit for all of us to hear the old tales again. Grown, with children of our own, we've forgotten their wisdom and learned instead the polite defenses that society teaches to mask the unspeakable meanness felt toward more handsome rivals. Last night's rage, for instance, disturbed our sleep, made us late for work this morning, those horrible dreams having something to do with the dinner party during which our husband agreed with his lovely dinner partner instead of with us, smiled at her in that conspiratorial way that is "our" smile, smiled it too long at that woman whom he later said was truly boring but whose hair and eyes and splendid clothes had strangely put to shame our own finery, magnificent when we left home.

The rage at him in the car driving home was out of all proportion to what had happened, which was nothing, after all, a smile, a few words. How to name out loud the humiliating feeling, the envy of the Wicked Queen toward the more beautiful Snow White, something painful but acceptable in our own mother's voice when we were little but totally disgraceful, mortifying for an adult. Raised to deny the power of beauty, we must also deny the envy that rides alongside it. And so last night we slept badly, the fear of loss of love to a rival buried. But the burial didn't work. Last night's dreams were of demons who promised a return to the powerlessness once felt in childhood, rage toward brothers and sisters that couldn't be admitted out of fear of abandonment, which, at that time in life was indeed death, or so it felt.

What happened today at the office was affected by the dreams, the loss of sleep to them; our usual competitive drive was unbalanced. We behaved badly, or did we do brilliantly, knock off the competition with a cruelty uncharacteristic, or was it? These feelings, unresolved, disturbing; we find ourselves, at our children's bedtime, reaching for the Brothers Grimm. We love our children, want to protect them as our own parents once tried to protect us.

If the powerful forces of beauty and envy aren't confronted, their sting is not removed, and denial becomes a way of life; power is traded on, pain inflicted, all actions and intentions called by names other than what they really are. For the rest of their lives together, parent and child will play fact and fiction, the child knowing he/she wasn't loved equally, the parent denying his or her affinity for the lovely one. It is a family history of Rashomon, in which each time they meet, a new scene is played out in reaction to the earliest dramatics of their shared lives. Each time the child believes it will all be different because life has outwardly changed, the parent grown older, the daughter/son now independent and successful, with children of her or his own. Except that it is never different. The old family quarrels and disappointments repeat because they are rooted in opposing versions of reality, one of which was how the power of looks influenced love.

Bettelheim writes that children often believe they deserve to be degraded, "relegated to a netherworld of smut," because of their secret wishes or actions. Moreover, they hate and fear their siblings and others whom they think free of such evilness and worry that, like Cinderella, they will be demeaned by their parents should their secrets be discovered. "Because he wants others—most of all, his parents—to believe in his innocence, he is delighted that 'everybody' believes in Cinderella's," he writes. "Since people give credence to Cinderella's goodness, they will also believe in his, so the child hopes . . . which is one reason it is such a delightful story."

To me, it's all of a piece, the fears of rejection and the promise of love in an omnipotent caretaker's adoring gaze, won by dint of dimple and curly hair. The fact that my own hair is straight and my feet too big has led to the nightmares of which I speak: the lost suitcases, the doorways in which I stand alone watching couples in one another's arms. I'm so accustomed to dreams of abandonment, I no longer question why intellectual understanding hasn't changed them. This, I have learned, is the unconscious, relentlessly playing its old familiar song.

Here, then, is what conscious intellect has taught me, that without the straight hair and the absence of the adoring gaze, I would never have become the little overachiever, a woman unafraid to seduce a man. It has meant a lot of closets and more shoes than I could ever count. But here is my husband, who I know loves me dearly. My husband who was chosen one day in the fourth grade to be The Beauty's favorite. "For one magic day," he says, "I was treated and looked at differently by all the other girls and boys because I stood in the beauty's magic glow. And then on another day, for a reason as indecipherable as the reason she chose me in the first place, she dropped me." He "forgot" the story until we met. My adorable husband, to whom I've promised that one day we will travel with one small suitcase.

Sibling Rivalry:
"What Is Beautiful Is Good"

I have no memory of myself as a child wanting pretty dresses, playing with combs and brushes, being held up to a mirror. Only in adolescence did this change totally and overnight. How early was it made, the choice to find ways other than beauty to get myself noticed? When did I decide to be a performer, to act a certain eye-catching way so that people who might otherwise pass me by would stop and smile, take me in and pick me up?

So early did tiny eyes take in the landscape, assessing my chances at survival in a house of pretty women, that I sit here today convinced I was born inventing an identity to take the place of beauty. I never expected to be loved, like my sister, by dint of just standing there.

Let me toss in badness too, a villainous feeling that I was not as nice as my lovely sister. This is a secret I've jealously guarded, and I tell it because my "secret" tallies so well with behavioral studies on appearance. It isn't just the early caretakers who single out the pretty babies; little children do too. Preschoolers will tell you which class-mates are cuter; they prefer attractive children as friends and expect them to be friendlier and less aggressive, less likely to hit without good reason. By the time little children enter kindergarten, they rate the more attractive kids as smarter, friendlier, nicer, more self-sufficient and independent than unattractive children; by contrast, unattractive children, particularly boys, are seen as more aggressive and antisocial.

The Ph.D.'s who study appearance call it "The Halo Effect." Pretti-ness, by virtue of itself, is good, so simple and loaded with potential. Think about all the dewy-eyed heroines in fairy tales; the goose girl didn't punch, nor did Cinderella give her wretched stepsisters what they deserved. Nor did my sister. But I went after her aggressively in every game of cards and hopscotch I could inveigle her into. She lost so readily, cared so little for winning that I wanted to shake her. It was as if she knew that the game didn't matter, that win or lose, there would be someone to take care of her. When she reached out to cuddle me, I shoved her away.

Am I being too hard on myself? Remember Melanie Klein's classic defenses against envy—idealization and devaluation—for I surely envied my sister's closeness to my mother, which I must have per-ceived to be in part due to shared beauty. Without doubt, I idealized my sister, elevating her in beauty and saintliness into the stratosphere beyond my killer envy; and here I sit still devaluing myself by creating a self-portrait far meaner and unattractive than it probably was.

There is a basic instability of threesomes within a family, or in any love relationship. "One sibling is always more prominent, eliciting pas-sionate feelings of hate or love," says psychologist Stephen Bank, whose special area of interest is sibling relationships; "rarely are such feelings distributed evenly." It is a theory that holds true in friendships (three little girls can't play together), and is characteristic of the psychology of love too, when the sacred dyad cannot bear interference from another. In any such threesome, "Two people will inevitably seek closeness, even fusion, leaving the third person to fend for himself or herself."

The Halo Effect describes perfectly how I saw my sister/my self. Because she was prettier, I thought she was a better person. *She was good and I was bad.* There are no photos of me before the age of four. Very well, here is what I remember: I am four, the straight, lank hair is tightly braided and my right eye, which has not yet been operated on, rolls inward—rather like Charles Laughton's Quasimodo—behind my steel-rimmed glasses. Beside me stands my sister, whose hair curls softly around her pretty face, so similar to my mother's. Was this the reason I always shoved her away? Were there unflattering comparisons made that I overheard from the cradle on? Judgments that decided my life, that I would not be like "them," my mother and sister?

I looked like someone from a different family, very well, I would act that way too, so originally that there would be no basis for comparison with my mother and sister. As far back as I can remember, I put different things into my body, refusing to eat fish, coconut cake, apple pie, all of which they enthusiastically endorsed; I even demanded that Miracle Whip be stocked, claiming I couldn't stomach their Hellman's on my peanut butter sandwich. They being so good (and pretty) and me bad (and ugly), I proceeded to flesh out my badness by lifting candy bars from stores at a very early age, filching small change from my mother's purse. When screen doors were inadvertently left open, I would toddle out alone, knowing it was forbidden but also searching, I am sure, for gazes that would record "the real me," the sweet darling disguised by necessity as a thief, forced to tell lies. Luckily, when I was four, the people I ran into on sidewalks turned out to be unimaginably kind; they took me home for chicken noodle soup and peanut butter sandwiches until much telephoning revealed to whom I belonged.

How I hated being dressed in that little yellow version of my sister's larger pink dress; until adolescence I would stubbornly avoid glass mirrors, preferring people's eyes, which I knew how to light up by standing on my head. If I could pin a crime on my sister I would, and felt justified in my revenge, though I cannot think of any bad thing she did to me. How could she comprehend my revenge, which went back to the beginning of life? How could I "remember" crimes from the cradle?

In *Diary of a Baby*, Dan Stern describes how a four-year-old has access to feelings dating from infancy. Are any memories from our distant past more constantly used, updated, and, therefore, as Stern says, "reworked and kept alive" than ancient feelings surrounding how parents and siblings loved or didn't love what they saw in us; judgments linked to smiling, touching, holding, kissing, then as now, now as then? Where else, no matter how old we grow, does the intensity of emotion come from at family reunions? Stern's description of memory takes these never forgotten feelings out of the unconscious and explains our acute sensitivity today to loss and rejection with family and lovers.

Don't mistake my self-portrait for self-pity, for I would not exchange this life for any other. The way it has turned out has everything to do with how it began. Those qualities I honed back then to gain visibility are now my most trusted self. I'm no one's fairy godmother, but I'm not the wicked child I painted myself to be when I was small. Early invisibility fascinates me not because of its sadness but rather because of its high drama, a testament to the little child's earliest determination to survive. The lesson is this: We must stop denigrating ourselves, devaluing not only whatever pleasant appearance we may have but also whatever goodness we possess. We are not as bad as we think we are.

Certainly my early adventures with danger, and sometimes the law, were "acting out" in reaction to the surety that my mother loved my sister more because she was prettier and sweeter. "Very well, if you will not love me, then I will be the bad person you think I am." Sitting on the stairs one afternoon I overheard my mother and her sister discussing how "kind and generous" my sister was. Did they say that I was *not* "kind and generous"? Did this really happen? Did I become bad because I envied her beauty and was/am badder than anyone else?

"Sibs are marvelous for learning about revenge," Dan Stern once told me. "They are good for learning all the realities of the legal and penal system. They work that way much better than parents do. What they often give you is a much better indoctrination into daily reality than your parents."

So there we were, the three of us, and though I never remember a cruel word from either my mother or sister in those early years, the anger and anxiety at feeling excluded from what I "perceived" to be a bond between them, very much beginning with their similarity in looks and temperament, determined the direction of my life. Let me add, however, that my foolish efforts at "revenge" have left me deprived of more good times and good things, because "they" owned them or did them, than I would care to count, not the least of which was my rejection of piano lessons because "they" both played. My writing table here, now, sits exactly where my dear friend composer/singer Peter Allen used to have his piano. I would wander in and out of his apartment, adoring the sight of that man sitting barefoot in his Hawaiian shirt, composing songs of unrequited love. No one could write them like Pete.

If ever there was a time for telling fairy tales, it is now. The real world is scary. All deals are off. Resentment, anger, and envy rule where traditional codes of behavior, ethics, and manners once dictated. Enough "beauty is as beauty does." Today beauty is a player, out there stalking the streets, bare-breasted, stiletto-heeled, fly unzipped with a massive hard-on. And you want to read your child *The Little Engine That Could*? Reach for Grimm. Grimm is how it is, and children desperately long to hear reality spoken out loud.

Still close to purity of emotion, children recognize in their bones exactly what the wretched stepsisters feel toward the more beautiful Cinderella, having felt the same murderous cruelty that very day toward their own brother or sister, whose golden curls, once again, won the last cookie on the plate. Nor has the pretty one escaped awareness of what the golden curls get you: killer sibling envy. When mother doesn't honestly acknowledge the meanness and fear inherent in the cookie incident, when she simply tries to make nice and pretends that everybody loves everybody else all the time, then children fall into caricature wherein they see themselves and others as exaggeratedly evil or angelically good.

Fairy tales divert children from these overly harsh accusations by giving them events and characters who represent and play out everything the child is feeling; the child no longer has to internalize the bad feelings, turn them against himself. The stepsisters in "Cinderella" not only get what is coming to them, they are so very evil that they make the child's own hatred mild by comparison.

"Since [the child] cannot comprehend intermediate stages of degree and intensity, things are either all light or all darkness," writes Bettelheim. "One is either all courage or all fear; the happiest or the most miserable; the most beautiful or the ugliest; the smartest or the dumbest; one either loves or hates, never anything in between.

"This is also how the fairy tale depicts the world: figures are ferocity incarnate or unselfish benevolence. An animal is either all-devouring or all-helpful. Every figure is essentially one-dimensional, enabling the child to comprehend its actions and reactions easily. Through simple and direct images the fairy story helps the child sort out his complex and ambivalent feelings, so that these begin to fall each one into a separate place, rather than being all one big muddle."

If beauty did not play such a major role in our lives, it would not feature so prominently and so often as the theme on which fairy tales turn. Pretty babies do get picked up first in the broadest sense of the phrase. Eyes are pulled to them, voices warm at the sight of them, sighs and loving words are drawn from the mouths of caretakers who can't help themselves, feasting their eyes for just a moment on the adorable one. Other little children take in this reality, a more powerful truth than the later recorded, "I love my children equally."

Being seen is everything when we are little, a truth that endures until it's time to tell a story to our own children. Long before fairy tales were written down, this memory of what really mattered in the nursery is what parents told their children. It is what they chose to remember. They could have made up prettier stories representing the admirable life they dreamed of for their child; instead, instinctively, they protected their babies with tales, not about how life might be, but how it *feels*.

Whether we provide for ourselves, choose to love another woman, or live alone, beauty prevails because childhood was beauty's kingdom and no one, boy or girl, forgets eyes that passed over them to fasten adoringly on another. It is far, far more generous and wise for feminists to encourage fathers to enter the nursery than to write newfangled fairy tales that suit grown-up agendas; father is another pair of eyes, arms, another dear voice, smell, touch, another source of love and another opinion of beauty. Now that would be a richer life.

And invariably in any tale of beauty comes the plot of cruelest sibling rivalry, made extreme for a purpose: to give the child a wide-screen version of emotions her parents are calling by other, more civilized names, but also to let the child off the hook a bit. Cinderella's stepsisters, for instance, are so grotesquely evil, it is okay to hate them, to recognize that you don't want to be that terrible, and last, to acknowledge that you aren't as awful as you feared. When children associate goodness with beauty, they simultaneously rank themselves, with their imperfect looks, as mean, bad, the worst, which becomes their secret selves, the blackness they will grow up to try to hide. Those of us who were the plainer ones often try to conceal this "bad character" with pretty finery, an exaggerated effort to please, behind which lurks the suspicion that when the phone doesn't ring or the invitation doesn't arrive, the world has seen through our lovely exterior to the blackness within.

Children love to hear fairy tales told again and again, as confirmation that they aren't "the only ones" to harbor dark, cruel emotions. It is the grown-ups who forget and now flinch at the horror of fairy tales: "Dear, dear, how can you tell a child that?" How can you not when it is the only honesty around?

Transformations are the stuff of fairy tales, their promise to the listening child, near sleep but never far from her own desires and/or overly harsh self-judgments; to the child there are no shades of gray: The bad self wars with the good self. The fairy tale is part of the resolution, allowing her to sleep, promising good will prevail and is in her, alongside the bad, but that ambivalence must be learned, meaning we can make choices.

"It is, in the final analysis, love which transforms even ugly things into something beautiful," writes Bettelheim. "It is ourselves alone who can turn the primordial, uncouth, and most ordinary content of our unconscious—turnips, mice, toads—into the most refined products of our mind."

The promise of the "beauty makeover," the hottest hour on television at any hour of any given day, isn't simply the physical transformation of the sad-looking woman in the third row. It is also the belief, hers as well as ours, that, for being lovelier, she will be a better person with a better life. The Halo Effect. Yes, we want to be beautiful, but like the child about to go to sleep, we want to think better of ourselves by getting rid of the enviously mean-spirited thoughts that make us want to strike out at someone like a sibling. It is a shame we stop reading fairy tales so young; we should, in fact, raise our children to read them back to us once they are able. It would be an interesting exercise to hear, in their voices, how well they still apply to all of us.

It all happened so long ago, we refuse to believe that nursery rages have anything to do with our reactions today. Why, we have children of our own, how can you suggest that what went on with my brother/sister still influences me? Where else would you look for reasons to explain the influence of looks over life today, the many trips to Bergdorf's, the orders made too often from catalogues, all that junk from QVC? Everywhere we go, eyes are judging us, pushing that memory button that calls up feelings from the first years of life, comparisons made. When our beloved looks at another person "in that way," our overreaction is not due to an act on his part—nothing happened—but to that "frequently used and updated" feeling we experienced when the new baby brother first entered our lives.

Intellectually we know why and how our beloved feels about us. Where then does the inappropriately overwhelming rage come from? The fact is, the feeling of being "the plain one" never gets a rest, never goes away. It remains "highly available" with all the intensity felt by a powerless, dependent child.

You and I, we don't believe compliments offered by loved ones— not as readily as we would an evil story about us; we've spent half our salary to put together the person in the mirror, but she is a fabrication, only good until the wind blows. The judgment of Paris is the first assessment, the one we swallowed whole when we were totally dependent, when being seen as our selves, and not someone else's fantasy of how they wanted us to be, meant life.

All we want, we say, is to create an image of ourselves with which we can live more happily, as if it had to do with hiring an image consultant, when it is more likely buried in battles won and lost long ago opposite a brother or sister who stole the focus. "Do you love me?" we ask our new lover, whose fervent "Yes!" isn't credible. We can't see anyone lovable in the mirror and so we press again, and again he repeats, "Of course I do, yes!" until finally we triumphantly find a loophole, some flaw in his protestation: "No, no, you don't love me!" we cry, filled with despair but a speck of self-righteousness too. "You're right," he gives up, agrees. "I don't."

Here in Key West, it is Christmas morning and I am in my garden, prowling barefoot among the palms, the *Phoenix robellini, Monsteria deliciosa,* the *Cocos plumosam,* looking for my beauty makeover, the double white hibiscus that I will wear in my hair today.

One perfect day of beauty, that is the life of the hibiscus. Not a long life, but not a bad one. Born in the morning's first sun, voluptuous by noon, the flower shrivels at night and falls from its stem. Unless, of course, I chill it until evening, prolonging its life and mine too, for I feel like a different (better) person wearing one, two, sometimes three. I move the pots according to the sun's orbit around the garden whenever I get up from my work. I want my crop to reach perfection. Plucked at their peak, stored in the fridge until the pumpkin/carriage arrives that evening, I wear hibiscus from ear to crown. I only wear the enormous double white version, which when perfect has exquisite tones of palest pink and Devon cream shot through its petals.

This is my favorite image of myself, not just because I borrow the hibiscus's beauty, but because flowers in a woman's hair connote easeful femininity in a sexual liaison with nature. It is a fairy tale transformation from the way I see myself by day: a flowerless, driven, ambitious, impatient, not always kind, less lovely and therefore less good person. The truth is, a little beauty probably does make most of us better, even nicer, seeing ourselves transformed in the mirror. The representation is confirmed when others hesitate and look at us in a different way; and we, seeing them see us, are grateful. So the exchange goes, each working the beauty transformation through their individual systems until something characteristically said or done breaks the spell, reminding us that it is only a flower or a dress or a new hairdo, and that underneath we are still the less than beautiful people we always were. Which doesn't mean we should dismiss the power of the transformation, for it is omnipresent. Someone, somewhere, is always slipping into a dress of gold thread woven by elves.

For me, a woman seldom at rest, who draws heavily on her masculine genes, it is deeply rewarding to accentuate the feminine. Three double whites in my hair may be exhibitionistic, but unlike a transparent blouse, flowers are disarming; who can accuse you of drawing attention to yourself, of arousing envy, if you have simply borrowed from nature?

In the morning I find the dear, shriveled corpses of my hibiscus from the night before on my bedside table, on the floor, or lying in a brandy snifter; they are always full of memory as with orchids from a boy long ago. But in giving the hibiscus to myself, I am distanced from that powerless girl who was totally dependent on the boy. These flowers are my chosen accomplices, implicated in the pleasures I initiated the night before, not just my own good times but generous acts performed for others, kindnesses I wouldn't/couldn't have performed as effortlessly without the flowers' beauty transforming me from the Bad Nancy.

I have never doubted that my exhibitionism stems from competition with my older sister, the child beauty. (That my own share came when I was about nineteen is beside the point; it was far, far too late to be believed in.) I told myself as a child that I didn't mind failing that silly contest, having gone on to invent, and win, other competitions in which I starred. When the looks arrived, this early pattern of exhibitionism on the playing fields had already been taken in and learned. It was part of me, who I was. Wearing these exotic, enormous flowers in my hair in make-believe Key West has the most soothing, benign effect; the nervous edge of not measuring up is gone, pffffft!, as fast as a fairy wand.

Today being Christmas, I say a little extra prayer that nature has been bountiful while we slept. I shall need at least nine blooms to get me through the three acts of Christmas Day, the first being breakfast with our dearest friends and neighbors, Dick and Bob, whose garden adjoins ours. I part the giant shards of a bird-of-paradise and there they are, a magical harvest of dewy hibiscus blooms, three for now, three for Jimmy's brunch, and three for David's dinner on the roof of the old Kress building. I retire to the kitchen to scramble eggs, fry rashers of bacon, and heat pounds of Entenmann's pecan coffee cake and brioches from the French bakery on Duval. The StairMaster will wait until tomorrow.

We always make an extra fuss over Dick during this ritual to compensate for a Christmas when he was four. That morning he donned his little blue blazer with the red piping, his knee socks and short gray flannel pants and, good little boy that he was, stood at the top of the stairs in full expectation of a perfect holiday. Instead, he looked down upon his beautiful mother being carried out the front door in the arms of the chauffeur, her lover, never to return to his father's house. Dick was promptly sent to his room, his presents left unopened.

He is an only child, which doesn't mean he has been spared sibling rivalry. His mother covers all the bases, sibling and Oedipal. It was his father who had wanted "a beautiful son and heir," and had thus selected a perfect, much, much younger specimen as mate and mother to his boy. "He used to hold me, toss me in the air, and kiss my tummy, making me laugh," Dick sighs. But when his mother walked out, his father never held his son again.

As in fairy tales, it was his warmhearted grandmother who presided over her son's house and nurtured her little grandson. Periodically he would visit his mother, The Ice Queen, but when his grandmother died, he was bereft of the only love he'd known. On Sundays his father's brother, the poor relation, would come to dinner with his Brunhild wife and their "no-neck monster" children, as Tennessee Williams would write in *Cat on a Hot Tin Roof*. They would compete for his father's attention/money. Bitterly resenting Dick, the beautiful one, the evil uncle and cousins would eventually connive to have him disinherited.

Twenty years ago, Dick's mother invited him to lunch at the Westbury Hotel's Polo Lounge in New York and kissed him off forever. She was about to marry for the fourth time, and she was sure he would understand "that no one would believe I had a son your age." Never mind that Dick is a man of exceeding good looks; a woman who trades on her beauty feels that her power is jeopardized if the wrong numbers, any numbers, are attached to it. She was only seventeen when he was born, and she hated his beauty, seeing it as a threat that would draw admiring eyes away from her. When he grew into an adolescent of eye-stopping appeal, and one particular lover's eyes abandoned her and rested too long on him, she curtailed his monthly visits. "Mother will call you when she wants to see you," she announced with near sibling rivalry.

That day at the Polo Lounge, she added, "Oh, and don't ever telephone again. Don't ever try to reach me."

Now we pile far too many splendidly beribboned boxes under the tree fashioned of boughs of bougainvillea, and while Tony Bennett fills the air with songs more seemly for seduction than Christmas, we toast the beauty of the day and our good fortune in having one another. As we unwrap our gifts, family members telephone to wish us well, but no family calls for Dick.

One of our calls is from my cousin in Charleston to say how much the children love our gift, a bound set of fairy tales on video. "We must have rented *Snow White* from the video store a dozen times," she says. "Now they have their own copy. Guess who loves them the most? The two-year-old."

Two years old and hooked on beauty, love, and killer envy, the stuff of life when you're two and want the straight poop.

"Beauty is as beauty does," mother murmurs the ancient mantra in her dear voice, wanting to keep baby humbly in her place, but also to ward off the evil eye and teach the ambivalence of beauty power. "You shall not escape me," cries the evil witch who tries to murder her too pretty stepdaughter in the Grimm tale, "Sweetheart Roland." This is the secret of ancient mantras, in a couple of words they say it all.

Barely off mother's milk, the two-year-old records the contradictory mantras so reminiscent of what life is really like. Beauty is power. The lesson has been learned and, along with it, the etiquette every beauty must practice if she is to survive in women's world; the possession of beauty already places you so far ahead of all the other girls—especially those in the family, in the next bed—that it is only proper, only safe, to downplay your own.

By the time the little girl is four "beauty is only skin deep" will be so deeply imprinted on her brain that the words will not have to be repeated. Other children will have taught her their own ambivalent feelings regarding her gift; they will seek her out, as drawn to the serenity of her lovely form as any adult. Should she acquire more power, admiration is transmogrified into the envy that was always waiting in the wings. The beauty's portfolio can be devalued in an instant, worse, she can be put at risk, and no one is more aware of her precarious power than she. How to survive in women's world, even little women's world, if you have the gift? Play it down, be careful, already having so much, don't try for too much more.

By the time a child reaches the advanced age of ten or eleven, the defense system against envy has become so practiced that when a study was done on fifth-grade girls, more than 75 percent of them, including the prettiest, graded themselves as the least attractive in the class. It is a remarkable finding, so rich in implications that one doesn't know where to begin. How can the minds of ten-year-olds be so programmed that they dare not acknowledge reality? And we wonder why women never believe in their beauty, why our closets are so filled with clothes that promised beauty but never delivered.

I'd thought twice about sending that collection of fairy tales on video to my cousin's children. Being read to was what I'd loved as a child, the adult's physical presence close to me, the sight, the smell of this dear person giving me exclusive attention, their time, and then the familiar voice repeating the stories that were called "make-believe" but which felt closer to life than anything real.

The Brothers Grimm collection was a heavy blue volume when I was a child, and the raised, ornate, gold scroll on its cover promised convoluted tales that never disappointed. I would thrill in my bones at the terror, probably recognizing my own rage as an envious child with a beautiful older sister whose tie to my mother seemed to leave no room for me. Perhaps more than anything I loved the idea that my own mother had been read to from the same book, for inside there was a printed plate that read, "From the Library of the Colbert Children." Imagine!

Myths and folklore offer the child imaginary resolutions to the real contradictions in life. Transformations and disguises do not so much confound as explain. Ugly frogs turn into handsome princes, kindly seeming grandmothers become crones who torture small children. Yes, it feels right, because to a child, the adult world is rampant with contradictions. Adults do not call emotions by their real names. Their interpretation of what is going on around the house is at odds with what the child experiences. They say they love you when they don't, and lie about the value of a pretty face. The fairy tale is closer to reality than what mother says. Even as I write this I become aware of how the belief in my secret evil childhood self grew into a portrait I brought to every important relationship later in life; once again I had to appear to be someone I wasn't, someone who was nicer than the Bad Nancy. As for my sister and mother, well, I have only recently demythologized them, allowing them some of the badness that as a child I had monopolized.

Whatever is right and true, neither today's intellectual understanding, nor kindness and spontaneous generosity, no, not even love for my darling husband seem to purge my suspicion that childhood envy has marked me as a Bad Girl for life. When a dear friend writes a malicious review of one of my books, I am beyond consolation. My husband tries to tell me that it was envy that provoked her. But other people's envy doesn't lessen suspicion of my own. The self-portraits we draw in childhood are overly harsh to protect us from them and them from us. Without today's Zoran, earrings by Ted Muehling, and storebought blond streaks, I would be recognized as who I am. To trace our midlife disguises to the early years of life is as obvious as follow-the-dots.

I have tried to understand the anxiety in that house I was brought to from the hospital. My young mother was economically dependent on her domineering father, who was so opposed to her marrying the man she loved that they eloped. Then he went away, my mysterious father, gone, never to return again. Of course she had no time or inclination for baby pictures. But I have the inner eye of memory, snap-shots from my bank of dreams, which tell me I correctly sense that my exhibitionistic life grew out of the earliest possible hunger for visibility.

Memories of my father. I have none. I grew up believing he was dead, though no one ever said the words. Someone must have, but when? "Oh, my daddy's dead," I would cheerfully reply when strangers asked of his whereabouts. Nothing more, for I knew nothing, also not to ask, not even to wonder about him, so forbidden, so loaded with terrible consequences was the subject of him. From the earliest days I assumed that he was the source of mother's anxiety; she sighed a great deal, and on those few occasions when she, instead of my beloved nurse, Anna, braided my hair, her sighing behind my head was frightening proof that I was a terrible burden to her. Other times when I heard her sigh, I assumed it had to do with his absence. I put two and two together and knew that if it weren't for me, she would still be with him.

I've always suspected that there was a time, before I came along, when "they" were all happy—my mother, sister, and father. My sister had known him, been held by him, seen herself in his eyes. And surely my mother was happy then. It was my *feeling* that my mother and sis-ter shared this family romance, a bond between them. I must have envied it bitterly, although I totally denied that envy until recent years, until writing books brought it out of me. Rivalrous with my silly older sister? Absolutely not! Was I not the most popular girl in class, the brightest, the funniest, she who was welcome in any house in town?

Looks weren't even on the list of what mattered in my young life; I worked at my happiness by winning love outside the family in any arena other than beauty. My defenses against the recognition of my envy of my sister for having known my father, and for resembling my lovely mother, were impenetrable.

Now I find that in studies conducted among very successful women, the majority admit to an early sense of feeling themselves to be the less attractive sibling. When I did my own national survey with pollsters DYG Inc. in 1990, 75 percent of the women surveyed said that being the less "pretty one" in the family made them determined to prove themselves.

Well, then, we might conclude, perceiving yourself as the plain kid has great advantages; but wouldn't the best of all possible worlds be one in which the family went out of its way to praise intellectual curiosity, independence, wit, and bravery, and gave beauty its due too, acknowledging its powerful force so that you became competent at handling it in yourself as well as in others.

Why would so many popular fairy tales turn on rivalries between brothers and sisters if beauty, simply by virtue of its luminous power, was not the issue that more than any other the tiny child wanted to hear told, and retold so that his or her own feelings could be recognized?

Once upon a time—this is a real story—a man gave me a wide gold ring on which he'd had engraved an illustration of the fairy tale of the princess on the glass mountain whose father, the king, had said, "He who can climb the glass mountain will win my daughter and the kingdom." There was a family of three brothers, the eldest of whom charged arrogantly up the glass mountain on his horse and failed miserably. The middle brother tried the same tactic and failed. It was the youngest, neglected brother who was able to ascend the slippery mountain on foot and win the princess's heart. Sure enough, if you looked very closely at the ring, there was a tiny princess on a hill, and each of the three brothers.

The man who gave it to me was the youngest of three brothers, they much older than he who was his mother's darling. Until a sister was born, the much desired only daughter, who took his place. How he hated that sister, an envy that I now recall explains his solitary comment on what he referred to as the "breakthrough" in his analysis. Until now, his words have always puzzled me: "The beauty of women is important." Never believing in any looks I got, I accepted the ring and wore it; I still have it. He was such a tough guy, that lover, an intellectual encased in defenses of iron. Imagine allowing himself to create such a gift. Imagine me never believing, ever.

Here is a little rhyme with which to close this section on sibling rivalry. It was collected in England by the same people who gave us my all-time favorite, "I one my mother . . . I ate my mother." It is noted by the authors that small children chant this while swinging:

I went to my father's garden,
And found an Irish farthing.
I gave it to my mother
To buy a baby brother.
My brother was so nasty,

I baked him in a pasty,
The pasty wasn't tasty
So I threw it over the garden wall,
I threw it over the garden wall.
   Die once!
      Die twice!
Die three times and never no more,
And never – no – more!

Learning to Be Clean (and Beautiful)

A modern puzzle: Why do women, who are famous for disliking the sight, smell, and touch of genitals, their own as well as men's, continue to be that sex that toilet trains the human race? We know that our most lasting impressions of our genitals are laid down in the earliest years, feelings that we carry into our sexual lives and which are painfully hard to change. With all the love in the world, what does a woman bring to the teaching of self-love, the whole self, including what lies between the legs?

What do her eyes, facial expressions, her voice and body language communicate when she parts the little legs to clean the cracks and crannies? Is she impervious to the smell of shit? Can her lifelong approach to fastidious hygiene, her fear of humiliation regarding loss of control in all functions related to the genital area bring a relaxed, not overly critical approach to bladder and sphincter control? In the end, can she have any more regard for her daughter's vulva, hairless and pure as it may look, than she does for her own, which she may once have allowed her husband to kiss but now hates for him to touch?

Along with the grim but expected dysfunctions that our society has tried to avoid discussing for hundreds of years, we now have an epidemic of unwanted pregnancies as well as sex-related diseases that end in death. We have heard and read that the attitude we have about our genitals determines our sexual behavior. Our feelings, conscious and unconscious, are also going to predict how our children grow into adulthood, *if* they reach maturity.

Even if women could leave the workplace—an unrealistic possibility—we would never again be able to infuse "mother" with either the omnipotence or grace she once had; we've now seen too many women who act like men to ever again believe in the idealized mommy of yesteryear who, by women's own hand, has been brought down to earth, a hand as big and sometimes as cruel as any man's.

This leaves the door to the nursery fortuitously ajar. Women's workload, grown prodigious both in and outside the home, demands that certain tasks be reassigned; to each person should go that job for which he or she is best qualified. Given the top priority of teaching tiny children genital respect, the obvious candidate is a man, father. Training a child to control his or her bladder and sphincter, even as he or she sleeps, is where genital respect begins. If it is done with ease, with reward and not punishment, everything "down there" is not freighted with disgust, fear, and the threat of loss of love. I'd give anything to have been toilet trained by a man.

I realize that this is not going to be a popular discussion. Though it has nothing to do with accusing women of being bad mothers, it will be taken as such, the usual defensive tactic used to make things go away. I will be labeled a mother blamer and taken to task. But I am on the side of the angels here. This subject is at the very heart of this book: Our feelings about our genitals, the image we have of them, which began even before toilet training, is an unavoidable lens through which we see every other part of our body. How could it be otherwise?

When women look in the mirror, what we see that is unattractive, that is never right, is the dirty secret between our legs, something that we know is ugly and not clean. Aren't women, first and foremost, "clean"? Consciously, our genitals may not come to mind, but they are like a disfigurement that no amount of beautiful clothes, scent, or embellishment of other areas of the body can cancel out. Nor can any honey-tongued man ever persuade us that he loves "it," for we have a memory lodged in our earliest years in which the most important person in our lives imprinted upon us *her* feelings about *our* genitals.

Neither sex is born loving or hating its genitals more than the other. It is learned, all learned. And it is learned at a time when we are so tiny and impressionable, given our total dependency, that the lessons are never forgotten, freighted as they are with the promise of or withholding of love, meaning food, warmth, shelter, safety, life.

We women accuse men of being too much in love with their penises. We bitterly resent that love affair because it leaves us out, yes, even to the point where you could say we are jealous of the time he spends alone with "it." We don't necessarily want it, but that doesn't mean we want him to enjoy it, thus reminding us of our own failure as sexual people. In some part of our brain we women know that sex is healthy and natural, that there have been good times when we too enjoyed it, but not like him. No, he could do it, have it far more often than we. We're not just jealous he's left us out of his masturbation, we're envious too; though we would never admit it, we secretly admire someone who masturbates without guilt, maybe even with it. Imagine being able to feel guilt and have an orgasm too!

Since men and women spend so much of their lives out of sync with one another regarding the beauty of genitals, our own and one another's, the quandary is worth pursuing. Could it be, for instance, that women, seeing ourselves in mother the caretaker, unwittingly take on her attitude about private parts, and that boys, being mother's opposite, spend their lives proving mother wrong: denying and defying her? That so many men go through life measuring, masturbating, visiting "bad" women for forbidden sex, and that most do not abuse women but instead mask their anger, even turn it against themselves, says how very deep the cut was, that first estimation by the most important person in the world.

Think of the sad little volume that might be compiled of humiliating nicknames like "Sissybox" applied by a kind and loving mother to a little boy's penis. Let us be methodical about this, for the picture of our genitals with which we grow up is integral to the whole self-portrait: What does mother see or feel when she holds her boy's penis in the course of teaching him the ABCs of toilet training? Though this one is no bigger than her thumb, has she ever held a penis this close before, ever wanted to, or kissed one, brought it to full erection in her mouth? Yes, yes, this is her son and he is only two years old, *but this is a penis*, and, before you know it, he will grow up and away. She calls it his sissybox, not consciously clipping his wings, but clip, clip, nonetheless.

Of course boys grow up "programmed" to flaunt their penises in the company of other good fellows who share many interests but none of them quite as liberating as the sexual relief of having gotten away from the Giantess. The penis is the flag staking out territory won in spite of her; behavior with genital associations that once threatened the loss of mother love becomes a male playground and a source of pride. No little girl would dare to fart in class, but to boys the public breaking of Women's Rules is a defiant victory, all the more joyous when little girls (little mothers) wrinkle their noses in disgust.

Any hope that adolescent girls share the boys' interest in exploring the forbidden part of the body is dashed when female indignation informs him that girls are just like mother. The boy has the unhappy choice of acting like a girl or hanging defiantly with the boys, setting up the sad division between the sexes wherein each perceives the other as the beloved enemy, or simply, "the enemy."

How much more implicated are women in men's obsession with their erections than we would care to admit? Who can blame the boy for going to "bad" women for sex when he has been raised by a woman to separate love and sex? When he meets a female who adores his penis with an enthusiasm to match his own, after the initial, thrilling gratitude comes the question, Why? What sort of a woman is she? The old line about there being girls you fuck and those you marry hasn't been around this long without reason.

A majority of men's sexual fantasies grow out of a man's first love, when as a boy he was made to feel it was his mother's love or his penis. In his fantasy the man cleverly manages to get around mother's prohibition, in fact, to make her scary warnings about "bad sex" work for him. He imagines himself bound, chained, humiliated, and at the mercy of a Big Woman. She is in control, yes, but he wins. She may have the whip, but he gets his dirty little orgasm. Very clever.

Why should a man expect "nice women" to love his penis any more than mother did? Indeed, the woman who combines mother's niceness with an easy sexual familiarity with male sexual organs might be felt to have too much power. Should they marry, the man is often relieved when her sexual drive diminishes after childbirth. He prefers to find sex in a less complicated setting than home, where mother and children are once again present. Nowadays, she too may prefer to separate sex and marriage. It has everything to do with issues of control and love, the portraits of ourselves as either sexual or nice, conflicting images that are the emotional fretwork of what is fondly called The Battle of the Chamber Pot.

Listen to a man writing about how his mother taught him to "pee into the bowl like a big man." It is this event, he contemplates, that causes him in adult life to be "torn by desires that are repugnant to my conscience, and a conscience repugnant to my desires." The passage, from *Portnoy's Complaint*, by Philip Roth, was written almost thirty years ago, when the world was so in tune and Roth so funny and fine a writer that even the prissiest of readers saw something recognizable in it:

I stand over the circle of water, my baby's weeny jutting cutely forth, while my momma sits beside the toilet on the rim of the bathtub, one hand controlling the tap of the tub (from which a trickle runs that I am supposed to imitate) and her other hand tickling the underside of my prick. I repeat: *tickling my prickling!* I guess she thinks that's how to get stuff to come out of the front of that thing, and let me tell you, the lady is right. "Make a nice sis, *bubala*, make a nice little sissy for Mommy," sings Mommy to me, while in actuality what I am standing there making with her hand on my prong is in all probability my future! Imagine! The *ludicrousness!* A man's character is being forged, a destiny is being shaped. . . .

Poor Vagina, a Rose by Any Other Name . . .

When I went to be fitted for my first diaphragm—long after I should have, silly virgin who played with intercourse, "losing" my precious jewel by centimeters—I sat in the doctor's office with my new rubber disk and watched without seeing as he described the ugly pink model on his desk of a woman's reproductive organs. I didn't want to see, be informed, though pregnancy terrified me. I could not watch where his pencil lines had traced for hundreds of other blind women the trail from cervix to urethra, to bladder, and oh, no! not the anus. I had never seen either urethra or anus, and while nothing brought me closer to heaven than a man's mouth in that area, I didn't want to know about it. That was essential to the magic, I am sure, that he, my lover, wanted to put his mouth "there"; somehow, it made him powerfully male and dirty, allowing me, the innocent female, to be overwhelmed into orgasm by forces beyond my control.

I've mentioned that there is an unthought-out way we tend to imagine everything "down there" as one hole, one aperture through which everything exits our body: the cloaca, Latin for sewer. To this day gynecologists tell me that many women still don't know the precise location or the difference between the urethra and vagina; great strides have been made, however, since the invention of the vibrator, as to the location of the clitoris. That so many women prefer to masturbate lying under the pure water from a bathtub faucet isn't surprising; not only is it a fine system but it eliminates having to touch oneself, promising cleanliness as absolution in the very throes of orgasms.

"I don't think penis envy is inborn, as did Freud," says my mentor, Richard Robertiello, "nor do most people in the field today. I don't think a woman's born feeling she has a defective organ." But like others in his profession, Robertiello feels that little girls, because of overly strict toilet training, because of mothers who are self-deprecating or masochistic, along with a perception that females are valued less than males in the family, well, it all adds up to a feeling that "there is something wrong with them, which is their genitals," he says. "Women grow up displacing this 'disfigurement' onto their thighs, their breasts, their flabby arms. Have you ever met a woman who didn't think there was something wrong with her physically?"

I shake my head sadly, wishing I had a good argument. Robertiello and I have had this conversation often over the years. The more I write, read, think, live, the more convinced I am of the cloaca's spillover, as it were, smearing the rest of our body. When we are little girls, we don't want the penis as much as we want the control it represents. If we should also grow up witnessing mother's erotic attachment to our brother, our conviction that he has something desirable we don't is enhanced. Whatever differential treatment the boy gets, from family or society, can seem to have its source in that area of the body that we little girls feel is inadequate. I didn't have a brother or a father; nonetheless, I learned this as far back as I can remember. As far back as "explicit" memory goes, I tried to pee standing up, rather unsuccessfully. As for my body: unacceptable!

The fact is, most men do not have women's lifelong dissatisfaction with their bodies; they may worry about the size of their penis, but they do not think of the penis and anus as a sewer. When young boys learn to disparage the vagina, referring to it as a "gash" or a "slit," it is an intended slur, learned in part from girls' own sensitivity about their "deformity." The boy may have some envy of his own regarding women's breasts and their ability to bear children, but he is best informed by the girls' own self-consciousness regarding their genitals that here is a perfect outlet for male resentment: Disparage the girl, and in putting her down, get back at women who boss you around!

When the boy eventually learns women's absolute control over whether or not there will be sex, his crude and embarrassing remarks to girls increase; what he would prefer, most of the time, is simply to adore the woman's body. When he is abruptly put in his place and made to feel like an animal, well, he responds like one: Two men stand talking to each other on a street, all the while their eyes drawn to a woman walking by, all splendor. Feeling their gaze, she glares at them. Awe turns to anger: "Hey, Harry," one guy says to the other, "look at those jugs!" "Crude brutes!" the woman says, consoling herself, hunching her shoulders forward.

What sort of a war is this? When does it begin, and why? Men should not yell rude remarks at women, but they are playing on a sensitivity that has always been there, at best a fear of inadequacy that women learn from other women. The irony is that men have found the chink in our armor, a valuable weakness to know when, in fact, it is women, in the boy's mind, who have all the power.

"When patients come to me and say, 'Body image is the size of my nose, my height, my weight,' I try to get them to see how complicated body image is," says psychologist Ann Kearney-Cooke. "Body image is *not* how you think about your body, talk about it. It's about how you feel sexually; it's about issues of control, which begin in how your body functions, beginning with the earliest lessons you had in controlling those functions."

Our earliest sense of our identity comes from how we feel about our body as children, how we are raised to see ourselves, how "they" saw us. "Your body is the house you live in, and if there is something going on inside that you feel is not right," says Kearney-Cooke, "then the way you see your body is negative. When you began to crawl, to walk, everyone clapped. Learning sphincter control, to be toilet trained, this too is what gets you either love or a sense of failure. The more control you feel of your body, the more control you feel of yourself as a child, which translates into a good body image."

Control. Probably the last thing we would think of as key to body image; but think of its opposite, loss of control, soiling oneself, drawing attention to one's self when we aren't absolutely sure every little hair is in place. It is only, in fact, when we can *control the observer*, meaning attract his/her attention at the very moment when we are absolutely positive that we look perfect—as in a living tableau—that we are comfortable with being seen. Control, control, control.

Where do we women learn our need—which men hate—to control the world? We learn it early, in the nursery and then in the adjoining room, the bathroom, where there is the toilet, on which we are placed to control sphincter and bladder, and thus win love, approval, or not, meaning we have neither control over ourselves or sureness of the love of those dear people without whom we cannot live. Suddenly love, acceptance, image rest totally on our ability to control the flow of urine and feces.

"Girl babies are plopped on a toilet, they're not to look at themselves, they're not to touch themselves, but they are instructed that this is a body function they must manage, control," says sex educator Judith Seifer. "Girl babies are given a consistent message of contamination, that what you have down there is dark, it's dirty, you don't touch it. After they do urinate the next thing they are taught to do is to wipe themselves clean with lots of toilet paper, and then to wash, wash their hands until clean. Boys, on the other hand, are taught to hold their penis, to aim it, and we give them great praise when the stream of urine hits the toilet bowl."

Let's take our brother's penis—so to speak—which is an external organ he can literally direct and aim. He may not be expert at learning the rigors of sphincter and bladder control, but to us, his sister, he has a unique advantage in winning mother's praise and love. (It wouldn't be called the battle of the chamber pot if it weren't about her love.) To the girl, the manipulatable gadget he holds in his hand is like the handle on the faucet that turns the water on and off. If there is envy of the penis, it is acquired envy of something perceived to control functions in such a way as to make mother happy. Seated on the toilet, her genitals out of sight—no handle there anyway—the girl must assume that this place between her legs is unmanageable. If it were not so, mother's face and attitude would eventually be relaxed and satisfied regarding everything to do with her daughter's bodily functions.

In a recent study of ethnically and socioeconomically diverse mothers with one- to four-year-old children, it was found that fewer than a third of the children had received accurate words for their genitals, learning instead expressions like "bucket," "dinkie," "garage," "peabuggy," "potato," and "twattie" (for girls) and "aeriel," "dingadoo," "jugjug," "peeper," "schmuck," and "wormywillie" (for boys). Some were given no word at all. And lest you think we improve with age and education, in the teaching programs of two different medical universities, pediatric residents "performing routine well-child care examinations either omitted examining the genitals, proceeded through the genital examination in silence, or prefaced it with comments such as, 'Now, I'm going to check down there'; [a similar study] found that pediatric residents included the genitals in their examinations approximately half as frequently for girls as for boys."

Occasionally I was bathed and toweled in my mother's pretty bathroom, and I'm sure I assumed that one day I would inherit all those lovely bottles and vials with their sweet-smelling elixirs that made mother so pretty and clean. The very look and scent of our future is in these carefully packaged accessories decorated with flowers and bouquets chosen to promise women, anxious about their odors, absolute success at daintiness. Being clean, smelling nice, different from our brother, has much to do with the toilet and the different manner in which we approach it; he stands holding his penis and chatting with chums when he urinates and doesn't wipe but leaves drops on the floor. (Imagine if we left a puddle on the floor!)

It is a riddle to a girl child who sees her brother both cleaner in his ability to control urine and yet dirtier in his habits; soon, the boy will work at outdistancing his sister in dirtiness, making himself as different as possible from her and mother-whom-he-loves-too-much. Before she even enters school, the girl will stand alongside mother tsk-tsking her brother's muddy footprints on mother's clean kitchen floor, identified with mother in clean floors as well as in the vials and jars of cosmetics in the cabinet over the bathroom sink.

She may not yet understand their application, but she has grasped that they mask a woman's unmentionables, make her pretty. One day, in full ignorance of its function, the little girl puts a sanitary napkin between her legs, playing "grown-up lady," a ritual of daintiness, which has more to do with the sewer than she would want to imagine. Oh, no, not blood, not *there*! In time, everything the girl puts on her body—clothes, lipstick, lovely lingerie—is camouflage, a veil, theatrical makeup to please the eye, to divert attention from the birthmark, the blemish, the sewer.

"Over the years, many patients of all ages and backgrounds have asked me during their pelvic exams, 'How can you do this job? It's so disgusting,'" says gynecologist Christiane Northrup. "The most common reason that women douche, moreover, is their mistaken belief, handed down from mother to daughter, that this area of the body is offensive and requires special cleaning."

It is demoralizing to think that our intimate relationships as adults are reactions to what we had with Mommy: Nowhere do women fight so hard to love our bodies than in our erotic reveries, where the desire to feel sexual does battle with Mother's Nice Girl; nowhere is women's anger quite so misplaced as when it is deflected away from mother and projected onto the Bad Men of sexual fantasy, who "force" us to feel what we have always dreamed of, the orgasmic pleasure that originates in his penis, his hand, better still, his mouth, on that dark, forbidden, dirty place.

Long ago—it seems like another lifetime—when nice women were identified and graded by their roles as homemakers, television commercials projected Mr. Clean into the kitchen, catching housewives off guard as they used the wrong detergent and warning them that their floors weren't clean at all. Bad, dirty women! To attain the Good Housekeeping seal of approval, every woman needed a jolly giant product of one sort or another, a "big man" for a "big job": cleanliness.

Today's commercials are aimed at the New Woman, who runs between office and home, frantic that she isn't fulfilling any of her jobs adequately. These go straight to that area that Mr. Clean only symbolized: Ladies, you're not getting it really clean! You may be doing a man's work, even paying your own way, but you've overlooked home base: Douche it! Spray it! Massengill Douche has put Mr. Clean in the closet.

How wonderful for a little girl to be bathed, powdered, and toilet trained by someone who doesn't think the sight and smell of excrement are loathsome, someone who doesn't see the vagina as a sewer that must be scoured again and again. Most men's idea of cleanliness isn't absolute, nor do they feel their own identity is at stake, that the world will judge them if a child touches her genitals, as babies do. What about the history of masturbation if it were left in Dad's hands instead of Mother's? Imagine growing up masturbating when you felt like it, naturally, learning the rules of privacy, feeling entitled and therefore more responsible for your sexuality?

When the former surgeon general, Joycelyn Elders, was asked at an AIDS conference what she thought were the "prospects of a more explicit discussion and promotion of masturbation," she replied, "I think that is something that is a part of human sexuality and it's a part of something that perhaps should be taught. But we've not even taught our children the very basics. And I feel that we have tried ignorance for a very long time, and it's time we try education."

Brave and well-chosen words that sadly hastened President Clinton's request for Elders's resignation. I've never been more disappointed in the man for whom I voted. It is unforgivable that a country drowning in the loss of lives to sexual ignorance should deprive its young people of knowing that they have the right and obligation to own their bodies. My only difference with Elders is her choice of the

word "teach"; we don't need to be taught, but were we *allowed* to masturbate without fear of the loss of love, we would.

We don't want to think about preadolescent sexuality; it makes us
uncomfortable imagining small children as sexual—just look at what it
did to Freud's career in Victorian Vienna!—but we are also loath to resurrect our own earliest sexual stirrings in our parents' house, where
watchful eyes gave us no privacy. There we were one day straddling
the arm of the sofa, rocking back and forth as we often did, except that
this time we felt an exciting sensation that began between our legs,
coursed through our bodies from toes to fingertips and up to the brain,
where pictures of pirates holding us hostage told us this was scary.
Though we were only four years old, we knew from the place of origin
that what we were doing might be wrong, but it was mother's sudden
appearance, her voice and the expression on her face, that warned us
that we must never do it again. But do what? Was it the rocking on the
sofa arm, what we were imagining, or the warm glow spreading
through our bodies? Was it that we must never touch ourselves
"there," or was it that she knew what we were feeling, that she had felt
it too, once, and that it wasn't nice at all?

Mother's disapproval is now woven into our sexual feelings. She is
good—of that there can be no question—and therefore we and that
nice feeling aren't nice at all. If we give up the feeling, she will never
leave us. We disavow it, or try to, and quarrel with its return for the
rest of our lives. Even the faintest stirring of sexual arousal, ten, twenty
years later, comes mixed with anxiety that tightens muscles against it
in our belly, slams doors shut in our brains where passion has already
begun to trigger surrender; we don't remember the incident on the
sofa arm but when our own child is four we recognize our anger when
we catch him touching himself, and we feel closer to mother. We forgive her and scold him.

If there had been another source of love, equal to mother's, in the
house when we were little, someone who wasn't against rocking on
the sofa arm, we might like our bodies more. I realize that not all men
are comfortable with sexuality, especially when dealing with their own
daughters, but part of men's discomfort with both sex and women
comes from their own female-dominated childhood. This discomfort
would lessen over time if father were a second caretaker, a different
voice. Children wouldn't fear mother's disapproval so totally. Her
occasional criticism wouldn't loom like doomsday, and we would

come to love her for her self, a person who was both as good and bad as any other human. We would not automatically incorporate the parts of her we hate—her anxiety and possessiveness, her asexuality—in order to prove our love. "Mom is wonderful, but I am a different person and I love her for allowing me to become who I am."

You have noticed the amazing effect of great sex on appearance. Women's faces acquire a radiance, a glow, an easing of the lines of tension we didn't even know we carried, so constantly are we on guard. Have you ever gone out, say to a restaurant, while that flush is still present and noticed your postorgasmic power over the room, how grateful the maître d' is, the waiters' faces adjusting and softening in response to your including them in your magic circle? It is a terrible waste of natural resources that we don't go out of our way, especially in these strained, difficult times, to educate more women to beam postorgasmically upon the world. Imagine if all women were raised to enjoy great sex, responsibly: what warmth, what happiness, what a dream.

That women, instead, spend so much time and money on beauty and so little in bed, which is free, explains the iron hold of the antisex rules on which we were raised. Think of the roots of our rage at having denied ourselves sex, our hellish bad temper that is barely contained so long as all women subscribe to those rules. Damn any woman who spreads her legs more than the rest of us and wears that postorgasmic smile, for she mocks our forced goodness, reminding us of what we have sacrificed.

Even the recent economic success that women have won doesn't lessen the resentment at the sacrifice, begun long before adolescence, of sexuality. I often think women's rage is even worse today and grows, commensurate with the increase in our economic power, as if to say, "Here I sit, mistress of my universe, and I *still* hate my body! Damn those Big, Bad Men who are responsible!" Poor men, always a safer target when they probably had nothing to do with teaching us to loathe our bodies. Men didn't bathe us, toilet train us, or teach us to think of our genitals as dirty. However, to face the origin of self-loathing, the person for whose love we abandoned sexual identity, is today as fraught with anxiety as when we were children. It is demoralizing. The only thing that makes it better is when we repeat with our own children exactly what she taught us; her behavior comes to us easily, automatically. By becoming her, we forgive mother. See, I don't hate you, Mommy! Am I not just like you? Now I understand: This is how mothers are!

It is childish to avoid this interesting dialogue on the grounds that it is blaming poor old mom. How can a mother who has abandoned her own sexual life be overjoyed when she finds that her daughters are sexually curious? I don't mean sexually active, simply open, self-accepting. There is great envy attached to people, yes, even one's own daughter, who appear to be more sexually at ease; they awaken awareness of what we gave up and we hate them for sparking that memory of what might have been. When women tell me stories of mothers who angrily berated them for masturbating when young—"No decent man will marry you!"—I hear mother's envy talking.

What makes women's policing of sexuality so devastating is that it becomes necessary to control not just their children but the world around them as well. Owning our sexuality is vital to a sense of completeness, of feeling whole, the awareness of oneself as sexually alive. When others partake of the forbidden fruit, it is unbearable. Sexual self-loathing and abstinence can only be lived with when everyone agrees to go along with it. The right-wing, antisex community—men and women—get their extraordinary energy from envy, the rage that has no end.

To suggest that even the most adoring mother is going to teach her daughter love of her vagina, her son love of his penis, when she doesn't share these feelings, is asking her to invent a new kind of mothering. It is asking her to act like a man, or to invite her husband to help her change women's antisex legacy by joining her as an equal in the nursery. We should think hard about why we are so willing to concede that women have a right to enter the workplace, but question men in the nursery. Some men can run a nursery as well as some women can an office.

It must become acceptable to say this, talk about it; it should be one of those discussions lovers have when they talk about their future, about marriage. Both may want a family, but she shouldn't feel guilty admitting that she doesn't fancy raising children. It would be an important reason for her choosing a man who loved the idea of full-time fathering, or part-time, while she worked outside the home. We choose partners for religious reasons, economics, looks, a shared love of old movies and fishing trips. Why shouldn't a match be made on grounds as significant as who is best at raising children and/or earning money? Twenty years ago, all hell broke loose at the suggestion that there is no such thing as a "maternal instinct." Well, there isn't. Love is learned by parent and children.

The return to the idealization of motherhood in recent years is obvious in the relentless standards of perfection celebrated in the new crop of Mother's Day cards. Meanwhile, advertisers wring their hands as to how to appeal to the "typical" mother. "Advertisers are so afraid of offending their best customers," said Barbara Lippert, the advertising critic for *Adweek* magazine. "If they show mothers staying at home, the working mothers tune out. If they show them as frantic working mothers, the stay-at-home mothers tune out."

Imagine a generation in which both sexes bring their own unique qualifications and life experiences to the care and education of a tiny child; imagine growing up loving one's amazing sexual parts, seeing them as beautiful, the vagina, the penis, the anus, the works. Are any of the problems surrounding men being more intimately involved in the raising of their children more daunting than those women confronted twenty years ago? What could be tougher than getting men to abandon their monopoly on the all-male workplace? Legally, morally, we women were in the right; even men saw this, and many fought alongside us for our equal rights. Well, the success of getting men into the nursery—as moral and ethical an issue as women in the workplace—lies in women's hands. Men will not enter that area where a woman once totally controlled them until we relinquish absolute control and not just invite men to share responsibility, but demand it of them because it is what is best for their children.

Change will not come easily. Perhaps this is why I am so touched by a scene from Saul Bellow's novel *Herzog*, in which Moses Herzog, packing a pistol, drives to his former wife Madeline's house to seek revenge on her and her new husband, Gersbach. Looking through the bathroom window he observes a hand—a man's hand!—reaching into the tub to shut off the water. Then the hated rival Gersbach playfully, kindly, orders his stepdaughter "to stand, and she stooped slightly to allow him to wash her little cleft. . . . Steady and thorough, he dried her, and then with a large puff he powdered her. The child jumped up and down with delight. 'Enough of this wild stuff,' said Gersbach, 'put on those p-j's now.'" With that, all of Herzog's rage is dissipated, and he leaves. "Firing this pistol was nothing but a thought."

I've thought often of this scene of a man who comes bearing a gun and is disarmed by the sight of his rival tenderly washing his daughter's "little cleft." I love that. So bombarded are we by stories and statistics of male abuse of children, we begin to believe it is latent in all men, which is no more true than it is of women. A woman kisses a baby boy's penis and the world shrugs; a man does the same and is jailed.

A poll dating back to 1977 found that 51 percent of the husbands surveyed would spend more time with their families if they had a shorter workweek. The *Los Angeles Times* conducted a poll in 1990 that found 39 percent of the fathers surveyed want to quit their jobs to have more time with their kids; 74 percent of men in another survey would prefer a "daddy-track job" over a "fast-track job." We also have studies that indicate that men who have been intimately involved in the raising of their children think better of themselves, which translates into higher self-esteem; and these men are less abusive. It seems so obvious. Why aren't planes writing it in the sky? Doesn't it also suggest that a boy raised by a male as well as a female might grow up to be less abusive?

Until we design a new agreement between the sexes, which includes men's rights as well as women's, our men will grow ever angrier, and women will too, even as we edge toward economic parity while retaining the trump card, the ability to bear the human race and shape it without men. The coming Matriarchy.

A hundred years ago men and women had a dozen offspring to compensate for the inevitable mortality rate among little children. Now that we have medicine and technology, our problem is that we have children, but no parents; and we have lost the extended family of grandparents, uncles, and aunts who once provided not just extra hands but laps and additional loving eyes that reflected a child to himself or herself. Adult attention, says Penelope Leach, "is one of the scarcest commodities in our materially rich homes." Children ". . . cannot *be* themselves with no attention at all. They would rather have disapproval, anger, even punishment, than be ignored and will often provoke negative attention if that is the only kind available to them."

What a bitter irony that we have made such medical and technological strides and lost our humanity in the process. We give our children more things and less of our selves, perhaps because we place more value on possessions than we do on ourselves. Intellectually, we know that life's patterns of thinking and behaving are laid down in the first years. Only two, three years old and already veterans of some of life's most impressive battles. By then, our children will have the bedrock of a sense of self, identity, separate from us, or they will not. When they look in the mirror, they will see someone who is fine just as she or he is, someone "good enough," loved enough so that later suspicions of not measuring up don't arise. Otherwise, their reflected image will be distorted by humiliating defeats, hidden behind the defenses of memory, battles lost to more beautiful siblings, to the plain sister whose envy was feared, or to caretakers who tried to make them into their own beauty ideal. No one ever saw them as finished: "Go, my child, you are perfect just as you are."

3

The Years of Invention

===

Freedom, Ah, the Feel of It, the Look of It!

There is a chapter that is strangely left out of the telling of life's story, as though it had no drama and simply didn't matter. Yet, if I were to pick the time when true self-image came most in focus and I felt like the heroine of my own story, I would turn to these exhilarating years bookended between mother's all-seeing eyes and the strobe lights of adolescence.

We are how old—maybe eight, nine?—and we are out of the house, relatively unfettered compared to what went before and lies ahead. It is unfortunate that Freud called these years The Latency Period, making them sound boring, as if we sleepwalked through them, when, indeed, there is greater potential for creativity and optimism than we will ever have again. Nor are we devoid of sexual feeling as the word *latency* suggests; it is rather that, after the bad opening night reviews of our Oedipal years, we have learned to keep sexual stirrings to ourselves.

Yes, we are young, but we have a unique combination of curiosity, bravery, and the infallibility of innocence; we may have been hurt in the competitive struggles within the family, but those losses have the advantage of being framed within the walls of home. As far as the brutal weeding-out process that will soon go on in adolescence, where we will be labeled for life, well, who at nine or ten can possibly comprehend its enormity?

Once we get beyond our lawn, we discover with a thrill that no one outside the house knows of our defeats opposite siblings. For now we bicycle or walk away from home base, where we return to refuel, physically and emotionally, but which is no longer our entire world. Beyond our house there is a new audience of eyes that perceive us in a way that we have never before been seen: Until now, everyone has viewed us within the context of our parents, looking from them to us, us to them. "You look just like your dad," they have said. "You have your mother's eyes." This is very nice, but it is not *us*.

On our bicycles, on our walks, at school, and in the homes of friends, we are seen for the first time as separate from our family. An unexpected window opens. How could it be otherwise? These people don't know our dreadful family nicknames; they have no expectations of us. The man at the filling station where we get air in our bicycle tires, the woman behind the counter at the store where we buy candy, the way they see us comes from *their* lives and has nothing to do with us, which is oddly freeing. They could care less, which gives us room to practice a posture: a way of talking and walking that captures their attention. For maybe a minute they stop what they are doing, and if we are sufficiently winning, we see their pupils dilate as they focus *on us*.

Us. It dawns on us that we can make ourselves up! As in the fairy tales read to us all these years, we can be the hero of an adventure, at the very least we can effect and accomplish, not just be acted upon.

It is a moment in literature, film, life when someone outside the family informs the parents of their own child: "What a wonderful storyteller your son is. What a charming kid, so funny, so kind, so adorable." The parent is enlightened, maybe thrilled, but not always. Although they will deny it, some parents don't relish being instructed about their own children by a stranger; not having been let in on this side of their child's character gives them an odd sense of failure, almost of betrayal, that the child didn't show them first. But the child sees the disappointment and suspicion of disloyalty in having given something special of herself outside the familial bond, and so decides to keep these new, secret identities just that.

The private quality of much that goes on in these years can be our way of protecting parents as well as ourselves. That certain adventures are kept to ourselves for "their" sake forges a newfound sense of responsibility. It is the growing child's version of the adults' whispering to one another, "How can you tell a child that?" What the boys in the film *Stand by Me* learn is that the adventure they have just been through is best kept private; it doesn't just knit them together in camaraderie but binds them with an oath of protection of parents, the beginning of the passing of the torch. They emerge from their adventure feeling different about themselves, and looking different too, less childish, more self-assured.

Someone may be prettier than we, but there are other assets that count now, count as they never will again, given the later sovereignty of looks. We match our intelligence, speed, inventiveness, bravery against a pretty face and come out a winner! Well, at least equal. Practiced again and again, these abilities become ours, become in time who we are. Believing this, we begin to look like the athlete, the actress, the leader. In earlier years, uncertainty dogged our features as our personality was being formed by constant comparisons within the family. Now, with luck, the baby face with its lowered and sad look comes alive and takes on character. We don't need to look in mirrors; we have begun to embrace internally the knowledge of who we are, and in our own mind's eye it is how we look.

Our parents and siblings may notice that we have begun to walk and talk as if we were playing a part; indeed, a brother may accuse us of "showing off," a sister advise us to "stop trying to be someone you aren't." With newfound bravery we brush off their criticism, keeping our new selves to ourselves. Things may never change within the family portrait, where brothers, sisters, parents may for the rest of our lives continue to see us as we were placed in the earliest hierarchy. "John is the handsome one," they will say twenty, thirty years later when, indeed, we have become far better-looking than John. When a parent has invested his or her own image in a specific child early on, there can be a refusal, conscious or not, to alter that favored child's position in the family; to do so would diminish the parent.

Try to force a reevaluation today at a family reunion and we walk into a minefield. So they called us "Tubby," "Four Eyes," "Shorty" and refuse to acknowledge what we've accomplished in our lives. Let it go, I advise you. Dump the old baggage of sibling and/or parental injustices, for there is nothing that sucks out joy more than arguing old family judgments in an endeavor to force them to see us as we have become. Take the anger, look at it in its age-appropriate frame, and let it go.

Had I not become a writer I would never have unearthed that young girl I was in my preadolescent years, she who has been the positive force in my life. In every book I have written in the past twenty-five years, I have grieved over abandoning her when adolescence overwhelmed. But she never actually went away. Her basic optimism worked on an unconscious level all of my life until recently, when she took conscious form and I remembered myself running along those high walls that contained all the lovely secret gardens in that wonderful place where I grew up. Once I was big enough to bicycle away from home, where I felt invisible, it was thrilling that the eyes of the people I met reflected a different me, an inkling of myself I'd always had. Now, just being myself was enough to win love.

When I stood atop my walls, soft bricks crumbling underfoot, and surveyed the world below, the sadness of not being able to catch my mother's eye was gone. My sureness of self came from a newfound sense of borders, safety. I believed I could take care of myself. While it was not actually true, what I felt was belief in the world as a good place, the open heart of the boy hero in fairy tales and novels as he strides away from the parental home in search of his fortune. What did I know of gender lines, the stereotypical roles that lay ahead, where everything that made me feel alive—initiative, bravery, competition—would be denied me? How could I anticipate how the love of boys, the desperate need to have them see me, would make the surrender of my twelve-year-old self immediate and overnight? For the rest of my life I would never have as agreeable a self-image as I did then. I suppose it was what drew me, and millions of others, to Saint-Exupéry's *The Little Prince* in the early seventies. "This world of childhood memories," as he would write, "will always seem to me hopelessly more real than the other."

This period of time we get between being tied to mother and adolescence is a small picture, a camera shutter briefly opening and closing. But time doesn't matter as long as we pin down the important character features that describe us. These years are money in the bank.

We spend so much of life fulfilling what family and society expect of us, although it may not be how we see ourselves. While it is necessary to learn to support ourselves economically, and perhaps a family too, do we really need so much baggage, possessions, clothes, and makeup as we are programmed to want? When we look in the mirror, saddled with all these acquisitions, we do not like what we see nearly as much as the sight of ourselves when we were ten and stood on top of the world.

The bicycle comes to mind as the symbol of these years. Learning to ride it is mastery, but short of owning a horse—my dream image, cowgirl—the bicycle was my companion in opening up the world I'd never explored beyond my house, streets, neighborhood. Being alone for the first time on a bicycle is an experience of control and adventure unlike any other, until perhaps the first car, even greater mastery as the world's boundaries open farther still and the camera lens widens to show us moving into territory ever more distant from the first judgmental eyes. Strangers enter our lives. Strangers can turn into anything, become anyone, as can we in their eyes.

I see me on my green Schwinn, no hands, singing, wearing jeans and a sweater of no particular color or style, for what did I care of mirror images? I felt who I was, in motion, flying past mere pedestrians, covering familiar ground that had become mine in repeated trips to school, suddenly hooking a right, experimenting with a new route, getting lost, getting found, doing it on my own, proving I could, proving, proving, proving. Legs, muscles, coordination became a sense of self in motion, totally in control. In my mind's eye I imagined others witnessed my passage and power. So what if they hadn't even noticed? Hadn't I left them in the dust? Reality was unimportant; it was the picture of me in my eyes and in theirs that reinforced mastery, the look of it. I had entered their world and left it at will.

The ingredients for happiness were so limited then, and I had them all; take one bicycle, add one girl, cook until done. I could have lived on that. I still could, if I could get back that feeling of being good enough. Was I ever that happy again?

The magic of these years for all of us is that for a brief time we are free to explore, to imitate admirable others, practice genetic treasures for which we find we have a natural talent, to which we bring a skill. Suddenly we are special. A teacher says, "Why, you have a real eye for drawing!" Someone has recognized us! Try me on! Be this! Act thus! inner voices urge; spontaneity is king as it will never be again, not with this unique freedom from judgmental eyes, slotting us. Just around the corner waits adolescence with its ironclad rules of behavior, a straitjacket compared to the leisured informality of the noncritical world of the nine-year-old.

What better time in life to find out who we want to be? An audience is waiting, and while there may be stage fright, it will never again be less daunting. Do it now. Be whoever. The time to find out what we want and who we are is upon us. Nothing succeeds like invention. No one is more inventive than a nine-year-old. Quick, before adolescence, when sameness is everything and uniqueness is death! Think of *The Red and the Black, Tom Sawyer, My Life as a Dog, Stand by Me*. We love these young heroes because we see ourselves in them, and though I would wish for more nine-year-old heroines in films and books, I nonetheless can look at Robert De Niro's *A Bronx Tale* and lose myself in that little boy, sleeping with his bed pushed under the window so that he will miss nothing in the street below that is his world. I too used to sleep with my pillow on the window ledge, so sure was I that my life was happening out there, everywhere, life without limits, and I didn't want to miss any of it. And there were no mirrors.

In those years I was not the least self-conscious. Free of physical comparison with my sister and mother, I grew on the love I was able to inspire in others. A feeling of great generosity was born in me, a desire to give that was as big as my need. How did I lose that, where did it go? Dear God, what a totally different person I would be today if the creativity of those years had been stoked instead of shut down by the tyranny of adolescent beauty.

It never occurred to me to question my love of romantic music. Riding the green bike, I would sing full throttle the ballads I had learned from my mother's recordings of Broadway musicals. Heartbreaking love songs flew from my lips as I rolled along those sweet, narrow streets of my youth, melodies that opened me in a way I didn't yet understand, pulling me into their yearning; maybe romance was taken for something else in my youthful mind, but maybe not. Romance, after all, is not sex; in fact, the very essence of romantic love, as originally understood by the troubadours, was the unattainable beloved. Pure yearning.

Certainly I was desperate to get lost in someone's arms, which, now that I think of it, was one of my favorites, "I Got Lost in His Arms," from *Annie Get Your Gun*. I could sing it for you now, every word. His arms, her arms, what did I care? Being held was what mattered and I didn't even know it, couldn't let myself acknowledge it for fear of being rejected, again.

I can still give myself to romantic music like no one else, except, perhaps, my sweet neighbor Peter Allen, who commanded the entire stage at Radio City Music Hall, kicking as high as the Rockettes. He sang his love songs on the terrace that we shared for twelve years. No one could write love songs like Pete. In the summer, I would sit on the terrace listening to him compose, feeling my life had come full circle that I should have this music man within singing distance. The summer before he died, we had his piano wheeled onto the terrace, and with Manhattan as the backdrop, the full moon over the Carlyle Hotel, Pete sang love songs, nothing but love songs.

Peter was like the brother I never had. It had always seemed sad when I was growing up that I didn't have a brother, since I would have flourished in the role of kid sister, so like a boy was I with my height and love of all things adventurous and, of course, my disinterest in mirrors. Identifying so little with my mother and sister, perhaps I cast myself as the brother. Surely I identified with my grandfather and, as I mentioned earlier, felt an obligation to be "the man of the house" given my mother's and sister's propensity to tears, as my sister's deepening adolescence exacerbated my mother's anxiety and competition. Someone had to be seen as in charge, and though I couldn't pay the bills, I vowed to bring no anxiety into that house and not to cry "like them."

This relaxation of gender roles is what I relish in these preadolescent years. Mother's imprint of how a little lady should look is still there, may always be there given her bedrock in the unconscious, staring at us critically from today's mirror as we pose in our Wonderbra wondering why we don't like what we see. What wars with mother's overly harsh judgment of our adult sexual look is the preadolescent flash of self-assured independence and bravery. When else in a woman's entire life is she given a respite from the judgment of men and women because, not yet being sexual, she is considered to be "not at risk"? Most of us will never again have this opportunity to invent ourselves or will dare to take it for a thousand different reasons, none of which, though they may feel that way, is insurmountable. And so we die untested, who we really are tightly curled inside, an embryo of what we might have been.

If we see more boyish bravado in young girls than we see feminine qualities in boys, it is in part because society is so tough on males, so rigid in defining what a man is. It's the boy's job to deny the very qualities in mother he loved most by fleeing everything female to find what is masculine. What a woman is, he knows all too well, firsthand and up close, but what is a man except a disciplinarian with a briefcase? Boys meet, gather outside the home, each identifying with images of men learned from television: Schwarzenegger, Rambo, whoever the boys' heroes, somehow none is as credible as woman/mother power. To make himself bigger than she, he must belittle women.

And the fewer fathers, the bigger the mother looms, meaning the greater distance the boy today must race to see himself as different from her. He forms a band of other boys who also need to prove they don't need women. Together they practice new ways to act, feel, speak, all the while casting off, right and left, female attributes. Picture young boys racing toward a summer lake, throwing off their clothes pell-mell until they are together in the water, naked reborn, as in Eakins's painting *The Swimming Hole*.

Gladly I would have joined those boys in the water, so eager was I not to be like the women in my home, who were timid, in tears, and so involved with one another. Despite the fact that I had neither father nor brother, or even a friendship with a young boy, I nonetheless acted like one. And I did it without conscious imitation, which I find optimistic; but then, as I've said, I like myself more at this age than at any other.

Let me tell you about a summer vacation with two girlfriends and their family on Ocracoke Island, off North Carolina. On my arrival, one foot barely off the boat, my friends race to me, collide, saying all the while, "Oh, Nancy, Nancy, we've told them that when you get here you'll show them, you'll punish them!" In their eyes I was some kind of avenging hero, for the people I was to take on were a group of rowdy boys. I remember feeling thrown off balance by *how they saw me*. Was I so formidable? If I was, it hadn't been planned. I also remember on several occasions that summer locking myself in the bathroom and trying to pee into a glass. Was I practicing being a boy? Perhaps. I don't recall how the confrontation with the rowdies turned out, or even if it took place, but I do remember the not altogether unpleasant sensation of trying to contain my stream in that small glass pressed tightly against my vulva.

My mother has always dismissed my grown-up memory of how I looked in those years, saying, "Why, you were so cute in your pigtails, climbing those walls in your jeans." But I wasn't cute, and that is why I climbed, to prove that I was a winner at something other than beauty. It doesn't matter that other members of our families have their indelible impressions of how we were; for you, for me, the people we are today grew out of our own feelings of how we were seen within the family portrait. When I want to think well of myself today, here is the ten-year-old I remember:

I get up in the morning, so early that night hasn't altogether left the room. Clothes folded on the chair from the night before I take out of the bedroom I share with my sister and into the bathroom. On the back of the door hang the stockings and the slip of a grown woman, my mother. The mirror over the sink reflects pigtails, a high forehead, freckles, braces, and the garments going on over my head have no coordination of color or texture. In fact, the mirror is unexamined until I pick up my toothbrush, get it halfway to my mouth, take in my mother's and sister's brushes, and defiantly wet my brush under the tap and put it back in the rack. Not brushing my teeth or waiting to have my hair re-braided is a minor victory, a stamp of identity: Different from Them. That no one will notice the toothbrush or the hair is understood, but the rite is performed nonetheless.

Downstairs I collect Raisin Bran, peanut butter, and toast, sit at my place at the table and eat, playing all the while with pages from a notebook spread before me. I am writing songs, well, actually new words from already existing popular melodies. These I will teach to the other members of The Slick Chick Jivers, a foursome of fifth-graders destined that very day to perform at the Upper School, the magisterial mansion on the far side of the playing fields from the Lower School, which I attend. While I eat, I hum, rehearse a few hand motions, once or twice stand and execute a tricky step remembered from the latest movie musical at The Gloria.

What I like about my girlish self (and grieve that I have lost) is its utter lack of guile and self-consciousness. Books in hand, I mount my trusty Schwinn and pedal like the wind away from that house of timidity, slowing only to wave at the women setting out their flower baskets at the foot of the post office steps, and the men delivering ice in their horse-drawn wagon, which I used to ride alongside (until my mother's friends reported me). By the time I have reached my friend Joanne's house, I am ready for another breakfast, especially since this one will be with a full family, meaning a father at the head of the table.

I am welcomed as one of the family, and literally come to life, smiling, charming.

Joanne, being my best friend, is one of the Jivers, and we readily suggest giving the family a preview of our act. I stand, and with my arms around her—she barely reaches my shoulder, but what do I care of height, what do I know of adolescence?—we do our song and dance, "You Wonderful You," as performed by Gene Kelly and Judy Garland in *Summer Stock*. The romantic words of the ballad blend perfectly in Joanne's sweet soprano and my alto. The sentimental yearning is all there in two little girls playing the roles of a man and woman in love. We are still children, and while we feel the longing for love—as we do at any age—we are not yet awakened to the sexual undertones of what we are singing.

All that was required in those brief years was that I turn up at home for meals and be in bed at nine. And even these demands were waived when I telephoned from one of the many homes all over town in which I was welcome. I owe so much to the families that laid another place for me at their tables. Did they see me as a lost soul, the only child in our circle without a father? I have no idea. If they did, their pity never showed; instead, praise, acceptance, and love were reflected back. I have not paid this debt of gratitude, and it bothers me sorely. Perhaps it is too great. Or perhaps I've had to live this long to appreciate the enormity of my debt to these people, this school, in memory, the whole idyllic town.

These preadolescent school years replace the narrow confines of home. If our parents and siblings have always seen us as The Quiet One, it is difficult to change their opinion. Opposite our older, outspoken brother, yes, we are silent, but without that comparison, we are now, for the first time, heard fresh by teachers and classmates. The power of our voice and new reflection in their eyes shines back at us. This voice is ours, this new respect, and we cosset it, a treasure on which to build.

And so there were two of me, the achiever at school for whom they engraved a silver cup for leadership when I graduated—it holds the pencils beside me today—and the person at home, where invisibility began to suit me. My whereabouts were never questioned, which left me deeply ambivalent, for while not being missed hurt, it did give me the chance to re-create myself endlessly.

My school, that wonderful place where I grew and lived more

hours than I spent at home, was my Garden of Eden, a place of endless delights, in which I would rehearse plays, practice baseball, write musicals, be a leader. Some mornings I would arrive so early that only the caretaker was there, and while I waited for the rest of the team to arrive for practice, I would shoot baskets, perfectly happy just to be there, my school, mine. I cared deeply for competitive sports, and if they became a bit too important, there was a reason. In the South, girls weren't supposed to compete hard, meaning to win, which drove me a little crazy given that winning was the point of the game.

I must add that this was an all-girl school, for which I have been eternally grateful; had male companionship been available, I'm sure I would have been desperate for boys' eyes to see me as a likable/lovable girl instead of becoming the athlete, the scholar, the leader. For when boys did enter my life, I gave up all the rest for the love of them, though to be fair, they never asked me to.

Well, there is my preadolescent portrait, one that I admire more wholeheartedly than any memory of myself between then and now. I was kind, I was good, I was ambitious, fair, competitive, eager, articulate, a leader, and I abandoned it a few years later for the portrait of The Nice Girl, a portrait that didn't fit.

Seeing Ourselves on the Silver Screen

Few memories are as indelibly linked to these years as the discovery of our secret selves at the movies. If the bicycle offers physical mastery of the outer world, movies awaken our imagination, opening us to dreams we might never have had, given how we saw ourselves, and others saw us, in our small world. If fairy tales mirrored the turbulent emotions that rocked us as small children, the experience of the big screen picks up where the Brothers Grimm left off. As we sit in the movies, the perimeters of life extend infinitely; we see beyond home and school, imagining ourselves wherever the camera takes us. Yes, it is make-believe, but to some of us it feels more real than anything we have experienced, or even read about. We are not beautiful, we cannot dance up and down flights of stairs, but neither could the heroine in the beginning, until—until what?—until someone saw her differently because of a song, a dress, a kiss.

For some young people, the movies are simply entertainment; they are only ten but are at home in their skins; they see themselves in time becoming their parents; given their temperament and life experience so far, what they want is already familiar. For others, movies are where life began. Think back to your own childhood at the movies. Can't you separate out the people you grew up with who lost themselves in the big screen from those for whom it was an experience that began and ended with the movie?

For ten-year-olds like myself, movies, with all their make-believe, were where life began. I think it has everything in the world to do with earliest visibility within the family, with whether or not we are seen and warmed by the most important eyes in the world, our parents. If we were *their* movie, the person in whose beloved features they lost themselves, then our own days of stardom absorbed our need for visibility. We have been sufficiently adored at the proper time, the beginning. If we have not, I believe the movies—and I don't mean television but instead, the big, big screen—give us an image in which to lose ourselves. Staring at the screen, we may be the voyeurs, but the magic of movies is that they take us in.

I'm not surprised that I share this obsession with my closest friends who, like me, saw every movie that came to town. What draws us to one another isn't precisely our religious attendance at the movies but our shared inclination toward exhibitionism: the predisposition to put ourselves on the line and take chances.

Like the little boy in the film *Cinema Paradiso*, having seen one movie, I had to see them all. I would scavenge in my mother's coat pockets and handbags until I found the necessary small change—less than a dollar, as I remember—then walk the few blocks to the drugstore on the corner of King and Broad Streets where I would meet my friends. Having already decided between the film at The Gloria or The Riviera, we would stop at the bakery to fill brown paper bags with jelly doughnuts and chocolate éclairs to be devoured in the sanctity of the darkness that encouraged the surrender of our naked selves, transformed into the people on the big screen. Eyes riveted, we sighed with them; mouths filled with sugared dough, we died with them; we were them. This is what is missed on television; the giant size of the people and their passion, which overwhelmed and included us.

If no real adult in our young lives has as yet fleshed out the heroic feelings inside us, these giants who live for an hour on the screen of the movie theater fill the void, reflecting what feels and looks like someone we could become. To sit in a large dark space—amid strangers!—and experience our most private and unacknowledged feelings *publicly* is a revelation I've not since duplicated. We gasp and sigh in a group display of emotion, which is the flip side of Good Manners, mandating that we keep our feelings to ourselves. I suppose it was what the Greeks and Romans shared in their amphitheaters.

Oddly enough, it was akin to what the Church gave me: a feeling of being part of a larger-than-life emotion, shared with others publicly, a group image of ourselves. Certainly, I saw myself as a little Christian, mirrored in all the other nice, good Christians around me, but the Church Me was only a fraction of who I was. The Real Me was born at the movies, where I was introduced to all my selves, the smorgasbord of what life could be. This is where the seed was planted that would grow into an adolescent sureness that I didn't want to marry after graduation, like so many of my friends. There were experiences to be had, emotions to be felt in all their fullness, as I had felt them up there on the screen; oh, no, I wanted it all.

Movies also gave great comfort; here were villains far worse than my own evil suspicions about myself. Seeing Richard Widmark was terrifying, but the extent of his meanness made my own livable. Maybe I was not so bad after all. Elizabeth Taylor's beauty was beyond my wildest dreams, but instead of envying her, the glamour of movies allowed me to adore her. Strangely enough, her giant beauty as well as her suffering—they always suffered, the great beauties—made me think that beauty wasn't everything, that powers alternative to beauty might actually be preferable, meaning that there was hope for me. Yes, beauty was powerful, but movies gave you an eyeful of how close the envious have-nots come to killing the beauty.

Nothing, however, moved me so seismically as the great musicals of the late forties and early fifties: *Singin' in the Rain, Show Boat, On Moonlight Bay, Good News, Funny Face.* Hypnotized, I would sit in the dark, lips moving, body in motion, me as Doris Day pining for the boy next door, and when I left The Gloria after being Fred Astaire and Judy Garland in *Easter Parade,* I couldn't help taking the post office's flight of steps two at a time, imaginary cane in hand, oblivious to the smiles of the flower ladies below. The music in the movies that captured me would continue its spell long after I'd bought the records and learned every word. I didn't want to come out of the trance into which I'd allowed myself to fall, all sighing and longing and dying. The promise of happiness in song and dance.

How appropriate that the old musicals came back so strongly in the loveless eighties, when heartfelt romance was at a low ebb. Unable to manufacture new lyrics and music that captured romantic love, we rediscovered Frank Sinatra and Tony Bennett, who effortlessly created the sound of a breaking heart for a new generation.

When I say that movies saved my life, giving me a look and a promise of faces and roles I might try on, it is not an exaggeration. It mattered not a jot whether the emotions were felt by male or female; the movies opened my eyes to precisely what I hadn't been able to find in real life, where I'd been taught to hold back and deny the full expression of large steps and a big voice. Movies said it was more than all right, it was good to feel as much as possible, that you must never give up hope, like Black Beauty, like Leslie Caron, like Bette Davis.

Three Little Girls Can't Play Together

What we need when we are ten and imagining ourselves in all of life's variety is the heartfelt encouragement of our dear band of friends. We read a book, see a movie, meet someone who awakens in us a sense of mutuality. We are right to be shopping around, living with myriad balloons over our heads, trying on this person or that, to see who fits. There will never again be so few pressures to conform. If we had the nerve to experiment, to grow and change with full reinforcement from friends, we would hold on to these imaginary inner portraits so determinedly we might get through adolescence without abandoning our dream. Eventually we might grow up to become our own heroine: someone we admire instead of a woman unsure of who she is, how she looks, always adjusting, changing, altering her body, face, and hair to conform to a look that never stares back from our mirror as convincingly as we saw her in the pages of a book, a magazine, a movie.

If young girls could only champion one another, encourage individuality, originality. Oh, we form intense friendships with girls without whom we feel we cannot live, friendships that could support uniqueness. But the very love in these friendships leads us to betray one another and ourselves too. The love is patterned on the only kind we know, tight and symbiotic, with a dark side; the old anger we couldn't afford to show mother for fear of losing her is now affordable, is, in fact, irresistible. One day we drop our best friend, or exclude her.

Another girl has come along, setting up a threesome that triggered an undeniable urge to leave someone out.

It is a game women play, and it begins so early in life that it defines us as inevitably as breasts, as if to say, This *is* woman. In fact it is learned. By sheer repetition it becomes compelling whenever more than two females get together. There isn't a mother who hasn't gone through it with her own daughter: "Mommy, she was my best friend! What did I do? Why did she and that other girl giggle and run away and leave me?"

When, out of a clear blue sky, two little girls begin shunning another, they are flexing muscles, getting off on the misery they are able to cause, a pain they know well having been there themselves. It is such "girl" behavior, excluding one of our own, someone who was our nearest and dearest five minutes earlier. Two girls are absolutely fine, but a third, the alternate, affords the opportunity to create a thrilling dyad out of the misery of one girl by giving her "the treatment."

It begins as soon as we are out of the house, when we are practicing relationships, and it is patterned on the only love relationship we've ever known, with Mother. We want intimacy with our new friend, but we want power too, like Mommy's power over us, a desire to which we are reawakened when "the victim" comes along. Since we've had to play that role ourselves, there is an insurmountable urge to impose it on another. We want to play mother. It isn't that we've stopped emotionally connecting with our best friend; we have, in fact, confused her with us. Aren't we the same, meshed, just as we were with Mommy? Very well, let her suffer for a while, as Mommy made us suffer.

Being able to create a victim automatically makes the new dyad with our conspirator more alive and intense. It is real passion. The grimness of it is that even after we have been the abandoned one ourselves, when the opportunity arises, we will do it to another girl/woman.

If mother had allowed her daughter to go through the gradual process of becoming her own person, with the love between them internalized in the journey of separation, the daughter wouldn't be so afraid of losing love whenever mother turned to others in the family; there wouldn't be total dependency on mother for everything. With no safe perimeters of identity locked inside, the little girl remains frozen in a love/hate relationship with mother, which now extends to all girls/women. She loves her best friend in the only way she knows how. The sad irony is that in loving her, she cannot help making her suffer, as mother had with her.

These should be years of great friendships and the practicing of loyalty. And they are! But they are also the commencement of betrayal and the abandonment of the people we love.

The following letter was printed on the "Help!" page of *American Girl* magazine; it is such a frequent cry for help that at least one "left out" letter gets answered in every issue:

Dear *American Girl*,

My two best friends stick together like glue. I am always the one left out. I'm fine playing with them separately. How can we all be friends without being in a fight all the time?

We are nine, maybe ten or eleven. Our bodies are stretching, our capacity for emotions growing, and our faces opening with expectancy, a palette across which all the feelings of life should feel free to race without fear of censure. Mother isn't always present to tell us to calm down and be good. We should be egging one another on, applauding. Our eyes should be wide in anticipation of shared adventures with other brave, curious girls. What makes our big eyes narrow and shift nervously?

Fear. Apprehension. Anxiety over potential loss of love. The suspicion that if we go too far, win too much, get too happy, the other girls will abandon us. Where else do you think grown women learn to deflect compliments—"Oh, this old thing?" "That old one-hundred-thousand-dollar contract?" Threat of exclusion hangs in the air like the sword of Damocles over the dearest of little-girl friendships.

"Mommy, why did they hide from me? What did I do?"

She did nothing. Two little girls wanted to feel intensely close, and a third girl was needed to get them there, not unlike a fire that only bursts into flame with the added fuel or, in this case, sacrifice. The excluded victim may well be loved again tomorrow, but now, this moment, the irresistible urge can't be denied. Punish her, hurt her, defuse the stored-up anger! It worked. The third girl's banishment made the dyad madly inseparable, totally entwined and giddy on pain they had caused another. Something more complicated than love was wanted—for if two can love, then three can love more—and that was the rage/revenge/power still enmeshed in the girls' concept of love. Never weaned off infantile symbiotic love, wherein trust of self and another in a love relationship was learned, the tight dyad remained the only known, safe form of love: total ownership.

How then did this sort of love feel when mother turned away from the girl to father or to her baby brother, breaking the dyad? The girl was only one or two and so her rage had to be swallowed to keep mother's love; an exercise learned again and again as when the girl turned to father and felt mother's angry competition at her back. Forbidden by mother to display any signs of her own anger or power—a rule laid down more rigidly for girls than boys—the little girl would reenact the painful scene with her dolls, whom she punished just as she'd been punished: "Bad, bad, bad!" She loved her dolls, but by now integral to love were rage/revenge and the desire to own mother's power herself.

The psychoanalytic dictionary has an expression for this reenactment: It is called "Identification with the Aggressor." It works quite simply, as the words imply, and it is precisely what two little girls do to a third. The more intense the friendship, the more it awakens what went right and wrong with the most important woman in life. Competitive struggles over father, with brothers and sisters, get played out when three little girls get together. Competition is not named, but the air is filled with it. Since mother "won" all the unspoken competitions within the home, then her daughter identifies with her in this struggle between best friends for the ownership of love, meaning that someone must "lose." The other best friend is thrown to the wolves.

Little girls measure love and life as if there were just so much out there; when mother turned to someone else at home, there was always the feeling that there was less for us, for the left-out one. The girl envied father, sister, brother's power to take away mother's love, but her greatest teacher and competitor had never taught her to acknowledge that one could fight the good fight, be angry, compete, and that there would still be love afterward.

A little girl grows up instead with this sense of a priori defeat; why try to compete? She would lose anyway. Competitions therefore terrify her. Unless, of course, victory can be guaranteed. When the new girl approaches, she drops and betrays her best friend, siding instead with the newcomer, *but* competition has been avoided! It isn't necessary to strike out, actually to hurt her or to say anything evil. The avoidance, whispers, giggles, an emotional pulling away does it. Isn't she sobbing? Hasn't a symbiotic union been created, a victory scored?

If you confronted the two girls—as concerned mothers often do—they couldn't explain why they did it any more than grown women can. It goes on all our lives, we women whispering, conspiring, testing the irresistible urge to excommunicate another woman, conspiratorially drawing our heads together as we feel the adrenaline rush brought on by a friend's sudden look of misery. Oh, as time goes by Big Girls learn to do it deftly, with their eyes, just a signal across a crowded room. It's called The Look. In progress, The Look is smug, clandestine, and mean, indulged in by two or more grown women at a restaurant, for instance, after an unfortunate member of the party has gone to the ladies' room. Heads together, eyes narrowed like cats, the women are ten-year-olds in full makeup. They are deadly but cool, having handled this ammunition for years; deep in their gut, they feel the old rush as headily as ever. Two Little Girls Are Leaving Out One Little Girl, who was their best friend five minutes earlier.

The Look may sound like a minor piece of business, but it is significant, a flaw not just in our relationships with one another but in our self-image; we know we are untrustworthy, as capable of betrayal as of being the next victim in women's world. What do you think this apprehension, year after year, does to a woman's face: We are always at risk, the little trace lines of anxiety and tension never relax and so become incised; do others see us as "too flashy," too drab, too loud, underdressed, overdressed, *not just right*?

"Within the first years of life children learn to control some of these facial expressions, concealing true feelings and falsifying expressions of emotions not felt," says psychologist Paul Ekman. "Parents teach their children to control their expressions by example and, more directly, with statements such as: 'Don't you give me that angry look.'"

As we grow up, Ekman says, we learn "display rules" for the management of emotional expression, which operate automatically, altering our expressions without choice or awareness. Even when we become aware of our display rules, it is not always possible and certainly not easy to stop following them. "I believe that those habits involving the management of emotion—display rules—may be the most difficult of all to break," says Ekman.

In time, our faces become maps of our lives. More often, beginning in childhood, our emotional expressions lose their spontaneity, and what Ekman terms "masking" begins. Forcing muscles to conceal our emotions must make for a lot of wear and tear. The false face. Small wonder the cosmetic surgeon has become a staple in these years when there is more nasty emotion to mask, beginning in the earliest years when children have fewer mirroring eyes than ever to catch and respond to the look of love.

In our feminist, matriarchal age, women seem to have more power than ever over other women's looks. We respond, weather vanes to the slightest glance, not to men's judgment but to the critical gaze of other women, who decide our fate as they rule our little world; boys enter dramatically at adolescence, arousing sexual desire, but in most cliques The Girls retain dominance. Adolescent girls who switch allegiance to men are Bad Girls.

Women's rule over one another, established with just a "look," is a plot device in more than one Bette Davis movie. It goes on in the best of friendships; cumulatively, over the years The Look gains profound influence over how far we dare to go, how much to show, how much success, how much sex, how much beauty given the women looking, appraising, judging, their heads together, lips moving, though no words are heard or required, given their eyes on us. Some heroic women don't give a damn; they too are notorious in film and literature, the character played by Rosalind Russell or Katharine Hepburn, who didn't change her demeanor when other women were around; actually, with that kind of woman, men were around instead of women, which in itself tells a story.

After today's working lunch, for instance, telephone calls were made, gossip was shared regarding another woman's promotion, her new sexual conquest, her exhibitionistic clothing, her "self-importance," or so it felt to her sisters, whose lives now seemed less opposite her win. How dare she break the unwritten laws that keep all women equal? How dare she make us mindful of what we don't have compared to her? She has awakened the forbidden feeling of competition that lives, suppressed, at volcanic heat. Knock her off. Give her "The Look," or the silent treatment.

When Hillary Rodham Clinton got too big for her britches too soon after her husband's inauguration, men could never have sandbagged her without women's full cooperation. Make her suffer! Make a joke of her ill-advised wardrobe. The same women who admire Hillary watched her demotion with ill-disguised satisfaction. Better she had stayed in the frumpy clothes. Better she had turned a deaf ear to Annie Leibovitz's irresistible encouragement to show the camera eye the seductive power of beauty she'd kept hidden under a barrel. Better she'd kept the barrel.

If a man treated a woman the way certain women friends treat her, she would leave him. We cannot leave our women friends; next week, next month, this same woman who shunned us, whispered about us, and left us out of the dinner party will be the one who runs to our side in an emergency. Hasn't this been the ritual of our lives, a cycle of intimacy, exclusion, and pain that keeps the urge to compete at bay, though it is in itself a sick form of competition.

Girls and boys bully their peers differently, says a senior counseling manager of Childline, a telephone counseling service for children in England. "Boys try the macho, aggressive form of bullying; with girls, it's more likely bullying means exclusion from their friendship group."

In her novel *Cat's Eye*, Margaret Atwood catches the nasty taste of this girlish business when Elaine, the nine-year-old heroine, is trying to fit in with her first girlfriends: "I worry about what I've said today, the expression on my face, how I walk, what I wear, because all of these things need improvement. I am not normal, I am not like other girls. Cordelia tells me so, but she will help me. Grace and Carol will help me too. It will take hard work and a long time. . . . With enemies you can feel hatred, and anger. But Cordelia is my friend. She likes me, she wants to help me, they all do. They are my friends, my girl friends, my best friends."

Men can be rats. They forget to telephone and do not return our love. But women can live just fine without men; we are proving that in increasing numbers. If men live with less of this life-and-death drama in a love affair, it is because most have a stronger sense of self; most managed to separate more successfully for no other reason than the fact that they are a different sex from mother, who, like it or not, is enjoined by society to reward her son's independence.

One last comment from Atwood, who is so good on women: "I see that there will be no end to imperfection, or to doing things the wrong way," says Elaine. "Even if you grow up, no matter how hard you scrub, whatever you do, there will always be some other stain or spot on your face or stupid act, somebody frowning. But it pleases me somehow to cut out all these imperfect women [from the women's magazines], with their forehead wrinkles that show how worried they are, and fix them into my scrapbook."

Years later, we are still trying to paint the perfect face, wear the perfect dress, say the perfect things; does any woman honestly believe that our terrible anxiety, which men do not seem to share, has anything to do with what they have done to us? Even if men do leave us, it would hurt less if we believed in the possibility of another love, another man, if we hadn't grown up feeling that the breaking of the dyad was death, and competition a bad feeling for which there was no safe, practiced outlet.

How much suppression of anger can a body take? *Fatal Attraction* was a popular film for many reasons, not the least of which was a beautiful woman in high sexual gear very actively seducing the man; but the real attraction for the audience, I thought, was that we got to see modern woman, fury written all over her seemingly in-charge Armani image. She was deranged, but no more so than a lot of aggressive, seductive, in-charge women in designer suits on the brink of something-like-murder. The person who gets our rage, when the dam breaks, will be a man; do we honestly believe that the kind of titanic fury erupting all over town from women gets its roots in adolescence, when boys enter our lives? Oh, no. Women's rage today has far deeper, earlier roots. We don't dare show other women the kind of fury we can show a man.

I suppose the young boy is dear to my heart because I was so boyish myself in my preadolescent years, not just in dress and behavior but in my total innocence of what adolescence would bring. So determined was I never to be like "them," my very feminine mother and sister whose dyad excluded me, that age ten was how I planned to live forever. In the mid-eighties, when I was a writer in residence at the *San Francisco Examiner*, I wrote an article about the preadolescent boy's life, the bucolic years between mother and the power of young girls' beauty; why, I wrote, wasn't there at least one magazine for these boys, something to celebrate these years but also to prepare them for what lies ahead? There are dozens of such magazines for girls this age. The day after the column appeared, the publisher approached me and, laughing heartily, said, "If we had such a magazine, I'd call it 'Crybaby.'" Clearly, he didn't want his son to have it any easier than he had.

The preadolescent boy is making his own plans for an imagined life, seeing himself as athlete, inventor, interplanetary traveler, whatever suits his inner eye. The full weight of father's briefcase has not yet come into focus. A Good Provider isn't on his list. Girls? Well, girls are reminiscent of mother, whom he loves and still needs too much; if he is to be a Real Boy, the way mother/girls are is opposite everything he must become. Mom is Mom and she is great, but girls? Girls are absolutely not wanted in The All-Boy Club. Signs outside the clubhouse make it clear: NO GIRLS.

There is a truism in Hollywood: Both sexes go to boys' movies, but boys won't go to girls' movies. When *A Little Princess* was in the planning stages, it was suggested that the heroine be changed to a hero. When the film was screened, the heroine's gender intact, it got rave reviews, but the pundits had been right: Nothing much happened at the box office. The film *Pocahontas* may have had a budget that equaled the hugely successful *The Lion King*, but the former never measured up, "because of the girl factor," said one Hollywood insider. "Boys won't want to go to a girl picture." When you are a ten-year-old boy, all of life is focused on pinning down exactly what a boy is, and the first answer is: everything that is opposite mother/girls.

Friendships, camaraderie, trust, all matter greatly, for The Boy Gang pins down exactly what a Real Boy is. One boy may let down another, but their friendships do not form and re-form like garden worms, separating, rejoining, always excluding someone. And if there is a break in friendship, the boy can do something with the "left out" feeling; he has a voice for anger. Mother gave him more leeway than his sister to argue, disagree, raise his voice—"Such a little man, just like your father!" Boys fight, argue, challenge, but when there is a competition, be it a fight or a game, there are learned rules. You don't fight dirty.

The boy who doesn't play by the rules is left out, and he knows why. Games are about winning and losing; by definition, someone is always left out, today him, tomorrow another boy. Both winning and losing must be accepted and dealt with. After the game, hands must be shaken. Unlike his sister, the boy grows to believe that life is an ongoing game with endless winnings.

Boys can be cruel, but they encourage and applaud bravery. The boy leader of the pack is followed because he has outstripped the others. He breaks records set by heroes before him on the playing field, and bends overly rigid rules that prohibit freedom. Other boys may feel angrily envious and competitive, but if they don't learn to lose in these years, to shake hands in the belief that today they lost but tomorrow they may win, they are not eligible to be part of the gang.

Boys have close one-on-one friendships, but they belong to a larger club. Sometimes the club is organized and has a headquarters, a tree house, someone's father's garage, a basement. And there are No Girls! A free-floating feeling of camaraderie stirred up outside an enormous stadium becomes a club. Men get to be part of it by learning to win and lose. In time, of course, it becomes the Men Only Club on the corner of Main Street.

Male bonding isn't akin to that of a girls' group, which is based on sameness and the avoidance of open competition. Ask a child psychiatrist; young boys don't come home crying, "Yesterday he was my best friend. Why did he run away from me with that other guy? What did I do? Why won't they talk to me?"

Women have so much more power over one another than a man can ever have over us. We are one another's great permission givers, and we are one another's jailers. These powers will greatly accelerate in adolescence and will never let up. The potential to excommunicate another woman from women's world is what hinders women's networking professionally. The juice is extracted from healthy competition because buried in the challenge to compete with another woman is the dilemma: If I win, will she still love me, or will she kill me? The two are not so far apart.

Girls who work hard to live up to an inner drive that propels them toward their unique identity cannot help but feel in opposition to mother, even if the older woman says nothing. Without healthy separation, she is inside our heads, or so it feels when we act differently than she. Guilt is our middle name. There would be less guilt in women's lives for betraying mother if there were a father as dear and close as she. Listen to Bettelheim's splendid advice:

> The child begins to feel [herself] as a person, as a significant and meaningful partner in a human relation, when [she] begins to relate to the father. One becomes a person only as one defines oneself against another person. . . . Some very rudimentary self-definition begins with defining oneself in regard to [mother]. But because of [the] deep dependency on the mother, the child cannot move out into self-definition unless [she] can lean on some third

person. It is a necessary step toward independence to learn "I can also lean, rely, on some person other than Mother" before one can believe that one can manage without leaning on *somebody*.

Who better than a father to be the first "significant other" for a daughter, to teach her how competition works safely, that there is life beyond the dyad? Father presents an alternative. "When the father first emerges to offer the girl a tie that can supplement . . . the tie to the mother," writes Dorothy Dinnerstein, "he makes available to her a new way of handling . . . the ambivalence at the heart of the infant-mother tie." Father has a "clean slate," says Dinnerstein, unmarked by "the inevitable griefs of infancy," with mother. By attaching to him, the little girl "gains a less equivocal focus for her feelings of pure love, and feels freer to experience her grievances against her mother without fear of being cut off altogether from the ideal of wholehearted harmony with a magic, animally loved, parental being."

Until girls are raised from the beginning to feel there is great reward in becoming a unique individual, someone who is her mother's daughter but not her clone, we will go through life seeking other women's approval, fearing their disapproval. Let there be arguments without fear of reprisals, anger without fear of loss of the relationship, and let there be healthy competition with her who is our born teacher in learning how to win and lose. Until this happens, three little girls will not be able to play together, work together, be together, without fear of exclusion.

I understand women's professional need today to be included in men's clubs, but I feel some sympathy for men because they are losing their "rooms without women." Men still need to reconstitute their sense of self, whole maleness, in a world where, even at the height of Patriarchy, they feared women's power. When I say this to my egalitarian husband, he reminds me of the business deals executed in these places from which women used to be excluded. Yes, I understand. Nonetheless, not all of life can be explained in terms of fairness in business.

Men and women need their separate rituals and places that allow us to coexist socially and sexually as well as professionally. I've always been aware that women's happiness with men, and theirs with us, becomes more wholehearted after men have had a period of time away from us. It goes back to the first years of life, where the baby boy was totally dependent on the Giantess, leaving him with all that infantile rage still focused on women.

Put more men in the nursery and I predict that women will be more gracefully received in the all-male club, and less rudely treated, less harassed, in the workplace. Until then, men will feel even more trapped in a world where women's power, already considerable in men's eyes, is now greater than ever. Men will find places somewhere, somehow, to be alone together, without women, if only to be able to love them.

Don't let there be another generation of women who are one another's vigilant jailers, determined that no one woman should get more than any other. When I was a girl, it was difficult to rouse a team of competitive girls who played to win. Giggling and dropping the ball was applauded. It drove me crazy. Watching women's sports teams today makes my heart soar. These young women take another woman's victory as a benchmark to be matched, a safe outlet for the fires of competition. When the University of Connecticut's girls basketball team, the Huskies, had an undefeated season in 1994–1995, it was a beautiful sight to watch that last game, the picture of the players and of the crowd too. I felt that I was seeing the turn of the century.

And if the runner, the skater, or the basketball player is beautiful too, how do other women and men react to this accumulation of power? How does she? It is appropriate that today, beauty, unbound, runs the streets like a loose electric wire, alive with current. What to do with it? Women no longer have an exclusive on beauty; as we become more competitive, men become more beautiful. Styles for males and females of all ages fluctuate constantly, as if life is caught in a revolving door. Kids on the street, men and women in offices, lengthen, shorten hems, hair, swapping generational as well as cross-gender styles.

Looks and sex are inseparable and become that material with which we reinvent our societal roles. Just as when we were children and put on our parents' clothes, aping their voices and mannerisms, today we grown-ups, and children too, try on everything, all the costumes and sexual poses. Understandably, the archconservatives are nervous, remembering what happened in the sixties and seventies, on which they would blame today's chaos. But they might as well blame the ethos, the winds of change, since the sixties and seventies themselves grew out of the rigidity and bigotry of the fifties. And so it goes, or went.

Whatever we do, we must pay close attention to beauty and sex, which are moving us mysteriously across the Ouija board; we have been given a rare opportunity to create a new way to live and should see the passing fashions and gender poses not as the end product but as a means to the end. We want to be the creators of our future, the molders of the clay and not the clay itself. The looks on the street are telling us something: Unlike our parents, we can consciously choose how much importance to place on beauty, how to use its power, which by extension includes all other forms of power too: love, sex, work, the lot.

To choose wisely we should call in all the chips, use everything in our memory banks, not the least of which are these so-called Latency Years. We just might find in them our favorite portrait of ourselves, inside and out, not a fashion slave, or a slave to money, but a young person who never looked in mirrors because what we trusted was how we felt about ourselves internally.

The Search for an Ego Ideal

Between the confinement of home and the equally restricting Nice Girl Rules of adolescence, I had two heroines, two loves, who for this brief period took me over, so thrilling were the images of them, and of me in them. Each awoke me to a promise of a life as yet undreamed of. They need do nothing, just be. Each had the power to break my heart, so enamored was I, wanting to be near them, to stare at them and imitate what I recognized as ways in which I wanted to move, talk, act, look. One was my creative, the other, my erotic muse. One was adult, the other, just two years older than I. Both were female, and to this day I recognize their imprint on me.

My aunt Pat came to live with us when I was nine. My mother's youngest sister, she arrived as an interplanetary visitor, so beautiful to my eyes in her originality of look and behavior. She was like no grown woman I'd ever seen, like no one's mother, like no teacher. She was a born heroine. It was easy to stare at her—tall, like me, and a blood relative—and find both a portrait of myself and a pattern to follow. I was certainly not glamorous like she was, with her red hair swept up in deep waves of curls, her billowing skirts cinched with wide belts, her ballet shoes, but I adored her differentness on sight, knowing in my heart that I too was different from all my comrades, an otherness that went beyond my not being a born Southerner and the only girl without a father.

My aunt, an actress, painter, and writer, threw her head back when she laughed and smelled of a musky perfume that seemed to come from the ancient Greek coins she wore on her wrist. I followed along beside her to the waterfront, where she furnished a studio on the second floor of an abandoned warehouse. There she set up her easel, threw shawls and pillows over old sofas, stoppered Chianti bottles with candles, by which light she and her actor friends read aloud from *The Lady's Not for Burning, The Voice of the Turtle,* and *Bell, Book and Candle.* And I, this nine-year-old, was allowed to join in, even given parts to read. The generosity of them, the kindness! I have never forgotten.

Some nights we would go to the Dock Street Theatre—the oldest theater in the country—and I would watch the man she would later marry direct her, his leading lady, in Shakespeare, Wilder, O'Neill. On summer days we would go to the graveyard behind St. Phillips Church, where she taught me to use watercolors, and very soon it began to feel as though I couldn't live without her. School was out during that first summer she lived with us, and I would lie on my bed, suffocating in the heavy magnolia air outside my window, because it seemed I couldn't breathe until I heard the sound of her footfall on the gravel path, the squeak of the big iron gate. She was back!

I was in love, and the wonderful part of the story is that Aunt Pat allowed me to love her; she wasn't the least self-conscious of my worshipful gaze and must have recognized the pain I felt when away from her, for she included me with her adult friends whenever possible. Sitting in the dark of a movie theater, I would allow my arm to be close to hers, feeling in the physical contact something like, but not exactly, what I would feel in a few years for boys.

Her interest in me let me believe that in time I might look, even become, like her. She embodied the first hope, no, more exactly, the first real desire I allowed myself to dream of looks and of being looked at. What gave me this faith was her vision of me as being someone worthy of imbuing with great ideas of accomplishments. There were reading lists drawn up, acting lessons, and pride in height and posture was taught. Mostly, there was the sight of her typing a play on a card table set up in my bedroom, where she would write of an afternoon, her gold cigarette holder wafting a trail of dreamy smoke, carried on the light summer breeze across the room where I would take it in, the whole picture, as I watched, not even pretending to read the book in my lap, so in love was I with the image of this lovely young woman, the first person in my life who had ever seen me and made me feel loved.

Simultaneously, I met and fell equally in love with Poppy, a girl two years older than I, whose family had bought a house beyond our garden wall. In these years I traveled around my neighborhood on the brick walls that surrounded the lovely gardens in our part of town. A few had shards of glass along the top to discourage trespassers, but I was not dissuaded nor did I ever feel unwelcome in the yards into which I unceremoniously dropped. Those in residence seemed to be expecting me, by which I mean, they were never taken aback or angry if they walked into their yards and found me playing with their pets, or sitting in their trees. Perhaps it was my friendliness, for I never questioned their hospitality and had long known the power of a smile and a good story well told.

Mostly it was the time and place. Charleston was still "the best-kept secret in America"—my uncle's words—and the people, well, they were certainly not Empty Packages, hollow souls desperate for expensive clothes, labels, jewelry, or fancy cars that drew attention. Filled to the brim with kindness, character, manners, and an inherited sense of who they were, they peopled my childhood and made it blessed. The high walls along which I raced, instead of confinement promised compartments of adventure like chapters in a book of fairy tales. DuBose Heyward had once lived several walls to the west, and it was said that the scene for his *Porgy and Bess* was near our maze of walls; just south of our house lived one of the last black families in the neighborhood, and the children would sit on their porch railing, shaking their heads in disbelief as I waved from the three-story wall skirting their property, a crumbling free-standing structure whose bricks broke loose underfoot, alerting the Dobermans on the opposite side to crash through the underbrush, barking furiously. Where did I get my fearlessness, and where did I lose it?

One day I dropped from my bedroom window onto our wall to discover that two yards away a new family was moving into our community. Which is how I met Poppy, whose opening greeting was, "Who the hell are you?", an expression I'd never heard a Nice Girl use, but which had in its power to shock a definite come-hither quality. I swung down into Poppy's yard and was instantly infatuated, for she was more hell-bent than I and, along with her family (who, people would say, came from the wrong side of the tracks), had the most obvious sexuality I'd ever encountered. I sensed it, smelled it, felt it before I knew its name was sex, though I would soon learn the word from Poppy and her three older sisters, each of whom wore a shade of lipstick that marked them: Bad Girls.

I was unaccustomed to a girl near my age outstripping me in bravado, to which Poppy also brought the customs of her blue-collar world, making my private girls' school environment tame and straitlaced. I didn't know how much I'd missed the steamy side of life, embodied in the look and feel of Poppy's entire family, until I fell into their midst. Their house was not well kept, nor did boughs of magnolia leaves decorate the fireplace in summer, or candles light the table at supper; in fact, they ate in the kitchen and communicated with one another by yelling. But mostly, it was the sexual thing, something my other heroine, my aunt, didn't impart, but which now had instant appeal.

In my Girl Scout shorts I would sit for hours—which is what it took—watching Poppy's sisters prepare for dates with the Citadel cadets who waited downstairs for these bosomy young women, heavy, with blond hair and makeup. All their beds were in one large room, and sandwiched between the four of them were dressing tables, copious mirrors into which they would stare at themselves for hours, plucking hairs, slowly, skillfully applying makeup, mascara, rouge, eyebrow pencil, expertly blending colors, licking their fingers to smooth errant hairs. Then the nail polish, the fingers spread across the naked knee, the blood-red painted on as delicately as priests must have drawn the *Book of Hours*. All the while, the Citadel cadets downstairs waiting, expecting, hoping. I wanted to say to these deliberately slow women, "Hurry, hurry, or they'll leave!" But they knew better.

My mother and aunt wore very little makeup, while these females had drawers jammed with jars and bottles of ointments, lotions, pastel-colored creams, and on their crowded dressing tables were so many brushes of all lengths, curling irons, combs that whenever anything was picked up, clouds of powder billowed up and swam around them, shaven gold, giving the whole scene a surrealistic magnificence.

I knew they were preparing for something so momentous that it made my heart race; someday I too would be a part of this, and I studied them as closely as I studied my aunt. Here were two sides of becoming, and they were, if not contradictory, certainly complex to combine into one: There was my aunt's handsome world of accomplishment, with its promise of creativity and applause; and here was this world of forbidden sexuality, with its equal guarantee of eye-catching visibility, something for which I had a decided appetite, nourished by years of invisibility within my family.

One sleep-over night that began like any other, Poppy crawled into my bed and took my hand, moving it over her breasts, showing me, directing me, before crawling between my legs and putting her mouth and tongue all over that part of my body I had never touched except to wipe myself clean. It was an exciting feeling made all the more so by the known badness of the act. I was only ten, but I knew it was forbidden and that I could not tell the other Nice Girls about it. But I have always loved forbidden sex.

My aunt did not approve of Poppy. One day she caught me furtively applying hot-pink lipstick behind an azalea bush just inside our big iron gates; I was in my jeans, old flannel shirt, and with my pigtails and braces, I must have been a confusing image. "Why do you see that girl?" Aunt Pat asked. If I'd been able to read my yearnings, I would have answered, "Because she arouses in me a way I want to feel, something inside that is as much a part of who I am as what you have brought to me." But I said nothing; rather, shamefaced, I ran, moth to the flame.

Adolescence hit Poppy overnight, and I became useless to her. She disappeared from my life as abruptly as she'd arrived. She was surrounded by boys who were in heat over the look and musk she had been raised to emanate. In the steps of her sisters, Poppy went forth to attract men with the same allure that had attracted me. Heartbroken, I returned to the company of the girls I'd known all my life. I became one of them again, but inside, I was different.

The most generous gift my mother gave me was not to judge or in any way limit my adoration of her younger sister. It is not at all unusual for some women, even though they are totally disinterested in mothering, to resent their daughters fixating on another grown woman, but my mother allowed me all the closeness in the world with my aunt, whose friends followed her down from the North. They were women, like Pat, cast in a unique mold; in New York they edited magazines and wrote books. Men too arrived, tall, handsome architects, poets, playwrights, all proposing marriage to my aunt; one made two trips on a Greyhound bus for this very reason and was twice rejected; years later I would meet him in New York, where he is still one of

Broadway's leading directors. I would live in my aunt's shadow until the day adolescence struck me too like a fever and I was off, into the next chapter.

What I took away from this love affair with Aunt Pat was an image of a way to look, not in the sense of fashion or makeup but of an internal way of seeing myself that came from her. Of course, it never erased the infantile fear of being abandoned for a prettier other. The two do battle to this day: a powerful belief in self, which she gave me, and the plain child who never measured up. Ambivalence.

From Nancy Drew to Thelma and Louise

Ambassadors for ourselves, we ten-year-olds go looking for alliances, our credentials being the trust we get from our families. Do we go with their blessings to find models other than them of how to be a woman or a man? Do our parents love to hear the stories we bring home of the wonderful people we have met, the father of our friend, who is teaching us to fly-fish, the beautiful teacher who says we have a gift for languages, painting, for maybe even being a great soprano and going to Europe to sing at a place called La Scala?

Or do we get a sense of treason, a whiff of disloyalty? What we need at ten is permission to lovingly imitate others beyond the family; we need to hear from the people dearest to us that they genuinely want us to be open to alternatives, models beyond themselves. Actually, we've needed this generosity from them since the beginning, from mother's urging us to move toward father, her smiling on the portrait of our love for and our closeness to him, feeling it took nothing away from her.

If instead, for instance, we felt that our affection for an older brother, an uncle, was taken by mother as a betrayal, we clung more tightly, feeling her unspoken pain at our disloyalty. Mother, father would deny that they resent our alliances beyond the family; the sense of ownership a parent has is so easily called by other names: responsibility, concern, fear of the outer world, which is indeed real. But knowing the difference between real and imagined danger is the parent's role.

How do you tell a father or mother that it is one of the greatest acts of parental love to encourage a child to get close to other people? Children are naturally drawn into the world to find themselves, which is why we love the old stories of Tom Sawyer and Huckleberry Finn and their adventures with colorful characters they meet outside the home, people who change their thoughts and lives. Young girls need heroines too, now more than ever, given the choices that lie ahead, decisions that will be hard to make if choosing to be different from mother is experienced as treason. The variety in the world beyond home is looked forward to when mother's and father's spoken encouragement has convinced the daughter and son that going their own way is a good thing and in no way diminishes love within the family. Women have been waiting for this larger stage for years; today our variegated world has been thrust upon us and these are the prime years to prepare for it.

We are nine or ten, desperate for heroes, not even knowing it until they arrive, awakening us from the torpor of confinement that was home and family, whom we love but have outgrown as regards imitation. We know them inside and out and want more. We have pockets of different kinds of love uncalled on by our parents. The loose skin of our life lies in folds, waiting to be filled; we need instruction in the form of heroes who have practiced ways we too want to be. In our minds, a vacuum of cells waits for the inspiration of an admirable other who invites us to see our identity in him or her, a picture to put in the cellophane envelope of our new wallet. Who are we? We don't even know the question exists, but it presses us out into the world.

In theory, separation is something we complete between the first and second years of life, but in fact it is something we work on all of our lives. We are never too old to expand identity, shore up our feeling of safety unto our selves. If we have the love of family internalized, we have fuel to move on. As for children who miss out on the security of unconditional love, well, in these few years there is still an eagerness to find someone, people "out there" who will embrace us, will look us keenly in the eye and recognize our spark of individuality. Adolescence will anesthetize us; the time is now.

What is wanted from parents is the spoken encouragement to form other close ties, something along the lines of "I think it's wonderful you've found someone who appreciates your love of reading, of tennis, languages. How kind of him to give you his time and attention." Do parents realize how many opportunities small children turn down out of a fear of disloyalty? With our parents' goodwill at our backs, we feel free to walk, talk, think, dress like significant others, and, lo and behold, we discover that our new self hasn't cost us a drop of family love. We have grown.

Each time we fall in love, the initial excitement is at being seen as someone unique. When that excitement of giving someone our special self changes to fear of being abandoned, we lose our separateness, usually without any decision to do so. Who would choose to lose identity? We fall back into the baby's unseparated, symbiotic neediness: "I'll die if you leave me!"

The Years of Invention stand out in many women's memories because they were that thrilling time between need of mother and need of men. For a while, we were free of rules, free of all-seeing eyes, free to invent a self. Of course women are angry today; look what was given up.

None of us wants to be left by a beloved, but when we read desertion in the slightest turning away—when he just looks at another woman—our anger terrifies us, and him. If we never learned that anger is part of love, its inevitable other side, then it lives at its original killer heat. If it were not allowed to be expressed during our growing years, aired, and the terrible words allowed to hang in the air until they dissipated, the air once again cleared between us, then this is how anger always feels, titanic. It is a dangerous world, but nowhere near as dangerous as many grown women imagine; I think of myself as fearless, but all my life, whenever I am alone in the house at night and hear noises at doors and windows, I imagine killers; Robertiello says it is my own rage, never aired when I was a child, that lives on in the unconscious, only to be projected on to evil forces "out there."

What attracted me, like millions of other young girls, to Nancy Drew was her bravery. She didn't hear murderers shaking the windows and doors when she was home alone. I read every book in the series—each won for perfect attendance at Sunday school—and it wasn't her looks I wanted to emulate. It was the determination with which she intuitively met injustice and opposition. She didn't waffle— "Oh, dear, what will the other girls think?"—she acted. Nor did danger make her pause and reconsider—"Oh, I couldn't possibly go in that big, dark house alone!" She went in. So did I at ten. Big empty houses, railroad cars down by the waterfront, high trees all beckoned; the element of danger didn't hold a candle to the reward of mastery. It was only in my mother's house, when I was alone at night, that I feared the unspeakable threat in the dark beyond the windowpane.

My own rage projected outward, projected on to killers who would destroy me: "I one my mother, I two my mother . . . I ate my mother."

Conversely and simultaneously I practiced courage like a swordsman, daring my band of friends to climb higher onto the brick walls that surrounded the secret gardens between our houses, until we could see every belfry in our lovely city of churches. Even now the unexpected appeals more than comfort, in which I feel uncomfortable. It is certainly not everybody's choice of a life, but given today's unknowns, courage is not a bad thing to teach a girl, and there is no better time to practice than the tenth year.

It was that same Nancy Drew adrenaline that grabbed me when I saw *Thelma and Louise*, a film, you may remember, that stirred up the most amazing brouhaha in 1991, was on the cover of *Time* magazine, and got the drawers of many feminists in a twist. Disillusioned, unfulfilled, closer to the end of their lives than the beginning, the two heroines fall into an adventure that reunites them with their libidos, their courage, their expansiveness. They sling guns, rob a few stores, blow up a truck, and generally "act just like men." So? Isn't this a movie, make-believe, and aren't we already acting just like men, except for bravery?

My, my, what an uproar that film created, especially among those Matriarchal Feminists who like to keep all the badness in the world blamed on men. Women were telephoning one another all over the country for days, arguing, yelling, some furious, others laughing, but alive! It was a good feeling to have the argument out there, and the movie was the first of many in which female leads stalk the streets, blowing up buildings right and left. But because it was written by a woman, *Thelma and Louise* got an especially rough reception from certain feminists who flapped their wings and scolded, like film critic Sheila Benson, who saw it as a betrayal of feminism, which "has to do with responsibility, equality, sensitivity, understanding—not revenge, retribution, or sadistic behavior." Oh?

Each of us takes away from a film what *we* saw; what I saw in *Thelma and Louise* and have seen in more and more films since are moving-picture allegories of women in roles in which we have never been seen. But we know the cruelty, we've felt it in real life, women's rage as well as the kindness. It is freeing, reassuring, sometimes entertaining to see the bitch in us. It tells us that we, the voyeurs, are human; it tells us to take off that frozen mask that we think hides our cruelty—I'd far rather see the whites of my enemy's eyes—and it reminds us to make a more conscious choice the next time we feel sadistic.

To take these films any more literally than the standard stories of male heroes, to see them as an incitement for women to become gun-toting outlaws is to miss the beauty of the message. This *is* who we have become, maybe not literally, but we didn't take Clint Eastwood taunting, "Make my day," literally. We accepted that men, some of them, were killers; well, so are women. Do these finger-wagging feminists think the rest of us need a Set of Rules to follow, *their* rules, because we are too unformed to make our own life choices? Feminists are "sensitive," "understanding"? Puh-leeze!

For me, *Thelma and Louise* was the perfect grown-up sequel to the preadolescent years: the image of women being wild, ready for action, aroused too much envy, not in men, but in that breed of feminist who simply cannot abide another woman racing down a sexual highway with the top down on the convertible, gun in hand, ready to face oblivion rather than go back to a life of rules and regulations. It's a road the inhibitors know they will never travel.

These are the same feminists who would urge you to "Take Your Daughter to Work" and leave your son at home, to take resources from the educational system at the expense of young boys on the bogus accusation that gender bias in the schools has created a debilitating loss of self-esteem in America's schoolgirls. The fact is that the majority of experts in the field of preadolescent development simply do not acknowledge a vast gender difference in self-esteem. "Shortchanging Girls, Shortchanging America"—the academic study that prompted "Take Your Daughter to Work"—is flawed research with rigged statistics so dramatically presented that it drove the media into a feeding frenzy that hasn't ceased.

Have you spent time at a college lately? Are you aware of the matriarchal rule on these campuses where your sons as well as your daughters are being fed female-victim rhetoric that gains its fuel from the assumption that sleeping men will continue to back off from women's rage? Wake up, men!

It baffles me why men continue to cave in at the slightest murmur of victimization of women. Is it guilt, fear, or the traditional shared male belief that if you go along with women's wailing long enough, they'll wind down? Don't count on it, men. That was your father's reaction. These women don't need or want you. Your sperm is of no value; they can pick up a vial at the nearest sperm bank. You are nonessential in their world.

Since the Anita Hill affair, Matriarchal Feminism has sucked more profit out of victimization than anyone would have imagined, and it still goes on. I was no fan of Clarence Thomas or that congressional caricature of an all-male jury. But don't assume that women's rage will ever be voided on men alone. The giant heart pump of women's anger-that-never-dies is the bottomless reservoir that goes back to our first years. It is anger not at men, but at women. Given our inability to express it then at the person we loved and needed, infantile omnipotent rage never went away at all. Today women have a voice and no safer target than sleeping men. What woman dares name the real source of our rage, who is also the target of our love . . . "I one my mother, I two my mother . . . I ate my mother."

The Power of the Negative Role Model

Opposite those people we idolized were those who represented a way of acting, looking, living that we hated and swore we would never imitate. Perhaps it wasn't conscious then, but in our souls we swore we would not grow up to be like an overly critical father, a complaining mother, or a cruel sibling. Still dependent on our family, we couldn't afford to say the words out loud, but the vow was made: I will not be like them! And we aren't.

When we look in the mirror today we don't see certain physical similarities to an overly boastful uncle, a cranky grandparent, a physically abusive older brother. A cosmetic surgeon tells me that patients will look at their reflections, pointing out features they would like to change, never seeing the bump on the nose, the drooping eyelid; these were the characteristics of the negative role model. We vowed we would never be like them, and in our own eyes, we aren't!

I was captured by Doris Lessing's depiction of her parents in the first volume of her autobiography, an image of the way her own life would *not* turn out: "There they are, together, *stuck together*, held there by poverty and—much worse—secret and inadmissible needs that come from deep in their two so different histories. They seem to me intolerable, pathetic, unbearable, it is their helplessness that I can't bear. I stand there, a fierce unforgiving adamant child, saying to myself: I won't. I will not. I will not be like that. I am never going to be like them. . . . Remember this moment," the young Lessing warns herself. "Remember it always. Don't let yourself forget it. *Don't be like them.*"

When was it that I vowed I would be economically independent, seeing the price my mother paid for her dependence on my grandfather? He was my hero, but like many grandparents who can build ties to their grandchildren, he was unable to be anything except a critical disciplinarian with his own children. He was a wealthy man, but his Calvinistic rigidity demanded that my mother work for him in partial "repayment" of the funds he laid out for her and us children. Maybe that sounds reasonable today, but when I was growing up in the South, no woman from "our class" worked; what I learned from my mother wasn't the admirable image of a working woman—she resented that job—but her anxious air of resignation. I swore never to wear it. The sadness on her pretty face frightened me, especially at the dinner table, the battleground of so many families. When she was with her friends, at parties that often spontaneously happened in our house, then I saw her happy and laughing, but it was always with a sigh when she turned to me, or so it seemed.

I would never sigh like that, I swore, and I never did, not over money problems, not ever. Like most children I accepted that I was the cause of those deep sighs, and it didn't require much figuring out to conclude that their source was her dependence on her father. Never me, I decided. I will never wear that look of capitulation. Should I catch anything bordering on it today while passing a store window, I take a quick, deep breath and relax the muscles. I may have consciously resolved to be different, to be independent, but there are certain characteristics, looks, we cannot help but inherit for dozens of reasons, not the least of which is proof of love—"See, Mommy, I don't hate you, I've become you!" My family smiled at my lemonade stands, at my rummage sales, at the plays I produced on our back terrace, using bedsheets as curtains, with one child collecting pennies at "the door." It was considered unfeminine, unladylike, even to think of money.

All this began at about age seven. I saved my money in a glass bank shaped like the world. As I watched Portugal, then France become opaque behind my pennies, nickels, and dimes, I imagined these coins buying my ticket to voyage to the brightly colored countries on the postage stamps my grandfather sent from his travels. That my bank was a globe mattered, for as I can recall, I dreamed of moving on, travel, adventure. I just couldn't repeat my mother's life.

I would come to have enormous sympathy for what my mother went through, but when I was little, I didn't know the background of her unhappiness. My father, whom I'd been taught to believe dead, was actually still alive; she lived with that, along with the chagrin of her reliance on my grandfather's "largesse." I saw only the exasperation, and what I read as a lack of joy when she saw me, her shoulders rounding in resignation. And so I brought home straight A's always, and won awards, trophies, games, was elected captain, president, of everything in sight. But she took no delight, and so I resolved never to bring problems, or prizes, to her door. I tried to be responsible for myself.

That is how I grew up and remain today, economically and emotionally. No one has ever paid my rent or bought my food or clothes. It is not a proud manifesto, simply a given. I remember the first man who bought me a piece of what I suppose is called "serious" jewelry. He was an Italian film producer whom I met in Rome in the sixties. "Is this real?" I asked ungraciously, pulling away from it, a gold pin encrusted with tiny diamonds and rubies. He was taken aback. I protested that I had no intention of prolonging our love affair, that I was returning to New York, to another man, but he laughed out loud and put his hand over mine. "Nancy," he said, "it is just a little gift." When I look at that pin today, I recall my fear that taking the pin might be read to mean that I was surrendering some degree of my independence; I understand what the younger Nancy felt and feel it still.

With all our celebration of successful women, there remains a deep, traditional resentment in our society of women who have succeeded economically. The System applauds a man "having it all," but when a woman accrues wealth, fame, looks, and power, she is cut down to size, even in Hollywood.

Between my aunt, the positive role model of independence, joy in the creative life, and my mother, whom I fear I represent unfairly as only a negative role model, an emotional blueprint developed that still applies. What has changed is conscious awareness that my mother's laugh, her zest and competitive spirit are mine as well, both genetically and by way of imitation. I was too angry for too long to admit how much I owe her; the gratitude was suppressed along with the rage. She didn't see me when I was little. That grieved me deeply. She is my mother. In Key West, when I see her with my friends, drinking martinis around the pool and leaning seductively toward the man who is my dearest friend, I see myself.

And when she sees my life, the way we live, fly around the world, the clothes I wear, she says, "My, my, aren't you the woman of the world." It's all right now. I can live with her envy because I understand it: Genetically and temperamentally, she was as capable as I of having my life or any other; she simply didn't have as good a negative role model as I did.

Ambivalence. If I could make that fact of life acceptable—that those we love most get our hottest rage—I would have accomplished something.

The Tree House Versus the Sleep-Over

That preadolescent girls and boys, once out of the house, head in such diametrically opposing directions states the urgency of their business: Each sex is eager to find people like themselves, to form friendships, groups that replace family intimacies with look-alike, carbon copies of what a girl is, what a boy is. We are desperate for another face and body our own size and with our own needs.

Girls nest together in sleep-overs, touching, talking into the night, reassuring one another that each is like the other, loves the other. The last thing the boy gang wants is a pretty chintz bedroom. Better to sleep in a tent, a tree house, and to compare, compete on a baseball diamond; it is as opposite from his sister's grouping as his body is from hers. The preadolescent boy *must* find contact with other boys for no other reason than to get away from the sight of himself in the eyes of women/mother, whom he loves but who has dominated him from the time he was born. Who am I? he wonders. What do I look like in eyes other than hers, which cannot really see me, her body being so different from mine, and I am beginning to believe that her thoughts and needs are also different. Therefore, while I love her and must protect her from my secret self, I must find other people my size, who look like me, in whom I see my self, and whom I can trust.

The entry of fathers into their sons' intimate lives isn't keeping pace with the number of women raising boys totally on their own. Are we surprised that boys/men so often come off sounding, looking, and behaving as if they were antifemale? Just for a sample of "what might have been" or "could still be," let me quote from a recent article in *Esquire* about a study by Robert Sears, who documented a group of men for several decades and who found that "those who were best able to resolve conflicts through compromise when they were twenty-three were raised by parents who shared equally in child rearing when they were five ... their fathers were as engaged with them as their mothers. When the same men were assessed for empathy at age thirty-one and their social relationships and intimacy were measured at forty-one, the greatest determining factor turned out to be the level of their fathers' involvement." Given a choice, I'd prefer fathers involved from day one, but I'll take what I can get in this contentious but crucial debate on shared parenting.

Left to themselves, preadolescent boys form The Boy Gang, prototype for the future poker game, all-male club, saloon, any place or time boys/men can hang together without girls/women.

Now, on playing fields, in secret clubs, dark, dirty places chosen specifically for their rankness, their dank, smelly, rough quality, so antithetical to females, a new language and posture is fashioned, practiced. Learned so carefully, at such risk and with so much promise that many men never unlearn it. "Shit! Fuck! Puke! Who farted?" They yell it, they do it, masturbating, farting, shitting together, anything that doesn't look female. If boys exaggerate it is because they are desperate to be opposite from us. In a few years, a young boy will be expected to have mastered the seeming manliness of having everything under control. Be a man! Make that goal! Storm that beachhead!

I loved the scene in John Irving's *The Hotel New Hampshire*, in which John and his sister Fanny shit together on the path that the football players take on their way back to the gym and then wait to see them step in it. That would have been grand, thought I, wishing for the thousandth time that growing up, I had had a brother. Or a penis—not now, but back then when I fully appreciated the boy's fixation. The penis is such a unifying symbol, so out there, so graspable and clean.

What else do boys have that better distinguishes them as different from women, who have up till now dominated their lives? Of course they douse the campfire in a communal piss, cavort naked in locker rooms, and play masturbatory games of who can shoot the farthest. Joyfully breaking mother's strictest rules and getting away with it injects them with bravado. It is an act of defiance and victory. The boy is proudly claiming ownership of that part of himself that, a few short years ago, she controlled but didn't like. This is something he has that she doesn't, and there are few objects of which this can be said. Every time a boy masturbates, it is an exercise in separation from women and a declaration of maleness.

How many chances does a boy have to see himself in another male, to admire and love the sight of the beautiful, young, male body? Girls/women touch, look, adore, lie down together without threat. But the boy has but this brief, shame-free period of time in which to allow himself to adore someone who is like him, a kind of hero worship. Soon enough will come terrors of homosexuality at just thinking of another man, "Oh, my God, I must be gay!" A 1969 movie titled *If* contained a scene that memorably captured this picture of hero worship: The older boy swings effortlessly on high gymnastic bars, his elegant, disciplined body in perfect coordination. The younger boy, watching, is clearly in love with the perfection of form and prowess, perhaps in love with the other man, who might in time be he.

A boy's decision to forfeit looks in favor of alternative means of getting attention is part of his separation from mother. Earlier admiration of his long lashes and blond curls is now brushed off in favor of near-miss feats of courage, which would alarm if not disgust mother, but which gain points with the gang. Losing her adoration of his beauty is a trade-off for the ground he has won as a man. Beauty's power has become an inferior girlish asset, and if mother should now smooth his hair and gaze upon him—"Let me feast my eyes on you"— he would push her away, saying, "Aw, Mom." His standing in the eyes of the gang has planted in him a sureness that strength, badness, might is how he proves maleness, his distance from mother/girls. Within the gang, beauty does not count.

Appearance becomes intentionally disheveled, even dirty. Television commercials that portray his mother as a laundress focus on her gratitude to detergents that get out the young scoundrel's dirt. The note of pride in her "little man" is apparent—"Now try not to get so much mud on my nice clean uniform!"—is said with fond resignation, an acceptance of boys' dirt that does not extend to her daughter. Not all boys are athletes—of late, the nerd with the plastic "nerdpak" has become an alternate hero—but for boys who have the ability and courage, sports are still where the preadolescent most successfully identifies himself as male.

It will be interesting to see what happens to the evolving look of the ten-year-old as appearance becomes an increasingly important part of the male makeup. It isn't just grown men who are getting deeper into fashion and grooming, enjoying the power that comes with looking good. Television has made male beauty an increasingly profitable business. According to my friends with young sons, looking good has trickled down to their boys' age group. Hair gel, mousse, the right Nikes, the correct shirt and jeans can matter deeply to a nine-year-old. What confuses the boy are the girls telephoning him, following him home from school; he is dressing to be part of his gang of friends, not for girls, not yet.

Today, the look of the Beat Generation is back, reminding me of a book by Joyce Johnson that came out in the early eighties, in which she describes her life with such Beat luminaries as Jack Kerouac and Allen Ginsberg. She understood that the look and feel of the Beat movement was that of the "boy gang" gathered round the sacred fire. Women like Johnson were allowed to be there but were excluded from the inner sanctum; women never really belonged. At one point she writes of how her friend Elise "watches wistfully as they [the men] play their dangerous games, killing time between now and the final disaster."

Girls in Each Other's Arms

Contrary to boys, young girls bring to their intimacies with one another the same passionate symbiotic glue they had with mother. Girls come to life in sleep-overs, nights of sharing everything they can dredge up from their short lives, any secret, any bit of self they can offer to show trust, in the hope that the other girl(s) will return the confidence, thus sealing the oneness between them. Yes, we want to live our own special life, but the only pattern we know is the dyad. We never walked alone. Try as we might to be different from mother, we are saturated with her, how she was with us and how we have perceived her all these years.

Little girls crawl into each other's beds to whisper, giggle, tickle each other's backs, hug, touch, look. We cannot look too deeply, for the other girl is us and we are she. We begin to love ourselves. This is what a girl is, not mother, not sister, but the best friend who is so like me that when we are apart we remain connected by telephone, so desperate are we to hang on to this new image of self. Mother was our mirror, but now she is too tall, too old; her clothes closet is exciting, but her dresses are too big, her dressing table fascinating but too complicated to grasp. Our dear little friend, however, she is our new reflection! No matter that she is brunette and we are blond. We are soul sisters, she the bridge to the great unknown, the totally trustworthy "other" who supports our tentative steps away from home, her hand in ours, her eyes shining back to us a sureness of self. Until she betrays us with another girl, leaves us out and without our self.

The world doesn't want to think of the nine-year-old as sexual; puberty comes soon enough, and our dogged refusal to accept a child's sexual feelings from life's beginning reflects our own fear of sex. If we don't think about it until adolescence, when reproduction can occur, then we don't have to worry. It is pathetic that we deny what science consistently tells us and instead raise young people to suppress a vitality they might otherwise use in areas of growth other than sexual intercourse if only *we* could come to terms with our own sexuality.

Sexual energy is fuel to be applied to learning, to sports, to social communication, to all talents and skills; children are capable of learning this, and also that early sexual intercourse could ruin a young life. We cheat them by not educating them on the age-appropriate uses of sexual energy. By the time adolescence arrives, there is little desire to take responsibility for something so "bad" that no one dear to us ever acknowledged how exciting it is; in fact, their blindness to what we have discovered, the thrill of sexual feeling, makes it something "they" couldn't possibly understand. And we wonder why children tell us nothing of their sexual feelings.

More than our brothers, we girls have internalized mother's anti-sex attitude, given that we are the same gender and she our unavoidable model; but when we play our sexually exploratory games with other little girls and boys, the notion of mother with her wagging finger and threats of withdrawal of love if we are caught only makes the game more exciting. "We sat on the edge of the sandbox," a woman tells me, "we were maybe eight or nine, girls and boys, and I'll always remember the grunting noises we made, like little animals as we pulled down our pants and showed ourselves to one another." The thrill of the forbidden; it is the cornerstone of the sexual fantasies that women will continue to embroider for years.

The most popular erotic daydream among both heterosexual and lesbian women today is of sex with another woman, and the earliest memory of such real sexual exploration goes back to these Years of Invention. Of course the memory of first arousal stays with us, the touch of a finger the same size as ours, the awareness that this is another little girl's, who shares our thoughts, up till now kept secret. We believed we were the only ones, that all females were like mother. But here is this darling companion, who softens mother's rules until they melt. Together, partners in mind and deed, we distance ourselves from mother. On the one hand, it makes us mother's protector, we will not tell her; secrets are part of separation, but simultaneously, the forbidden element of breaking her rules becomes endemic, so deeply associated with sex that for many grown women "forbidden sex" is the only kind that excites; after marriage, sex loses its kick.

Another prevalent detail within adult women's sexual fantasies is intimate talk, the sharing of secrets, hours of words building an erotic bridge to the act of sex. Men don't understand women's fondness for the verbal preamble of hushed conversation before sex, words and words that build to trust, loosening antisex constraints, allowing the door of the cage to open and passion to soar. Little girls lie in bed and tell secrets; big girls want a candlelit dinner, low voices sharing intimacies, and, maybe later, romantic music, more words of love that make them wet with longing. Once we were promised we would be loved forever if we were good little girls. To break this symbiotic agreement with mother and be sexually free we want our lover to be more persuasive than mother.

When we are little, when we are nine, we have already internalized the picture of our genitals as untouchable, except when it was necessary to wipe ourselves clean. We have never seen our genitals, but we know it is not a pretty picture. Here with this other little girl is a chance to discover that perhaps mother was wrong. If the other girl wants to touch us "there" and wants us to touch her, then the secret is no longer dirty and no longer a secret. Our vagina, our clitoris can maybe begin to be thought of as a part of us, part of our self-portrait. How hard it must be for men to understand this unique access women have to one another, the ability to persuade each other that our genitals are thrilling to touch, delicious to taste, and beautiful to see. We want to believe men, but they cannot imitate women's persuasive voice.

Some women "forget" their preadolescent adventures with other girls until, years later, the unconscious releases a feeling during intercourse or masturbation, which is the excitement felt in our first sexual self-discovery. Now in the grown woman's fantasy during sex is a picture of a female with beautiful breasts and pubic hair, attributes not yet developed in the girls of our preadolescent sleep-overs; they are mother's breasts, mother's pubic hair, but in fantasy, today, she merges with our erotic playmate of the ninth year of life to form a whole woman.

Many young girls would never dream of touching another little girl, lying on top of her, exploring her body. Should they do something bad, such as pee together in the tall grass, they are sure someone is watching and are filled with anxiety. Never having practiced separation, internalized mother's love—"My daughter, right or wrong"—the girl has incorporated mother's all-seeing eye. Years later, when she lies in bed with a man and her mother telephones, she is sure mother "sees" him naked beside her, the sheets soiled. The adoring eye of infancy still watches from a celestial height, monitoring everything she does and leaving her wondering, "I don't know why I'm so guilty!" Standing in front of the mirror, she puts on and takes off the sexy new dress, her indecision rooted in an inability to believe in the erotic vision of her self, never separate or different from her mother's critical view of her. Today mother's opinion destroys her as effectively as it did when she was two, nine, or forty.

Twenty years ago, women's sexual fantasies of one another were relatively few in number. Today they are the most popular theme. Women, in fact, are sexually drawn to one another in real life as well as fantasy, drawn in numbers so universal that they lie down in each other's arms in fashion ads, films, everywhere. It is a given that women move in and out of one another's beds without a second thought. In a way, it seems the most logical thing in a world where women are reinventing who a woman is and how she looks. We do men's work, but we are more desperate than ever to look like a woman. Who is she? What is a woman? We turn curiously, eagerly, to one another for close scrutiny and confirmation of what it is to be female, just as we did when we were nine.

Do women ever stop and think what an advantage we have over our brothers in our ambisexual ease at entering into experiments with either sex without fear of loss of gender sureness? I've seldom heard women of any age condemn themselves with the kind of overly harsh indictment a boy/man feels for just thinking sexually about another man: "Oh, my God, I must be homosexual!" The spontaneous fantasy of sex, or real experience, with another female may enrich a girl's self-portrait, but for the boy, the doors slam and the portrait narrows.

Straight men don't dare play with fantasies of other men; instead, the most prevalent theme in men's fantasies remains the one that shows how very deep, often unconscious, is that first woman's power over her son and his rage that she never recognized and blessed his sexuality. "There are an awful lot of men, especially if they're heads of corporations or very powerful in their day-to-day existence, who want to relinquish that power," says Norma Jean Almodovar, head of COYOTE, the sex workers' union in California. "And they want to do it in a very safe situation, where they would trust the person to whom they are giving power over them. They want to be tied up and told what children they are; they're into the words, more than any physical abuse."

In erotic dreams of degradation, the man turns his rage at women against himself; infantilized at the feet of the Big Woman, the dominatrix, the groveling man gets back at women/mother; he gives her the whip, the power of authority over him, but he triumphs with his dirty little orgasm.

Some young girls accept mother's sexual rigidity so completely that they will never grow beyond her dislike of all things sexual; oh, they will enter puberty, marry, have sex, and become mothers, but they will never see themselves as sexual people. When they look in the mirror, they will not imagine a man responding to the curve of their lovely breast, length of leg; they will never have seen themselves in that way. The sexual feeling was given up long, long ago and will never be missed.

You have seen these women, you know them—and some men too, though they are fewer in number. They have a look, a way of dressing, a cast of features that warns: Do not look at me as a sexual person. They are called Latency Women, which means they never emotionally experienced the sexual coming of age that is adolescence. They aren't lesbian, they simply aren't sexual, and are more comfortable with other women than with men. In marriage, they may try to set up with their men what they had with mother, but most men fear losing themselves emotionally in a soft, tight merge. Very well, their women decide, if you won't form a symbiotic union with me, I will remain your wife but feel most relaxed and happy in the company of the other girls.

So long as these Girl Scout women keep their antisex attitudes to themselves I wish them well; it is when they turn their judgmental, holier-than-thou eyes on the rest of us, demanding that we live as they, that I regard them as the enemy. Give up riches, give up the eating of meat, dancing on Sunday, but give up your sexual center and you will grind your teeth at night imagining others partaking of the forbidden fruit. Sexual abstinence is only tolerable if everyone else abstains.

Antisex men are as mean-minded, nosy, and critical as their women. I have never doubted that the Radical Right Wing gets its ramrod of envious rage from the insufferable vision of others enjoying what they, the abstemious, self-proclaimed God-fearing haven't enjoyed in years. Nor do I doubt that the most religious readers of pornography are those who, after reading, rush forth into the world to seek absolution for their own dirty orgasms; they find forgiveness in their red-faced condemnation of any damned soul who reads the book they just soiled.

When I write about the coming Matriarchy, I see its most obvious roots in the female-dominated homes today where a man's absence isn't questioned. It is, in fact, preferred. Total control of her children may feel good to a woman, but without a father, girls and boys arrive at adolescence with no feel whatsoever for a man. The boy will lean all the more heavily on his all-male group; the girl expects intimacy with a man to mirror the only love she's known, mother love: Men's eyes are expected to reflect her as mother's have. It is a doomed expectation of boys, to say the least.

Many of us women do not want to live in a Matriarchy; we fear women's rigid rules and restrictive power as much as, if not more than, Patriarchal Society's. But children growing up only surrounded by woman power don't have our adult choices. Instead of love of men, they get a daily dose of anger at terrible men, reinforced by their depiction as abusive, cruel, and brutal on television and in print.

When a fatherless boy grows to manhood and responds obnoxiously to the unexpected arrival of a woman in an all-male environment, it is the ten-year-old's overreaction to women's power, the knee-jerk reminder that to be a Real Man he must act the opposite of mother. A boy isn't predisposed genetically to be a voyager alien to women. But men will not stop preying on women's vulnerability until the boy gets the feel of an empathic man's power from day one and the grown man rediscovers his capacity for compassion in caring for his own dependent child.

Fascinating, isn't it, that we learn about the life-determining need for early intimate parenting at the very moment that we lose the extended team—mother, father, grandparents, the lot? Not that having many pairs of arms around the house automatically guaranteed perfect oneness and separation. Nonetheless, we look at Woody Allen's *Radio Days* or Neil Simon's *Lost in Yonkers*, and sigh for the eccentric but lovable aunts and uncles who used to live in the family spare bedrooms.

I've been thinking about the people I love and admire most, probably because so many of them have died recently. They didn't get oneness and separation, but they did have someone like my aunt Pat, who focused on them. It wasn't a perfect solution, but that person's admirable image and love was fuel enough to move out into life on a kind of charming crutch. Ironically, it was the lack of early symbiotic love combined with the crutch that gave us a peculiar talent for getting ourselves seen and picked up.

That so many of these people grew up to become actors, dancers, composers, writers, directors isn't surprising. That so many of the best of them died early of AIDS says, to me, Who wouldn't want to lie down with them? Long, long ago, they made themselves irresistible in order to survive. They wrote songs, plays, and books about finding and losing love because that is what they knew best. Up and down passion's scale they zoomed, falling in love with people who were unattainable, who betrayed them or whom they betrayed. Passion and agony always rode alongside. And when they died, the memorial services at the theaters were jammed with those of us who cried for ourselves, having loved them precisely for who they were.

It always comes back to the old existential argument with Robertiello: "Would you rather have been born beautiful and loved as the Christ Child and never let go, or invisible and had to invent alternative means of survival to get yourself seen?" Me, I always choose the latter; it makes for very high highs and lows you don't want to know about, but the very young beauty gets cheated too: It doesn't last, whereas the talents learned from an Aunt Pat, or a fascinating uncle who was a ventriloquist, a violinist, an opera singer, well, they can last a lifetime.

What I hope is that young people will read this chapter in particular, and even if they don't see themselves will recognize the untapped possibilities that are out there, opportunities unique to the eight- or ten-year-old to get close to some admirable other. We never get this precious time again in which we are so malleable and free of the demands of family, their projections, and how society wants us to be and look. Even if we forfeit our fine ten-year-old self in the hall of mirrors that will be adolescence, the victories of these years remain intact, inside us.

I can assure you that it is never too late to go back and claim an image created when we were nine or ten; upon examination it still fits perfectly because it is internal. Ten years ago, I finally came of age; by which I mean I shed the skin in which I'd lived my adult life, stopped trying to create with men what I hadn't had as an infant. Where I went to find the skin that fit just right was here, in the enchanted years.

Remember to mark this spot in life, as pirates marked the buried treasure on their maps. We must know where we left the admirable person whom adolescence overshadowed.

4

The Dance of Adolescence: Girls

====

Pretty Babies Get Picked Up First, Again

No one forgets adolescence. No one.

On a day that begins like any other, an almond-sized section of the brain called the hypothalamus signals to the body that we are now ready to begin sexual maturation. Awakened by a need that lures us from our childhood games with people in whom we've seen ourselves for years, we turn to meet the judgmental eyes of the opposite sex. Drawn to them, we look for a new reflection. Do we suit them, do they like what they see, are we all right, good enough? Whatever self-esteem we've acquired, we feel dependent now on how they grade us. We wait to dance.

If I were to choreograph adolescence—dance being an appropriate art form in which to express these years—the curtain would rise on the slow and easy last days of childhood. Imagine the stage evenly lit, boys in their group stage left, girls right, a sheer curtain between them. Neither group is mindful of the other, so engrossed is each in its own dance. Movements are full of unencumbered life, a lack of self-consciousness, big stretches that extend bodies so that they almost seem to grow in front of us. They follow one another, imitating, challenging, especially the boys, who are far more competitive and combative in their interplay than the girls.

On the other side of the curtain, the girls dance together to a different music, some in each other's arms; they comb each other's hair, whisper, read together; others play a game of ball until a dispute arises, competition threatens, and the game dissolves. Suddenly a gaggle of girls comes apart at the seams and a girl is tossed out, left to stand pitifully alone and then just as abruptly swallowed back into the group. They are intensely loving, quickly mean; ambivalence labels their play, expressing a desire to break away from the sameness of the group and at the same time to be contained and comforted by it.

We see a few girls approach the curtain to spy on the boys; they invite them into their game, but the boys are mindless of the girls, even disdainful, so intent are they on their own dance.

The competitive energy of the boys' movements is constant, and when it builds to a pitch that threatens to destroy the camaraderie, the most powerful, cleverest boy reaches out his hand in a formal gesture, a handshake that is repeated by all the boys until all the daring movements of the leader have been imitated by the gang, taking them to a new level of communal excellence. The excitement of the all-boy team is a clash of energy and challenge carrying the entire male ensemble higher and higher in developmental skill until a height of breathtaking flawlessness is reached. All the while, the athletic beauty of the chorus is seen to be held together by the repeated handshake, the motif that constantly quells disruption.

At a moment when each of the groups is at its most definitive and different, when we least expect it, a howling wind blows away the curtain between the sexes and propels the girls, the boys, into two rigid formations facing one another, each visually riveted, staring at the people opposite who have been so near but of whom each has been oblivious. What do they see in one another? They do not know but they cannot turn away, cannot return to their individual dance, though one or two are seen to try, and fail. Instead they now respond to a demand that they accomplish a mutual dance, one for which they have had no preparation, but which they cannot deny. How to begin?

One of the more extroverted girls begins to rush happily forward, initiating her own dance toward the boys, only to be hastily pulled back into the ranks and scolded by the other girls, who now have a more intuitive sense than their former leader of how the dance will progress. And, indeed, from out of the chorus several exquisite girls, who have been quiet in the background until now, emerge and dance, *ensemble*, the birth of sexual beauty out of the soft limbs of childhood. So exquisite are their movements that they seem to inform the boys' ranks, selecting the several heroes who have been seen to be more athletic, handsomer, and more developed than their fellows. Crossing the line where the curtain had been, the male leaders move assuredly away from their gang, which obediently falls back to let their heroes perform what is felt to be their destiny: the most physically accomplished to lead the dance with the most beautiful girl. This is how I remember the choreography in *Seven Brides for Seven Brothers*, *West Side Story*, and *Oklahoma!*

Writing these words, I feel this dance as painfully as when I first went through it. Substantial a minute ago, I am airborne, imagining adolescence's promise to answer my prayers, the needs of an infant who had never been held or loved. Such is the magic of romantic music and dance.

Over the years I have written of that night at the Yacht Club, our first formal dance in the grown-up world of "the older crowd," and of my shock, as though I were witnessing something as inconceivable as death, for how could I at thirteen possibly imagine my world, my self, disintegrating and falling apart? All my lovely years of invention blown away like the pages of a calendar in a movie, suggesting time passing. But for me, time was racing backward not forward as I stood in my horrible dress, shoulder blades pressing into the wall, watching my dear friends whose leader I had been dance by in the arms of handsome boys; and all the while that frozen, ghastly smile on my face, denying that I needed to be rescued. Why, even the girl who couldn't shoot a basket for the life of her danced by. Though they all whispered to me to hide in the ladies' room, I stood my ground.

Whether it was that night or shortly after, I abdicated my role as leader, throwing in with it my bravery, intelligence, wit, speed; everything practiced for years now proved useless in my desperation to be held and led in the dance of adolescence.

I've a photo of myself taken in our yard on what looks like The First Day of Adolescence. Someone has cut my hair into a lank pageboy with bangs; it makes my long face even sadder as I sit there in a white wicker chair, hunched forward, staring at the ground, hands tightly clasped in my lap, swathed in the loser's agony of defeat. Who took that picture? I have no idea, though I remember the box camera aimed at me and that awful skirt and sweater, which had been my sister's, as had the dress at the Yacht Club, fine for a beauty, but oh, so wrong for a tomboy.

Adults whispered to one another, "It's just a phase, she'll get over it." Psychologists still use these words, as though the pain and contradictions are inevitable. Are they? I am not convinced. I believe we all, men and women, give up far more than is necessary to fit the rigid standards of adolescence. The biggest mistakes I've made in life, the roads not taken and opportunities not seized, I am sure, today, might have been avoided if only I'd been able to take into adolescence the girl I'd been just prior to it. Reining her in, forcing her to obey the restricting rules by which all girls had to live made me acutely self-conscious, overly cautious, unsure of myself, second-guessing everything for the rest of my life. And angry, don't leave out anger at abandoning myself, teeth-grinding anger that I dutifully swallowed and "forgot."

The rigid rules of adolescence turned me, like almost every woman I've met, into a very controlling person. Leading a little life when you naturally hunger for more is bearable only if all the girls suppress their appetites as well. It is perhaps the major reason that I decided long ago not to become a mother; I didn't want to control another human being, to demand from a child the perfectionism, the rigidity I acquired in those years.

And please don't tell me that my voluntarily acquiescing to the stereotype of the Nice Girl was due to the dictates of bad and brutish Patriarchal Society. Men had nothing to do with the setback of my adolescence except that I wanted them desperately and made the mistake of believing that what they wanted was what women's world demanded: passivity and beauty. Yes, men want the beauty, but they want other things in a woman too, such as warmth, kindness, a full heart, humor, initiative. It is we women who pin everything on beauty, on achieving whatever degree of it we can, only to disbelieve what we own, never trusting what we see in the mirror. And so, more today than ever, the competition over beauty unto death continues with the judgmental eye remaining other women's.

Adolescence caught me without a mirror to my name. For years I'd passed them by without conscious awareness of their power. The glass over the bathroom sink might as well have been a painted wall. So sure was I of who I was, seeing myself in people's eyes, what need had I of glass? What people reflected back to me was approval and enjoyment, their pleasure in my presence. I felt their kindness and so stayed a moment longer, warming myself.

Now suddenly I had to appraise my assets. I closed the bathroom door and stared at the tall person in the full-length mirror; as in the tests at school, I added up my hair, face, body, but this time I failed. Suddenly, I wasn't even a contender. Used to winning, scholastically and athletically, I knew the skills and deficiencies of all my friends, having played basketball and baseball with them all my life. I was used to choosing teams and would never have picked myself for this new contest, which, to my grief, felt more significant than anything yet attempted. On the spot, overnight, I buried my fine inner self-portrait and threw all my energy into imitating the prettiest girls' mannerisms, posture, dress; I even acquired a teeny, tiny voice.

Suddenly, inside my own house there were unavoidable images of success at beauty: my lovely mother soon to be remarried and my sister The Beauty. The arguments between the two of them at the dinner table, heated disputes over makeup and tight sweaters, were loaded with significance. Until now I had prized my invisibility, sitting there between them, figuring myself well out of their competition. Now, I wanted them to stop bickering and bring to my plight their considerable know-how in this business of looks. Perhaps I would have rejected their offers of help, but I was so desperate for a beauty makeover that they would have found a willing candidate had they pushed past my childish defenses.

Do I exaggerate? I don't think so. My friend Molly's mother took one look at me and made me a pretty skirt and blouse to wear to dancing class. I put them on and returned once again to the mirror for a verdict; bending my knees under the full skirt made me shorter, which helped. Now I was able to put my head on the boy's shoulder when we danced, but the bent knees had to be maneuvered in such a way so as not to collide with his and give away my "secret": that I wasn't really a little, adorable person.

Looking back, I fully understand the plight of the anorexic, desperate to control everything in life, which is so out of control; only her wasted body obeys her. Very, very thin was not in vogue when I was growing up, but in the South, very small was. Had bound feet been in vogue, I would gladly have hobbled with the best of them. We were in a race, we girls, a struggle to outdo one another in a negative competition, the goal of which was to be less, not more. Even intellect, especially intellect, the good grades for which we had competed, was not something of which we could boast. Boys didn't want a "walking dictionary," our snide nickname for the girl who simply couldn't help reading everything in the library.

Before adolescence, what life had taught me was that anything practiced long enough could be mastered. Now my task was to unlearn everything, to slow down, speak less, think less, be less. It would be many years before I could again trust myself to speak my thoughts fluently, so expertly had I ruptured in adolescence the circuitry between brain and tongue. How many times in college, throughout my twenties, and, yes, into my thirties would I launch into an opinion only to feel a dizzying panic, a creeping paralysis that I was losing my train of thought; all eyes were on me and I was on the brink of humiliation.

Twenty years later I would go through countless hours of therapy to realign my spine, which has never recovered from the bent leg posture I mastered in the art of being less. Mostly what I missed for years, however, was the absolute sureness of self, the bravery that I owned prior to adolescence, that self-image inside that made every door I opened an optimistic adventure; why would people not love me? Neither professional success, great friendships, nor the love of men helped me to recapture the degree of self-confidence, the inner vision, and, yes, the kindness and generosity I owned prior to the external mirrors of adolescence. Not until my house burned down could I begin to rebuild, though you can never fully regain the momentum that builds to what was originally in the making; some things are just too age appropriate to be fully recaptured later in life.

Until the world changed, so quickly did adolescence happen, winning love had come to mean accomplishment. The realization that I could gain visibility and admiration through intelligence, humor, excellence in a variety of fields had been the most wonderful growing experience. When a teacher writes a congratulatory note on a paper we've composed, when we're elected by our peers to be a captain, the leader, the president, we have been seen by them as someone different from the child within our home whose growth never changed the original assessment of the family gaze. "Carpe diem!" cries the Robin Williams professor to his sleeping class, awakening them to life in the film *Dead Poets Society*. Was there a member of that audience who didn't resonate, remembering the lost potential?

Only in the past few hundred years have we been able, literally, to afford these years called Adolescence, to give our children a chance to grow instead of toiling in fields and factories only to become parents themselves by age fourteen. Why the gift if we do not recognize *them*, gaze at the miracle of their physical and intellectual growth, as we gazed at them in infancy? Granted, they no longer have the infant's beguiling dependency on us, which made us feel Madonnaesque; quite the contrary, adolescents can be maddening, crawling into our laps one day, demanding adults' rights the next. It would be humiliating for them to request the loving reflection of themselves appropriate to an infant, but it is precisely what is wanted—The Gaze—when they aren't demanding total privacy. Too much to ask of a parent? Then why the gift of these years?

The morning paper is filled with stories of adolescent crime and pregnancy; photos of beautiful fifteen-, sixteen-year-olds in the latest fashions dominate the pages. We have created a monster out of what should be a valuable time period in which to prepare for life.

I could weep for what we give up to fit the stereotype, today just as it was in my day. And in this abdication I would include the beautiful girls too, who come to believe totally in the ruling power of beauty. How could they not, given how the world bowed to them? How do you tell the heroes and heroines of adolescence that their few moments in the sun may be just that? I would answer that we must teach them the role of beauty, instruct them in how it works, pointing out beauty's power but also showing them how to weigh the longevity of intelligence, wit, and compassion opposite the brief reign of looks/appearance so that these learning years are not squandered.

We've been remiss, dangerously so, in denying how beauty operates and is traded on behind homilies and platitudes. Instead, we hype beauty in every medium and count the bucks we make on our young. Today's birthday parties for nine-year-olds take place in beauty parlors, where group makeovers include manicures, hairstyles, makeup, the works; top modeling agencies advertise videos for the youngest adolescents on "How to Become a Model."

If I were setting up a curriculum for preadolescents, I would prepare them for the new appraisal of and by the opposite sex that is just around the corner. I remember adolescence as a door abruptly opening, and there they were, boys. I didn't even know what I'd missed until I saw them and the music began; then, all the desperate yearning rose from the earliest days of my life to demand satisfaction. Every song I had sung on my bicycle, arms outstretched as in dances at the movies, now had a purpose.

Until adolescence my childish exhibitionism had been to win attention and approval from the world at large. Now, from the moment that small, almond-sized part of my brain dropped and spread its elixir throughout my bloodstream, I recognized my true audience: boys. Only they could take me in, love what they saw, and in that gaze return me to myself. The Gaze. Never experienced at the appropriate time, The Gaze of infancy now swam up from the toys in the nursery to demand another chance, this time with boys instead of mother. The unfortunate catch was that sexual desire was confused in my thirteen-year-old mind and body with the infantile yearning for symbiotic bliss.

The libidinal energy now available to intellectual and social development was detoured and rerouted to service my irresistible need to be held. Had intellect and leadership been prized in these earliest mating rituals, I might have continued growing. No one said a word, but one quick assessment of the boy/girl lineup told me that if I were going to dance, be held in a boy's arms, then silence and smallness would serve me best.

And only one boy would do. In my eyes, only one had the power to awaken me. Malcolm, leader of the pack, James Dean, Elvis, alter ego to my little-girl self buried inside the self-confident, I-can-take-care-of-myself shell I'd built. What did I know of the difference between sexual desire and the need for oneness? To me, Malcolm, the tough guy in the windbreaker, the sleeves on his T-shirt rolled high above the muscles in his arms, his eyes and shoulders unyielding, to me he was the rock to which I would cling, the unattainable prince for whom I would slay any dragon. A contradiction, but such is the character of adolescence.

But Malcolm didn't even see me. He looked right past me to a girl I'd known all my life, who couldn't hit a baseball, climb a wall, or lead a class. A girl who was beautiful, of whom today's researchers in beauty ideals would say had the perfect alignment of large eyes, narrow chin, broad cheekbones, childbearing hips, and, of course, breasts.

Did I envy her? On some preconscious level I'm sure I did, for I never lost sight of Malcolm in those adolescent years, never stopped desiring him, the unattainable one, the very essence of romantic love. But I couldn't afford to hate the girl he chose, who was my friend and would vehemently have denied that I felt competitive. Boys were the goal, but my crowd of girls was home base. Instead, I employed one of the finest defenses against the recognition of envy: I idealized my rival. She was beautiful, perfect, so far out of my league as to be unthinkable as a rival. I smiled in her presence, hugged her as close as ever, and told myself I was happy dating one of Malcolm's lieutenants.

If I was no longer my crowd's leader in this new game of desirability, I would be the most imitative in collective identity. Though my entire dream life, waking and sleeping, was now taken over by love of boys, I would never question home rule. I applied my competitive spirit to outdistancing everyone in the Nice Girl Rules, which said No Competition and No Sex; try as I may, I cannot recall anyone ever saying The Rules out loud or suggesting that breaking the antisex rules would automatically eliminate you from The Group. But they existed more strictly than any perimeters I've known since.

My crowd of girls was the collective bosom on which I laid my head, the Big Mother that stood in for her disciplinary eye; though I've always felt that no one in our crowd desired boys more passionately than I did, simultaneously, no one held more vigorously to The Rules than I did. I've occasionally thought of telephoning and asking the girls of my youth if they tasted the forbidden fruit. Was I the only one, dying to cross over, to give myself utterly to the beloved boy in exchange for love, who abstained?

Actually, what I found to take the place of sexual intercourse was quite fulfilling in its way. I would go so far as to say that some of the most passionate, extended hours in life were spent in parked cars, romantic music on the radio fueling the sense of lost boundaries, of floating out of my body, of somehow creating the most orgasmic sense of entering the boy's self so completely that I willed myself into a state of semiconsciousness. The more I study women's orgasmic potential, the power of fantasy alone to create orgasm without any touching whatsoever, the more I'm convinced that this is what passion achieved in those cars of my youth. I never did understand why my pretty white cotton panties with the lace trim were soaked through when I returned home. My breasts were not allowed to be touched, nor my genitals; it was all in my head.

Sexual satisfaction does lie more between the ears than between the legs. I could live without penetration, which loomed like Hell itself with its threat of ostracization from The Group. What did we foolish virgins know of how pregnancy actually happened? It was my cognitive promise to myself that worked better than any store-bought device: a "mental rubber" determinedly planted inside my head by my aunt and teachers, along with the books I'd read and the movies I'd seen, which determined me to see the world, to be an adventuress.

As consuming as was my love of boys, whose arms promised the symbiotic oneness I'd missed in the first years of life, more powerful still was the prospect of many men, many adventures, all of which would be forfeited by pregnancy, which meant repeating my mother's life. Ah, the power of the negative role model. For the moment, the drug of choice was loss of self to the sound of romantic music.

And yet I do not think of my teenage years as the Great American Tragedy. The people in that wonderful place where I grew up were kind, and in memory filled with acceptance and love despite my doomed efforts to become small and cute. No one demanded that I turn myself into this bad reproduction of a Girl Girl. The tragedy is that it has taken me most of my life to break out of that role. By the time I left for college, I believed I was the happiest girl in town. Wasn't I voted the most popular girl in my graduation class? Years later, when I returned with my former husband to those lovely, narrow streets, he was told by people he met, "Everybody loved Nancy Friday."

They did. The smile that hid my anger at having abandoned my self became who I was. The gold circle pin that all we Nice Girls wore said I was one of the club. Just lying in a boy/man's arms and feeling adored made it all worthwhile, and when in my early twenties I did eventually have sexual intercourse, I was my most acquiescent: I gave him full responsibility; I used no contraception. It was not the behavior of the dependable girl I'd been before adolescence.

More strongly than words, women's sexual irresponsibility says to mother that we're still her little girl: "See, Mommy, I'm having sex, but I'm not an equal partner. I've given this man/boy ownership of my body just as I once gave it to you."

Puberty: "A Farewell to Childhood"

G. Stanley Hall, a psychologist at the turn of the century, wrote of adolescence as "a second birth," a time of heightened creativity.

According to Hall, at no other time in life do we get such an opportunity. In these years, either the next generation's future is developed, advanced in terms of civilization, or this precious time is lost.

So much of our future will be experienced in reaction to what happens in adolescence; were these years a peak after which life went downhill or a distressing period of adjustment, which, in retrospect, motivated choices that determined the rest of life? So painful is the realization that some of us do not measure up to the demands of adolescent accomplishment—not the least of which is beauty—that the ground lost in these competitive years is never regained.

As psychoanalyst Peter Blos explains, "There is a progressive awareness of the relevancy of one's actions to one's present and future role and place in society." Quoting Inhelder and Piaget, Blos writes that nothing distinguishes the adolescent from the child more than that "he thinks beyond the present . . . he commits himself to possibilities."

Why then do we tend to denigrate adolescence, choosing to see it as something between a comic opera and a troublesome period of adjustment? Adults smile or weep over the emotional extremes of teenagers, waiting for the problematic years to pass; we act as if we don't remember our own adolescence vividly, which may explain why we are so reluctant to give our adolescent children the patience and understanding they deserve and which no one gave us. Could it be that we envy them? Here, we have literally bought with our hard work and prosperity these years so that they might more profitably go through the emotional/intellectual/biological stages of "the second birth" instead of having to labor and become parents themselves at a too early age. We give them the years but no mental tools on how to best use them. Yes, I think we do envy them.

How else to explain why the role of adolescence, compared to the first years of life, has until recently been so neglected by modern behaviorists? English philosopher John Locke viewed the adolescent as waiting to be formed into an adult by education, literacy, self-control, and a sense of shame; in the eighteenth century the French political theorist Jean-Jacques Rousseau's romantic vision of adolescence was as that time of life when we most closely approximate the "state of nature." But today, in our very technologically advanced times, I would choose the words of Peter Blos: "Western democratic, capitalistic society provides hardly any uniform processes or techniques to define the adolescent role, nor does this society recognize ritually the adolescent status change. . . . During adolescence, in sharp contrast to early childhood, the lack of institutionalized patterning is striking. Society, so to speak, abandons youth and lets it fend for itself."

"A second birth." We are the only primates with this long developmental period in life called adolescence. Lower primates are born, grow until they can reproduce, and automatically do just that, again and again until they die, just as the generation before them. "Physically mature beasts simply are not welcome in the family den," writes sociologist Virginia Rutter; "sexual competition makes cohabitating untenable. But for animals, physical maturity coincides with mental acuity, so their departure is not a rejection."

Imagine if we were thrown out of the house once we'd reached puberty; in fact, it isn't far from how life used to be roughly three hundred years ago. It wasn't just prosperity, the Industrial Revolution, but education, primarily the invention of the printing press, which in turn required the setting up of schools that created a body of years called adolescence. From then onward, the young had to learn to read to become adults. "Because the school was designed for the preparation of a literate adult," writes Neil Postman, "the young came to be perceived not as miniature adults but as something quite different altogether—unformed adults," or adolescents. Do you recall the paintings of the sixteenth and seventeenth centuries I mentioned earlier wherein little children were indeed drawn as "miniature adults"? Well, book learning, reading, schools, education, prosperity altered the depiction of a young adolescent person in art just as in real life.

Given all this trouble we've gone to, why have we so tenaciously avoided the psychological, moral, and sexual understanding of the adolescent? We have dozens, hundreds of fine books on infancy, the needs of the baby, physically and psychologically, and also volumes on parental roles; but where is the library on adolescence educating adults and young people to the complicated changes going on chemically, physically, emotionally, preparing parents to best assist their children?

"Only a few years ago it was an open secret among serious students of human development," writes developmental psychologist Urie Bronfenbrenner, "that the field of adolescence was something of a shambles. There were, of course, a substantial number of elegant and exciting studies, but much of what passed for research was pedestrian at best." Since 1985 and the establishment of the Society for Researching Adolescence, this has changed; but it is late.

Where are the compassionate Drs. Spock and Brazelton of adolescence, the TV documentaries on how it feels to be thirteen, fifteen, dramatizing how these years are going to shape and determine so much of the rest of life? When did you ever see a how-to manual for parents of adolescents on the bestseller list? We manufacture an already flooded market of products sold to teens, which garners millions of dollars annually—nearly $100 billion a year in 1994—but we do not have the time or inclination to study their development as closely as when they were babies. We have an ever growing world of geriatric specialists to balance our world of pediatrics, but where are the "adolescentiatrics"?

My quick but honest answer would be that we envy our adolescents. We resent the picture of their beautiful sexuality, the fact that so much of life is before them, and in contrast so much of our own behind us. Seeing them, we cannot help remembering our own adolescence with its promise of infinite life. Oh, we love them as well, our darlings, love them intensely, which is exactly why we also resent their going off into the night hand in hand, so young, so full of expectation, so reminiscent of our youth.

The world of the adolescent grows increasingly complex and dangerous; why go to all the trouble and expense of caring for infants and small children only to abandon them, misunderstood, on the shore of puberty? Opposite lies adulthood and, alas, the line between teen and adult grows ever more blurred as adolescents become stars of adult movies, are top-earning models, MTV superstars, and idols not just of their own generation but of ours too. Just maybe—unconsciously, of course—we don't want our adolescent children to outdistance us, remind us in the fullness of their burgeoning sexual lives that we are old.

It is a paradox filled with ambivalence, and it is ruled by sexual beauty. We love our children, and perhaps at no time more than when they are little, dependent, "ours." The possessive pronoun doesn't apply to the adolescent, who is full of contradiction, demanding to be heard one minute, pleading for solace the next. The world today, the media, the fashions, the films, the marketplace, everything is focused on beautiful young people, as if these sixteen-year-olds were the center of the universe. It can be very disturbing to a parent on many levels. Setting rules for an adolescent is difficult in the best of times, and these aren't.

Parents aren't immune to envying their children. We save our hottest resentments for the people we love most, whether they be lovers, parents, or children. The ambivalence of love knows nothing of familial ties or chronological age: The baby loves the breast, the baby bites the breast that has all the power; the man loves his wife, the man shoots his wife because only she could arouse so much rage, having so much power over his happiness, and the police will approach him first, so notorious are loved ones as first suspects in a murder.

We wish our children well, have sacrificed for them, but when we beam on the fullness of their adolescent life, the picture of their beauty, their social, intellectual, and sexual success that takes them away from us and is beyond what we ever accomplished, we feel a mean prick of envy. Denied and called by other names—"I'm only doing this for your own good"—the terrible *grrrr* of envy only grows worse.

Adolescence is sufficiently complex to require three developmental stages: preadolescence/early adolescence/adolescence proper, or, if you prefer, pubescence/puberty/youth. Listening to the names of the hormones marching through the adolescent body—androgens, estrogen, testosterone—I am reminded of Roman armies: *"Insula est parva,"* for these were the years when we girls were learning our first Latin from dear Mrs. Jervey. Reading about the adolescent body secretions— fluids, chemical energy "triggering a growth spurt," "alerting" pubic hair to sprout, I imagine a scene from Charlie Chaplin's *Modern Times*, machine wheels, conveyor belts methodically marching in all directions.

The boy sleeps and still the march continues, stimulating the descent of testes, growth of penis, every bone, organ, tissue pushing, growing, demanding more space. One morning he awakens with semen on mother's sheets. "Oh, my God!" A friend tells me of nights in adolescence when he would stagger to the refrigerator for milk, bread, fuel for the advancing army inside him that was himself becoming. Another day his voice changes, an unsolicited erection occurs on the school bus.

And there sits the girl, reading, dreaming, listening to romantic music as her armies initiate growth of clitoris, vulva, breasts, hairs, and, of course, pimples. One day in class she bleeds, soiling her dress. "Oh, my God!" From a child's body a woman's body, capable of carrying another child, is being formed. She raises her arms to look for the first hairs, spreads her legs when she wipes herself clean to see if a hair has sprouted, stands sideways before the mirror in the hope that breasts comparable to her friends' have emerged. She has dreams and fantasies that signal her body to discharge fluid; daydreams too, longings for an intimacy that are a refrain from the days of infancy, which she cannot remember "explicitly" but which are nonetheless abundant with the nostalgia of being dear, precious, and protected. Remember Dan Stern's description of a two-year-old's memory of earlier infancy, not exact, not precise, but a "feeling" of having been here before, felt this way before. It is a process of associations that go back in time, and if we were to ask our parents, they would not remember, for they did not feel as we did.

This is what the adolescent goes through, a recapitulation of earlier childhood. Opposite these tender reminiscences there is a defiant, rule-breaking teenager; clothes, hairstyle, a new lingo, a new dance and music invented to distance him or her from vulnerable feelings of "the second birth," and to distance them too from us adults. That we buy our adolescent children's disguise so wholeheartedly speaks of the complex emotions that parents feel in the presence of their newly sexual children. In an earlier historical age, parents would shoo them out of the cave or off the farm, get them married, or let them get pregnant. But we have bought our children this gift of time; we have advanced up the ladder of civilization, haven't we?

We give our children a gift of years but act like children ourselves who cannot bear to part with the lovely gift we have brought to another's party; sullenly we hand over the years but hold back instruction on how to use them, how to make the gift work. Without *our* understanding of their adolescence, and our very good wishes too— "Happy second birth, my darling!"—the gift is awkward and, often, dangerous.

No, it is we who want to be young and beautiful with another shot at adolescence! "We're best friends," the mother says, not wanting distance between her daughter and herself, she in the role of older, wiser parent, disciplinarian. Still in need of closeness with mother but wishing for someone wise, the daughter smiles agreement but misses the rules that only an elder can enforce. Today's adults don't want to look parental, cosmetically or behaviorally. They want their children's looks; the most loving of sons and daughters must, on some level, resent it.

What happened to the optimism of the eighteenth-century intellectuals' idealistic vision of the adolescent as being in a "state of nature"?

How did we get to the verge of a twenty-first century and our view of adolescents as greedy consumers and irresponsible sybarites? It is our doing. If adolescents are self-obsessed, it is because we adults have made them into shoppers who spend on anything that will give them an identity; poor little Empty Packages, they replicate their parents, who also feel invisible unless they wrap their hollow selves in the latest, hottest, new signature clothes. Look at me! See me or I will die!

The latest Calvin Klein advertisements posed young children in underwear for the eye of the errant pedophile and were greeted by so much brouhaha in the press that Klein's sales went through the roof. This is precisely how the marketplace works, and our adolescents know it and laugh at us rather than question the morality of the event. On the contrary, they will take the mercenary Klein himself as a role model.

We don't raise children to move beyond the love of self to a love of the species; they certainly haven't seen anything in us approximating this selfless behavior. Our society is consumed with unhealthy narcissism; adolescents see us wearing our identity on our backs, our self-worth and morality in our adornments and possessions. They see our unscrupulous, duplicitous national and international leaders on the evening news. Rousseau would tell us that these are the turning years, the moment for the young mind to question, challenge the culture's standards, to probe itself, analyze, question, contribute. Already self-absorbed, adolescents should be, could be—in spite of us—the very people to further their own cause. They are their own great hope for the future. What better obligatory course at school, college, for the adolescent student than "Know thyself"?

Referring to adolescence as that period in life when the next generation was either advanced, in terms of civilization, or lost forever, G. Stanley Hall went so far as to declare that he did not believe it was possible in later life to make up for what was lost in "the second birth." I would agree. Although I sentimentalize my own adolescence, I realize the amount of ground I did indeed lose then. I never regained that momentum; I accept that a higher level of thinking might have been mine had I not forfeited so much to the immediate satisfactions of these years. I would have been intellectually richer, more ethically organized, had I been able to take with me into adolescence the achievements of childhood.

I remember in early adolescence returning briefly to my beloved dolls; I resurrected Lulu from the basement and with my friend Daisy retreated once again to her attic where we "played house." But it wasn't like before. This time around they weren't babies; instead, we invested our dolls with a language and an identity separate from us. We told ourselves we could hear them talking and moving around in the attic, enjoying a life secret from and not the least dependent on us. We would creep up the stairs to catch them in the act, convincing ourselves we saw them move. I haven't a doubt that this brief episode was both my saying good-bye to childhood and allowing Lulu to act out my own next independent phase of life; Lulu had to live without me as I knew I had to live without my mother.

No one had spoken to any of us in my group of friends about what was happening to our bodies. There was no sex education at home or at school, or we girls who had known each other most of our lives would have discussed it. If biology was unexplained, certainly these years were not framed for us as they should have been, with the rewards of continued intellectual growth spelled out dramatically as a far more exciting future than a too early marriage, a too early pregnancy. We should have been the generation that would take society the next step up the ladder, go beyond our parents, build a better world. Society must not have wanted that or it would have happened.

Superficially, today's adolescent world bears little resemblance to the world of my youth, and yours too if you are over thirty. But the inner picture of self—which interests me far more than the package's wrappings—remains the same: turbulent, vacillating, and desperate for recognition: "How do you see me so that I may see myself?" Our teenagers awaken us to our own adolescences, the lost opportunities, the sexual excitements we denied ourselves. When we were young we didn't understand that sexual energy also fueled intellectual and social development; but on some unconscious level we know it now, that much was lost back then, not just sexual adventuring but the whole world that we never got to taste, the loss of which we are reminded of by our own adolescent children.

Having focused all of our punitive energy on the suppression of young sexual activity—as though we have the power to stop it—we shut down the whole machine. Unless we chain them to the wall, we can't police teens to keep them from having sex. It is our refusal to supply them with sex education and protection that guarantees that they will not outstrip us or remind us of our own paltry world of social and sexual fulfillment. Today, teens face increasing rates of depression, suicide, substance abuse; close to 30 percent have had sexual relations by age fifteen. It's true that birthrates among teens were higher in the mid-1950s than they are today, but in those days pregnant adolescents tended to marry, "and the economy was such that even a non–high school graduate could support a family," says youth advocate Margaret Pruitt Clark. "What people are really concerned about today is teen pregnancy that results in welfare dependency."

Those who preach that giving young people information about sex is giving them permission to have sex reduce their children to the level of trained animals. In refusing to believe that a young person can come to see his or her body as a temple worth protecting, says Virginia Rutter, we show our hand: "It also hints at the negative feelings Americans have toward adolescence—we consider it a disease."

There are good reasons not to have sexual intercourse at an early age. As powerful as the sexual fantasy may be, a teenager is quite capable of putting an even more dominant pressure into play: his or her own dream of the special life ahead that would be ruined unless sex were postponed or contraception used. When a principled adolescent chooses to subordinate sexual gratification to The Grand Scheme, but a parent neither trusts nor assists him or her, then the dream of the responsible self can be irreparably damaged.

When a girl feels emotionally betrayed by a mother who is rivalrous, or has not prepared her for adolescence or recognized her daughter's sexuality, then pregnancy is waiting to happen. "Almost always, in an unwanted teenage pregnancy there is an unconscious wish to be reunited with mother," says psychiatrist Louise Kaplan, "and a rebellious vengeance toward the mother who took her love away."

Adolescents today don't perceive us as admirable models whom they want to emulate by pressing mind and body to grow beyond our achievements. Working hard so that our children would have a better life than ours was what the famous American Dream was all about. Today, it is a disaster. More than 1.6 million young people ages five to fourteen are left home alone each day. How many of our adolescent sexual surrenders that end up in unintended pregnancies happen out of a passionate cry of "Take care of me! Adore me!" rather than a desire for sex, which could be had responsibly? Giving up responsibility creates the dependency of infantile oneness never enjoyed. Not having taken in the feel of one's life being witnessed in the first birth, the hungry child reaches the second birth of adolescence and snatches a moment of symbiotic bliss in another adolescent's arms rather than wait for some factitious, untrustworthy promise of an adult life.

We have addicted our adolescents to the power of The Image. They have felt our envy of their youth and beauty and watched us steal their adolescence from them, their fashions, their music, their dance, everything they invent to separate themselves from us. Shameless, guiltless envy—all learned from us—has become their mindset.

Temple or Sewer?
Today I Am a Woman, or Is It a Curse?

At the very moment when beauty matters most, we are awakened as from a nightmare to the shocking awareness that we have no control over what is happening to our bodies. Our breasts grow, the clothes that fit us yesterday are this morning too short and too tight. And then one day we bleed and soil ourselves.

We have been here before. This feeling of unavoidable shame awakens a chapter of our history buried years ago. The scenario of the first years of life's defeats reemerges: loss of pride, scared little baby stuff we thought we had conquered for good, forever, with the recent accomplishments of childhood and our years of invention.

Just when we thought we had found our place on the ladder among our friends, shifted our identification from mother to people our own age and size, the undertow of a tidal wave of physical and emotional change drags us back in time to nursery humiliations. The blood of menstruation reawakens fear of loss of control from the first years of life, a sense of bodily filth learned from another woman, who feels that way about her own body. We have always known that mother didn't like her body; now we understand why. It is an ugliness that may happen only once a month for a period of five or seven days, but in the other days of the month, we wait, always aware that we are only clean until we are dirty and unlovable once again.

Whatever self-image a young girl has built prior to her menses, that portrait will now change; the negative feelings that accompany bleeding will put in question the beauty of every part of her body. So emotionally profound is menstruation and all of its attendant rites and rituals that the girl will never again look into a mirror and see herself as optimistically as she did prior to her first bleeding, when face, hair, thighs, and upper arms were good enough. In rearousing the feelings of loss of control from the first years of life, now capped by bleeding that soils, smells, and defies control, menstruation becomes beauty's most feared enemy. And it needn't be so.

When I was growing up, the only references to feminine hygiene were the full-page ads of beautiful women in elegant gowns and in a corner the discreet message, "Modess Because." Because what? Prior to that first blood I didn't think about the mystery of menstruation, though I would say today that its polite message had been incised on my brain. But when I began to bleed, I "knew" without being told that if I didn't keep my dirty little secret to myself, like the elegant lady in the photo, I would never qualify for Niceness. Foolish me to think I wasn't impressed by these ads; didn't I circle the counters in our neighborhood pharmacy until there was a woman free to sell me a box of Tampax, so ashamed was I to ask a man?

How must it feel to young girls today, growing up bombarded by feminine hygiene commercials that enflame the issue to epidemic health proportions? Gone is the understated "Modess Because," which was bad enough given that it left everything unsaid; in its place are visions of happy teenagers on the beach, of mothers and daughters walking in fields of cornflowers, grateful that they have made it through another month without humiliation thanks to one or another of the dozens of feminine hygiene products the marketplace offers. Women in advertising, some of them no doubt cum laude graduates, write prose for feminine hygiene products that acknowledges women's loathsome spectacle of our genitals; why do we not turn it around, create a true revolution in women's self-esteem?

Long before her menses, the girl has come to terms with the fact that she can control her bladder and sphincter, yes, even as she sleeps; all the childish fears that her brother had more control than she because of his "handle" that could turn things on and off, well, that has all been forgotten. Or has it? There is no way to control the onset of monthly bleeding, no way to know when it will begin or to be absolutely sure that this time we won't spot our clothes in public. To make it worse, we now realize that the area between our legs is the source of sexual pleasure as well as of imminent shame. How can we even think about the conflict?

For years we have seen the familiar boxes of Kotex and Tampax, whatever mother uses; we've seen them but cannot imagine their function until it happens. How could we? I can remember one day, having a few odd moments, taking a Tampax out of the blue and white box under the basin, unwrapping it, disassembling it, and another day stuffing a Kotex into my underpants and strutting around the bathroom. Ha!

I must have accepted these items as my future, but I didn't dwell on it. Riding in the branches of high trees, exploring empty buildings with No Trespassing signs, now these were investigations worthy of my time. No detective work deterred me except the close scrutiny of my own body. Masturbation should have been on my agenda but curiously wasn't.

"We are not equipping women to be responsible for their bodies," says Judith Seifer, who has studied puberty and taught adolescent sexuality for more than twenty years. "In sex education classes young girls are still not told they have a clitoris. I've been fighting with two drug companies for eighteen years, Ortho and Wyeth, both of whom make plastic models that are used in doctors' treatment rooms. The Ortho model is a little pink and blue thing in clear plastic originally designed to show where a diaphragm goes. I have never seen a female model produced by a drug company for sex education that has a clitoris on it. The girls in my classes who are in the sixth to ninth grades pick these models up and look at them and if they have been lucky enough to find their own clitoris and they don't see one on the model, they will never believe another word that comes out of my mouth."

We reach puberty earlier than ever before, largely due to better nutrition, meaning that we are big enough to carry a child. For instance, in fifty years the hipline of a size 10 dress has grown from 34.5 inches to 37 inches to accommodate today's larger population. Since the mid-1800s, puberty—the advent of sexual maturation and the starting point of adolescence—has inched back one year for every twenty-five years elapsed. It now occurs, on average, six years earlier than it did in 1850—age eleven or twelve for girls; age twelve or thirteen for boys.

"When I was growing up in the late fifties and early sixties, it was twelve years and eight or nine months," says Seifer. "Pre–World War II, it was probably age thirteen plus. The reason ten- and eleven-year-old girls in the inner city are beginning to menstruate so early and getting pregnant is that many of them have more body fat than previous generations; they eat foods that are not necessarily healthy but which produce fat cells, and estrogen is stored in fat cells."

As our menses begin ever earlier, menopause grows increasingly distant, leaving us with thirty or forty years in which to bleed, and worry. It will happen to every girl, menstruation, and there is consolation in that; indeed, if it doesn't come soon enough, we begin to fear that it never will. One of author Judy Blume's most popular characters speaks for every little girl when she urgently prays for her first period: *"Are you there God? It's me, Margaret. Gretchen, my friend, got her period. I'm so jealous God. I hate myself for being so jealous, but I am. I wish you'd help me just a little. Nancy's sure she's going to get it soon, too. And if I'm last I don't know what I'll do. Oh please God. I just want to be normal."*

Now, more than ever, sameness is what life is all about; when the humiliations associated with menstruation loom, sameness binds us together in tight groups; we share our best friend's mortification when she spots her dress, for we know it could as easily happen to us. Control alone can save us. We must watch ourselves, each move, guard against loss of control at every moment.

We become mistresses of control once our periods begin. The Rules that used to command our group of friends, unbreakable rules that could get you ostracized but that kept us all equal, now become more ironclad than ever. This new controlling goes beyond the pool of blood as if to monitor everything we girls now do. Fastidiousness/purity/control was always there, of course, not just in early toilet training but subsequently in mother and teachers always reminding us to lower our voices, modulate our raucous laughter, slow our full-throttle running; and then, of course, came The Group's control of dress and behavior, everything.

Now, with boys, there is also control of passion, unspoken rules that today in certain groups may allow for sex with one boy, but when a girl has two boyfriends while everyone else has drawn the line, she is punished, labeled, shunned, left out. The threat of excommunication from The Group takes on added grimness and loneliness after the arrival of menstruation and its unspeakable partner, humiliation.

There is no part of my nature I hate more than my controlling side, no accusation from my man that brings me closer to tears than, "Stop trying to control me!" It was that side of my mother I swore never to inherit.

How bitter that we have successfully stormed the barricades of the all-male workplace and have done nothing to help ourselves celebrate the most natural thing in a woman's life, her bleeding. "It's learned behavior," says Judith Seifer. "Girls still don't like their period. They still call it 'the curse.' If you grow up in a household with women who hate the experience, who disdain it and pathologize it, have cramps and who are taking over-the-counter pills for it or going to bed with a heating pad—what are *you* going to do in an attempt to mimic adult behavior, other than the same thing?"

Writing Seifer's words, I remember the shot glass of gin being carried upstairs to my groaning sister by my mother. From behind closed doors, the moans resonated throughout the house twice a month, mother and daughter. One day in history class, my period arrived; suddenly, I was doubled over in pain. I rose dutifully from my desk, asked to be excused, and like the hypnotized son in *The Manchurian Candidate*, I stumbled across the street to my friend's house, only to find the door locked. Faithful to family tradition, I broke a kitchen window to get to the gin.

"Primitive menstrual taboos were not necessarily a male invention," wrote Susan Brownmiller in her 1984 book *Femininity*. "Seclusion in a menstrual hut, avoidance of sex and of men in general, and relief from agricultural and cooking labors were pragmatic ways of dealing with cramps and a copious flow.... Put squarely, menstruation is a nasty inconvenience ... a dripping, bloating, congestive mess.... [It is] an imposition of cautious caretaker concerns: secure protection, check against leakage, carry the extra tampon, change the pad, or suffer the mortification of the drip, the gush and the stain."

I would not pretend to make a rose out of a cabbage, but why do Brownmiller and that earlier pugilistic feminist Simone de Beauvoir act "like girls" when it comes to that function that more than any other signals our childbearing power? Smells, as either good or bad, are learned, and the sight of blood, when soaked through the bandages of a warrior, for instance, is worthy of a salute. Why then is our blood not a triumphant banner under which women march in celebration of the life force that is ours alone, we the powerful sex that continues the human race?

Instead, here is my heroine, de Beauvoir: "The sex organ of a man is simple and neat as a finger; it is readily visible and often exhibited to comrades with proud rivalry; but the feminine sex organ is mysterious even to the woman herself, concealed, mucous, and humid, as it is; it bleeds each month, it is often sullied with body fluids, it has a secret and perilous life of its own."

Shame is attached to a splotch of our blood, the mark of a curse, announcing the woman has not kept her house in order and has been negligent in self-control; the humiliation of it sends her running from the room to weep inconsolably, soothed by other women who can only be grateful that it didn't happen to them. By not being sufficiently cautious and superhumanly controlling the magic of her menstrual cycle, which of course defies control, she feels less a woman.

Some Jewish friends tell me they honor their daughters' menarche by celebrating her bat mitzvah, the equivalent of the boys' bar mitzvah. This is good, but only a beginning. The societal message must be reversed and soon, for leaving The Curse just that renders women too intensely focused on bodily imperfection. Today our work is in public, meaning that eyes are always on us, mirrors and reflecting surfaces surround us, distracting us with reminders that we are too fat, too short, too tall, and perhaps unaware that we have spotted our clothes. In the eyes of the anorexic, mastery over loss of flesh is a great blessing. Sufficiently emaciated, she stops bleeding altogether. Once the blood is gone, only the starved body, symbol of triumph and total control, remains.

Before we expose girls to the competitive rigors of the workplace, why not an advertising campaign to set the record straight regarding menstruation? We might sell red armbands to wear proudly on those days we bleed. Twenty years ago I wrote that if men bled monthly, if they were the sex that could carry a child, give birth, propagate the species, they would honor it as publicly as possible. If the emission of blood were a male rite of passage, it would be marked by bravado, the shooting off of cannons. Instead of a wad of cotton strapped as inconspicuously as possible between his legs, the adolescent boy's penis would be adorned, festooned with an amulet, an artful apparatus to catch the blood, package it to be used, you can be sure, in some religious or money-making scheme.

I've read that menstrual blood is excellent food for plants, gardens; now, if men menstruated and knew this, they would have cornered the market. The smell would be inhaled deeply, like Chanel No. 5, applied to the body as an aphrodisiac, signal of sexual power. Oh, yes, I do think that if the roles were reversed, bleeding once a month would be a celebration to which the boy looked forward.

We raise our daughters to believe that they can accomplish anything but saddle them with our miseries regarding menstruation. The taboo is so embedded in my own unconscious that as I sit here surrounded by recent literature on ceremonies, books, classes, rituals on how women might initiate their daughters into a healthy, even joyous, acceptance of menstruation, half of my brain says Yes! and the other half, Witchcraft! Intellectually, I believe that no physical handicap inhibits women more than the mindset regarding the bleeding female body. What good is an equal wage if we see ourselves flawed, always at risk unless we control everything?

"Designed to stop accidents before they start," reads an advertisement for menstrual pads in a teen magazine. "The bus is late and you've got killer cramps. You're retaining so much water you feel like a baby beluga . . . ," reads another, the closing line of which promises, "As good as it gets until it's gone." What is "it"? Maybe 20 percent of our childbearing years, those days, lost, ugly, and at risk, if you believe the advertisements that continue to brainwash young girls and their mothers.

Just as beauty's sovereignty in women's lives reemerged in the mid-eighties—after years of dark blue serge Dressing for Success—the full-page ads for feminine hygiene products also began to soar; in 1986, $23,974,600 was spent on magazine advertising for these products and by 1994 the figure had risen to $40,931,300. Even more startling were the television commercials that suddenly filled our living rooms, popping up like ugly jacks-in-the-box when we least expected. Today, more than a decade later, the ads and commercials proliferate, making the curse more personally hideous and threatening than ever before. It will be fascinating to see how subsequent generations of en masse working women with their own bank accounts deal with the increasing demands of beauty in the shadow of The Sewer.

"We don't know how to mark the physiological and psychological changes of becoming a woman or how to celebrate it," says Tamara Slayton, director of the Menstrual Health Foundation. It was her own unintended pregnancy at the age of fifteen that set Slayton on the path that led to a government grant to fund the courses she teaches on fertility awareness and the celebration of the menarche.

"When I began working with pubescent girls," she says, "I found that they saw no redeeming value in menstruation. So deep was their hatred of bleeding that many young women, I felt, subconsciously wished to get pregnant in order not to have to deal with their periods. In our culture, pregnancy is seen nowadays in a positive light, even out of wedlock, while menstruation remains a negative experience. The hormonal changes going on in the body at this time lead to behavioral changes, but we don't have any way of marking that. Girls come up to the challenge of the physical body, of making decisions on their own, of directing their own life, but they do it through an early pregnancy. So this whole pregnancy phenomenon in young girls may actually be taking the place of a rite of passage that could be instituted at first menstruation."

Not only are teenage mothers accepted, many receive the benefits of welfare and food stamps along with the respect of their peers, who see them as "beauty ideals," meaning they have turned the ugliness of bleeding into an advantage. The preposterous idea of orphanages as a solution to the epidemic of teen pregnancies is a cruel nonsolution to a problem that has its roots in women's attitudes about our bodies, the societal view of the menstruating women as unclean rather than beautiful, proud, and in charge of her body. It is sex education that is wanted, beginning in the home and emphasized in school.

"If a mother feels negative about her body, she shouldn't talk about it around her children," says Ann Kearney-Cooke, a psychologist who specializes in appearance issues. "Early in life children begin identifying with their parents, to borrow from their self-esteem. A parent must try to understand her own body image history so that she doesn't project an aversion to certain parts of her body on to her child. Mothers who are ashamed of their sex, their breasts, their genitals, without saying a word transmit this to their daughters."

I'd go a step further and urge mothers to tell their daughters honestly how they feel about their own bodies and about menstruation; the girl already knows. It is hearing mother say it out loud that begins to free the girl, especially when mother adds that she wants her daughter to have a better self-image than she. If she can't say it and mean it, then the Good Mother should arrange for the girl to talk with someone who does have a healthy attitude regarding menstruation. That, to me, is one of the great mother/daughter gifts.

I agree with Tamara Slayton that we have a "silent initiation into shame, in which the young girl is given a very clear picture of what it means to be female and how to ignore her rhythms as a source of strength and inspiration." This silence that surrounds our bleeding also cuts into our vocal cords, making articulate twelve- and thirteen-year-olds mute, embarrassed by our bodies, which we no longer trust; yesterday's well-spoken, inventive girl is now unsure, reluctant to draw attention to herself, afraid of speaking out before she's checked the sentence in her head as well as her physical image, smoothing her skirt, fluffing her hair, and tentatively checking the back of her dress to be sure it is clean. What if she drew attention to herself at the very moment her body betrayed her? Better not to speak at all.

Familial and societal silence that surrounds the menarche explains the negative makeover at puberty of once lively, self-assured girls. Add to this traditional setback today's exaggerated spotlight on beauty and appearance, and we have a generation of young women raised to earn their way in a competitive workplace where they will remain pre-occupied with menstrual anxiety.

Centuries ago, the menstruating woman was considered blessed; the word *blessing* derives from the Old English *bletsian*, or bleeding, according to Webster's dictionary. From Aristotle's time, writes Barbara Walker, author of *The Woman's Encyclopedia of Myths and Secrets*, humans were thought to be formed in the womb from congealed menstrual blood, a belief taught in European medical schools until the eighteenth century. In Middle Eastern and other creation stories a goddess created mankind from mixing clay with her menstrual blood; the influence of this belief can be found in the Old Testament name "Adam," from the Hebrew word *adamah*, or "bloody clay." However, when Christianity spread through Europe, the idea of women's menstrual uncleanness spread with it.

Somewhere between the ancient worship of menstrual blood and today's hysteria regarding women's menstruation lies sanity and acceptance. "Young girls today learn that they can't trust their body," says Judith Seifer. "They say, 'I can only rely on my body to make me smelly, dirty, crampy, achy, and bitchy.' Now PMS is officially labeled a psychiatric disorder. What is the difference between that and what went on in Victorian times, when female hysteria was assumed to come from a woman's menses? It was involutional or it was cyclical. Women were institutionalized for it."

Whether we are age five or fifty-five, the number one predictor of self-esteem is perception of our physical appearance, says developmental psychologist Susan Harter, who has been studying issues of self-esteem for twenty years. Here is the girl on the brink of adolescence, when romance, love, and beauty occupy her night and day dreams. She has never been more sensitive about her looks, which will bring her love and romance, kissing, holding, the re-arousal of oneness and weightlessness in the boy's arms: "Take me, hold me, never let me go," sings the dreamy voice on the car radio.

When he moves his hand between her legs, the Swept Away feeling is shattered. Since she began to menstruate, she thinks of that place as doubly untouchable, and he wants to put his hand where the blood gushes, the smell originates? How can he ruin everything by making her feel ugly just when she was feeling loved? Her inner picture of herself plummets: Not just the romantic moment, but her whole self-esteem is now zero.

Adolescence is precisely where this discussion belongs; here is where the self-loathing begins in earnest, genital abhorrence inherited from mother who learned it from her mother. Ah! Now we understand why mother hated her genitals. We have become links in the generational chain that will be passed on to our own daughters, the sad, dark disgust regarding menstrual blood.

Most females think they bleed in a great gush of blood, an unstoppable flow, when the truth is that most bleed about six tablespoons of blood during any one period. If we exaggerate the amount of blood, it's understandable why we also imagine that the vile drainage has disfigured other parts of our body. Adolescents obsess about their fleshy arms, fat stomachs, bulk of thigh. Very well, if they can't control the flow or smell, they can control their weight; whatever curves they desire can be developed at the gym if, of course, they have the energy to exercise.

What do young people today think of Rubens's masterpieces of fleshy women, bulging with rolls of fat, painted in gardens, with swans, in men's arms, riding on the backs of bulls, animals/men who carry them off for sex? Sex, with all that fat? How gross! Today's beauty icons, whom adolescents and their mothers emulate, are so rail thin as to be embryonic, some with eyes bulging, their faces waiflike, emaciated. It is not for men that we starve ourselves but for the approving eyes of other women, who respond admiringly to the success of she who has managed to turn the lovely roundness of her body into sharp angles.

I can't remember when it was born, this mental picture of my mother standing in front of the fireplace in the house where we lived when I was eleven. It is the cocktail hour, and she and a man are talking, laughing, and I am sitting on the sofa watching them. Suddenly I see that there is a pool of blood on the floor where my pretty mother is standing and I am horrified, as speechless as is she. It is the man who goes quickly to the kitchen and returns with paper towels to mop up the blood. He is not in the least uncomfortable, but we two women—for I am now united with her in bleeding . . . at this point, the camera in my mind jams and will not proceed with what happened next, if indeed this incident ever did occur. I've never known for sure, and my mother, whom I've just telephoned, is aghast at the story. It is all in my imagination, the nightmare of humiliation of the eleven-year-old who has just become a woman. Or is it? Memory, wrote Oscar Wilde, is the diary that chronicles things that never happened and couldn't possibly have happened.

Some men handle women's bleeding bodies better than we and I cannot help thinking fondly of those lovers in my life who have readily purchased the emergency box of Tampax in a crowded pharmacy; their lack of shame informs me, as have the men who genuinely loved my body during menstruation, withdrawing their bloodied penis, soiling the sheets with it in an abandon that told me something . . . something important, but what? That my shame might be unlearned? I have never doubted, as I said earlier, that if it were men who bled monthly, instead of we women, every day of the month would be a red-letter day. What bitter irony that we successful working women create the advertising and plan the marketing that enables the highly profitable feminine hygiene industry to hype the image of ourselves as dirty.

I can remember twenty years ago when my aunt—my heroine when I was growing up—told me of her idea to write a book on menopause, which she had just entered. "I telephoned your mother," she added, "but she didn't want to talk about it." She never wrote the book, but in recent years other women have. Almost daily an article is published on yet another new piece of research on women's health; as we live longer and become more affluent, new divisions of companies are established to manufacture an ever growing line of women's health products. And yet, our inquisitive minds stop at the edge of menstruation as though it were the River Styx. Rather than understand the origin of the loathing of our bodies, we dedicate ourselves more than ever to the pursuit of beauty, a pretty, empty package that would deny what is inside. Is our chosen ignorance a way of holding on to our own mothers and grandmothers? As our lives change at the rate of geometric progression, is ignorance how we cling to the past?

Almost fifty years ago de Beauvoir wrote: "It is not easy to play the idol, the fairy, the faraway princess, when one feels a bloody cloth between one's legs; and, more generally, when one is conscious of the primitive misery of being a body." When Brownmiller quoted these words in *Femininity*, I wished she had corrected de Beauvoir, brought her up to date with a new feminist appraisal, linking menstruation with the full, powerful spectrum of fertility.

In Carol Gilligan's *Meeting at the Crossroads*, which documents the dramatic changes in preadolescent girls as they move from one stage of life to another, this Matriarchal feminist avoids altogether any mention of menstruation. What kind of avoidance is this? According to an article by Susan C. Roberts in *New Age Journal*, the private girls' school where Gilligan and her colleague Lyn Mikel Brown did their research, "frowned on explicit mention of such subjects" as menstruation. Unmentionable? How can you write a book on the passage from latency years into adolescence and leave out menstruation, which is *the* symbol of The Crossroads?

The other reason for the omission, however, is sadder still, namely that Gilligan wanted to avoid flak from other feminists "for supposedly implying that women are 'essentially' different from men," says Roberts. "Were they to begin emphasizing menarche, they would be accused of joining the backlash against feminism, cloaking the old sexist argument that 'anatomy is destiny' in up-to-date garb."

And so, a major feminist, a brilliant thinker whose words carry enormous weight in women's world, omits mention of menstruation for fear The Other Girls will ostracize her. The tyranny of men can't hold a candle to that of women over other women. It is exactly *by omission* that these feminists emphasize "anatomy is destiny"; to bleed monthly is our destiny, symbol of our power to continue the human race. It is precisely female denial—and not Bad Patriarchal Society— that has led some women to obliterate their bleeding through starvation. If we don't soon salvage menstruation from the sewer and learn to celebrate it, we will have missed meeting at the crossroads.

In Praise of Masturbation

Imagine the difference it would make if we grew up thinking of our genitals as an elegant design and a natural source of pleasure;

what if the taboo were removed from that part of our body that is a lifelong reminder of contention and filth? We know from studies by Simmons and Rosenberg that boys and girls have roughly equivalent self-images until adolescence, when self-esteem changes dramatically along gender lines, and far more girls than boys become highly self-conscious. Asked "How good-looking are you?" early adolescents were less likely than younger children to answer "Very good-looking." And the more they cared about their looks, the worse their self-consciousness.

Because of the physiological changes taking place in these years, it would be unusual if adolescents weren't more conscious of the mirror. At this age, girls and boys tend "not to distinguish between what others are thinking and their own self-preoccupation and therefore assume that their peers are as obsessed with their behavior and appearance as they are," says psychologist David Elkind. It is hardly surprising that the primary basis of friendships in these years is outward appearance.

We would prefer that our adolescent children value kindness and generosity more than looks; our morality is in the right place, but we forget that we were no less "appearance conscious" when we were their age. Nonetheless, there are ways we can help them past surface assessment, beginning with the encouragement to accept their bodies, especially their most intimate parts. Adolescence is late, but better late than never to allow a young person to explore his or her own genitals (no one needs to be taught how to masturbate) until a warm, loving feeling has been aroused, the likes of which there is no other. Imagine how natural it would be for a girl to learn to respect and protect this area that brings her so much pleasure; sexual responsibility should be discussed until the light of recognition dawns in an adolescent's eyes. If the parents can't do it naturally, easily, credibly, then they must find someone who can. That is their duty.

For all of its being written about in recent years, self-esteem is at heart a good opinion of one's self. We mistake arrogance, vanity, and pride for self-esteem, when more often the grandiose person's boastfulness hides a very bad opinion of herself. Simply put, how can we have a good opinion of our selves if we think of our genitals as ugly, meaning that we harbor a sewer? If a female, young or old, cannot touch her genitals without revulsion, her efforts at self-respect are doomed, no matter how she may flaunt the number of suitors who pursue her.

When the person who cannot pleasurably put her dainty fingers on her clitoris has sex, she will be disinclined to get involved with the insertion of a diaphragm; the very image of her hand "there" is alien to the fantasies in her head of being swept away by this prince who now holds her in his arms.

Masturbation is something we would have naturally come to in the exploration of our bodies over the years, had the unspoken rules against it not been so freighted with dire consequences. In the first years of life the tiny hand went between the legs because it felt good. Unless someone important repeatedly took the hand away, murmuring negative noises with furrowed brow, we would have continued learning about our anatomy. In time, we would also have learned the simple rules of privacy.

Nowadays the statistics on unplanned pregnancies appear frequently in newspapers and magazines. Every year, twelve percent of all fifteen- to nineteen-year-old girls become pregnant. Knowing this, how can loving parents not prepare adolescent children in every way possible? Whatever the adults' own opinion of masturbation, personal or religious, if it helps prevent pregnancy, which would derail their child's future, what can possibly weigh against it?

I would do everything in my power to persuade an adolescent to postpone pregnancy. The risk of pregnancy and disease aside, there are such sane, persuasive arguments in staying on our own, open to growth, the mind and imagination expanding as it only can when we are independent in this amazing period of becoming, which is adolescence; there is a glory to the way we grow, a time-specific miracle that occurs in these years, and it simply doesn't happen if we become part of a couple, meaning marriage or parenthood. We can't regain it, can't make up this growth later; with a child, a husband, life is experienced as a couple, meaning ideas, feelings, possibilities are filtered through this merge of self with another.

I'm not saying don't fall in love in your teens. I'm not crazy. It is intercourse and the outpouring of emotion that it triggers, even when we are twenty or thirty, that a fourteen-year-old simply isn't prepared for, especially a young girl who is likely to be programmed for symbiotic oneness. When we give our bodies over to sex, we can't help feeling that this precious gift to the boy is something he recognizes as just that: We are his.

One minute we are growing intellectually, socially, physically, and then suddenly, in a moment of Swept Away passion, a boy puts his penis inside us and the miracle of a young girl becoming a unique individual is interrupted by a wave of abandon that goes back to infantile neediness. "I want you/I need you/I can't live without you!" is how we feel, clinging to the boy, who wonders what has happened, where the sexual heat went and where this baby girl came from. Believe me, young girls, believe me in this if in nothing else: Adolescent sex isn't worth what is being forever lost.

Was there anyone more starved than I in adolescence, more vulnerable to "that feeling" boys aroused when I was held and kissed? Had I let them enter me, had the emotional floodgates been opened by sexual intercourse, I would have become enslaved. Nothing would have mattered except being with him again, and again, for he had the key to my life, or so I would have felt. As stupid as I was about contraception back then, I knew I would never realize my dreams if I let him "put it in." I was right.

Would that I'd been encouraged—no, would that I had not been discouraged—to learn about sex from my own body. Most adolescent girls still don't understand that sexual intercourse isn't just the insertion of the penis into the vagina. If the girl has not learned from self-arousal that her sexual feelings reside in her alone, and are not something another person has the power to ignite in her, then the magic belongs to the boy. She confuses love and sex. She becomes addicted to "his" magic, what his hands and mouth can do to her.

Until she discovers that her own hand touching herself unleashes some of this same feeling, it will be the boy-prince who holds the key; she will sit by the telephone and wait and wait in expectation of the next magical moment when he holds her in his arms and "makes" her sexual. That so many girls and so many grown women give into "his" magic and eventually allow full intercourse, without contraception, has everything to do with who's got the magic.

And we castigate men for being overly proud of their penises. Who teaches them the magnificent power of erection? Yes, the boy likes his genitals more than girls do theirs; he thinks the world of his penis. But we women give him his summa cum laude. "Wow," thinks the boy, seeing that his penis has transformed the reluctant girl into his love slave, "I knew it was good, but I didn't know it could do *that!*"

The adolescent girl wrestles with her own desire for love and the boy's desire to touch her "there"; how can he want to explore the sewer with his fingers, his mouth! Doesn't he know what goes on there, can't he smell it? Hasn't he seen the commercials on television? But the media have also informed her of the ecstasy of oral sex and its promise of orgasm. Behind her self-loathing there is the wish to feel this mysterious ecstasy she has read about and seen repeatedly on the rapturous faces of beautiful television and film heroines. How does she reconcile erotic desire with the ugly mental picture of "it"?

The touch of his lips solves her dilemma. Like the fairy tale frog who turns into a prince when kissed by the princess, the unloved sewer becomes less hideous when kissed by the prince. He who accomplishes this for a girl becomes adored: She forgets the lack of beauty between her legs when his brave, hungry mouth is on her. What an animal he is! How desirous he makes her feel, wanting sex so much he will do this unthinkable act and bring her to orgasm too. The magic, however, is in his mouth, not her clitoris. "Just let me go down on a woman and she's mine!" I've heard men boast. But if she gives his mouth all the credit for *her* orgasm, she will hand herself over to him body and soul. Now, when he moves to insert his penis, her infantile desire for symbiotic love automatically awards him full responsibility for her little self.

It is distressingly ironic that for some of us it is easier to let a man's mouth touch us "there" than to explore ourselves with our own fingers. In my own case it was a honey-tongued Citadel cadet quoting Baudelaire who got me past "No!" He sweet-talked me beyond self-loathing into orgasm. I've never forgotten his mouth, the feel of the sand on the beach, and to this day he and the essence of forbidden sex wander through my fantasies.

Why did it take another ten years to discover I could accomplish "his" magic with my own hand, by myself? I believe I simply didn't want to be alone with my orgasm. Mine was the mindset of a little girl who refused to learn to braid her own hair for fear that her beloved nurse Anna, feeling unneeded, would leave her. Even as we revile men and blame them for all the wickedness in the world, this is precisely what we girl/women do with the boy/man: We leave the key to our sex in their hands; we don't want to masturbate and bring ourselves to orgasm, for this would say we are independent, and we aren't, not emotionally. The vagina unexplored, clitoris untouched by us, we lie there like a lox, waiting: "Give me an orgasm! Make me sexual! Don't leave me or I'll die! Take care of me, for I am a little thing and helpless without you!"

Call it self-respect or self-love, our opinion of our genitals is central to the image of our entire being. Thinking we have a sewer down there influences how we see ourselves, clothed or unclothed. We don't admit it consciously, but when we look in the mirror or imagine how others see us, our unconscious takes the sewer into account and our self-image is distorted by the ugliness hidden between our legs. Like the taint on Lady Macbeth's hands that can never be washed clean, our genital disfigurement is displaced onto other parts of our body, becoming the ugliness of our underarms, the fleshiness of thighs, the nose, the feet, the legs, wrong, wrong, wrong!

Why do we stiffen with anxiety at seeing the workmen on the sidewalk up ahead? When they stare and whistle, commenting among themselves, we automatically assume they are disparaging us, mocking us; we thought we looked good in the mirror before leaving the house. But their X-ray Gaze reminds us that we are never at peace with the way we look; our slip is showing, our skirt too tight, something is wrong! Something is always wrong. Bad men!

Anger: "Not a Pretty Face": Swallow It

I had stood, all eagerness and impatience, while my sister's old evening dress was pinned on me before that fateful dance at the Yacht Club. I didn't even know enough to look critically at the mirror and see that the strapless gown didn't suit me, especially after the dark brown velvet straps had been added to keep the dress up on my flat chest. I placed no value on looks. Having not had this rite of passage explained to me, I hadn't a clue that beauty was *the* prerequisite to adolescent stardom. Certainly, the new longing for boys had made me awkward in their presence; but I'd noticed that they were awkward too. Accustomed to being chosen first for any team of girls, I didn't question success that night, couldn't remember failure, so carefully had I buried nursery angers under trophies of recent accomplishments. Had the boys been hesitant in the choosing of partners this particular night, I'm sure I was prepared to solve their problem by taking the initiative myself. Assuming responsibility was who I was. In recent years my life had been a great adventure, in which there had been no comparisons made to my mother and sister. In my mind, they were boring, tediously arguing over my sister's looks and her evenings with boys.

That night at the Yacht Club marked the end of childhood, the finish of an adventure story with me as heroine. In one fateful night I took it all in and made my concession speech to myself. I watched my friends, whose leader I had been for years, watched them happy in the arms of desirable boys, and I recognized what they had that I lacked, saw it so clearly that I can re-create the film today, frame by frame: They had a look that went beyond beauty. It wasn't just curls, breasts, prettiness but, more important, a quality of acquiescence, the agreeable offer to be led instead of to lead; a submissive appeal that cried out, "Take me, for I am little and cannot live without you." My own face was too eager, too open, too sure of itself. I needed a mask. I needed a new face that belied the intelligent leader inside and portrayed the little girl, no, the tiny, helpless baby who hadn't been held in the first years of life and had been waiting all these years for what boys now offered.

Miserable as I was that night, I acknowledged the work ahead: The girl I'd invented, who had become me, who was so full of words waiting to be spoken and skills to be mastered, she had to be pushed down like an ugly jack-in-the-box, the lid sat on. No boy was going to take on a package like me. Deny me, hide me, forget about me.

Ready as I was to pay whatever price for the love of boys, a part of me must have been filled with rage at having to abandon what I thought to be a fine person. That rage would have been titanic, commensurate with the infantile need for love. What did I do with all my fury? I had no voice for rage. I belonged to a family of women who wept, and by not weeping, I'd made myself different from mother/sister.

That night I became a woman; I wept and wept after someone's father drove me home while the rest of My Group went off into the night to a late party with boys. I showed my grief but not my rage. I had no model of a girl/woman who took rage in hand, shaped and transformed it into constructive energy. I did what most women still do; I swallowed my anger, choked on it—no doubt triggering a series of physical problems that would manifest years later after repeated swallowings; I bowed my head, in part to be shorter, but also, like a cornered cow, to signal that I'd given up.

The shame of my bankruptcy at the Yacht Club dance was all the worse for being so public, for I stood there the entire night, shoulder blades boring into the wall behind me, refusing on principle to hide. Even more destabilizing was the immediate throwback in time to a feeling of being very little and unable to catch my mother's eye. Once again I was invisible! This time around there was no denying that what I didn't have was beauty, a power I may have been able to devalue in the past, but no longer. Now beauty reigned supreme.

By morning, I'd buried and mourned my eleven-year-old self, the wall walker, and had become an ardent beauty student. From now on I would ape my beautiful friends, smile The Group smile, walk The Group walk, and, what with hanging my head and bending my knees, approximate as best I could The Group look. But I was very, very angry; not then, not consciously, but I can recognize it now. How could I not be, me and every other girl who doesn't fit the mold?

On the eve of adolescence I put my anger in the same hermetically sealed room in the unconscious where I'd stored the ancient anger at my mother. Of anger at mother I would emphasize that some of that anger is as inevitable as the dark side of any love affair. The clue to understanding adult rage is to return to the earliest source; if we deny anger at mother and try to understand rages at people we love later on, we lose the key. As much as today's beloved may be to blame, if our anger is out of proportion to what just happened, the volume of our unhappiness and rage does not spring from what they have just done or not done. Look further back.

The angers of infancy and their recapitulations in adolescence stoke the furnace of the dark side of our adult love affairs, when we want to strike out at our beloved, hurt them, maybe kill them. They are called crimes of passion and in some countries are grounds for clemency, so close to love's passion is murderous rage.

We can't consciously remember infancy, where the patterns of love and rage are first laid down, but adolescence, when all these themes are rearoused, is available to us. Find the umbilical cord of anger in adolescence and follow it back as far as you can to the nursery, to infancy and mother, original source of The Gaze. Did you get The Gaze? Adolescence is when we try again. Did you get it this time around? Were you lovely at adolescence, beamed on, seen, reflected? Were there angry competitions over beauty within the family or outside it?

Certainly there are alternatives to beauty; men have always had elective talents and skills to practice. Now young women can pursue these same options, but we still practice beauty, more than ever. What does it mean? Follow the umbilical cord. Try not to question too dismissively the foggy pictures in the mind from the first years of life; remember that while that portion of the brain that stores memory isn't fully developed until around age three, we still have impressions from before then that have stayed with us all our lives. Mark Twain called these fuzzy recollections "stretchers," meaning that they were caught somewhere between fact and fiction. They can be some of our most valuable memories. I have discovered quite a few "stretchers" while writing this book; after pestering relatives from my earliest years, I've managed to confirm most of them as reality. It's a great relief discovering that there are real reasons for my lifelong rages, denied until I became a writer.

What a fistful of rage I must have swallowed at adolescence. All that bravado, intelligence, and wit I'd previously acquired of no use whatsoever in winning love. My strengths were exactly what was *not* wanted, were in fact *masculine*. The boys in my adolescent life must have been overwhelmed by the intensity of my passion. Grown men have been. How could any of them have known that they were holding a baby, not a young woman? With my eyes closed, my body embraced, I did indeed feel very small, all needs being satisfied with kisses of deep oral satisfaction.

The lyricists of romantic music, the really good ones, are clued in to the infantile needs of adult passion. Did you know that studies have been done showing that nothing is more arousing to adolescent girls than romantic music? Not movies, not pictures in magazines, but the pictures/feelings in our heads when we listen to Take Me–Hold Me music. "Extraordinary how potent cheap music is," wrote Noel Coward in the 1930 play *Private Lives*. I've never doubted that Coward's aching sophistication hid a besotted romantic.

Dear Peter Allen had his own brand of irony, but his music and lyrics were a dead giveaway to the susceptibility of his heart; he wrote a song, wrote it right here where my typewriter now sits. I was lying on the sofa behind him, listening to him sing—"I'm falling fast, why can't we stay together"—and I thought how some of us just can't get enough of that broken-heart feeling, don't even require a specific beloved to get high on the sighing/dying/crying feeling of the lost loves of adolescence.

It is the essence of adolescence that we can will ourselves weightless, captured by romantic music and words; we are in love with love, desperate to give ourselves to sexual arousal, oral passion, sensory deprivation, though we call it romance.

So many adolescent songs hang on The Gaze. When we buy a new dress, our first high heels, sleep on painful rollers in our hair at night, our objective is to find ourselves in The Gaze of the unwitting lad who hasn't a clue to his power. Poor boys of my adolescence, how could they possibly have known how I wanted them to see me when I didn't have a good enough internalized image of myself? All the dresses over all these years could never elicit for more than an evening what I wanted then, what I want even now: to possess it for no other reason than to walk away and honestly say, "Enough. No more dresses. No more mirrors."

In my rush for adolescent beauty there is nothing abandoned that I regret more than my power of speech. I suppose I was aiming for an appealing Little Girl neediness. It wasn't a thought-out master plan. But I disavowed the thinking/talking me, the girl who had stood repeatedly at the head of the school in assembly, taken the lead in plays. I swallowed my tongue, turned off the circuitry between brain and the formation of words. It wasn't a conscious ruse to deceive boys. On the contrary, it was the most unconscious of surrenders. But it was certainly part of the eventual surrender of self that would lead to lack of responsibility in my first sexual experiences. The anger that became the dark side of my love for men wasn't fury at them: "After all I gave up for you in my adolescence!" My rage was that I never could get men to love me as I'd wanted my mommy to love me. Poor boys/men, how could they know this passionate girl/woman wanted to be seen as The Christ Child?

Speech in motion is obviously a part of our look, how others perceive us. An articulate girl/woman's face is alive, her whole body involved in the act of forming thoughts into words. Silent women who wait for others to speak for them, order for them in restaurants, make their decisions on weighty matters such as investments and wills, their faces are windows with the shades pulled down. Masks.

Speech, I have always known, was the saddest forfeit in my life. Words release anger, humor, inspiration; grabbing our thoughts, forming them into words, all the while the mind racing ahead to capture a subsequent thought that only came alive as the last words were leaving our lips; is there anything more exciting than good talk, individuals sparked by the electric current of one another's words and our own? We grow in these exchanges, we become, we reinvent ourselves. And until recently women had lost all this in adolescence. Thoughts kept inside, words swallowed, bring down the corners of the mouth, build to a look of resignation, behind which is anger, ahead of which is sickness, physical and mental. How could it be otherwise? Speech is power. If we do not speak, others do not know who we are, and neither do we. One day life ends and they write on our tombstone: She was a nice person.

Learning to speak our anger should have been part of our earliest separation from mother in the first years of life. Found manageable in the presence of the person upon whom we are dependent for life, we would learn to trust how we handled anger; in the process we would find that anger need not lose us love. It is one of life's most important lessons. If we didn't learn it then, we remain terrified of anger, for it always feels as destructive as in infancy. All our life we will keep trying for perfect love, the reward mother promised if we swallowed anger, as she had swallowed hers with her mother. In our eyes, because nothing was ever mother's fault and all ours, the seed of anger remains our disease, the cancer grows. Mother remains perfect; we are the bad ones.

In adolescence we imbue the romantic object with mother's perfection, she being our model of love. Now, this boy will adore us in that perfect way we have always longed for. He is our reward for being a Good Girl. When he is less perfect than the way we have programmed him to be, when we do not see ourselves constantly adored in his eyes, we die. We could kill him, or so it feels, but this rage cannot be felt in the conscious here and now. Again, we bury the anger, turning it silently against ourselves.

The most successful films about these adolescent years resonate no matter what age we are; they capture young people's inability to get themselves seen by parents, society, as who they really are. These are films like *Splendor in the Grass*, *Rebel Without a Cause*, and one of my favorites, *Dirty Dancing*, the low-budget sleeper that struck an international chord. In each of these films, the adolescent's inability to get his or her internal, real self recognized had led to a "false" face, a mask behind which he or she hid anger at the outside world's rejection, until, of course, the hero/heroine could no longer repress real feelings and identity.

Until these sexual years, everything was noticed and commented on within the family. The adolescent waits with faith for confirmation of what is happening to her. What is so terrible about sex that it cannot be admitted along with everything else that is happening to mind and body? The adolescent feels the lack of trust, that while all eyes are focused on her sex, it is dishonestly handled. Very well, the girl feels, if what I am going through is so forbidden, I will act accordingly and write the truth only in my diary. But diaries are often ferreted out by anxious parents who excuse their invasions of privacy on the grounds of "doing it for the girl's own good."

That she has neither privacy from mother nor a separate life of her own teaches the girl a grim lesson. "My mother is always in my room," a teenage girl writes to *Seventeen* magazine. "She goes in while I'm at school or out with my friends. I always find things moved, borrowed, thrown away, or just general signs of her snooping. I feel like my privacy isn't being respected. I've tried talking to her, but her response is either, 'Why do you care? Are you hiding something?' or 'It's your room but it's *my* house.'"

What we need when we are young is an outlet for anger within the family, good arguments that build and then subside, allowing all to see that no one has been killed, that anger is another one of life's emotions. Melanie Klein's example of how the omnipotent rage of the infant is assuaged over time by the awareness that while mother may not respond instantly to the child's demands for food, warmth, holding, she does eventually arrive, again and again, offering the breast, pulling up the cover, holding her darling baby and beaming her adoration into the baby's eyes. In time the infant learns that while mother cannot be omnipotently controlled, she is "good enough," a feeling that inspires gratitude and, eventually, love.

In a way, this earliest practice in rage and love is what must be repeated in adolescence. Now the child's needs are for recognition of a more mature self, one who has opinions, rights, a need for privacy and an assurance that love remains even when resentment is aired. Love always remains, it must be felt. If we cannot say our piece within our family and have the meal end with a verbal handshake, smiles all around, we will not trust our anger, ever. Rage will remain stuck at that infantile, omnipotent stage. We suck anger back inside until enough of it becomes manifested in a twitching eye, migraine headaches, the herniated disk.

"Just like your father," murmurs mother at her son, not loving his contradiction, his angry refusal to comply, but "This is how men are." She would like to hold on to him, but society will grade her a "bad mother" if she doesn't let him go. Her daughter is another matter. Mother will not tolerate "that voice" from her girl.

When The Group replaces mother as lifeline, the girl finds that dissension is not allowed among these "little mothers" either. One-on-ones via the telephone may hiss anger across town, but when The Group again forms, loving faces are required. Girls become experts at denying anger—"Oh, we love her, she's our best friend!"—which gives itself away in the frozen smile, the ever narrowing lips. The standard of excellence in adolescence—beauty above all—is limited to so few that envy is inevitable. Envy is resentment is anger. We swallow it, we smile, and like wax dolls we chorus, "Who, me, angry?"

The Ugly Denial of Mother-Daughter Competition

Twenty years ago, to suggest to a mother that she was in competition with her adolescent daughter would have aroused either an angry wall of denial, or stupefaction. Well, perhaps she would admit that her girl's entry into puberty rearoused memories of her own youth and, yes, it did make her feel older. But in an era when thirteen-year-old girls looked their age and mothers were matronly, even these admissions would have been a stretch: "Compete with my little girl? You must be mad!"

But today is another story. Our reverence for youthful beauty in women of all ages sets a more predictable stage for a mother/daughter face-off; suddenly there are two sexual females in the house. A face-off isn't necessarily competitive, but it requires that the older woman look at her daughter in a new light, for the girl is now recognizable as society's beauty icon, the model wearing the clothes that mother admires in her favorite magazine. Nonetheless, most mothers would claim that "nothing has changed" regarding how they feel about their girls; it is what mothers were taught by their own mothers. Competition between women, especially mother and daughter, is the smoking gun women still refuse to acknowledge: "What gun?"

I know women who had highly competitive mothers and others, like myself, who remained invisible to theirs, but whether we were vaporous or threatening in her eyes, how she responded to our second birth, separation from her, shapes the rest of our lives.

I would have told you until this book that I felt myself well out of the rivalry between my mother and sister, but it would be a lie. The truth is that upon reaching adolescence, my once valued ability to move in and out of the house without catching her judgmental eye now made me feel inferior; what had been a plus, invisibility, was now confirmation of my failure at holding the ticket to adolescence: beauty. It cut so deep that since failing at beauty in her eyes in adolescence, I have entered and left rooms self-consciously, simultaneously desperate for recognition and blind to any I received. The first years of life had set the mold; now adolescence cast it in bronze.

How ironic that I was the first in my crowd to menstruate, even before Julie and Rose Anne, who had beautiful breasts. The shock of the telltale stains on my white cotton pants demanded my mother's involvement, she more embarrassed than I at having to strap me into the ugly sanitary belt (interesting choice of word) that I'd often seen in the bathroom drawer and associated with her other female accoutrements that had kept me happily, or so I convinced myself, separate from her. Now I was one of them, she and my sister, and I didn't want to be, though the truth is, I'd never been invited in.

To my grief, I suddenly felt included in the competitive issues that made up my mother's complicated relationship with my sister. For years I had sat at the dining room table—unfortunate setting of too many family arguments, not to mention eating disorders—and witnessed their strained debates over my sister's dress, her late nights with boys, painful bursts of emotion that erupted out of my mother's inability to deal with her oldest daughter's lush beauty. In memory, these were also my mother's most beautiful years. That my own arrival into puberty went all but unobserved was no doubt due to my bearing no resemblance to the two of them, with my straight hair, braces, and flat chest.

I loved my mother, had always needed her, now more than ever, but my chosen role was that of the strong, uncomplaining one; as far back as memory goes, she had told people, "I've never had to worry about Nancy. She can take care of herself." And so I did, until adolescence, when the world changed and group sameness required that I wear a bra, regardless of having nothing with which to fill it. I refused to ask for one after her amused comment to my aunt that I was lucky that I was "flat." While her observation was true, my humiliation was such that when eventually I did require a bra, I shoplifted several from

Belk's Department Store. Nor did I ask her for the kind of pretty pastel dresses my friends wore, instead taking cold comfort from my sister's hand-me-downs. I was in a pitiful game of refusing to ask for anything in the hope, I suppose, that one day my mother would turn around and see me.

Eventually, when my looks did arrive, she never noticed; when her friend Betty commented ten years later in the ladies' room at the 21 Club that she thought I had become the prettier daughter, my mother looked at her friend as if she were daft. To alter her opinion of my sister would put in question many of the decisions she'd made regarding her own life. It never changes, the family grading system. I accept that my mother will never focus on anything I've achieved; there is a bright side, which is whatever success I have had with looks, men, work has been fueled in large part by her blindness to me.

According to psychologist Laurence Steinberg, a child's adolescence is typically that time when parents find themselves reviewing their own lives. While it is especially painful to the parent of the same sex, mothers and daughters generally have more difficulty than fathers and sons. "In either case, the children tend to serve as a mirror of their lost selves," Virginia Rutter summarizes. "[The adolescent's sexuality] can raise doubts about [the parents'] own attractiveness, their current sex lives, as well as regrets or nostalgia for their teenage sexual experiences. . . . Parents of a teenager feel depressed about their own life or their own marriage; feel the loss of their child; feel jealous, rejected, and confused about their child's new sexually mature looks, bad moods, withdrawal into privacy at home, and increasing involvement with friends."

The analogy of adolescent separation to the earlier separation in the first year of life is readily apparent; emotional and physical drives pull the adolescent forward, out of the house, only to have her return and crawl into mother's lap, lie beside her in bed. Granted, we are not giant babies now grown sexual, but when the adolescent vacillates between demanding her own space and hanging on mother's neck, she is in the throes of something as precarious and brave as the baby's first steps into the next room. She needs rules, yes, reasonable rules that set safe boundaries but also encouragement and affirmation of both her new separate self and her parents' ongoing love—"Go, my darling, with my unconditional love, my daughter, right or wrong!"

If so many of us get stuck in adolescence, never becoming responsible adults, it is due in part to a lack of faith in the future, in ourselves, meaning an inability to let go of the past. We work at separation all our lives, but there is no time more uniquely suited than adolescence in which to invent our identities out of the daydreams of our futures.

Beauty has always crowned adolescence, been that prize for which we compete. But beauty today drives males and females of all ages; the more youthful, the better. With mother and daughter sharing the same objective and the girl younger than mother, how is the important business of healthy competition to be recognized, much less discussed?

One of the most destructive and backward moves of recent Matriarchal Feminism has been the effort to restore the ancient idealization of the mother/daughter relationship. These mothers' children comprise what the demographers call The Second Baby Boom. They may be working outside the home, unlike their own mothers, but they want with their little girls the very thing we worked to outgrow in the seventies: togetherness with Mommy. The rewards of individuation are now disparaged.

Now, as mothers, the "letting go" of their daughters is overwhelmed by a stronger yearning to set up with the girl the tightest possible relationship. For many of these mothers, the daughter is their nearest and dearest relationship, maybe their only one. Because these women are providers as well as caretakers, they often have an added sense of "entitlement"; perhaps it isn't thought out as such, but making the money and raising the child on their own boosts their sense of ownership and control. Didn't the role of breadwinner make men feel that they "owned" their women?

What chance has a daughter to find her unique identity if her so-called feminist mother is against letting her become her separate self in the full assurance that mother remains on her side? Instead, mother will preach equality but will stamp her girl, like a cookie cutter, in her own identity. These young daughters of the nineties are reminiscent of girls from the fifties, the "good girls" who "share all their secrets with Mother. . . . They are, and usually remain, carbon copies of an idealized version of Mom—imitating the way she combs her hair, dresses, eats, talks, walks," writes psychiatrist Louise Kaplan. "'We were never as close as we are now,' brags her proud mother. . . . Even after [the daughter] is married, her best friend is Mom. Mom is her confidante, her ally against her husband. No man can come between this mother-daughter intimacy."

Our culture never has stopped smiling on this kind of glued-at-the-hip relationship between mother and daughter, preferring to see a desexualized woman, a clone, rather than a daughter with her own strong identity, standing equal, loving—but separate. Today no one keeps us from fulfilling what we started twenty years ago more doggedly than other women; the loudest and most influential are those who control Matriarchal Feminism, which is anti-men and antisex.

Making competition synonymous with betrayal gives a grown woman permission to deny her own rivalry with an adolescent daughter at a moment when youth and beauty are center stage. The beauty contest is all about competition. Adolescents and grown women walk the street in short, body-revealing, nipple-baring clothes. "Look at me!" their outfits demand. But no one looks because everyone is in the competition for the eye. Asked by *Seventeen* magazine, "How do you see your generation?" 60 percent of the adolescent respondents answered "competitive." These girls can name the emotion, but they have not been raised to deal with it, and so it rages out of control.

Today's supremacy of looks/beauty/appearance leaves adolescents with the untenable anxiety of competing hard against other girls and their mothers, all the while fearing that competition destroys love. It is an either/or paralysis learned early in life from our dearest rival. If mother doesn't go through the stages of healthy competition with us, again and again until we believe it is exciting to vie, to win, and that we are as good friends as ever afterward, then when/if we are forced to compete, it is with fear and rage.

I believe the mother-daughter tie can be women's greatest source of strength, but not if there is a nasty worm called denial at the heart of the lovely red apple of love. I've seen veiled competition over beauty in the most seemingly perfect relationships; it is all but invisible until "something happens." When I was in my mid-twenties I visited my lover's family. It was a weekend, and we were to go to the country club for dinner. My lover's mother was a beautiful woman in her early sixties, very carefully turned out from top to toe. The daughter could have been equally attractive had she not been dressed in a shapeless garment with dowdy accessories to match. The loving closeness between the two women was evident, but so was the understanding as to who would be the star.

Our photograph was taken that night, and when we all looked at our likenesses on our next weekend together, the daughter retired to her room, in tears. Her brother, knowing full well what was going on, told me, "My mother buys all my sister's clothes. She's always dressed her that way, even when she was in college. I think the sight of you and mother looking so great together and her in that awful dress . . . well, what is she to do? It can never be discussed."

This mother loved her daughter; the daughter loved her mother. But there was no room for two beauties in the family. It was an arrangement that could be lived with until a photo made an inadmissible truth all too clear. Today the daughter has daughters of her own and dresses them in the clothes from her own childhood that her mother kept in the attic. These women speak every day on the phone; their love may be real, but it is at the cost of suppressed rage.

When a daughter such as this grows up and marries, it is still mother's world; the other woman on the tennis court, the other woman at whom her husband stares automatically becomes the competitor against whom she could not win; an a priori defeat. Why be responsible, adult, when the ground has been preempted by the person who has always controlled life and whose loss of love would feel like death? Let mother take responsibility for her sex life, her genital disease, the problem with drugs, or let men pick up the slack; she gives herself over to passion and assumes that he, like Mom, will take care of everything.

If the workings of beauty aren't discussed honestly, along with sex, which is so allied to adolescent beauty, then mother's denial is taken by the girl to mean that these are areas she cannot control and over which she has no responsibility. Boys learn early on that promises of love and repeated assurances of the girl's beauty—telling her that it is so overpowering, he must have her, cannot help himself—melt her defenses. Finally hearing what she has always wanted to hear, that she has indeed attained that consummate goal in women's lives, the power of beauty, she puts herself in his hands.

A 1992 study showed that girls with "traditional values" had sex earlier than those who didn't, and were also less likely to use contraception. What was meant by "traditional values" were such beliefs as the following: "Most women can't take care of themselves without help from men"; "Most women are [not] very interested in their jobs and careers"; "A husband should be smarter than his wife."

Because mother works out at the gym and watches her diet, she can wear her daughter's clothes. The new, hot music on MTV, her daughter's channel, is the identical music in mother's beauty parlor, on the radio when mother drives to work, and if she is divorced or a single parent, it is the music mother dances to at her clubs, her favorite bars with her date, who is possibly younger than she, somewhere between her age and her daughter's. The latest fashions in the store may look more appropriate for the daughter, but do we expect mother to dress like a matron? Out of the question; these are the best years of her life, or so she was feeling until her daughter's sexual beauty began increasing daily.

Mother loves her girl, still feels like her guardian, keeper of the rules, disciplinarian, the "woman" of the house. What does she do with feelings of competition, for which she was not prepared by her own mother, and which even now she would not call by that awful name, competition. She uses everything in her arsenal to deny the nasty feeling, beginning with, "Compete with my daughter? Why, we're best friends!"

Science and economics have converged to make youth available longer to all who can afford it; still, no one wants to take the *grrrr* out of competition with learned rules that teach women that it is a human emotion, one they will encounter in the workplace and which is best practiced in the first competitive relationship at home. "No!" mothers declare, reaching instead for the Band-Aid of mother/daughter look-alike togetherness. Fears of feeling older opposite the sexual beauty of her daughter are put to sleep; doesn't everyone say they look more like sisters? Which one is the mother?

We say we are raising our adolescent girls to believe that they are architects of their futures. Consciously, they take this in, but in response to unconscious pressures they act like my generation, which waited to be asked to dance, waited for him to advance the seduction as choreographed in our imaginations, as we would do it if we were in his place. Of course he does it wrong. The new generation may invite the boy to a movie, to dinner, but when it comes to sex, she hands responsibility to him.

My friends who have teenage daughters bear no resemblance to the mothers of yesteryear. I look at photos of my own mother when I was in my teens, and while she was lovely, she was obviously older by a full generation. When today's media applaud the mother-daughter sister team, who has succeeded, the younger woman in looking older or the mother in turning back the clock? Obviously the latter. There is something so deeply disturbing in the interchangeable mother and daughter, especially today when the value of looks has replaced civility: The beautifully wrapped package is empty.

What does today's adolescent girl do to set herself apart from the mother whom she loves? How to announce her exit from childhood and arrival on the brink of a new generation she and her friends will create? There are profound reasons for adolescent dress, music, dance, and vocabulary that traditionally shock and bewilder the outraged older generation. We are desperate to be seen as ourselves in adolescence, to feel inside that our "difference" has been publicly noted. It is a period of great narcissism. Coming out from behind mother's shadow, we emerge, childhood behind us, feeling so unique inside that we go to extremes. "We, as a group, are different from you," the group's look declares to the elders. Should they, the "old" generation, refuse to acknowledge the passing of the torch, the wilder the look and action of the new generation becomes: "God damn it, look at *us!*"

The elders are meant to be aghast at our look; in its way, it underscores the incest taboo: Keep off the grass, stay away. Today, when grown-ups imitate their young people's look, they are forgetting who they are; they don't have to look and act old, but they should not cross the generational line. Stay young and healthy-looking as long as possible, have a surgical nip and tuck, but respect the distance between generations, which serves a purpose. An adolescent hasn't the resources to demand that mother maintain this distance between them.

It is mother's role to honor privacy, to be the one who makes the "sacrifice" of looking and acting like the older, responsible generation. Adolescents are compulsive self-doubters whose comparison with other females is automatic. The last person a daughter needs to be judging herself opposite is her own mother, who looks better in her "teen fashions" than she. If mother wins the contest, grabbing the spotlight for herself, the daughter will go through life calling competition by every name other than what she honestly feels, conceding defeat and secretly hating her rivals for "winning."

If men once "wore" their beautiful women to bring attention to themselves, then surely this is what parents do today. So children grow up with the importance of appearance thrust in their faces. For more than a decade now, the older, parental generation has preempted their children's celebration of adolescence by grabbing their styles, their music and mannerisms as quickly as they are invented. The latest adolescent "group look," intended for the purpose of separating parents from progeny, is stolen overnight by the manufacturers of clothes, videos, music, magazines; these manufacturers *are* the parents.

Mass-produced on the streets, in stores, on billboards, the purloined adolescent look of the moment is re-created by expensive high-fashion designers and sold to parents whose co-option now forces their kids to invent yet another look. Manufacturers of both teen and high fashion make billions from both markets as each generation searches desperately for a look, an identity, something that will give it visibility in the age of The Empty Package.

Clothes were always a badge of identity, but today's adolescents have been raised to see themselves as the center of attention. So greedy is the economy to get rich on young people's enslavement to beauty that The Look changes constantly; so fleeting is the fulfillment found in a new pair of jeans, the latest footwear, jewelry, that happiness must be constantly recharged, repurchased, for there is nothing internal, no sense of self to fall back on. The unchecked rage that walks our streets, rattles the dishes in homes, anger that used to be governed by grown-ups who knew and acted their role, is now taken on by younger people whose identity is stolen by adults.

Adolescent sexual fever fuels to a frenzy the desperation to be seen. Daughters who starve themselves engage in the darkest competition of all, for the winner dies. Girls/women eye one another enviously, comparing the diminishing diameter of ankle and waist, crowing, "Oh, you look wonderful, you're so *thin!*" It is ostensibly about being more beautiful, this competition, but it has nothing to do with men. Binding women's feet, cutting off our clitorises so that we have no sexual feeling, may have kept us in our place, but anorexia and bulimia grow out of the unspeakable issues between women.

The emergence of adolescent supermodels, who are aped and adored by adults, puts the ordinary adolescent in an untenable position. The model, the cultural idol of the age, *is* the adolescent. Why grow up?

Several fashion seasons ago a glowing review of the designer Donna Karan's DKNY collection for fall appeared in the *New York Times*, where the critic wrote, "the designer insisted that fashion today is multicultural, that mothers can wear the same clothes as their daughters and that fashion is as important on the job as it is in the gym, at clubs and at parties."

Three days later, on the opposite coast, the lead singer of Nirvana, the grunge rock group that had sprung to prominence four years before, killed himself. Kurt Cobain came from a working-class background, a family broken by an angry divorce, and his songs, which attracted an entire generation, were of a primal rage, death and alienation, filled with psychic damage. It is bitterly ironic that his obituaries noted that he is given credit for having invented The Grunge Look, a recent fashion craze, which copied the singer's torn, faded, totally "unrespectable" look.

I remember the summers at Sullivan's Island when my group was growing up. The place where we used to meet was called The Pavillion, our dance was the Shag, and my own invented uniform a pair of regulation white navy trousers, bought at the navy surplus store and taken in so tightly that I could all but hear my mother's gasp when she and her friends drove by. "Nancy, those tight pants, the way you were dancing, that loud music!" she would sigh the next morning at the breakfast table, which I would summarily leave, taking with me a new feeling of satisfaction because I had at last gotten my mother's attention. When she rolled her eyes like that, heavenward, other grown-ups around the table would smile and so would she, and so would I.

Fortified with a box of chocolate Mallomars and a Coke, I would spend the entire day on the beach, religiously tanning my too long body into a deep golden hue, which the mirror had shown me to be transforming. The magic of that lovely Pocahontas shade that I mastered on beaches around the world made me one of the great sun worshipers. Restless by nature, I could spend whole days standing knee-deep in oceans, lakes, seas, at peace, totally content in the knowledge that I had found my special beauty secret, a way of getting noticed. Feeling lovely when deeply tanned, I walked with terrific posture, up and down the world's beaches, basking in the heads that turned to see me pass. In one admonition my mother was right: I did irreparable harm to my skin. Nonetheless, these were some of my favorite years, in which I learned the power of conquest.

During those adolescent summers, my mother's disapproval of my clothes, my music, my dancing, my hours in the arms of Citadel cadets in the big rope hammock, all was reassurance of my becoming me and her remaining part of the past, loved but distanced. In this distance I had engineered and she honored, I recognized a growing sense of responsibility for myself when I was more and more out of her sight: If

I wasn't going to look like her or behave like her, I had to take care of myself.

How can I emphasize that in the adolescent's creative effort to set ourselves apart from our parents is born the opportunity to establish a set of self-protective rules? "It is an odd fact that what we know now of the mental and emotional life of infants surpasses what we comprehend about adolescents," says Louise Kaplan, "these older children of ours who could—given the opportunity—speak so eloquently about their sexual and moral dilemmas."

There is no room for healthy competition between a mother and daughter who are "best friends." Such a goal leaves the girl in the position of having to yield to the older woman; she never takes responsibility for herself, never challenges another woman—or perhaps challenges women at every step. When there is no father in the house, a man who might more readily recognize competition, there is virtually no one else to help the adolescent girl beyond symbiotic attachment and into her own life.

When we argue, when we disagree, when there is a contest with safe rules, competitive feelings don't destroy love; it is when competition exists and is denied that we are paralyzed. Let it be a mantra: It is possible to love and compete. I would take it further; there is a surge of camaraderie when the competitive struggle is honestly played out, with a winner and a loser, followed by the embrace, the handshake that says, We played our best, by the rules, and we are better friends than ever.

The Good Mother finds her "best friend" outside the mother/ daughter dyad, which is inappropriate for confidantes. A best friend should be a peer, and mother's voice, in reaction to whatever secrets are told to her, sexual and otherwise, carries a judgmental authority rooted in her role as the Giantess of the Nursery. Even if she says nothing in reaction to her daughter's confidences, the younger woman knows exactly how mother feels, has always known. As for the beauty contest, the daughter can't afford to outdistance mother, for in winning she loses the only person she has been raised to believe really loves her.

The Group—The No-Compete Clause

Where were the boys of my adolescence prior to that fateful day when they stood on the horizon, suddenly imbued with all the power and glamour of the sun, moon, and stars? I suppose they'd been around, shooting baskets, just like me. But I hardly remember them prior to adolescence. We girls had been inseparable, sleeping together in one another's beds for years, our friendships completing each other, our reflections in the others' eyes making life whole. Now our mutual appraisals demanded that we judge one another through the eyes of the opposite sex. Suddenly boys were the judges and we, unquestioning, lived by their scorecards; how they rated us made us see one another in a different light.

Certainly we girls had taken into account the value of a pretty face during our latency years; but comparison and competition were easily folded into the more powerful emotion of togetherness. Now, the male selection of certain girls from our group, the reasoning behind the most desirable boy's choice of a particular girl, set up an undeniable new pecking order.

Requiring no explanation, we went along with boys' preferences for breasts, blond curls, and pretty legs. The supremacy of adolescent beauty had awakened our memory of beauty's power from the earliest days of our lives within the family. The latency years had been a significant respite from the tyranny of looks, but now it was back and fueled by nature's most powerful chemical: sexual desire.

Male and female, we move to it, moth to the flame. Beauty is the currency of the land. It buys everything. It matters not that the beauty is our own sex; she has the elixir and we want to be around her. We absolutely understand why the best boy chooses the prettiest girl. We would do the same. Indeed, my own closest friends through both the latency years and then through adolescence were the prettiest girls; I must have felt that just to be near them was to be warmed. Standing in their radiance, I probably hoped that some of their afterglow would reflect on to me. Maybe one of the beauty's rejected suitors would settle for me.

"Starting in the third grade, perceptions of appearance for girls goes down the tubes, whereas boys continue to think they look fine," says psychologist Susan Harter. "More than intelligence, athletic competence, and other areas of self-content, how people think they look is highly related to their self-esteem. It is true for groups as varied as the male and the female, the handicapped and the gifted. Among all these groups, the evaluation of one's looks takes precedence over every other domain as the number-one predictor of self-esteem, causing us to question whether self-esteem is only skin deep. Why should one's *outer* physical self be so tied to one's *inner*, psychological self?"

We are not alone in giving our looks influence over our whole selves; as in kindergarten and the latency years, friends and teachers too imbue the lovelier ones with special talents: A 1987 study found that "the classroom teachers of the early adolescents rated physically attractive students as more scholastically, socially, and athletically competent . . . than physically unattractive students."

Without any discussion, we girls reshuffled the deck according to the seismic workings of beauty in our lives; the leaders of the latency years automatically took a backseat to the adolescent beauties, fully aware of the appropriateness of natural selection. The tragedy was that, opposite beauty, our mental, physical, and social skills looked to us to be so paltry, sometimes even a deficit, in the erotic, romantic dance in which we now yearned to move.

The irony for adolescent girls is that while we may desire our image in the boys' eyes, the judges who still rule life are The Other Girls, whose eyes are no less harsh, no more tolerant than mother's. A boy's eye can be caught, but there is a higher power without whose approval we cannot live. When The Other Girls' eyes judge us as having gone too far with a boy, shown too much in our exhibitionism, we are inconsolable. Not even the beloved boy can bring us back to life; only when we are forgiven, restored to The Family, do we feel whole again. Living on Girls' Rules while attaining the love of men is a balancing act that has nothing to do with the adventurous, creative girl of the latency years just previous, who is now all but useless. Yes, friendships with girls were important then, vital, but boys have introduced an intensity of sexual competition between us for which we are totally unprepared.

Thrown into sexual rivalry with the girls who have been our life for years, we become passive zombies, waiting, waiting to be chosen, because to take the initiative with boys puts forbidden competition into play. At their heart these friendships have a powerful No-Compete Clause, a red light that switches on whenever we feel the urge to outdistance another girl. It is the same No-Compete understanding we had with mother, to whom we always tearfully capitulated. It was never a true competition, for winning meant losing her.

I'd grown up with the boys of my early adolescence; I'd wager they would have been pleased if I'd telephoned them, made the first move. But taking the initiative was totally taboo then, unless, of course, we did it as a group. I would sit by the telephone, staring at it, waiting, praying for it to ring. Forbidden to reach for the boy's hand at the movies, I placed it in its most pleading position on the chair arm between us, or in my lap, and prayed. Teen magazines today say that the majority of both girls and boys think, "There's nothing wrong with a girl asking a guy out." That is a plus, but the same polls agree that, "Girls who go out with more than one guy at a time get reputations as sluts." It's the same old Zero-Sum game: If you get more, that means there is less for me.

Just yesterday our best friend was our world; today, The Group takes her place, spreading its wings over all of us like a mother hen. In fact, The Group is a big mother, a source of love and identity as well as the sometimes overly harsh tribunal. After school our group ritual was to drive around, up and down those lovely old streets until we found the boys, generally on one or another playing field. We would never do this alone, but Group courage was huge.

A driver's license could be had at age fourteen, and the designated driver would pick up each member of The Group until seven or eight of us were crammed into the car. Oh, the anxiety of waiting by the window for my friend's car, fearing I would be forgotten, though it never happened. It was a fear I'd conquered in prior years, when pitching a game of softball I would encourage my more timorous friends to be brave. Now I was back in the waiting position, and while no one ever mentioned my lack of beauty, I'm sure it was the cause of my rearoused fear of abandonment.

Had I been able to take my comfort with competition with me into adolescence, I surely would have found something in my abundant character with which to vie with the beauties. But given the supremacy of beauty in the South, I fell back into my noncompetitive role within my family, where I had always been invisible. There, I'd been able to persuade myself that I didn't need "them," my mother and my sister, but I needed my group with all my heart.

"Adolescence is another stage of trying to become an independent, psychological self," says clinical psychologist Jeanne Murrone. "You get it at eight months, at age two, again at four and five, and in adolescence. The way adolescents still negotiate this stage of individuation is not to be totally alone, but to have a substitute family, the peer group. For the first time in life, your peers are probably the most important people, rather than your family."

I've confused love and sex most of my life, finding in men's arms far more than they bargained for. Once kissed, I was enslaved to a passion that had nothing to do with the boy/man. He was merely a figurehead, a mythological solution to my errant heart's lifelong search. Twice kissed, and I felt equal in beauty to the girls whose looks moments before had made me feel inferior. Now I too had arms to hold me; I was a genuine member of The Group, where beauty and its prize, the prince, were prerequisites for membership.

I loved my adolescent years, dancing to beach music, the hours in the drive-in movies. But the intensity of romantic yearning dumbed down my brain; I lost the rhythm of the accelerating process of mental growth. Considering how much energy was focused on group beauty/sex standards and the distance I felt I had to run to keep up with those ideals, I had no fear so rigorous as the judgment of the mirror. What was demanded was that I abandon Rousseau's opportunity to move beyond "love of oneself" to a "love of the species" and be reborn into a mirror reflection of a popular adolescent Girl Girl.

Once boys had moved into our tight ranks and plucked us girls from one another's arms to take us off individually into the night, our loyalties were strained. We longed to be chosen and went happily, but boys' offers of love and praise would never be invested with as much influence as the voices of the other girls.

We felt more comfortable with girls because we all shared a lack of belief in boys' love. Drowning, we clung to one another, despairing that boys could not make us believe they loved us and that they could walk away. Of course this kind of love didn't restrain us from also, on a summer day of intoxicating girlishness, giving one of our dearest friends "the treatment." We loved her/we wanted to punish her; love and rage, the earliest and most important model of intimacy.

Standing out from The Group, being different, being "more," can mean rejection and isolation, says sports psychologist Cheryl McLaughlin. "To be accepted, particularly during the late junior high and high school years, girls have to be like each other, dress the same, have their own slang, everything. Choosing to stand out by showing your talents often has serious consequences. On high school tennis teams, talented players often choose to hide their skills, lose matches to their friends and then play the number three spot because they don't want to risk losing their friendships. Girls and women at all levels tend to back away from competing for such reasons as,

'How can I feel OK winning when it means the other person is going to lose?'"

When we do compete, it is with stealth, denial, and in the dark. We love our best friend but sometimes we just can't help ourselves, the iron hoops that keep girls/women together are tested: "I lost my virginity last year," a young woman writes to *Seventeen* magazine, "and since then my best friend has been trying to compete with me. If I sleep with one guy, she sleeps with two. It seems like every time we compete, she sleeps with that extra guy to win, and she always rubs it in my face. I don't know what to do. Am I stupid for using all these guys in this ignorant competition?"

Competitiveness is a natural feeling; it is we who are ignorant because we have not been prepared to handle it with safe rules. There is no area in which rivalry is more inevitable than where beauty abounds, and that time in life is adolescence.

Similarly, a young man tells me of an incident in his school a few years ago when his best friend's girl got pregnant. She was one of the prettiest girls and belonged to a particular group who were the school's cheerleaders, as well as the brightest in their class. They were a tight clique, dubbed The Vestal Virgins. When it was discovered that one of their own had broken the cardinal rule, they banished her. The boy chose to marry his girl but not before he had walked into the cafeteria and, in front of the entire school, announced to The Vestal Virgins, "How dare you turn on my girlfriend! Let me tell you who else in your holier-than-thou midst has had sex with me: You and you!" He pointed to two girls. The group blew apart, never to be mended.

One of the great female sexual fantasies, beginning in adolescence, is to seduce a man. Grown women dream of what it would be like to return to adolescence and, breaking The Rules, to approach the adored boy and show him all the forbidden forms of seduction. Whatever the rules when you were growing up, the most rigid were probably those that regulated how a girl could display her body.

We go through life buying beauty, dieting for beauty, mutilating our bodies to acquire a power look that we never believe in. Even the natural beauty doesn't permit herself to show too much pleasure in her advantage. It's luck, just good genes she got from her parents, Cybill Shepherd would have us believe, tossing her gorgeous blond hair in a TV commercial for L'Oreal. "Yeah, right," we say enviously, feeling a wee bit of pleasure when we read that her marriage has fallen apart.

"Don't hate me because I'm beautiful," pleads another film beauty from the pages of a women's magazine, which is more to the point.

Here is a lovely quote from William Faulkner's *The Hamlet* that captures The Beauty just as I remember her:

> Eula Varner was not quite thirteen. . . . Her entire appearance suggested some symbology out of the old Dionysic times—honey in sunlight and bursting grapes, the writhen bleeding of the crushed fecundated vine beneath the hard rapacious trampling goat-hoof. She seemed to be not a living integer of her contemporary scene, but rather to exist in a teeming vacuum in which her days followed one another as though behind sound-proof glass, where she seemed to listen in sullen bemusement, with a weary wisdom heired of all mammalian maturity, to the enlarging of her own organs. . . .
>
> Through that spring and through that long succeeding summer of her fourteenth year, the youths of fifteen and sixteen and seventeen who had been in school with her and others who had not, swarmed like wasps about the ripe peach which her full damp mouth resembled. There were about a dozen of them. They formed a group, close, homogeneous, and loud, of which she was the serene and usually steadily and constantly eating axis, center. There were three or four girls in the group, lesser girls, though if she were deliberately using them for foils, nobody knew it for certain. They were smaller girls, even though mostly older. It was as though that abundance which had invested her cradle, not content with merely overshadowing them with the shape of features and texture of hair and skin, must also dwarf and extinguish them ultimately with sheer bulk and mass.

To enter adolescence without looks can be a reversal of such proportions that many women never recover from their sense of inadequacy. Looks may arrive ten years later, but the reflection is never believed. Beauty's tyranny holds us back because it has at its heart the denial of competition.

Only in whispers, in secret with another woman who shares our resentment, can we vent our spleen. When an adolescent girl sees two other girls' heads together, their eyes narrowed, the electricity between them sizzling, she recognizes meanness escaping. In their way, these occasional ventings of envy help The Group to hold. The beloved boy may be the goal, but if he breaks our heart, we know that The Girls will circle round, console us.

We struggle in adolescence to be loved by the opposite sex and simultaneously not to lose our ties and identification with The Group. Can we have both? Why does it mean that for females it must be either/or? All too soon the expectant faces of young girls begin to record the anxiety of rejection by boys but also the suppressed rivalry with the people who are the bedrock of our world. The look of adolescence becomes tentative as we try to control the emotions that used to run across our faces naturally. Emotions such as anger and fear must be facially censored. A muscular pattern of expressions begins to be etched into our faces; the lines and wrinkles that we will later hate seeing in the mirror over the basin are being laid in. In time our faces become the road maps of our lives, not unlike the deep creases of a suit in which we've sat for a long time, creases that won't smooth when we stand up.

"I think that character does show through," says Lynton Whitaker, head of plastic surgery at the University of Pennsylvania Medical School, "because the mimetic muscles of the face are unlike any other muscles in the body: they attach directly from the bone into the skin. Therefore they show what you're feeling in the way that you individually show it. It has to be recurrent over a period of time long enough to create the etching, like an etching in glass. It has to be done several million times, probably, before the lines become imprinted permanently. Maybe 20 to 30 percent of the people who come to me for cosmetic surgery ask me specifically to remove something that would be characterized as an emotion: sadness, anger, anxiety, fatigue. There's no doubt that these wrinkles start in some people in the teenage years." Imagine the muscular control demanded so that at all times the look of hate and anger doesn't come through our pretty little faces!

As for sexual self-acceptance—not intercourse, but comfort with our new sexual self—a lifelong pattern also forms. If life under mother's roof did not earlier promise that she was on our side, that competition could be aired but that love always remained—"My daughter, right or wrong!"—then arguments and rivalry with both girls and boys whom we love will always feel like a threat to love; happiness is only possible in glued-at-the-hip togetherness. The near-death feeling in the tight, best friendships of our latency years, when two little girls abandoned a third girl for no reason, this anguish is not far from what The Group feels now when adorable, irresistible boys select out one or two girls.

A boy wants the girl he didn't even know he'd been dreaming of until last night, and there she is, she of the demure smile, white skin, lovely breasts, she who arouses in him a feeling that says, Dance with me. He doesn't mean to break up the Girl Group or put down the also-rans; he has had to deal with choosing and losing for several years. In luring her away from her friends, he is unaware of the risk, as well as the power, that she accrues.

The tragedy for The Beautiful One is that more than likely she was just another girl until adolescence, when the swan emerged. While a part of her acknowledges success in the eyes of boys, she is wary of placing too much weight on her triumph. The look in the eyes of the other girls who love but also envy her requires that she lose in some way so as to balance her win. To moderate her new powers, she doesn't try to excel in other activities, already having so much. The love of boys is wonderful, but the support and love of The Girls/Mother is the adolescent's lifeline.

Though we may have longed to be the homecoming queen or king, the inevitability of their union moves us deeply; we understand totally why they belong together. Power drawn to power. Together they reign over us, their role uncontested, until, of course, there is a chink in their perfect armor, revealing their vulnerability, inviting our envy. We insert the blade and release some of resentment's mean steam, thus learning the reverse side of beauty's power, that it encourages cruelty in the have-nots.

Gossip is the plot device in popular adolescent films, whispers of scandal that embroider something overheard into exaggerated rumor; around the school the rumor flies, "Kill them! Knock them off! Feel a little better in their pain!" By the movie's end, we rejoice in their reunion, their vindication, their beauty. Ambivalence.

So intensely has smothered rivalry over beauty bubbled in women's traditional world that the no-compete rule had to extend to everything in life. These anticompetition laws only began to melt when beauty was no longer our only source of power. Nowhere is this more apparent than in girls'/women's sports. What a beautiful sight it was to see the Connecticut Women's Basketball Team top their undefeated season by winning the NCAA National Championship. To watch these young women in competitive play was breathtaking. The healthy hiss of competition in sports, the flat-out effort of the players restrained only by good rules, is music to the ears and eyes. And to see young women playing as hard and gracefully as any boys' team, to watch them rejoice in victory and shake hands with their competitors, who know they may win tomorrow, this, for me, was feminism at its best. My kind of feminism. It is wonderful experience for the workplace up ahead, and for motherhood too, should these young women choose it.

"The biggest problem girl athletes have in the beginning is going all out against their own teammates during practice and then remaining friendly with them off the court," says Geno Auriemma, who coaches the Connecticut team. "One of the first talks I have with them is, 'Listen, there's not going to be any of that girly stuff. No *She said that you said that they said,* that is so associated with girls.' And they know exactly what I'm talking about. Let's say two guys on a high school team are vying for the same position. During practice they absolutely kill each other; the intensity level is sky-high. Practice ends. The two guys get together and go out, maybe grab something to eat. And they come back tomorrow and do it all over again. And that's called competition.

"Girls have a hard time doing this. They carry the competition from the court off the court. 'I'm not going to talk to her.' Or, 'She's trying to beat me out and that means she's my enemy.' It's difficult to teach girls that someone *should* try their hardest in a competitive situation. The game is about playing your best, not about 'Who's my friend, who's my enemy.' Playing your hardest doesn't ruin the friendship.

"I've got a girl on my team, Jennifer Rizzotti, who is without question the most competitive person I have every coached, male or female. We need women like that. 'I want it now and I'll work for it until I deserve it,' she says. She is confident, fair, competitive, and a great team player. She's probably the best point guard in the country this year. And she's five foot five.

"I think women will work longer and harder than men. But they have to learn to work as a team instead of always leaving someone out. They have to believe they can compete their hardest and then go out and have a drink afterward. The same at work when they get older. People say, 'Women can't handle competition, they're too emotional.' Baloney. Women are stronger than people give them credit for.

"Young women who handle responsibility well are the most competitive. 'Gee, you have six players on the dean's list,' people say. Of course we do. That's why we're the national champions. If you can be great in competitive sports, that means you have discipline and commitment. Women can handle anything. Anything. They need permission to be competitive, that they can beat the other girl and still be friends."

To whom, then, do young women listen, to the clarion call of healthy competition or to the old party line as laid down by the Matriarchal Feminists? Steinem has said that competition is detrimental to feminism and alongside her, Carol Gilligan asserts that women's superiority resides in our innate reluctance to indulge in competition.

In fact, it is the lack of safe rules of competition that makes the tyranny of beauty so deadly. Instead of acknowledging beauty's power and the inevitable competition it arouses, we revert to a sameness, which seemingly protects the beauty from resentment and supports the Have-Nots. Rather than deal with competition, the group dress and group look announce, "See, I'm not angry, I look just like you, I feel just like you, talk just like you, walk just like you. I don't want to be unique. I want to be a replica of you and you and you." That original person, fired by the sexual growth unique to these years, is never created in this Second Birth of adolescence.

There was no one day on which we discussed The Rules that dictated how we should live our adolescent lives. I only know there were things I wanted to do that I did not. It was as though The Fairy of Adolescence had visited each of us in the night as we slept and whispered The Rules. One day we got up and dressed for school and we were less adventurous, more watchful of one another, though a spectator might have called it more intimate/symbiotic. Fear of being left out, more than anything, glued us together.

So dependent on one another were we girls who had grown up together, we now approached adolescence, boys, sex, our arms linked, a kind of aquatic gene pool. The Esther Williams school of ballet. We never broke the magic chain that was our support—and our guarantee too—that no one girl swim off with more than her share of the forbidden fruit. We got our first menstrual periods on days in different months, but we were emotionally on top of one another in each girl's experience of everything.

So few of us fit the stereotypical look of youth demanded in that time and place where we grew up. Years later we look at the old photos and laugh at everybody's penny loafers, the cashmere sweaters with pearls or the miniskirts and poor-boy sweaters, the sameness of hair, long, short, ironed, frizzed, beehived, whatever was essential to belonging. As powerful as the need may be to be recognized and loved by boys, the restraining tug of The Group keeps us in check. No one girl getting any more of the pie than any other is what makes the Nice Girl Rules bearable. We may not be ready for sexual intercourse, but we crave more life than the wagging fingers of the girls allow. We miss the loud voices we had in latency, the intellectual stretch at school, the pride in athletic achievement. Everyone loses when competition over adolescent beauty is not dealt with. The irony, of course, is that the competition goes on regardless, denied, disavowed, and called by other names.

No one had actually said precisely what you could and couldn't do with a boy. Maybe this was what made The Rules so portentous: They left each of us unsure as to exactly what the other girls were doing in the dark, meaning only that we had gone too far in a moment of passion and must therefore write our own ticket to hell.

I've always felt closer to men in my sexual drive than to women. It is not a boast, but a suspicion, a fear, that I am not "normal." Why should I even care? There is no Nice Girl Club today from which I can be tossed. But you see, there is. They never really go away, The Girls. Every now and then something happens to jolt me into an awareness of women's ability to condemn me to hell, their lifelong hold on me.

One summer in the mid-sixties, I was at Fire Island, lying naked in a bed with my lover, Stan. It wasn't our bed, but Stan loved to fuck in forbidden places, and the party in the adjoining room roared in our ears, the cloud of grass hanging in the rafters. Remember, these were the years of No Rules, the only rule being to break any you ran into. Not just Stan and I but everyone on the other side of that door was deeply into rule breaking. Fucking on the fringe of the crowd was bringing Stan close to orgasm when suddenly a woman's voice rose above the rumble of the party, a definitely critical voice meant to reach into my erotic fantasy and yank me back to reality with the terrible indictment of a judge's gavel. "Guilty!" it said, though in fact her words were, "Nancy is in the bedroom fucking Stan."

True. But it was the tone of female censure; or did my overly harsh conscience twist a matter-of-fact comment into a term of banishment in the never-ending Nice Girl/Bad Girl identity problem? The Nice Girl Rules will go with me to the grave. I take to heart their public censure in the media whenever I write about sex. Though I anticipate their prissy criticism, indeed use it as creative fire in writing my books, feeling my words punching them in the nose for spreading sexual guilt among women, nonetheless, they reach me. I like to think that this is changing; the new generation of young comediennes, for instance, The Bad Girls on The Comedy Channel, they spit in the eye of girlish censure with every bawdy joke they tell, heralding better times.

Looking for My Father's Eyes

My father. The words are so foreign on my lips, my fingertips, laying them down on paper. A kind of treason, breaking the unspoken vow of silence. Even now it seems dangerous, writing about him, meaning the lack of him. As a good girl, it was my duty never to ask, "What happened to him? Where did he go? What did he look like?" So loaded was the subject, my mother never said his name, ever. His name was Walter. There, I've written it.

It is time to speak of him, especially in this chapter, which cries out for fathers; he has taken up too many frames in my dream sleep of late. I know that his absence, especially in my adolescence, was a profound omission, as it must be for every fatherless girl. Until that abysmal night at the Yacht Club, when no one chose me, I'd made do without a man in my life, except for my grandfather. I had, in fact, tried to take my father's place within the family by being responsible, uncomplaining, brave opposite my wilting, anxious mother and sister, or so I chose to see them. Now, overnight, I wanted to be a star member of that sex from which I'd walked away, that private club of womanly women to which my mother and sister belonged and which I'd never been asked to join.

Having no father in the house to bless my femaleness, I set out with some desperation to find male approval elsewhere. I suppose this is what psychiatrist Leonard Michaels meant that day years ago when I interviewed him at Payne Whitney: "A child who grows up in a house without a father never stops being hungry for a man."

By nature, I am a father's girl, a lover of men and "mannish" in my determination always to prove myself. Though my love of men stemmed in part from the desire to find in their eyes the adoration I'd missed with mother, the twin to that need was to become my man's soul mate, thereby fulfilling his adolescent dream of a girl who would meet him halfway in everything. I have always known that if I could just get a man to lower his defenses and let me in, he would recognize me as the woman who accepted him utterly. I would be the mirror reflecting back to him the self he feared no woman would love; knowing there was nothing he showed me that I would not accept, he would surrender. He would never leave me. Where would he find me/himself again?

One hot day in my adolescence I did see his picture at the bottom of my mother's lingerie drawer. I remember the stillness of the house, the sunlight on the dark wood of the mahogany bureau that I would one day inherit. It wasn't the first time I had explored my mother's closet and bureau drawers, for I was always searching, rummaging when she was out of the house. Consciously, I didn't admit that it was for clues of my father that I searched but suddenly, under the pretty lace slips, there he was, looking up at me, a handsome man with dark hair in a suit and tie. My secret father, the person of whom no one spoke, the missing link in our family and in my life; the eyes I had always missed seeing me, taking me in, approving of me, loving me.

"Your father was a great favorite with the ladies," one of my mother's sisters would tell me years later. "He was what we call a 'womanizer.'" Of course I have always assumed that I would have been his chosen one, as my sister was my mother's.

Would his presence in my life have lessened the competition I felt involved in, not just opposite my mother and sister but now in adolescence with my childhood friends? If he had been there to hold me and love me, perhaps the old nursery sibling defeats would not have risen so starkly from the grave, reducing me to tears when my role as leader within my group was surrendered.

Of my gender identity I was never in doubt; what I died for was to see my desirability confirmed by the opposite sex. The tragedy was that I did not look as female as I felt. By the time some looks arrived in my late teens, the die had been cast; the mirror has always shown me the failed-in-beauty girl of my thirteenth year; sometimes I smother her in store-bought glamour, but without the paint, she reemerges. I've never doubted that my exhibitionistic need for approval in men's eyes is a reaction against having lost the beauty contest to my mother and sister.

One day during my therapy sessions with Dan Stern, that year after my house burned down and I'd separated from my ex-husband, I selected from the back of the closet a dress I hadn't worn in years, a bright yellow, full-skirted ingenue number with an off-the-shoulder neckline that wasn't my style at all, nor an appropriate garment to choose to wear to a session with one's analyst.

"Are you wearing that pretty yellow dress for me?" were his opening words, as gentle as a father's to a child and with the dearest smile on his face.

He had seen through me, knew my intentions better than I. Yes, of course I was out to seduce my analyst, had been at it from the moment we'd met; my favorite position during our sessions was to lie on the floor on my back, and while we talked I would run my stockinged foot up and down his leg. In my defense, I will say that I have a bad back and often lie on floors, but I am dodging the obvious; I was crazy about my father/my analyst, and the yellow dress incident caught me up short, for I was playing the seductress not as the adult vamp but as an adolescent girl.

"Haven't you read Proust?" I asked haughtily in a hasty attempt to salvage my sophisticated composure. "Half of *À la recherche du temps perdu* is about what Albertine was wearing. Clothes advanced the plot."

"And what plot are you trying to advance, Nancy?" he asked.

"Our affair, of course. Which you refuse to recognize. Instead you leave me to go off on your stupid boat." It was almost August, national vacation month for analysts. And then we laughed, though mine was half-hearted. No one knew better than Stern the influence of my absent father.

"I'll be back," he said to his big baby in the yellow dress.

I was not convinced.

It is remarkable how readily we accept a father's absence from his adolescent daughter's life when it is so obvious in what ways he might help her, he being male and therefore knowledgeable about boys, on whom she is now so fixated. Imagine a father humanizing the male sex for his girl and at the same time explaining, far better than mother, the powerful effect of her sexual beauty on boys. If father were close to his daughter, he would tell her of the boy's insecurities, his dreams, his fallback on the macho role because he is unable to handle his emotions in opposition to the girl who, to him, seems to have all the power in the world.

The whole world is raised by women who know nothing about men. Ours would be a different world if it were customary and expected that men, like women, remain as close to their adolescent children as they had been in the child's infancy. Leaving adolescent girls solely in the hands of women guarantees that they will grow up with no more understanding of the opposite sex than their mothers had.

In adolescence, father's eyes are new territory for a daughter to conquer; she would light them up as this dear person she has known all her life recognizes what has happened to her. Standing before him, hanging on his arm, she waits for his verdict: "See me," she would say. "Let me know that I am doing this right, succeeding as a pretty girl. You're the only person whose opinion I can trust."

"Leave your father alone, you're a big girl now," mother says. If mother interferes, if father retreats at this crucial stage of the father/daughter relationship, the girl learns that closeness to men loses her the beloved ties to other women. And father will relearn what he has always known, that his wife jealously guards her ownership of the children, and of him.

If he does withdraw from the competition between the women in the house, he fails his daughter. So many women remember being "dropped" by fathers who had been close companions until adolescence. "I was my daddy's girl," the story goes, "his favorite person, who went with him on fishing trips and sometimes traveled with him on selling trips. But when I reached adolescence, he dropped me."

Where to put the confusion and anger, the sense of betrayal? How not to think that what has happened to her body has something to do with it, and that it's bad if it loses her the most important person in her life? And how easy to shift her father's infidelity on to all the subsequent males in her life: "That's how men are! They leave you."

That so many of us, for a variety of reasons, entered adolescence without father's loving approval of our sexual awakening is a loss that never stops kicking back. The adolescent girl doesn't actually mean to steal father away from mother so much as to test her skill at flirtation on the only man she can trust. If he recognizes what she needs and knows his lines, he will say with genuine love in his eyes, "You have grown into such a beautiful young woman." Recognizing that he means it, she will believe him. The gift will have been exchanged. If I'd had such a father, my life would have been different. Of one thing I am sure, I have inappropriately looked for him in all men, never totally believing their words either of love or their assurances of my beauty.

I can remember no girl from my adolescence who had a strong

relationship with her father. Not one. I may have been the only father-less girl in our group, but at this stage all the girls might as well have been. There was no paternal advice or knowledge that any one girl passed on to the rest of us, and when I visited friends' houses, fathers were like ghosts, shadowy figures reading newspapers in wing chairs.

In a study done on teenage girls who had grown up either with or without fathers, one group came from divorced parents and hadn't seen their fathers since the divorce, the second had widowed mothers, and the third group had both mother and father at home. There were no distinguishable behavioral problems among the groups, but there were definite differences in how they reacted to men.

As part of the study, each girl was shown into an office where she was interviewed by a man. There were three chairs in the office for the girls to choose from. The daughters of divorce usually chose the chair closest to the man and sat in an open-legged, sprawling position; they were flirtatious, talkative, and leaned toward the man, looking into his eyes. The girls whose fathers had died chose the chair farthest from the man and sat stiffly, their legs together, neither smiling nor making eye-contact; they were shy and timid. Girls from two-parent homes acted in a manner between the extremes and were much more at ease with the man. *When these same girls were interviewed by a woman, these differences didn't show up.*

When the researchers studied the girls in relationships with other males, they found that girls from divorced families spent much of their time in places where young men hung out and tended to use their bodies to get attention; they dated more often and had sex more often and at an earlier age than girls in the other two groups. Girls whose fathers had died dated later, tended to avoid males, and seemed sexu-ally inhibited. In the study, psychologist E. Mavis Hetherington writes, "For both groups of father-absent girls the lack of opportunity for con-structive interaction with a loving, attentive father has resulted in apprehension and inadequate skills in relating to males."

The findings indicated that if a father isn't part of the family, his absence has a strong influence on the daughter's attitude toward men, which continues long past her adolescent years. "The women from intact families made the most realistic and successful choices of hus-bands and reported more sexual satisfaction (including number of orgasms) in their marriages than did women who grew up without fathers."

Does the above study come as a surprise? The fact that it makes sense is the saddest reaction of all, for it implies that we have always known the influence of father deprivation on young girls but chose to live with it as part of the silent trade-off of power within Patriarchy. To keep men focused on the wheel of industry, father's role of good provider was idealized just as mother's monopoly on home and children was elevated to Madonna status. Today, either sex can be a good provider, and we have a societal imbalance.

If we continue to portray the role of the caretaker as powerless, fathers will not push to demand a share, and mothers will continue to raise the human race while also competing with men in the workplace. What is wrong with this scenario? Women prefer to take on more work than we can handle rather than demand that fathers be part of their children's lives. Men are going to have to press for their paternal rights as doggedly as women demand equal power in all areas still dominated by men.

All the weighty judgment of the first years of life should not rest in women's eyes alone. When adolescence arrived, father should recognize his daughter having crossed the threshold into young womanhood; instead of turning away, he should be there to urge her continuing to practice intellect, speech, and all the other preadolescent skills she'd mastered. He should talk to her about sex, explain boys as real people, with their own inadequacies and strengths.

Why should a girl have to wait for an opinion on her success at beauty from another adolescent, a boy ill-prepared to grasp what is being asked of him, when she has the perfect judge at home? If he neglects this ceremonial appraisal of her rite of passage, the importance of peer approval becomes too weighty. When the adolescent boy does offer the praise she's been longing to hear, she will read so much into his adoration that she will offer herself to him in gratitude.

Parental compliments may be shrugged off as part of the adolescent's break with the past, but the words must be spoken, for they are indeed heard. "It's very clear that for most adolescents parents continue to be the major influence," says Jeanne Brooks–Gunne, president of the Society for the Research of Adolescence. "Even though peer influence gains in stature during these years, when you look at studies of the importance of academic achievement, importance of grades, post–high school goals, even things like smoking and drinking, parents still matter more than peers."

Father's recognition of the growth that goes on even as the adolescent sleeps—Sleeping Beauty—will be the mantra pinned over her bed, the last thing she sees at night, the first in the morning, reminding every adolescent girl who cried herself to sleep that father's trusted judgment is right. Eventually, when she awakens from the torpor of adolescence and is in need of a promise made long ago, his faith in her will be remembered, will have always been remembered.

The daughter who lacks beauty will learn from father that not all men are looking for a beauty; he will make her believe that other qualities and attributes are important to men. It may be cool comfort, but she will take it in nonetheless, more than she would from mother, because he belongs to that world of boys/men to which she is so drawn. His advice to her not to abandon talents that have nothing to do with the mirror will have weight. She will believe him because she has learned to trust what she sees in his eyes.

Until now, women have believed that only other women's eyes could judge beauty; that monopoly derived from women's total dependence on mother/women all our lives. As more fathers continue to help raise their daughters from birth, their eyes and verdicts on appearance will be as credible and sought after as women's/mother's. The answer to the old saw, "For whom do women dress?" will be "Men and women."

Asked what an adolescent girl needs most, Judith Seifer replies, "She needs to have a nonseducible adult male around with whom to try on social and vamping skills. She can't do this with her girlfriends. And yet the very culture that is not giving this to a woman is also teaching men that all women are potential sex partners. Women and girls are so eroticized in our culture that the only way most husbands or fathers in a household can deal with their adolescent daughters is to deny their sexuality. When father withdraws, *she* doesn't understand why this person she loves is pulling away from her. We punish young girls for growing up. If father doesn't endorse the physical changes his daughter is experiencing, *in a nonseductive way*, she has a whole line of boys out there who are all too willing to endorse them."

Why do we assume that fathers are less capable of dealing with a daughter's sexuality than mothers with sons? Why should a man be less able to restrain himself from crossing the incest line? I sometimes think our readiness to see men as unable to control their sexuality, in all areas, has become a self-fulfilling prophecy. We look at a man who is responsible for a beautiful young girl and automatically have ideas of his molesting her; what is wrong with us?

The given of paternal incest has gone on for generations because it suited society. Erotic fantasies of people in our families happen, but a fantasy is not a predetermined act. If society didn't want fathers to retreat from their daughters, didn't choose to see men's lust as uncontrollable, we would have educated men, raised them to understand fantasies as ideas and images that come to mind, just as thoughts of murder sometimes do; we don't commit murder/we don't commit incest.

By keeping men at a distance from their children, out of the home, society focused men totally on their role as providers, neatly balanced by women's monopoly on everything domestic. The assumption that "men are sexual beasts" further inflated men's image as powerful and dampened women's own original lust. You may have noticed that we don't live this way anymore. How can we look so squarely at women's new rights to equal opportunity and keep our vision of men so skewed? Leaving the care of children to "good" mothers, to the exclusion of men, was a bad setup in olden times, but it certainly doesn't wash today.

We choose to think that mothers are devoid of incestuous thoughts, that mother/son, mother/daughter incest doesn't occur. Of course it does. As women's economic power has grown, the full range of our sexuality has come more and more to light. If the only way to get fathers more deeply involved with their children is to expose the dark side of women's sexuality—we being no less human than men— then I am for it. The biggest impediment to a daughter having a close relationship with her father is feminism's refusal to put women's sexuality on the agenda, to see the whole picture.

Maternal incest has been swept under the carpet because society needed idealized caretakers. The behavioral world denied that women even had sexual fantasies until thirty years ago. If society balked at accepting the fact that women even *thought* about sex, clearly the idea of maternal incest, thought or deed, was out of the question. We've made paternal incest such a juicy news item, the very stuff of daytime talk shows, and we turn away in horror at the suggestion that mothers not only have the incestuous thought, but actually commit the deed.

What constitutes incest? By definition, it isn't simply intercourse. The mother who kisses her baby boy's penis after she's bathed and toweled him isn't going to see her act as incestuous. So ironclad are maternal rights that bystanders watching this act would neither comment on it nor do anything about it. In her loneliness, mother crawls into her son's bed while her husband is away on business. She sleeps with her arm around the boy, nothing more, but it is "something" to the boy, who lies there with his erection and remembers it for the rest of his life. A mother's sense of entitlement includes physical contact with children long after the age when it is appropriate.

We hear little of maternal incest because boys/men don't tell. Mother loved him; some part of him enjoyed her lying beside him. The sexual feelings are his fault; he feels terrible guilt at the erection he got as he lay in her arms; mother is good/he is bad.

Grown to a man, the son feels it would be unmanly and ungrateful for him to discuss it, even think about it; in fact, most men do "forget" such incidents. Weren't they committed by the person who gave birth to them, cared for them all their lives, and to whom they are joined by knots of steel? The hundreds of men who have written and spoken to me of mother incest do not do so in a judgmental voice. Most prefer to think of it as love, and yet what can be more sexually confusing to a son than a mother who sleeps with him by night and plays rule maker opposite him by day?

The sexes are composed of shades of gray. The rage that women used to dutifully swallow and turn against themselves today flies in the air, seeking other targets. Men are getting more than their share as women shrink from venting their spleen on other women, who are scarier than men. Younger women are especially quick to accept the new Bitch/Killer as a recognizable heroine to put in films, books, television, and cartoon strips. This is progress. It is healthy to show women as equally guilty of badness as men.

"We've been acculturated to see mothers as loving and caring, totally self-sacrificing," says psychologist Jeanne Murrone. "But there are angry mothers, some of them abusive, who struggle with 'I don't like this kid. I had mixed feelings about having this kid. Nobody ever told me it would be like this. I'm not crazy about this at all.' As a culture we don't talk about things like that, it's not permissible."

We know that more than one million of the United States' nine million girls between the ages of fifteen and nineteen get pregnant each year; we know that teenage girls who grow up without their fathers tend to have sex earlier. It seems obvious that without a man at home, an adolescent girl is going to idealize men, to imagine how much better the "problem areas" in her life would have been had there been a father who had seen her as she would have liked to be seen. Of course she is vulnerable when she sees herself "that way" in a boy's eyes.

Once upon a time, a boy would press a girl "to go all the way," but if she resisted, he would usually stop. Thirty years ago there were more fathers at home providing at least a semblance of an example of manhood to their sons. But today's adolescent girl, as eager as ever to be taken care of, finds herself in the arms of a boy who has formed his image of manhood from television. Until adolescence, the fatherless girl has survived in women's world; now she needs a mirroring image of her successful transition from childhood to young womanhood. She reads that image of herself into the boy's eyes just as she reads into the feelings he has aroused in her the idea that he loves her and will take care of her; she gives herself to him, without any form of contraception, which in her eyes makes him responsible.

"Daughters *really* need their fathers during adolescence, when the man's awareness and approval allow his daughter to accept herself physically, her whole body image," says psychologist Henry Biller, who has been studying fatherhood for thirty years. "But what the daughter wants is so simple: confirmation that what has happened to her physically and emotionally is good and admirable, and that in his eyes she has succeeded. She has become a lovely young woman."

Unfortunately, we have no father/daughter "tradition," as it were; there are no stories, no wisdom passed down through generations in a family so that fathers today know what their responsibilities are in terms of an adolescent daughter. The modern father is inventing himself. His wife reinvented herself in the male workplace, where her mother may not have worked; very well, fathers must take courage in hand and, when they see, for instance, that there is competition between mother and daughter, they must involve themselves. Sounds terrifying? Well, the days of father retreating from "women's business" are over.

Books for fathers are waiting to be written, and one of the most daunting chapters will be on how father should deal with competition between the women in the house so that it is acknowledged, lived through with neither mother nor daughter feeling that they have lost him or one another. Not even the master, Dr. Freud, handled it well in his own house. His most famous daughter, Anna, grew up feeling that she could never get her father's attention, and she knew it had to do with her lack of beauty. It was Sophie, her older, beautiful sister, who caught Freud's eye. Anna Freud never did have a sexual encounter in her life, leaving us to wonder if having lost the beauty contest in the family led her to choose her father's profession, given that she lacked the essential "feminine" quality that had drawn him to her sister.

Today's adolescent girls will soon face competition with both sexes in the workplace. They need to learn the basics beginning with the fact that the competitive feeling is all right, that it can be aired, argued; that there are rules that protect, and when it is over, you shake hands, knowing that next week you may need today's adversary as an ally. Behavioral studies are showing that girls who play sports have a better chance at succeeding in business because they learn teamwork, cooperation, and risk-taking, all of which translates into networking in the workplace. This is what father knows best. We have a great resource; who better than father to bring his daughter into the next century?

When I was single in the sixties in New York I avoided the corporate jobs offered me; I preferred jobs that required intense work but that had a beginning and an end. I would have given you all sorts of answers back then as to why I turned down high salaries in big companies, but I know now that I feared my competitive spirit. I would have been a success, but how could I appeal to men if they saw me as someone as powerful as they?

It is a wonder that I didn't marry one of those boys who held me close and remain a child/woman; the intoxication of being loved, finally, by an exotic "other," so male, so much what I'd been missing in the house of women. If I idealized boys, it was because I'd had a life in which to imagine them in the absence of my father. Of course I filled it with an ideal. Though I must add that in reality I have found men to be more generous, fairer, and more appealing in their neediness of women's love than most feminists paint them.

Even without a crown of beauty, I loved my adolescent awakening to men. None of my early loves was The Boy Divine, Malcolm, he whom I would have chosen had taking the initiative been something A Nice Girl did. Had I put my hand in his, however, it wouldn't have been a proper fit; I didn't own the appropriate beauty to match his leadership, nor could I disobey The Nice Girl Rules. He had rules too, and sex was what he wanted. He told me that, the only time I ever lay in his arms, the night before I left for college. When I pushed his hand away from between my legs, he said, "This is why it wouldn't work,

Nancy. This is what I want." He said it in a nice voice, making it sound fair, like a man older than his years. Well, he was the leader of the pack. Malcolm/father.

How I had the heart to deny myself what I wanted most, I'll never know. I was such a besotted, lovesick teenager; though I called it romance, it had a heavy dose of pure sexual desire. But the rules I'd made for myself were overly rigid in their self-condemnation; in the absence of my father in our family, I'd made myself the responsible one. Of course I was always chosen to be the leader at school.

One spring day in my sophomore year at college, I decided I didn't want to continue my career as class leader. I didn't want to be the rule maker who said you couldn't drink beer on the lanes around the lake; I wanted to drink beer with my date on a Saturday afternoon. More exactly, I wanted the choice, wanted to be more emotionally involved in what I chose to do with men. I longed to drop the Nice Girl Rules and be myself, whoever she was.

My decision confounded my faculty adviser. It may sound like a minor event, but it was a turning point, and it had a lot to do with sex and a need to invent a life with men based on new rules. Rules are important, the making and the breaking of them. Rules are especially important to a girl who grows up without a father, always hungry for men.

I understood the full significance neither of that glass bank in which I'd saved my nickels and dimes nor, foolish virgin, my biology, even as I played with penises and near-insertions in parked cars. As for the power of beauty, while those were still the days when beauty was the paramount price for the best prince, all these enormous influences that had ruled my young life—economics, sex, and looks—would not be fully grasped until my house burned down in 1980.

Young women today don't have the luxury of my own extended naive youth; my generation was the last to know the basic optimism built into the Protestant work ethic, which prevailed for so many generations. Today we no longer trust that if you raise your children to work hard, believe in God, that they will have a higher standard of living. The work ethic, optimism, inner beauty, morality are gone.

The naked power of money, sex, and external beauty all come together in adolescence. More than ever before, father, a "nonseducible adult male," is very much what is wanted in an adolescent girl's life.

Without him, without any feel of a man growing up, my own

determination to take care of myself economically got seriously twisted; I became an excellent earner, a good provider, but when I married that first time, I handed the money over to my husband. I didn't want to understand how economics worked. In a bargain that said I was the child and he the daddy I'd never had, I simply endorsed my checks over to him. When he mentioned totals in the bank, my brain went fuzzy. It wasn't until that fire and my talks with the nonseducible Dan Stern that I began to separate the powers of money, sex, and beauty that adolescence had confused.

5

The Dance of Adolescence: Boys

═══════

The Look of Boys: Beloved Enemy

One night on the cusp of adolescence we girls and boys who had grown up together played a game for the last time on the broad beach of Sullivan's Island. It was called Red Rover, a game in which two teams faced one another, girls and boys holding on tightly to one another's arms, creating a human chain that members of the opposite team attempted to race toward and break through. A person who broke the line got to take back to his or her team a member of the opposing line. We'd played the game for years, but that night there was a new excitement, something not altogether different from what we felt at our recent introduction to the dance at Madame Larka's classes at the Hibernian Hall, where we also stood opposite one another, waiting to choose, if you were a boy, or be selected, if a girl.

But tonight, true to the nonsexist rules of the game, having broken the line, I was entitled to take back whomever I chose. I looked at the boys. Without thinking, I said, "You're all so beautiful, I don't know who to choose." These may not be the exact words, but they are close enough and were no sooner spoken than I was overwhelmed with shame. But they had come from the heart. I have always been a lover of men and of their beauty. From the awesome pleasure I take in their faces and forms, I imagine how much men have to gain in seeing themselves as I do.

While I yearned for boys' love in adolescence, I recognized, if only unconsciously, how much was being asked of them. So like a boy was I in my leadership, height, and courage that I remember wanting to help them, even as The Rules forbade it: "Here, let me assist you with this wooing business, for I am besotted with you and know exactly where the dance is heading, so desperate am I to be held."

The power of beauty isn't new in adolescence, for we have all been here before. Though we have tried to turn our backs on early childhood, pushed the painful memory of mother's preference for our lovely brother or sister into oblivion, now, in the supremacy of sexual beauty, it all comes swimming up again: the old jealousy, envy, the memory of loss. Does the boy dare try again to win the beauty, is he good enough, does he have the prerequisite looks, the power to match hers? Dare he risk defeat in front of his comrades?

For five, six years now his need of women's/mother's love has been lessened by a growing solidarity in the camaraderie of other boys, the powerful identity it gives him as different from women. Abruptly, which is how it happens, the beauty of girls sweeps all before it, demanding ascendancy by its undeniable effect upon him, reducing the strong, developed, self-assured boy into a slavish, gawky suitor; yes, the attraction is exciting but fraught with fear. He may not consciously associate girls' power over him with what he felt in opposition to his mother, but it is there, somewhere in his memory.

In his awakening to the beauty of girls, is the boy really so different from Sleeping Beauty? Forget sexist roles for a moment. For some of us, there is no sight more heart-stopping than that of the youthful male body; the Greeks had their heads on straight. It is all a matter of training, of the eye becoming accustomed to faddish styles of dress, fat versus thin, and ideal beauty as male or female. In my mind's eye, I see the adolescent boy extending his hand to the girl, he all perfection, not unlike Michelangelo's male nude figure at the dawn of creation. No, more precisely, at the dawn of *being* created, for in that elegant male outstretched hand there is the expectation of mutuality, that the girl will meet him halfway. In his eyes, she has so much power and he, having been away from the female touch for several years, is in need, once again, of being seen, being visually regarded and found acceptable in his self.

His memory of beauty is mother, who had all the power in the world; while he lived in her domain, his need of her eyes on him was total; he grew on her gaze, fed off it, took comfort and strength from it. In time he squirmed under her loving fingers, combing the hair away from his eyes so that she might look more deeply, see him. Now grown to puberty and cowed by the beauty of girls, he rubs the sleep from his eyes, abruptly remembering something of female power. While he can't remove his gaze from the girl's beauty, he is as much in need of being recognized as she is. How could he not be? Had it not been written that males must be the voyeurs and females the exhibitionists, this adolescent dance might be more cooperative. As it is, the boy rudely learns that no one sees him, no one really looks at him. And we wonder why men sometimes stare at us with anger in their eyes.

Imagine being the invisible sex on whom no adoring eye, filled with desire, fastens. The Gaze, with its restorative powers, was life's first feeding tube and never loses that power. But men are taught to turn away, it being unmanly to be seen basking in The Gaze. Instead, the boy sees the girl's eyes go past him to his car, his prowess on the playing field, his status, her eyes totaling his worth like an adding machine and searching for envy in the eyes of the other girls.

Yes, today she makes money of her own, but she wants her old options as well as the new. Should she reject him, he must appear to be impervious. Girls have a monopoly on showing pain, and he wouldn't want his comrades to see him with a chink in his armor. It hasn't turned out the way he'd dreamed before adolescence, when he had plans, wide horizons. Now he understands the power of the briefcase, that leather box that made his father seem old before his time.

He is only thirteen and is learning to pose, hoping to pass as something he isn't. Girls have expectations and judge a boy differently than other guys do. Girls know what they want; while they are both formidable and mythic in their beauty, they want to be skillfully led. What does a thirteen-year-old know of escorting a goddess who has been practicing The Goddess Walk? What does he know of her fantasies of him, of the access to her self that she will give him—but only if he convinces her of his mastery? In his recent monastic life he had thought himself well off without women. Now, here they are, wise in the lore of girls' magazines, practiced in the fine art of intimacy but nonetheless demanding his mastery. Lead?

It wouldn't occur to the girl that the boy hasn't been anticipating her arrival, hasn't rehearsed the requisite skills, hasn't been conjuring up the vision of her that she is so desperate now to see in his eyes, the mirror that will show her to herself as unblemished. Never having been emotionally distanced from the first years of life, she has kept alive in memory the Golden Beam between hers and the caretaker's eyes. Now, she reactivates that bliss of being adored and cared for, deftly substituting the boy for mother.

How can the boy, having been on a totally different journey, comprehend that the girl wants to feel like his beloved baby whose thoughts he can read and over whom he has total mastery? Why, to him she has all the power! Hasn't she controlled every move so far, allowing him access inch by inch? He reads her acquiescence in his arms as the meeting of peers, with her having the edge, meaning that only she can make sense of his sexuality, humanizing the brooding masturbatory dreams that until now had no heart.

For her, the lowering of her drawbridge to him has said, I am yours, meaning that he will make her sexual and take responsibility for her. How can the adolescent boy comprehend the significance of her surrender and the expectations she now has of him? Yes, he is grateful, perhaps even loves her, but wasn't it a joint venture? What does he know of how intimacy has totally changed her vision of herself and her new expectations of being transformed in his eyes? What does he know of mirrors? He has taught his eyes not to give him away, not to betray him. He sees her globally, while to herself she is an assemblage of parts, each imperfect until now, until him.

Now that he has transformed her, she needs his eyes on her alone, recognizing when she is unhappy, when she has parted her hair on a different side, when she has a pimple or wears a new sweater. This is how mother/girls look at her. When he fails, she cries, You never loved me! Once again she learns that only women know how to appraise one another; only women, she deduces, know how to love.

Men's eyes are seldom as credible as other women's, except perhaps in literature, as in Isabel Allende's *The House of Spirits*, where she describes the adolescent Alba, who has fallen in love with Miguel:

For the first time in her life, Alba wanted to be beautiful. She regretted that the splendid women in her family had not bequeathed their attributes to her, that the only one who had, Rosa the Beautiful, had given her only the algae tones in her hair, which seemed more like a hairdresser's mistake than anything else. Miguel understood the source of her anxiety. He led her by the hand to the huge Venetian mirror that adorned one wall of their secret room, shook the dust from the cracked glass, and lit all the candles they had and arranged them around her. She stared at herself in the thousand pieces of the mirror. In the candlelight her skin was the unreal color of wax statues. Miguel began to caress her and she saw her face transformed in the kaleidoscope of the mirror, and she finally believed that she was the most beautiful woman in the universe because she was able to see herself with Miguel's eyes.

What of the very handsome boy, seeing himself in mirrors, hearing people comment on his beauty? Under the Old Deal, men were forbidden to parlay their looks; yes, they saw their reflections, knew women were attracted to them. But like the adolescent girl who must walk more slowly and be less, the boy must give up knowing too consciously what his beauty buys him. How very twisted.

I regret that I did not give the boys of my adolescence more awareness of the power of their beauty. It would be years before I admitted even to myself how their look intoxicated me, activating parts of my body in ways I probably attributed to indigestion, so stupid was I of how male beauty could make you crazy. No one had prepared me. No female spoke of the excitement of gorging one's eyes on the spectacle of male beauty. So profound was the silence, I suppose I took it to mean that looking was verboten.

The societal deal of female beauty in exchange for male protection had blinded us as surely as men were defended against their wanting to be seen. Of course men are angry, as angry as we women; deprived of the healthy narcissistic pleasure of being seen, adored, taken in by loving eyes, men act like the invisible creatures we have made them.

My earliest awareness of the beauty of the male form, the arousing experience of looking at men's bodies—seen but not seen, mind you, for visual lust was forbidden—was the spectacle on the parade ground at The Citadel. In a ritual that Charleston girls observed on Friday afternoons, we parked our cars along the perimeter of the field and perched ourselves prettily atop the front fenders as the cadets marched past to the strains of John Philip Sousa. We girls saw ourselves as the confections, the center of visual regard, waiting in our cashmere sweaters and pearls for the cadets to break ranks and come choose us. What a farce.

Is there a more sexually exhibitionistic spectacle to watch than the collective beauty of a corps of cadets in their fitted uniforms, the skintight jackets with their seductive dark stripes down the back, the S curves that splayed the shoulders, hips, and asses of our sweethearts. How strange that none of us spoke of it, our hypnotic enslavement to that sight, its imprint on our fantasies. So rigid are the sexist roles of exhibitionist and voyeur in the South, that we girls twitched in self-conscious awareness of our own beauty, crossing our legs so as to be sure that we would draw the men to us.

Last night we watched the 1949 film *The Heiress*, with Olivia de Havilland playing the plain daughter who is disdained by her cold father for her lack of looks and is rejected by the handsome fortune-hunter when he discovers that her father had threatened to disinherit her should she marry him. This morning my husband is bleary-eyed. "I was disturbed by that movie all night," he says. "They were so cruel to her. What an awful father, and Montgomery Clift was no better. Why, she was the only person in the film you would want to spend time with. Just because she was plain . . ."

"You identified with her," I say.

"I guess I did identify," he says. "There she was, perfectly happy in her simple life until her looks suddenly became important." My husband has never forgotten the disruptions and rejections of adolescence; no amount of success washes it away. He never believes in his later-found looks. None of us does.

Raised on two different planets, boys and girls meet in adolescence, the one without knowledge of the other. While he may initially feel ineffectual, her dreamy vision of him as the in-charge initiator is a role he would very much like to fill; it is grand to be seen as larger than life when you are all thumbs. He woos her. Only afterward does he realize the full scope of her expectations. He feels bad. She feels betrayed.

Young women sacrifice so much at the advent of adolescence and then hate men for not rewarding us adequately for everything we gave up for them. But boys did not ask it of us. We did it, drank the Kool-Aid and then hated boys for not raising us from the dead with a power they never possessed in the first place.

Girls never consider what the adolescent boy has left behind in his yearning to be loved by us. In the years just prior, he had come to believe through the fellowship of other boys that males had a strength equal to mothers; not all boys like one another, but a sense of ease had come to be expected when good fellows got together. "Men Only" wasn't initially directed against women but was for themselves, a need born in the female-dominated first years of life. Now, in adolescence, here come the girls! As thrilling as girls are, boys learn quickly what they must bring to the bargaining table if they are to win a beauty.

It is scarier than ever to be an adolescent boy these days, to have to deal with the very knowing, demanding young women raised on a Matriarchal Feminist agenda that sees the boy as Public Enemy Number One. The word *feminist* need not even be applied; the girls growing up in Fort Worth with a mother who repudiates the women's movement are still part of a culture shaped by its antimaleness. But fathers still refuse to address the plight of their sons, their adolescent predicament at finding themselves totally unschooled in behavior opposite The New Girl of postfeminism. I have to assume that the neglect is one of choice.

Behaviorists tell us that parents see themselves in their adolescent children, that this age in particular reawakens their own experiences. If a father went through hell in adolescence, does he want to make his son's life any easier? Maybe he thought the hard knocks he took are what made a man of him; maybe he's envious of his son's having all the things he never enjoyed, which only his hard work has won. Yes, this is the reason he worked so hard, but now that the boy is on the brink of life, at a time when father suddenly feels his age, the older man also feels envy, resentment.

Patriarchal Society taught father that men are expected to be powerful and in charge, devoid of "weak" feelings; let the son suffer in these years, which are a kind of boot camp for life, father decides. It probably isn't conscious, but it assuages the envy of youth. However, today's adolescent girls aren't what they were in father's day; they aspire to become economically powerful too. The boy's future isn't at all certain; the definition of a Real Man isn't what it was in father's day.

Without parents, teachers, popular literature of his own that informs him of what lies ahead and how very complex and contradictory The New Girl is, the boy is worse off than his father was at his age. At least father had a societal deal in which women saw him as necessary to their economic survival. It wasn't a great deal, and we're well rid of it, but that still leaves today's adolescent male doomed to stumble with girls who are as emotionally needy and demanding as ever but who can, ultimately, survive without him.

What can the young man today ante up to match the girls' power? He aspires to the traditional male power of wealth, but he works on his looks too, consults his mirror, buys more clothes and beauty products than any generation before him. The power of women's beauty, now buttressed by their recent acquisition of what used to be male power, forces adolescent boys to reevaluate the influence of looks for themselves. It is a wise boy indeed who understands the currency of beauty.

If young men are getting into looks more readily today—like my friend Joni's eleven-year-old son who religiously mousses his hair every morning and checks himself repeatedly in the mirror—it is because the danger of male vanity has been removed: A male is no less male for being handsome, wearing great clothes. Feminism has done this for men, has steadily, slowly opened the closet door to reveal a wardrobe increasingly varied as any female's.

As the period of adolescence grows ever longer, giving our child/men more and more time to grow out of childhood and to imagine a future superior to that of their parents', we the older generation should better understand the potential of these years; they might, with our help, move beyond our loveless world and create a new moral order. Instead, our eyes reflect envy of our children's youth; we no longer act like adults, tutors, respected disciplinarians.

Having created our children as spenders, we make more money than ever from them, not just addicting them to spending but then turning around and stealing whatever it is they have created in their effort to be unique. Adolescents are going to require more than their age-specific moral and genital passions to step over us and change the world they have inherited.

Today, boys'/men's rage spills over in all directions, sometimes upon women: More than one million incidents of domestic violence occur in America annually. There is no question that one reason men strike out has to do with how women see them. As much as women's lives have changed, we still want men to bite the bullet and take care of us too. It is nowhere more obvious than in the adolescent.

"Be a Man!"

In those brief latency years between dependency on mother and the arrival of adolescent girls, the boy has weaned himself from his adoration of the female form as part of his separation from mother. In the company of other boys he learned to "forget" his love/envy of the body that once contained him, its power to sustain him. He built with his own hands and imagination a world of Boy Power that reinforced his newfound sense of independence without woman. Instead, he visually fixated on the perfect older boy. Hero worship.

And then, one day, comes adolescence. Suddenly, the girls who were invisible and useless to him yesterday are seen in all their magisterial beauty, awakening his almost forgotten yearning for the female body; but this new longing compounds potent memories of the beauty of the breast, the female skin and smell, with sexual longing.

"It seems to me that many men fix on their object of desire at a place that is deep in the recesses of childhood," writes Paul Theroux. "Their libidos are coded at an early age. The childish aspect of lust is for most men the hardest to admit or come to terms with. It is the childishness that all prostitutes and role-players know . . . [it] is based on an infantile or adolescent memory," which is why most men are reluctant to reveal the source to a woman, "because revealing it to you will give you power over him."

Such a wise admission, this memory of Theroux's, which goes back to his own early adolescence when he walked into a friend's summer house one day and saw the boy's lovely young mother sitting in her loose shorts, barefoot, wearing only her white bra:

> The cone bra like an icon, the day's humidity, the bare feet, her eyes, her smile, her skin, her posture, my wolfish breathing . . . I was not supposed to be there. That was part of the thrill—that I had entered a house that was not my own and saw my friend's mother, who was more naked than I had ever seen any woman. . . . I desired her. Though the word desire was not in my vocabulary, this was my ravenous awakening. . . . Being away from home . . . was a distinct part of the thrill. I am sure that my urge to travel began that day. . . . Is it any wonder I have spent almost 35 years wandering? The word wanderlust is one of the truest words in the language. . . . There is no such thing as mature desire. The feeling is rooted in a man's youthful unconscious.

And Theroux was only ten at the time. I would wish that every woman would read this entire essay and feel for the ten-year-old, better to understand the boy grown to manhood.

Given that we all, men and women, begin at the breast, the adolescent girl has no infantile unconscious of a male body, is not awakened to sexual urgency when she looks at boys her own age. Should she walk into a friend's house unannounced and see a grown man almost naked, would she be aroused, remember the shape of the man's penis beneath his shorts as "an icon" inspiring her to *wanderlust*? I doubt it.

Instead, she must create a new vision out of the beauty of the male form, with its roots in the here and now of age twelve, thirteen; and if the ground is not ready, welcoming, and fertile, if she has not been raised on the love of men, her imagination will not accept the erotic vision of young men. Her life's training under women's rules, her lack of familiarity with her own body, leaves her even less inclined, less stimulated by the vision of the male form, and less likely to be a voyeur. Never having seen her mother visually enjoying the appearance of men, in adolescence the girl does not share the boy's awakening to the erotic stimuli of looking. Her libido is not "always loaded and cocked," to quote Theroux. It isn't just that she lacks the boy's external organ announcing arousal; it is deeper, meaning older, going back further in time. The boy begins life in love with the texture, smell, and sight of women's bodies, especially the lovely conical breast in its "chaste white bra." We women like to look at her too.

(I love Theroux's comment on wanderlust, his sense that his own desire for forbidden, exotic experiences offered in travel was "an escape from the strictness of home." It is an idea to which I too respond, having always known that the feel of sex wasn't present excitingly in my mother's house, and therefore when I first felt it in unfamiliar surroundings, sexual excitement was commingled with the forbidden; to be experienced, to be lived through, and not just imagined, I had to journey, get away.)

What does the smitten adolescent boy have to offer in exchange for female beauty? It doesn't occur to him that his own looks are even worthy to put on the scale opposite the girl's face, her body; nor do her own eyes fasten on him, loving the look of him, awakening him to his worthiness, learned in her eyes. He feels powerless. It is the girl who will teach him what *she* wants, which boy *she* feels weighs in opposite her beauty. Alas, she makes this decision blindly, without full awareness or even consideration of what the boy feels, of her effect on him; oh, she knows he looks at her, but she has no sympathy, no empathy.

And much to his unhappiness, she is repelled by the sight of his penis. In time, it will be her decision as to whether he can kiss her lips, touch the breast, the contour of which awakens him in the night with an erection. The girl doesn't realize the extent of her power, but what is also missing from this scenario is that she doesn't see his beauty. Nor has he been raised to acknowledge it, but surely he yearns to be taken in. Isn't this what women do—love you with their eyes?

But no. We abandon adolescent boys to struggle with their bankruptcy opposite the supremacy of female beauty. I suppose it is meant to toughen them—"Be a man!"—so that they more quickly learn their role as provider and problem solver, the purchase price of beauty. The grim side effect, however, is that it has always left men very envious of the power of female beauty.

We must reactivate admiration of male beauty, teach lazy eyes to awaken to the hypnotic curve of the male torso, which is all over town, on playing fields, in gyms, standing over there at the bar, his foot on the brass rail thus accentuating the beautiful ass. It is already happening. In 1995, 73 percent of boys from twelve to nineteen said they either "try hard" to keep up with or "care somewhat" about keeping up with the latest fashions. Aren't we all a bit sated with the power of female beauty these days? Time for male beauty, and none is lovelier than the adolescent.

We leave adolescent boys at a terrible disadvantage, many of them knowing, having come from fatherless homes, that girls, like their own mothers, can do without men. This leaves the boy to deal with his vision of the all-powerful girl, who has aroused feelings in him from he knows not where, urges and desires that he must attempt to hide, since they are so one-sided, the girl obviously not suffering, not looking at him.

My own memory of an adolescent night: We are parked on the beach, at the drive-in. The memory is so sensory that I could play it for you better on a musical instrument, a feeling of my silent prayer that he will turn his head and bring his mouth to mine. My eyes are closed, my lips wait, my tremulous hands, which might have reached up and gently turned his head and brought his lips to mine, are clasped in my lap. None of this passivity was *me*. Let me add that this anxiety, fear, holding back was not him either. He was as jellied by the power of female beauty as boys are today. I was not allowed to initiate, to make the first move, but isn't this precisely what feminism has won for our adolescent girls, not just the *right* to take the initiative but also a shared responsibility for it, which includes the courage to risk rejection?

We adults, who have not taken sexual responsibility for our own selves, are poor candidates to teach our sons to see themselves clearly in the mirror so that they might enjoy a share of the power of beauty, learn to use it wisely, and be accountable for what it provokes. Believing this, the boy would enter adolescence as a contender instead of feeling whiplashed by the dismissive toss of the beautiful girl's head. Having something of his own, he would not take her rejection, knead it into a ball of rage to use against her one night when she is vulnerable. We haven't even taught our daughters the uses and responsibilities of beauty power, much less raised them to appreciate the beautiful line of a male torso.

Doesn't the experience of women's beauty awaken the young man to the full spectrum of life itself? Theroux links his own earliest awareness of female beauty to his lifelong desire to see the world, to feel everything. What an amazing door our beauty opens to men! In recognizing men's beauty, couldn't we teach our daughters to give men a reflection of themselves that they are literally dying for?

If we can teach young people the workings of money, why not explain the currency of beauty: how it has been traded under Patriarchal Society for centuries, how its rate has evolved under modern feminism. With women in the workplace doing what we used to call "men's work," the return of male beauty power has been inevitable. It would be a good thing if we adults, along with our children, understood beauty's powerful exchange. No more "beauty is only skin deep."

Tell the boy why he turns to Jell-O opposite lovely girls and why the girl who has chosen him has turned his friends into rivals. Uneducated, he sleepwalks, nods his head dumbly at the inevitability of the pairing of the prettiest girl with the athletic hero, the school leader, the guy with the car, the money. There is valuable information we now have that might explain to adolescents how these things work; for instance, early physical development, meaning broad shoulders, the growth of a beard, height, and a deep voice, translates naturally into psychological maturity, meaning leadership for the boy.

According to psychologists, the same parallel doesn't hold for the adolescent girl, where the early development of breasts, wide hips, and the onset of menstruation isn't a forecast of leadership within her group. It is a difference between the sexes that resonates; the early developed boy, the leader, for instance, chooses the most beautiful girl. We know why, and yet we don't. What this did in our group when I was growing up was to make judgmental eyes very envious indeed when our "best friend" blossomed before the rest of us. Very well, we accepted nature's law that she should be chosen by boys, but within The Group she had to watch her step, not let her breasts go to her head, so to speak. Not surprisingly, psychologists have discovered that girls who develop earliest have the most psychological problems in adolescence.

It is a meaningful imbalance between the sexes, this correspondence of physical and psychological growth. How each sex recognizes its members and leaders is a lesson we take into the rest of our lives. That so many physically unendowed boys, the nerds, pursue economic success with such dogged diligence may not be by chance; that so many of today's successful women report feeling themselves "the less pretty one" growing up also resonates. Those who are underprivileged in beauty compensate with other talents. Are The Nice Girl Rules in women's world today still demanding that no one woman get any more of the pie than any other really all that different from what we lived out through our teens?

Only recently have we discovered that some of us, both male and female, are genetically more assertive than others. It is in the bloodstream. Once upon a time, boys had hormones on their side—or so they thought—meaning chemically, biologically, girls weren't supposed to act aggressively. Today, we know that androgens and estrogen, once thought to be strictly divided between males and females, exist in shades of gray in both sexes. It seems that there is nothing the boy can call his own, not even testosterone, to back up self-confidence in picking up the telephone, risking rejection. Ten, fifteen years ago, feminists were quick to deny aggression in women: "No, no, men are aggressive and competitive, women are conciliatory."

Yet, one look at the sinister Bad Girls who grab the lead in today's films and run all over men says that boys will have to look elsewhere for their "naturally" superior muscle. Only yesterday a girl saw hair on her upper lip as failure as a woman; what man would want to take care of a bearded lady? Today's adolescent girls, without losing one ounce of womanliness, pursue boys, maybe share the price of a movie and watch beautiful Sharon Stone flash her pubic hairs.

When today's girl finds herself, no, *puts* herself in the arms of a boy whose hands explore her body, she is caught between two worlds. Her mother, for instance, never told her about her clitoris; very few mothers do. When the boy discovers it for her, his image is transformed into that of Prince, and she has gone from assertive New Girl into Love Slave.

"When we don't educate young girls about their bodies, we leave them vulnerable for other people to reveal them to themselves," says Judith Seifer. "I guarantee you, as God is my witness, if the girl hasn't found her clitoris herself, and no one's encouraged her to, she is going to think she is in love with the first guy who trips over it. 'Oh my God, this is what love feels like!' And of course it doesn't have a thing to do with love. Back in the halcyon days of sex education in the seventies, we really thought we were making a difference. But I realize, in today's explosion of unplanned pregnancies, that we haven't made an inch of difference in the way we raise our children."

As confusing as it is for the girl, imagine, twenty-five years into feminism, what a boy feels. It has always seemed to boys that girls have all the power. And yet, when he brings her to orgasm she becomes his baby, his Swept Away darling. *He* knows he didn't do anything masterful, that the magic is her own. How empowering is this for the boy? It's rather like being mistaken for someone else, or something else, meaning that *he* knows she could have accomplished the same thing with her own hand.

Boys today have to look cooler and more in charge than ever; with so many markets focused on the billions of dollars they spend annually, we forget that the person standing in the $135 Nikes has been growing close to twelve inches in four years, growing as much as three and a half to four inches a year by the time puberty is over. Girls get their growth spurt earlier than boys, around age twelve; the boy's doesn't start until roughly age fourteen, but these inequalities matter more today when the boy is as eager to be admired as is the girl. The culture has no sympathy for the male experience. The feminist rage at men has become the culture's rage.

With fewer fathers at home than ever, no model of a man to emulate, the boy's invisibility and lack of power opposite Big Women leave him to identify more than ever with his peers. The boy invents his own look, language, and behavior out of the raw desperation of adolescent anger. Is it so surprising that with so much woman power making him feel small, he tries to bring us down a peg, denigrate the beauty by mocking her in ways that keep her and her formidable power *in her place.* "Her body's beautiful, so I'm thinkin' rape—shouldn't had her curtains open, see, that's her fate," rap the Geto Boys. When rude men make disparaging remarks at women on the street, it is envy crying out; when young rap singers mouth the crude, ugly lyrics about women's bodies, our most sensitive parts, their nasty resentment is the voice of people who feel insignificant opposite the women who today act as if they don't even need men.

Read these disturbing lyrics by the group Nine Inch Nails, and tell me if they don't protest too much. "i am a big man (yes I am). and i have a big gun. got me a big old dick and i, i like to have fun. held against your forehead, i'll make you suck it. maybe i'll put a hole in your head. you know, just for the fuck of it. i can reduce you if I want. i can devour. i'm hard as fucking steel, and i've got the power. i'm every inch a man, and i'll show you somehow, me and my fucking gun. nothing can stop me now. shoot, shoot, shoot, shoot, shoot. I'm going to come all over you . . . me and my fucking gun, me and my fucking gun."

How Girls Project on to Boys the Ugliness of Sex

One of the first things a boy must learn in adolescence is to hide his insecurity; while girls may seem to have all the power, they want to be led, to be taken care of. Self-consciousness opposite girls is a new feeling, and his ignorance of what they want must not betray him. Therefore, he must cast his features, the muscles of his face and his body in such a way as to belie feeling anything. Imagine the amount of muscular control that goes into facial denial, the mask, when he is off-balance as pretty girls approach. Within a few years the stonewall look will be natural, and a few years after that the deadpan similarity of successful men's photos in the newspaper will be baffling.

"What are you feeling?" women ask, looking impatiently at the impassive male face. "What are you thinking?" Women get exasperated with men, who give nothing away in their look, while we, the emotional sex, can be read like books. In time, the boy/man becomes stonewalled inside too, sensitive reaction quickly suppressed. The adolescent heroes in today's films never give themselves away; they stare into the wind, their faces hardened and lined by the elements, not by tears, not ever.

There is a reason adolescent boys hang in clusters to practice voyeurism: It is too scary alone. This urgent demand to give large parts of their attention to staring at girls instead of shooting baskets is new. Even earlier fantasies of sailing to Africa are taken over by dreams of female bodies. When girls walk by, his jaw drops; what does he know initially of girls' sensitivity to being stared at? We know nothing of his involuntary reaction to the sight of us, neither understanding nor sympathizing. Had our infantile sensory pleasure and dependency been focused on a male body, so that we came to anticipate the sight, smell, and dearness of men, we might stare back at boys in adolescence, recognizing in them our new erotic selves.

Since we refuse to recognize him, the boy picks up on our discomfort. Sorely missing the eye contact, any mutuality of a shared gaze, he combines our powerlessness with the chink we have shown him in our armor, and he gives us "the look" that we hate, that up-and-down appraisal. It is, however, a rare boy who will stand alone and gaze; by the time he has grown to manhood he may look at women on his own, always hopeful that one will smile back, but in adolescence, the full tribe is required. The old gang's camaraderie takes on new meaning in adolescence when the powerful sight of girls makes the boy too small on his own.

Having paid scant attention to his own looks, he is unaware of girls' self-consciousness regarding fat thighs, stringy hair, the pimple on our nose. He thinks we are Mistresses of the Universe, and we give him weaponry he didn't know he had. Add to our lifelong care about appearance the recent arrival of The Curse, and every inch of beauty is now in question. All at the very moment when sexual desire fires our need to be wanted, chosen.

On his part, the boy hasn't been held, or wanted to caress anyone, for years; this is what he spartanly taught himself to do without. Now he desires the girl, that very one with the pimple on her nose, which he doesn't even notice. Out of practice and ill-equipped to assume the role of leader in courtship, he desires her, and she doesn't even look his way. Feeling invisible and rejected, the boy takes the power she has given him; the fear in her eyes at being appraised, along with her wilting passivity, emboldens him to stare.

He does it crudely, with too much braggadocio so as to conquer anxiety. It is not at all how girls would have done it, were the role of initiator ours. We know how to kiss, stroke, cuddle, love, and certainly we know how to appraise other females. When his inept advances fall beneath our standards, we reject the gawky boy. We do not do it nicely, being angry at having to be so passive. He too stirs anger into his next effort. By the time he has conquered the art of looking at girls, there is a lot of hostility in his stare, most of it learned from us.

Outside Schwettman's drugstore, the boys in their windbreakers leaned against the plate-glass window through which I could see the soda fountain, my favorite retreat just the day before. Today, not even the promise of a chocolate nut sundae could induce me to brush past The Judges. The boys were just passing time, doing nothing, but I was twelve, and to me they were a tribunal, a bank of eyes that had all the power in the world. This was my accustomed route home along King Street after the afternoon movie at The Gloria. I'd walked it hundreds of times, and now, overnight, it was a nightmare.

Ordinarily I loved a challenge, but here was a promise of failure that no amount of courage could match. To tell you the truth, I don't even know if they looked at me, or if they did, what was in their eyes, but I felt their a priori rejection so keenly they might have been a firing squad. Oh, I walked past them; to detour around *my* accustomed route home was unthinkable. But I died. The odd thing is, I didn't despise them; they hadn't invented what I was feeling, this ancient failure to catch my mother's eye.

I can barely remember how the boys themselves looked in these early days of adolescence; so keenly did we girls feel the focus of their orbs that it didn't occur to us to use our own eyes. And so sure were we of inadequacies, so full of hate of our own bodies, that we projected self-contempt on to them. We filled their eyes with weaponry that we then assumed they used against us. A self-fulfilling prophecy. Where else could a boy learn that he had the same power his mother's eyes had once had over him? He doesn't consciously remember, which would be unmanly; instead, he decides that this is what men do: check out babes.

Nowadays I approach the sidewalk gauntlet with a mix of curiosity, a modicum of belief in my self-image, and, God knows, some left-over anxiety too. A rude remark, deliberately mean, my face grows hot. But I separate the mean bastard from the others lounging on the sidewalk eating their lunch; the bastard is the exception, I have come to believe, and not the rule.

Yes, boys chase girls, stand on corners and look at us, but first and always they hang out. Their intactness, their self-sufficiency without us, is maddening. When I was growing up, we would sometimes meet at one girl's house and wait for the boys to find us: "Waiting for the boys." Sooner or later they arrived; they always found us, but it was in their own time. We were meshed, we girls, but come adolescence, strangely incomplete without boys. It was our lack of autonomy, which we hadn't practiced in the first years of life, that left us needing boys in that deep, emotional way that boys didn't "need" us. Men love us, want us, don't do well living on their own later without a woman, but they do not have that life-and-death fear that, beginning in adolescence, grips females.

Other afternoons we girls stood on the sidelines of the boys' playing field, watching them engrossed in their game, content to finish it before they turned to us. Sometimes we stood for hours, unable to go home happily without them. What did we think we were feeling? It certainly wasn't the excitement of the game that held us there giggling, waiting, pushing, pulling one another. We didn't call it erotic desire. Moving to the boys' playing field was simply a geographic transfer of our claustrophobic sleep-overs. Eros may have called us, but we were still joined at the hip; and while we looked at the boys, we kept a far more judgmental eye on one another.

Was it painful, reining in the inclination to take the initiative? What hurt most was the waiting, waiting, waiting for the phone to ring, for the boy to kiss me, for something to happen that I wanted with all my heart. It became my theme song, my explanation to myself for years and years after adolescence as to why I didn't want to marry, not yet, and why I traveled, knowing always that there would be another interesting man around the next corner: "I'm waiting for something to happen." What I was waiting for, I would learn, was to regain my natural talent as initiator.

I would imagine that if girls were raised to take the initiative with boys, share it, we would more naturally assume responsibility for ourselves sexually. All that waiting makes a girl/woman indolent, lazy, childish, and irresponsible. It would require years before I learned how wholeheartedly a man responds to a woman who will shoulder half the risk, but first I would have to learn to recognize that kind of man. That kind of man doesn't want sex with a little girl. It would be a man who taught me to take responsibility for my sexuality. It was eye-opening. It was also he who awakened me to what I'd abandoned in adolescence—speech, speed, intellect, all of it—my little gift to boys.

Have women any idea how it feels to be rejected again and again? Sometimes the boy awakens in terror—the thought being the deed—

from erotic dreams of people of his own sex. He doesn't know it is natural to have such dreams; to him they often signal his failure at not
"measuring up" to girls. The boy labels himself and says: "I must be
gay." Maybe he is, but maybe he isn't. Women have wildly erotic day
and night dreams of one another all our lives without putting our heterosexuality in question. The double standard isn't always in men's
favor.

The girl doesn't have an external organ that tells her when she is
aroused. She has never seen a penis up close and associates everything
between the legs as ugly and dirty. When he tries to guide her hand
there, when he puts her hand on his naked penis, or shows her that he
wants her to put her mouth "there," she is repulsed. He is confused,
hurt, rejected. He would worship at that place between her legs, just to
touch it.

"No!" she commands. She hasn't touched her own genitals,
explored them with her fingers, and if she has masturbated, it has been
with great guilt. That he, her romantic hero, who has just ignited her
with his kisses, should now ruin everything by drawing her hand to
the hard bulge in his trousers, or by exposing that big, red, ugly
"thing" . . . why, she could weep. Maybe she does. Thus the boy learns
how very different males and females are: He is bad and she is good.

This is how she sees him and herself. Very well, at least it's better
than being seen as the wimp he sometimes feels he is. Being "bad,"
tough, sounds masculine. Therefore, if he is to further invade her
citadel, he must play the dirty, sexual aggressor and she the princess;
he must woo her with this not altogether unpleasant business of kissing, tentative touching, slowly winning a bit more ground, a bit more
trust as her restraining hands put up less and less resistance.

Until adolescence he has not associated love and sex. In fact, given
his love of mother and her dislike of his masturbation, he has separated love and sex. The boy is absolutely right; it is wonderful when
they come together, but sex and love *are* different. The nicest of boys is
now put in the unenviable position of learning what turns girls on; the
irony is that she believes the magic in her sexual arousal is in him. He
has the key, *is* the key.

It is the boy's job to introduce her to her forbidden/dirty/bad sex,
while also remaining her Prince. She splits him in two. It is she who
teaches him that no doesn't always mean no. When she murmurs,
"Oh, no, don't do that!" even as her body curves into him, it is the sig-

nal for The Brute Boy in him to press on, to insist, even as, in his role as Prince, he whispers in her ear, "Oh, God, how I love you, you're so beautiful, so sweet, oh, yes, please let me touch you, please, please, I love you so much . . . !" And so it goes, she wanting the sexual feeling but not wanting the responsibility for it unless sex is disguised as love. Meanwhile, the ugly penis, which is bigger than both of them, demands its reward, not unlike the troll that lived under the bridge.

After that night, whether or not there was intercourse, she will lie on her bed and re-create what she felt with the boy to the sound of romantic music, replacing herself in his arms and sensing it all again, he the powerful, dark force and she a lovely will-o'-the-wisp, and as the violins soar, the words in her head are: "Take me, bend me, make me feel 'that way,' out of my skin, out of my mind, high, Swept Away, Yours!"

The dreamy surrender in the best of romantic music is background to her fantasies of being taken, made to yield to his mastery, which pushes her past her "No," making her a victim of love (her word for sex). She imagines herself wooed, captured. And he? She sees him as overcome by her beauty, the effect of it like a drug on his accustomed strong, withdrawn, tough self, maybe a little Sean Penn–ish, so bad and animal-like is he, for he must be hungry enough for both of them, meaning determined to thrust past her "No!" When he doesn't telephone the next day, of course she accuses him of betrayal, imagining him prowling the streets in his lust, as she would if she were in his place. Men are starved for sex: projection.

She waits for his telephone call; how can he not want to reconnect? When the phone doesn't ring, when she sees him with another girl, or when she is pregnant, she cries to him, "But you said you loved me! You said I was beautiful! I would never have done those things if I didn't think you cared." But he didn't say he loved her, and even if he did, he didn't know what she meant by love. In fairness to the boy, he sees the mutuality of their passion as an example of her knowing precisely what she was doing; *he* did.

In time, with repetition, the boy learns the sad truth: Girls, like mother, don't like his penis; in fact, they think it is ugly, sinister, which isn't too far from their opinion of sex itself. When he grows up, when he marries, the female image of the male erection is incompatible with the clean, nice, maternal image of his wife. For good sex—meaning dirty—he goes to whores.

If we girls take any initiative with men, we are divided from our friends. If he wants us, he must seem to pull us away from the other girls, who will then understand that he is an irresistible force, dark, mysterious, alien to women, but nonetheless our future. Girls must be seen by the other girls as leaving them only against our wills—*The Rape of Europa*—overcome by something against which we have no control. The confusion of "bad" sex that takes us away from Mommy/girls becomes a given; when men hurt us, or leave us, we return to women, who circle round and console: "There, there, that is how men are."

The adolescent boy wouldn't have a clue as to his mastery if we didn't project it on to him in adolescence; when men later force us into sex, they are carrying out women's opinion of them. And it will never change until girls are raised to understand and take charge of their sexuality, to give up the pose of the drowning nymph whose helpless body requires rescue. Instead of swooning, drifting, undulating in our provocative little dance in front of boys, girls must be raised to grab hold of their sexual selves with authority. Masturbation, as I've said, is a great lesson in responsibility, for it teaches girls that they and not the boy hold the key to their sexuality; having given herself an orgasm, the girl doesn't transfer the power of *her* sex on to him, his kiss, his embrace. She is not good and he bad. They are equal.

The boy may not be proficient in sexual responsibility, but he has probably masturbated and before adolescence may have come to believe that his own magical fluid that spurts when he ejaculates has a power of its own. He knows that his seed is in his semen, and that while women carry the child, there can be no pregnancy without him—well, at least until sperm banks. Of course the boy fantasizes that the girl likes his ejaculation, his fantasy being her drinking it, and it remains one of men's favorite fantasies throughout life. The "come shot" is the cherished climax of stag movies, showing men in their glory.

The adolescent boy may not have seen a stag film, but "the circle jerk" may have been part of growing up, leaving him ill-prepared for the girl's repugnance to the suggestion that she might like to put her mouth on his penis. In Hunt's study on sex in 1974, twice the number of young men had masturbated by age thirteen (63 percent) as had young women (33 percent). Since Hunt, various studies on adolescent sexuality have reported a range of figures, which show an increase in masturbation by girls, but what remains constant is that far more boys masturbate than do girls.

"Obviously . . . masturbation is not as reinforcing for women as it is for men," commented the researchers in a 1993 study. "The usual explanation for this sex difference is that women have been socialized more than men to associate sex with romance and relationships and emotional intimacy. To be interested in sex solely for physical gratification is supposedly more taboo for women than for men . . . the recent effort to encourage women to take more responsibility for their own sexuality and the explicit suggestion to masturbate more has not altered this socialization process."

Masturbation plays an interesting role in fairy tales. According to Bettelheim, the tale of "Jack and the Beanstalk" allays the boy's fears that he will suffer terrible punishment if his masturbation is discovered. In another version, "Jack and His Magic Stick," there is the implication that the stick allows him to stand up to his father for the first time, as well as to win the competition with other suitors for the princess; eventually Jack takes possession of the princess when The Stick beats off the wild animals. This is some stick!

All in all, Bettelheim assures us that the various tales of Jack and his stalk or stick make the boy feel better about his erections and masturbation while also teaching him that "after puberty, a boy must find constructive goals and work for them to become a useful member of society," which I suppose means that he shouldn't lie around all day and masturbate.

While Bettelheim reiterates that these fairy tales speak to both girls and boys, I am left to wonder how the girl finds acceptance and permission regarding masturbation in tales of sticks and stalks. Come to think of it, is there any comforting fairy tale for girls on masturbation?

Growing up without a man in the house, I have no memory of early images of penises, hard or soft. I grew to love the feel of one against me when we danced, but I neither pictured it nor gave a thought to what part of my own anatomy was so excited rubbing against it. For years, the penis would remain disassociated in my mind with the rest of the beloved boy, in the sense that until I held one in my hand and became familiar with it in my mouth, it bore no resemblance to the beauty of the rest of his form. Like oysters, the penis would be an acquired taste. What helped this to happen was the realization of the man's gratitude, along with my own sense of power at being able to give a man so much pleasure.

Today, I study Mapplethorpe's amazing photos of penises with unending curiosity; what a work of art is a man! And how tragic that the sexes, designed physically to fit together so beautifully, should psychologically have such a hard time of it. But here is the rub: Aside from anxiety regarding size, men tend to find their own design acceptable and ours divine, whereas we hate the sight of our own and are divided on any given day as to whether or not we like the look of a penis at all.

Alas, sex has never been a chapter in modern feminism. Masturbation, the joys of it as well as the responsibility and self-esteem it teaches, are not an accepted part of growing up in mother's house. Girls still think our sex is something men bestow on us. Since we denigrate our sexual parts and the act of sex itself, it follows that we see men—who are the sexual people—as bad, dirty brutes. No honey-tongued man will ever convince a woman of the beauty of her body as well as she could instruct herself, and we hate them for failing. We look to boys and men to be our good mirrors; when they fail at convincing us that our breasts and cunts are beautiful, we are given all the more reason to remain with the authoritative and altogether negative opinion of other women. As for men, they are all the darker for liking their penises.

June Reinisch, director emerita of the Kinsey Institute, says that when asked what they want in a partner, men's number one answer is "to be loved." "Boys only want one thing" isn't true; it is our projection, and in doing this we disregard everything else the boy desires— closeness, comfort, friendship, love. Already damned, he might as well live up to the image; what does he have to lose?

The girl projects on to the boy everything she would do if she were in his place, if the world did not forbid girls to be sexual self-starters. All of her life she has known that her breasts and her genitals have an innate imperfection. These are the very parts the boy wants to touch. What is she to do? To save herself and avoid the dilemma, she puts herself in his hands; he is both inventor of her bliss and responsible for whatever may come of this union. To him it was sex, to her it was an act of love; she is his. Her refusal to protect herself contraceptively is in keeping with her projection onto him of both the dirtiness of sex and his liability for her.

Perhaps the boy does love her, but he cannot comprehend how

very much girls genuinely confuse love and sex. What does he know of women's love, from which he ran away, so tight were mother's arms? The boy is as unfamiliar with the girl's definition of love as she is with his acceptance and understanding of sex.

Adolescence has taught him that girls control sex. Soon enough he learns that they have the same low regard for his genitals that mother did. This person his own age may love his face, his shoulders, his chest, but she turns away from that part that defines him as male, his penis. Her low opinion puts him on the defensive and makes him angry. He thinks less of his overall self-image, which throws beauty's power even more into women's court.

"High school girls are less comfortable with their sexual experiences than are their male counterparts," announced a nationwide survey in 1994. Is anyone surprised that boys enjoy sex more or that "while 81 percent of the sexually active boys said that 'sex is a pleasurable experience,' only 59 percent of the girls said they felt that way"? We wouldn't be surprised if the same figures turned up in men and women twenty years older. We still don't expect women to enjoy sex as much as men do, giving such reasons as men's insensitivity to women's needs, when the truth is that most women still expect men to make us sexual.

"If the boy really accepts women's opinion that his penis is an ugly, dirty part of his body, then the girl who really loves to make love to him is also not a very nice person and certainly not somebody you would want to marry and have kids with," says Reinisch. "It's very unconscious. It may sow the seeds of the Madonna/Whore idea."

The plight of the adolescent male used to be the stuff of books and plays. The character Marty, for instance, in the classic film that bears his name, was a young man who physically and emotionally felt that he didn't measure up to society's expectations. Eventually he finds his kind of girl, his type. We have all known Martys, who never go out of style. But the hero in Bill Inge's *Picnic*, played in the movie by the young William Holden, is less in vogue these days. Society doesn't respond so eagerly to the irresistible male sexual force embodied in the tough young stranger who hops off a freight train one hot summer day and into the lives of a family in a small town. In the late fifties, when *Picnic* appeared, we didn't automatically associate villain/brute/rapist with an erotically powerful young man.

No woman in this family escapes his musk, from the Old Maid

schoolteacher, to the adolescent girl who understands, in the purest sense, exactly why her lush, beautiful older sister responds to him in a way not aroused by the Nice Young Man who is her steady beau, a fine fellow but lacking heat.

Before the stranger arrived, the lovely sister was just that; but she is not quite alive, not as she will be when the stranger's threatening sexuality ignites her. When it happens, appropriately after she has been crowned the town's beauty queen, we feel his bad lust making her bad too. But we cannot blame her, for Inge's skill makes the audience cheer for her lust; the hero has seduced us all.

Whether or not we recognize it, Inge is telling us that great sex is only made evil by our own convention. Yes, the hero almost destroys the family, the whole town, but he has done nothing, merely appeared, as sex does in our adolescence. We make it ugly, and no one recognizes this more plainly than the adolescent young sister. In a recent interview, Paul Newman mentioned that he was rejected for the lead role in the film *Picnic* because he wasn't "threatening enough."

No one writes plays like *Picnic* nowadays. Young men like Brad Pitt are sexy but don't own the kind of musk that comes packaged with this warning: Danger. Feminism should have split the musk between the sexes, giving women our due share along with men. Instead, it chose to leave sex in men's hands, sex being such an easy foil for evil. Men and women aren't as sexually excited by one another nowadays because we've lost the Satyr, the beautiful male force who is the other half of our sexual beauty. Instead, we raise another generation of foolish girls to wait for a boy's key to reveal them to themselves.

A Farewell to Penis Envy

You don't hear much of penis envy these days. There's a dated ring to it, bittersweet, as in 1940s movies, conjuring up images of men in gray flannel suits bringing home the bacon, protecting women. These were the heydays when just the word *envy* triggered the prefix *penis*.

Personally, I never liked the expression. I was too in love with men, too needy of them, and therefore defended against any envy of their power over me. The mere mention of Freud's name made my lip curl; I looked down on people in analysis, whom I saw as weak characters, squandering time and money. Then I became a writer, never expecting that I was about to meet someone scarier than Freud— Melanie Klein, who would teach me that there was something far more powerful than the penis, namely, the breast.

Long before modern feminism, no one but the strictest Freudians still believed that women wanted to exchange their vaginas for penises; psychiatrist Clara Thompson's famous paper, "Penis Envy in Women," published in 1943, had set the record straight: Penis envy is primarily symbolic in that it demonstrates women's feelings of inadequacy in patriarchal society. "Cultural factors," she wrote, "can explain the tendency of women to feel inferior about their sex and their consequent tendency to envy men . . . so the attitude called penis envy is similar to the attitude of any underprivileged group towards those in power."

Today things look bleak for the endangered penis. Lorena Bobbitt's butchery on her husband isn't precisely what I mean, though it doesn't altogether miss the mark. That Ms. Bobbitt was found not guilty is baffling, though it reverberates with Nice Girl Feminism: "We're Good and They're Bad!" Yes, Bobbitt was an abuser and deserved due punishment; but you just don't slice off a man's penis when he is asleep.

What has really buried the supremacy of the penis is the rise of Breast Envy, growing by leaps and bounds. Opposite the power of the breast, the penis as symbol simply isn't holding up. Breast Envy is big all over town. It was always there, but now it's won celebrity status. Men of old, safe in the knowledge that the penis was king in patriarchal culture, used to ogle, not envy, women's breasts. "I'm a breast man," a guy would say, meaning that he ate nails for breakfast, so secure was he behind the Teutonic defenses of Patriarchy. A man could safely lose himself in pictures of women's breasts and masturbate happily, knowing he was in Marlboro Country. "Envy" a woman's tits? Hell, no.

Today women push men aside to worship at the breast, to gaze rapturously at what has come to mean something more significant to women themselves than to mere men, who couldn't possibly understand the real message of the breast. The role that breasts now play in women's lives has nothing to do with men. Women get hot looking at other women's breasts. In their sexual fantasies they describe in great detail the size, shape, taste of the other woman's breasts; they want to lie on them, *own them*. Just as women buy sperm, they can now buy breasts. Who needs a man?

Naked breasts, breast implants, breast reconstruction, push-up Wonderbras, breast-feeding on park benches . . . there have never been so many breasts and so little milk of human kindness. There was a day when a man could "steal" a feel, nibble on a nipple as The Nice Girl pleaded the required "No, no!", meaning yes. Today she instructs him to suck harder, to knead her breast this way or that, to do it better, faster, like the other woman does it. Men are having the power of the breast thrust in their faces.

In last year's Fantasy Fest here in Key West, the man who used to be my housekeeper yelled to me from across the street, "Hey, Nancy, look at my breasts!" There he was, cross-dressed as a raging tart, with breasts the size of Jayne Mansfield's. But it wasn't just drag queens who stole women's breasts, there were college guys, straight men with pointed conical breasts strapped on their hairy chests, along with "pregnant" men, including one who lay on a table and delivered a live chicken.

As more and more women take their proud, pregnant tummies into offices, where they compete with men for their jobs as well as demand maternity leave and extra benefits, how do men feel? Fairness and justice for women aside, how is the disenfranchised man supposed to react to this display of breasts and pregnancy on the streets, naked on the covers of magazines, advertised as THE fashion statement? Even macho male film stars get in on the act, donning full drag attire plus huge falsies in a movie about three outrageous queens on a cross-country journey, where they win a drag beauty contest and actually look more beautiful than some of the real women in the film. The poor old penis doesn't even have a bit part.

This is what we must remember as we try to understand the adolescent boy's rage at women: Our most intense envy/resentment/rage is directed at the people we love and need the most. If the boy feels that mother/girls' power makes him small and groveling, well, of course he is going to be ambivalent about women; he cannot afford to hate mother, and so his rage/envy of the power of the female body goes out toward girls whose breasts and genitals have become the objects of his adolescent desire.

Young women are no better educated regarding the power of their bodies than are the men who desire them. In patriarchal days we didn't raise either sex to be cognizant of women's power; the penis was all. Now we have a society that bears no name, and we still refuse to acknowledge the influence of women's bodies—breasts, genitals, skin, smell, texture—over all our lives. Today, no one is feeling that power more acutely than the adolescent boy.

Look at the beautiful young women dancing topless at bars like Stringfellows. They massage their enormous breasts, self-absorbed, in love with their own flesh. They get sexually heated running their hands over the fullness of breast, and when they press their rosy peaked nipples between dainty fingertips, little sighs escape. Obviously aware of the hungry stares of the mesmerized men, the women's self-love says, "Yes, I understand why you want these beauties; so do I. Eat your hearts out."

Male habitués of the burlesque parlors of yesteryear have described to me the mutual adoration that used to be parlayed between performer and voyeur; the joints weren't as posh as today's clubs, but the exchange between audience and stage was far warmer: The men were grateful for what the women showed, for letting them feast their eyes, and the naked women let the men see how much they loved being taken in.

We live in the age of denial. Denial is the first defense against envy. Women are accustomed to denial; during our long-standing disenfranchisement, denial was our middle name: "Who me, angry? Who me, beautiful, envious, resentful? Oh, no!" But men are not accustomed to denial; when they feel anger, they act, especially adolescent males who are trying to be men, the long-standing definition of which still remains powerful, strong, and in charge. The young boys watch the neighborhood girls in their Wonderbras parading independently up and down the street, their message as flagrant as the naked women at Stringfellows: We don't need you guys; we can do just fine without you.

The boy takes hunger and rejection in hand and masturbates not only with longing but also with fury. His music gets louder, wilder, the lyrics speak of girls as whores and mouth contempt of women's evil-smelling bodies, and no one has the time to tell the boy what is working on him. Instead, television shows him the emotion-free thug, the man who kills and rapes women without blinking. And he watches the new Bitch heroine in her crotch-high leather skirt who competes with The Terminator in murder. He has nothing left to call his own, not even emotion-free destruction. We look at rising statistics on adolescent male crime, drugs, imprisonment, suicide, and chalk them up to everything but the seemingly soft subject of the power of women's sexual beauty.

I take breasts very seriously. Melanie Klein says that the destructive power of envy begins with the infant at the breast; the infant loves the breast/the infant resents the breast's power. If we don't ameliorate envy's nasty destructiveness so that we arrive at gratitude and love for the mother/breast, then bitter envy remains with us throughout our loveless lives.

We have turned society on its head in the past twenty years; we choose to think our confusion is all about jobs, money, politics, when, in fact, we are hungry for the nurturing that women once embodied. We have all lost our mommies, including we women, which is why so many turn to other women instead of men. Give me a breast to lie on! Of course the penis has been replaced by the breast. Of course women pump up their breasts and stare as hungrily as men at other women. We're all starved. And no one more so than the adolescent boy who hasn't even had a taste, a memory of the good things that we unintentionally lost in the past twenty-five years.

The Look of Anger

Slowly, inexorably, as the onset of puberty grows younger and the average age of marriage older—today almost twenty-five for women and almost twenty-seven for men—adolescence stretches on and on. It could mean more time in which to develop intellectually and socially before the responsibilities of marriage and motherhood. What better period in all of life to grow and experiment? It is hard to navigate adolescence when the look of the adult culture, its beauty ideal, is adolescence itself. Where is the adult? Far from finding something in us to emulate, adolescents resent our intrusion, and rightly so. With no visible boundaries between us, they assume the privileges of adulthood, become sexual too soon, drink and take more drugs than their parents, and carry weapons. We have put them in angry competition with us.

When we accuse our teenagers of acting beyond their years, assuming privileges before they are of age, we should take a look at ourselves overstepping boundaries, backward onto their turf. We are as irresponsible as they—more so. We don't discuss the tragedies of adolescents as our own creations; to admit it would mean how avidly we are against aging, not just getting old, but even becoming middle-aged.

Does anyone feel emptier than an adolescent inheriting our world? What if we were fourteen and all we'd ever known was today's exhibitionism and voyeurism, where everyone is so afraid of being invisible, having nothing inside to fall back on? More than anyone, an adolescent is desperate to be seen. "The parts of the body do not all grow at the same rate or at the same time during puberty," says Laurence Steinberg. "This . . . can lead to an appearance of awkwardness or gawkiness in the young adolescent, who may be embarrassed by the unmatched accelerated growth of different parts of the body."

These are also the years of increased introspection, self-consciousness, and intellectualization. Appearance has always been important to adolescents, but today's teenager also sees an idealized version of a male adolescent as the hero of TV sitcoms, the lead singer/dancer on MTV, and looking very good on the covers of magazines. All eyes are on an idealized version of him, or so it feels.

Men used to call women's wagging finger and accusatory voice "nagging." But it rolled off men's backs then, when they held the power. The nagging wife/mother was the stuff of comic strips, accepted with good humor and dismissed; it made women angry, but women had no voice for rage then. "Aw, Ma," the adolescent boy would complain, dutifully accepting mother's efforts to control him, which is how he had seen his father respond. Having given his mother a hug, the boy would proceed to bend her rules, being careful, like Dad, to keep his "badness" out of her sight.

Somewhere in between "bad" men's control of society and "good" women's efforts to control men, a set of ethical rules was created, a morality and code of manners which were very much a product of this goodness and badness that men and women owned. It was not a healthy system, but it worked for a long time.

Today, women are as "bad" as men, but we retain our right to blame men for all the wickedness in the world, part of which is our own, but even that is explained away as being "men's fault." No man feels this more harshly than the adolescent boy, still very close to the feel of mother's power, compounded by the demands of adolescent girls. The young man feels women's anger spewed onto him and seeks cover. How should he look, what should he wear to protect himself from the fallout from females who already own so much but nonetheless want his balls, blame him for not giving them his job, for not providing the kind of love girls want, for not taking their verbal abuse, for not, in sum, rolling over and letting girls control him?

Males commit many crimes and the statistics escalate, yet no one asks why our men, increasingly young men, act this way. It is verboten to suggest that feminism's afterbirth has left any havoc in its trail.

Every revolution, even our glorious women's movement, leaves a mess in its wake, but the Victim Feminists want no responsibility. Women's traditional privilege of blaming men is still in place. Maybe a grown man can roll over, but the adolescent boy is vulnerable; there is one grim thing he can do when the pressure gets too tough: Between 1960 and 1992, suicide rates for white males 15 to 19 increased by 212 percent compared to the female rate, which increased by 131 percent.

As we go about our business of making money, marrying, divorcing, buying more clothes, more "things" to cover our emptiness, do we think our children don't take this in? When home, community, society have no rules but are instead places where every bargain has been broken, beginning with that between once-married parents, what should adolescents hold on to? Adult rules are suspect if they cannot even support those who invent them. There is no basic tenet between grown men and women that holds, and no conscience, private or public. The one constancy that society offers that seems to bear fruit for young people today is the promise of power in beauty. What future is there for an adolescent when all the likenesses on billboards and magazine covers are of sixteen-year-olds, the adolescent's own age? Why grow up when your image, tarted up to inspire envy between grown-ups, is the cult image?

Adolescent boys as well as girls are aware of the outrageous incomes of the runway models. There it is in black-and-white and Technicolor: It is wonderful to be a beautiful woman and be rich too. Men much older and more powerful than the teenage boy squire beautiful young girls, taking in warmth from their reflection. The boy cannot help but look at his lovely female peers, but he must camouflage desire, for they are more powerful than ever today. The boy is reacting to the genetic, erotic pull toward lovely girls while trying very hard, as did his father, to appear cool.

Because feminism refuses to acknowledge the power of female beauty, to understand how the dark as well as the bright side works on us, we leave our adolescent children at a terrible disadvantage, both sexes tyrannized by beauty. Yes, we expect a preoccupation with looks, but today we have elevated beauty as the power that rules us all. It is bad enough to be middle-aged and motivated by beauty's mysterious force, but it is untenable when you are fourteen, eighteen, and more motivated by external appearance than by any moral structure.

What does "Be a Man" mean? The boy must learn to appear in control, to hide emotion. Young men invent a fad, a way to dress, which others quickly copy. Thirty years ago, they let their hair grow, demanded the Beatle Look even as their fathers winced. There were numerous cartoons of dads and sons going through this ritual at the barber's. But today's look is not cute; the adolescent boy is desperate for a look that can stand up to girls' power over him. Not just clothes, but behavior, a stance, a certain kind of walk and facial expression are required to hide the anxiety within. Perhaps he is not yet aware of Political Correctness, but its disdain of him has trickled down. He learns to wear a false face.

As physiologist Paul Ekman notes, when a person is wearing such a mask he will sometimes betray his feelings in an expression that lasts a fraction of a second; sometimes, if a true expression begins to leak out, the person will squelch it. Using antagonistic muscles to cover a truthful expression—forcing lips together to hide a smile of pleasure is an example of "Masking."

Last night, I thought of Ekman's masking research while leafing through a copy of an Italian *Men's Vogue*; there were maybe eight full-page shots of adolescent boys, most in underwear, posing nearly nude for a photographer who sometimes caught the "mask" of their seemingly cool faces. Other times, what leaked through was the sweetness and vulnerability of a boy obviously aware of his genitals on display. These pages were photographed by Steven Meisel, who also shot Calvin Klein's campaign of nearly nude adolescents wearing his fabled underwear.

What are Klein and Meisel pretending to do? Show us Boy Toys, Pinups, and if so, are they for the voyeuristic pleasure of other males, as it would seem they are? I can't help but wonder about the impact of these suggestive photos both on the young models and on us voyeurs who don't know quite how to take them.

There is another predicament a sexually unsure young man must face, which is how to respond to the new lesbian chic on college campuses. I've mentioned this before, but in the context of the adolescent boy, it very much warrants amplification. The New Lesbianism, on and off campus, is not so much a product of Gay Liberation but of Matriarchal Feminism; women's new economic freedom allows young women to be able to choose another female as sexual partner rather than look for a husband. The New Economics has written the New Lesbian Chic.

Across the country, feminist teachers in classrooms occupied by males and females often paint the world in shades of Them and Us, meaning "Them" as the Bad Men, the rapists/harassers/enemies of "Us," the good, virtuous women. In many classrooms, anything created by dead, white, male intellectuals is rejected. One feminist teacher even demanded that a reproduction of Ingres's nude be removed from the wall.

I can see where the grown man might mistake the Lesbian Chic for a real-life enactment of his own erotic dreams. It is one of men's most popular, has always been a dream come true when a man could persuade two women into his bed. But some of today's daughters of modern feminism are quite different in their turning to one another; certainly the men their own age don't always look upon female-to-female kissing, oral sex, living together, as just another turn-on. These women don't need men, not at all, a message that puts a young man's sexuality, as well as his future, into question.

After graduation, many of these college lesbians fully expect to enter into heterosexual relationships; their earlier sexual affairs with women are irrelevant. It is an option not available to young men: Two women lie down together and the world shrugs, but when a man even thinks of sex with another man, well, he labels himself harshly. A man is either straight or gay, but for a woman, the world is our oyster.

Male homosexuals prize the act of sex. Once made, it is a decision not easily reversed, at least not in the man's mind. But the lesbian sorority can be a sisterly choice that isn't life-defining so much as it is an inclination to stay where the young woman has always been, close to women.

Once upon a time, the male adolescent saw the female breast as his goal, the shape and texture of which was so appealing he could not help but look, desire, admire. He didn't tie his fascination into nursery dependency, but saw the breast of the adolescent girl as whole and new. Today, The Power Bosom, clothed in the Wonderbra, is not flashed at him but at other girls. Young women, much more consciously than their mothers, look to other women's eyes for approval and desire too.

Is the boy then in competition with other men or with other women for that beautiful breast across the room? Should the boy live out his father's favorite fantasy of two women having sex, how does he fit into this complete couple, who don't even look at him, see no beauty in him, whereas he, being heterosexual, yearns desperately for female beauty, for their eyes to reflect him to himself.

The so-called Lesbians Until Graduation—or LUGs, as they are known—may come and go, but the sorority of women with women grows steadily, leaving men to wait, and wonder, it being unmanly to protest women's sexual affection for one another. When an article on college lesbians recently appeared on the front page of the second section of the *Wall Street Journal*, not one man I know brought it up. "Look, the way I figure it," one LUG commented in this piece, "today everything is so tough with trying to find jobs and being as successful as your parents—to let love pass by because of something like labels of someone's sex just seems really stupid."

Sexual selection is stupid? In another newspaper that day, there is an article on a gay man being hounded out of the military. Young men read these articles and know full well that their own futures in the workplace might be in jeopardy if they acted like the woman quoted above. But the women in the *Journal* article give their real names and likenesses, and tomorrow they have the privilege of returning to heterosexual life and a man who will think no less of them as a woman. What a privilege! I wouldn't take it away from them, but what of men's rights? What of an adolescent boy who grows up in the heat of woman power and sees his elders shrugging off the privileges of LUGs, a sexual selection that would have very different implications for him?

In his book, *The Father Factor*, Henry Biller writes, "Your son's relationship with girls . . . will be based on the quality of his masculinity, which you have influenced by the example you set with your wife and with other women. . . . Your son will also learn from observing how you react to the sexual attractiveness of women. . . . Boys who do not have a strong relationship with their fathers or who suffer from father absence or neglect . . . may have problems relating to girls and women. Without a solid gender identity, they are less likely to feel secure with females." Given that nearly two of every five children in America do not live with their fathers, "the absence of fathers is linked to most social nightmares—from boys with guns to girls with babies."

"We wonder where the violence, shoplifting, stealing, and mugging among adolescent boys is coming from," says Jeanne Murrone, a clinical psychologist who treats adolescents. "Our culture breeds a sense of entitlement. When a teenage boy puts on television, what he sees advertised is a pair of $120 Adidas sneakers. He can't afford $120 shoes, but to be accepted, he can't wear Fayva's $20 shoes. 'I have to get the Adidas $120 shoes,' he thinks. 'I'm entitled to those shoes, to that down jacket. I'll get a gun and put it in somebody's face and take them off his feet.'" Today's adolescents would laugh at Rousseau's vision of them "struggling with moral tensions." How are they to understand morality and idealism when there are no mature, rational, respected adults?

A study released by the Centers for Disease Control and Prevention states that the annual rate at which fifteen- to nineteen-year-old men were being murdered soared 154 percent from 1985 to 1991. We are quick to blame drugs for what goes wrong in our society, tracing the evil back to the seventies. In fact, the evil is in us, and whether our emptiness began in post–World War II consumerism, in the fifties with McCarthy, or in the sixties and seventies with Vietnam, or whether we choose to blame it on the greed that crescendoed in the eighties, the fact is that we have lost our best selves. Rather than confront the horror of our emptiness we dress ourselves in fancy wrappings and scuttle out of our once perfect Eden.

Was it around the time of Watergate that integrity and kindness began to disappear, along with shame and guilt? In my memory it was the early eighties, and I was at breakfast with the *Miami Herald* and yet another front-page story on yet another high government official, another captain of industry who had cheated, stolen, lied; nowhere in these articles was their resignation mentioned. By the end of the decade, I and everyone else had ceased to be dismayed that neither thieves, liars, cheats—national figures all—apologized nor removed themselves from office out of shame. Nor did the public seem to expect them to. We'd gotten used to The Empty Package.

Nowadays it is an anonymous man/child on the front page, killing himself or someone else without regret. When the highest leaders of the country break the moral code and community leaders cheat, lie, and steal, there is nothing left inside the gutless culture. We have become terrified of our own emptiness; how are we to judge ourselves and one another when the invisible traits that once identified a person no longer exist? Look to what is on the outside of the package, the wrappings. Dress it up! Hollow and frightened, we walk the streets, catching eyes, drawing sight lines, demanding attention. "Look at me, God damn it, or I'll kill you!"

"I Am the Father That Your Boyhood Lacked"

The above line is spoken by Odysseus to his son, Telemachus, after twenty years of separation. How simple the words, like an inscription on a tombstone, as if there were not space or possibility to capture in a greeting all that twenty long years had comprised. I found the quote in a faded newspaper clipping from 1984, in which the poet Stanley Kunitz remarked that the Oedipus myth "holds less meaning in 20th-century America than the myth of reconciliation represented by the meeting of Odysseus and his son. . . . 'And even when physically present they [the fathers] are spiritually absent. . . . The father is as lost in life as he is in the Army, the factory, the marketplace.'" In his own poem written fifty years earlier, Kunitz wrote, "'Father,' I cried, 'return. You know the way.'"

What does the young boy today do, growing up without a desirable male image that can stand up to the powerful look and feel of women? Where can he focus on an admirable man whom he would like to emulate, one who would make him feel he had arrived at adulthood among his male peers but who would also be attractive to girls? A year ago, "Take Back the Night" demonstrations on college campuses were all the rage. A headline on an Ellen Goodman column read, "Safety for Women? Try Removing Men."

Is it surprising that boys copy the look of Trent Reznor of Nine Inch Nails, whose second album shot to number two in 1994? His jet-black hair, black clothing, and pasty-white skin may not be precisely mimicked, but his attitude, along with the lyrics of his music, speaks for his generation; he sings of madness, suicide, the pointlessness of life and the reality of pain, and the crowd goes crazy; inside and out, he mirrors what they feel.

In this age of adolescence, we have created our own poor Frankenstein, who lumbers about dangerously, terrifying the populace with his gaudy, noisy appearance, all the while looking for the daddy who created him. Mary Shelley's Frankenstein was inherently good, capable of great intelligence, but so desperate for love and so doomed by his appearance to ever find it that the poor creature struck out furiously at all around him. His father had left him. Shelley created her monster out of the political, social, and economic turmoil at the last turn of the century, a classic Romantic hero who resorted to violence only as a last resort because of the treatment he'd received from fellow living beings.

When a boy grows up without a father, not even a memory of him, an inkling of who might have loved him, maybe chosen him to be his favorite child, it shapes his whole life. With all the love in the world showered on him, how to comprehend his mother's decision to leave men out of her life and his? Since he is also male, is there a hidden rage in mother's heart at him too? What is so awful about people of his sex? He can't grow up to be like mother, a woman. Who is he to be?

Yes, bad men abandon their children and walk out on child support. They are morally wrong and I join in the public outcry for their punishment. But I also fault those women who intentionally deprive a child of a father from conception. It is a selfish act. So far, men have reacted to this exclusion with relative silence; but it has to have influenced the recent years of male brutality, as much against themselves as against women. If we don't need men in the human race, well, they might as well act as if they were superfluous.

When fatherless brute-boys meet fatherless young girls, says psychiatrist Frank Pittman, "girls are likely to choose boyfriends who are violent and highly seductive."

Robert Bly, in his bestselling *Iron John*, looks at the increasing power of women as requiring grown men to aid the younger generation in ceremonial gatherings separate from women, where they can "bond" and assume their lost masculinity. "It seems to me that Bly has framed his cure the wrong way round," comments educator/author Marina Warner, continuing, "The monsters of machismo are created in societies where men and women are already too far separated by sexual fear and loathing, segregated by contempt for the prescribed domestic realm of the female, and above all by exaggerated insistence on aggression as the defining characteristic of heroism and power. . . . The presence of fathers will only reduce the threatening character of maleness flourishing around us if sexual polarities are lessened, not increased." In any case, what is clear is that boys need more time with men.

Today's adolescent boys grow up learning what it is to be male from films, television, comic books, video games, and the new modern myths and/or fairy tales. What is the look of the male hero? "Fear of men has grown alongside belief that aggression—including sexual violence—inevitably defines the character of the young male," adds Warner. Gone is the witch, the traditional scary intruder. Instead, she says, there is a "new fascination and unease surrounding men. . . . Boys are not raised to be cozeners or tricksters [as in old myths and fairy tales]—it'd be unthinkable to train the future man in lures and wiles and masks and tricks; they're brought up to play with Action Man, and his heavy-duty, futuristic Star Wars arsenal; they're taught to identify with Ninja Turtles, as crusaders, vigilantes, warriors . . . the Terminator, Robocop. . . . I'm not advancing the con man over the soldier, or the cozener over the honest gentleman—that would be absurd; I'm observing a trend toward defining male identity and gender through visible, physical, sexualised signs of potency rather than verbal, mental agility."

Studies tell us that close to three quarters of young criminals in state reform institutions come from fatherless homes; such young people are also more likely to drop out of high school. In a sad way, the better a single mother is at doing everything a man can do, the more the boy is left to wonder why women need a man at all. In contrast, there are positive findings that fathers involved in their sons' early lives get as much from the relationship as the boys. The Glueck study, for example, tracked 240 Boston fathers and their children for four decades. It determined that not only do fathers who participate in their sons' development produce higher verbal and social skills in their boys, but that the fathers too are rewarded with greater career advancement, marital stability, and happiness in middle age.

What if there was a noncompetitive father who had been with his son from the beginning, had held and bathed him, had shared the love of him so that the boy felt himself seen and adored by both a man and a woman? And what if separation from them had not been fraught with the desperation boys feel, when there is just a woman representing all love and intimacy, making these emotions something he must renounce in order to be male?

Wouldn't there be less need for the boy to overemphasize his difference from women/mother, the person who held, fed, bathed, and gave him the only safe haven he has known? Her power was extraordinary, and now he, only age eight or nine, must turn away from her to be opposite, to pretend he has power when it feels as if she still has it all.

It is a Herculean task for a boy, something he can only seem to accomplish over the years with braggadocio, a show of might and muscle. How different it might be if a man had shown his son from day one that a man can be tender and loving as well as strong. If there were identification with father from the start, and an effort on the older man's part to temper competition, wouldn't adolescence and the years just prior be less intensely colored by the condemnation of all things female?

In adolescence, perhaps the boy would not fear the desire for intimacy, but instead, like the girl, he would feel he had come full circle, back to something long ago for which he'd once had a talent: love. He would understand what the girl wanted and not be afraid to gaze at her in that personal, intimate way she desires. He would enjoy losing himself in her beauty instead of needing the safe distance offered by objectified photographs of women in *Playboy*. No one, in my opinion, but a father can raise a boy to be this kind of man.

Until their teens, "boys and girls express emotions equally," psychologist Warren Farrell points out. "It is adolescence that ... pressures American boys ... to withdraw emotionally." The beautiful girl becomes what Farrell calls "a genetic celebrity." Boys compete for her attention as if she were a star and the "genetic celebrity becomes entitlement dependent. As difficult as this is for girls, I believe that something is happening to boys during this time," says Farrell, "that makes suicide a greater possibility."

Males as villains seem to be the only viable models around these days. Given the almost total lack of women in the imaginary world of the video games and films that occupy preadolescent boys, the male's sense of apartness, of alienation, ill prepares him for the spectacle of adolescent girls. With all the desire and ambition in the world, how can he measure up to the hero she has in mind? An adolescent learns from watching his parents' marriage. When his father looks at his mother, how does that exchange work, how does it seem that his mother fills his father's eyes?

When today's father was growing up, there was not so much power in the adolescent girls' camp; physical beauty wasn't so openly parlayed the coinage it is today. How then does father assist his son in this new power exchange? According to the Glueck study, "Fathers who provided high levels of intellectual-academic support during both childhood and adolescence, as well as high levels of social-emotional support during childhood, had sons who achieved greater educational mobility."

Paternal support in this study was measured in three critical domains—social/emotional, physical/athletic, and intellectual/academic—and it was found that it is impossible for fathers to be overinvolved with their boys.

What happens when feelings of competition arise? Yes, we expect athletic and intellectual success to stir envy in the older man, but what of the son's sexual success, his superior physical development, which draws the eyes of women of all ages to him? Especially today, when a man of any age would have to be blind not to recognize the new ascendancy of male beauty.

If the New Fatherhood continues, and a father's involvement in his son's life accelerates, we will hear more of the paternal envy of a son's physical attractiveness and sexual success, given how rapidly males of all ages are moving into the mirror. Competition over beauty between father and son—now there is a new version in the tired old debate between mother and daughter.

Why do men not write more of the adolescent boy's dreams? Perhaps it is too unmasculine to dredge up these memories, which must also be filled with anger at the sacrifices made along the way. Maybe men don't want to make youth any easier for their sons. In *Winesburg, Ohio*, novelist Sherwood Anderson wrote a wonderful description of George Willard, a male adolescent on the brink of life, saying farewell to childhood after his mother's death:

There is a time in the life of every boy when he for the first time takes the backward view of life. Perhaps that is the moment when he crosses the line into manhood. The boy is walking through the street of his town. He is thinking of the future and of the figure he will cut in the world. Ambitions and regrets awake within him. Suddenly something happens; he stops under a tree and waits as for a voice calling his name. Ghosts of old things creep into his consciousness; the voices outside of himself whisper a message concerning the limitations of life. From being quite sure of himself and his future he becomes not at all sure. If he be an imaginative boy a door is torn open and for the first time he looks out upon the world, seeing, as though they marched in procession before him, the countless figures of men who before his time have come out of nothingness into the world, lived their lives and again disappeared into nothingness. The sadness of sophistication has come to the boy. With a little gasp he sees himself as merely a leaf blown by the wind through the streets of his village. He knows that in spite of all the stout talk of his fellows he must live and die in uncertainty, a thing blown by the winds, a thing destined like corn to wilt in the sun. He shivers and looks eagerly about. The eighteen years he has lived seem but a moment, a breathing space in the long march of humanity. Already he hears death calling. With all his heart he wants to come close to some other human, touch someone with his hands, be touched by the hand of another. If he prefers that the other be a woman, that is because he believes that a woman will be gentle, that she will understand. He wants, most of all, understanding.

Basic trust, optimism. I carried it with me when I left Charleston for college, as did the boys I met there. We had that look. Yes, we had George's sense of loss, but it was offset by our expectations that we would meet our mate, who would also be our match. It is harder for today's adolescents to feel that optimism. Their parents' faces reveal the hopelessness that permeates much of society, and they are told to brace themselves for a lower living standard—something no other generation of Americans has ever anticipated. As for finding understanding in the opposite sex, it takes extraordinary optimism to rise above the alienation between the sexes that is so pervasive on today's campuses.

Psychiatrist Peter Blos, who quotes Anderson at length, himself writes that in the farewell to adolescence, the boy/man feels "the limitless future of childhood [shrinking] to realistic proportions, to one of limited chances and goals; but, by the same token, the mastery of time and space and the conquest of helplessness afford a hitherto unknown promise of self-realization. This is the human condition of adolescence which the poet has laid bare."

6

Feminism and Beauty

===

"The Girls in Their Summer Dresses"

Being a single woman in the sixties was a gift of time and place. To live through the sexual awakening that came with reliable contraception and the independence it offered, especially in an era when men and women seemed to coexist happily, well, if you'd been there, it might help you to make sense of our difficult present. For me, those years are the bedrock against which everything subsequent is referred. If you became sexually active in the sixties, you probably grew up in the fifties and experienced the birth of the current War Between the Men and the Women in the old regime.

It all happened in a decade, less, for until Jack Kennedy died in 1963, taking with him the promise of a new world, we didn't realize how much we'd counted on him to carry us to the climax to which we'd been steadily marching since the end of World War II. And so the dead father's broken promise further embittered all those other revolutions: the Civil Rights Movement, the uprising against the war in Vietnam, the Feminist Movement, the hippie counterculture, the drugs, all of it.

I am not saying that Kennedy was the cause of our bitterness but that we grieve for ourselves even now when we see his picture. He stood for the best of the past brought to fruition in him; he was the promise of the future. If you were not there when it happened, when it was A Happening, as we called Big Moments in those days, it must be hell trying to figure out What It All Means. Even with the pieces of the puzzle, it is hard to comprehend because it is so sad, not just his death but the unfulfilled promise to grow beyond what we had been.

Kennedy, the adolescent hero, was the dream of every young girl and the way boys longed to look. In him we saw our selves as we might have grown into maturity, having reached that higher moral level of which Rousseau wrote, if only JFK hadn't abandoned us. We'll never know about that, of course, but the rage since his death is that of inconsolable adolescent orphans who remain furious at father for walking out.

Since the end of World War II we have been the richest country in the world, but the rest of the world—they, so much older than we, so much more jaded, having been around for so many centuries, been invaded so many times, been betrayed and repeatedly sold out to foster parents/countries—looks at us and wonders why, like spoiled, rich children, we have squandered our inheritance. Well, we lost our daddy; with Kennedy we lost our image of ourselves.

Prior to the Revolutions of the sixties and seventies, just before the world changed, I had come to live in upper Manhattan, where everything looked pretty much as it had for generations. The grown-ups in those fine old families with whom I dined on Sundays resembled their parents who, in turn, resembled theirs. Only the fashions in the photos on the polished sofa tables changed. For a few moments I belonged to that world still seamless with the fifties, and for this I am grateful, for it remains my point of reference to this day for everything that followed.

I had been raised in a world of sameness, in which everyone had good teeth, a certain income, and education instantly recognizable by their Episcopalian niceness, good hair, affable expressions. Manners were important, very important; I think I miss them more than anything. But women were the custodians of manners, and when eventually we began snapping at polite men who held doors and chairs for us, they began to stare more fixedly at us in that way we say we hate. "Very well, if you tell me in that rude voice not to hold your chair, bitch, I'll look at you any damn way I wish!" This is not to say that women are responsible for our mannerless world, simply that revolutions have their spin-offs.

New York in the early sixties still had an innocent look, as did the girls on the Upper East Side, where I shared an apartment with two other virgins. There were three twin beds in the room where we slept, one clothes closet, and a telephone answering service that recognized the voices of the men to whom we didn't want to speak. Gristede's left our groceries on the back landing, and the doorman's presence assured our parents that no harm would come to us. There was less traffic, less noise, less garbage, and the white glove counter at Bonwit Teller did a brisk business. Not a picture some feminists or politically corrects would smile upon, but it did last a long time and many enjoyed it.

My roommates and I were in a constant state of romantic love, and though the objects of our affections changed regularly until we had each in our turn lost our virginity, no one had a diaphragm. That one of us would get pregnant was inevitable. Maybe innocent isn't the right word to describe us, but "stupid" is too harsh a word for my beautiful roommate, with whom I walked to the corner of Second Avenue one Saturday morning and with whom I wept as she drove off to an abortion that would leave her bleeding and in excruciating pain for days. Soon after, she married.

I was careful whom I slept with. I appreciated how profoundly a man who had been a friend would become an addiction after sex: As powerful as I felt working my magic on a man standing up, I became enslaved once supine; it was my mouth, my body, my cunt that gripped and drained him, but he would rise, postorgasm, rejuvenated, would do a better day's work, while I would lie mesmerized, unable to function until he telephoned or, better yet, returned to give me another fix. I knew my addiction to romantic music was partly self-induced, that the perilous sense of mortality I felt had nothing to do with the individual man, who merely turned the key into my secret garden, but for me, as for all addicts, intellectual understanding didn't lessen the craving.

We girls in the East Fifties and Sixties were different heights and weights, but there was a practiced, interchangeable look among us that I would say in hindsight was our way of avoiding competition. Nothing accomplished this so readily as the way we dressed; no one stood out in an exhibitionistic way so as to catch men's eyes. Men were the goal for which we'd been raised, but landing one had to be accomplished without seeming to try too hard. Earning money, being so competitive and time-consuming, meant the last thing a man needed was an exhibitionistic, seductive woman. Yes, he wanted a beauty, all the better to signify his economic success, but once married, he wanted her siren song turned matronly; a working man had no time for jealous suspicions.

When they were away from home, traditional men knew they didn't have to worry about their women wandering. Women policed one another, making sure no one got more of the pie than her share; envy of a sister's sexual appetite would have made the Patriarchal Deal unbearable for all the others. Pre-Sexual Revolution, the world was distinctly divided into Good Girls and Bad, and nothing drew the line more obviously than a sexual look that Hollywood had down pat. There was Doris Day and there was Marilyn Monroe. In those days, a girl's clothes, makeup, hair, shoes, and certainly the way she cast her gaze—never too directly at a man—said everything.

Nothing captured this moment in time like the snowy day Jack Kennedy was sworn into office, that march with pretty Jackie in her pillbox hat up Pennsylvania Avenue that climaxed the American Dream. All previous historical lines converged here, the look of how we wanted to think of ourselves inside and out, our Camelot. They were both so beautiful, so clean-cut, she with her little voice that allowed his words to embrace our highest ideals. This was what a woman did: "Take care of my husband, the President." That he was an adulterer, that there was a long history within the Kennedy family of crime that seems, still, to have no end, didn't and doesn't matter. In preserving them, the look of them, somehow we preserve ourselves, the promise.

When Jackie died in 1994, we huddled together nationally—no, internationally, as when her husband died and the world mourned; once again we stared at the old photos with nostalgic grief, yes, but also to see if they might tell us who we had become. We resonate to their look, because it is how we once wanted to be, a look that said who we were inside. Where did it go, the feeling of being good people? Never mind that it was often a sham, we want it back, the look and the feel.

When I tried to recapture my impression of life on Fifth Avenue in the earliest sixties, what swam up from memory was the title of Irwin Shaw's short story "The Girls in Their Summer Dresses." The words evoke how I imagined life had always been in New York, the seamless change of years as summer followed spring and men got out their seersucker Brooks Brothers suits to stroll with pretty bare-armed girls in pastel dresses. Actually, Shaw's story was published in 1939, not in the sixties as I had thought, and it took place in Greenwich Village, not Midtown. Well, that's memory for you. However, I never mistake the precise time when we girls threw away our underwear and shortened our skirts to the crotch, when the look and feel of Nice Girls changed to New Women, when we began paying our own way and initiating sex.

Whatever went wrong back then, we'll never get it right until we assimilate the past with which we are so absorbed, and consciously decide if there aren't some things—politically incorrect as they might seem—we'd like to have back. You and I, with our intellectual dogmas, can do without, but when my editor tells me that her ten- and eleven-year-old sons can't get enough of the reruns of *The Adventures of Ozzie & Harriet* and *The Dick Van Dyke Show*, we should listen. When children today stare hypnotically into a screen, watching the same thing again and again, they are hungry to understand, "What does it all mean?"

The past is with us as never before, and no one feels the itch for the old more than the young, who never knew a society of lavender-scented grandmotherly bosoms. They should be wanting something absolutely different from the past world, but they can't move on until they get our mess straight. They know this better than we who threw out the invisible things they are looking for, like courtesy and patience. Teenagers put on the fashions we wore thirty years ago, reinvented by grown-up designers who don't question why they imitate instead of create. Children inherit the black holes we forgot to replace because there is nothing with which you can replace ethics.

Today's mail brings the latest *W*, the fashion bible, in which Cary Grant, Kim Novak, Grace Kelly, and Sophia Loren are featured in a section titled "Before the Brat Pack, before the Jet Set, there were the Beautiful People . . . in the Fifties." "They look so chaste and old-fashioned," says my husband. But we stare at them as if for a message. A few pages on is the latest fashion statement, The Slip. Not a dress that looks like a slip, but a slip like women used to wear in the fifties and early sixties. Only this one is sheerer, though it is intended as outerwear. Sophia and Grace probably had one on *under* their outerwear. This is not prurient criticism. What strikes me is the look of past and present: Somewhere in time they meet, today's emaciated teen model in her insubstantial slip and the fleshed-out movie stars of the fifties/sixties who look strangely younger.

Jax Pants and the Twist

I'd arrived in New York looking and dressing pretty much as I had throughout college, where my luck had changed. I was seen differently in the North. Perhaps it was that the men were taller, or were looking for someone with a quality I possessed that was as yet unknown to me. I've never understood why, at our first college mixer with Harvard men, the handsomest fellow in the room cut a path through the crowd to me. There I stood, smiling that phony smile I'd learned to replace the natural grin, expecting the worst. He was a hero, a star athlete, and I became his maiden, wore his enormous maroon crew sweater with the big "H."

To my surprise, I was light-years ahead of him in the sexual dance, meaning prolonged hours of kissing and fondling, and was also used to fending off the Southern boys raised to go as far as they could with a girl. This prince, however, had been raised in a cold climate, and strangely enough, it was disappointing to find myself more heated than the man. It was as though we danced to a different beat. Though he begged for marriage by our second year together, I had lost interest. I'd found that there was more to a man than a pretty face.

In him I discovered I had the power to attract men. Perhaps I also learned from what he lacked, that I should/could display my own preference. In any case, I began to look for sheaths rather than full skirts. I would have blushed had you said that I wanted to be noticed, for it wasn't thought out; only in hindsight do I recognize where my life as an exhibitionist began. Virgin that I was, and would remain for several years, I nonetheless wanted to wear my true colors.

The girls I knew in New York had inherited our mothers' philosophy on dress; we all wore Nice Girl clothes and sensible shoes that quietly signaled one's station in life. There was a respect for "good clothes" that one was expected to wear for at least a few years; winter wardrobes were stored with the dry cleaner and brought out the following year with an addition or two. That was how I had grown up. When a box arrived from my great aunt Mildred containing elegant dresses and suits from Hattie Carnegie that were barely worn and beautifully kept, my mother was thrilled. Dior's famous New Look may have made international news in 1951, but the vast majority of Charleston women in "our class" dressed sensibly.

When I got my first paychecks I wandered through Saks and Bergdorf Goodman looking for something that was Me, but when the polite saleswoman approached, I had no words to describe what I wanted, who Me was. Then I discovered Jax, just off Fifth Avenue on Fifty-seventh Street. Jax explained why the Nice Girl dresses at Bergdorf's didn't satisfy. So unschooled was I in fashion that I had never studied my body, never appreciated what I had until I saw myself in the mirror in Jax pants. Something awoke, a slumbering realization that I too had the power to draw people's eyes to me in that way I'd seen other girls being taken in, visually adored. It was exhilarating.

In their not so small way just minutes before Pucci, Courrèges, and the miniskirt, Jax pants signaled the Sexual Revolution brewing at sea. Those amazing lengths of wool jersey and checked gingham were cut narrow, straight, stitched in such a way as to make a well-turned ass and long legs irresistible. I've known women who say their lives began in Jax pants; I would number myself among them.

What bliss to twist at the Peppermint Lounge in Jax pants, a mix of music, sex, and a look that came together by design. To twist in sensible clothes would have been self-defeating. Not everyone who grows up feeling invisible, losing early battles within the family to more beautiful others, automatically turns into an exhibitionist, but that there are so many of us today, male and female, parading in search of latent voyeurs who will see us, pick us up, and love us, is not surprising. As single-parent families have multiplied, so have short, tight, transparent fashions.

My lovers in the early sixties were as distant as I could get from the Nice Boys with whom I'd gone to college. Was my choice of men of whom mother wouldn't have approved in retaliation to her refusal to recognize me, even to see me? Perhaps. Or was I following in my admirable Aunt Pat's path, seeking the company of architects, painters, actors, and musicians? Perhaps. But unlike my aunt and mother, I wasn't looking for marriage, and the possibility of motherhood was so distant as to be unimaginable. Marriage, motherhood, meant stopping. Life was just beginning.

To me New York seemed a woman's town. On the arms of different men a girl could move nightly from uptown to downtown to crosstown; men, on the other hand, seemed confined and defined by their individual milieus, where their circle of friends seldom changed, a group pretty much determined by their work. To my eyes, men were like the desmoiselles of Amsterdam, each offering his unique specialty in his unique milieu; men were happiest with their own sort, and each group—Wall Street, advertising, music, art—had its own appeal, publicized by the speech, dress code, and professional expertise in that particular world. Socially speaking, men seldom left their communities; Greenwich Village types didn't turn up at Upper East Side parties, nor did Wall Streeters frequent the West Side lofts of filmmakers.

But a woman, ah! On any given night she could accompany a man into a world where she had never been, where she would meet people who led totally different lives than she had ever known, who would bring up topics never before discussed and, most of all, who would see her in a way that she had never been seen before.

I was an anomaly, a nice girl from a nice family tripped by adolescence into a state of semi-retardation; like Humpty Dumpty I was trying to get back on my wall. Men helped me. Men were my postgraduate course in areas of living and study I never knew existed, and they were patient teachers to a good listener. Especially the men I met on the West Side and downtown, who didn't look like the Harvard and Yale men from my past. They had a reckless way about them, as though they had dressed in the dark and didn't own a mirror, by which I mean there wasn't a Brooks Brothers suit in sight, but their eyes looked at you without apology, taking you in like a good meal. There was no masking of emotion on these faces.

The most interesting were Jewish. They expected you to have opinions, and listened as you formed thoughts never before expressed, no one having ever asked. Their laughter was loud and spontaneous, and the eagerness with which they argued, the volume at which they laughed, all told me that I was wise and lucky not to have married after graduation like all the Nice Girls on the Upper East Side. I had been formally educated in fine schools, but in the eyes of these people I was uneducated, and I wanted to learn, explore their worlds, become like them, relaxed, easy, assertive, and self-supporting. Much more than other women, these men were my role models.

On the back of my lover's Honda I wore my Jax pants below Fourteenth Street, once the significant line of demarcation above which many prided themselves on never going, so boring, so life-inhibiting was the uptown scene considered. The formidable women who held court downtown referred to me—not quite out of my hearing—as an "uptown chick," meaning that I was overdressed. These women made a religion out of not dressing, which was, of course, a fashion statement in itself. They were five minutes ahead of The Sexual Revolution, deeply into Norman O. Brown and Timothy Leary, and their parties took place under an omnipresent cloud of marijuana. The drugs in the bedroom were the first mescaline and psilocybin I encountered. If I drew the line at group sex, it was more out of the terror of losing my beloved to another woman, or man, than morality.

What gave me courage and allowed me to stand my ground in that mysterious world were my newfound looks. Intelligence, wit, social graces had been mine, but I had grown up watching eyes pass over me and arms reach out to the beauty standing next to me. When my looks arrived, it no longer mattered a bit whether I was right or wrong about the past. Because I radiated belief in my new sexual self, this is what others saw. "What's it like to be you, pretty girl?" a woman whose sculptures hung in galleries asked me one night. Another woman had never called me "pretty." Confident in my Jax pants, I felt equal to these amazing people on West Thirteenth Street, pioneers in the various revolutions about to happen. I bloomed. The more confidence I gained, the more sexually exhibitionistic my look became.

One day, walking west on East Fifty-fourth Street—it was morning, maybe 9:00 A.M.—I saw a bright tangerine silk shirt and traffic-stopping fuchsia skirt in a brownstone window. I stood outside until the boutique opened, only to enter and discover that there was a coat of the reversible colors as well. Thus was I introduced to Rudi Gernreich and serious fashion, meaning I began to save my money. When I eventually slipped the rainbow over my head, edging the narrow skirt over my hips, the look was transforming, as in a fairy tale. The colors of clothes may seem a strange way to proclaim one's separation, but given the significant role of sex in establishing identity, Gernreich's tight, bright clothes became my racing colors. In wearing them, there was no longer any waffling as to whether or not I wanted to be seen.

The following year I found a Gernreich white silk/jersey tube, sleeveless, floor length, and with a V in the back so deep that underwear was out of the question. An architect who was my date that New Year's Eve had given me a dazzling white feather boa to complete the picture. Upon entering our first party of the evening, an older woman accused, "You used to be a pretty girl," convincing me that I had for the first time in my life aroused the envy of beauty in another woman.

The following year, 1964, Gernreich made history with his topless bathing suit. The bra-burning protest, four years later at the Miss America Pageant, generally gets the credit for convincing women to throw away their bras, but it was Gernreich's topless black suit with its little suspenders that started it, that memorable photo of the model, black hair cropped, that tells us what time it was in history. As Robin Morgan states in her collection of "Historical Documents" in *Sisterhood Is Powerful*, published in 1970, "Bras were never burned. Bra-burning was a whole-cloth invention of the media." Women may not have bought Gernreich's suit, but we certainly bought the symbol.

The colors of the early sixties were like nothing that had gone before. Since then, we've periodically recycled all of our once meaningful statements of freedom. But for those of us who were there the first time around, the brazen colors and exhibitionism were a "look" we had never seen our mothers wear.

We abandoned traditional beauty as a slave might his or her chains; we were tearing up the deal that had regulated the exchange of our beauty for men's wealth. Though no one I knew had yet read Betty Friedan's *The Feminine Mystique*, which had been published in 1963, its message was in the air. The role of the miniskirt and bralessness in the sixties was meaningful in more ways than anti-men, antisex feminists want to count. As novelist Tom Robbins wrote:

> I can think of two material items from the 60's and 70's that ought to be honored: the miniskirt, for its glorious debut, and the brassiere, for its martyrdom, its retreat. The widespread donning of the miniskirt and doffing of the bra symbolized the rebellion against constraint—sexual, cultural, political, economic and religious—that characterized the era. Our culture was being re-feminized, and unharnessed women in abbreviated loin-wrappings ... expressed this in a way every bit as direct and immediate as men in waist-length hair.... Women might protest an unjust war or battle for civil rights, but as evidenced by their attire, they refused to let the issues of the day make style victims of them or drag them down into despair.... Short-short skirts have come back several times since then. But you know I'm right when I say it's not the same.

It has often been pointed out that Proust used clothes to speak for his characters; just so, we imbued our clothes with meaning, and they returned the favor. The walls here in my writing room are covered with the fashion revivals of the past four years. They say absolutely nothing new.

The various revolutions on the horizon foreshadowed by clothes, music, art, and dance made me hungry for a voice of my own, a voice that had once been mine, prior to adolescence. I began to seek out men at parties on whom I could practice talking, something at which I'd become rusty since swallowing my tongue at adolescence. I'd noticed that people who were at ease in phrasing their thoughts spontaneously had a more open look, an unaffected stance. I wanted to lose the Nice Girl rigidity, and men's relaxed posture while talking suggested that there was more to gain in opening up the conduit between brain and tongue than just words. Men didn't say brilliant things all the time, but they were easy in their skins.

I don't exaggerate this business of relearning speech—it cannot be said often enough—but it was perhaps the major building block in putting myself back together. I found that some of the best talkers were older men who were not lovers, men who had lived in Burma, fought in World War II, directed films abroad for USIA. I recall standing at a bar in the Village—standing at bars and talking used to be a great pastime—and discussing something with a man, saying it spontaneously before all the juice had been edited out, and how he cocked his head and looked at me more closely, saying, "Where did you learn to talk like that?" He said it with such admiration and cool curiosity that my face burned with pleasure. If there were a moment in time when the rigidity of holding back, compressing myself into a small Girl Girl that had begun in my eleventh year changed, it was then.

There has been so much written against men as profiteers of women that I would like to paint them as I saw them in the sixties, which is pretty much as I see them today, people as likely to be as kind or abusive as the people of my own sex. When I walk around my house today, I recognize men who were friends, lovers, teachers. My gratitude for what they gave me isn't for physical gifts so much as a love and appreciation of art, cooking, music, books, along with an addiction to building, leaving me unhappy without the sound of hammers and saws. They made me think beyond the printed pages I had studied at college, made me want to fill pages with my own words. There is a university education, and there is life. "How did you get away?" a man asked one night at a party, recognizing the Nice Girl school behind my remarks. The truth was that I hadn't yet gotten away. When I eventually did, that success was greatly due to the kindness of men, their generosity of spirit, intellectual encouragement, and the praise they were not too envious to show me in their eyes.

Women who love men know that they are more mutable than we, their empathic emotional expression having been capped early in life so as to appear manly, and that there is nothing more exciting than removing that cap, freeing them from their "compartmentalized" life wherein they only dare show masculine feelings. I have remained friends with most of my old lovers because the gratitude has been so deep on both sides.

Wonderbras and Power Suits

The way we looked back then, on the cusp of all the revolutions, was the way we were. Nice Girls looking for Nice Men to take care of them had a virginal look that promised continuity to would-be suitors; as advertisements for themselves, women knew that they must project their side of the societal bargain by reflecting outside what they were inside: good mother material, meaning kind, submissive, noncompetitive. This projection allowed the man to fulfill his side of The Deal, to enter the grimy, unkind marketplace and bring home the bacon.

Women packaged themselves for the eyes of men so as to capture their protection and power. "I'll die if you leave me!" wasn't just a line from a 1950s movie heroine, it was real life, how it felt. On their side of the bargain, men in their gray flannel suits looked providerish, permanently planted in the ground in their heavy, dark shoes, a look that promised women that all their years of denial of independence, adventure, speech, but mostly sex, had been worthwhile.

Gregory Peck, Charlton Heston, and, yes, Jack Kennedy had that look down pat. They were substantial. Even short, far less handsome men broadcast security to dependent women. Divorces happened, and they were often grimmer than today because most ditched wives had no work skills. But there was pressure to stay together; divorce didn't look good on a man's résumé. Companies liked family men. As late as 1970, my husband remembers what a scandal it was in Detroit that the president of General Motors had divorced his wife to marry his hot-looking secretary. A man's adultery was preferable to divorce, and women lived with it. The women with whom a married man took up, sexual women, had a recognizable look.

When I lost my virginity—meaning complete penetration and not just the tip of the penis in the vagina—I went immediately to the mirror to see my new self, so sure was I that sex changed a woman's looks. To my surprise, I looked the same. Luckily, my years as a sexual single girl happened on the advent of what would be called The Sexual Revolution, into which I threw myself wholeheartedly. Now I could look like The Real Me, the girl who had always died to be seen, to be desired.

The advertisement of my sexual self didn't sit well with my Nice Girl friends on the Upper East Side, but that didn't deter me. It was "beyond my control," as the male character in *Les Liaisons Dangereuses* said, defending his erotic adventures. Having been strictly raised on The Rules of Nice Girlhood, I was well aware of the penalty, real or imagined, that I paid for having changed my look. The phrase that summed it up was one I would hear from men in the sixties who would smile and wipe their brow after a hot twist on the dance floor, handing me back to my date with, "Too much woman for me!" It didn't sound like a compliment. What did it mean? I assumed there was no such thing as "too much woman" for a man; I didn't yet understand The Deal, which meant that even economically powerful men were put in a vulnerable position by a Bad Girl who visually advertised sex. Success, money, to the man in the dark blue suit meant that there was an even greater distance to fall should he be cuckolded, should the hot woman by his side show him to be a weak sister who couldn't hold on to his woman.

As much as this may sound like ancient history to women in their twenties and thirties who never saw the early sixties, be assured that these deep feelings don't go away in the speck of time that is thirty years. Women today may wear their underwear out to dinner, and men too may flash their sexual beauty in a way their fathers couldn't, but a man looking for a mate still shrinks at the cuckold role more than anything. Approximately 25 percent of young men still want a virgin bride, and that percentage hasn't wavered much since researchers started counting.

Was it yesterday when I saw the review from Milan of men's fashions for next winter? Never mind the exact date; since beginning this book, fashion's revolving door is out of control. They are now calling it

The Power Suit, Armani's new large, broad-shouldered jacket, not exactly what Gregory Peck wore in *The Man in the Grey Flannel Suit*, but close enough. "Why can't men be glamourous in a masculine way?" Armani asks. To which I respond, "Here, here!" It has been suggested that what has prompted men to seek a more powerful image in the mirror is "the Wonderbra-clad, stiletto-shod, boa-draped, disco-hopping vixen that women's fashion has been promoting so brazenly." Meaning that if women were going to up the ante of their sexual exhibitionism, men had to balance the picture.

"A full bosom is actually a millstone around a woman's neck," wrote Germaine Greer in 1970; "it endears her to the men who want to make their mammet of her, but she is never allowed to think that their popping eyes actually see her." We may have dismissed the full bosom in the late sixties as the signature of enslavement to men—making it impossible to find a push-up bra for thirty years—but they are back, not in answer to men's demands but to women's. Women want big, big bosoms again and eye their owners with obvious envy.

Society once felt cheated when people appeared one way and acted another. "She looked like such a Nice Girl! He looked so responsible, not at all like a man who would walk out on his wife and children!" We still expect people to live up to their advertisements of themselves, which is why fashion continuously recycles. We don't have a New Deal between the sexes to replace the old, an understanding that would enable us, via what we wore and how we wore it, to flash our suitability, our content, to a prospective partner. The question is, do we have any content at all, beginning with, what is masculinity if women are also good providers?

Wonderbras and Power Suits. Yes, I can see why yesterday's "deconstructed" suit for men didn't hold up opposite a woman in six-inch stiletto heels that throw her lovely body into a devastating S curve, reminiscent of naked women being "taken" by satyrs. Huge breasts and a spinal curvature that cries out for penile insertion makes men in deconstructed suits that flap in the wind look like pubescent, ineffectual boys. When the Wonderbra hit the news pages—the fashion page alone couldn't contain it—I blinked; had I not owned lovely bras like this in the early sixties, when the little pads were insertable so that one could push up breasts or let them lie?

When the Council of Fashion Designers of America announced a Special Award for "the Wonderbra, for its contribution to fashion," I thought, Hold on, this is a revival, not an invention. And to prove my point I searched the basement of our barn until I found the trunk containing memorabilia from Great Nights of the Past. Sure enough, there they were, a collection of lacy push-up confections purchased at Saks in the sixties. I have little else from those years except for some remarkably large black shades, which along with my Wonderbra and nothing else would make a very contemporary fashion statement.

Thank You, Dr. Guttmacher

The problem was, I fell in love too easily. The problem was, I didn't know the difference between love and sex. Once my looks arrived, the opportunities for both multiplied, trouble just waiting to happen.

I lived on oral sex and the teeniest, weeniest bit of penile entry during my first years in New York. I knew the risk and, when my period was late, would return again and again to the ladies' room, praying for the spots of blood signaling that I had been spared the nightmare that, more than any other, terrified me. However, once out of the woods for another four weeks, I returned to my play with penises, orgasms, partial entry, until the man ejaculated. As Sally Belfrage said in her memoir of growing up, "No penetration, as they put it later, one in a million, but there you are: you're pregnant."

I was a very intelligent young woman in everything but this, even though I had plans, wonderful dreams of a life that didn't yet include marriage and children; I paid my rent on time, never wrote home for money, did my work professionally, but in this one thing I failed repeatedly. The promise of that Swept Away feeling in a man's arms spit in the eye of intelligence; as for all the promises to God that I would never take the risk again if he would just save me this one last time, well, it is a puzzle of infinite magnitude, which we still refuse to discuss.

Somehow, foolish as I was, I escaped pregnancy; perhaps it explains my dedication to preaching the educational benefits of masturbation in all my books. If someone had informed me early on that I could give myself an orgasm, that my sex was my own and not something The Prince awoke in me, I would not have succumbed to "his" magic so readily. Exploring the labyrinths of my genitals would have been a valuable geography lesson, a primer course in self-esteem that would have taught me that the sexual beauty I sought in my twenties began not with the seductive wrapping I bought in boutiques but with the mystery between my legs, not a sewer but a flower as erotically bewitching as any of Georgia O'Keeffe's.

My early professional routine was to take an exciting job requiring eight or nine months of intense work, jobs that had a beginning and an end. I wasn't looking for a career or marriage, just enough money to pay the rent and allow me to travel abroad until the money ran out, at which point I would return to New York and meet someone, usually a man, who would offer me a new job. I met men on dance floors and at parties, and none ever asked for a favor in exchange for the job.

I always traveled alone, my first European adventure having taught me that two women sitting side by side were a formidable prospect for any man to approach. I'd ended that first trip in a hotel near the Étoile in Paris, a tiny bordello frequented by prostitutes and their johns who fought at night in the narrow stairwell. It was very cheap. In my cramped room there was a washbasin and a metal bidet on a folding stool, a scene I drew in my sketchbook when I wasn't reading *For Whom the Bell Tolls*. I ate peanut butter and waited for something to happen. That is what I wrote in my journal, "I am waiting for something to happen."

Each day I walked the rue du Faubourg-St.-Honoré collecting posters from the art galleries; since I had little money, only my ticket home, I told them I was an art critic for a small newspaper. At night I sat in bars with men who kissed me and whom I kissed back, some more passionately than others, but when the money was gone, I boarded a ship and sailed home, a virgin by centimeters, still "waiting for something to happen."

Getting that advantage I'd envied in others all my life, looks, should have been an unexpected inheritance, power to spend. But looks-arrived-late are thoroughly unreliable. When you were invisible as a little child and had to build a world wherein talents other than beauty were honed so that people beamed on you, and then you lost it all in adolescence, well, people's admiring eyes become untrustworthy.

I desperately wanted to believe. I smiled back at men, relishing the desire in their eyes, and became increasingly choosy as to whom I allowed to pay for my dinner. Finally, as the mirror convinced me that my new packaging was involving me in too many risky adventures— penile tips slipping deeper and deeper into the tunnel—I walked the two blocks one morning to Dr. Aronson's office. Lying on the table, feet in stirrups, being fitted for a diaphragm had none of the thrill of trying on a new pair of shoes. What I should have felt was, "Oh, boy, now I can safely fuck a million men, live up to the promise of the Jax pants, the Gernreich tube of silk that forbade underwear when I twisted my ass off at Le Club. Afterward, in Dr. Aronson's office, I held the ugly rubber disk, the blinds drawn in front of my eyeballs, as he traced on a plastic model with his pencil tip the various canals and caves of my reproductive organs.

If our sexuality hadn't been stigmatized as Bad, perhaps the diaphragm might have served women better. If we'd been raised to think well of ourselves as sexual, we would have taken our diaphragms with us as automatically as the keys to the apartment. Instead, a Nice Girl had to remind herself to carry the nasty-looking thing in her purse, "just in case," like carrying an umbrella on a sunny day. If she came home and hadn't used it, she felt like a failed Jezebel; if she did find herself in the throes of Eros and had to disengage herself from passion to retire to the bathroom, squat, and insert it in her now moist canal, she was reminded that it wasn't foolproof; doubled over like a fortune cookie—Good luck!—and pushed up into the vagina, a woman still had to pray it would spring into proper formation around the ravenous cervix, always hungry for the intrepid do-or-die sperm fighting their way upstream like crazed salmon.

What a stupid virgin I had been, waiting too long to get fitted for a diaphragm and, once owning it, never taking pride in it, still letting myself get "swept away" by passion. Like many young women then and now I was a total contradiction, part independent explorer eager to see the world and fuck any man, but reduced to being a baby whenever I fell in love, meaning whenever I had sex.

Here was the good doctor teaching me how to protect myself, as a drill sergeant might instruct a recruit in how to save his life. Didn't I fear pregnancy as death itself, and wasn't marriage a distant possibility only after I'd finished my Odyssean adventures? The new reflection in the mirror was the power I'd always yearned to enjoy. And this rubber disk, wasn't it my ticket to travel, a bulletproof vest that promised I could lie with any man I desired, be the seductress I'd been dreaming of becoming? Well, your honor, I would argue that the sexual gift of being able to seduce a man doesn't automatically empower a girl to stand up, postorgasm, and walk independently away.

I often chose to go to parties alone, all the better to practice the effectiveness of my new looks, to leave with a man of my choosing. Automatically my eye went to the most unattainable man in the room, he with the sexual self-sufficiency and unapologetic stare; Malcolm, the inaccessible, the distant, emotionally cut-off dream of my thirteenth year. Now, however, I was not only ready to lie down with a man but had learned the appeal to a man like this of a woman who wanted sex for sex's sake, not his heart, not his soul. I understood that the offer of sex without strings is catnip to men.

I was playing a game for which I was ill-equipped. It was exhausting, and it was a lie. I haven't a doubt in the world that the allure of the unattainable man was born in the fathomless mystery of my father.

The games we play. Power was only mine until a man's penis, mouth, lips, inquisitive tongue and hands brought me to orgasm again and again; I gave as much as I took, but men are not raised like we women to respond to symbiotic oneness. Before the night was over, I'd lost myself in him, floated into him. Houdini couldn't have done it better.

It must have been perplexing for a man to be seduced by a young woman in a sexy dress, whose assertive body said that she, being so independent, would never hold him down, only to wake in the morning and hear her ask, "When will I see you?" He would do a better day's work, feeling stronger, more powerful, while I lay bankrupt, the sight on the floor of my former armor—the little Jax dress and high heels a puddle of powerlessness—now that love, oh, desperate love had taken me over.

This post-sex enslavement scared me far more than it worried the men. It infuriated me that I could not control this witchy transformation. What good was beauty and sexual power if the union I had initiated destroyed my good opinion of myself, made me feel like a beggar while he, lucky Prince, had become such a potent addiction that I would remain glued to the telephone, waiting, praying, not even daring to go down to the store for peanut butter. What if he called when I wasn't there? Better to starve. As for intellect, giving myself a rational talking-to, well, nobody ever put it better than Dorothy Parker: "Please, God, let him telephone me now. Dear God, let him call me now. I won't ask anything else of You, truly I won't. It isn't very much to ask. It would be so little to You, God, such a little, little thing."

Damn it, this business of women's addiction to symbiotic oneness, especially post-sex, should have been one of feminism's first pieces of business, teaching women the difference between love and sex. Lesson number one should have spelled out the origin of our neediness in the lack of healthy separation from mother in the first years of life, a dependency reawakened by adult intimacy. What good is equal opportunity in the workplace if we still lose our identity in sex?

Instead of teaching us that we could have love, work, and sex, some of which are nice together but each of which is separate, feminism chose to keep women ignorant, leaving real safety only in ties to other women. Feminism distances itself from sex, knowing that if women were sexually free to genuinely love men, their total allegiance to Women's World would be lost.

How to describe the drama of going from a girl with a diaphragm to a woman on the Pill? It wasn't just the fear of pregnancy the Pill removed, making each day without bleeding like water torture, given how untrustworthy that little devil, the diaphragm, was. No, what the Pill accomplished was to question the Nice Girl's role in sex, or to put it another way, what was not nice about sex? The Pill erased that frozen Nice Girl smile from my face and with it the iron barriers through which I had to blast each time I approached orgasm. That my fascination with women's sexual fantasies began just a few years after the Pill entered my life is not without meaning. With its freedom came my first awareness that I even had sexual fantasies.

How could a little pill, taken daily, extend the perimeters of life, altering how I thought about myself? For many of us, the Pill was what the first Ford automobile had been for men fifty years earlier. It was our ticket, our wheels, our way out of a restricted life: This was when we women began to initiate sex, to approach a man, to seduce him, a feeling unlike any other.

It was 1963, and I'd never even heard of the Pill until my lover groaned one morning, referring to my diaphragm as "fucking uncomfortable." I trusted this man, especially in matters sexual, where he had opened doors and encouraged my entry. "Read this," he said, handing me an article about Dr. Alan Guttmacher and the new contraceptive pill. Having no great love myself of that little rubber disk, its feel, its smell, not to mention the messy creams and the ongoing uncertainty regarding pregnancy, I made an appointment to see the venerable Dr. Guttmacher, was examined by the great man himself, and given a prescription for a new life. I owe a great deal to that lover of mine.

Uncertain as to just where I would be at the appointed hour when

I took my daily pill, I carried them in a gold bracelet from which hung a tiny hinged globe of the world. Feeling in charge of my sexuality changed how I walked down the street. I wore higher heels, not just to be seen but to look, to catch a man's eye, or try, discovering in the process that this was how a man felt. If you are the active one, prepared at all times, and not the passive person waiting to be chosen like a lottery ticket, then you get to take the initiative.

"What women responded to in the Pill was that it distanced the act of contraception from the sexual act itself," says Jeannie Rossoff, president of the Alan Guttmacher Institute. "We know from experience that the more remote a method of birth control is from the act of intercourse, the more likely it is to be effective." To this I would add that the Pill's influence went beyond contraception; in hindsight, it allowed me to feel like a sexual person all the time, not just when I was with a man. My sex belonged to me instead of being something a man ignited. The magic was mine and, by extension, mine to apply to intellectual and social growth too.

It wasn't the chemical makeup of the Pill but the fact that one's preparedness at all times for sex removed the antisex rigidity inculcated into women from an early age, an anxiety we carried with us physically, emotionally, and intellectually. It was a remarkable transformation, not visible or precisely understood at that time, but I believe I had always known that the sexual feeling was energy. I certainly was happier for having it to spend.

There was nothing reckless in my new exhibitionism, the exhilaration of walking along on a summer evening in a sea-green Pucci dress, a wisp of a garment you could hold on the tip of a pinkie nail and under which I wore only stockings and a garter belt. If men hadn't looked, I would have been disappointed. Choosing to be visually appraised, drawing eyes to my body, and by my choice, gave me a surge of control. I knew exactly what I had put on and why; I accepted that it was my job to be responsible for the waves I had set in motion.

Walking east on Forty-eighth Street to the bar where we gathered after work was a march and farewell to that poor young thing at the Yacht Club who'd stood the entire night with her shoulder blades pressed into the wall, watching her friends dance by. Every day between five and six, no matter where I was, opposite whatever man, I would open the globe on my responsible little wrist and swallow my pill. Feeling safe, the captain of my ship, I stopped waiting to be asked and approached men who caught my eye. It was an exhilarating experience the Pill gave, perhaps the most liberating in my life, and I never missed a day.

You had to have been there to appreciate how much the Pill felt a part of our times, a natural extension of the music, the clothes, the dances, the revolutionary feeling in the air that extended to Civil Rights and the antiwar marches. The Pill was our defense system. That we looked so different from previous generations wasn't just attributable to fashions. You couldn't expect the virgin Breck Girl to be part of this, she who had smiled passively from the pages of magazines all my life, so squeaky clean, so pure, so asexual. The Breck Girl epitomized the Good Girl/Bad Girl split, a depletion of energy, a confusion of identity we could no longer afford.

The Pill set us apart from our mothers in a way that was almost tangible. I couldn't imagine my mother on the Pill. Before the Pill, women were divided into Jane Russells and Grace Kellys, meaning that sex was so recognizable you could spot it a mile away. That was the past. We may not have used all our new freedoms as responsibly as we might, but it wasn't the fault of the Pill. We were, on some level, and still are, our mothers' daughters, and fathers' too, for all of society is at fault for not applauding sexual responsibility in women.

Society had never before given women a prescription for sexual freedom. Along with the IUD and other new contraceptives, the Pill offered women permission to think beyond patriarchy and matriarchy too. No more "waiting for something to happen"; now the only thing that kept women from "making something happen" was fear of other women's judgment. The Nice Girl Rules had been set up not by men to control women, but by women to control one another at a time of limited resources; only one man to a woman, only so much sex, no more to one woman than another. Well, the resources weren't and aren't so limited today. All women ever needed was the support of one another, the raising of the tyranny of banishment from Women's World. Neither the Pill nor any other form of contraception will ever be perfect until women want and approve of other women enjoying sexual freedom.

For a while, maybe a decade, it felt like, looked like, we were getting there. I sometimes think that is what the fashion designers have been trying to recapture in today's revivals of the clothes we used to wear: our optimism, the promise of sexual relationships evolving into a future where women and men thought of themselves as equals, partners in a dance that either could initiate and in which each is responsible. If the Pill wasn't perfect, it was the optimism we had back then that we were achieving not just economic, but sexual independence too that gave us that look: on top, chest out, proud, sexual. If subsequent economic achievements feel hollow, it is because Matriarchal Feminism has eliminated both the love of, and sex with, men.

The Looks of Revolution

The sixties were so thick with change that it is difficult to disentangle the revolutions. Their fever was all-consuming, making it easy to think of your impassioned crusade for your own high goal as the only parade in town. Watching the evening news with the sound off, it was impossible to discern whether the on-screen marchers were Students for a Democratic Society (SDS), anti-Vietnam War demonstrators, Civil Rights marchers, Feminists, Hippies, or another wave of as yet unnamed revolutionary zealots. Those days, the look of the land was a sea of jeans, T-shirts, boots, long hair, pony tails, Afros, the women sometimes indistinguishable from the men unless in profile. The one thing the revolutionaries had in common was not to look like the establishment.

Even so, it was possible to go through those years as your parents had done. Eventually, the cumulative changes wrought by the sixties would affect all our lives, but at the time, the vast American majority (who were not on television) didn't want to know about The Sexual Revolution and bitterly resented the counterculture's takeover of the airwaves. The Hippies, the Flower Children, the students staging a sit-in at Berkeley in 1964, the music of Jefferson Airplane, such oddball pronouncements as Andy Warhol's "In the future everyone will be famous for fifteen minutes." The media's fascination with these sights and sounds made mainstream America feel left out of some secret, which was exactly what was intended: You were either In or Out, an expression we thought we'd invented but which I've since discovered has been around for centuries.

When the antiwar demonstrators spit on the flag and jeered the boys going off to Vietnam, it understandably infuriated people who thought of themselves as true Americans; it was a different resentment than what they felt when their children adopted the Beatles' music and hair and demanded the miniskirts hot off the fashion pages in 1964, but it was resentment nonetheless. Something foreign to The American Way was taking over the land, and those who didn't like it felt invisible. It was a division that has never healed.

In time, the anger of the Invisible Majority would include the bitterness of traditional women, who felt denigrated by the national spotlight on the new feminism, which not only looked down on their values, but obliterated them. To my knowledge, no one has written sympathetically about the anger and resentment of the men and women who were not part of the many overlapping rebellions of the sixties and seventies; I am not just referring to the older generation, which was automatically outraged, but to the people in their twenties, and younger, who fought in Vietnam by choice, the women who chose to marry, work at home, raise children as their mothers had. Eventually, many of these traditionalists would become the backbone of today's Republican Right Wing.

If you weren't there watching the fifties being shelled from all sides by the SNCC march in Maryland in 1963, the Watts riots in 1965, the bloodshed at the 1968 Democratic Convention in Chicago, the march on the Pentagon in 1969; if you didn't sing the songs, wear the clothes, smoke the smoke; if you missed all that, you may be puzzled by today's revivals of everything from those years, the TV series, the films, the music, and especially the revolving doors of fashion. I was there, and I'm puzzled.

As I write, there is an Andy Warhol retrospective. I remember *Empire* the first time around, an eight-hour static shot of the Empire State Building as time passed and passed, until we ambled from the screening room out onto the balcony, smoked marijuana, and stared down at the city until Andy appeared and walked among us. You see, it doesn't tell well, the whole point of the "happening" to be nothing happening at all, to be "laid back"; to understand this, you had to be In; to question was to be Out. Nonetheless, empty or filled with meaning, here it is again, not just the film but a continuous reemergence of Warhol's inner circle, one by one turning up in lengthy interviews in newspapers and magazines, looking and sounding old, tired, and empty thirty years later. Why do journalists seek them out? I suppose it is for the same reason that designers reinvent little Courrèges skirts and the cropped, tight, poor boy sweaters that Edie Sedgwick— another of Warhol's superstars—wore.

I take the clothes of today's runways very seriously indeed. Like

Nelson Thall, president of the Marshall McLuhan Center on Global Communications, I too believe that "our clothing is an extension of our skin, just like a hammer is a technological extension of our hand." Clothing is also an extension of what we feel, including our unconscious feelings. What we wore in the 1960s and 1970s was meant to carry messages. Some of those looks were antifashion, some antiestablishment, anti–Vietnam War, antisegregation, antimaterialism. But clothing as political statement was very different from today's clothing, which serves more as a desperate plea for recognition.

What are we looking for in those years? Fashion may revel in revivals, but recent years have been a desperate bad dream, as when something is lost, like a key, and to find it we have to go through all the clothes, the closets, the pockets. Writing about the sixties I'd hoped to find a clue as to why history blames today's ills on what happened then.

In his review of the 1995 Warhol film retrospective, critic Stephen Holden wrote, "The esthetic running through Warhol's films is an icy voyeurism. . . . Again and again, one has the feeling of confronting people with limited inner resources, desperate to be noticed at any cost. . . . Taking it further, the Warhol superstar can also be viewed as the forerunner of the thousands of ordinary folks who seem more than eager to disclose their most intimate secrets on talk television."

To which telling observation I would include the people on today's streets in their exhibitionistic dress, who are also "more than eager to disclose their most intimate" physical parts, so desperate are they to see themselves reflected in the eyes of strangers walking toward them. But everyone is sated by outrage; we are jaded. The potential voyeurs have by now seen everything; fully aware of what is wanted of them— their eyes lighting up, the gasp of wonder—they will be damned if they will give the exhibitionists the time of day.

Warhol himself was not a nice person. His genius was in recognizing society's emptiness, the human hunger to be seen. He tapped those individuals who would gladly, eagerly, do or show anything that would get them seen. He was the master tailor of the modern fairy tale, convincing the players that their nudity and sexual extremes were filled with meaning; he then hoodwinked the audiences who watched his films and bought his canvases into believing that they now had content. His fascination with women's shoes—notebooks filled with drawings—and his collections of antique toys has, in my mind, always fixed Warhol in the nursery. His talent was in recognizing his own emptiness in everyone else, and putting it to work for himself.

Many people carried things too far in those years. Some died from overindulgence, and a great many who marched against the Establishment, smoked and fucked at the Sleep-In in Central Park went on to become rich or famous or more conservative than their parents. My friend Joanna spent several nights in jail for various of the above offenses in 1968; fifteen years later she was senior vice president of a major Wall Street firm, which she left in 1990 to return to full-time mothering and work at home. Today, she and her little girl wear mother/daughter look-alike dresses.

Because we marched in different parades on different days of the week, many of us had complicated wardrobes. My friend Kate, who worked at Grove Press, which had published Burroughs's *Naked Lunch*, and then at Random House, which was publishing Stokely Carmichael, Abbie Hoffman, and Tom Hayden, vividly remembers the complexity of looks: "I had one whole closet full of short, sexy dresses from Paraphernalia and The Electric Circus that I wore to Max's Kansas City or Le Club, and then I had my torn bell-bottom jeans, with the little scarves to tie around the leg, and the shrunken T-shirts with no bra underneath for the rallies in Central Park." We laugh when I remind her of the night a friend's father had looked at us as we left the house for the rally; cupping Kate's lovely face in his hand, he said, "You'll never get away with it, not with a face like that." Did we ever feel subversive in our costumes? "Not a bit," says Kate. "What held it all together was sex. Everyone was getting laid. We were on the Pill, or had an IUD, something. Whether we were marching or dancing, we were all having sex."

Even when the revolution was stridently against looking good, the look that emerged as symbol of that particular rebellion became as obligatory as what was being replaced. For all the singing of freedom and "do your own thing," the Hippies and Flower Children with long hair and wearing Salvation Army castoffs, who were involved in nudity, drugs, and sexual excess, were absolutely rigid about anyone whose look didn't fit the mold.

In the late sixties I was in Haight-Ashbury with a camera crew filming the scene and remember people being thrown out of parties because they looked "wrong." Wear something found, torn, dirty, wear a blanket, just don't look like "them," a demand that was as much a uniform as the practiced look at Mom and Dad's country club. In the words of Timothy Leary, "The essence of the 60's was a populist movement, but there was a dress code among the hippies that was stronger than the ones at West Point and Park Avenue."

One night in the fall of 1967, Michael Butler telephoned to invite me to a musical at Joseph Papp's theater downtown. Michael had given me my first job in New York editing a magazine called *Islands in the Sun*. I'd never written an article, much less edited a magazine, but he hired me with the same spontaneity with which he acquired *Hair*, a musical that was about to close and disappear into oblivion. From that night on, all of our lives changed, no one's more than Michael's, who would never again wear one of his custom-made suits.

The night before *Hair* opened on Broadway, a group of us sat in Casey's Greenwich Village restaurant, the director and producer finally conceding that it would be left to the individual members of the cast as to whether to emerge naked from under the tarpaulin at the end of Act I. Opening night, the stunned audience gasped as a cast stood, stark naked, for the first time on a Broadway stage. The next morning, drama critic Clive Barnes had this to say about the show: "Fresh and frank . . . likable . . . rock musical that last night completed its trek from downtown, via a discotheque, and landed, positively panting with love and smelling of sweat and flowers. . . . So new, so fresh and so unassuming. . . ."

Hair made theater history; at one time a record twenty-one companies were performing it around the world; but more significant, *Hair* put to popular music the schisms in our society over the issues of homosexuality, drugs, the Vietnam War, racial and sexual freedom, schisms that still exist. *Hair* didn't create the problem, it opened the window that gave us a clear view back into time of what had been brewing for years. *Hair*'s use of nudity and long hair was no theatrical trick; these looks have remained with us for almost thirty years because of what they still represent. What *Hair* did with bare breasts and buttocks was to strip the human package on a Broadway stage at a time when we were morally and intellectually empty. It showed us to ourselves.

Hair called itself the "Tribal Love Rock Musical," when, in fact, there was little love among those most deeply involved in the production. "Peace and Love" was on everyone's lips, but it was not a self-fulfilling prophecy. Like the Warhol family and other In groups around town, members got a lot of warmth from exclusion: "We are In and you are Out." It's an interesting game that people play and gets much of its nihilistic anger from the nursery.

As much as I loved the sixties, I remember the cruelty of the contemptuous looks of certain Insiders, who just five minutes earlier were Out; it was so like those girlish cliques when two little girls leave another out, or like sibling exclusions, or Oedipal games. But that we practiced In and Out so cuttingly in the Age of Aquarius says how ill-equipped the children of affluent Post–World War II and, yes, McCarthyism were to build a society on love.

Around the mid-sixties, a depressing, different vogue began that has never let up. People were wearing other people's names and initials on their clothes. One day I walked into Saks Fifth Avenue to see a mad commotion around the Yves Saint-Laurent scarf counter as women grabbed at the big beautiful silk squares, fighting over them. Yes, they were lovely to behold, but "YSL" was all over them. Why would someone pay hundreds of dollars to put another person's initials on her body, like buying bed sheets with a stranger's monogram? Soon it became impossible to find even a T-shirt that didn't have someone else's initials on it.

Until then, the "LV"s on the Louis Vuitton luggage that my great-aunt Mildred carried were the only initials I'd ever seen used this way. Today, Vuitton luggage, once only carried by the wealthy, is everywhere; secretaries save their money to buy one of the ubiquitous LV tote bags so that people on the street will recognize them; meanwhile, Vuitton's luggage becomes increasingly ill-constructed as the profit margin replaces pride in product. Hermès, Gucci, and Ralph Lauren's customers would feel cheated if the recognizable initials were removed from their socks and shirts. Who would know who they were? How would they know who they were?

People are so happy to be In, to have an identity and feel substantial, that they eagerly take up the aloof, haughty arrogance of a hollow celebrity, forgetting that until their own recent purchase they were Out. It is the knowledge that others see them, enviously watch them, even as they pretend to be oblivious to the voyeurs, that give the In people the substance that makes them high.

As John Berger observed, "The happiness of being envied is glamour. . . . Being envied is a solitary form of reassurance. It depends precisely upon not sharing your experience with those who envy you. You are observed with interest but you do not observe with interest—if you do, you will become less enviable. . . . It is this which explains the absent, unfocused look of so many glamour images. They look out *over* the looks of envy which sustain them."

The values that the sixties revolutions rejected were long overdue for questioning, but when the dust settled and time passed, we wondered if we'd replaced emptiness with emptiness. When feminists barked at men for holding the door open, they outlawed a civility that may have been an empty gesture when women had no real power. Now we have power but have lost not just the chair and door-holding but all the other manners, kindnesses, seemingly empty gestures of politeness that are the ground rules on which a society rests; a civil conversation regarding peace, dénouement, reconciliation, détente, the preservation of a marriage, can only be held with manners. Once women were the custodians of the invisible virtues; now no one has the time or inclination to demand and practice the civilities, out of which word "civilization" is coined; instead of manners we have "icy voyeurism" and desperate exhibitionism.

In his 1994 Encyclical, Pope John Paul referred to the 1960s as the beginning of all that is evil in society today—the breakdown of the family, AIDS, the spread of homosexuality. For some of us, however, Howell Raines's editorial in the *New York Times* summed up those years more accurately:

> The 60's spawned a new morality-based politics that emphasized the individual's responsibility to speak out against injustice and corruption . . . to raise their voices to end America's most disastrous foreign military adventure, the Vietnam War. On this level, the Sixties saw an exercise in mass sanity in which a nation's previously voiceless citizens—its young—overturned a war policy that was, in fact, deranged. . . . At its essence, the counterculture was about one of conservatives' favorite words: values.

The Sexual Revolution Versus The Women's Movement

I suppose it's because they happened simultaneously that we tend to think that The Women's Movement and The Sexual Revolution were one and the same, a magnificent march for freedom across the board. At the beginning I assumed we were all on the same side. Certainly we all looked alike in our jeans and T-shirts proudly punctuated by our recently bared nipples, making it easy to assume that it was one historic movement, along with the Civil Rights marches and those against the Vietnam War.

To this day, many who were there presume great sex was on the Women's Rights agenda. Nothing implied this more than the arrival of the contraceptive pill, an obvious declaration of sexual independence. Along with the highly visible and vocal Pro-Choice Movement, whose banners trumpeted a woman's right to control her own body, it was blatantly automatic to assume that feminism was pro-sex.

Disentangle these assumptions and you will find the fine print that became the genesis of today's War Between The Women: at first, the two camps looked like the traditional women with families who chose to work at home versus The New Woman in the workplace. However, in recent years new schisms have splintered us into other divisions, as victimism in particular has divided feminists to the point where the new generations of women are reluctant even to call themselves feminists, even to use the word. As the debate boils, the subject of sex becomes increasingly important as to how you want to define yourself.

We will never know how much ground we might have won over the past twenty-five years if women hadn't been so divided among ourselves. In hindsight, I'd say the schism between The Women's Movement and The Sexual Revolution was our Achilles' Heel, especially when sexuality, not just the sexual act, is viewed as an essential part of our humanity. The rigid, exclusionary demands of antisex, anti-men, Matriarchal Feminism didn't just lose the Women's Movement the membership of women who felt pressed to choose between the love of men and The Sisterhood. It weakened card-carrying feminists who felt alienated from their sisters for being less loyal by continuing to sleep with the enemy.

Betty Friedan's 1963 *The Feminine Mystique* went to the core of what was wrong in The System that feminism attacked, a system that manipulated women to find their only role and identity as wives and mothers. She never painted men as the enemy but instead saw them as victims of the same system, controlled by big business, advertising, the universities. If women shrunk themselves to fit the stereotypes presented by women's magazines, men died at their desks of too early heart attacks in the race to live up to their side of the bargain.

Among the women I knew in New York and London, where I was living in the early seventies, sexual freedom was very much what the new feminism was about. What woman would not assume that our new politics of freedom embraced the erotic, an enhanced union between the sexes to which we women would bring our newly awakened sexual desires, different from men's, but not alien. Nothing had controlled our lives more rigidly than sex, an openness to which could ruin a woman's life. Now everything around us—films, books, clothes, music, dance—encouraged women to grow, expand, to become that sexual person they had perhaps secretly dreamed of being. Surely, this was the core of the new feminism.

Not precisely. Perhaps it was naive, but in the beginning some of us eagerly set out to be card-carrying feminists, fighting for economic and political equality, and loving men too. The new erotic horizon and feminism were commingled in our minds; I cannot exaggerate how heady a mix this was, feeling part of a world of women pushing the boundaries. For the first time in history, we controlled contraception. Publishers were frantic to sign women to contracts for books, poems, articles that elaborated how women felt; we were the new undiscovered continent. As our works were published, as more and more women joined the workforce, rebelled, dropped out, or "did their own thing," there was a tacit understanding that no idea was so obscure, or "unladylike," that it would not be acceptable to our sisters.

I had never heard or read about other women's sexual fantasies. Very well, I thought, if the world really wants to know what women think, what we are like sexually, why not a book on these secret erotic thoughts? It was 1969. My own fantasies, long suppressed, had only recently swum up from the preconscious in answer to the permission that was in the air and the blessing that the Pill had automatically given our sexuality.

The first hint that I had entered territory more taboo than ever imagined was the wall of denial I ran into when interviewing some of the most sexually adventurous women I knew. "What is a sexual fantasy?" they would ask, looking at me blankly. They wanted to be part of anything sexual, wanted to contribute to my research, and were pained that there might be something they were missing. But women having sexual fantasies was something of which they had never heard.

These were halcyon days in London, and sexual reality had never been livelier; I would try out the topic over drinks at the Aretusa or Annabelle's, where the initial response was eager titillation. But when a married woman ventured to describe the images that ran through her head during sex, her husband's stunned reaction silenced the table. Or another woman would stop her with, "Oh, I thought you were very happy in your real sexual life, sweetie. I didn't realize you *needed* fantasies."

For some reason, the internal engine that stoked erotic fantasies aroused envy in women and anxiety in men, as if it were being suggested that having a fantasy diminished a woman's *real* sexual life when, in fact, quite the opposite is true. Nothing is quite so sexually thrilling as the forbidden, erotic ideas, the earliest associations of which go back to the first years of life. Breaking those rules, which once would have lost us mother's love—or so we feared—takes us over the moon. When men go to prostitutes, they don't ask for "ordinary" sex, they want the forbidden. Now women too were swimming down into the preconscious to play in the same dark waters.

But it took awhile. After four years of interviewing women, writing articles, placing ads in *New York* magazine and the *Los Angeles Times*, I discovered that the quickest method of putting women in touch with their fantasies was to tell them mine as well as other women's. Permission. We were raised to be such Nice Girls that the idea of thinking of another man while in our lover's arms was tantamount to out-and-out adultery. Once a woman read or heard other women's fantasies, however, permission overcame denial, the unthinkable became acceptable. When I tell this story to young women today, they look at me in disbelief, so sewn into literature, film, advertising, even conversation, are women's erotic dreams.

My own experience in writing the text for *My Secret Garden* was no less daunting. I might as well have been violating everything I'd learned in Sunday school. So tense did I get at the typewriter, I'd have to leave the room where I was working, go to another part of the house, and lie on the sofa until my heartbeat returned to normal. I'd thought of myself as fully liberated; had I not invented the idea of this book, despite what analysts and therapists had told me, including *Cosmopolitan* magazine's house psychiatrist—"Women do not have sexual fantasies"?

When I sent the galleys of *My Secret Garden* to an editor at *Ms.* magazine, a woman with whom I'd partied in the halcyon days of the sixties, I assumed that she would find the material, at the very least, interesting. Her own unabashed sexual exhibitionism in those days was legend. What I received back was a one-sentence, terse reprimand stating, "*Ms*. magazine will decide what women's sexual fantasies are."

That was my first taste of feminism's antisex stance. A few months after publication, a review of *MSG* appeared in *Ms*., where I was accused not only of making up the entire book of "subterranean sadism," but also, and let me quote, "Anybody who could write those thoroughly reprehensible sentences isn't a feminist, of course; and that's one of the troubles with this book."

Twenty years later I can smile at this rough scolding, but at the time it took my breath away and, I regret to say, humiliated me, which, of course, was the intent. But it taught me a lesson about The Sisterhood that I have never forgotten: You play by their rules or not at all. Until a few years ago, I proudly called myself a feminist, refusing to abandon allegiance to a movement in which I'd always played a part. But recently the victim, anti-men, anti-sex Matriarchal Feminists have so misappropriated the word *feminism* that I, along with other women, many much younger, have hesitated to use the word, though we have no other. It is absolutely intolerable to the *Ms*./Dworkin/McKinnon camp that other women enjoy the forbidden fruit while they, for reasons of their own, abstain.

One of the early slogans of feminism was "Women's freedom will be men's freedom too." During the seventies, when I lectured on college campuses, I often quoted this slogan, elaborating on how the changes in women's lives would also liberate men. But the anti-men sentiment had already heated up, as some feminist leaders realized they needed a scapegoat not only for society's injustices against women, but for women's against one another. Dump it all on Bad Men was what it came down to. It wasn't unusual at those college lectures for angry young women in the audience to stand and shake their fists at me for being sympathetic to men. "We don't give a damn about men!" they would yell. "Why are you talking about *their* freedom?"

The other dead giveaway that one's heart was not true to The Sisterhood in the seventies was the pursuit of a kind of beauty that advertised a sexual interest in men. "How can you say the feminist things you're saying and dress that way?" a confused student yelled at me at a small university in Indiana. My words of political equality excited her but my gray flannel pants and cashmere sweater cried, "Mirror, Mirror!"

One of my earliest memories of the rigidity of feminism is of something that happened at a party where my friend the late actress Joan Hackett and I had wandered into a room apart from the rest of the group. Hackett, as she liked to be called, was a brilliant conversationalist, and we were in the thick of it when several men entered the room. When they left, she turned to me and said, "You change when a man comes in the room." Though I loved her dearly and admired her courage as much as any woman's I've known, that night I felt that the lack of understanding lay with her. It was criticism of me as a feminist: I had been engaged in talk with a woman and had altered my expression, or my speech, when men approached.

How many times have I gone over this incident; surely, just as we "change" when an older person or a child enters the room, we reflect the arrival of a person of the opposite sex. Not to change when a man enters the room—not to do whatever is natural and spontaneous—doesn't make you a better feminist, it desensitizes you, robs you of the genuine reaction.

We've needed more than the one word *feminism* to define us for a long time. The argument over sex and beauty has for twenty years not just divided the ranks but has deepened within each of us individually the Good Girl/Bad Girl split. As with our relationship to mother, we fear we can't be our selves, sexual and separate from her, and retain her love too.

A few years ago I was lecturing at the YMHA in New York and happened to mention women who lived out their exhibitionistic fantasies, one of which was to "flash," to ride the bus with knees apart and no panties. A group of self-proclaimed feminists in the front row yelled, "Yeah, a woman can do that and no man has the right to lay a finger on her!" I commented that I felt this particular fantasy might be one of those best left safely in the mind. All hell broke loose in the front row, the women angrily insisting that women can do anything they want and vile men can't touch them.

This is what feminism has come to, not safety in an unsafe world, but omnipotent thinking that allows women, in the guise of rightness, to do whatever they choose, and should Bad Men attack, well, that too is a victory, for it only goes to show how really evil men are as opposed to us poor little victims. Feminists have it backward; the lesson to be learned isn't that All Men Are Brutes, but that women must take responsibility for our selves. The columnist William Raspberry caught this behavior precisely, writing of "feminist leaders who find it

impossible to acknowledge serious progress toward gender fairness—
not because there has been no progress but because their power
derives from their ability to keep portraying women as victims."

Herein lies my argument with The Sisterhood: If my face gets
warm, my eyes light up, my pulse quickens when men enter a room,
why should I have to prove my feminism by reacting to men as though
they were women? As the differences between the sexes diminish, I
celebrate everything that is opposite in us. My dear friend Hackett was
an angry woman; over the years she had told me about her childhood,
her mother whom she loved but toward whom there had clearly been
a great deal of rage. Like many of us who cannot easily accept anger at
mother/women, she found it less painful to hang it all on men.

Separation of sex and sisterhood continues to grow. In the eyes of
certain feminists, you cannot have your primary union with men and
be a feminist too. It is as if The Rules of adolescence never went away,
wherein any one girl who had more sex than the others was ostracized.
This exclusionary clause is a direct outgrowth of the childish adage,
Three Little Girls Can't Play Together, because two always gang up on
one and leave her out. Men/sex/beauty arouse competition and thus
destroy The Group.

How many millions of potential members has feminism lost,
women who would eagerly have joined an organization that celebrated women's rights, including the right to love men, to work at
home, and, yes, to pursue beauty too? "It is often falsely assumed . . .
that sexuality is the enemy of the female who really wants to develop
these aspects of her personality [like initiative and ambition]," wrote
Germaine Greer in *The Female Eunuch*, "and this is perhaps the most
misleading aspect of movements like the National Organization of
Women." Pretty soon The Rules get to be what the revolution is all
about. The Rule Makers get so proficient at patrolling to be sure no
one person steps outside the limiting boundaries that they become
dictators.

Almost twenty-five years ago *Ms*. magazine declared in its first
issue, "The Sexual Revolution and The Women's Movement are polar
opposites in philosophy, goals and spirit . . . the so-called Sexual Revolution is merely a link in the chain of abuse laid on women throughout
patriarchal history." In separating itself from The Sexual Revolution—
no, let me correct that—in separating itself from sex and men, feminism won the battle and lost the war.

Had feminism embraced sexuality, it would have become the great educating force in sexual responsibility, teaching women to love our bodies so that we automatically taught our daughters the beauty of the female form and, in particular, our genitals. What more obvious piece of business could there be for feminism than to celebrate the beauty of sexuality, our greatest power, the ability to give life? Had the slogan for women been, "We will protect our bodies, respect our genitals, so that we may be responsible for our sex, and enjoy it," women would be less susceptible to unintended pregnancies.

Chastity would also have value; preserving one's virginity out of regard for one's whole self, mental and physical, until that time when a woman was ready for sex, would be thought of as a spiritual act.

And if feminism had kept to the original promise that "Women's freedom will be men's freedom," then men would have felt kinship with our revolution, seen what was in it for them. It would have allowed both sexes to adjust to the awareness that the Patriarchal Deal, set in place generations ago, was a dead end for men as well as women. Men would have recognized that, while there would be competition with women in the workplace, they would have less of the onerous job of constantly providing.

If that had happened, more women would have embraced feminism, bringing their men along with them. We would have family feminism. Without the rigid definitions of what was men's and what was women's work, each of us would more naturally choose that area of work we felt better suited for—home or workplace, or both.

Today's twenty- and thirty-year-olds, benefactors of our various revolutions, play with issues of sex, competition, and beauty. That both sexes will remain in the workplace is a given; but they are handicapped by our reluctance to address the years we know best, having been there, been the ones who changed the status quo, turned the world on its head thirty years ago. It's all of a piece, then and now. Here, today, are the fashions we wore, back in the stores again. When a new generation of young women puts on bell-bottoms and stumbles down the street in platform wedgies, it is more than fashion reinventing itself.

Last night I went to a book party for a young woman's first novel. The story, set in the seventies, is about a woman whose life has been overshadowed by her older sister's, a flower child of the sixties who died mysteriously in Europe. "Why have the sixties been such an inspiration and a burden to generations since?" read the copy on the front flap. "Only by dispelling the ghosts of a romanticized past does [the heroine] come into full possession of her world ... a journey essential to all of us."

It is precisely what the clothes, the look, the revivals from that era are about, an effort to understand what happened then, so as to understand today. Was there really a Sexual Revolution, and if so, why is there so little love between the sexes now? Why do the feminists from those years, who were there, attack men so angrily? What happened to Peace and Love? Young women today are confused by feminism's ongoing tirade against men and sex.

The loss of sexual joy is separate from the plague of AIDS and venereal diseases. The latter have blighted sex in their own way. But women control sex; without our consent there will be none. If the sex that we do have is irresponsible, accompanied by accusations of abuse and harassment, along with a dramatic increase in women choosing to have sex with other women instead of with men, feminism has something to do with it.

Think of The Dress, the one in fairy tales, which has magical properties. Only in fairy tales does the power of beauty win out over the envy of the evil sisters/bad women. In reality, we see ourselves in the magical dress, but we do not buy it out of fear of other women's disapproval. Wasn't freedom the goal of feminism? When men were our meal tickets, and women our whole emotional world, the rivalry between women that sex and beauty aroused was a very real problem.

Now we pay our own way and can have as many men as we want; even with the scourge of sex-related diseases, we could practice safe sex. But we don't. Venereal diseases today are as epidemic as unintended pregnancies. Clearly, sex isn't what women really want. If so, they would be responsible and have more of it. The fact is, in divorcing feminism from the joy of sex, the old-line feminists maintain their control over women's world by making men the enemy and keeping women under the censorious control of other women.

Never in my lifetime have clothes had the burning significance that they have today. The sexual look has replaced the sexual act; as in Vogueing, the goal of being seen, looked at, is the crowning achievement. A new look must be created every five minutes, a fashion world gone haywire, ultimately tearing the clothes apart, exposing the seams as in an act of search and discovery, as exemplified by the deconstructed look that was hot for a season, only to be trashed and replaced by bras, corsets, underwear sewn onto the outside of the garment. What are we looking for?

In bad old Patriarchal days we wore the same clothes for years, took care of them. What we had on our backs was not as important as who we were inside. We have not yet found a substitute for The Patriarchal Deal. Feminism would have us believe that their antisex, antimen formula is the Final Solution. But the young generation is not buying it, which leaves them with a problem of identity.

In a 1992 *Time*/CNN poll, 50 percent of women surveyed said that they did not believe the Women's Movement reflected the views of most women. In an *Atlantic Monthly* article that interviewed the editors of the top women's magazines, the issue of readers' identification with the word *feminist* was decidedly mixed.

We read a book, listen to the babble at a cocktail party or on television, memorize the latest revolutionary rhetoric, even act on it, and think we have become new people, moved light-years beyond our parents. But the deep, unconscious feelings we took in from our parents, the sense of right and wrong that they got from their parents—which is our conscience—these feelings change slowly, if they change at all. Neither men nor women realized thirty years ago how long it would take to begin to change a way of life in which each sex had found its identity for hundreds of years.

Not even the man most committed to feminism, as burdened as he might feel supporting a woman economically, sexually, and socially, wants to lose his job to either another man or to a woman. The number of women today who are returning from the workplace to their mothers' roles, or who would like to if they could afford it, says how slowly the deep, often unconscious feelings of right and wrong change. That so many of the near naked revelers of the sixties and seventies have become conservative pillars of today's society says that the roots of real change are still shallow. Nothing underscores the slow pace of change like the tragedies associated with sex, mistakes that perhaps could have been avoided if sex had been put at the top of the feminist agenda along with equality in the workplace.

Feminism Versus Beauty and Men

It was inevitable that beauty would be jettisoned within the Women's Movement. It wasn't simply the mechanics of marching in high heels carrying large purses filled with cosmetics. Lovely beauty was women's greatest bargaining chip in a system feminism sought to overhaul, a system in which men had all the real power—economic. A woman's face, her body, were her meal ticket, a certificate to marriage, a name, home, and sustenance. You saw a beautiful woman and expected her to be with a powerful man; you recognized the arrangement. Women thus pursued looks as doggedly as men died at their desks from too early heart attacks, pushing the envelope to prove their manhood.

A mother looked at her baby daughter's face and saw her future. But even the loveliest woman soon realized that her days in the sun were limited. Married at twenty (the average age of marriage in 1960), the young wife rose in the morning to see the sun already waning.

Beauty had to become politically incorrect if women were to imagine ourselves whole and independent, without a man at our side. In our mind's eye, we had to see not every hair in place, but a life in which we clothed and fed our selves and paid for it, an image diametrically opposed to how our mothers looked and lived. What was essential was that we no longer saw ourselves as trophies for men.

Woman's greatest power, however, was and remains that she bears, raises, and shapes the human race. But it was power that, as such, could not be realized. So long as women were totally dependent on men's money for survival, of what value was conscious awareness of motherhood's power opposite the fact that mother and children died without "his" food and shelter? The equation of his money for her beauty and child-bearing power was too loaded even to think about. Women ruled from behind the fan; women ruled through manipulation to the extent that we ruled at all. And should a financially successful man awaken to an awareness of his increased power, entitlement nudged him toward a younger, more beautiful woman as his prize.

Not every man traded up as his fortunes increased. Many loved their wives and families and felt the woman's role to be very powerful indeed, reminiscent of what his mother had once had over him. Couples often called one another "Mother" and "Father." President Reagan called Nancy "Mommy." Nevertheless, there was no discussing how the Patriarchal Deal looked on Libra's scale.

Women resisted seeing the role of motherhood as powerful. They still do. Consciously, it didn't feel like power, wasn't how the woman's own mother assessed child-rearing; to this day there remains a suspicion that, if motherhood is portrayed as "power" rather than as the preferred "sacrifice," women might lose their monopolistic hold on the nursery.

As for discussing "his" money, it remains the surest sign of imminent argument, a chink in the armor of a marriage. To this day, divorce lawyers have a hard time convincing the jilted wife that she must ascertain her departing husband's net worth. Her arm may be in a sling from the last battle, but she clings to the belief that he will take care of her.

When I was growing up, Nice Girls never discussed money. It was bad manners to mention the price paid for a car, a house, even a dress. Even when we women, the owners and practitioners of beauty power, set modern feminism in motion, there was never an honest, open discussion of how we might now use beauty power to our own benefit. It was too hot to handle. Instead, feminism simply outlawed beauty in the early seventies, banned the use of it, the enjoyment of it. Women who came to the rally in makeup, who smiled too invitingly at men, were given "the treatment" by their sisters.

It is the nature of revolutions to be intolerant. Much of the steam required for the march is gotten from the electric charge of exclusivity that binds the revolutionaries. Rejecting those who didn't have the right fit, the proper look, the precise political feel, tightened the ranks of The Women's Movement. It wasn't just what you said, how you acted, it was also very much how you looked in what you were wearing.

My own awareness of feminism in the late sixties was gradual, but what I read and heard resonated on a deep, personal level, the visceral response being, "Yes, absolutely, yes!" The feminism that evolved from Betty Friedan's *The Feminine Mystique* arrived at a time when many sirens competed for our eyes and ears. The world as we had always known it was changing rapidly, and those of us who wanted to change with it believed that for the first time in our lives originality, not conformity, was the rule.

Feminism's focus on economic equality made it my kind of club. Who could argue with equal pay? When I was a little girl, hadn't they made fun of me for saving my nickels and dimes, much as they had questioned why I didn't want to marry one of the "nice boys" I brought home on vacation? It was essential to me that I pay my own rent and be free of economic dependence on my family, knowing that every dollar I took had strings attached.

It would take some time before I understood the animosity my Halston suede pants aroused at a rally. I refused to give them up. As time passed and the anti-beauty rules became even stricter, I watched as leaders of The Women's Movement rejected offers of assistance from powerful women who worked in films, actresses who were beautiful. There was clearly more to feminism's anti-beauty stand than met the eye.

"The problem that has no name," Friedan wrote, "that American women are kept from growing to their full human capacities—is taking a far greater toll on the physical and mental health of our country than any known disease." When I reread *The Feminine Mystique* today, what jumps out is that Friedan did *not* write into her agenda the anti-men, antisex, anti-beauty stance that would later characterize feminism. Perhaps it was inevitable that some women would focus on men as the enemy of all the injustices we women endure, but it should be remembered that it did not begin this way. Many of us who were happily dancing and sleeping with men throughout the sixties would awaken in the seventies to find ourselves labeled traitors, women who were not "real feminists."

To my knowledge no one spoke it out loud, put it in writing, but eventually any attempt at beauty, at drawing attention to one's body, one's face, was outlawed. Sex and beauty cannot be divorced, therefore any man who turned up at the rallies in the early seventies had to have a strong stomach, since anti-men, hate dialogue was the order of business.

But there were men who were good feminists and who fought for women's rights. One of them recalls a political rally in New York in the seventies organized to promote the election of a certain feminist. "There were several hundred women there and maybe a dozen men besides me," he says. "For two hours different speakers attacked the male establishment in a way that made me, how shall I say . . . nervous? When it was over, the candidate leapt to the podium and cheerfully cried out, 'Now, let's all join hands and sing, "What the world needs now is love, love, love."'"

The Feminine Mystique didn't get its brief review in the *New York Times* until three months after publication, and then the reviewer took exception to the author's "sweeping generalities," saying it was "superficial to blame the 'culture'" for women's "depression and emptiness." It made the bestseller list for only six weeks that year, never surpassing *Happiness Is a Warm Puppy* by Charles Schultz. But by November 1963, *Life* magazine would call it "an overnight best seller, as disruptive of cocktail party conversation and women's clubs discussions as a tear-gas bomb."

My earliest memory of one of these cocktail party conversations was a topic I'd never before heard women discuss, speech. It was a tenet of Patriarchal Society that Nice Girls don't talk, never raise their voices. As far back as the Middle Ages, writes Marina Warner, "the seduction of women's talk reflected the seduction of their bodies; it was considered dangerous to Christian men, and condemned as improper *per se*." Women's voices, like our sexuality, had to be suppressed.

Now, for the first time, I stood with other women and talked about the problem of getting our voices heard, forming our thoughts in our minds and speaking them before the thought had vanished. It may sound basic today, but in the late sixties it was exhilarating to stand with a drink in my hand hearing other women say exactly what I'd been living through since adolescence, when I'd first begun to bite my tongue before the spontaneous idea was verbalized.

"By the time I form a sentence in my head," one woman said, "the conversation has already moved onto another subject." We all nodded agreement, and another woman added that wasn't it strange that when a woman said something interesting, no one heard it, but if a man's voice said the identical thing ten minutes later, all eyes would turn to him and both women and men would say, "Why, George, what an exciting idea!"

That was grassroots feminism at work, a reaction to Friedan's book that had spawned a revolution. You needn't have read the book to respond to what was in the air. Three years after publication of *The Feminine Mystique*, in 1966, Friedan was at a luncheon with a group of women who were discussing the deliberate nonenforcement of Title VII of the Civil Rights Act, which barred sexual discrimination. At some point in the discussion, they decided to form an "NAACP for women." "I wrote the word 'NOW' on a paper napkin," she said. "'Our group should be called the National Organization *for* Women,' I said, 'because men should be part of it.'"

Friedan would remain president of NOW until 1970. Since her original "friendly to men" concept of feminism would not prevail after her leadership, let me quote Friedan's 1983 epilogue to the twentieth anniversary edition of *The Feminine Mystique*; just maybe, given today's renewed interest in looks/fashion/beauty, it would be helpful for those who have forgotten, or who are too young to remember, that there was a moment in feminism when women believed we could have equality along with pleasure in both beauty and the love of men. We still can. Here is Friedan:

> I couldn't define "liberation" for women in terms that denied the sexual and human reality of our need to love, and even sometimes to depend upon, a man. What had to be changed was the obsolete feminine and masculine sex roles that dehumanized sex, making it almost impossible for women and men to make love, not war. . . . It seemed to me that men weren't really the enemy— they were fellow victims, suffering from an outmoded masculine mystique that made them feel unnecessarily inadequate when there were no bears to kill.

Looking back at the way things were in the late sixties, the anger and rebellion that was already in the air from all the other revolutions in the streets, it is easy to see how feminism tapped into the look of rebellion—jeans, boots, long hair, the total antifashion statement. You could march against the war in Vietnam and for women's rights in the same afternoon, changing neither expression nor clothing. My friend Molly was in the front line of the bloody 1968 Chicago riots, and she never traveled without her heated rollers. By 1970, in the Fiftieth Anniversary of Woman's Suffrage March down Fifth Avenue, women led the march of 50,000, but men also marched. It was still possible to be a good feminist and love men too.

Psychologist Warren Farrell, who became active in the women's movement in 1969, served on the board of directors of the New York City chapter of NOW for three years. "Men were in almost every women's movement that took place, either joining individually or in auxiliaries like 'Men for ERA,'" he reminds me today. "Betty Friedan and Karen DeCrow—NOW president from 1971 to 1974—were always very, very, very, very committed to *equality* between men and women, not just women's rights."

When feminism eliminated men from our struggle for equality, we took a road that eventually led to today's victim mentality; we also strengthened the divisive War Between the Women. Modern man didn't invent the Patriarchal Deal so much as inherit it. Men too suffered from society's demands. Yes, they controlled the money, but you didn't have to be clairvoyant to see that most men were barren of the kind of feelings that sustain life, caring, loving, tender, empathic emotions. In the early seventies, sociologist Jessie Bernard would write of the heightened rate of alcoholism, suicide, and death among men who lived without women.

The woman who would follow Friedan as acknowledged leader of the Feminist Movement, Gloria Steinem, at some level clearly believed this too. Men, as lovers and friends, have been at the heart of her life and never seemed to interfere with her feminism. Steinem is the key to any understanding of feminism's absence of comment on how looks should function in the world we have so dramatically altered. She knows men, knows how to use them to get what she needs politically and personally. This is not a criticism. We use whatever resources we have. Why should the trade-off of money for power be more acceptable than the uses of beauty? Would a member of the Kennedy clan hesitate to use the family name to gain advantage?

When Steinem needed a powerful name to pen the foreword to her first book in 1963, titled *The Beach Book*, a lighthearted collection of songs, puzzles, chess problems, instructions on how to get a tan, peel a sunburn, build sand castles, she called on aristocratic John Kenneth Galbraith. He obliged. "Except that I like this book and the girl who put it together, I could seem a most improbable person to write this introduction," he begins.

But he did write it. Thirty years later I heard that her lover, Mort Zuckerman, would lend *Ms.* magazine $1.4 million. In the years in between those favors, men as well as women would personally and professionally assist Steinem for a variety of reasons, not the least of which was and is that she is lovely to look at. Why must an asset, any asset, go unacknowledged, regardless of its association with a time when beauty was our only ticket to power?

If there were a face to be attached to modern feminism, it would be Steinem's; a portrait on a postal stamp honoring feminism, it would be hers. We can't possibly understand today's ambivalence on issues of men and beauty and omit what Steinem herself stood for. She cannot be left out of the discussion because she was the feminist army's general and Pinup Girl. Her face alone triggers our memory of feminism becoming popular. The fact that it was and is a great-looking face matters.

"Personification of womanpower" was the caption under a photo of Steinem in a *Time* magazine article in January 1969. "One of the best dates to take to a New York party these days," the article opened, ". . . one of the most arresting names to drop—is Gloria Steinem. [She] is not only a successful freelance writer . . . she is also a trim, undeniably female, blonde-streaked brunette who has been described as 'the thinking man's Jean Shrimpton.' She does something for her soft suits and clinging dresses, has legs worthy of her miniskirts, and a brain that keeps conversation lively without getting tricky."

In a photo that accompanied the *Time* article, Gloria sits, long legs bared, worthy of a centerfold, not the costume or the pose assumed when she traveled the country raising "money and consciousness for the still amorphous and revolutionary state of mind called the Women's Liberation Movement." This is not to criticize the dual persona; there is, as our parents always told us, "a time and a place" for the power of sexual beauty. It helped influence wealthy, powerful men but it was not wanted at the diverse feminist rallies at which Steinem was speaking, often as a team with a black feminist partner.

"By speaking together at hundreds of public meetings," she wrote in her book of essays, *Outrageous Acts and Everyday Rebellions*, "we hoped to widen a public image of the women's movement created largely by its first homegrown media event, *The Feminine Mystique*."

To Steinem's thinking, Betty Friedan's book was aimed at "white, well-educated, suburban women" and as such had limited appeal. Though Friedan would eventually endorse Steinem's leadership, acknowledging feminism's need for a young, articulate leader, bad blood remained between them. That Steinem was a beauty didn't hurt her candidacy; feminism had gotten itself a name in the media as being an army of disgruntled, unattractive women who were acting out their anger at the men who rejected them. A stupid disclaimer but useful nonetheless to a media controlled by Patriarchal Society.

Gloria Steinem was heaven-sent. While she may describe herself in her autobiographical *Revolution from Within* as a woman who never outgrew her sense of herself as a pudgy, unattractive little girl, she flew in the face of adversaries of the movement, as proud and beautiful as the masthead on a fine schooner.

"One could argue that for a few years during the late 1960s and early 70s, there were two competing feminist movements—liberal feminism and women's liberation," wrote Flora Davis in *Moving the Moun-*

tain: The Women's Movement in America Since 1960. Among the latter were the New York Radical Women, the Redstockings, the Feminists, Cell 16, Bread and Roses, and SCUM (the Society for Cutting Up Men); they were a younger group of feminists, mostly in their twenties, many of them rooted in the Civil Rights Movement, campus radicalism, and opposition to the Vietnam War. "When it came to tactics," wrote Davis, "they thought in terms of civil disobedience—revolutionary tactics designed to force revolutionary changes."

Gloria Steinem provided what was needed; she was good for the cause, good for the ever hungry media. "We tangled a lot," said Friedan in a 1992 interview, referring to her relationship with Steinem. "I was really opposed to the radical chic, anti-man politics she espoused: 'A woman needs a man like a fish needs a bicycle.' . . . I didn't like it when she went to the League of Women Voters to support the ERA and, in her speech, said that all wives are prostitutes. I thought it was politically unwise, and I fought it within NOW and within the women's movement generally. I fought attempts to push the women's movement out of the mainstream, and that put me in opposition to Gloria."

In time Betty Friedan would be accused of being too soft on men. The organization she founded, NOW, would move ever more toward militancy, and by the early seventies, Gloria would be feminism's leader. That she was articulate, charismatic, and a beauty, even with the dark glasses, the hair curtaining her face, made her even more of a standout figurehead: "Eat your hearts out, guys, she is ours!"

As the more radical fringe groups began dying out in the early seventies, NOW (and other moderate organizations like the AAUW) began to absorb the radical women who had nowhere else to go. Thus, these organizations were pulled toward the matriarchal (anti-male) left; by the mid-seventies fully half of the nation's NOW chapters were opposed to joint custody as a starting assumption in a divorce.

In 1970 Kate Millett appeared on the cover of *Time* magazine, which excerpted her *Sexual Politics,* and in the same year Germaine Greer's *The Female Eunuch* was also published. A group of women writers and editors decided "that a glossy magazine that appeared every month on newsstands around the country might make feminists of thousands of women." In 1971, *New York* magazine offered a preview of *Ms.* magazine, and in January 1972 the first issue hit the newsstand and sold out in eight weeks.

Now media decision makers began to take the complaints of the women's movement more seriously. "As they began to treat the movement with more respect," writes Flora Davis, "they abandoned the more militant radical feminists. . . . By the mid-seventies, most of the radical feminists who had written the books and lit up the talk shows were no longer heard from."

No one has been more of a political savant regarding the ticklish feminist issue of beauty than Gloria herself. It is an interesting sidebar to modern feminism that its most recognizable leader has managed during the past twenty-five years to juggle beauty with "being taken seriously," while simultaneously maintaining intimate relationships with various wealthy, powerful men.

"Steinem's expressed attitude toward her own loveliness is that she just wishes everyone would ignore it—with the implication that anyone who responds to it is simply treating her as a Sexual Object—but things are a little less clear-cut than that. 'She doesn't like this idea of being thought of as a sex symbol, yet she seems to ask for it in a way—perhaps without realizing it,' says *New York Times* woman's news editor Charlotte Curtis."

Steinem's fondness for the mirror has been obvious throughout her career, and she has succeeded in making it seem that her being beautiful was inconsequential. Having put away her miniskirts in the early seventies, she chose to see her new feminist self as a woman in jeans, hair falling across her face, face hidden behind large shades. But what the rest of the world saw was a beautiful woman in tight jeans with wonderful hair and glamorous tinted glasses who also spoke persuasively and was followed worshipfully by an army. The packaging mattered all the more for being equaled by its content, a genius at leadership of women who publicly disdained men and other women's pursuit of beauty. What a coup.

I sat opposite Steinem in a videotaped interview we did in 1989, when I was beginning research for this book. She couldn't have been more agreeable, nicer. I was constantly in jeopardy of falling under the spell of her line of reasoning, so contagious is her geniality, the—well, yes—motherly tone in which she seems to persuade you away from your own point of view. When I asked her bluntly about her beauty, how she used it, felt its power or hindrance, she answered with a story: "There was an assignment at *Life* magazine in the sixties that I was eager to get. I arrived with my portfolio to be greeted by a man who looked up at me and said, 'We don't want a pretty girl, we want a writer.' I didn't get the job."

The considerable heat Mort Zuckerman takes in *Revolution from Within* may be the price one pays for falling in love with a saint; Zuckerman used to tell her that it was harder living with a saint than being a saint. In the end, after quarreling with herself over the luxury of limousines, the big house in the Hamptons, the genuine pleasure of being the companion of one of the most powerful men in New York while simultaneously representing the feminist movement, Gloria voted in favor of The Sisterhood.

It is a fine decision. I genuinely believe that these will be Gloria Steinem's happiest years, and her most powerful. She has declared herself free of the subversive temptation of beauty maintenance and of men. Her followers now have her all to themselves, though I always believed they never doubted that her heart was theirs and that they relished her ability to use her looks to gain them ground, perks, influence.

While Gloria was pushing her politics and denying her beauty, Helen Gurley Brown was publishing her brand of feminism, which never wavered. Looking beautiful, getting laid, and making money never made the Cosmo Girl any less a feminist. From the day Brown took over as editor of that ailing magazine in 1965, she stuck to her formula, creating one of the great legends in publishing history. The Cosmo Girl—please note that she never became a Cosmo Woman—was created from Brown's own rib.

More the girlfriend of *Playboy* than a version of a *Playboy* for women, the Cosmo Girl invites the eye to pause, to peruse, to plunge the extra quarter inch toward the nipple, toward the pubic hair, but don't look away, don't *not* look at me as a sex object, she challenges. Does it bother Brown that her brand of feminism collides head-on with *Ms.* magazine? Let the near-naked Cosmo Girl reply from her typical full-page advertisement:

Am I a feminist? Yes. Feminism means you want the best for *both* sexes, everyone gets the chance to be his or her most achieving self. Have there been inequities for women? You bet, but our sex is *getting* there . . . lawyers, doctors, scientists by the thousand and we've just begun. My favorite magazine says equality and achievement are crucial for women but you don't have to stop loving men while you get there. *That's* being *feminine.* I love that magazine. I guess you could say I'm That COSMOPOLITAN Girl.

The only thing that worries Helen Gurley Brown, for whom I wrote my first published magazine article, is circulation, whether she is keeping up with the successive generations of women who buy her magazine. Circulation just climbs and climbs, edging toward 3,000,000, making *Cosmopolitan* "the largest-selling young woman's magazine in the world." It is more than five times the circulation of *Ms.* With great reluctance she has accepted a forced retirement in 1997 at the age of seventy-four, after thirty-two years at the helm.

Gloria and Helen have sat crosstown at their respective magazines for years. According to my research, *Ms.* has never taken on the Cosmo philosophy. The silence probably irks Brown, a tough competitor. Gloria wisely doesn't argue with America's favorite women's magazine: how to blame big-bad-men-the-brutes for forcing women to buy their monthly bible of sex, fashion, glamour, and advice?

Locked into its narrow formula, *Ms.* magazine often struggles to survive. There is little humor and, of course, little regard for the human craving for beauty and sex. Describing women's devotion to romance as a "displacement" was pretty much how Steinem would instruct her followers regarding women's devotion to beauty; it has always been an open secret that Gloria loved the mirror, but political leaders are famous for their glaring inconsistencies.

It is maddening that Gloria cannot enlarge her vision of her feminism to include other voices, dissension, healthy argument. She is a highly competitive leader, but alas, her brand of competition is filled with denial, a kind of mother-knows-best refusal to let her children disagree, grow up, maybe usurp her throne. The new generation of feminists does not blindly accept her absolutism; but when they argue against such Steinem "truths" as the one below, their books and articles are shelled by the heavy hitters who still control the media:

"It isn't that women attracted to pornography cannot also be feminists," Steinem wrote in "Erotica vs. Pornography," "but that pornography itself must be recognized as an adversary of women's safety and equality, and therefore, in the long run, of feminism."

Since beauty and sex are so intertwined, it is not surprising that Steinem is no less peremptory and absolutist regarding beauty's role in feminism: "So women who 'ooh' and 'ah' about clothes and make great fuss about them are playing into the image so many men like to have of us—of 'fluffy little things.' To play into that role is actually to help in the dehumanizing of women, and we should stop it." How then to explain her own pursuit of beauty's power?

Over the years, feminism has lost hundreds of thousands of members because women in Middle America didn't see themselves as part of the movement. Ordinary women wanted equality but balked at the man-hating look and speech of a feminism that would have separated them from their husbands, sons, and lovers. It is a major reason for our having lost the ERA in 1982. We lost it for other reasons too, but for me, the sad nonsense of it was the inability of feminism to relate to women who choose the traditional style of living. Feminism was not the look of a life that they wanted; many of them didn't so much agree with Phyllis Schlafly as disagree with the bossy arrogance of the toughs who dictated feminism, Big Girls who, just like nine-year-olds, weren't going to let you play unless you played by their rules.

As novelist Anne Tyler said in 1982, "A lot of the failures of the movement are built into the people who are speaking for women. . . . Basically I agree with everything they say, but I find myself wanting to disagree because of the way they say it. If people like me, who are pro-women, are put off by it, imagine other people."

In 1980, women like Raquel Welch were rejected by Feminist Headquarters when they offered to lend their considerable support to the passage of the Equal Rights Amendment. Was the fear that the loyalist membership would be undermined by a subversive interest in beauty maintenance? Feminism's concern with the illegitimacy of beauty continues for no other reason than the fact that beauty arouses competition, that emotion that cannot be discussed.

Absolutism has soured feminism since the late sixties, not healthy argument, but imperious women's voices, each claiming ownership of the word *feminist*. In the April 1992 pro-choice rally in Washington, in which 500,000 people marched for choice, Betty Friedan, mother of the Women's Movement, wasn't even asked to speak.

Says Friedan, "I'm not going to lie. I'm very hurt when I feel trashed by the leaders of the organizations that I helped to start. But I'm not going to indulge in the media's delight at exacerbating the divisions between us. I do admit that I was really hurt that I wasn't asked to speak at the rally. . . . It's sort of a de-Stalinization of the women's movement—their attempt to write me out of history, though I don't think that will happen."

The "banishment" of Friedan was tawdry and vindictive. Can't these women see how it makes "their" feminism look when they exclude the woman who pioneered modern feminism? When a Susan Faludi charges Friedan with "stomping on a movement that she did so much to create and lead," and consequently becomes Steinem's new acolyte, one must look more closely: Faludi is meek in self-presentation and possesses a tiny voice, close to a whisper. She is no challenge to the queen; but Friedan—well, she may not be a beauty, but she believes in its power, is an honest lover of men, and has a strong voice.

Why did a book like Naomi Wolf's *The Beauty Myth* rally women from college campuses across the country? It offered the standard panacea for all of women's ills: Big Bad Men made me pursue beauty, starve my body. As much media coverage as the book received, it didn't detract women from the heated pursuit of beauty that had started up again in the mid-eighties. Nor did it deter the author from fondly including men in her next book, who turn out to be beloved, wanted, needed.

Beauty/sex/men will be that route by which we exit the old feminism. It is a good road; well argued, written about, and practiced, it is already taking us into a more modern feminism. Writers like Camille Paglia, Katie Roiphe, Christina Hoff Sommers, and Nadine Strossen, to name a few, have already put their published voices on the line; puffballs of smoke from the old feminist headquarters label them "pseudo" feminists, post-feminists, "faux" feminists, silly girlish names that betray the weaknesses of the old guard. However, one great victory may come out of this name-calling: It will eventually get us out of the Semantic Jungle.

Gloria, "America's best-loved feminist," sounds no less girlish when she excommunicates Camille Paglia from The Group. Because another woman does not agree with her, and because she is brilliant and much in favor of beauty, power, and sex, Steinem banishes Paglia in print from "her" feminism. "What's important is that we have progressed enough that being a feminist is no longer seen as some fringe activity," says Steinem. "It is mainstream enough for anti-feminists like Camille Paglia to need to say that they are feminists." It is a damning remark, but filled with vanity and arrogance too in its sweeping power of random banishment.

Paglia can be difficult, dictatorial, and egocentric too, but if she is not a luminous feminist, a warrior consistently sharpened by her own brand of fierce intellectual debate, then I do not understand feminism.

She certainly lacks Steinem's ability to please, but that is precisely what makes her a powerful contender; she belongs to that generation of feminism that speaks its mind without apology, without smiling The Nice Girl smile. Isn't this what we fought for, a feminism that encourages debate so strong it can swell and contract like a heartbeat, even on disagreement from its members?

If Steinem were not so narrowly focused on controlling her leadership of a small band of feminists but instead reached out to the millions of women eager to be part of feminism, she could still win the day. But she doesn't know how to lose, a prerequisite for a healthy competitor. The fear of loss strangles her, pushing her to an ever more rigid position. It is not competition that she hates so much as the inability to handle defeat gracefully.

She often quotes Alfie Kohn's book *No Contest: The Case Against Competition*; Kohn would eradicate the competitive ethic altogether. But, as one reviewer wrote of the book, "Kohn is describing competition in its pathologically excessive form. For many of us, the pleasure of the contest makes the outcome unimportant. It is meeting the challenge, not beating the other guy, that lifts the spirit. Games do not just socialize for the lust to win, they also teach the idea of impartial rules and fair play. . . . Implicit in [Kohn's] analysis is the idea that if we could get rid of competition, we could enter paradise. . . . The more likely alternative to the right to compete seems to be the loss of rights altogether."

On her side, Paglia loves the competitive debate. Intellectually, she is a wizard at the powerful workings of beauty throughout history, having written often about it, and clearly recognizes Gloria's conflict over beauty and competition. From a stage in Manhattan, in front of the *60 Minutes* cameras, Paglia delivers her challenge to Gloria: "I hate victimology. I despise a victim-centered view of the universe which, you know, is symptomatic of current feminism." She goes on to accuse Steinem of "keeping down dissident female voices over the last twenty years."

When the *60 Minutes* camera crew turns up at Steinem's own panel discussion crosstown, they are barred at the door. "No, you're not going to ask a question for your show about an antifeminist woman," yells Gloria from the dais. "We are not going to contribute to the dissension. This is our night. . . . Turn the cameras off. We don't give a shit about what she thinks." It was the only time I have ever heard Steinem lose her cool. Her often denied competitive spirit was on fire. She is not going to give up "her" feminism gracefully.

An exhibitionist at heart, Paglia fairly loses control when a camera focuses on her, a public demonstration with which I sympathize, knowing too well the invisibility the writer feels, alone for years in a room, leading some of our profession to an over-the-top desire for applause. But Camille Paglia is doing an impressive job of being in her own words, "the Paglia cigarette boat that goes POW, POW, POW. I put so many torpedoes into those . . . big heavy, lazy battleships [of feminism] . . . they're slowly sinking and they don't even know it."

Women's Ink/Women's Blood

There was a group of women writers to which I belonged in the mid-seventies, which in its small way reflected the best and worst of feminism, unspeakable contradictions that in the end dismembered our club as cruelly as a bomb planted at its center. We called ourselves Women's Ink and met informally at a different member's apartment each month to socialize and to exchange professional ideas.

Not only do writers live inside their heads, but most spend the day alone in a room, dealing with thoughts that in one form or another also end up in our dreams at night. Professionally, we have a naive attachment (no doubt growing out of this isolation) to our agents and editors, whom we choose to believe have our interests foremost in their parental minds. While they may like our work and even us, the agent/editor/publisher alliance comes first to each of them. You can see how many voids a group like Women's Ink might fill, giving us a setting in which to gossip, find consolation, and discuss the convoluted workings of contracts, royalty statements, and book tours.

There was from the start, however, a rivalrous electricity in those big West Side apartments where we gathered, which sent many of us home feeling as though we'd just been through a sorority rush. It was hard to put your finger on it, but in hindsight I'd say it was the cliquish Girl Grouping of the eighth grade; there were the "stars," the much published women, and we lesser mortals, or so we felt.

About four months after our launch a power struggle erupted over leadership, not an openly aired and argued competition but something far more insidious, like a whisper campaign in school against a sacrificial lamb. There were midnight telephone calls, secret meetings of the so-called Steering Committee, the objective of which was to blackball this one assertive woman, to exclude her in the style of Three Little Girls Can't Play Together.

I do not mean to portray myself as innocent, for when asked to attend these clandestine powwows, I went. But I would return home shaking; I was writing *My Mother/My Self* at the time, and women's cruelty to other women was precisely what was filling my waking and dreaming hours. I suppose I was flattered to be included, but to this day I am not sure exactly what crime The Accused One had committed, the pretty blond one whose head was on the guillotine. Certainly, the real argument was over power, something we couldn't say out loud, being women raised by women. Because we had not been taught to compete in a healthy way, these meetings were not about open, honest argument.

Here we were, seasoned, card-carrying feminists, and rather than hold together a group that would aid us all professionally, we were going to disembowel it. One woman had the audacity to question the group's leaders. And she was very pretty, and tough, and had genuine leadership ability herself. The most cardinal of her sins: She had broken the no-compete rule. In a final letter she wrote:

A few years ago Nora Ephron wrote an essay about vaginal sprays. One reason they sell is: you can always make people believe something is wrong with them. Hit them where they hurt—in their sense of fear, their sense of being ugly, their sense of smelling bad. You can always make people feel that if they are assertive, they smell. . . . Raising one's voice . . . good anger, and confrontation are not *my* problem. They *are* the problem of many on the Steering Committee. Instead of being complimented on aggressiveness, I was told I needed vaginal sprays.

It was a nasty piece of business, that campaign to spray her, an ugly little war waged by grown women. There was no enemy "out there," no evil men upon whom we could dump our badness. The enemy was within, a cruelty that each of us had felt at one time or another, seething inside, just waiting for a victim. And here she was: Spray her!

The linkage between women's ink and women's blood might sound obtuse, but it is integral to this book. What we women allow ourselves to say, to write, is constrained by our deepest feelings about our bodies. The constant need to appear clean, to not humiliate ourselves, censors even what we allow ourselves to think.

Men don't spray women. Other women have the art down pat. *Time* magazine's review of my book on women's sexual fantasies, *Women on Top*, is an example of one woman's spray job of another. The article was titled "Batteries Not Included." The line that most revealed the reviewer's insecurities was "Gone are the appealing men, comfortable settings, clean sheets and room service of prefeminist fantasies." "Clean sheets"? Pray, madam, how do you have sex and keep the sheets clean? In meek response to *Time* magazine's denunciation, my publishers hastily removed the Simon & Schuster logo on the next printing of the book.

It's been almost twenty-five years since Nora Ephron wrote that essay, practically the life span of the women's movement. You would think that as women grew professionally and economically we would become impervious to The Spray Job, that our self-image would have moved beyond the niggling fear that the taint of our genitals had once again fouled the environment. I regret to report that the genital spray industry has never been more profitable.

Ephron's article, titled "Dealing with the, Uh, Problem," was published in *Esquire* in 1973. Since the "problem" is key to women's self-image, let me reprint Ephron's quote of psychoanalyst Natalie Shainess: "These [feminine hygiene] products further paranoid feelings in women and in men about women—and the way they're advertised presents a horrendous image, of women being inherently smelly creatures. It undermines the sense of self and ego even as it's supposed to do something about it."

The quote above is as applicable today as when first printed. We will put a woman on the moon and in the Oval Office before we will address the unspeakable issue of how we women feel about our genitals. The only thing that has changed since 1972 is that the market for all feminine hygiene products has flourished, and nothing has contributed more to sales than the very knowing supervision of women who now run the focus groups and write the advertisements.

There is nothing harder than convincing women that this subject pertains directly to self-perception, image, how we feel about and see ourselves in the mirror. So much is suppressed, denied, "forgotten," a whole lifetime, beginning at birth, in which our hands, eyes, and thoughts have been directed away from that area that is the heartbeat of our gender. We compete with men in the workplace, live with or without them by choice, but at any moment of any day we are vulnerable. As the persecuted woman in my Women's Ink group said, "We can always be made to feel that there is something wrong with us, that we are ugly, too assertive, too loud, that we smell bad."

All the success and power in the world are as dust opposite the fear of unexpected humiliations, bad odors, the sense of failure as a woman. We buy our own clothes, care deeply about our looks, but what chance has the pretty new dress, the lovely hair, the shapely legs against yeast infections, odors, menstrual blood, an entire zoo of microscopic germs threatening to overtake our vaginas and expose us publicly: "What's that smell?"

"Put our fingers in there, put something deep into ourselves when we're bleeding and then remove it when it's full of blood? Absolutely not!" said a focus group researching a new product that would allow women to enjoy sex—"without a mess"—during their menstrual periods. "They simply didn't want a product that involved them having to understand where to put something inside themselves," said the market researcher. "They didn't want to have to reach in and remove it, come in contact with the menstrual flow." Nor were the added days for sexual activity seen as a bonus. "I'm used to getting ten days a month off from sex," was a common comment. "I don't want those days for sex, thanks very much."

Most men have no clue as to the extent of our genital anxiety. Even we are distanced consciously from how that sensitivity affects everything else in our lives. The next time you read the cautionary text of a feminine hygiene ad, consider what buttons are being pushed; in reminding other women of the communal Cloaca we all share, the sameness of our lives is being emphasized. In their way, these ads and commercials, which now enter our living rooms via television in living color, are warning us that any woman who thinks she is smarter, faster, prettier than any other had better think again. In the reminder that we are all alike in this one unfortunate matter, the competitive woman is tripped up. A woman needn't be warned in so many words that she has soiled her skirt; all women need do is leave another woman out, give her the treatment as in my Women's Ink group, to let her know she smells bad.

How easily we are deceived by the New Women's looks, the wrappings on the seductive exhibitionists who stride the city streets, hems up to the crotch, nipples discernible beneath the cropped, tight sweaters prescribed by this season's fashion dictators. Not just men taken in, but we women too, convinced that a woman who can dress that authoritatively, broadcast that domineering look, is absolutely sure of herself, down to the bone. Anyone with that kind of attitude obviously has her life under control. Oh?

I sometimes think the hard-earned money women invest in looks nowadays is a last-ditch denial of how we really see the most intimate area of our bodies. We are left to wonder which vision of womanhood is today's Real Woman, the constant reminders of our vulnerability or the new Bitch Heroine?

It is all of a package, The In-Charge New Woman is inseparable from the insecure child, is still slave to her genitals. If we are ever to get the look right, interior and exterior lined up, it will be the most important missing chapter in feminism: We will learn to protect ourselves contraceptively. Among thirty- to thirty-four-year-olds, 41 percent of pregnancies are unplanned. And this age group is the fruit of our labors of the past twenty-five years. Nothing will change until we explore our deepest, unconscious feelings about our genitals.

As sexually voracious as books, films, and television may portray the new Dark Heroine, the beautiful bitch who kills and fucks "like a man," the lie is at her center, as evidenced by the gigantic, female, genital cleansing industry. She is more technological product than an organic New Woman who has created herself from the inside out, meaning on the unconscious level, which is where real change occurs. She is a media event, born of our new economics. Her look was inevitable when our recent accomplishments could no longer be contained within the Dark Blue Dress for Success Suit. We women wanted something to show for our hard work. So there she/we stand in our Armani suit, self-confident, a dash of arrogance. But we bleed once a month, emit an odor in crowded elevators, fear we have a dark spot on our skirt.

The new heroines may fuck men to death on the screen, push their naked breasts in men's faces, and leave their panties at home, but what women honestly think about our bodies is hammered at again and again in television commercials for vaginal sprays, douches, disinfectants, anti-yeast creams, all of which promise to make a garden of the sewer. The new Bitch Heroine is long overdue; she represents the very real dark side of women denied in our earlier idealization. "Shoot the women first," Interpol instructs its antiterrorist squads, because female terrorists are considered more dangerous than male terrorists. Is anyone really surprised?

Audiences accept Linda Fiorentino killing men without losing a lift on her stiletto heels. It is real life that is scary, real women acting out their venomous resentment and bitchy rivalry, all the while smiling and saying, "Oh, no, we love one another!" Women's rage is in the air, the Harpies are everywhere; screenwriters give us Killer Mommy movies and killer adolescent movies too, such as *Heavenly Creatures*, the story of two girls who bludgeon to death one of their mothers. The real event took place in 1952, when there wasn't an appetite for such films; today, people want to see it like it really is.

Notice that the beautiful Bitch Heroine is almost always without child. She is more weapon than woman and probably doesn't bleed at all, couldn't/wouldn't conceive. Her loathing is gathered into a ball aimed at men who have created all the evil in the world. There are many reasons she despises men, not the least of which is their failure to convince her of her beauty, an accusation she would never level against other women.

Men are such easy scapegoats; we blame them for the brevity of our functional lives, hemmed in by the onset of youthful beauty, our reproductive ability, and the cessation of both, and we blame them for not listening to our voices. And yet, I haven't a doubt that our primary contention over power lies not with men but with one another. Nowhere is this more obviously played out than in the beauty arena.

Today we have alternative powers, but we have returned to beauty with unparalleled intensity; beauty is where the answers are, the reasons we do not feel like the powerful women we have become. Women have important business to settle among ourselves. Until we accomplish it, we cannot take up seriously with men.

The word *lesbian* doesn't quite describe the sexual curiosity women today have about one another. They are like each other's archeological dig, in which the excavation of genitals, breasts, the taste of skin is where they look to find what is missing in their lives, something men cannot give them. Having inherited the rights of feminism, they wonder why they do not feel equal, not so much equal to men, but to other women.

Forget men's protestations of their beauty; it is *her* voice they trust and her beautiful body with which they want to identify. Any day, any month, any year, they may choose to enter into heterosexual love and sex—which is women's privilege—but first they need to hear this lovely other woman tell them in her womanly voice that she finds their genitals delicious, sweet to the taste, perfection in design. Given that she too bleeds once a month, her voice is credible.

In Alice Walker's 1982 Pulitzer Prize–winning novel *The Color Purple*, two women become lovers, Celie and Shug, after Shug introduces Celie to the beauty of her own genitals:

> She say, Here, take this mirror and go look at yourself down there, I bet you never seen it, have you?
> Naw.
> And I bet you never seen Albert [Celie's husband] down there either.
> I felt him, I say.
> I stand there with the mirror.
> She say, What, too shame even to go off and look at yourself? And you look so cute too, she say, laughing. All dressed up for Harpo's, smelling good and everything, but scared to look at your own pussy.
> You come with me while I look, I say.
> And us run off to my room like two little prankish girls.
> You guard the door, I say.
> She giggle. Okay, she say. Nobody coming. Coast clear.
> I lie back on the bed and haul up my dress. Yank down my bloomers. Stick the looking glass tween my legs. Ugh. All that hair. Then my pussy lips be black. Then inside look like a wet rose.
> It a lot prettier than you thought, ain't it? she say from the door.
> It mine, I say. Where the button?
> Right up near the top, she say. The part that stick out a little.
> I look at her and touch it with my finger. A little shiver go through me. Nothing much. But just enough to tell me this the right button to mash. . . .
> Albert and Harpo coming, she say. And I yank up my drawers and yank down my dress. I feel like us been doing something wrong.

In women's sexual fantasies of other women, the woman may call herself lesbian, bisexual, or heterosexual. Women these days express little guilt or ambivalence in either thinking about or being with another woman. Erotic interest in one another permeates the fashion shots in major women's magazines, in film, and in clubs such as The Clit Club and Lesbo-A-Go-Go: When Lesbo-A-Go-Go opened several years ago, groups of older feminists marched in to lecture their younger sisters that they were demeaning themselves. A near-naked beauty yelled back, as quoted in the *Washington Post*, "I'm very much a feminist and it's *not* degrading. . . . I like to get the crowd excited, to see their mouths" gape.

"A lot of what women don't like about their bodies is an area they never look at," says psychologist Lonnie Barbach. "Because they think it's ugly, it grows out of proportion in their minds until it develops a kind of largeness. The ugliness of their genitals becomes the heaviness of their thighs, too small breasts or too large, whatever they're criticizing in their body."

There were few erotic thoughts of sex with other women in *My Secret Garden*, published in 1973, but somewhere in the eighties, women changed their minds about oral sex and their partner of choice, in real life and in fantasy. Even women who have no actual desire for lesbian sex dream of having another woman's mouth explore that part of the body that more than any other disqualifies them from the beauty contest. As expert as a man's mouth may be, the fact that he is male and therefore can't grasp what is wanted in this exercise—to be made to feel that we are beautiful and delicious enough to eat—makes him second-best. Mother was our first Permission Giver; only someone who has a vagina and a clitoris can alter mother's opinion.

The sensations many women describe during oral sex come close to loss of consciousness, and the cry of orgasm is near tears, as at a long journey's end. That time to which oral orgasm returns us was when the bargain was first made to give up love of our body in exchange for the love of the person upon whom we were dependent for everything. The goal of the fantasy is to push past her "No," deny it. The scene of the fantasies during oral sex often go back to adolescence, when the rigid antisex rules were first tested; we are in parked cars, on beaches, in public rooms where discovery is imminent and the thrill of the forbidden so intense that it carries us over the top. For women, sex *is* breaking mother's rules, which is why the mirroring effect of another woman's genitals, another woman's mouth, has so much power. She has known The Sewer at its worst, when it bleeds and the stench is unbearable.

Most of us learned silence at our menarche. This business of bleeding flows alongside the lost reverence for women's voices. It must be very dark indeed, this blood, if no one speaks of its mystery. Silently, we too learn to count the days so that the unspeakable bleeding doesn't catch us unawares. In our cautionary muteness we swallow the spontaneous outburst that used to be our custom. What if we made ourselves the center of attention at the very moment our body betrayed us?

Time's 1970 Kate Millett cover story referred to her as "the Mao Tse-tung of Women's Liberation." In her book *Sexual Politics*, Millett elaborates on how the Patriarchal System confers on to women the dark, evil, *unclean* aspects of sexuality while keeping for itself the higher attributes of sex as symbolized by fertility through the Phallus:

> Patriarchy has God on its side. One of its most effective agents of control is the powerfully expeditious character of its doctrines as to the nature and origin of the female and the attribution to her alone of the dangers and evils it imputes to sexuality. The Greek example is interesting here: when it wishes to exalt sexuality it celebrates fertility through the phallus; when it wishes to denigrate sexuality, it cites Pandora. Patriarchal religion and ethics tend to lump the female and sex together as if the whole burden of the onus and stigma it attaches to sex were the fault of the female alone. Thereby sex, which is known to be unclean, sinful, and debilitating, pertains to the female, and the male identity is preserved as a human, rather than a sexual one.

I understand the black-and-white nature of Revolutionary zeal, but twenty-five years later women have sufficient power to address the shades of gray, which is really how we live. In this middle ground, can't we see who is most assiduously keeping alive the belief that we women represent the dirtiness of sexuality? It is we who have been raised to recognize the filth of our sexual parts, learned from other women, meaning that only women can change the image.

Men are not born hating women; it is learned. There are reasons for men abusing and raping women, reasons for the anger that fuels harassment. Is it not more important to know the reasons for men's rage, even if it involves some understanding of how it must feel to men that we no longer need them, that we want their jobs, their balls, everything?

One night during the Winter Olympics in 1994, my husband and I were lying in bed watching the women's figure-skating finals, oohing and ahing at the skill and beauty of the athletes. Still awash with admiration at the spectacle's conclusion, we switched channels to *Saturday Night Live*, where comedian Martin Lawrence was beginning his opening monologue.

Is it possible that two jaded adults in this day can still be shocked?

It wasn't just by what was said but by the fact that it appeared on a network show. Well, as the title of the show says, it is "Live," meaning that unless you were watching the original broadcast, you missed a lot of Lawrence's monologue, which was quickly edited. Let me add that it wasn't easy to obtain a video of the unedited show; even the NBC executive I telephoned, a friend, had difficulty getting this for me, so eager was the network to bury the evidence in response to the reaction of offended viewers.

Lawrence and others customarily do similar routines on cable shows, but this was a network first. Men, especially young men, are angry with women and have found ample ammunition in the television commercials that advertise women's humiliation. May I present Martin Lawrence:

> See, I'm single. I'm a single man. I don't have nobody; I'm looking for somebody.
>
> But I'm meeting a lot of women out there—you got some beautiful women, but you got something out there, I gotta say something: some of you are not washing you ass properly. . . . Now, I don't know what it is that a woman got to do to keep up the hygiene on the body. I know I'm watching douche commercials on television. And I'm wondering if some of you are reading the instructions. I don't think so. 'Cause I'm getting with some of you ladies, smelling odors, going, "Wait a minute! Girl, smell this, this is you. Smell yourself, girl!" [Then, to the camera:] Smell yourself! I'll tell a woman in a minute: "Douche! Douche!" Some women don't like when you tell them that, when you're straightforward with them. "Douche!" . . . I say, "I don't give a damn what you do. Put a TicTac in you ass! Put a Cert in your ass! This looks like a good damn place for a Stick-Up up in your ass!" . . . You know, I'm a man; I like to kiss on women. You know, I like to kiss all over their bodies. But if you're not clean in your proper areas, I can't kiss all over the places I want to kiss. Some women lets you go down, knowing they've got a yeast infection. I'm sorry. Sorry! Come up with dough all on your damn lip! Got a bagel and a croissant on your lip! "Anybody got any butter? I like jelly on mine."

The comic delivery only heightened the anger behind the insult. Since that night I have heard or read enough rap lyrics to get the message: Young men aren't going to take it any longer, our Woman Power, our disdain of them.

The New War Between the Men and the Women builds; each sex reaches for its weapons. Fashion has become the theater in which we costume our anger. Last year's models, dressed in the leather bustiers of the dominatrix, carried jeweled whips and knives as they strode down the runways in killer stiletto heels. Full-page fashion shots in the major women's magazines featured naked models, male and female, presumably making love, or was it war? A threat of violence, danger, was emphasized, but also the sense of lassitude as though it all didn't really matter. Smartly dressed models posed behind men standing at the urinal, the transvestite was everywhere, and it's all become so ordinary no one discusses it.

A recent Diet Sprite TV commercial shows a "career" woman walking up to a bar, sitting next to a guy, and saying, "All men are liars. They say they love you, but they don't. They say they love kids, but they forget to mention that they already have two. They tell you that the bandage on their ring finger's from a fishing accident. Yeah." Then she takes his glass, has a swig, and asks him what it is, to which he replies, "Diet Sprite." She throws the drink in his face, calls him a liar, and stomps out. The Diet Sprite people tell Maureen Dowd of the *New York Times* the ad is aimed at "independent" women who "follow their instincts."

More than twenty years ago, in a book called *Sexual Suicide*, conservative George Gilder warned that if women didn't go back into the home, leave the workplace, all hell would break loose, pretty much as it has. Given the scope of the revolution, which is still ongoing, how could we expect less? Having freed woman from the constraints of Patriarchy we see that she is in many ways "just like a man." The Dark Heroine, the bitch, the leather-clad dominatrix, the rage, was always there. What happens next will depend upon women as we zero in on the target of our rage; sooner or later women have to face one another. But at least it's out there, the rage, not swallowed like it used to be, until it made us ill.

Last week's Sunday *New York Times* was a revelation. I had not realized the extent of the new women's "underground comic universe," there in living color on the front page of the "Arts and Leisure" section. According to journalist Roberta Smith, "The female underground began to approach critical mass in 1990. . . . Their work may constitute one of the 20th century's most accessible, most psychologically detailed portraits of the many forms of female life and life style. . . . Everything from artistic crises to bodily functions is fair game. . . . Taken to extremes, and usually with a drawing style to match, the comics can be a wonderful outlet for the emotions. Nearly every woman cartoonist has used the medium for venting some form of female rage.... In one memorable Di Massa strip, a heavyset man sits next to Hothead on a park bench, carelessly letting his leg touch hers, an experience known to most women who ride subways. Fulfilling an untold number of rush-hour fantasies, Hothead simply whips out an ax and chops off the offending limb.... [Women cartoonists] offer evidence that women are subject to the same feelings, torments and desires, and capable of the same unspeakable acts and fantasies as men ... their work removes women from either doormat ... or pedestal status and seeks to put them on an equal footing with men."

This may not be politically correct, but in a new medium for women it reflects another portrait of The New Feminism. The Sisterhood prefers to gain its ground by projecting men as brutes and women as good, and there is very little humor. But comedy, along with fashion, has always been a form of expression of social upheaval. The look of the new generation of comediennes who appear regularly on the Comedy Channel is another exciting indication of today's fractured feminism.

Twenty years ago, I was searching for examples of women who dared to risk the humiliation that every comic must face. Only Phyllis Diller and Joan Rivers qualified. To put oneself on the line publicly, to gamble with the possibility of shame instead of adulation, which is what a comedienne must do, is tapping into that wellspring of embarrassment that surrounds the menstruating female body. What if she stood on that stage and "stained" herself, made an outrageous, dirty joke that fell flat? The new generation of comediennes doesn't just make fun of sex and violence, they also get into menstruation and abortion. Unlike Martin Lawrence, they are making fun of themselves.

"Traditionally, women who make people laugh are not feminine," says Gail Singer, the director of a documentary on women in stand-up comedy called *Wisecracks*. Stand-up comedy is "not the proper place for women to have that kind of strength and wit." Comedienne Robin Tyler explains, "All of a sudden she's got the center stage—and she's not a ballet dancer being caught by a man, and she's not an opera singer waiting for the guy...." As veteran comedienne Phyllis Diller put it, "Look, comedy is an aggressive, hostile act, and men are brought up to be aggressive and hostile. Women are brought up to be gracious and self-effacing." When male comics finish their acts, says

Singer, there are groupies, women fans, waiting for them at the stage door, but "there is no parallel for the powerful, effective, successful woman comic."

When I watch two comediennes tell the following jokes about menstruation—in front of an audience—I see history in the making. If you don't find them amusing, take heart in the knowledge that enough airing of the "unmentionable" will contribute to less tension on women's faces. Remarking on the new menstrual pad with wings that actually flap in the TV commercial, as if they are about to take off into the sky, one comedienne swings a leg up over an imaginary pad and pretends to ride it as if it were Pegasus. Or this one: "'With Kotex towels, no one will ever know you're having your period,'" Jenny Lecoat quotes from an advertisement. "Oh sure! Until you sit down in front of the class and you're three inches higher than everybody else! . . . Do you remember the new ones they brought out that were toilet flushable? We all fell for that one, didn't we? Flush a sanitary towel down the toilet—like you might flush a *television* down the toilet!"

I hear these jokes and The Nice Girl of my adolescence confronts the ten-year-old exhibitionist on her high walls, and I feel made whole. Comedienne Joy Behar points out that there are, however, certain jokes men can get away with that women cannot. "There is a male comedian working today who is absolutely filthy and absolutely graphic," she says. "He starts things with, 'So she's sucking my dick,' or 'So I had my tongue up her ass.' . . . If a woman ever said that, she'd be driven out of town."

Perhaps there will come a time when women will tell jokes as filthy as the ones men tell, but that should be the woman's choice, and ours to listen to her or not. We aren't there yet; the Nice Girl Rules still punish sisters for not doing things they should, and doing things they should not.

In the last twenty years' effort to show that we could do the job as well as any man, we have lost sight of our gender differences that make women mysteriously powerful, and men too, in their variation from us. The knee-jerk reaction to women who preach the holy mysteries of the fertility cycle is that they are California Earth Mothers. One advertisement for washable cloth menstrual pads reads, "Many women share that [after washing their menstrual pads] they spontaneously return this rich soaking water to their plants and gardens for amazing results." A little extreme? But isn't it somehow more positive than Madison Avenue's pretty young woman on television who recounts her humiliation when her sanitary pad failed and she had to tie her jacket around her waist?

Are women going to continue to bury our self-esteem in humiliation and disgust regarding our bleeding? A Victory Garden fertilized with menstrual blood isn't everyone's choice, but the heart sinks at the prospect of yet another generation of women raised on advertising that plays to their disgust at having to touch their genitals during menstruation.

What does it say when the Women's Tennis Association recently turned down a $10 million offer from Tambrands (makers of Tampax) to replace Virginia Slims as its sponsor? It seems that women can live with cigarettes that kill but not with a reminder that we bleed once a month, and oh, how humiliating if one of the women on the court stained her lily-whites!

Once upon a time women's bodies were worshiped. "The great annual festival of Aphrodite in Argos was called *Hysteria*, 'womb,'" writes Barbara Walker. "Megalithic tombs and barrow-mounds were designed as 'wombs' to give rebirth to the dead. Their vaginal entrance passages show that Neolithic folk went to considerable trouble to devise imitations of female anatomy in earth and stone."

Back in the seventies Betty Dodson got a name for herself by painting large canvases of vaginas and teaching classes in masturbation for women. Never officially accepted at feminist headquarters, she still teaches masturbation, a vocation that grew out of her own silent coming to terms with her body as a child when a nonverbal message from her mother was communicated that her genitals were ugly and ill-formed. Dodson was convinced that masturbation had stretched the inner lips of her vulva, disfigured it. Until she was thirty-five and divorced, she was too humiliated to let a man see her disfigurement; then, a lover, "a connoisseur of cunts" as she called him, persuaded her to let him look, up close and with the lights on, and pronounced her beautiful. "He got a stack of girlie magazines and showed me pictures of women who had genitals just like mine!" she says. "It was an enormous transformation for me to realize that I was normal. I still have workshops where women have never looked at their genitals!"

It is all of a piece, this business of bleeding, masturbation, sexual intercourse, and contraception. When one is dirty, all are dirty. Because the sexual revolution and the feminist revolution were simultaneous, and because some of us marched for both, we think they were one and the same. The truth is that feminism turned its back on the physical, on sex, on men and beauty too. It is time to move on.

Dressing for Success

"I haven't a thing to wear!" Women's ubiquitous lament since Eve left the Garden took on new significance when armies of women began entering the workplace in the 1970s. It was no longer a joke, a despairing woman standing at her overcrowded closet.

After generations of dressing to get men's attention, women were faced with what to wear when we wanted to be seen as equals, fellow workers. How *not* to be seen as a sexual woman, but instead, to be taken seriously? For starters, how were we to look in the mirror and imagine a New Self, an image, up until this moment, totally different from the look of the women in our families and among our friends? It wasn't just men's eyes that we had to train not to look for breast and leg, we had to train our own. And we had to cease comparing ourselves to other women, pitting our looks against theirs. Enter John T. Molloy and "The Dress for Success Look."

We've been so deeply into fashion madness in recent years that Molloy has slipped into oblivion when, in fact, his Dress Code for women, while not beautiful, was a godsend nonetheless. There we were in the mid-seventies in jeans, minis, short shorts, maxi skirts, costumes invented in reaction to the high glamour of previous decades, when suddenly the feminist rhetoric, all the marching and banging on the doors of industry, paid off: The doors opened. Well, perhaps it wasn't that sudden, but women were keenly aware of being improperly garbed, of not having anticipated that while we didn't want to be seen as sex objects, we did have to wear something.

Molloy's Dress for Success Suit will be remembered as *the* look of women entering the workplace, armies clad in sensible shoes, briefcases clutched at our sides, all wearing the dark blue power suit, white shirt, and, as Lily Tomlin put it, "wearing something around your neck that looks sort of like a scarf and sort of like a tie and sort of like a ruffle and doesn't threaten anyone because you don't look good in it." Ours was obviously the female version of a man's business suit, and the alacrity with which women bought it demonstrated the desperate need it filled, the dilemma at wanting to be seen as a serious business person, not the sexy woman in tight pants and cropped sweater, not the Courrèges Girl in white boots, not the Halston Glamour-puss, no, no, no, not any woman ever seen before, but a New Woman, equal to any man at getting the job done. You couldn't be on an airplane in the mid-seventies and not notice that half the women aboard were studying Molloy's book.

Today we resurrect all those pre-Molloy looks, as if in once again putting on the bell-bottoms and the whole Courrèges bit we can explain how we got here, why we feel incomplete, angry; something is missing, was left back there in the sixties and seventies, and we don't know what it is. Which is not to say that Molloy was wrong. He was a genius. His suit got us in the door comfortably, and it still works well for many women.

But the sexes have the occasional itch to flash one another. Animals can show off their genitals, raise their tails, curl their lips, expand their bodies, swagger, send a scent. We wear clothes, use their language to telegraph messages; in wearing today's stiletto-heeled, lamé boots and leather bras we are trying, in a simple way, to say that men and women would like to work out a New Deal. That we dress in the styles of the past, repeating it in every possible variation, might suggest that to find our way again men and women have returned to the looks we were wearing when the mating game stalled, when women went to war.

Molloy's uniform for that war conveyed a state of mind: Don't look at me as a woman or a sex object but as a working person; take me seriously. At a glance, it was meant to undo generations of visual appraisal. Women as well as men judged and valued women by what we wore, imagining the size and shape of the bodies beneath. We women were as voyeuristic as the men, and though we've just begun to appraise men unabashedly, we've always critiqued one another shamelessly. Feminist literature would have you believe that The Dress for Success Suit was solely aimed at men, but the competition over dress that it eliminated among women was equally important.

John Molloy had begun his research on the influence of wardrobe when studying the careers of men and women in academia, where he discovered that what a teacher wore had a lot to do with how much respect and attention she/he received from students. When he broadened his thesis to include the workplace, he found that high-level female executives had difficulty in getting respect, leading him to deduce that to have authority, one must look authoritative.

What Molloy preached to his readers was that when a man wore a suit, it was as if he were wearing a sign that read, "I am a businessman worthy of respect." In the 1970s, women had no such easy solution in their closets; Molloy's uniform for women promised to do for them what Brooks Brothers and the gray flannel suit had done for men.

After extensive testing around the country of coworkers' first impressions and reactions to certain styles, Molloy settled on the specific colors, fabrics, patterns, cuts, and styles of clothes that had produced the desired effect on peers and superiors in the workplace. Thousands of women assiduously followed Molloy's lists of what was In and Out, his commands on what one must Never do as well as the Always list.

As Molloy's book climbed the bestseller list to the number one spot, his Success-suited followers around the country pledged, in effect, to "do this so that women may have as effective a work uniform as men and therefore be better able to compete on an equal footing." It is easy today to spoof the look, the attaché cases specified to replace the feminine handbag, but this was war. Molloy understood that it was the women who had to be trained to see and think of themselves as people who wouldn't get a second glance on the street; these women were the first wave of the invasion.

But by the mid–eighties, women were longing to slip into something more exciting than Molloy's formula; perhaps entitlement describes what a woman feels when she has worked hard, earned the money, and wants a reward. There was an itch where beauty had once been. Women began discovering that it was a heady experience paying for one's self-selected wardrobe: "This is *me*," she would say, selecting something more fashionable than the Dark Blue Suit.

"But the fashion industry trammeled the experiment in creating businesswear for women," scolded Naomi Wolf, "and they lost the instant professional status and moderate sexual camouflage that the male uniform provides. The shift in fashion [away from Molloy's suit] ensured that the fashion industry would not suffer, while it also ensured that women would have simultaneously to work harder to be 'beautiful' and work harder to be taken seriously."

Is Ms. Wolf telling us that working women are mere pawns and made no conscious decision when we returned to fashion? Her words do us discredit. As anthropologist Lionel Tiger says, "I've never believed in the brainwashing theory of women. That they do things because they see ads, because they see people on television, because they're told to believe certain things. I think they do what they want, and when women didn't have much power they still wanted beauty. And now that women have more power, they want more beauty. That should tell us something; it should tell us a lot."

My first suspicion that women weren't being sufficiently nourished by The Dress for Success Suit was The Invasion of the Nail Salons. It was the early to mid-eighties. In its subtle way, it was a touching beginning, this inevitable return of beauty sneaking in by way of the fingertip. So swiftly did they spread, these clandestine nail boutiques upstairs, downstairs, sandwiched in between larger shops, that I awoke one day and they were everywhere—today, nearly 35,000 of them. Prior to feminism, the only place you could get a manicure was in a beauty salon; now women of all ages were waiting in line for the forbidden touch of blood-red sensuality. The Success Suit was excellent coverage but, like an army blanket, its rough texture made women mindful of that missing part of our selves. Before fashion's revival, first came long red nails. And sexy lingerie.

Ah, lingerie. The word itself cannot be translated. Lingerie is not underwear, or "intimate apparel," which was all we had in this country, at least in my lifetime, prior to feminism. In America there were rows and rows of blah drip-dry, stolid, bland bras, panties, and uninspiring slips that served no sensual purpose.

It wasn't until my first trip to Europe that I saw what I'd always longed for: sexy lingerie. In Paris and Rome, in countless tiny shops, they would custom-make you garter belts of lace the color of café au lait, pale-blue satin slips with straps of tiny rosebuds. The Duchess of Windsor wasn't the only woman with a passion for beautiful sexy panties, lacy camisoles, and delicately sculpted bras that cupped the breasts as might a lover's hand.

Today there are many designers of sensual lingerie, and Victoria's Secret, which opened its first stores in 1982, now has 601 stores nationwide. But Fernando Sanchez deserves the title of El Primo. Was it in the late seventies when I first saw his black velvet and marabou wrap in *Vogue*? On first sighting, something awoke in me deep, deep, wherever orgasm begins; it also touched a corner of my heart, as in tenderness, as few things do. The sleeves were slit from shoulder to wrist and banded in black satin, which also tied the waist. There I sat, as today, at my typewriter in the oldest, shabbiest pair of trousers and worn-out sweater, my writing uniform; perhaps like the woman in her navy Success Suit, I longed for the touch of velvet, silk, and satin against my skin. My work fed me generously, but the other me saw myself in that black velvet creation, even though I had no place to wear it, so informal was my life. I bought it anyway.

I wore it while I cooked for my friends, me in this Harlow-esque creation, the steam curling the marabou as I served dinner at a long refectory table where men and women loudly argued the politics of the new world we were creating. To those of us addicted to sexy lingerie, peignoirs, bustiers, it mattered not a jot that friends shook their heads and smiled at the sight of me engulfed in steam at the stove. I was taking care of many things at once, my work, my play, and not least, my sex. I still have that marabou robe.

I praise Sanchez as I would the poets. He was an innovator of sexual beauty at the height of The Dress for Success Suit. And he was right; we can have both, which is what we are still working on—the mix of work, love, and sex. Ironically, nothing provoked our critical need for something so deeply feminine as beautiful lingerie as did our mass entry into the workplace. Women were desperate for reassurance of our sexual selves as we elbowed deeper and deeper into competition with men and one another. Those who would blame the fashion industry for turning women off from the bland blue suit show their ignorance of what makes us women powerful.

Do you remember my dance of adolescence, a description of how young girls awaken to their sexuality? Imagine, then, another dance, one of a grown woman awakening in the early morning to go to her job, appraising the dark suit designed effectively to hide her lovely contours, to repel the eye and focus attention elsewhere, for instance, on her many accomplishments. Before she dons her armor, however, she reaches for a black satin teddy, steps into it slowly, allowing the weightless bit of fabric to glide up over her thighs, her hips, her breasts, until the tiny straps are in place. She looks at herself in the mirror, appraising the beauty that no one else may see, that no man may ever admire. But all day long as it moves against her body, she is reminded of her sexual center.

There is something tender but also proud about a woman spending a lot of money on a silk and lace camisole that she alone will see. It is a private luxury, all the more complex in its powerful return on the investment when we buy it with our own money, for it speaks of our identity; we feed on our sexual image much as we require bread. Buying our own beautiful lingerie, responding to it, says, I am sexual all by myself, the star of my own erotic fantasies, and if I choose to share them or myself with another person, I bring the power of my independent identity to that liaison.

By perpetuating The Male Brute mentality, we make our understanding of how we might use beauty far more arduous than is necessary. It has always been precarious for women to balance what used to be called "beauty and brains." The woman who chooses to buy an elegant, stand-out Gianfranco Ferré suit with her hard-earned money and to wear the killer outfit to her place of employment has her work cut out for her.

She should know this consciously, that she has every right in the world to wear it and also that others are going to react, which is normal; she should be prepared to handle what she sets in motion in a way that neither disrupts business nor her own peace of mind. She has put envy and desire in play, maybe even harassment from both sexes. (Yes, women do harass other women, sometimes sexually, sometimes rivalrously.) Instead of educating women to their rights and responsibilities regarding the uses of beauty in the workplace, we allow men's sexual harassment of women to grow into a national plague.

Nor have men been raised to handle women's sexual beauty in a work environment; since it is we women who now choose to involve our sexuality in that asexual environment, the weight of responsibility falls first on us. Having brought dynamite into the office, it behooves us to understand the danger. No man should violate a woman. But what is our role in the drama? Sexual beauty is a force *meant* to excite, to arouse, certainly to demand attention. Sexual beauty is built into the mating ritual.

Now we have the mating ritual in the competitive office and men totally unschooled from birth as to how even to look at a sexual woman, much less speak, act. It is no good ordering women to go back to the Dark Blue Suit. It is certainly no good blaming men for their inept reactions and leaving women totally blameless. We are all involved. Women's entry into the workplace is an evolutionary step and should be addressed as such.

One of my heroines in early modern feminism was attorney Flo Kennedy, whose heart was true but who refused to blather some of the witless slogans or to abandon certain beauty accessories. "Nail polish or false eyelashes isn't politics," she said in 1974. "If you have good politics, what you wear is irrelevant. I don't take dictation from the pig-o-cratic style setters who say I should dress like a middle-aged colored lady. My politics don't depend on whether my tits are in or out of a bra."

At a rally at the glamorous Four Seasons restaurant, to which we had all trooped in jeans and boots, the thrust of the speeches on getting women into political office was that women, simply by being women, would automatically bring honesty, goodness, and peace to the entire world. Unable to take the rhetoric any longer, Kennedy stood calmly and said, "Please, let's cut the shit." She also refused to abandon her long red nails or her purple fox coat until it was, in her words, "stolen at a rally."

If we women don't learn to use the power of beauty more effectively, men will soon take beauty as their own and have a much better time with it. Men have had to come to terms with beauty's power since their days with mother, when they felt very keenly that their need of her beauty reflected on to them. In time a man learned to win a beautiful woman of his own, but today we women not only work alongside him, we compete for that monetary power that was once only his. Having felt beauty's potency, knowing it well, he will now use it like a pro. While women fight among ourselves over who is the holiest feminist, men will run off with the beauty crown, leaving us to compete for them, maybe provide for them, work our little fingers to the bone, ruing the day that we never learned to use beauty more profitably.

Feminism should stop debunking and begin studying beauty. Conferences, panels, symposia should be arguing the many uses of beauty, defrocking the old denials. We are no longer as powerless as we were under Paternalistic rule, when beauty was all we had to trade. Think of what we might do with beauty, how much more we might enjoy it, if we understood it and mastered competition so that it didn't level us.

If we don't stop attacking one another because of what we wear and don't wear, we will lose sight of precisely what we marched against twenty-five years ago, that limited life wherein we edited our thoughts before we spoke, stood in front of the mirror buttoning and unbuttoning our blouse, unsure of how much cleavage we dared show. Then, as now, it wasn't men's censure we feared so much as other women's.

Who is so mighty that she should draw a line regarding how a feminist should look? Of course some of us have returned to beauty. What we should be asking is why some can't stand it when one of us is the center of attention. Envy is nasty but can only be dealt with when recognized. Here we are, paying our own rent, running for public office, managing corporations, but still grousing because Madonna, Streisand, whoever, is hurting feminism by dressing up and showing off.

Madonna invented herself and never apologized for her sexual exhibitionism. Instead, she created an empire and an enormous following of fans who take courage from her. Envy flies around a woman who couples economic success with sexual exhibitionism. Whatever her next incarnation may be, Madonna's greatest success was with young people who saw in her a more honest brand of feminism with which they could identify. In a society that compartmentalizes each, there is a powerful political force in a woman who can combine intelligence, beauty, and sexuality and make them pay off.

Another woman who got caught up in the conflict between beauty and economic power is Diane Sawyer, who has a restraint typical of pre-feminism years. Before she became a star on CBS on *60 Minutes*, she had been a speechwriter at the White House. One autumn day in 1987 she turned up in an absolutely gorgeous double-page photo in *Vanity Fair*. Ha! thought I, now here is a truly beautiful woman enjoying the pleasure of exhibitionistic glamour, allowing herself to do it because she has professionally earned it. Photographer Annie Leibovitz had posed her in a languorous, horizontal shot, wearing evening pajamas (not transparent), head flung back, the famous long blond hair cascading.

It didn't take long for the combined forces of envy and competition to muster and then to confront Sawyer—who was, at that moment, negotiating a new contract—with the pronouncement that she "had gone too far," exposed too much sexual beauty, been "unprofessional." The man with whom she was then living said that she had feared the criticism, had come home that night after the photo shoot wringing her hands, lamenting that she had let the seductive Annie Leibovitz talk her into the glamorous pose.

One night at a dinner party, I commented on how hopeless I thought her critics were. From the press she was getting, you would have thought she had posed nude. My dinner partners, all media and publishing heavies, turned on me roundly: "An anchorwoman, someone who reads the news and wants to be taken seriously, cannot, should not show her beauty so, well, so profusely! It will ruin her career!"

In fact, Sawyer went on to sign a $7 million contract with ABC, a big increase over her previous salary. Did the photo help or hinder? You decide. As for Sawyer, alas, she quickly cut her magnificent hair, which I saw as penance on her part. But I miss it, the playing out of her beauty power—definitely magnified by the hair—along with the economic and professional status. It will take another generation, those of you now ascending, male and female, to knit our collective resources of power into one life.

Be assured, there will be human sacrifices along the way, much hairstyling, as with Hillary Rodham Clinton, whose politics and tresses became entangled. Interestingly, her odyssey from Fashion Innocent also included crucial time in Annie Leibovitz's glamorizing lens. Off to a rough start at the beginning of her husband's Presidency, she emerged victorious on all fronts, including beauty. But Hillary Rodham Clinton is no ordinary First Lady. She belongs to a generation of women who look as independent, opinionated, aggressive, and competitive as any man, some would say even more so. She looks this way because she lives this way. To put this family, in particular, to put *her* in soft focus, would be a lie.

Hillary Rodham Clinton's story is so interesting because her looks dramatically changed in front of our eyes and, more specifically, in front of the eyes of the press and television cameras. Because she is the first First Lady to go through such a transformation, you might say a public Day of Beauty, it is tempting to speculate on what turned this "unfashionable" woman into such a looker. "I would grind my teeth and wish I could sit Hillary on the edge of my tub and give her some makeup lessons," said the President's mother, the late Virginia Kelley, a self-proclaimed exhibitionist. "Show her how to bring out all that natural beauty she was covering up by going natural. None of that mattered to her, though. She was too busy getting educated and doing good things like starting youth-advocate programs. Makeup didn't mean a whit to her."

Well, it does now, and I would imagine that a woman who has so successfully accrued power over the years must find it interesting, if not also pleasurable, to experience the power of beauty after having eschewed it for so long. Stylists who worked on her appearance early in her husband's administration commented that she never looked in the mirror during their ministrations, so fixed was she on her pre-television notes.

But there must have been compliments, smiles, a new look in people's eyes when they spoke to her after that speech, after the eye-catching Annie Leibovitz photo of her in the sexy Donna Karan dress. This is the stuff of fairy tales. Hillary was accustomed to praise for her achievements, but there is nothing quite like the healing warmth of praise for one's person.

Hillary Rodham Clinton's saga is like a morality tale in reverse; before she became beautiful, we already knew she was no idealized household nun. This is a modern woman, arguing, fighting her way through a political drama, sometimes winning, sometimes losing, but using her full arsenal. Now she is also beautiful. We have a full, working portrait of the de-idealized woman, good and bad. This is just what the doctor ordered; we've needed for a long time to surrender the image of women as kinder and more virtuous than men.

For generations women have disguised the many uses of beauty, just as we devalued our power in the nursery, making it into a sacrificial role rather than the magisterial one it is. In a society where women had no real economic power, manipulative power was granted us. It is time to get off the pedestal, drop the victim guise. It is good that in our living rooms on the evening news we are seeing that the most powerful woman in the country is learning the power of her beauty.

The Denial of Competition

I could not write this book if I had not grown up seeing beauty at work prior to the sixties, when the world changed. Once the feminist army was under way, we couldn't have women competing for the mirror. If we were to get our share of the economic pie, which was owned and operated by men, then that currency with which we had once bought a nibble had to go. Starting in the late sixties and building through the seventies, men and beauty were suspect.

Then in the mid-eighties, suddenly—or so it seemed to me—exhibitionistic beauty returned with a vengeance. Something was brewing: When I turned on the television the women reading the news were wearing sculpted jackets in brilliant primary colors; one day in 1985 I opened a fashion magazine and there was Donna Karan's first collection, featuring a red cashmere bodysuit and wrap skirt, very sexy and very eye-catching. I reacted the way I had to the Rudi Gernreich fuschia and tangerine skirt and blouse I had spotted in a window twenty years earlier: I had to have it!

The replacement of the harmless Dress for Success Suit with beauty power made me wonder, How are women going to deal with this new sexual look in the competitive workplace? Will they be aware of what they are setting in motion when they enter a room in a drop-dead exhibitionistic outfit? Will they know how to defuse envy? And when men stare at them, will they be wise enough to accept this as what their sexual look "naturally" does?

I also wondered how men would react when women walked past them in those narrow, ass-hugging, short skirts, alerting testosterone. Some of these men and women were too young to remember sexual beauty the last time around. How would they handle work and sex simultaneously? Even we veterans hadn't experienced such an erotic cocktail, not in the workplace.

"In the modern workplace, men are drones, and women are queen bees," writes Camille Paglia. "Men's corporate costume, with its fore-and-aft jacket flaps, conceals their sexuality. Woman's eroticized dress inescapably makes her the center of visual interest, whether people are conscious of it or not. Most women, as well as most men, straight or gay, instantly appraise whether a woman has 'good legs' or a big bosom, not because these attributes diminish her or reduce her to 'meat' (another feminist canard) but because they unjustifiably add to her power in ways that may destabilize the workplace. Woman's sexuality *is* disruptive of the dully mechanical workaday world, in which efficiency means uniformity.... She brings nature into the social realm, which may be too small to contain it."

Sexual beauty's return was exciting, yes, even more so in the work-place, for surely now its power would demand feminism's full focus on the issues of competition, envy, jealousy, which we had initially sidestepped. But no one mentioned competition. Instead, the sexual fashions accelerated, leaving competitors to push and shove for any mirroring eyes that weren't already preoccupied in their own search for a mirror. Everyone wanted to be seen, and there were no safe rules.

I felt a conflagration coming on, something historical that went back in time to when I had first arrived in New York. Having so recently left the writing room's isolation, I couldn't face another three or four years on a book. But I couldn't get the idea out of my head; I compromised and telephoned various friends at the major fashion magazines.

How about a photo story, I suggested, with pictures of curvy models strutting through corporate offices and captions asking all the questions this vision had prompted in my mind. A working woman who has spent half her salary on a suit, Manolo Blahnik heels, and half an hour applying her war paint has her work cut out for her: Other women's *grrrr!* must be defused: The stirring in the groin of the men whose papers are ruffled by her perfumed passing must be calmed. The room must be brought back to normal, as it was before she entered. It was a lot of responsibility, even for a trouper, much less a thirty-year-old who was new to the game, new to The Gaze. These younger women were raised on a feminism that had enjoined women to dump sexual beauty so as to embrace economic and political power. Well, Donna Karan's bodysuits were flying out of the stores, and women were crying for more.

"What do you mean 'Beauty Power'? What does envy and competition have to do with fashion?" the magazine editors asked. Unwilling to write the full-length article they sought, I invented other ways of approaching this subject. I produced a ten-minute video, pitched a television series on the subject, set up symposia in three different cities, did some consulting for a major cosmetics firm, and, in partnership with DYG Inc., the market research firm headed by Dan Yankelovich and Madeline Hochstein, went to work on a series of focus groups that culminated in a national survey.

I invited men and women—psychologists, sociologists, anthropologists, and other academicians—to speak at these symposia. They were of an age to remember beauty's role prior to the sexual and women's revolutions. Wouldn't it be useful to young women, I thought, to hear and see how their mothers had used beauty in the days when it was the ticket to survival?

"Thinking of myself as an intellectual, I feel uncomfortable with the idea of discussing beauty," said film critic Molly Haskell at that first symposium in 1989, which was titled "The Power of Beauty." "A woman's relationship to beauty—to the mirror—is one of the most personal, individual, even secret, mysterious, relationships there is."

I'd invited Haskell to speak because I admired her work and had always seen her as a woman who recognized her beauty. Yes, I saw her as an intellectual too, but I've remembered her words because they go directly to the heart of the discussion: Can a woman have beauty and any other power as well? Why should an intellectual not also be beautiful?

Under the old laws of Patriarchy, a woman who was beautiful was not expected to possess other wealth. If she did, she should have the good grace to play it down. I wonder if Molly Haskell would still say those words today, years later, when there are so many beautiful women who are also brilliant thinkers and speakers. I have talked with many of them, and they know precisely what I am saying; it is as if, even today, the old limits are imposed; if you possess beauty and great success in your work too, you walk on eggshells.

Because women are raised to deny beauty so as to ward off others' envy, we never really learn its full power, its effect on people, how we might better use it. "Lying, of course, is a way of gaining power over other people through manipulating them in various ways, and this is something that children learn. They also learn to keep secrets," says philosopher Sissela Bok. "I believe we almost have to *un*learn that. If we are to mature, we have to unlearn any enjoyment of that power, any benefit from it. . . . On the whole, how can you try to lead your life so that you communicate with other people without trying to manipulate them?"

The other warning I hear in Bok's words is that Matriarchal Feminism must stop preaching to women that competition is evil, when it is evident to all that modern feminism survives on competition, that in the most obvious sense, it refuses to tolerate argument. The old-line feminists are mistresses of manipulation.

The fact that women are now economically and politically entrenched in an international market built on competition even as feminism continues its old soundtrack, "We will not compete!", would be laughable if it weren't so destructive. It leaves women to compete with one hand tied behind our backs, not unlike the way we always handled beauty, using it while denying we even owned it: "What beauty? Haven't you seen my awful nose, fat thighs, stringy hair?" By mannerisms and verbiage, working women smile the Nice Girl smile as they push ahead, blind to whoever is trammeled underfoot. "Hurt her? Oh, no, she's our best friend!"

Men push and stomp too, but they don't deny their power. Some of the most belligerent people I know are women; they just don't call it that. Some of the most caring people I know are men, but they still aren't encouraged to embrace that description of themselves for fear it is not manly. We women are as much involved in discriminating against men at home, as caretakers, as they are in wanting to keep us from taking their jobs.

The most competitive women I've met, and whose books I've read, are members of feminism's old guard. When it comes to belligerence and rivalry, these women set a new benchmark. Nina Auerbach set off a media firestorm with her efforts to torpedo Christina Hoff Sommers's book, *Who Stole Feminism?*, in the *New York Times*, so unprofessional and biased was her review. Sommers says that Gloria Steinem called Connie Chung personally to keep Sommers off the air— although Steinem would not agree to be interviewed on camera with her criticism. These women are free to mount their rivalrous campaign; it is their duplicity with which I quarrel.

What I find galling, especially from feminism's earliest marchers, is the promise that love awaits those good girls who "kick the competition habit." "Whether by virtue of full breasts (literally or figuratively) or a devastating hostess gown," wrote the editor of *Ms.* magazine, Letty Cottin Pogrebin, "we women have long been engaged in the enervating game of going every other woman one better. While this invidious habit is more widespread than name-dropping or nail-biting, until recently it has been every woman's dirty little secret. Now, the lid is off. Women are trading secrets with one another. And the real revelation is that our competitiveness is not a dirty act of treachery but the survival tactic of a second-class human being. . . . Once you kick the competition habit, prepare for a new high: liking women. Really liking women."

Feminism hasn't budged from its Big Mother Knows Best position since it began: Be Nice, don't argue, be a good little noncompetitive feminist and Big Momma will always love you. The No-Compete Clause of feminism is itself a direct steal from Patriarchal days, the very law that kept women in our place for so long. If we ever did "kick the competition habit" altogether, we would find ourselves ruled, dominated, and controlled by a Matriarchy so competitive in its absolutism as to leave Patriarchy in the dust.

It is inevitable that as it grows, feminism should splinter over such issues as competition. A movement as large as ours must divide as special interest groups are born and our objectives separate us from one another. To break doesn't have to be any more acrimonious than separation from mother. But there is an adolescent level of girlish spitefulness and cruelty in feminism. Leaders never do like to lose control, though some great leaders have understood how benevolence ensures the goodwill of the separating factions, that in allowing them to go their way, a bond is maintained through gratitude. The Good Mother learns this with her children. The Bad Mother, in binding her children to her, thinks she has kept her power, but the "love" felt for her is more angry dependency than gratitude. Our modern feminism, in its refusal to encourage and praise healthy competition, acts precisely like the Bad Mother.

For those of you who missed the early years of modern feminism, I wish I could paint an emotional picture of how it felt before women began preaching to other women what they could and couldn't do or say, who was a "real" feminist and who was not. Now feminism is buried in The Semantic Jungle. We have become as hard on one another as any Patriarchy; given that Women's Rules are more prohibitive, our punishments are more painful.

My Mother/My Self had begun as an investigation into the source of women's guilt about sex. It grew out of *My Secret Garden*, which had left me dumbfounded as to why women felt so guilty in just thinking about sex—not doing it, simply imagining, privately. Who was going to know what they were thinking? Two steps into the barbed wire surrounding what went on between mothers and daughters, I ran into competition.

Unraveling that dark mystery in women's lives involved tangling with mother. In fact, one of the most destructive and backward moves of recent Matriarchal Feminism has been the effort to restore the ancient idealization of the mother/daughter relationship. It fits neatly into the script that would pose women as morally superior to Big Bad Men. How ironic and cruel that at this moment in history, when women are most in need of practicing the healthy rules of competition—rules best learned in opposition to mother so that they are readily available in the workplace—we have a feminist clique of mothers who would undo Margaret Mahler's work.

Every seat a woman takes in the workplace means one less for a man or another woman; every seat a man takes is seen by both men and women as one that could have been theirs. It is a complicated, competitive war, one made all the more complex as men and women also compete for one another's hearts. "One of the reasons we are so confused these days is that the workplace has changed so dramatically," says psychologist and professor of management Lisa Mainero. "Beginning in the early eighties, corporate norms regarding dress, image, and appearance became more dynamic. One of the most influential changes is that the workplace has become the place to meet, date, and relate to the opposite sex. Among the women I surveyed, 76 percent said they had either been personally involved in or had known about an office romance that had occurred in their firm."

Mainero spoke at the third and last symposium I conducted, which was held in Chicago and titled "Beauty in the Workplace." It was 1990, a year before DYG Inc. and I had completed two years of focus groups, culminating in our national survey on beauty among men and women. One of the most interesting findings was that women rated appearance as the top quality affecting their self-image; 76 percent ranked it in the top five of fourteen qualities and 34 percent ranked it number one, above intelligence, job performance, sexuality—even though more than three quarters of them were working women.

Mainero's research findings, that men and women both fear that attractive women have an unfair advantage in the workplace, would line up precisely with what we eventually found in the DYG survey. In the past five years, the many new studies on beauty/sex/appearance in the workplace have multiplied, and one particular change of attitude stands out: In studies such as Madeline Heilman's in 1979, the finding was that being good-looking was a plus for men, but a plus for a woman only when the job was lower-level. The assumption was that attractive women in managerial positions seemed more feminine, thus victim to all the female stereotypes of passiveness, timidity, and so on.

By the late eighties, however, two studies were showing that each additional attractiveness point translated into an additional $1,000 on a male's starting salary, and while a good-looking woman gained no immediate advantage until on the job, once on board, each attractiveness point was worth more than $2,000. By 1993, people perceived as good-looking—men and women—were earning at least 5 percent more than those labeled average-looking. In a 1993 McCall's/Yankelovich survey, the great majority of women, of all ages surveyed, agreed that "most people judge you on the basis of the way you look."

"We American women want to be loved for ourselves, for who we are," says fashion writer Holly Brubach, "and if it so happens that we're pretty, that's a bonus. This attitude may have its origins in our Puritan heritage, but the feminist movement has recently given it a big boost by reinforcing our conviction that it's wròng for a woman to trade on her appearance. Also, the worship of beauty doesn't sit well with the tenet that good looks constitute an unfair advantage in a society in which all women are supposed to be created equal."

Our Puritan heritage may be responsible for our traditional admonition not to judge a book by its cover, but feminism's warning that it's wrong for a woman to trade on her appearance has far more to do with women's taboo against the competitive itch, which, once scratched, would invite healthy debate, disagreement, and the eventual unseating of feminism's most powerful players.

The fact is that young women today, freed of the tyranny of beauty as their only power under Patriarchy, recognize, nonetheless, the very real influence of looks over their lives. In our survey, 86 percent of the women and 76 percent of the men chose self-confidence as the reason for beauty being important to women. When feminists denounce furthering the healthy understanding of competition so that women might better use it as the potentially profitable tool that it is, they deprive women of self-confidence. Admitting to the importance of beauty in their lives, while having little practice in the known, safe rules that govern competition, leaves women vulnerable beyond measure.

Beauty/sex/competition, all are entwined and play off one another; all are currently in high gear and are frowned upon by feminism. The more sexualized beauty becomes, the more envy is aroused, the more dangerous things grow, as everyone pretends that their exposed sexual parts have no effect on the status quo. Fashion cries out in its sexual extremes for comment. But the funding for scientific research on everything related to sex has dried up.

It is as if our envy of the power of women's sexuality has silenced any analysis of what is happening. Opposite the classic beauty, women may feel rivalrous, but the heightened threat of a sexually liberated woman who is also beautiful arouses a growl of resentment that gnaws. Even if she is not beautiful, women know that men are drawn to the sexually accepting woman, for to be with a woman who loves her body, and by extension loves the man's too, is to lie down with the Good Mother.

When Streisand appeared at Clinton's inaugural in 1993 wearing an elegant, dark, man-tailored skirt slit to the knee, the vest showing a bit of cleavage, Anne Taylor Fleming dashed off a bitchy column on the "Op-Ed" page of the *New York Times*. What infuriated the writer was that Streisand was "letting us know that underneath her peekaboo power suit, underneath all her bravado and accomplishments, she is still an accessible femme fatale."

If there had been no flesh, no slit skirt, no cleavage, the power suit would have been fine. It was the mixed message that made the writer so furious: "What the slit says is: We may imitate your wardrobe and ask to be let into your male-only chambers, but, rest assured, underneath we are still your centerfolds, your MTV dream girls. . . . [The suits] exemplify society's effort to keep women off balance, to keep them beholden to the new sex-object imagery: male on top, seductress underneath."

Clearly, not only beauty, but sexual message too is in the eye of the beholder. I thought Streisand's look terrific, in-charge, top-of-her-form, balancing beauty and brain. But Fleming's fantasy as she watched Streisand was very different; could it be envy? To the critic who couldn't resist venting her resentment in ink, Streisand's costume sent "a disturbing signal to—and about—American woman." Oh? I don't think so. In fact, it did quite the opposite. It said to women and men, "Recognize your suit, guys? I'll borrow it and give it something you never could, a woman's legs and breasts." It is why so many women love to wear the real thing, a man's tuxedo, and why men and other women love to look at the power of the exhibitionist who can pull it off. That Streisand can amass her various powers and present them in an elegant, sexual manner says to me, Here is a model to be admired.

Streisand's a good example of the underground minefield women must walk in feminist land, especially if they have accomplished something *and* are beautiful too. Are we to believe this once ugly duckling doesn't know firsthand the killer fire of envy? She turns it all around to become not simply a *jolie laide*, but someone whose body of work so moves us that we have come to see her as beloved.

When asked in an interview whether women pursue beauty for men, Norman Mailer, who has spent a lifetime in the company of and writing about beautiful women, said:

> No. Women dress for other women; women do their hair for other women. It's competitive as hell. Reminds me of the way jazzmen used to be in the early sixties, when the musicians stopped

paying attention to the audience and started playing for each other, getting into more and more elaborate riffs each night just to show each other how far out they could get. That's what goes on now with women's fashions. Among every hundred women, there will be a few who set the trends. The rest follow like slaves, and all complain that the men are getting superficial. We men go for beauty because we have no option. All the women pointed us toward it. It's not easy for a man to say, I'd like to get out of this rat race and settle down with one woman who has virtues.

There is nothing virtuous in abandoning the pursuit of beauty, and I cannot imagine worse advice to give women today than to promote the false concept that "good women" will not compete like "bad men"; for the first time, we are all in the workplace and in the mirror too; healthy competition must be practiced in order to make it safe. Some of us, women and men, are by nature, genes, temperament, background more competitive than others. Those women who preach the philosophy of women as superior by virtue of being noncompetitive do their sisters a terrible disservice.

In *Revolution from Within* Steinem urges women to abandon competition and to think instead of a noncompetitive union with other women as akin to quilt-making. "Rather than finding a source in competition, self-esteem and excellence both come from the excitement of learning and pressing individual boundaries; a satisfaction in the task itself; pleasure in cooperating with, appreciating, and being appreciated by others—and as much joy in the process as in the result," she says. "As each person completes herself or himself and contributes what is authentic, a new paradigm emerges: circularity. . . . If we think of ourselves as circles, our goal is completion—not defeating others. . . . If we think of work structures as circles, excellence and cooperation are the goal—not competition."

To support her view, Steinem embraces author Alfie Kohn's eccentric view of competition, quoting at length his assertion that "superior performance not only does not *require* competition; it usually seems to require its absence. . . . *We compete to overcome fundamental doubts about our capabilities and, finally, to compensate for low self-esteem.*"

Making quilts and hoping for a tie in competitive games and situations is an escape from real life. Here we are, desperately in need of instruction in how to compete, and feminism offers us "circularity." It isn't necessary to preach competition, the feeling exists from the earliest days of our lives. When we feel we are about to lose something or someone vital to us, the anxiety, the fear, the anger that grip us are, in part, competition; the person who would take away what we love and need is our competitor. Even before the Oedipal triangle, a child feels competitive with anything or anyone who takes away mother's eye. The child's goal is to win mother's attention back from father, from a sibling, or from her work.

These intrusions are inevitable, and how we fared in them back then sets the stage for how we respond to competitive threats in the Oedipal years and, subsequently, how we feel when competition arises today. You might say that pre-Oedipally we learn to fight back. When sex enters the competition in the Oedipal years, bringing guilt and the fear of retaliation, this is when we learn how to inhibit competition. Integration is the goal: to compete but to do it within safe limits.

In replacing the healthy competitive spirit with Steinem's "circularity," in which "progress becomes mutual support and connectedness," these feminists draw kindergarten smiles on women's faces, pushing us back into the nursery, where mother's law was, "Everybody loves everybody equally." We didn't believe it then, and we certainly don't now that we've had twenty-five years in the real world. Most of our mothers didn't know how to teach healthy competition; no one had taught them.

But life, in particular the workplace, has taught us that human nature comes in shades of gray, not black and white. We are all a little good, a little bad, sometimes. Competition is not something only men do, nor is it an imposed male conceit that we superior women can remove. There is one job, one contract; quite a few of us want it and only one will get it. Destroying other people, lying, cheating, is not the answer, nor is circularity. Doing superior work, proving one is better suited for the job, winning the job, the contract, that is safe, healthy competition. Women must learn how to use it in a nondestructive way, bringing to the contest genetic skills from women's work, which improve competition as practiced by men, making it a better game, but competitive nonetheless.

The obstacles that have confined women to second-class status have been talked to death; now it's time to admit to problems among ourselves, the issues of envy and competition, which have silently kept women afraid of outstripping our mothers, our friends, all other women.

When my husband was managing editor of the *Wall Street Journal*, he set a precedent for hiring women, promoting them to the top levels. Some performed better than others, but all had a problem with criticism, competition, the eventual one-on-ones in his office, which often ended in tears. These women would fight for their objective, compete like gladiators, but when criticized, they would sit opposite him teary-eyed. It wasn't that he questioned their competition but that criticism itself was felt to be punishment.

If competition, aggressive behavior, were permitted forms of female behavior, they would have been sanctioned by mother; because they are usually not part of our loving relationship with her, every subsequent "boss" who scolds us awakens the terrible reprisals we felt would be our due as children had we broken the rules. Thirty, forty years old, we burst into tears when criticized because we feel like bad little girls who are no longer loved. Male bosses sit opposite weeping women who ten minutes earlier were fully in control and wonder what they did to bring about this transformation. They did nothing. It had all been done years ago and was merely reawakened.

We enter rooms convinced that eyes are judging us. Maybe they are, maybe they aren't, but this is who women are, judges and the judged. It is what we did as little girls and has become what we expect, to be appraised, accepted, or rejected. Even women who love us, judge us, perhaps they more than others, for if we surpassed them, their fear is that we would leave them for a more elite circle of friends.

How can we admit to our own competitiveness when our first love, our model, our first competitor never admitted to hers, nor had her mother, or hers? If we were raised to feel that our accomplishments, achievements, including our beauty, aroused something in mother too evil to be named, we learned to distrust outdistancing her, and other women too. Nothing encourages us like praise, first from mother, to go beyond our presumed limits, exercise intellectual curiosity, or take genuine pleasure in the reflection we see in the mirror. She does not have to speak for us to know what she is feeling; we know her inside and out. Pressed to put a name to what she feels when people praise and admire our beauty, we would call it anything but the dreaded word *competition*.

"How does a daughter deal with her mother's competitiveness with her or jealousy of her accomplishments?" asks psychologist Paula Caplan. "Often, she does one of two things (or tries both at different times): She reduces her efforts to achieve (or at least begins to conceal them from her mother), and she puts emotional or physical distance between herself and her mother."

Perhaps this is why I couldn't wait to get away from home, couldn't wait to travel, put distance between myself and the unacknowledged competition in that house where I grew up. I'd always thought it was my rivalry with my sister, the pretty one. But I am certain now that even more than this I hated and feared the complicated, mysterious intensity of what my sister aroused in my mother.

I have come to understand why no amount of success and certainty of my beloved's love for me can eliminate the competitive fires fanned when another woman tries to capture his eye. It isn't just the rearoused sibling rivalry, but what I witnessed between them, usually at the dinner table during those years of my sister's ripe adolescence, when the air was alive with unspeakable emotions, so unacceptable to my lovely mother, so blocked and unutterable, there was nothing for her to do but leave the table in tears, followed by my sister, also in tears. I considered myself well out of it, but I see now that that too was a defense; in truth, I was as lonely as a cloud, for I didn't figure in their drama, being of so little beauty, was ineligible.

I encourage you to understand today's problems with competition by coming to terms with what happened in your earliest years. Does it help today knowing the root of an a priori sense of defeat when a rival looms? Yes, absolutely and certainly. Just knowing that it isn't the proud, exhibitionistic woman that I am who is feeling defeated before any battle has even begun, but a child, the child that I once was, this puts the situation in perspective. I feel the sickness rise, and I grab it by the throat, wrestle it down, and speak, for there is nothing like hearing one's own strong voice to restore reality. I will wrestle with it till I die, but power is knowledge.

Women share this sense of a priori defeat, when the mere hint of loss is in the air, unless they had mothers who taught them the safe rules of competition, who aired the poisonous feeling so that the word didn't have that slanderous, unfeminine sound. It is all right for a mother to feel competitive with a daughter, and nothing makes it safer than admission, discussion, the good humor, the hug, the sense of winning and losing and life going on, love intact.

What disappointed me in Naomi Wolf's book *The Beauty Myth* was the lost opportunity for a beautiful young woman to discuss the forbidden subject of competition. Instead, she used trumped-up statistics to lay women's pursuit unto death of beauty at the feet of Evil Men. The women-as-victims mentality that pervades her book galvanized another generation to see men as the root of a problem that, more than any other, can only be solved within women's world. Perhaps the decision to omit from the dust jacket a photo of the very pretty author was made on the corporate level, but clearly someone, somewhere decided that intellectual credibility and book sales among feminists would be at risk.

Men see no inconsistency between competition and networking, since they believe both expand opportunity. Women, unskilled at and wary of competition, also struggle with networking in the workplace. We hesitate to bring one another along as we advance up the ladder, fearing our assist may open the possibility of the other woman becoming our equal, even outstripping us. Our anxiety is based on the belief that, unlike men, we have limited resources and limited opportunity.

Mother raised us to believe that without her approval and love, we would die. We must never compete with her. When you are raised to fear competition and to believe that there is only so much love, only so many jobs, only so much beauty, then every grain a rival gets is that much less for you.

Men don't bring along the guy under them because they are good and generous people; they do it because in networking, they hope, lies loyalty and gratitude. The debt will be remembered, paid back in various ways, something we women don't believe in because it hasn't been sufficiently practiced and proven. As the coach of the Connecticut Women's Basketball Team said, women haven't yet learned to leave their competition/anger behind when the game is over, they carry it with them, still hating the other person who beat them.

The man who doesn't learn to shake hands and buy a round of drinks in the spirit that tomorrow the victory may be his is considered "unclubbable," meaning that he hasn't learned the rules of competition. This is precisely what competition and networking teach, that in time a chain of people learn to rely on the others for the vote, cooperation, teamwork. Men make better networkers than we because most of them are more at ease with competition; the past has taught them more about circularity—returning favors—than quilt-making ever could.

The handshake takes the sting out of losing, opens the door for a communal reunion, allows for a decent night's sleep. The other guy's victory becomes fuel for winning the next bout. Men's lips don't get mean and narrow, as ours do from sucking in all the swallowed venom. Men make war, but so do we. Thatcher and Golda Meir are the tip of the wedge. Women may live longer, but if we continue to swallow our bile, heart attacks, ulcers, not to mention the loss of beautiful hair, will be on the rise among women.

Give me women's strong voices raised in argument any day over quilt-making. What we need is more dialogue, the freedom to disagree, open, healthy competition between as many of us as choose to enter the fray. Women must experience in the workplace that it is possible to argue, to get a new contract that another woman also wants and still have lunch together; unlike traditional women's world, the competitive workplace demands that hatchets be buried and the wheel of commerce be kept constantly in play. Networking is always a gamble; the person helped up the ladder may or may not be loyal, but the risk must be taken. That's business. As a recent cover of *Fortune* magazine put it: "So you fail. So what?"

Imperious as a Camille Paglia may be, she *is* the new wave of feminism. So are the antiliberty forces like McKinnon and Dworkin, not my favorite people, but any woman's strong voice is good to hear in a competitive society. It forces us to think more exactly about our own beliefs. Steinem's old guard may still get the sound bites, but as younger, equally poised, articulate, and, yes, beautiful women continue to speak up, we will have a more contemporary sound and look, which is a feminism that has many competitive voices and faces.

7

Men in the Mirror

===

My Grandfather's Closet

In my childhood there was nothing so mysterious as my grandfather's dressing room. He was my hero and my model. In studying this elegant chamber, so intimately his, everything in it made to his measurements, perhaps I thought I would associate myself more personally with him. I was a girl and interested neither in clothes nor in being male, but I knew this sartorial room was at the heart of the man I adored, whom everyone in my extended family feared and loved, and whose eye I was determined to catch. Some deep, personal communion went on in here amidst the smell of fine shoe leather and cologne, something that he enjoyed and that made him even more powerful.

I knew every inch of my mother's closet, had rummaged through it almost daily searching for small change with which to buy ice cream or stamps from the old man on Broad Street. That tiny store was filled with the miniature pictures of faraway places that I pasted into the stamp album my grandfather gave me on my ninth birthday.

I had climbed up onto his bed that morning—a rare treat—and propped myself beside him against the mountains of pillows, where he read his *Wall Street Journal*; together we leafed through the big leather-bound volume he'd already decorated with stamps from his own international voyages. (And I wonder where my "wanderlust" originated!) But there was no mystery to my mother's closet, not a drop. While I loved my mother, I had no intention of ever growing up to be like her, a lady in a nice house with nice children and a nice life. I wanted to be like my grandfather, a self-made man who had built his fortune in the steel-alloy business in Pittsburgh, lost everything in the Depression, and then gotten it all back.

During the summers when we were in residence at his estate on the banks of the Niagara River, I would slip into his bedroom on hot August afternoons and quietly open the door-that-made-no-noise into the paneled room designed for the presentation of his wardrobe. The concealed lights would go up, as on a stage, and there would be his splendid, regimented suits hung shoulder to shoulder like an army, shirts of the loveliest soft fabric laid in mahogany drawers as if on display, rows of hats, dressing gowns, and in tiny velvet-lined drawers, rings and cuff links, every imaginable accessory to enhance male splendor.

Up to a certain height the walls were mirrored, and then above hung photos of my grandfather's possessions, his horses, houses, boats, and family. To this day I have a navy pea coat designed at Dunhill, along with gray flannel trousers and Top-Siders, clothes he had ordered for his five children when he purchased his last boat, *The Duchess*. How his children hated to put on their uniforms for summer cruises on Lake Ontario; how eagerly I longed to grow big enough to wear them; "hand-me-downs" from my grandfather were precious ties to him.

Portraits of him by my grandmother, his first wife, now hang in my house. In them he is still young and handsome, with red hair, and he bears a striking resemblance to the young F. Scott Fitzgerald. I remember him older, grown portly, a John Huston arriving in our quiet town with an entourage of secretaries, business associates, all encamped in a suite of rooms at The Fort Sumpter Hotel. In his white linen suit, Panama hat, cigar clamped in his teeth, he was like no man I'd ever seen.

What magnified him even more was the deferential respect shown him not just by us grandchildren but by his adult children as well. My mother and her sisters grew meek in his presence, and a harsh word wounded them visibly, yet they adored him and craved his respect.

Critical of everything they accomplished, from the role of my uncle, the admiral, in the Bay of Pigs to my mother's posture—"Shoulders back!"—he was also uncommonly proud of the beauty of The Clan arriving at the country club, scrubbed and dressed to the nines, no one standing less than five feet eight.

I especially loved my grandfather's ease, his big laugh, the energy he brought into a room. The way to his heart I had learned was not to hold back, but to brashly climb on his knee, give him a kiss, tell him a story. And show him my straight A's, my prizes and ribbons from school. Ah, how he loved accomplishments. Loved them too much, no doubt, but he set me an objective. Having unconsciously decided long ago that, since my mother wouldn't look at me, I would childishly tell her nothing of my successes, I sent my report cards to Daddy Colbert, as he liked to be called. His letters of praise and encouragement, dictated to his secretary, John, were my reward.

My high school graduation gift was an initialed set of Hartmann luggage, along with the promise of a trip to Europe when I finished college. "Buy the best," he told me. "It is always worth the investment." Those were the days when "good" things were well made and fine luggage was "meant to last." The subsequent pieces of Hartmann luggage I would buy ten years later would be poorly constructed disasters. As for the original set of Hartmann, it is in its fourth decade, still used by one of my nieces.

Can a woman learn her look from a man? Absolutely. It was not my grandfather's pale cream corduroy custom-made suit, which he so fancied in Palm Beach, that I aspired to own; it was my reflection in his eyes. The look I began to create for myself in my twenties was the invented image I saw as worthy of the woman on his arm. I can say this now, though at the moments of purchase, my careful choice of clothes was based on something unidentifiable. There was no woman in my family who dressed as I always have, with an eye for the beauty of the fabric and construction as well as the eye-catching effect. They are more conservative in their dress—not the least exhibitionistic the way I am, my grandfather's direct descendant.

I cannot tell you how revelatory it is, writing this. Until now I have never understood the pattern. Today, as men enter the mirror in as thoughtful a way as they enter the workplace, I would imagine that there will be more young girls who, like me, grow up studying the men whom they love, perhaps learning much if not more from a relationship to his image than to a woman's. Not all women like the mirror, either the reflecting glass or the eyes of others upon them. But my early world of invisibility is common today, there being so few reflecting eyes at home, and the place my grandfather filled in that void, not as fashion plate but as a substantial alternative to the sea around me, well, he saved my life.

When he visited Manhattan in the sixties, he never bothered to alert me in advance. He would call from The Pierre or The Plaza, tell me where and when to meet him for lunch or dinner. "I'll be waiting for you at 21 at one o'clock," he would say, and I would happily cancel any other plan, select my outfit carefully, and make my entrance, looking for his eye as he stood, open-armed, to embrace me and proudly introduce me to his men friends. He took such delight in the fact that I was "a working girl," that my jobs took me to Europe and the Caribbean, and that my presence among these men made them sit up straight.

After lunch we would stroll east, he smoking one of his big cigars, to one of his favorite haberdashers, Sulka or Dunhill, where his entrance was greeted with a flourish. I would be given a comfortable chair, a glass of white wine, and then a performance. My grandfather's love of excellence extended to the most esoteric details. A fresh cigar would be lit, and items would be brought forth from the inner sanctum, a fabric, for instance, that presumably no one but he, Charles Colbert, would appreciate. He and the shop's manager would lose themselves in the turn of a lapel. He would ask my opinion on everything—ties, sports coat, dinner jacket, fabrics for shirts—pointing out to me subtle differences that accounted for superior craftsmanship.

Proudly, he would announce once again to the manager, as he did to everyone, "My granddaughter is a working girl," thoroughly enjoying the man's uncertainty as to our real relationship. It delighted me that they might think me this old man's "poopsie." I would recross my legs and smile, knowing I had made him happy and that the world had come to this. After all, hadn't I learned it all from him, to work, to provide for myself, to finally be seen?

On the day he sold the company he had built, then lost and rebuilt, he telephoned me at 6 P.M. and in his usual peremptory manner instructed me to meet him at The Plaza Hotel for dinner, never questioning that I might have other plans. I bid farewell to the man on my sofa, taxied crosstown, and found my grandfather in his stocking feet in the middle of his suite, tired but ebullient. He was seventy years old.

We sat together on the deep sofa looking out at the pale spring treetops in Central Park and toasted his success. He didn't yet know what it would be like not to work, to be devoid of responsibility and power; how could he? He had worked since he was a boy, had supported his own parents, for my great-grandfather, much to his son's confusion, was a man who cared more for people than for money, couldn't press a man to pay a bill if he didn't have the cash, and so went bankrupt half a dozen times. Almost from the day he sold his company, my grandfather's health would deteriorate, like so many men who, with retirement, lose their identities.

But for that night's celebration, our last alone together, he was on top of the world, proud of the trust he had created for his children and grandchildren. "Better than that foolish trust Mellon set up," he boasted, and pressed me to ask questions as to the workings of the trust. But I was chilled at the thought of anything that took its life from his and begged him to talk instead of early days in Pittsburgh, when he and Mellon and Carnegie dined at The William Penn Hotel, competed at Steeplechase, and drank bootleg gin.

He told me about his first job interview, how he was late and running across the fields, ripped the new pair of high-top black patent leather shoes on a wire fence; he told me about his dates with Delores, who sang with a band and who would become Bob Hope's wife, and how there used to be a white linen runner on the stairs leading to the ladies' section of the exclusive Duquesne Club.

There was a moment over drinks when the bellboy knocked at the door and my grandfather anxiously shooed me into the next room where I stood in my bare feet, amused that he had feared the bellboy would see me as "a bad woman," a projection, no doubt, of my grandfather's own fantasy.

That would be the last night I would dance with him. When we entered The Persian Room he pressed a bill into the maître d's hand saying, "John, this is my granddaughter, and I want you to always take good care of her." As far back as I could remember, John had stood at this door at Thanksgiving reunions, had ushered our family to a table at the edge of the dance floor where we would watch Ethel Merman or maybe Bobby Darin while the adults drank martinis and ate food, such as frogs' legs, repugnant to me. John no more remembered me as the plain child with the braces than he believed I was this elegant old man's granddaughter.

My grandfather and I drank champagne, ate oysters and lobster, and danced every dance, for my mother's father was a superb dancer. That he held me too close and put his hand on my leg under the table, though I repeatedly removed it, all but brought me to tears; my grandfather was celebrating the end of his life.

"You are the only woman in the family who sees your grandfather as a man," my step-grandmother would tell me years later, just before his death. She also confided that he was a wonderful lover. He was a great womanizer, my daddy Colbert. Married three times, he managed to remain in the Catholic Church and, in the words of his last wife, was "the greatest catch in Palm Beach."

If, near the end of his life, he saw me as a sensual woman, I am sure I became that way, in part, for him. I was his child, he was my hero, my model of how to live life on a big scale. My fondness for the company of men, my inclination to think of them as no more evil than women, comes from him and from the mystery of my own father, in whose enigmatic absence was created an idealized image of man, the missing parent who would have loved me and seen me as his girl. Those women who would choose to leave men out of their children's lives should remember this.

The Good Provider

Until recently, most men and women in our culture and throughout the world defined masculinity as a Good Provider. It cannot be exaggerated how succinctly this definition summed up a man's masculinity, his unquestionable success at being A Real Man. Being a Good Provider was so much the stamp of a man that the more he provided, the more money he made, the less anyone questioned anything else about him. His personality, his coldness, his kindness—if he succeeded at providing, he succeeded at being a man.

This definition, on which generations of men were raised, was so vital to the stability of the world—Atlas holding up the globe outside Rockefeller Center—that all other roles were arranged beneath it, beginning with the definition of womanliness as The Caretaker. Under this Patriarchal Deal, children might grow up with dreams of alternative lives, but they were almost always abandoned as the reality of The Deal took precedence.

Ideally, a man didn't have a "look" at all. You might say his success went before him in the images of his wife and children, handsomely turned out, or the fine spectacle of his house and car; but when we looked at him, whether he was fat or thin, bald or bearded, what we saw was power, and power in itself was, and still is, very attractive.

When a man wore a beautiful woman on his arm, we would look at *her* fur coat, *her* alligator handbag, the elegance of *her* face and form, and having totaled her assets, we would read the bottom line of his prominence. While we complimented her on her fine accessories, our deepest respect went to him.

As the feminist army entered the workplace, the way we saw women changed, and I can't imagine that we will ever go back to the traditional definition of womanliness. The Caretaker may, in part, define women, but our partial appropriation of what used to be called masculinity has left men exposed. Meanwhile, we continue to judge men's status by the attractiveness of the woman on his arm.

"Men seek attractive women as mates not simply for their reproductive value," writes psychologist David M. Buss, "but also as signals of status to same-sex competitors and to other potential mates." Buss's research, using photographs of men with women of differing physical attractiveness, led him to conclude that "people suspect that a homely man must have high status if he can interest a stunning woman." Psychologist Susan Harter found a corollary: "Men's attractiveness is often associated with power, status, wealth, position. The man who has these commodities is often judged to be attractive even if physically you may not think that his features meet some classic definition." One survey that drove that home for Harter came right after the Gulf War in a woman's magazine article that asked, "Who Is the Sexiest Man in America?" It was General Norman Schwarzkopf.

Under Patriarchy some wealthy men, like my grandfather, had a touch of the peacock and dressed more elegantly, choosing fine suits and linens, shoes that were recognizably well made, but they required a panache to carry it off; a man had to watch himself where showy looks were concerned. In the nineteenth-century industrialized world, it just didn't do for a man to put appearance above performance. Better to err on the side of invisibility. High-ranking military men, like Generals Göring and Patton were famous for flourish, but mere mortals knew better. A "fancy man" advertised that he had been with his tailor instead of behind his desk.

Men's withdrawal from the mirror was a momentous historical reversal. Until the advent of capitalism and the rise of the bourgeoisie, men's clothes had been more splendid than women's. In the eighteenth century, men had dressed to draw attention to their person; the finer the cloth, the more admired the man. But near the turn of that century, men renounced fashion, elegance, and beauty and donned a new uniform, the dark suit, in which they entered the capitalist factory. In exchange for this public power, the role of being gorgeous was given to women, a private power, yes, but very much controlled by men.

Superficially it sounds like a good deal for men, but wearing beauty in the form of a woman on your arm, and owning none yourself, is like eating food with all the flavor chewed out of it. As my old friend psychiatrist Richard Robertiello once remarked, "Men get a lot of nourishment from people's eyes admiring the beautiful women they wear. We identify with her exhibitionism, unconsciously, of course, but we get our vanity fed when people savor her beauty."

"Secondhand admiration doesn't sound very filling," I replied.

He shrugged. "Which is why many men resented the power of women's beauty and put them down. Men loved it, and they envied it too."

In terms of healthy narcissism, the Patriarchal Deal was healthy neither for men nor for women, who were encouraged to be lovely objects, but worn like pretty flowers, with a brief life span. When we look back on those years, it is tempting in today's chaos to think of them as a better time, more ordered. But order was precisely what drove The Deal; sexual roles were regimented so rigidly that what didn't fit was smothered in denial.

Men couldn't afford to admit to themselves how powerless, aroused, and intimidated they felt opposite women's beauty; it would have defeated the commercial demands of Patriarchy before it got started. Therefore, women had to be domesticated, their potent sexual beauty neutered so that the man might comfortably leave the little woman at home while he went off to stoke the furnaces of the industrial world.

Knowing full well what had attracted him to his woman in the first place—her breasts, full lips, beautiful legs—how could he leave this tempting sexual being at home, unmonitored, miles away from his place of business? What if another man saw her, smelled her, got his foot in the door? Why, the husband would be cuckolded, the worst thing that could happen to a man.

Wasn't the wife his property? A crass thing to think, but he did pay for everything, and a casual fuck with the plumber, the postman, anyone, would diminish her value, much as a splintered leg ruins a fine Chippendale table. A man would lose face appearing in public with a woman another man had sexually "used." Better to desexualize her after the marriage, encourage her to lengthen her skirts, let her hair go back to its natural color. Best to dim his own view of her as sexual.

Men complain that women turn off sexually once the honeymoon is over, but these highly significant adjustments are usually in tandem. A family man didn't want to think of the kind of "dirty" sex he craved with the mother of his children, the woman he also called "Mother"; for this kind of sex, he went to Bad Women, who had their own look, one you can be sure was very, very different from that of a Caretaker.

In cutting her sexual beauty short, he limited his own enjoyment too, but it made The Good Provider's life easier. He who couldn't "control" his wife was seen by other men, and women, as limp. In time, moving a wife to the suburbs, where there were only other women during the long days, was as consoling to modern man as the chastity belt had once been to the crusader departing for the war, which was how men saw the marketplace.

Prior to feminism, society was structured in such a way as to eliminate anything that impeded economic progress. Those who interfered therefore had a look signaling trouble. The unsettling effect of a Bad Woman—the character Lana Turner portrayed in movies like *The Postman Always Rings Twice*—was that her exaggerated sexuality—high heels, short shorts, and a turban—threatened the status quo. From the second this "type" entered the film, the music took an erotic turn, telling women viewers in their full-skirted dresses what they already knew: that they were in jeopardy of losing their men to women such as these. The entire town would go to hell when a Gloria Grahame or Marilyn Monroe walked down Main Street, turning every man's head, as the music went *va-va-va-voom*. Looks told us everything.

Growing up under this formula, I saw myself as neither home breaker nor nest builder, nor did I recognize my kind of man in a gray flannel suit that promised security. Once I arrived in New York, I found the look of men who were *not* Good Providers to be exciting. There was a siren sexuality in the unruly hair, the slouch, the absence of the dark blue suit, the way "forbidden men" held their cigarettes or a glass of scotch. A girl knew they had no money and were driven by other, far more fascinating goals—oh, boy! Their faces were animated with the thoughts about to spill out, and when they looked at a woman, they saw her. In their regimented way, most men's lives were as narrow as women's; we'd all been set on tracks early on and nothing advertised where we were heading like the way we looked.

Men get little sympathy from women who still see them as having all the power, when in fact most men are in the business of making themselves dull, dependable, closing down all horizons except those that lead to economic success, which still describes a man. To women interested in settling down, the blue-suited look of surrender to the capitalist harness is the mating call.

That I went the opposite way was a mystery to my mother, though she never worried about me. When I took my various men home for the holidays, she didn't mention the absence of the blue suit and sensible shoes. Musicians, writers, artists, drifters, none of the lovers who accompanied me to Mother's house dismayed her or provoked comment, except the occasional, "He's Jewish, isn't he?" They were, almost without exception, smart, funny, and obviously sexual, which I think my mother also sensed.

There was a gift I gave to every man I loved, which was what my grandfather had given me: I introduced them to the mirror. Not to the dark blue suit, which they so clearly had disavowed, but to the finest version of whatever it was they chose to put on their backs. It is a powerful gift to open a man to his vanity, very heady, as in fairy-tale awakenings. A woman who applauds a man's narcissism, giving him permission to pursue it further, well, a man does not quickly forget such tutelage. A certain dependency is born, wherein the man feels a more pressing need for that woman in his life. She is now the sun, without whom there would be no one to take him in, see him. Giving a man this gift puts meat on the bones of love, a word begging for definition. "Ah, my love, I love the way you see me!" Now, *that* has meaning. We women are the permission givers, beginning with that first woman in his life, who loved his adorable shape or didn't; either way, this is what the grown woman ignites in him, the sight of himself as adored in her eyes.

There was a certain writer I took to a tailor, whose magical threads would be sewn in such a way as to alter the way my lover saw himself, and me. We were in Rome, on vacation. In his one suitcase he had packed some extra jeans, shirts, and one blazer, but it was mostly filled with the yellow legal pads on which he wrote and with the books he was reading. I loved him madly and wanted to give him a charm that would bind him to me. One morning I announced I was taking him to Mastroianni's tailor. "Think of it as an experience to write about," I said by way of persuasion.

Even after a long martini lunch in the Piazza Navona he was as nervous as a bridegroom, and so we walked to the Via Condotti until we were just a few doors short of the Spanish Steps. There we turned into a small courtyard, went up a narrow flight of stairs, and entered a shadowy suite of rooms, the shutters half closed against the afternoon sun. Bolts of fabric lay haphazardly unfurled on cutting tables and were stacked on high shelves, the only sound being the fountain in the courtyard below.

"*Buona sera*," purred the magician tailor, a study in the elegant unmade-bed school of masculine fashion. While his attendants took the measure of my man, the maestro spoke in the gentlest tones, sensing that he had a novice in his hands.

My lover was an arrogant fellow, prone to masking any sign of discomfort, but his performance that day was like a virgin slowly, expertly, being seduced. The twist in the assignation was, of course, that he was falling in love with his own image. As with my grandfather, my pleasure came from being the voyeur, watching his defenses fall. It has struck me that most men tend to fix their faces in an almost pained, unnatural portrait when they look at themselves in the mirror, like little boys, which is not inappropriate given their lack of practice.

"When a man looks into a mirror, he looks anywhere but straight ahead," a mirror salesman is quoted in *Esquire*. "It's as if he thinks it's wrong to look at himself, as if he's afraid of being caught." My own early invisibility had made me sensitive to men's need for praise of their physical selves. I understood the loneliness of feeling eyes pass over me.

By the time the blazer and cavalry twill trousers were finished, the man in them was so at home with being fitted, pinned, admired in the tall, three-way mirror, well, he was as infatuated as any animal seeing its reflection in a still pond. His relationship with his tailor when they parted was such that they were trading jokes and cigars.

It was a gift I would exchange with other men, but only after I recognized that they loved me in part for my exhibitionistic self, something they wanted to share. I didn't want a man who wore me on his arm, getting his own exhibitionism fed secondhand. Better to be that powerful conduit opening him to his own healthy narcissism. Men who feed on their women's looks in time begin to envy the woman's power, or they tire of its flavor and look for new women, new tastes. No resentful escort for me; rather, a twin in the power of being seen. Returning a man to the beauty of his own reflection is a magic charm required by those of us who fear rejection.

Only recently have the terms *voyeurism* and *exhibitionism* slipped into polite conversation. The experts caution me that the words are only properly used when referring to pathologies, where the looking or the exhibitionistic act are replacing sex. But the gurus also concede that we've not yet coined words to express what has been happening in recent years as more and more people walk around half naked. Today's craze to draw attention to one's body sums up where the world is voyeuristically/exhibitionistically; nothing has influenced this more than men's reentering the beauty contest.

"People use the words much more generally nowadays," says Robertiello. "Men are definitely more voyeuristic and women infinitely more exhibitionistic in terms of their physical selves. Some men today are more into looking good, showing off their bodies, but it's a relatively late development and still doesn't apply to most men." Twenty years ago, the behavioral gurus wagged their fingers at me, warning me that only men were voyeurs. Having stared at men all my life, I bit my tongue and bided my time.

Today, wise women like Judith Seifer admit, "Of course women are voyeurs! What is it other than voyeurism, the way women look at other women and recall with elephantine memory precisely what each other wears? There are porn videos today made expressly for women." While William H. Masters emphasizes that using the term *exhibitionist* in psychotherapeutic terms still means you're talking about a male, most behaviorists agree that both words, *exhibitionism* and *voyeurism*, are slipping more and more into popular usage. There is a difference between the male "flasher" in the dirty raincoat and the woman who wears a transparent dress on a public street, but the shades of gray multiply.

In the seventies, Kate Millett described what Charlotte Brontë's heroine in *Villette* feels when she looks at men: "Their beauty, for Brontë is perhaps the first woman who ever admitted in print that women find men beautiful, amazes and hurts her." Can it be true, I wondered, that women have been so reluctant to speak and write of the power of male beauty over them? Is our reluctance to share with men the power of beauty any less determined than men's to give up their economic and political power? Money power is so obvious that when it changes hands it demands discussion; beauty is no less powerful, but we have dismissed its reigning influence for several hundred years because the Patriarchal Deal, having denied it to men, couldn't publicly afford to put women's beauty on the scale.

Women's ownership of beauty, under Patriarchy, led to a lot of nasty behavior among those men who could not economically afford the beautiful women to whom they felt drawn, even entitled. It is the stuff of literature, the little boy who grows up adored by his mother, seeing himself in her eyes and identifying with her beauty. But he hasn't the wealth for a beauty, or her family is looking for a better match. Now when he sees lovely women who will never be his, he hates them, tries to bring them down a peg or two, not unlike the more competent and thus disgruntled wife who hates her husband for being a failure in the marketplace.

Even the wealthy man with a great beauty on his arm often isn't satisfied; the beauty is hers, not his. And so men act with contempt toward women, who own all this power, though they would never consciously acknowledge why they stand on street corners and make rude remarks, their rage as nasty as some feminist's fury at men.

Imagine how women's entry into the workplace and our providing for ourselves has altered the way in which men see themselves. Leave women's entitlement to work out of the discussion, for the unconscious knows nothing of fairness. The not-so-merry-go-round of fashion images that men and women put on our backs reflects the dramatic change in how we define masculinity and femininity. We are all trying for a look that goes far deeper than mere clothes—not that clothes are ever "mere"—trying for an image of our lives with which we can sanely live. It is very disturbing to exist without the anchor of identity, which includes visual image.

Burdensome, stultifying, and suffocating, the traditional roles of Good Provider and Caretaker accomplished more than we like to admit; without our social roles, men especially are left in a gray area of what it means to be a man. We spare no time or ink probing women's roles, women's problems, women's lives. For men, *not* questioning manliness may be the only totally male thing left to them. This is excellent for women who hate men, and that number grows, I fear. Most men seem to plod along, perhaps in the belief that the past twenty-five years will go away, that right-wing Republicanism will restore the status quo.

My sympathy for men may influence my optimistic belief that the original disparagement of such groups as the organizers of the Million Man March and The Promise Keepers will soften. You would think that the soaring rate of homes without fathers, along with the unprecedented rate of the imprisonment of young men for crime, drugs, abuse would make us ask, Why? Why have we lost so many men, so many fathers? Instead, Matriarchal Feminists berate men even more.

Our uncontrollable rage, our ability to love, as well as our need to be seen, begins at birth. Neither the abuser, nor the rude sidewalk gawker, nor even the near naked beauty he is verbally abusing wants to believe that our needs are rooted in the nursery. If there is an unconscious cry embedded in his catcall, it might be, "I hate you for being so beautiful, so powerful, and so blind to me who feels so small and needy opposite you: 'I one my mother, I two my mother, I three my mother ... I ate my mother.'" Which is exactly what angry men's/boys' eyes do: They devour us, some barbarically, some lovingly, a variable decided by the man's earliest history: whether or not mother's eyes lit up when she saw him. Need I add that the same is true of the woman's reaction to men's looking: She will be warmed by their eyes or hate them for what she thinks they see.

"What Does She See in Him?"

How did a woman thirty years ago see her man? Certainly not as a sex object or as a creature of beauty. When a woman's existence depends on a man who works outside the home, an unknown place to which he goes in the morning and from which he doesn't return until evening, her image of him is colored by absolute need, much as a child's glorified image of mother is surrounded by a halo even when she is a bad mother. Onto the man was projected the woman's own ambitions, everything she had ever wanted but was forbidden to pursue herself. A certain heroic shading was inevitable; he stood tall, probably taller than he was.

His weight, the sagging jowl, the premature balding, the aging, didn't occupy her image of him so much as did the prospect of his return to the home, her workplace, in which she took care of him, fed him, washed and ironed his clothes until the next day when he would leave again, taking with him everyone's destiny. When the commuter train was late, when she found a matchbook in his pocket from the Bide-a-Wee Motel or the other women whispered of his extramarital affair, her desperation wasn't the image of him as a sexual object—which she had lost sight of since the early days of marriage; instead, she prayed for the door to open, just to see him, solid and dependable, making her life whole again.

Until the mid-fifties, married couples in films slept in single beds and husbands wore their suits buttoned up until bedtime; in *The Man in the Grey Flannel Suit*, *Leave It to Beaver*, *The Dick Van Dyke Show*, even in *The Honeymooners*, husbands looked dependable and solid even around the house, emphasizing their role as provider. If a man did well by his family economically, no one asked, "What does she see in him?"

His magazines talked of business and politics. Her magazines advised her to put a little mystery into their evenings, light the candles, make a special casserole; the worst thing that could befall a woman was to lose her man. To that end, she could not afford to "let herself go." When women wanted to dream, escape, they read Harlequin romances. Since 1906, Harlequin and its subsidiaries have been fleshing out the look of women's dream men. In the fifties, sixties, and most of the seventies, "the Alpha Man was the embodiment of what women wanted," says Harlequin's Katherine Orr. "He was big, strong, imposing, a brooding type whose thoughts she couldn't read. He either owned an estate where she worked, or he was a doctor. There was a lot of nurse/doctor back then. The doctor was seen as an exciting, powerful figure. But here again, mysterious and quite brooding, because he was under a lot of pressure. And wealthy. Always wealthy."

Whether he was fat Jackie Gleason or a swarthy Alpha Man, he had to be a Good Provider. Otherwise, it made no sense; if a woman had no money of her own, what was the point of dreaming about handsome, sexual men, who were exciting but dangerous, given that sex outside marriage could rob a woman of everything. Another favorite image of 1940s movies was the story of a woman fallen prey to a man's sexual glamour, movies such as *Back Street*. Women simply couldn't afford to respond to anything in a man except his providership.

The film and paperback novel industries fed women's romantic fantasies, but there was no erotic industry for women, nothing specifically conceived to arouse them, make them think of masturbation or sex outside marriage. Romantic music filled a void, but since women didn't think of themselves as sexual unto themselves, alone and without a man, the sexual feelings they were actually having were called "romance" by them and everyone else.

Until twenty-five years ago, women didn't think they had sexual fantasies, nor did the rest of the world. What, therefore, was the point in men thinking about their own image, trying to catch a woman's eye if all women cared about was the man's ability to provide? It was a given that women didn't look. Men were the voyeurs and women the exhibitionists. The significance of men today getting into looking good extends beyond the obvious. It implies that women, now less economically dependent, are looking at them, judging them.

In a 1994 University of Chicago study titled *Sex in America*, 30 percent of women ages eighteen to forty-four and 18 percent of women ages forty-five to fifty-nine said they found "Watching partner undress" to be "Very appealing"; not a bad percentage, given that Nice Girls didn't look. As for men, 50 percent of the eighteen to forty-four age group and 40 percent of the forty-five to fifty-nine group found it "Very appealing" to watch a partner undress.

"Men more often find themselves in the position of sex objects today than in the past," says Warren Farrell, "but what is still true is that they are first and foremost seen as 'success objects' by women." As some women become disenchanted with the workplace, they have the option to leave, return to a husband and let him provide, to marry, or to work at home themselves. It is not an option most men have. Men realize that the same woman who competes with him at the office, who may even be his economic equal or superior, still grades him on his wage earning.

Yes, there are marriages in which women earn more than their men, but studies on family arguments, the breakdowns of marriages and relationships often point to "the money argument" as the beginning of the end. Even if the woman puts his lack of providing aside, the man cannot. The younger the man, the more likely he is to accept the investment in a beauty product, a new suit; these men are the tip of the wedge, and the male fashion/beauty industries are holding their breath. Will women buy it, buy *him*, the new beautiful man? Will women's eyes be amenable to sharing the mirror?

Meanwhile, from out of the west comes the new male hero at Harlequin books, never to be underestimated as a predictor of the future of the sexes. Enter the Western Cowboy, today's favorite fantasy hero, whose image is emblazoned on the covers of millions of books worldwide. Forty-six percent of the entire mass market paperback sales are romance novels. Worldwide, there are fifty million romance readers, and each of them reads more than one book a week. Barnes & Noble figures that the average reader spends $1,200 a year on her paperback fix. What kind of hunger is this feeding?

"His look says to the woman that he is strong, that he can take care of her," says Katherine Orr. Sounds suspiciously like The Good Provider; according to Orr, the Cowboy is no ordinary ranch hand, but owns hundreds of acres. "This immediately tells the woman, married or single—her average age is forty-two—that he can rescue her from the confinement of today's world," says Orr. "But while he is wealthy and strong, it is his focus on her, his attention to her that is most important. He talks to her. Women always want to communicate, men don't. Romance readers want dialogue. Because he has a lot of employees, he can walk away from his ranch and focus totally on her."

A Good Provider who talks. Still every woman's dream. After sex in real life, the man rolls over, having spiraled down from orgasm more quickly than the woman. He is ready to disconnect and sleep. She wants to maintain the intimacy, is still coming down, psychologically and chemically; she wants to be held, to talk. Pre- and post-coital conversation is high on women's list; even in fantasy, women emphasize the importance of words, the extended talk that builds trust, literally opening women up. How clever of Harlequin to hit upon a talking cowboy who is also rich.

Women accuse men of seeing us as an assemblage of parts, tits and ass. Is The Prince of Parts in women's romantic imagery all that different? There is a paperback hero "look" for every type of woman. Are these bits of pieces of men not like the naked women at whom men stare, first this part, then the other? True, men's photographs are on paper, and ours fleshed out in our minds; but even this is changing as more women can allow themselves—can literally afford—to see men, pecs to buns.

We are slowly training our eyes to take in the naked man in X-rated films, allowing ourselves to feel the electric charge that begins with the eye and courses down through our sexual circuitry to become the moisture between our legs. There was a great stir in the literary world and beyond, several years ago, when an esteemed woman writer, Sallie Tisdale, wrote an article in the equally esteemed *Harper's Magazine* titled "Talk Dirty to Me," relating her adventures in the X-rated video stores that she frequented. Imagine: an intellectual woman liking porn! So eye-catching was the idea that Tisdale extended the article into a book.

We women are learning as we look. The men in the first sexual fantasies I collected from women in the seventies had no identity; "I don't know who he is," the women would say. "I can't see his face." Being anonymous meant that "the faceless stranger" would not judge her, would disappear after the fuck, which he usually "forced" (her words) upon her. Therefore, she could show him her hidden, wild, erotic self, and since it was "rape" (again, her words, though there was no pain, no humiliation), she would emerge, her Nice Girl reputation intact. Today we can afford to see him; we want to look, and men, feeling our eyes on them, pump up their biceps, mousse their hair.

Some women denigrate men who masturbate while looking at naked women in *Playboy* and *Penthouse*, as if a voyeuristic connection with their penis were dirty and unmanly. The great majority of women don't have fantasies of men satisfying themselves because they would say to the woman that he doesn't need her; in this scenario, his penis is our competition. When I was in my twenties, I awoke one night and found my lover on the living room sofa, masturbating. I was furious, envious; just hours earlier we had had sex, and here he was with this other person/thing, doing it without me. In some strange way he had betrayed me. I looked at the wasted sperm on his belly like an ugly puddle; in fact, the whole man looked less attractive.

I often think part of male excitement during masturbation is that they are breaking mother's antisex rules, inculcated since they were little boys. Isn't this what the naked women in the magazines arouse in men, along with the extra kick that he is having his dirty little orgasm while looking at her looking back at him? She *sees* him "doing it." Eye-to-eye contact was Hugh Hefner's contribution.

"We may have some sexual tastes that come from our distant past," writes anthropologist Helen Fisher. "Some men are voyeurs. Some like to look at visual porn. . . . In fact, men's sexual fantasies are regularly aroused by visual stimuli of all sorts. Perhaps these partialities are, in part, directed by their more spatial brains. Women like romance novels and soap operas on television—tepid, verbal porn. Maybe these inclinations arise from their sensitivity to language."

Cosmopolitan recently published another male nude centerfold, approximately the twelfth since Burt Reynolds first appeared in the buff in 1973. Clearly, Helen Gurley Brown registered the popularity of the recent Coca-Cola commercial in which the women stare from an office window at the hunk construction worker on the street below. They giggle and mention his pecs. But do they get as moist as a man would get hard looking at naked women?

The answer is yes according to erotic film producer Candida Royalle. "I find that many women like seeing male genitalia. Women may not be admitting it to their men because they haven't yet admitted it to themselves. But tests have been done where receptors were hooked to women who were being shown a variety of erotic material. Interviewed afterward, most of the women said they had not been excited, but the receptors told a different story. They simply were not consciously acknowledging their physical reactions. 'Nice girls' still don't look."

To this day, the man who "forces" the woman to have sex remains one of women's most powerful fantasies. He arrives, he does the deed, he leaves her an "innocent" victim. And we women say that men see us as "objects." All we want from our fantasy lover is his strength and his cock. Are these fantasies any "nicer" than the naked beauties in *Playboy* who tempt men to be Bad Boys and masturbate? When Madonna and Sharon Stone assault men with their bodies, are they so different from the men who objectify women in the workplace with their sexually harassing words?

A man from my past comes to mind while writing the above. I realize now that I didn't "see" him, didn't even notice him for the first two nights I was in his company, having dinner with five other people. I looked right through him, my mind elsewhere, on another man. It wasn't until the next day that I looked at him, and then, what I saw were his sexual parts, which triggered an erotic response.

It was the mid-sixties, and I was in Palermo writing a travel article for a magazine. The days were passing slowly, uneventfully, until one morning the photographer with whom I was traveling suggested that it would be polite if I rode in the car with this man, an architect whose hotel we were going to visit. Grumbling at having to get back out in the heat and travel with a man whose name I didn't even remember, I consented to ride with him.

There we were, this stranger and I, flying along the Sicilian coast in his Alfa Romeo, silence hanging heavy in the summer heat, for he spoke no English and my Italian was rudimentary. *Vrroooom!* roared the powerful motor as the man controlling it took me faster and faster, up, over, and around the dangerously narrow road, past the painted carts with their high wheels, past other, slower, lest masterful drivers. Now I looked, looked down at the back of his widespread hand, shifting the gears up and back, and my eyes followed the dark hairs on his suntanned arm, reminding me of all the masculine hands and arms that had driven me off into the nights of my life. Only now, as his bronzed, sandaled foot pressed onto the accelerator did I look up at his face, see the whole man and know that before the day was over we would be lovers.

It was the sighting of his "parts," those masculine objects—hands, feet, arms—that pulled me into focus with him, a picture of me beside him, he all control and power and me, well, taken, of course. Though I would orchestrate the seduction along with him, *due virtuosi*, it would always remain that initial reawakening to the seductions of adolescence that triggered our month-long affair, crisscrossing Sicily, Rome, the Amalfi coast, Capri, his wife in hot pursuit.

Being in a car, alone with a man whose hands were on the steering wheel, whose arms and legs and feet were controlling my ride to a sexual rendezvous, this was what I was raised for, a Prince of Masculine Parts. Raised in a home without a man, all men by definition were an assemblage of lovely parts imbued by me with needs, desires, sexual fulfillments.

A man in a car was a prince on a horse. Hadn't I grown up in cars, in drive-in restaurants, in drive-in movies, parked on beaches? At the onset of these erotic adventures, the individual man was almost interchangeable with any other man whose objectified function was to drive/protect/direct me, little, powerless creature that I was; eventually, I would grow to love the subjective, whole man, but there has never been a drink so potent, or music so heartbreaking, that would shift me into sexual gear like being alone in a car with a man at the wheel.

That day in Palermo I awoke to an erotic fantasy like a woman in a trance, a triggered response. "Autolove" was what I called it in a short story I wrote ten years later.

Men's Hungry Eyes

In the compartmentalized life of a man, there is no need for romance novels, no door marked dreamy and soft, soft being the enemy of hard, which is how a man must get to perform sexually. Women want to be Swept Away, a man can't afford it. The Job of Sex has always weighed heavily on men; women may see it as power and resent men's sometimes clumsy efforts at seduction, but for a man who is not temperamentally suited to being a Don Juan, this business of erections and maintaining them is crucial to identity.

Women may say contemptuously that men are in love with their penises; we have no sympathy for men who look at naked women and masturbate. But what if the penis didn't get hard at the sight of a naked woman *in his bed*, not in a magazine, but lying there, expecting him to make her sexual, keep his penis hard until she is hot, and then "give" her an orgasm? Embarrassing as it is to get an unexpected erection, even worse to ejaculate in one's trousers, imagine how a man feels not getting an erection or losing it.

When Patriarchal man owned the world, he encouraged women's sexual ignorance, which made us boring partners in bed, but protected the man from our visual and intellectual sex education. We didn't look at our own genitals, and we didn't look at his. Women saw men as providers and protectors, to the degree that we looked at all, and men went to burlesque, to whorehouses to look at women and to fuck them in ways they didn't want to fuck their nice, clean wives. Men also looked at pictures of naked women because the human eye is born with a taste, so to speak, for the female body. One could say that looking at naked women was good practice for the penis, for that circuitry between brain and erection that men needed to keep well oiled.

There was at the turn of the century a fashionable school of painting that played with men's voyeuristic needs while abiding by the strict antierotic rules of the Victorian Age. In these canvases by some of the most eminent artists of the day, Childe Hassam, Robert van Vorst Sewell, Josef Englehardt, and Charles Chaplin, naked women sprawl on riverbanks, in verdant fields, on sun-bleached rocks, and under the boughs of trees, their lovely, strangely ethereal bodies seemingly involved in the very evolution of nature. One of our favorite restaurants in New York, the Café des Artistes, is famous for its murals of young nudes frolicking in the bulrushes, splashing in the brooks as if nature was their home.

It is quite a tour de force, this fin-de-siècle period of art that gave a Patriarchal gentleman the opportunity to stand at the Royal Exhibition and safely stare at naked women, satisfying his voyeurism as a patron of the arts, a student of the medium, religious in his reverence for the purity of woman. In fact, there is something very "unreal" about the naked women in these paintings. Yes, there are breasts and a cleft between their legs, but they seem to be without skeletons, almost spineless, barely able to support their willowy bodies as they emerge out of flowers or lie in a swoon as if fallen from the trees under which they sleep in one another's arms.

Today one might ask, What is going on here, so nonerotic are these naked women. It's fascinating how society always manages to feed the human need for the sight of the naked body within certain prescribed rules specific to the era, whether the beauty icon is male or female. All of a man's concentration was required to be a provider at the onset of the Industrial Revolution, but an outlet was nonetheless required for his erotic imagination. Patriarch and captain of industry, he had neither time nor societal permission to pursue beauty in himself. As for sexual excitement, Queen Victoria forbade it (leading, of course, to one of the most licentious periods in modern history). Nor could he afford to think of women as having any power whatsoever, including sexual beauty.

Women were therefore split neatly into two camps, the Good Woman who was wife and mother—whose total purity had to compensate for the man's necessary involvement in grimy immoral commerce— and the Bad Woman, she who was available to satisfy sexual needs. To combine Good and Bad Woman—mother and sex goddess—into one person was unthinkable, alarmingly frightening. Life was hard enough. Requiring respite from the crime and competition of the new marketplace, the Victorian gentleman was himself bound, at least publicly, by the asexual rules of the household in which he had been raised by his mother, "the household nun," and a withdrawn, tyrannical father.

What a perfect visual "feed" these paintings of nude, not quite human women were, a plethora of naked female flesh. In his club, or in his pub to which cheaper imitations quickly trickled down, a man found voyeuristic comfort in the bosom, quite literally, of the naked ladies who papered the walls.

I imagine Victorian man losing himself in the safest sort of erotic daydreams after a hard day's work in the bloodless mercantile machine. "To the late nineteenth-century male," writes Bram Dijkstra in *Idols of Perversity*, "nothing was as unwelcome as the thought of woman—even woman as the embodiment of nature—taking charge. *He* wanted to be in charge, it was his *right* to be in charge. To him, Henry Drummond assured him, had been 'mainly assigned the fulfillment of the first great function—the Struggle for Life.' It was woman's appointed role, even as the personification of nature, to float weightlessly in the breeze." And she floats in these paintings "because to walk is to act, and to beckon a form of invitation, a way of taking charge."

In Dijkstra's book there is a reproduction of a painting titled *Sleep*, in which several sumptuous nudes lie beneath a tree. "Out of the upper-right corner of this painting," writes Dijkstra, "crawls a peculiar little monster, half-businessman and half-slug, with the sunken eyes of the sort of male . . . found prone to self-pollution. . . . In fact, the peculiar creature . . . here only seems capable of contemplating the beautiful, self-sufficient women under the tree from a safe distance. The lower part of his body would seem to have melted away, as if he were a symbolic representation of the essence of voyeurism."

The voyeur and the beauty object, a rigid definition of sex roles for most of the twentieth century. Man the voyeur would be looked down upon for his masturbatory fantasies and actions, but nonetheless the "act" of masturbation remained his. Woman, the sex object, would eventually evolve into the Vargas Girl in the 1930s and '40s pages of *Esquire*, a long-legged sex goddess who had no more blood in her veins than the earlier nudes at the Royal Exhibition. But she and her less tony friends on cheap calendar art provided man with his necessary masturbatory tool: the safe, nude, female beauty object.

It would be Hugh Hefner, in the 1950s, who would take the revolutionary step of directly involving his naked centerfold, the Playmate, with her voyeuristic male companion. These women agreed, via their eyes, to enter the man's fantasies and invited him to enter theirs. As time passed, they grew bolder, touching their breasts and moving their hands between their legs. What her look said was "See, I am sexual like you." In her way, the Playmate was a step forward for women too, for she announced that the girl next door had a sexuality of her own. Not that Nice Girls initially identified with the naked centerfold, God forbid; but the door was open and the Playmate, Bad Girl that she was, gave permission to all women to be more sexually self-accepting.

There was outrage from feminists in 1979 when *Playboy* invited young women from the Ivy League colleges to compete for the privilege of taking off their clothes for the *Playboy* photographers, outrage against both the magazine and the women who did it. That it had come to this, that Very Very Nice Girls from the best next doors would pose nude, attested not only to men's voyeurism but also to women's acceptance of the joy of exhibitionism.

The Playmate, sexually blatant as she was, posed no threat to men, being inside the covers of a magazine. Even the Playboy Bunnies, invented to wait on men at their local Playboy Club, were untouchable, and the thick Rule Books by which these women worked were as strict as The Girl Scout Manual. They protected the Bunnies from lascivious men, but The Rules protected the men too.

Matriarchal Feminists still see the Playmate and the *Penthouse* Pet as degrading to women, an idea, in my mind, closer to men's Victorian image of women than to the sexual freedom we won in the sixties and seventies. But that is where we women divide, a problem between us that has nothing to do with men; the same women who picketed the Playboy Clubs twenty years ago today write against pornography as degrading to women, even when women write it.

I don't blame men for staying out of our furious debate on just how much a good feminist can show. Women who vilify other women for choosing to take their clothes off in front of a camera, for writing pornography or buying erotic videos so that they might go home and masturbate, these cranky sexual prohibitors are the direct descendants of the household nuns at the turn of the century. They hate seeing beauty and power in women's sexuality because it is not a license they allow themselves.

Once, long ago, these antisex women tasted erotic excitement; it is impossible to go through life never, even as a child, to have touched oneself. It used to be only Vile Men who reminded these witchy women of their suppressed sexuality. But now they hate sexual women even more for picking the scab where their own sex once lived.

Many men still enjoy satisfying their erotic needs just as their grandfathers did: alone in the dark. No orgasm was quite so thrilling as that during masturbation in mother's pretty powder room just feet away from the family dinner table. And no woman is so exciting as she whose fingers work between her legs, her eyes staring out at the man, inviting him to do likewise.

As men begin to appreciate their own beauty power, they will look at women differently. Being less needy, they will not stare at us with quite so much hunger. I wonder how women will like this, and if some won't miss the mirroring eyes many say they hate. Men know more about women and our beauty than we do. They watch us watching each other. We deny our competitiveness, but in literature and in film men have always seemed to be shaking their heads, amused, on the sidelines of women's competition for them, the male provider, but not really the prize, which was always in other women's eyes.

I welcome men's advance into the beauty arena. I want to stand on the street and cheer them forward to get the power and pleasure their male ancestors enjoyed two hundred years ago. If the fashions today dip into the fifties one day and the seventies the next, looking futuristic tomorrow, we should remember that the design of clothes is often ahead of our conscious day-to-day decisions.

As Anne Hollander says, "fashion tends to show us what we're really thinking rather than what we're saying." I think men are sick to death of women's posturing and preaching; maybe they can tolerate equality in the workplace, but to take their jobs, want their hearts too, and blame them for problems we are still afraid to face among ourselves? "I'll give you this, I'll give you that," many of them say, "but I'll take some of that beauty you don't even know how to use, and I'll show you how to exercise its power."

Men's eyes eat us up. When their stare is longer than a compliment, we hate them. How much looking constitutes a compliment? That decision has always been women's. When does a look of appreciation become a rude stare? Women critique men mercilessly for how they stare and hate them when they do not look. The man's eyes may have been drawn to the pretty woman as innocently as a passerby stares at pastries in a window, his thoughts on the business meeting to which he is heading. Men are hungry.

Having given us the power of beauty, which many men miss sorely—it being human and not gender-specific to want to be adored for one's self—men have needed to enjoy our beauty just as we needed their money. But rejected by women who hate their own bodies and so can't allow others to feast, men go to prostitutes, look at naked women in magazines, and release the longing and anger, which, it should be noted, is more often turned against themselves.

Most men do not pay prostitutes for sadistic pleasures but far more frequently play the masochist, the bad boy/man who gets his orgasm at the feet of the dominatrix. The statistics on men's abuse of women have risen along with women's entry into the workplace; men's brutality should not be overlooked or excused, but alongside should be the figures on men's mortality, their inability to live alone given their early training in suppression of emotion. We are all in this together. As premature aging and heart attacks increase among working women, maybe we will learn some compassion for "man the beast."

"The Copulatory Gaze"

No one took women's complaints at being ogled seriously in the old days; if men didn't look, there would be no selection/date/marriage/security. Women dressed to be seen so that we might be picked; men often took advantage of their role as voyeurs, "staring holes in us," but still no one taught boys how to look, the etiquette, how women felt being watched, or rejected. Our fear of rejection should be factored in, the heart-in-mouth quandary as we were graded, hating the examination but also praying that we wouldn't fail. To fail was to live unchosen, without husband or children. We hated men's eyes even as we dressed to the sound of romantic music and the fantasy of filling his eyes.

Let me quote anthropologist Helen Fisher at greater length, for her calm, intelligent voice is so full of reason and compassion for us poor confused human animals:

> The gaze is probably the most striking human courting ploy. Eye language. In Western cultures, where eye contact between the sexes is permitted, men and women often stare intently at a potential mate for about two to three seconds during which their pupils may dilate—a sign of extreme interest. Then the starer drops his or her eyelids and looks away.
>
> No wonder the custom of the veil has been adopted in so many cultures. Eye contact seems to have an immediate effect. The gaze triggers a primitive part of the human brain, calling forth one of two basic emotions—approach or retreat. You cannot ignore the eyes of another fixed on you; you must respond. You may smile and start conversation. You may look away and edge

toward the door. But first you will probably tug at an earlobe, adjust your sweater, yawn, fidget with your eyeglasses, or perform some other meaningless movement—a "displacement gesture"—to alleviate anxiety while you make up your mind how to acknowledge this invitation, whether to flee the premises or stay and play the courting game.

This look, known to ethologists as the copulatory gaze, may well be embedded in our evolutionary psyche. . . . Perhaps it is the eye—not the heart, the genitals, or the brain—that is the initial organ of romance, for the gaze (or stare) often triggers the human smile.

Men stare in a way that women do not. Fisher suggests that men's habit of looking comes from their ancestors, who squatted for hours behind the brush on the African veldt, watching for an animal on its way to the watering hole. The male brain addresses spatial action in a different way than does the female's. We women are just beginning to look in earnest, perhaps in answer to men's new interest in fashion, perhaps as reward for our own new economics.

Writer/editor Susie Bright argues that lesbians have the fine art of looking at women down pat and offers this advice to men: "Look at her. All over. Linger anywhere you like. When she notices (and she will if you're really looking), hold her eyes with yours. Hold them close. Every second will feel like a minute. You'll be tempted to avert your gaze but don't. . . . You'll know then and there whether she wants you or not. . . . If she does want you, she'll be thrilled by your look, because it says to her that she has your full attention. . . . The beginning of love is the promise of all that's to come—for boys and girls. And it all begins with a Look, which is nothing more than a Hope. If I can seduce a straight girl with the strength of my curious green eyes, then you shouldn't have any problem at all."

Oh? But he very much has a problem, beginning with the fact that a woman's gaze at another woman is felt quite differently than a man's look is. Women's eyes have always been the judges of our beauty; it is for women that we dress and for a woman's gaze that our tiny eyes searched when we were infants.

Men look from woman to woman, never satisfied, always seeking young, lovelier women when they feel bereft of beauty within. It is the wise woman who sees her man as her beauty subject, who awakens him to his belief in himself as physically lovable. He dare not lose her vision of him. Only she has the eye, the good mirror. Without her he would once again be relegated to the invisible drabness of men's world. Money is prodigious power, but it will not warm you. "Feed me! Feed me!" men's eyes bulge on the street, hungry that no one has seen them.

We would all stare less at women and more at men if we had seen ourselves in father's eyes from the beginning. When he is totally absent, the dependence on women is obviously exaggerated. In his fiction as in his life, D. H. Lawrence was ambivalent about women, an almost madness that originated in his intense relationship with his mother and the total absence of a father. It has been suggested by one of his many biographers that the women whom Lawrence treats with misogynistic contempt in his work represent a version of himself, that part of himself too tied to his all-consuming, adoring mother, perhaps too identified with her in the absence of a father. Lawrence could not abide any rival, and in his marriage with Frieda his unhealthy jealousy of her sons by a prior marriage often drove him to violence. Students of literature agonize over the "real" Lawrence as portrayed by the characters in his novels.

In strictly Patriarchal days a man grew up learning through observation the rituals of looking at women. No one suggested that there was an etiquette in voyeurism or that there should be. He observed his father and other men looking and commenting as women passed by, and since the men didn't mention how the women felt, being scrutinized, it didn't occur to the young man to master anything but the courage to fix his gaze. It was from us that boys/men discovered the chink in our formidable armor.

Consider the dawning awareness when a male, grown up under the monopolistic power of a woman's gaze, comes to the realization that his own eyes have the ability to dress and undress, excite or unhinge a person of his mother's sex. A man comes to this discovery about the same time he realizes his role as economic provider, meaning he has reassessed his father's influence, up till then understood to be less than that of the all-powerful mother. When a young man learns these various male powers, they help oil his way into the hitherto frightening world ruled by women.

Today women have traditional woman power along with economic power, and now we have become voyeuristic. If men have put a sharper edge on their voyeurism, there are reasons for it. Forever balancing power, men move like an army into the beauty arena, elbowing women aside in the mirror. It has nothing to do with fashion designers;

it is a genetic move and countermove in the evolving balance of power between the sexes. I do not mean to diminish fashion; clothes are very powerful window dressing, for they often say what the person inside is feeling. Today our clothes are way ahead of us.

In the olden days, a young woman might use the power of her naked body, "pretending" not to be aware of his hungry eyes; she used it to feel the thrill of power in his loss of control. There is in Carol De Chellis Hill's novel *Henry James' Midnight Song* a rapturous description of a young man outside the window of a young woman whose life he has saved while she was sleepwalking in the park. He is now watching her, naked in front of a mirror, playing with her breasts:

> He was dizzy with the spectacle . . . with the glowing wonder of that gold and rose and white white breast . . . and then her hand, three fingertips, reached up, brushed against it and scissoring went closed, then open. . . . Then she lifted her head and stared into the mirror, straight at him. . . . The girl stepped away from the glass, her face an unread smile. Had she seen him seeing her? . . . Had she known? . . . He knew somewhere that she knew he was watching her out there that night, pinned in the dark behind the glass. His breath had stopped when he saw her nipple there, and her smile and her leaning into the mirror, her back to him, her reflected face to him, and he had been so stung with beauty and desire.

Today we provide for ourselves, which frees us to enjoy the power of the bad, sexual exhibitionist; but the other girls, mother, The Rules, drain any real joy in our erotic omnipotence and we hate men, despise them for not solving our dilemma. We get back at men, punish them when we wear our exhibitionistic clothing in offices where we can get them fired, jailed, for not solving the good girl/bad girl split, a task that only we ourselves can perform.

There is no derogatory name for women who flash; in North Carolina and Mississippi, it is against the law for men to peep through windows at women but not for women to peep at men. We walk, near naked, on the street, stand in windows and undress, or we fantasize about the thrill of masturbating in the sight of the man next door: the thrill of the forbidden, as we spread our legs, feel his eyes on our genitals, with us safe behind our closed lids, brings on a shattering orgasm.

As women get more into looking at men, and we will, it would behoove us to learn from their mistakes, which we've complained about long and bitterly. When men try with their eyes to bring us down a peg or two, are they knocking us off our high heels because they think we are inferior? Could it be that, instead, they feel our dominance over them? When we complain that men's eyes "objectify" us, we make beauty ugly, when indeed "You are a sight for sore eyes," speaks of balm, the medicinal power of a restorative drug.

Part of women's surge of rage at the sidewalk gawker is that he hasn't gotten us past our own self-loathing. Weren't we told as small children that some day The Prince would come and recognize our beauty? Damn him, his eyes have failed us again, failed our efforts in front of the mirror before leaving the house, and left us publicly disgraced, fulfilling all of women's/mother's warnings: "I told you not to show off!"

Why does every positive choice regarding clothes, hair, makeup have its opposite, a warning that if we do wear that bustier, color our hair, we will be in danger? The Brothers Grimm wrote many cautionary tales: The beauty is haughty and earns a comeuppance; her stepmother and sister envy her and treat her cruelly; she is used to lure men to their deaths; and her own father is incestuously attracted to her. The elf/imp/animal in the fairy tale who warns the maiden not to wear the beautiful dress, the red shoes, is, in fact, mother/the other girls warning us that too much beauty will arouse resentment and exclusion.

Now, when the man's eyes undress us on the street, the cautionary tale cries, "You asked for it!" In truth, the man has said nothing. We have no idea what he thinks of us. He is only looking. The fear that we have gone too far, shown too much, is in us. When we arrive at our destination, we tell the other women of our experience on the street. "That is how men are," the women say in sympathy. However, maybe one will mention to another the unbuttoned blouse, the nipples discernible through the sheer fabric, the obvious curve of the ass. "She had it coming," they will murmur, a shared judgment that electrically tightens their friendship, leaving out the sacrificial lamb.

Perhaps what we hate in men's stare is that they have seen our worst self-assessment, or picked up on our fantasy of how we long to look, which is in great part sexual, precisely what we're not allowed to be. In that picture he just took, the click of the shutter of his blinking eyes, is our dress too tight, the bra too pointy? We were uncertain of our image in the mirror before we left home, but something in us loved how the outfit accentuated our curves, all the more prominent because we also abandoned the jacket, which we wish now in our discomfort that we had worn.

To be honest, when a man stares it isn't *his* opinion, but what his eyes have activated. We can't even see his eyes, don't dare to look, but we fear he sees the wench, the Bad Girl we have been warned to conceal and now have brazenly exposed, thinking we could handle it. We cannot, and we blame him for our failure. We hate him for seeing our bodies, which cry out for visibility, a caress, precisely what mother forbade. But it is our projection, taking our own bad, forbidden desires out of ourselves and placing them in the man, then accusing him for owning them.

The Fantasy Fuck

Only in fantasy do we allow ourselves to break mother/women's rules and soar into orgasm on the image of our bodies, our breasts, our cunts driving men mad, and ourselves too, for there is nothing like conquering the forbidden, stealing sex—"Yes, I'm breaking The Rules, fucking this man, these men, their bodies on fire at the sight of my beauty, faces buried deep in my cunt, which in their hunger they devour!" In my own life, nothing was more thrilling than oral sex in my date's car, just outside the dormitory door, the headmistress signaling only two minutes to curfew. To this day I love the memory of it.

The fantasy fucker—no "lover" he—accomplishes with his penis and mouth what no mortal man can: His tongue works against the image of our cunt—not a pretty sight—until he makes us come, our wrenching cry of orgasm partly out of gratitude for a few moments of self-love. A woman's fantasy of stripping in front of men driven to masturbation at the sight of her beautiful nude body frees her momentarily from the earliest learned lessons that her genitals were ugly. To reach these heights, women make men into brutes, for no ordinary Nice Man could overpower mother.

Men's erotic dreams are nowhere near as demeaning to women; in the privacy of their minds, where they might be and do anything, they are not the evil, mean, abusive louts that feminists would like to imagine. What the great majority of men dream is that a woman would adore their body, meet them halfway in sex, or take over the entire seduction, the job of it, thus removing all fears of rejection and giving the man the unequivocal approval he has always wanted from a woman. The woman of his dreams is hungry for sex, not a romantic dinner; she loves his penis, the sight and smell of it, and the taste of his semen is sweet nectar, swallowed to the last drop. She is everything that most real women are not, and she thinks of her own womanly body as he always has, a temple, every creamy cranny of which is to be explored by his mouth.

The fantasy of two women together, a perennial favorite, is something he dreams of fulfilling in reality, so exciting is the idea of women—two of them!—deeply enjoying each other's body, a living testimony that they are part animal, like he, and not the antisex people he has always had to work so hard to seduce into spreading their legs so that he might worship. Sometimes these fantasy women let him join them, and if he had the very good fortune and/or the money, he would make this erotic dream come true.

The last thing heterosexual Patriarchal man needed was the thought of sex with another man. It's fine for women to play with their own homosexual ideas, but the look of a straight man, from his physiognomy to what went on in his mind, had to conform to The Deal. To be a Real Man, one had to have a woman for whom to provide. Women's entry into the workplace has broadened the mirror for men; by taking on the role of the provider, women have freed men from their narrow vision of themselves.

Most men wouldn't attribute their return to the mirror to feminism. There are other contributing factors to the changes in men's lives, but to paraphrase Karl Marx, economics determines history. In this century, feminism is the New Economics. As men relax and proceed deeper into the mirror, I would imagine that their gender roles will also come to have more of women's fluidity.

My research shows that young heterosexual men's erotic fantasies of other men are just beginning to swim up to consciousness; unlike men before them, there is no guilt; however, the other man is usually anonymous, thus keeping the fantasy on safer ground. With so many men getting into beauty, how can the mind not wander into this once forbidden territory?

Beauty in the Workplace: Courtship or Sexual Harassment?

Were women aware of what we brought into the workplace twenty-five years ago, that in pulling men's eyes to us we were, in

Helen Fisher's language, "trigger[ing] a primitive part of the human brain, calling forth one of two basic emotions—approach or retreat"? Putting sexual beauty into the workplace was dynamite. The Dress for Success Suit was a form of armor that solved many problems, but when sexy fashions and high heels returned to the fashion scene, the people who were left to deal with this unprecedented event were men.

Women, according to feminist law, were allowed to do whatever they wanted with their bodies and men were forbidden to react. What background did men have in working alongside beautiful women who aroused them, confused them, and many times made them very angry by rejecting them?

Instead of educating women regarding the reactions we provoke when dressing in an eye-catching way, we give them outrage, the legal weapon of sexual harassment to use against any man who responds in a manner that makes the woman uncomfortable. We might have educated women regarding the language of clothes; instead, feminism declines even to consider that women, consciously or not, may be involved in their own harassment, that there are ways of dressing, walking, talking that signal to a man something that women may not have intended.

As women press deeper into the workplace, we compete with both men and women for jobs. Now we have returned to beauty competition, this time with both sexes, though most women would be reluctant to call it that. Instead, women call men's looks and speech that make us feel uncomfortable "sexual harassment."

Real sexual harassment occurs, and exactly what it is and how it should be punished are questions that will take time to resolve. After all, 80 percent of single women who get married while working full-time marry someone they meet through the workplace. It is one thing to ridicule men for looking and speaking to women on the street or in bars or at parties in a manner felt to be insulting and rude. Whether or not he was guilty, we could always walk away. But an office is confined, situation and feelings intensified by the compression of space, the chance that the look/words/touch could happen again, tomorrow, the next week.

We have brought the jungle into a fluorescent-lit space, leaving the human animals to work out the spectrum of male/female interaction. Everyone is bringing home his or her own bacon, everyone is competing, everyone is eyeing one another with desire, rage, envy, and competition, emotions that used to be spread across a dozen different stages, but are now all in one space with a waiting audience in the form of fellow workers.

"Women's freedom will be men's freedom too!" We said that. It was a campaign pledge twenty-five years ago. Did we understand how they would read that promise? Women have no idea of how men see us. Men are most relaxed in one another's company. When we peek at them in their locker rooms, on their playing fields, we envy the way they let go, so different from how they are with us and how we are with one another too; we want them to give us that trust they reserve for other males.

What do we give them? We are not yet men's economic or political equals, but we have taken a good chunk of their pie and, far from relaxing the rules of the war between us, we have become even more antagonistic to them. Instead of sexual harassment systematically being argued from the woman's point of view, why not question why the man is the only responsible party? Women are blind to our body image, clothed and unclothed. When issues of anorexia are raised, instead of attacking Patriarchal Society, why not question women's own contribution to the dilemma?

We are born and raised to be selected. What does our genetic heritage know of feminist alternatives? The heat that burns in our cheeks at the penetration of a man's gaze is a mix of excitement, humiliation, and rage. We have just broken The Nice Girl Rules. Never mind that in the real world we have outgrown them, that we are now economically independent and shouldn't even be thinking of mother's rules. Didn't we buy the dress, select it, and pay for it? Doesn't that separate us from her, still loving her, but very much our own person? These men are looking at us, not at the other woman; we have won the genetic beauty contest.

But before pride can settle in, there is a terror: We are on our own, all eyes on us and we are not part of a group! Without experience in handling the high of successful exhibitionism, the thrill of being the genetic star, we fear loss of control, humiliation. We do what women used to do and reach for haughty indignation. We cover ourselves with it like a shield. We act as women did before gaining economic power, which is where we still are emotionally; we love those books that buttress the platform that men are bad and women inherently good. We turn humiliation around and *voilà!* there is feminism, not educating us in the power of beauty and sex but encouraging us to dump all negative feelings on to Bad Men.

"What happens to women who haven't integrated their sexuality when they get into the workplace," says Judith Seifer, "is what so much of sexual harassment is about. They think, 'This is something I have to keep the lid on, I have to police, because men can't control themselves around it.' Instead, they should be thinking, 'Part of my energy, part of the thing that makes me so good in the workplace, part of the creative flow, has to do with my sexual energy.'

"I do workshops on sex in the workplace and the big issues today are the flirtatious, romantic, sexual, intensely personal relationships that go on there. Most women have had a good working relationship with a man, where they grow to rely on one another, read each other's minds, finish each other's sentences. What this often involves is a form of displaced energy. But whether the relationship between the man and woman is a working friendship, a personal friendship, or whether they become office lovers, the woman must acknowledge her own sexual energy. If it's never negotiated, it becomes a disaster waiting to happen; they're working late one night, they go to a convention or one of them is feeling needy, and here is the one person who understands and with whom they feel comfortable, and suddenly all that sexual energy that had been channeled into work goes into a sexual overture, or what we call sexual harassment.

"Women blame it all on men, but until women learn to recognize and separate out their own sexuality as an important part of who they are, they will never own it. I look at most energy as either physical or sexual. They blend and spill over. We don't teach our children this. A sense of control of our sexuality has to start in childhood. So far we've successfully robbed generations of people of a sense of personal control. Instead, we are raised to believe that if a woman gets a man turned on he will not be able to control himself. I know I can control myself, and so can men. But our culture at large has sanctioned the idea that 'Sex with men and sexual urges are uncontrollable. Sex is something that women have that men want, and we must police it.'

"This is why women think of themselves as victims; men don't make us victims, the culture, the way we are raised to disown our sexual energy, this is what leads to acquaintance rape and to sexual harassment in the workplace."

The burden of being male is just beginning to be discussed, written about, though the words stick in the craw, so wimpy, so unmasculine is it to change our picture of the Marlboro Man. Somewhere in the back of the Matriarchal Feminist mind there is the suspicion that if we allow men a humanity as vulnerable as our own, we women will become the brutes.

It seems that feminist headquarters will do anything to keep alive the proposition that men have all the power and women are nothing more than used Kleenex blowing in the wind. Last year, however, the Ms. Foundation went too far in preparing for its annual "Take Your Daughter to Work Day," urging teachers and parents to educate little boys on how it feels to be a girl: The boy should close his eyes and imagine himself living inside a cramped, dark box. "What if you want to get out of the box and you can't?" the written instructions read. "What do people say to girls to keep them in a box? What happens to girls who step outside the box?" Pressed to answer, I would imagine a boy would think *he* is more likely to be the one in a tight, dark box, given the amount of woman power at home, where as likely as not there is no other male, where mother/sister power is all he knows.

"Take Your Child to Work Day" is a great idea for both sexes. As young girls we do often abandon our best selves at age ten or eleven, but we would do it less if, from the day we were born, a man as well as a woman poured himself into us, his adoration, energy, voice, courage, everything. It is infuriating to imagine boys watching their sisters being honored, at their exclusion, being selected either by mother and/or father as The Chosen One. How will the boy see this? As he has seen life so far: women with all the power. And what about the splendid opportunity for boys to see women succeeding in the workplace, outside the nursery, and alongside men?

Why do we assume that our sons don't need as much of our emotional and intellectual focus? We have skewed our thinking to see men solely as negative models. I hear women in offices referring contemptuously to male colleagues as "Empty Suits"; how does a dear, sensitive boy grow into an Empty Suit? There will never be a "Take Your Child to Work Day" until fathers begin to tell their sons the full story, good and bad, of what it is to grow up male.

The definition of manliness is still so rooted in the strong and silent imagery of the tough guy that the relatively few men who have come forward to complain of sexual harassment by a woman are looked down on, as are men who claim to have been abused by a woman. Even many of us who write and fight for men's rights in the nursery admit to a vestigial twinge at the sight of a man with a baby strapped to his breast. We want him to love his baby, to do just what he is doing, but holding that baby, he can't take the bullet for us. This is precisely what must be discussed: Ambivalence.

The real world that young men today encounter in the workplace is not the world that Steinem and her sisters preach, in which women are powerless opposite Bad, Omnipotent Men. This isn't at all how young, and older, men feel. Neither sex is prepared for the relationships encountered today in the workplace. "There is often ambivalence," says Eleanor Maccoby, a developmental psychologist of gender studies. "You're not sure whether you want to be attractive to the other sex or just a colleague. That's when people have difficulty."

As a woman who is against real sexual harassment of women and men, let me quote Warren Farrell describing how men experience women's provocative dress, makeup, and flirting: "[Men] see these behaviors as an invitation to respond on a *non*-professional level, which leads them to take this woman's professional intentions less seriously."

As anthropologist Lionel Tiger put it in our first Beauty Symposium in 1989, "Beauty is a marketing tool for Mother Nature's most basic product—reproduction—which in turn depends upon sexual attraction and sexual success." When the beauty's initiative was successful, it led to marriage and the end of the woman's involvement in the workplace.

Colleagues of the beautiful woman know that every heterosexual male is vulnerable to her. She is what Farrell calls a "genetic celebrity." Male clients automatically offer her easier access. The male boss desires to mentor her, to show her the way and protect her from failing, to rescue her if she does fail; meanwhile, he also fears "playing favorites." Farrell's research indicates that the male employees who work for the beautiful woman fear that a genetic celebrity boss will be so used to being protected, she will not know how to protect them; they fear that she won't know how to "give and take" because she must be used to having her way. They fear that she has probably had little experience in being criticized.

Luckily, there is a growing number of women speaking and writing about working women's lives. "True, there are still far fewer women than men in senior management positions, but feminists don't acknowledge that this disparity is at least partly the result of women's choices," writes Laura A. Ingraham, a lawyer on the advisory board of the Independent Women's Forum. "The idea that women are constantly thwarted by invisible barriers of sexism relegates them to permanent victim status. It also stands on its head the cause that true feminists originally championed: equal opportunity for women. Equal access to the work force and advancement within it was never intended to guarantee that women would ultimately hold a fixed percentage of executive positions. . . . In 1992, women held 23 percent of corporate senior vice president positions as against 14 percent in 1982. From 1979 to 1993, women's wages increased by 119 percent. . . . By demanding real, not rigged, competition in every profession, women would fulfill the true goal of feminism. . . . Instead of whining about an imaginary glass ceiling, why don't feminists celebrate the fact that women in the work force are at long last pushing against a wide open door?"

Under Patriarchy, women didn't question a man's looks—the potbelly, sallow skin, loss of hair; if his bank account was healthy, his look of ill health didn't register. We have an investment in the image of men as indestructible; even as women have gained economic power, we resist looking at the figures on men's vulnerability.

In the past twenty-five years women's health issues have received long overdue attention; now it is one of the fastest growing areas of medicine. But I worry when feminism paints the picture of evil Patriarchy thriving at women's expense, when indeed, the facts are different. "In the latter part of the twentieth century women live about 10 percent longer than men," writes Dr. Andrew Kadar. "Throughout human history from antiquity until the beginning of this century men, on the average, lived slightly longer than women. By 1920 women's life expectancy in the United States was one year greater than men's (54.6 years versus 53.6). After that the gap increased steadily, to 3.5 years in 1930, 4.4 years in 1940, 5.5 in 1950, 6.5 in 1960. . . . In 1990 the figure was seven years (78.8 versus 71.8). . . . We have come to accept women's longer life span as natural, the consequence of their greater biological fitness. Yet this greater fitness never manifested itself in all the millennia of human history that preceded the present era and its medical-care system—the same system that women's-health advocates accuse of neglecting the female sex."

While swallowing our morning coffee, we read with aplomb the latest statistics on violence committed by men. Women's cruelty, however, is not as easily surveyed as men's; sons don't rat on their mothers, nor do most husbands on wives.

Some men, however, are coming forward. The morning paper recently told of a twenty-eight-year-old man who has lived uneasily all his life with a coroner's report that his baby brothers' deaths were diagnosed as crib deaths; having recently obtained legal action to have the bodies exhumed, he was right to have thought otherwise; twenty-five years ago his mother murdered her other two sons, and the judge, like everyone else at that time, refused to believe she did it. Mothers were idealized. More recently, Susan Smith, a South Carolina mother who drowned her two sons because they interfered with her love life, was quickly imprisoned. Medea grows more credible by the day.

Men have their work cut out for them: Paternalistic Society's protection isn't what it used to be. Women haven't just acquired our due rights, we can act as bad as any man, setting up punitive sexual harassment laws. While most men remain reluctant to press charges against women, there being so few definitions of manliness aside from Spartan silence, it won't last. Men are slow to confront feminism, but they aren't dumb.

When men's anger is voiced by the older patriarchal generation, as with Norman Mailer, we hear a startling revelation of men's fear of women: "If women ever take over everything, as they well may," Mailer is quoted as saying in an interview with Madonna, "and you get the equivalent of a Stalin or a Hitler among the women (and having had some contact with a few of the early women's liberationists, I can easily conceive of such a female), I can see a day when a hundred male slaves will be kept alive and milked every day and the stuff will be put in semen banks to keep the race going. No more than a hundred men will have to be maintained alive at any time. Men have a very deep fear of women as a result. It isn't that men think, 'Oh, there's a breast, I'll lay my head on it; it'll cost me nothing.' Rather, what they know is that in that tender breast there are chill zones of feeling, icy areas, zones of detestation, and if they have any sense at all of women, they know that approaching a woman is quite equal to climbing a rock face. . . . Not everyone thinks the same way I think, but men feel it instinctively, I'd argue."

What Mailer neglected in the above is that women, as well as men, have "a very deep fear of women." It is our fear of one another, our need for other women's approval, into which the *Ms.* form of feminism plays, the "don't you dare disobey me, disagree with me, compete with me" command from the Giantess of The Nursery. Women's anxiety over rejection by other women, the deep roots of our sadness that accompanies the feeling of being left out, gets its heat from that earliest relationship, which feminism naturally tapped into as a way to keep the marching army in line.

Early on, feminism preached that when women gained positions of real power, there would be less war. "With women as half the country's elected representatives, and a woman President once in a while," wrote Gloria Steinem in 1970, "the country's *machismo* problems would be greatly reduced. The old-fashioned idea that manhood depends on violence and victory is, after all, an important part of our troubles in the streets, and in Viet Nam. . . . For the next 50 years or so, women in politics will be very valuable by tempering the idea of manhood into something less aggressive and better suited to this crowded, post-atomic planet."

Women like Janet Reno, Jeane Kirkpatrick, and top Clinton adviser Susan Thomases don't exactly flesh out Steinem's prophecy that women would bring more compassion to positions of power. Nor has her forecast about women's looks come to pass: "Women with normal work identities will be less likely to attach their whole sense of self to youth and appearance; thus there will be fewer nervous breakdowns when the first wrinkles appear."

Oh?

Today, as women's incomes increase, so do the amounts we spend on fashion and cosmetics; whether new on the job or climbing the corporate ladder, in sophisticated pants suits or skirts eight inches above the knee, women in the workplace want to look good; maintaining a youthful appearance is very much a part of that portrait. Fashion designers may attempt with peripatetic designs to decipher precisely what it is that women want, but you can be sure that young men aren't going to just sit there and ogle the passing parade, taking whatever sexual harassment suits women throw at them. Instead, men will counterattack; they will compete with confused women and come up with a new golden age of male beauty.

Men will not be hampered by the "Who, me, beautiful?" defenses against envy that women hide behind. There is no girlish denial in men's style of competition; today, as men move more into using their looks within the power structure of the workplace, they assemble their arsenal—briefcase and great looks too, employing everything to get the contract. "When you control the resources [as men once did, almost exclusively]," says consumer psychologist Michael R. Solomon, "you don't worry about your personal desirability . . . [but the] influx of women into responsible positions in the workplace has shifted the balance of power." Men look around for what can give them back their edge and see how effectively women's looks work for them in the conference room.

A study finds that the city where men spend the most money on business clothing is not fashionable New York but Atlanta. A clothing executive tells *Newsweek* that Atlanta is "a city of salesmen and regional managers, 'just the type of people who must put their best foot forward.'" As manufacturer Hart Schaffner & Marx says in its ad for what they call "The Right Suit": [It] might not help you close the deal. But the wrong suit could easily close you out."

Nor do men, as you may have noticed, confine their new focus on fashion to the workplace. Norman Karr of the Men's Fashion Association tells *Newsweek* that men are accumulating separate wardrobes "for my public self and the real me." Sound familiar, ladies?

When the handsomely turned-out guy outdoes us in the boardroom, and it's obvious that all eyes are on him and not on us, will we cry harassment? When he blatantly uses his looks to get a promotion that we had wanted from his woman boss, how then will we feel about our ancient fear of other women's censoring our use of beauty? My money is on men accomplishing what we women could never do for ourselves: Their success with beauty—*our* area of expertise—will force us to learn how to compete or we will become the drab workhorses of industry.

"Get Outa My Mirror!"

After generations of grumbling that men undress us with their eyes, women are experiencing competition for which we are ill-prepared. The very people whom women used to chide are now our competitors. The contest for the admiring eyes of the world is no longer our exclusive turf. Women cannot acquire economic power without giving up something of our own.

Like the foolish virgins whose lamps ran out of oil, women are not taking men's return to the mirror seriously; so practiced are we in denial of competition between ourselves, we doggedly refuse to admit that we have new rivals in beauty, the very people who were once the prize. Did we honestly think men would let us take their jobs, the role that more than any other defined their masculinity, and not retaliate? And when he invests in the Calvin Klein suit, works out at the gym, and pays for a better barber, he will use the ammunition. No little dance of denial for him.

Women are either going to push past The Nice Girl Rules and learn how to compete, or we will lose the mirror to men, who will employ it with a vigor that will leave us in the dust. This new attention men are paying to looks reflects an appetite that was already there. If feminism hadn't carved out for women a piece of men's economic terrain— power that had identified men since the Industrial Revolution—perhaps the brilliant scarves, long hair, and jewelry affected by men in the seventies would have come and gone. But we women did take men's turf, and they are now seriously regaining that lost advantage.

Peacocks in the past, men will take the praise and wear it proudly. Their inclination to dress up and show off has more historic weight than our own. For almost five hundred years, men's form and face were *the* criteria of beauty. The pursuit of dressing up, owning great looks, is quickly relearned because its reward is so immediate. Exhilaration and a sense of well-being race through the blood when admiring eyes focus on us.

Women don't allow ourselves to get high on our beauty because of the instilled rules against competition, but men have no such fear. Soon enough women may find out what it was like to have been a man for the past two hundred years, wandering, invisible, in a cold climate, eyes searching hungrily for the nourishing sight of beauty.

When men embraced fashion, they had none of our maidenly protestations regarding the stares of the opposite sex. They understood the power of beauty and its many uses. "The erotic clothing men wore was partly designed to appeal to women, to provoke an erotic awakening in them," writes Lois Banner. "Europeans of these ages believed that love was a capricious passion, that it could strike at any moment. In this they believed that the eyes, and what the eyes saw, were crucial. What primarily provoked love was thought to be the quality of beauty, usually defined as the pleasing appearance of the person looked at."

For several hundred years now men have watched women's envious entanglements, knowing that nothing they can do or say will affect the power women have over one another. It is not very flattering to the man, but within the Patriarchal Deal the intrawoman business that kept women unaware of their beauty power allowed the man to pursue economic wealth in the knowledge, conscious or not, that The Other Women would keep his wife "in her place."

"Hey, looking good is a way of getting ahead!" say today's young men. A new kind of competition is at hand, one of which young women are still wary, but they nonetheless realize that men their age will steal beauty from them if they don't recognize what they are losing: beauty's power.

Likewise, men had better be alert to the devious way in which we women operate where beauty is concerned. "He was just an empty suit," a woman executive tells me about the beautifully dressed man she has fired. She is quite lovely, very blond, very successful at her work. We are having lunch to celebrate her having received the most prestigious award in her field, and though she didn't have to use her looks to get ahead, they undoubtedly helped.

In her tone of voice, there is an obvious dose of envy toward the handsome man who had intruded on her turf and was subsequently fired. As more women gain management status, will the men who work for them suffer the traditional woman's fate in the workplace, a resentful assumption that too much good looks translates into lower intelligence, drive, and ambition?

There is nothing like economics to force the most tenacious subject out of the closet. Good looks are no longer "just" an asset that women use to ensnare men. The kaleidoscopic happenings in men's and women's fashions, the meteoric rise of the model as cultural ideal, the spotlight on looks as never before in our lifetimes, all press the discussion forward.

The beautiful woman who fired "the empty suit" is about to meet her match, a "suit" who fights back. Men assess the opponent, advance, retreat, jostle for the lead, maybe even take their competitor as ally, building on their networking experience, but they don't telephone all the other guys and whisper to get the handsome dude excommunicated from The Group.

Fashions change even before we know what is historically about to happen; it is as if our practiced inner eye has sized up the distant landscape and is equipping us physically for what lies ahead. "By the end of the seventies, men and women were beginning to exchange their effects in earnest," says Anne Hollander. "We had women understanding how much they could use male costume—which was totally. Molloy's *Dress for Success* said, 'Do not dress as if you wanted the job. Dress as if you *had* the job.' And now what are the men supposed to do? They are going to use female effects for the first time in the whole history of fashion. Now men have a wonderful new ability to deal with the masculine tailored scheme in a way that was not possible until the shakeup of feminism occurred."

As the bottom line—always the true indicator—informed the male beauty industry that men were buying more clothes and grooming products, advertisers and manufacturers grew alert. They knew before the average man did where things were heading. Advertising in men's magazines informed the greater male population, activating men's imaginations to see themselves in a new way, in that double-breasted suit, thinner, more muscular, younger.

When prestigious Bergdorf Goodman built an expensive addition for male customers across from their women's store on Fifth Avenue, the manager told me that he had to conduct classes to educate his salesmen in how to get men to pay $1,000 for a suit. There was money to be made in the new world of men's fashions, but would men be willing to ante up the considerable sums that women are used to paying? The answer seems to be yes. Five years later, the Bergdorf ads read, "Without style, ambition is merely aggressive." Actually, I had hoped that such advantages as the traditional free alterations that men have always enjoyed would filter into woman's fashion world; instead, men seem willing to pay whatever it takes to acquire that degree of looks they desire.

Unlike women, men see beauty as something they can choose to pursue or not, realizing that if they are overlooked in the beauty contest, so be it. We women are not yet so independent. We may choose intellectually to be free of beauty's demands, a fine choice, but the time has not yet come when a woman does not have that memory of childhood in which female beauty played a considerable role; most of us do not yet believe in the alternative sources of power. If we did, women would not be so enviously damning of the beauty. No, not until we've learned to handle competition, recognize the feeling before it sours us, will we honestly choose to decline the pursuit of beauty. Attorney Susan Thomases, known as Hillary Rodham Clinton's "enforcer," may live easily with the nickname "old floppy-shoes" as she flip-flops in Washington power circles, hair unkempt, "suits often rumpled," and caring little for makeup, but she is sufficiently exceptional for the *Wall Street Journal* to have cited her for her lack of attention to beauty rituals.

Men have become as eye-catching as women. When we drive down the boulevard, do we stare at the billboard of the man with his near erection in his Calvin Klein underwear or at the block-long blowup of Cindy Crawford? When we arrive at our destination, whether we are man or woman, are our eyes drawn to the beautiful woman's cleavage or to one of the elegantly dressed, handsome young men who expect to be admired, who dressed in front of the mirror with the full conscious intention of being valued for their looks in a way that father never dreamed of?

Twenty, even ten years ago, men who spent too much time in front of the mirror were suspect. When I ask the most classically beautiful man I know—meaning that his features are so perfect he must always have been beautiful—what it was like to have such natural beauty and also be at the top of his field professionally, he answers, "It becomes very hard to be taken seriously." Today he is fifty. It is odd to hear a man say this, and I suppose it accounts for his reputation as a killer opponent, an aggressive intellectual. In the past, on those rare occasions when an article was written about very good-looking men, he was invariably interviewed. One of his closest friends says of him that any man as good-looking as he has always elicited the suspicion that he couldn't possibly be a man of any great intellect or business acumen. Clearly, he has worked very hard indeed to be taken seriously, for he was a star athlete in college, graduated summa cum laude, and went on to become a captain of industry. But his sons won't have that leftover baggage from strict Patriarchal World.

Most men proceed deeper into the mirror with caution, taking their cue from other men and from a constantly tested assurance that newly acquired beauty won't interfere with financial success. "Men never admit to what I'm about to say," writes a contributing editor to *Mademoiselle* magazine, "because it makes them feel a little weird—one of the great fears in a heterosexual man's life is saying the slightest thing that might give someone the reason to question his sexual orientation—but the truth is we men study the male hunk as intensely as women do. . . . We devour these stories only because we want to know why this guy is worshiped and we are not, why fame and money and women naturally fall down around him. . . . It seems to us as if he doesn't really need a purpose in life, that he doesn't need to do anything at all but wait—and great opportunities will soon present themselves."

He has a point; most of the straight male world is still edgy at the suspicion of seeming effeminate in dress. But it was the gay world that expanded and visibly enjoyed the fashion window that opened for men beginning in the late sixties. No gay man needs to be convinced of the power of beauty, visual signaling to one another being part of the gay courting ritual.

But all men today are indebted to the flamboyant, creative male look from thirty years ago that grew and diversified into the pastel-colored cashmere sweaters that are a staple in the wardrobes of most men today, regardless of with whom they sleep. The straight male culture no longer sucks in its breath nervously when they meander through Ralph Lauren's magnificent mansion of a store, where experimentation with fashion and color is the trademark of a style that men not only wear but with which they decorate their houses and offices.

Having criticized them for seeing us as "sexual objects" and argued them down in their workplace, we women have opened men's horizons. Do not be surprised if men not only make themselves more attractive but also wander into formerly forbidden pastures to find additional rewards for their hard work. We are accustomed to men leaving their wives for younger women, but today it could be a younger man.

Until recently nothing destroyed a man's life like the hint of homosexuality. Just a dream or fantasy of himself with another man, just thinking about it was enough to drive him to the analyst's couch. But a man's memory of childhood is likely to contain scenes of group masturbation, the erotic adoration of the older, beautifully formed boy athlete, dreams he was told to banish when the rigid laws of the male heterosexual world were learned. How do you banish a dream, turn off the unconscious?

I remember the morning last year when the phone call came with the breathless news that multimillionaire publisher Jann Wenner—he who had started *Rolling Stone* magazine—had left his wife and family and was ensconced in a suite at a posh East Side hotel with a male fashion model. It was indeed high gossip, but the world did not tremble as it might have twenty years earlier. Hesitations as to whether to print the story arose over concerns about the "outing" of homosexuals. By the time the story did eventually air, public reaction was mild, amused but tolerant. After all, some of the most powerful, wealthy men in publishing, in the film and music industry are gay. Wenner could as likely as not return to his wife and family tomorrow, appear once again with her in public, and there would be no scandal. We are a different culture where beauty is concerned, and beauty is linked to male homosexuality; as the power of beauty has shifted increasingly into men's lives, the star of homosexuality rises.

The world of fashion design has always been prominently gay; when we looked at beautiful women in gorgeous clothes we didn't automatically think, "Oh, no, a gay man must have designed that!" Instead, we thought, "Oh, isn't she breathtaking!" We still don't acknowledge our debt to the homosexual eye for having made our lives so beautiful; but we have allowed our men, all men, once again to draw attention to themselves.

Nothing speaks louder in our culture than money. Some may privately disparage Barry Diller and David Geffen, but the potent scent of their major bucks goes before them, turning big-mouthed homophobes into whimpering, envious pups. The spreading awareness of these powerful gay men infiltrates society's attitudes in all areas, as does the ascendancy of beauty, a world controlled almost exclusively by the gay sensibility. Suddenly, it seems we are less disparaging of a man, any man, who dresses in such a way as to command the eye; we no longer automatically label him gay any more than we would exclude Diller or Geffen or Jann Wenner from our dinner party, if only they would grace us with their presence.

More than work, more than marriage and a family, we need to have a sexual identity. In the privacy of erotic fantasies, men have always played with images of women arousing one another and in the women's coupling have found exciting permission for themselves; as forbidden, and therefore thrilling, as these fantasies were, the idea of imagining themselves with another man was not thrilling, meaning a limp cock.

Today, as evidenced in film, literature, erotic fantasies, and real life, the theme of gayness still triggers the forbidden thrill, but it is less daunting, the cock less limp, harder, as the thrill of the forbidden swims up from men's unconscious. In seeing the other man, the man looks at himself, stares as he once stared at other boys masturbating along with him when he was ten and needed a view of male power to stand up to his mother's, a time in life before looking at other men became tantamount to losing his manhood.

In last night's movie, *Heat*, Robert De Niro and Al Pacino are so intensely rivalrous and competitive in their game of cops and robbers that there is no room, no feeling or passion left over for the women in their lives; ultimately, they face each other down, and Pacino shoots De Niro, who holds out his hand in his last breath to the only person with whom he can identify. Pacino stands in the dark, flat space of an open field, holding the Bad Guy's hand until he dies, at which point we know that in winning, Pacino is now lonelier than ever without another man in whom he sees himself. Need I add that both men are swell dressers?

As economic competition with women increases, how will a man see himself in bed with that sex who wants to control him even more, wants his job, wants to police how he talks and acts, wants everything? Until now women were the prize for whom men competed. How well men performed sexually with women had its roots in the earliest years of life, opposite father, siblings, and that first great champion competitor, mother. This hasn't changed.

Patriarchal man ran from awareness of mother's influence in all areas. But the gay man, whose beauty is his meal ticket, is more cognizant of women's influence over him. Ten years ago my friend Dick's story, which follows, would have been strictly relegated to the homosexual world. I find it today a very modern parable for all men.

Dick's mother, you may remember, was a great beauty who was so rivalrous with her eye-riveting, four-year-old son that she couldn't bear to look at him. She walked out on him and his father, but on her infrequent returns for money and his brief visits with her, Dick became her student in beauty power. "I might as well have been invisible to her," he says. "I'd always been told I looked like her, and I couldn't understand why she didn't love me. But I watched how she used her beauty, and it was from her that I learned how to use my own looks. Very well, if I could not get her attention, I would beat her at her own game."

In a very beguiling, charming, and winning manner, Dick is one of the most competitive people I know. When Dick was thirteen, he was sent off for one of his formal, short stays with his mother. "She and her lover were just returning from Mexico," he says, "and they were wearing identical white outfits with red sashes. At one point, my mother left the sitting room. I flirted with him, was very aware of what I was doing, teasing him, touching his shoulder, his hand, and he put his arms around me. We were on the sofa and he was on top of me, kissing me, commanding me, 'No, no, open your mouth!' She walked in.

"I had never seen her so enraged. She sent me home, told my grandmother, who warned her that if she told my father she would never receive another penny. She rejected me and kept the lover. But I had competed with her and had won. I am sure she thought that. I was terrified at what her reprisals would be. Our visits became fewer and fewer, until they stopped altogether."

Since beginning this book I've thought often of his mother's refusal to see him again, even to speak to him by phone. "I don't think the reason she refuses to see you is because of your age," I said to him last Mother's Day when he was sitting, as usual, staring at the telephone he was forbidden by her to use. "I think it's because of her fear of competing with you, and your winning *again*."

"I've never thought of that," he said. "She was the most beautiful woman I ever saw. I only did it out of retaliation. She wouldn't look at me."

"Alas, you won the beauty contest."

A woman's genetic back goes up when a man nudges her aside in the mirror; his looks and behavior connote selfishness, not selflessness. Would he lay down his life for her? If he is gazing at his reflection, he won't see the grizzly bear. And when she is pregnant, during those nine months that anthropologists build into "natural selection" of a more powerful mate, how will he provide and protect if he is at his tailor's?

Never mind that she owns her own house, makes a better salary than he does, keeps a gun in the drawer of her bedside table to protect herself, and can now take out a breast and feed her baby in a restaurant where she is paying for dinner. (Now, that is breast power!) Her distrust of a narcissistic man is her maternal ancestors' suspicion of males who dress up instead of provide. Men say nothing, no "Help!" audible beneath women's layers of condemnation, not until it builds to a scream or a blow, so unpracticed are men in the emotional modulation of complaining.

"Women's Liberation has to be terribly conscious about the danger of provoking men to kill women," said Margaret Mead. "You have quite literally driven them mad." Very well, boys/men seem to be saying today in their growing reliance on muscle, on brute force, We will employ those traits you women have not appropriated. Marina Warner points out that in modern myths, such as movies and video games, young boys today are taught that size, that muscle building typify a real man. Force has become "the wellspring of male authority, of power," she writes.

One Matriarchal Feminist's reaction to the growing violence among young men isn't to question why but to write that men should be charged a "user's fee" for the prisons and rehabilitation they monopolize. "Men are expensive," psychologist June Stephenson writes. "We cannot expect men to police their own, to take responsibility for their contribution to the violence in this country. . . . Men are not their brothers' keepers. Except in male-bonding groups, men are not connected to each other emotionally in the same way women are. . . . Men must pay for being men."

Men must do something even more difficult than women entering the work world; and they must do it even as Matriarchal Feminism curses them for being innately violent and antipathetic to everything good and kind and feminine. When the man was a boy, these warm, soft feelings that belonged to mother, Ruler of the World, weren't felt to be meager at all. But when he walked out the door to join Boys' World, these powerful emotions had to be left behind. It was society that taught him that "masculine" emotions are superior. The other, "feminine" emotions, which are natural to us all, became suppressed.

Psychiatrist Willard Gaylin once told me, "If men don't have close friendships early on—boyhood, high school, college—later they don't have the talent or energy. The workplace drains them. They go through life with a sense of exclusion." I've lived with men most of my life, had two marriages and many love affairs, and I have never known a grown man who formed a new, great friendship with another grown man.

My husband tells me about a car crash, what he calls "a near-death experience" that happened when he was nineteen. The car was demolished. When his injuries healed, his father gave him his own car, saying he would buy a new one and suggested that his son use the insurance money to take a trip. "Invite one of your friends," he said. My husband asked his father to go with him. They had never spent time alone. His father was a successful, hardworking man, away days and often evenings too.

Together they went to half a dozen cities including Acapulco, Mexico City, and San Francisco, and they never talked. Oh, they discussed business, politics, news, but never anything to do with their personal lives, emotions, what was inside, invisible.

When I first met my husband, in our early intimate talks he often referred to his life before we met as "compartmentalized." Then I saw his collection of antique Japanese chests from when he lived in Tokyo. They were beautiful, and all had many tiny little drawers in which I imagined my sweetheart's emotions once secreted away.

Imagine a mother and daughter on such a trip as my husband and his father. Imagine them never discussing emotions, feelings. Impossible. It isn't written in stone, nor is it genetic that men must shut down their emotional selves as boys; it isn't women's "fault" nor our job to change men. It is grown men's job; compared to our fight to get into the workplace and political office—a struggle, but exciting, mature, even sexual in the energy and reward—this revolution is tougher still.

It is not easy for a grown man to dig into whatever he can find that is left of the emotional boy he once was so that he might talk his son into a different direction. For a grown man to use his own life as a template so that he might talk about what he might have done, could have done, to open up all these "unmanly" wounds and also include some understanding of women's world, well, it isn't something Freud or men's magazines deal with. And what of his competition with his son, speaking of Freud? If the boy doesn't learn from his father—who is the same sex and therefore the most trusted model—there will not be enough jails to contain the next generation, which would suit the Matriarchy just fine.

Such men's groups as Robert Bly's and The Promise Keepers are a beginning. *Ms.* magazine sent a female reporter "undercover," dressed as a male teenager, to one of The Promise Keepers conventions; while the author ended up applauding many of the organization's aims—"I don't see how society can change in the ways we want it to if men have no support to start acting less like 'men' and more like caring, loving, ethical, and nondominating human beings"—she obviously felt that her readers needed a mocking preamble: "Radiant, swishy men wave bright Promise Keepers flags as though they were batons," and, "Am I walking like someone with the signifier of power between my legs?"

It is an eye exercise to imagine how men's looks will change when boys grow up remaining open to emotion rather than moving through life with impassive faces, shutters closed, feelings compartmentalized.

"If you take the breeding power that you [women] have, the reproductive strength that you have, child rearing . . . and you try to get what's left of us," says television star Tim Allen, "you're going to get very angry men who will do very angry things to protect what little is left of their territory. . . ." What is it to be a man in an increasingly genteel, middle-class world where women have not only won power but have redefined the rules of engagement in their own terms? Allen continues:

> The birth of a child—my wife's going, "Ohh"—I see them in love in a room, and my eyes are like I'm looking in Macy's at toys I'll never own. I'll never have that! And the two of them: "Ah"—these little coos. . . . And I was like, "Whooo!" I shrank down to this little man. So what I have to do is somehow—I have to get some reason for them to need me. . . . "I have very little left, I have this little corner left. I have to be careful of your feelings; I gotta make sure that you're okay in the job market. And I'm not allowed to be an aggressive prick!" A warrior—my wife and I used to say, that's what I'm built to be. I'm a warrior . . . you [women] really don't want me to exist. Well, fuck you—I exist. And not only that . . . I will build an army, and I will crush you! I mean, if you get me that way, I'll do it. If that's what you really want—to have a war with me. . . . "You have picked the wrong mother-fucker to fuck with!" Because I know how to fight better than you.

The Short, Bald Takeover Tycoons and Their Towering Trophy Wives

My friend and I are sitting in the restaurant at the Bel Air in Los Angeles when she nudges me, alerting me to the entry of a little bald man in a dark blue suit who has just bought an airline, a country. He is indistinguishable from other men, but he stands tall, for he knows we are seeing his portfolio, his houses, his private plane and that they make him equal to and deserving of the most beautiful woman in the room, who happens to be on his arm. She carries an elegant Hermès briefcase and wears on her head a crown of beautifully coifed hair, which catches so much sunlight we are momentarily blinded. We don't ask, What does she see in him?

"He must have had a terrible adolescence," I say to my friend. It is written all over him: *rejected by girls in adolescence*. In that strange second half of the eighties, it was a line I used profitably when seated next to a scion of industry: "Tell me about your adolescence." The game isn't meant unkindly, for I throw in my own plight and fully appreciate why he worked so hard to get out of those years, to never repeat them again. Short, bald tycoons had a fiercer goal than the football heroes of their youth. They may have spent their Saturdays at their fathers' offices reading balance sheets when all the popular kids were at The Big Game, but invisibility and envy toughened them. In the end, they won.

At no time did The Short, Bald Men with Wretched Adolescences win more ostentatiously than in the mid-eighties. They were on the covers of magazines, or their beautiful wives were, their trademark Big Hair fanning out across the page. Even if they weren't beautiful, the hair made them seem so. "Hair is all," a friend of mine used to say, and these women had the budget to afford daily grooming from hair stylists who, along with the fashion designers, were the top beauty agents of the day.

It was an aging Debutante Ball, this self-outing of enormously successful men of no great beauty themselves, whose wives were more than trophies, for they too worked, ran their own companies, or devoted their lives to charity balls, which ran nonstop. The extravagance of the parade, such million-dollar parties as Malcolm Forbes's birthday party in Tangiers and Saul Steinberg's in the Hamptons, along with the gaudy, outlandish fashions, were Fellini-esque, a nervous high-wire act on the edge of implosion. Nothing caught it better than Tom Wolfe's *The Bonfire of the Vanities*.

A telling but tacky offshoot of the era was the avid, public discussion of money. Dinner table conversation focused on prices, dollar amounts spent on possessions. No one thought twice about asking how much was paid for an apartment, a dress, a summer house. If someone didn't ask, people felt compelled to tell what they had paid, as if you wouldn't see them without vast numbers attached. In my memory, the bad manners of talking prices got its start in the late seventies, when all the rules of childhood regarding polite invisibility of wealth flew out the window.

Was it Watergate on top of Vietnam, a communal shame leading to invisibility, which had made the goodness and kindness on which we'd been raised inadequate? Was this what drained us into hollow people, a society of The Empty Package, craving ever new fashions to cover the embarrassment? I am no priss, but the silence regarding prices was so firmly laid down so early in life that I never gave it a thought until dollar amounts were out there, zinging around the dinner table.

Beautiful women have traditionally been worn by men as signals to the outside world that they have arrived. But by the mid-eighties, the beautiful women—at least in Manhattan and other large cities—wanted their own portfolios. Feminism had made working chic, and wives of the richest men wanted to be In. Not just a job, but great success too was wanted by these competitive wives of the Very Rich, meaning that a Georgette Mosbacher wanted to carry her own briefcase and be interviewed by the press, not for her beauty routine, but for her business acumen. It would have been unthinkable to turn up for lunch at The Four Seasons or Le Cirque without their own clients. The Babe Paleys of the fifties who had lunched and dressed, and were worn by their husbands, were gone with the wind.

Financial need had nothing to do with the grueling daily routines of these women, their backbreaking schedules duly reported in *Vogue*, *Town and Country*, and *Harper's Bazaar*. That they raced from 6:00 A.M. workouts with their private trainers to their hairdressers and then to the office by chauffeured limousines was reported without tongue in cheek. For some crazy reason, they were, and still are, taken very seriously. Feminist headquarters has never touched them, either to praise or deprecate, though their competitive work-cum-play schedules were born in feminism's influence. It had become infuriatingly uncomfortable for a woman to appear at a social gathering and have nothing with which to answer the question, "And what do you do?" meaning, In what interesting work *outside the home* are you engaged?

Thus, The Power Couple was born, wherein a man, usually divorced, now chose a much younger, beautiful woman. Certainly, they were not the majority, but they were the darlings of the media. Where the first wife had stayed home and raised his children, this new young lovely bent herself to enlarge his image in other ways. Usually more socially adept than he, she taught him what clubs to join, what charities to enrich, what parties to attend and how to host them, as well, and, of course, she taught him how to dress.

She often spoke on his behalf; being more beautiful than he, she lent her lovely face to the cameras until her image alone invoked his name. The crux of The Deal was that she not make him look small, which would be untenable; instead, the public summation must be that he was quite a man to be able to take her on. On January first, they would sit together, filling in their Power Couple agendas to be sure their separate business schedules and combined social engagements jibed.

What an interesting alternative to invisibility feminism had provided them with: a working wife whose wealth certainly didn't match his own Fortune 500 status, but whose looks and, equally important, social savoir faire signaled to people that he was someone to be reckoned with. So fixated had their lives been on creating great wealth, these men were oblivious to the function of fish forks, reminder cards, and the blinding significance of being on the board of the Metropolitan Museum; eventually, some of them would have to wait in line for that prestigious museum to accept their ten-million-dollar donation, which bought entry to its board of directors.

We meet a little bald man in a dark blue suit, tailor-made but nonetheless indistinguishable from other suits, and we turn away until someone informs us of who he is, meaning what he owns. We turn back, see him anew, not as short but as princely and with a golden nimbus around his head, for now we remember how often we've seen that name, not just on the business pages of the paper, but the society pages of every periodical. Ah, now we understand the beautiful tall blonde crossing the room to glue herself to him. Everything falls into place, *click, click, click*, The Deal, the exchange of goods and services.

Many of these female thoroughbreds need never have married; they could have bought their own duplex apartments on Park Avenue. They could have afforded younger, better-looking mates, not necessarily gigolos but men who were closer to their age and interests, who did their dance and listened to their music. There are, however, persistent findings from studies conducted prior to and since modern feminism that indicate that women, regardless of the size of their own private economic resources, still prefer men with greater resources than their own.

"Evidence from dozens of studies documents that modern American women indeed value economic resources in mates substantially more than men do," writes psychologist David M. Buss. Going as far back as 1939, Buss's findings in 1956 and again in 1967 showed little variance. Nor did the sexual revolution of the sixties and seventies alter women's preference. Again, in the eighties, Buss went on to survey both men and women who "rated eighteen personal characteristics for their value in a marriage partner. As in the previous decades, women still value good financial prospects in a mate roughly twice as much as men do." A later study Buss conducted in 1994 and 1995, using "personal ads in newspapers and magazines confirm[ed] that women who are actually in the marriage market desire financial resources. . . . Female advertisers seek financial resources roughly eleven times as often as male advertisers do."

Buss and his colleagues proceeded to survey thirty-seven cultures on six continents and five islands, and once again found that "women across all continents, all political systems (including socialism and communism), all racial groups, all religious groups, and all systems of mating (from intense polygamy to presumptive monogamy) place more value than men on good financial prospects. Overall, women value financial resources about 100 percent more than men do."

Personally, I am disappointed in Buss's findings; while my anthropologist colleagues would shrug an "I told you so," I had hoped that women's dramatically increased earning ability since modern feminism would have freed us to look for characteristics that led to more intimate compatibility, a process of selection that outdistanced whatever genetic inclinations determine a woman's need for a mate who can protect and provide during her child-bearing years. Perversely, Buss's surveys seem to show that the most successful, educated women "express an even stronger preference for high-earning men than do women who are less financially successful."

A woman sees the rich man's balding head and potbelly in a different way than she sees the identical flaws in a poor man. Yes, it is his economic clout that transforms him, but if we trace the influence of power back far enough, isn't the man's bank account irresistible to a woman in the same way as mother's power? Mother, who had all the power in the world, was "beautiful" because we would die without her. Isn't this what is carried forward when the beautiful young woman with wealth of her own marries a short, bald tycoon who overpowers her economically? It is her implicit memory of being taken care of by the most powerful person in the world that draws her to power twenty, thirty, forty years later.

Professional studies notwithstanding, I hold to my optimism that beautiful, lively, self-providing women may stop selecting men twenty, thirty, forty years older than they and instead pick someone more in their own range of looks, interests, energy. To put it bluntly, when they lie down with these old men with their wrinkled flesh, aren't their fantasies of men whose erections last a little longer, at the very least? Beauty in a man has never topped my own list, but even when I had little money of my own, old men with potbellies, low libidos, and no hair were never on my horizon. As women's new economics digs deeper into our unconscious and women grow to feel a stronger sense of entitlement to someone who shares their energy and background, things may change. Certainly men's steady march into the mirror will affect how women look at men and choose a mate. Women's choice may never approximate the age difference between wealthy men and their adolescent brides, but it will change by the laws of economics, which have always shaped history.

Not since the Industrial Revolution has an historical event matched feminism's influence on every aspect of society. The repercussions roll on. In this morning's *Wall Street Journal*, for instance, there is an article on today's twenty-something generation of daughters of feminists, who grew up with mothers who were overworked, tired, and absent. These young women say they don't crave the kind of economic independence that drove their mothers but instead see something in between women's role under Patriarchy and what feminism created. If enough of them feel this way, they will certainly reshape feminism, as will their children's generation and the one after that.

If the little bald men introduced their wives to higher finance, their women brought them into the mirror. Already proficient in all aspects of high fashion, the wives in the Power Couple understood the meaning of an Hermès tie, a Charvet shirt, the tailor-made suit, Hunstman or Church custom shoes. Very quickly, the husbands learned to clock each other, noting shirt, tie, watch, shoes, brand names and prices toted up so quickly that the eyes barely moved.

I recall a certain short tycoon who, in his naiveté, was kind of endearing. Whenever I ran into him, he would scrutinize me from head to toe, starting at the top: "Who does your hair?" "Yves." "I love that jumpsuit. Who designed it?" "Geoffrey Beene." "Whose bag is that?" "Prada." "I bet those shoes are Ferragamo." "Right." One day when we met on the street, he asked me where I was going. I answered that I was on my way to see Yves, to get my hair cut. "Can I come?" he asked, and fell into step with me, taking big strides alongside me as his chauffeured Mercedes purred slowly behind us, not exactly like Cary Grant and Ingrid Bergman in *Indiscreet*, but it did come to mind. "How tall are you?" "Five feet, ten inches," I said.

It was clear that he was practicing getting the labels, prices, and look down pat. Here he was, fiftyish and finally going through adolescence, looking at women to whom he'd never felt entitled, and being seen by them, appraised, flirted with. He'd amassed his fortune in a smaller town well south of Manhattan, with a traditional wife.

He had bought a string of high-profile companies advertised by very tall, beautiful models whom he collected the way tycoons before him collected racehorses. Today, of course, models are the thoroughbreds of the age. What was likable about him back then, before the tall wife did him over, was his unabashed curiosity, his big-eyed wonder at the world into which he had dropped at a moment in history when the only asset he had—money—was the entity that mattered. Whenever I see his photo in the paper, that little round face, his latest racehorse on his arm, I wonder if he is still enjoying it, if the accessories of beauty ever make up for the anonymity of his adolescence.

In time, he would leave his second wife for an even more powerful, taller trophy, this one with political aspirations. It is one of the latest versions of The New Power Deal between the sexes, played in the tabloids by the Arianna Huffingtons: ambitious, tall, elegant women who need wealthy men to economically flesh out their own aspirations for power.

Other New Deals in which both partners work and have economic power mean that either can walk away at any time. This couple may never have children, may be of the same sex, but economic independence allows each of them to manipulate power—in the name of love—as a way of staying together in what psychologist Michael Vincent Miller calls "Intimate Terrorism."

Write sociologists Philip Blumstein and Pepper Schwartz, "New marriages where the wife is ambitious are less stable. It is not that an ambitious wife necessarily grows dissatisfied with her marriage or seeks greener pastures. Rather, it is her husband who does not want to live with such an ambitious or successful woman. Among married couples who have broken up, we find that the more ambitious the wife, the more likely that the husband wanted the relationship to end."

In a mere twenty-five years, feminism has reinvented the plot line of the universal story of a woman's life. It didn't use to matter what the man looked like or if he was old or mean. The objective was to find a provider, to not live alone, despised, rejected. Beautiful women seldom were Old Maids. No one uses that expression anymore. Nor do we look aghast at the lovely unmarried woman who has visited the Sperm Bank and who wears her fashionable maternity clothes without fear of censure. But when she went to buy her sperm, you can be sure she requested fluid with certain hereditary traits. "We don't get requests for short men," said the spokesperson for the bank my researcher called. No potential donor under five feet six need apply. Why do I think that if my short billionaire with the wretched adolescence offered some sperm, women would get down on their knees, so to speak, for a shot of that mogul medicine?

Nothing summed up the bad taste of the mid-eighties Power Couples gone berserk quite so brilliantly as the ballyhooed arrival in New York of designer Christian Lacroix, who came across the great ocean in November 1987 to dress The Trophy Wives. No one described the advent more richly, in all its misbegotten grotesquerie, than Julie Baumgold in *New York* magazine, where she wrote that Lacroix's fashions represented the same kind of ostentatious denial historically seen in dying aristocracies. "Clothes of such brilliant luxury and defiance probably haven't been seen since eighteenth-century French aristocrats rattled in carts over the cobblestones on their way to the guillotine."

There is something so like the fairy tale's lesson in humiliation and disaster learned from The Lacroix Experience, which followed the 1987 stock market crash; the clothes he brought to the new society women were ludicrous, some hilarious in their over-the-top extravagance. But the women who fought to buy them were blind to hilarity. A Lacroix concoction could cost $15,000, but women like Nan Kempner, Lee Radziwill, Blaine Trump, and Diandra Douglas vied and pleaded for the privilege of wearing these costumes, which were made of the most sumptuous fabrics, yes, but when worn made caricatures of the women wearing them.

Lacroix was, as Baumgold wrote, "the man who makes clothes of such extravagant, gorgeous excess as to divide the classes once and for all. The man who revived the mini, created the pouf. . . . The man who brought back tight bodices and bare flesh and who put across his love for weird, obsolete, rather bad-taste staples like cabbage roses, petticoats, bustles, fichus, panniers, and platter hats in clothes that are magnificent and visionary. His peculiar vision was flat out of his time, but he made it modern and daring. Especially daring, fit to dance on the lip of the volcano."

When The Dress for Success Suit began to itch, women wanted something to buy with our new money that looked like The New Woman. But who is she? Who she is can't be explained until we know who *he* is. Neither sex evolves alone. That our designers re-create instead of inventing originals doesn't mean that they have totally failed us. They are not psychiatrists. Until we get the present straight and discover where we left our hearts, we will continue putting on reincarnations from the past.

Fashion designers, alas, are not as wily as the magician tailors of fairy tales; they too are caught up in the past and recognize in the old photos that we looked more substantial. The right-wing extremists would have us believe that we lost our souls in the sixties and seventies. In fact, it was a time in which we were trying to strip away post-war materialism to find our selves. Today, our children put on the clothes from those years unwittingly, intuitively, and dance to our music.

Did the men who paid for the $15,000 Lacroix pouf dresses stop and reflect on what in hell their wives were doing with birdcages on their heads and hoops under their cabbage roses? They probably said nothing, assuming that their wives understood the social scene into which they had dropped like people from another planet. The little tycoons of the eighties were masters of the portfolio and little else; no one had taught them to samba. They relied on the trophy wife to navigate the tricky terrain of The New Society. They relied on her to teach them how to dress, or they hired an image consultant, a profession that boomed in the eighties and continues still as the internationalization of business spreads across the globe.

Today, getting ahead has put the businessman in the mirror opposite his European competitors, men who dress very well indeed; matching the competitor's look, maybe topping it, has reinforced men's return to looking good.

When an executive from Topeka flies to Turin, Italy, for a conference, he is advised that in the European business world a man's appearance is factored into the deal. The Association of Image Consultants International thrives not just on re-suiting the business person but on picking his shoes, cuff links, and ties, and also teaching him how to use the panoply of crystal and cutlery at dinner.

"When men meet around a conference table today," says consultant Camille Lavington, "they appraise one another as carefully as the prospectus on the table. Men want to do business with other men who understand the value of manners and appearance."

It is interesting that men's boredom with "the button-down look" began about the same time in the eighties as women's weariness with the blue Dress for Success Suit. "American men were suddenly earning lots of money to spend on clothes that would advertise their new wealth and enable them to compete with European and Japanese fine tailoring," says Lavington.

Along with the internationalization of business, sharp dressers like Don Johnson, in the top-rated television series *Miami Vice*, gave young men permission to move ahead on all fashion fronts: business, weekend, summer, winter. Men's wardrobes have come to demand the same dimensions of closet space that women's clothes occupy. Today, Hollywood and athletic stars, along with business moguls, set the male fashion standards, duly photographed and published, that the masses of men follow, either in the original high-priced line or in knockoffs.

Lavington's makeover instructions actually begin with eye contact, handshake, stance, posture. "The first thing you do is look somebody right in the eye; you can determine the quality of the person you are going to deal with. The second thing you do is to see if they are well groomed. In order, it goes haircut, clean shaven/beard, collar, necktie, the appearance of the clothes and suitability (in other words, whether they're well tailored), and then down to the shoes.

"How a man dresses says something of a man's power. In the international market, where you get off the Concorde and deal with the French and the Italians, if you are wearing short hose that show the skin on your leg instead of the long executive hose, these things are noticed. The decision makers, the people responsible for large amounts of money, conform to a certain recognized pattern of clothing and behavior."

Men's return to the mirror has not stopped with clothes. Nationwide, men made up 24 percent of plastic surgery procedures in 1993, up from 10 percent in 1980, reports the American Academy of Cosmetic Surgery. Men's pursuit of beauty now goes beyond face-lifts, nose jobs, and liposuction. From pectoral implants, which pump up the chest, to phalloplasty, which pumps up the penis, more men are now looking to improve more areas of their bodies. "Nationally, the procedures most often performed on men," says Jeffrey Knezovich, executive director of the American Academy of Cosmetic Surgery, "are hair replacement, rhinoplasty (nose job), blepharoplasty (eye-lift), liposuction and body sculpting, face-lift, dermabrasion, and pectoral implants."

My own feeling is that men's pursuit of looks won't be as compulsive as women's; our need of beauty was based on survival. Nor do I think that men are going to stop with beauty in their assumption of women's traditional privileges. Men's move into the nursery is going to take longer, but it is as inevitable, not so much because men want it—the role scares many men—but because the need exists. The New Father role will influence men's looks in a different way than image makeovers, plastic surgery, and bodybuilding, but in the end it will be a more profound and lasting transformation; a child will want to emulate the look of the good father because it was one of the most powerful looks in his life. How fascinating that all these changes in men's lives happen simultaneously and in response to one revolution: feminism.

"The Future of Men's Beauty Is Largely in Women's Hands"

When I was twenty, a lawyer telephoned to inform me of my modest inheritance. "From whom?" I asked. "From your father," he said, which is how I learned of his life and death.

Years later when my aunt Dot was visiting Key West, she said, "Your father was the handsomest man in Pittsburgh. He had a presence. People turned and looked when he entered a room." More recently, my mother told me on a visit that he was a bounder, a womanizer. After a lifetime of refusing to discuss him, she talked into a tape recorder that I had placed on the coffee table. Having waited so long for this—it happened two years ago—I still cannot bring myself to replay that tape. I want to finish this book without him, the way life always was.

No wonder I was never attracted to beautiful men. Not for me a man whom others would be tempted to steal away, whose looks signaled even a whiff of infidelity. Early deprivation had schooled me to seek out men who saw me as more than they had ever dreamed of winning. In turn, I gratefully became their good mirror, the eyes in which they would see themselves as the adored one. I love to watch my man dress and undress, and in this book I've come to understand why: Relegated to the role of voyeur—where he is often denigrated—man comes late to the mirror. I've known men who dressed without any mirror at all.

When I first met my husband in the early eighties, he was attracted to my display, my pleasure in dressing to be seen. When we walked down the street, he was aware when people looked at me and I was aware of his clocking this. I invited him into the mirror, took him to Bergdorf's, sat in a little gold chair, as I had for my grandfather at Sulka's, and watched him watching himself in the mirror as the tailor fitted his suit.

It was as if he'd never seen that man in the mirror. When we met, he owned six identical blue suits made in Korea. Buying him clothes is an investment in my own happiness. In the morning, he walks out of his dressing room and stands before me, awaiting my verdict. It is my eye that he craves, my judgment of a look he only allowed himself when we met. He wouldn't trust another woman's eye. Introducing him to his vanity has cooled my jealous nature. I am his best mirror.

I am not concerned that he will grow overly vain, so deeply planted in him is The Good Provider role. But when we walk down the street, no matter how splendid his own new threads, he is still more interested in how men look at me, which says something of the depth of value men feel in wearing a woman.

Other men tell me it is difficult to catch a woman's eye. "I'll be walking down Fifth Avenue with Nan," says author Gay Talese of his wife, "and I watch the women walking by and they don't even look at me, they look at her." What is it like to be the invisible sex? It can't be healthy and obviously contributes to the hunger in men's eyes when they stare at us. My friend Gay is a handsome man, an impeccable dresser, but women don't look at him. Women are not raised to look at men.

But young women are beginning to give men the eye, though it is unpracticed and will require time before voyeurism becomes natural. "One of the early analytic ideas about voyeurism has to do with the eyes being used as a mouth to take in something good," says Robertiello. "The experience of looking at a beautiful woman, savoring her body, taking it in and being nourished by the image is analogous to the feeding process."

No doubt this accounts, in part, for why women too like to look at women. In my DYG survey, the great majority of women listed men *fifth* in response to the question, "Why is beauty important to women?" Men, of course, put women as the number one reason they pursued good looks.

Will men's getting into the nursery bring to their children a sensory memory of the sight, smell, and texture of a man's body so that we are involuntarily drawn to it throughout life, just as we are to the luscious female body? Is the idea any more improbable than sperm banks once were or the egg and sperm of a couple deposited in another woman's body? True, a man cannot carry a fetus or nurse a baby, yet getting men in the nursery is the best tonic for the man/woman relationship.

As it is, we all stare at women's bodies. Women, as well as men, look with nostalgia at centerfolds of naked female bodies; we envy our friends' large breasts. We want to lay our heads there, and in women's erotic fantasies, this is precisely what we do. As maternal constancy grows scarcer, women grow up hating their own bodies more than ever, the flabby underarms that awaken breast envy and rage, the fleshy female buttocks and bellies that arouse nursery angers of deprivation.

A handsome salary cannot warm us in the cold recesses of the unconscious. Had a father shared caretaking with mother, then his skin, texture, smell, and touch might also be remembered; who knows what it might do for voyeurism in both sexes, but we would certainly be less angry with women.

Seeing only degradation in the eyes of men who masturbate while looking at women's bare breasts and genitals, angry feminists miss the point altogether. "The uninitiated think that men look at naked ladies to disparage them, or that the women hate the men and only do it to make a buck," says Robertiello, who used to frequent burlesque theaters. "But it's a love fest. We men worship. These women see the adoration in the guys' eyes. The men think the women are goddesses for letting them look. Their wives don't care enough to show them their bodies. These women live out the guy's suppressed dreams of exhibitionism."

"No catcalls?" I asked him.

"The few times that happened, the men were so disapproved of by the rest of the audience, they were thrown out of the theater. The stripper/audience relationship is a love affair, maybe even more important than a sex affair."

No one gives permission to men in all areas pertaining to beauty and sex like a woman, being that sex that denied permission in the first place. Now give it back. If he believes we mean it, if we turn him on to his own beauty, he will be ours forever. Without that first woman's permission to love his body, the threat of loss of love permeates a man's life, a weakness that must be turned into a strength. When he touched his penis as a boy, he was risking his life, or so it felt; grown older, the man still confuses fear, pain, and anger with love and erotic desire. The prostitute knows his fantasies, but his wife is in the untenable position of naysayer, which is how life began. If only women understood the power of permission. Giving it to men, drawing them into our world to share the powers of parenting and of beauty too, is a gift that never stops paying back.

Beauty may not precisely balance with economic wealth, but men's growing investment in looks is already righting The Deal between men and women. Women are looking seriously at men, maybe seeing them for the first time. And with young men using their looks to get ahead, women can hardly continue to deny and demur that we do likewise. Not having our history with beauty, men don't disclaim, "Oh, this old Armani suit?" Men aren't better people, but they are seasoned competitors, and don't live in the fear that the other guys will abandon them if they have more beauty.

Watching men use their looks competitively may encourage women to examine our own problems with losing and winning. Finding out that their whole identity doesn't hinge on economic power, perhaps men will learn from us that choosing a Good Provider in the form of a woman who loves the competitive workplace more than he is a far better life than what his father had. At the very least, the ameliorating rewards of looking good and winning admiration may take some of the edge off men's pursuit unto death of economic power, as well as lessen men's voyeuristic dependency on women.

As more women learn to enjoy looking at men, will pleasure lead to wondering why we denigrated men for so long for their voyeurism? As more of us appraise the beautiful men who work out alongside us at the gym, who buy their clothes from our designers, who now create for men too, will we see men as our beauty partners? Some women will look at men as "a piece of meat," our description of how they have always appraised us; other women, hopefully, will bring to voyeurism a natural talent, along with a memory, of how we always wished men would see us.

If women do start choosing beautiful men, men will work harder to make themselves more attractive. However, if we are to believe the women's magazines, there will be a testing period: "First, beauty is power, and men start off with enough of that," wrote a woman in an article titled "What If He's Cuter Than You?" "Second, physical perfection in a man always feels ominous to me. It's the lull before the storm. . . . The temper tantrum of my envy that I wasn't born perfect myself. . . . I saw Neil, as men so often see very beautiful women, as a fling, a plaything. In fact, it wasn't fair to say I 'saw' Neil at all. He was my hand mirror. I didn't care what lay beneath his surface. What I cared about was the reflected glory his beauty gave me: the picture of myself as the sort of woman who could attract that sort of man. And, eventually, the reflection that looked back at me came to seem predatory, and not at all pretty."

Will we ever get to that time when a hardworking, high-earning woman feels entitled to a great-looking guy and feels comfortable when people look at him and not at her? And will the division of power work for him too, when she is the one who brings home most of the bacon?

Again, economics determines history. There are no more sabre-toothed tigers to wrestle, no more wars fought with brawn; men's function has evolved. Some of us may still feel uncomfortable with the rituals of the new men's movements, but they are the tip of the wedge. Remember how they laughed at early feminism? One day, we will look back and wonder at our skepticism over men's early forays into beauty as well as women's reluctance to give men equality in the nursery. By then, a generation of women will have grown up expecting to provide for themselves, perhaps providing for a man too, and they will take that accomplishment as just that, a sign of success as a person who happens to be female.

Meanwhile, the man who approaches the beautiful woman still knows he is going to have to pay for her. He has learned this as part of his socialization, and he competes to do it, whereas a man who is focused on looks is anathema to a woman. Ambivalence. If he is too good-looking, the woman feels he may become dependent on his looks and expect her to support *him*. Women worry when a man's narcissism reaches a certain point; for the man in the same position, it is not a turn-off. So long as a man continues to provide well, what does the woman care about his balding head and extra weight?

"Women tend to like what they've got," says *Psychology Today*, reporting on a national survey on men's appearance, "whether he is bearded, uncircumcised, short, or otherwise 'off' the norm." Women who are more financially secure, however, and who see themselves as attractive: "This new and vocal minority," says the survey, "unabashedly declares a strong preference for better-looking men. . . . One of the most fascinating survey results was that women who rated themselves as more attractive tended to rank men's facial appearance and sexual performance higher. These women were a little older on average (mean age 38), thinner . . . and better off financially (almost half earned over $30,000 annually)."

Warren Farrell adds, "The difference between men and women who feel objectified as beauty objects is that the beautiful woman has been accustomed to celebrity status all her life, to men desiring her for her beauty. While the very handsome man may have grown up being admired for his beauty, other things were expected of him too, namely that he be economically successful. When the successful woman rejects him for failing economically, this is where he begins to feel like a sex object. It is a big difference between beautiful men and women, devastating for both, but dramatically different."

There is a new category of beautiful women today who are intimidating to a man, to the point of nonapproachability: These are the women who are both beautiful and successful. Successful women think men are put off by them, but Farrell's research disagrees: "Contrary to popular belief," he says, "the more successful a woman is, the more attractive she is to a man. But the man knows that a successful beautiful woman is much more likely to reject him than an unsuccessful beautiful woman is. She doesn't need him. She will Jane Fonda him. He will have to be her movie producer, presidential candidate, or a multibillionaire. Women say, 'Oh, men aren't attracted to successful women.' But that is simply not true. He wouldn't be intimidated at being rejected by her if he wasn't already attracted to her."

None of us wants to be rejected. Traditionally, we chose mates to make up for what we didn't have. Men had money and houses, which women didn't, but we had beauty, which men got by wearing us. Now that men are pursuing beauty to make up for what they have lost, they are more frequently showing up in doctors' offices. "I'm seeing more and more males who have body image disturbances," says Dr. Stephen Romano, director of the Outpatient Eating Disorders Clinic in New York. "They are compulsive exercisers, and there are a number of steroid abusers." Since 1987, the number of men exercising frequently has grown by more than 30 percent.

A lovely woman is a pleasure to look at, but so is a beautiful male body, once women, and other men, get used to looking at it. Today, among younger men especially, the hunger in their eyes when they gawk at women isn't just desire for the woman; men want some of women's pumped-up exhibitionism, that strut, that éclat for themselves. In a 1994 survey, 6,000 men ages eighteen to fifty-five were asked how they would like to see themselves. Three of men's top six answers had to do with appearance: attractive to women, sexy, good-looking. The stereotypical male traits—decisive, assertive—came in at numbers eight and nine. The same survey reported that 56 percent of the men agreed with the comment, "I'm pleased when people notice and comment on my appearance" (69 percent of men in their twenties agreed); six years prior, only 48 percent of all men had agreed.

Women haven't yet realized what we are losing; still focused on men as perverted voyeurs, the Matriarchal Feminist press won't acknowledge that women's beauty is an investment, a joy to own, even a weapon. The only obstacle that stands between us and our learning to use beauty profitably is the political jargon from women-without-men who still live in a world where they cannot bear the idea of a beautiful young woman enjoying what they never had. Long before we women have solved the competition between us, men may have found a way to recapture the beauty crown.

What do men born in the past thirty years care about the feminist attitudes regarding beauty, male or female? The sight of themselves in the mirror has deep historical roots; the pleasure of being admired is inherited from their ancestors, who played, not as bit players, but as stars. Some of these men move more deeply into the mirror in response to their genetic roots, a disposition, a natural inclination acquired or learned from parents. The display, the enthusiasm of being the beauty subject, runs in the blood.

History tends to repeat itself; until the late eighteenth century, the dressing-room mirror belonged to men. When the beauty of fashion was men's domain, they didn't employ women's denials of the past two hundred years. Nor did the uses of beauty, when men owned it, stop with courtship and sex. Men used their looks, flaunted them, competed with them to win whatever prize and power was to be had.

Anne Hollander describes a sixteenth-century summit meeting between Francis I and Henry VIII, in which "the descriptions of what everybody wore are unbearable! Everybody who was involved wore silver covered with diamonds, except when they were in cloth of gold and covered with rubies! Everything was lined in ermine and everything was 20 yards long, and there were plumes on everybody and so on. That's why that meeting was called the Field of the Cloth of Gold. Just as the poetry is filled with symbolic material and allegory, the clothing itself had that kind of material embedded in it. So the pattern woven on your sleeve in gold or in pearls had to have a certain strong effect. And if it didn't, you were less exciting than the fellow whose did, so to speak. They were in direct competition with one another, and so were their households, and the cohorts and entourage and everything else. They had to look more gorgeous than the others."

According to a recent study titled "Women: The New Providers," 55 percent of women contribute half or more to their household's income. This study has been called the most comprehensive look in fourteen years at women's views about work, family, and society. Women still average 73 cents for every dollar men make, but from 1974 to 1994 the number of households solely supported by a female earner increased by 114 percent. An interesting finding was that 48 percent of the women surveyed said that they would choose to work full-time or part-time even if money were not a consideration.

What remains to be seen today as women gain more of men's economic turf is how convincingly women also pursue men who are successful and/or attractive. This is what Warren Farrell means when he states that the future of male beauty is largely in the hands of women.

At this moment, we have no idea whether the sexes will share beauty, as we have begun to share economic power, or whether the younger male generations will pick up speed and outstrip women. Young men may be so fed up with feminism's anger, the Take Back the Night Marches, that they will simply look out for themselves, as women have been doing for the past twenty years. They will pursue a woman, want her, but will refuse to kowtow to her demands. If male beauty power continues to be effective in the workplace, this especially will bolster men's pursuit of it, making all other considerations inconsequential.

A man will compete with the woman for the job and not wait for her approval of his new tailor-made suit. If she rejects him because he is too pretty and thus steals her thunder, he will simply find another woman, one who sees him differently, genuinely loves his looks, his share of providership, and is not so centered on the mirror herself. A young man is now free to imagine a world in which his princess beams on his reflected beauty. She is out there, this woman who is not so envious, and it is his quest to find her.

Before long we will become accustomed to seeing handsome men with less beautiful women and seeing a beautiful woman with a man who is comfortable in her economically powerful shadow; of course, the old standby, the short, bald, wealthy men with towering princesses, will always be there. The mixes of economic wealth and beauty will be endlessly variable. This parlaying of men's beauty, now that it has started, is simply not going to go away. Like women's new economics, it will be factored into the New Deal.

"Men want to be powerful," says John Molloy. "Convince them that looks can gain them power, get people to do what they want them to do, then looks are great." The reverse of that is also true: Men will shun whatever reduces power. It was in 1675, when French seamstresses petitioned Louis XIV to allow them to make women's dresses, that men's interest in fashion began to wane. Instead of experimenting with the fundamental design of garments, as men's tailors were doing, female clothing makers' designs became studies in superficial excess. Fashion became foolish and ceased to be powerful; men's clothing gradually became more simple.

In her book *Sex and Suits*, Anne Hollander explains that near the turn of the eighteenth century, when tailors discovered Greek sculpture and the universal proportions of the human body, the Neo-classic movement and the male costume "made a radical leap in fashion."

The narrow-shouldered, big-bellied clothes we associate with portraits of George Washington and Benjamin Franklin were replaced by simpler designs that made the male wearers resemble the heroic figures of antiquity, with their shoulders broadened with padding, and legs now lengthened in appearance by full-length trousers. "The modern business suit [as we know it] stems from the late 1850s lounge coat, a loose, boxy jacket lacking the waist seam that defined the frock coat."

With the invention of power-spinning machines, power looms, and the development of the tape measure, clothes made on the Eastern seaboard of America in the mid-nineteenth century were available across the country by catalogue, creating a common national style of dress. Beginning in the 1880s, the influx of immigrants from Europe provided the cheap labor that spawned mass production in the garment industry. Before World War I, the ubiquitous three-piece blue serge suit had become men's uniform, so that the view of men pouring from their places of business seemed to make one class and profession of man indistinguishable from the next. By the end of World War II, The Deal was in place, and Girls in Their Summer Dresses hung on the arms of Men in Their Grey Flannel Suits.

Women haven't a clue as to the genius men will bring to the art of looking good. After two hundred years of owning beauty and demurring as to its power, we are about to see real peacocks on parade. We assume that men can't put two garments together. Think again. "Men came of age in the eighties in terms of using clothes as a form of communication," says menswear designer Alan Flusser, who has written several books on male fashion. "Women use fashion to communicate, but men use it in their own way. You had the emergence of the $1,000-plus suit, which became a regular phenomenon in stores. Until the eighties they hadn't sold that kind of expensive clothing to men. Men began buying more expensive clothing to represent the level of success they had attained, and for some men, the level of success they *wanted* to attain. There was an enthusiasm and encouragement toward men opening up their idea about what they can and cannot wear."

I agree with Flusser but would not diminish the impetus that came from feminism, when women's focus on economics left a vacuum in the mirror. The eye was hungry, and men were a natural. "It's clear that the fastest and sexiest advances in Western costume history were made in male fashion," writes Hollander, "including the initial leap into fashion itself in the late twelfth century, the shift into modernity which threw down the challenge to all succeeding generations."

As women have taken on more and more of men's work, we've assumed their fashions as well. Women put on men's trousers in World War II and never took them off. We now wear trousers into the workplace and the finest restaurants too. I remember a pants suit Italian designer Patrick de Berentzen made for me in 1963. It was the day after John F. Kennedy's assassination. I was in Rome weeping in the

Piazza del Popolo, and when he saw me he said, "Let me make you a gift. I've never designed one of these suits for women." As he measured me and selected the pale green embroidered fabric and diamanté buttons, he too wept. We all wept.

That New Year's Eve in New York I was taken to the 21 Club in my extraordinary evening suit; the maître d' debated whether I could enter. They had never served a woman in pants. But the suit was so beautiful they waved us in. The entire staff came from the kitchen to see a woman in a double-breasted "men's" evening suit.

Throughout the feminist years, we women have progressively put on more and more of men's fashions, which somehow have made men look less hard-edged. "It's clear that during the second half of this century," writes Hollander, "women finally took over the total male scheme of dress, modified it to suit themselves, and have handed it back to men charged with immense new possibilities."

At the opening night of *Hair*, in 1968, the men in the audience wore a wild variety of Nehru jackets, velvet pants, and silk scarves, along with necklaces, beads, the single earring. When I moved to London a year later, I frequented a shop on Greek Street where Thea Porter designed embroidered robes, caftans, and flowing pants of the most outrageous beauty for both men and women. In this morning's paper, the men's collection in Milan shows men in the same Nehru jackets, wide-legged pants. "Just as women are expected to willingly climb back onto stiletto heels and into clinging clothes," writes the *New York Times* fashion editor, "men are being asked to forsake an evolution that has made suits as comfortable as sweaters." Then she repeats something almost identical to what Hollander said, "The new male glamour features some strikingly literal appropriations of traditionally feminine allure."

Men will not wring their hands when they stand before their mirrors, fearing they have gone to an extreme in their dress. We women have hesitated to believe too deeply in our beauty, or to use it too overtly. Men don't fear exclusion from the gang for having used their looks to get ahead. When a man hears our whispered, "You are so handsome," he will look into our eyes and accept the praise far more readily than we have ever believed in men's praise or their love.

Love and beauty have a common history, which begins in the family. Today, preferable treatment given to a lovelier sibling in childhood and adolescence shapes a boy as much as it does his sister. The dance

in front of the mirror is as old as time; now men reenter to dance opposite and in competition with us, the inevitable reaction to women's
move into the economic arena. "Both sexes play changing games
today," says Hollander, "because for the first time in centuries men are
learning clothing habits from women, instead of the other way
around."

In my revision of the fairy tale, today's man is the sleeping prince
awaiting the kiss of the voyeuristic woman.

8

The Penis, the Shoe,
and the Vagina

===

The Penis: Past, Present, and Future

Shortly after I began this book, a poem arrived in the mail from
my aunt Pat, she who had been my heroine while growing up. It was
printed on a yellowed, raggedy piece of paper torn from a volume of
Cerberus, the annual collection of student stories and poems from my
beloved school. I have kept the dog-eared version, an appropriate talisman on this journey, pinned over my desk these past three years,
anticipating its inclusion here.

THE MAN WITH THE PAN

Once I met a man with a pan, pan, pan.
I didn't like the man with the pan so I ran, ran, ran.
That little man ran after me
But I was so smart I climbed up a tree.
That little man came after me
But I was so smart I climbed down the tree.

I ran home but that little man didn't come after me.
That little man was still up the tree.

NANCY FRIDAY, GRADE THREE

Several months after I'd received the poem, my family gathered for my uncle's funeral. The night we arrived at my aunt's big, antebellum house, we sat in a loose circle in the living room, four generations of us, for my great-aunt Marge, my grandmother's sister, had come from her nursing home. I hadn't been there twenty minutes when she turned to me and said, "Nancy, do you remember when you were a little girl and came running into the house saying that a man had exhibited himself to you?"

I don't think I had seen my aunt Marge since that day to which she'd just referred, and suddenly here she was, very old, very blind, and come to tell me about the meaning of this poem I'd recently been sent. When I'd received the torn remnants of "The Man with the Pan," I had read it with amusement, having no idea what was on my mind when, as a child, I'd written it.

Now I knew. Knew it because I was writing this book, which had penetrated the unconscious; knew it as clearly as I could now see the streets around that particular house where I used to roam in my curious way, looking for I knew not what, but always looking. This is where and when I encountered the man standing under a tree with his penis exposed. Three or four years later, when I wrote my poem, did I remember what he had done? I'll never know. What is magical, as in fairy tales, is that the old *Cerberus* was found in an attic, my poem torn out and sent to my aunt, who had forwarded it to me just as I was launched into this writing.

Certainly I wouldn't wish a Man with a Pan in any child's life, but he did turn up in mine and earned a place in this book about men and women in our unacceptable skins, the bodies we wrap in inviting, fashionable ways, hoping that we will inspire others to see and love those "parts" we cannot bring ourselves to look at. In my mind, there is a connection, be it ever so fine, between men who carry exhibitionism into appalling antisocial behavior and those who lie in their beds across the world, their hands on their unloved penises, their minds dreaming about a woman who, for a change, would look at it, touch it, taste it, adore it.

Raised by a woman, the man grows up accepting that in women's eyes there is nothing beautiful about the area between his legs. The sister receives the same education, leaving her to identify with mother for the rest of her life (unless a good man changes her mind), but the boy goes on to ally himself with other boys. Alas, it remains just that, men's shared determination, in defiance of women's opinion, to celebrate the symbol of their difference.

That men must work so hard at it says how deeply imprinted men are by that first woman's judgment. That men forgive women our scorn of the penis, that they go even further and try to persuade us of the beauty of our own genitals is, when you think of it, quite generous. Far from showing gratitude, we women disparage men's fondness for their penises.

Feminism should have taken up the penis years ago. Instead, fanatics like Andrea Dworkin spew such vitriol as her crazed ranting, "Violence is the male; the male is the penis; violence is the penis or the sperm ejaculated from it."

I know they exist, but in my twenty-five years of research I have never come across a man who had sexual fantasies of exposing himself. But mention the erotic dream of a woman who loves looking at his penis, inhaling the aroma, tasting the semen that spurts from it, followed by the final benediction, swallowing it! Well, hundreds of thousands of happy male eyes light up around the world. She accepts me! that fantasy says, she loves that deepest, sweetest part of me that women have taught me is repugnant, so vile that it makes them turn away from it and me, for we are interchangeable, inseparable, me and this penis with its magic fluid that most women, alas, want only for procreation.

Ironically, mother's guarded eye on his penis teaches the boy that it must be very important indeed, otherwise mother wouldn't lavish so much attention on it. As in fairy tales and video games, where the thing most heavily guarded is the most valuable prize, the boy comes to believe that his penis must be quite something or mother wouldn't protest so vehemently. In time, the forbidden is meshed with the pleasurable.

"It's not an accident we have so many men with erectile difficulties," says Judith Seifer, "or a loss of desire, or premature ejaculation. These are the very men who have been taught by mother that it's not permissible to be on good terms with their penis. The parents' way of dealing with any kind of erotic feeling or attitude is to deny or ignore it. Sex was considered nasty, dirty and a sin, or it was never discussed. By virtue of the guilt or the fear instilled in them, many of these men never go through the developmental preoccupation with their genitals that happens in puberty. These are not the kids who are masturbating, and that is exactly what ejaculatory competence takes. Practice. Starting in puberty, young boys learn that the longer they last, the more they feel. The more aroused you get before you let yourself come, the bigger your penis gets. This is the opportunity to literally take a good look at themselves, to get comfortable with how their equipment has changed and to learn how well it can serve them. Masturbation is a great teacher."

How disturbing it must be for a man to lie naked with a woman, inserting his penis into her and all the while knowing that she doesn't like the sight of it. It is a wonder men choose to be with us at all. And we resent that they go to prostitutes who know that the mouth on the penis is what men pay to enjoy. "It is the first thing men want, oral sex," says Norma Jean Almodovar, director of COYOTE, the prostitutes' union in California. "After oral sex, the most popular fantasy among all men is the ménage à trois. In that order." Two women adoring his penis! And neither of them is jealous of the other, now that is bliss!

"A lot of men, especially very powerful men, want to relinquish that power," says Almodovar. "They want to do it in a safe situation where they can trust the person to whom they give control. They often like to be tied up and told what naughty children they are. 'Bad boy!' Believe it or not, there are still an awful lot of women who will not give their husbands oral sex."

In men's erotic fantasies nothing registers higher than oral sex. "For men, oral sex seems to relate to their view of the entire relationship and to their view of being loved," says June Reinisch, director emerita of the Kinsey Institute. "For men it has great significance, beyond what it has for women. There is something related to the woman's acceptance, love, and admiration of a man's penis that he relates to an acceptance of the whole self, that all of him is appreciated and loved."

When he was a boy and his penis erupted in the night, soiling mother's clean sheets, his wish wasn't that he would never climax again but that he could get away from Women's Rules. He dreads dirtying mother's pretty towels in the bathroom where he masturbates, but his anger at the woman he loves must be internalized, where it wars with his need of mother/women. Men's sadomasochistic fantasies, please note, are rarely about abusing women; rather, the man debases himself at her feet, becomes her slave, and, yes, gets his dirty little orgasm too.

When men accept women's opinion that his penis is ugly, disgusting, and unkissable, they buy our verdict, not their own. Such behavior toughens men, separates them from emotion. When a couple argues, the man will walk out the door more easily, not because he hurts less but because life under Women's Rules has given him practice in the endurance of pain, in the prospect of a life without either beauty or feeling.

A man requires so little convincing, and he is so grateful when women beam at his elegant image. Why do we refuse to give back to men some of the pleasure they have given to us in the recognition of our beauty? Some men do carry voyeurism too far, but that is learned anger. Instead, our opinion of men's physical appeal never gets past our angry accusation of that part of their anatomy we hate: "The penis is conceived as a weapon," wrote Germaine Greer in *The Female Eunuch*, "and its action upon women is understood to be somehow destructive and hurtful."

Whatever women may think of the penis, the fact remains that we expect men to change our low opinion of our genitals, which we see as disfigurement. Read this scene from Terrence McNally's *Frankie and Johnny in the Claire de Lune*, and ask yourself how many women would give this gift to a man, this worshipful vision of his genitals:

JOHNNY: Open your robe.
FRANKIE: No. Why?
JOHNNY: I want to look at your pussy.
FRANKIE: No. Why?
JOHNNY: It's beautiful.
FRANKIE: It is not. You're just saying that.
JOHNNY: I think it is. I'm telling you you have a beautiful pussy—!
FRANKIE: I hate that word, Johnny!
JOHNNY: —alright, thing! And I'm asking you to open your robe so I can look at it. Just look. Fifteen seconds. . . .

(She agrees finally, and stands there talking her head off, embarrassed while he looks, then Johnny takes her hand, kisses it, rubs his cheek against it.)

Men cannot grasp our hatred of the very parts of our body they most worship; nor does either sex appreciate how this spreads and thus spoils our assessment of our other body parts. We push away men's hungry mouths, turn away from their eyes that would worship us, and call them pigs for wanting to look and taste. Perhaps when we first met we believed his words of adoration, but when attraction has turned into "love," our satyr becomes our caretaker. In our married roles of Mommy/Daddy, we see the two of us as we saw our parents, who in our eyes were never sexual.

And we wonder why men go to whores to find sex without strings, without love, which men have learned ruins sex. The man had thought he could have both, but now he settles for married love and purchased sex, where he can look at a woman's genitals and have his own tasted, for which oral satisfaction he accepts/expects punishment at the hands of the prostitute who whips him, steps on him with her high heels, spanks him for breaking Mommy's antisex rules.

I sit here trying to imagine what it must be like to be a man, to go through life with this penis that has its own separate life, its private connection with the brain that triggers its tumescence at will. Yes, other men accept the penis, even celebrate it, but half the world despises it. And even other men disparage it when it doesn't measure up.

Sex educator Betty Dodson says she has met very few men "who really like their cock and balls, and who really enjoy masturbating. When I published my first book, I tried to get cock drawings included to help the men along the same lines as I was trying to educate women, but the publisher wouldn't include the drawings. It's okay for women to be on display, but men? The salesmen refused to sell the book. Practically every man walking the planet doesn't think his cock is adequate or big enough. I ran a few groups for men, to get them to see the beauty of their genitals, but it was just impossible to get them to have a dialogue."

During the sixties I fell in love with a man who, when we met, had just left his restrictive wife in the suburbs. More than any man I've known, he celebrated sex and, in particular, his penis of a size so remarkable that when I eventually met Margot St. James, founder of COYOTE, and asked her if by chance she'd ever met my old lover, she paused only briefly. "Stan's got the biggest cock in San Francisco," she said.

The only story from his youth that Stan told me was that his mother destroyed the full-page advertisements for Hanes stockings that he had pinned over his bed. Was this female prohibition the beginning of my lover's fondness for sex in near-public places where we might be discovered: on beaches, under tables in restaurants, in swimming pools? The sixties were risk-taking years. Because he was the most articulate, well read, charming, and patient man I'd ever met, a born teacher, I followed him. I longed to lose my Nice Girl rigidity. From other free spirits in those years I learned that we Finishing School graduates often make the best candidates for sexual exploration. The Edie Sedgwicks were legion. Yes, she died, but many of us knew where to draw the line.

My parting memory of Stan was of a summer day at the corner of Fifth Avenue and Fifty-fifth Street, where he couldn't stand his invisibility any longer and called out, "Look at me!" He meant his cock, his jewel, which lay flaccid beneath his khaki trouser leg but, given its size and the fact that he wore no underwear, was dramatically bold in outline. No one passing understood his plaintive lament, precisely what it was he wanted to be seen, but I did. He and I would soon part company, with gratitude on both sides, Stan to go on to teach Tantra Love on a mountaintop near San Francisco.

There were quite a number of men who abandoned their underwear—liberated their penises, so to speak—in those years, a time we associate with female exhibitionism when, in fact, men too were trying to get past the culture's definition of masculinity, The Good Provider, just as we braless women were breaking out of our mothers' molds. Had we women been more aware of men's restrictive lives we might have helped ourselves in helping them. But most men were silent, so unaccustomed to complaint was the male voice, so unsympathetic were the ears of men and women. We still are. We neither want to hear their demands for rights in the nursery nor do we want to hear about their concerns regarding their penises.

Poor men. Relegated to having sex with women without dirtying the sheets. Poor men, who would gladly gaze at our vaginas for hours, clean them with their tongues like large tomcats. When men stare at naked women in magazines, women who spread their legs and let them have a good look up close, men pay homage to the centerfolds, homage that might have been ours if we weren't so priggish. But Nice Girls couldn't, wouldn't, consider letting him get close to the sewer that we have never investigated ourselves, and as for enjoying men's sticky semen jettisoned all over us—their "homage"—please, take that ugly thing away!

"It's remarkable how little women, even women who pose naked for magazines, know about male sexual response," says Gay Talese. "I was at the Los Angeles mansion back in the seventies when I used to spend a lot of time with Hefner. I was looking at the latest issue of *Playboy*, at the very beautiful, arousing Playmate of the month and suddenly she walked into the room. I was in the library having a brandy and we sat and had a conversation. She, of course, had her clothes on, but I had a very visual sense of her from just looking at that magazine.

"I asked her if she had any idea when she was posing for this photographer what effect her poses would have upon the audience that reads *Playboy*, three or four million men a month.

"'What do you mean?' she said.

"I said, 'Let's be very specific.' Remember, I was researching *Thy Neighbor's Wife* at this time. I said to her that 'the magazine is all over the country, in small towns, roadside motels, Holiday Inns, and possibly as I'm talking to you now in California, it is midnight in Newark, New Jersey, and in some Holiday Inn across the George Washington Bridge, after dinner some guy has gone up to his room with a *Playboy* magazine, and he's lying in bed with an erection. He's looking at these pictures, and he's masturbating. He's holding his hand on his penis, rubbing it up and down, looking at you. And he's about to have an orgasm. He's going to reach for a Kleenex, and he's going to stuff his penis into that Kleenex and he's going to come. He's going to essentially be having sex with you.'

"She said, 'I find this disgusting. This is really disgusting.'

"I said, 'I'm sorry it's disgusting, but what I'm telling you is true. I could well be that man because I saw that picture of you earlier and I think you're very arousing. And if I had any sexual energy left, I could easily be that guy. Not only am I that guy, but I am millions of guys like that guy.'

"So let me tell you what happened. This woman complained to Hefner, and he called me in the next day and said, 'Gay, I think you behaved badly last night, talking to her that way.' I said, 'I didn't behave badly at all. In fact, I'm insulted to have you talk to me that way. You are a man who has made millions out of masturbation. You are the first man in the history of the commerce of this capitalist country to make a million out of masturbation. This is where your fortune is made, not in those philosophic interviews you do.' He didn't want to hear it.

"I don't think women who pose today are any different. Even men don't know about men. There isn't an authority on the sexual lives of men. Henry Miller, John Updike, Philip Roth, they are literary pornographers. But they write fiction. They are hiding behind characters. 'This ain't me, ladies and gents in literary land, this ain't me.' But men? Men just don't write about their private sexual lives as women write about theirs. We really know nothing about the sexual lives of men. It's a dirty secret."

Today, as men move more steadily into the mirror, it is not surprising that the penis, along with everything else, is under closer scrutiny. Over the years when men have written to me, and thousands have, along with age, marital status, and profession, they have included their penis size, both flaccid and erect. I hadn't asked for it, but clearly it is a detail men thought I should have if I were to understand them. Clothed or naked, a man is conscious of his penis in a way that women cannot fathom. Women's image of The Sewer is an unconscious pressure, but for men, their genitals are very much a part of how they see themselves.

When June Reinisch was asked in an interview what men are most anxious about when it comes to sex, she replied, "Impotence is a big problem." She also listed disease, homosexuality, and achieving the "right kind" of orgasm. Then she caught a quick breath and added, "And penis size! Penis size is a real American male concern. People are suicidal about it."

In *A Moveable Feast*, Ernest Hemingway writes of men's insecurity about their penises. In it, F. Scott Fitzgerald tells Hemingway that he has never had sex with any woman other than Zelda, and that she had said "that the way I was built I could never make any woman happy and that was what upset her originally. She said it was a matter of measurements. I have never felt the same since she said that and I have to know truly."

To which Hemingway suggests they retire to the men's room and upon their return to the restaurant tells his friend, "You're perfectly fine. . . . You are O.K. There's nothing wrong with you. You look at yourself from above and you look foreshortened. Go over to the Louvre and look at the people in the statues and then go home and look at yourself in the mirror in profile."

"Those statues may not be accurate."

"They are pretty good. Most people would settle for them."

"But why would she say it?"

"To put you out of business. That's the oldest way in the world of putting people out of business."

But Fitzgerald never does quite believe Hemingway, at least not according to Papa; maybe it should be remembered that there had been a long and competitive tug-of-war between the two men. In telling this story is Hemingway as guilty as Zelda of putting Fitzgerald "out of business"?

All their lives men have compared their size with the other guy's in the locker room, the stranger standing beside them at the urinal. Nobody's size was more duly noted than father's, a lamentable comparison when you consider how young the boy is and how needy of images of manhood—many images!—that stand up opposite mother/women's powerful look. Once again, if father had been as intimately involved in his son's rearing as mother was, then the boy would feel as passionately about all forms of power, physical and emotional, that a man may possess. There wouldn't be this crazed obsession with size, anecdoted by author/actor Tim Allen in the following passage:

> My father would take me and my brothers to pee, and you're just dick tall, and your dad's is out. This whale of a penis would fly out, and you have a mushroom cap that two hands could barely pull out from your body. And your dad's penis would— thrrumm! And you'd scream at this huge, hairy beast of an ugly—"Goddamn! Aw, God!" And we'd leave the bathroom and all go, "Shit! Did you see that? Goddammit, it was all hairy, you know?" And we all prayed: "I hope I never look like that!"

Raised and toilet-trained by women, the sex that thinks everything between the legs is dirty, the boy looks to father for alternative signs of male power only to run up against a penis that resembles Gulliver's. A nurturing father would be part of what Helen Fisher calls his "love map"; during early childhood, he would have absorbed an unconscious list of what a man is like, what a man is supposed to do. Father's larger penis would not have to compensate for all the power owned by mother. The penis would still be admirable but would be seen by the boy as a promise of what was to come. Until men get into the caretaker role, the penis will never be big enough.

"After sex, every man wonders, 'Will I get hard again?'" says Gay Talese.

"And after sex, every woman wonders, 'Will he call again?'" I reply.

The comparison of men's and women's postcoital worries is telling: The man is responsible for performing, meaning getting hard, and also for initiating the next step in courtship, meaning risking rejection. In bed, women lie there, and later prefer to weep by the telephone rather than call him. Nevertheless, we blame men for being tactless and cold in their hesitation to connect with us, and we blame them for their sexual performance too.

It is not surprising in this era of women's new economics that penis enlargement surgery has also come of age. An article in *Vogue* magazine reports that between 1990 (when those operations began in America) until 1994, there were approximately 3,000 augmentations performed. In 1994 alone there were 3,000 more, and there are those who think that number may have doubled in 1995. Medical experts are alarmed, seeing genital cosmetic surgery as falling into a gray area between urology and chicanery. "We don't tell guys who pump iron that they're crazy, do we?" asks Gary Griffin, publisher of a newsletter called *Penis Power Quarterly*. "Men have always wanted bigger penises," adds Griffin. "The bigger the better. A big penis is a sign of masculinity, and men are competitive about that."

At a time when women are having more cosmetic surgery than ever, including breast implants, can we quibble with men who want to enlarge their penises? The figures vary on how women feel about penis size, whether it matters as regards performance, but one statistic stands out: "Women who rated themselves as more attractive were particularly concerned with larger size," reports psychiatrist Michael Pertschuk in a *Psychology Today* survey. "Of women describing themselves as 'much more attractive than average,' 64 percent cared strongly or moderately about penis width, and 54 percent cared about penis length. Women who rated their own looks as average were about 20 percentage points lower."

As men get more into overall attraction—clothes, cosmetics, body-building—and women respond to their physical beauty, will men be less anxious about penis size, realizing that there are other things, physically, that appeal to women? According to a *Glamour* magazine survey, the answer is no. Asked whether they would rather be (A) 5 feet 2 inches tall with a seven-inch penis or (B) 6 feet 2 inches tall with a three-inch penis, 62 percent of the male respondents picked A and only 36 percent picked B.

Of Feet and Fetishes

There are no absolutes in the research regarding the connection of the penis to women's shoes and feet, no final word as to what it all means, but as more women wander into X-rated video stores to get a glimpse of the naked penis, they are also buying more high-heeled shoes; men too have returned to their fascination with women's feet and shoes.

Here is a report from a journalist on returning from a recent fashion show in New York's Bryant Park:

> [The models] were mounted in ... dominatrixy ankle-high boots and belted stiletto sandals and spike-heeled, black patent-leather witch slippers—shoes that would be at home in any fetish boutique. There was envy and drama and beauty and death in the air, and it was not coming from the sea of telephoto lenses or from ... the orders being placed. ... It was not coming from the clothes, either. It was coming from the shoes, the true instruments of transcendence.

Nothing is by chance in the world of fashion; the return to the stiletto, simultaneous with men's padded underwear and penile implants, suggests this get-together is no coincidence. The flirtatious connection between penis, shoe, and vagina amuses and informs, so redolent are all three of fairy-tale connection.

"A tiny receptacle into which some part of the body can slip and fit tightly can be seen as a symbol of the vagina," Bettelheim wrote in his reference to Cinderella and her slipper. "Something that is brittle and must not be stretched because it would break reminds us of the hymen; and something that is easily lost at the end of a ball when one's lover tries to keep his hold on his beloved seems an appropriate image for virginity. ... Every child knows that marriage is connected with sex ... and it is quite clear that Cinderella is a virginal bride. ...

"Since for over two thousand years ... in much loved stories the female slipper has been accepted as a fairy-tale solution to the problem of finding the right bride, there must be good reasons for it. The difficulty in analyzing the unconscious meaning of the slipper as a symbol

462 / NANCY FRIDAY

for the vagina is that although both males and females respond to this symbolic meaning, they do not do so in the same ways."

I rather like the vagueness of the penis/shoe connection, the not knowing, for unlike other provable facts of sexuality, here is one that none of us has escaped or understood, the eye mysteriously drawn to women's feet and shoes. So rich is the history of the subject that I might have hung this entire book on its insoluble mystery, for the foot/shoe thing is integral to sexual beauty.

But let us start with Freud, who said that in dreams the shoe or slipper represents female genitalia, and that while the pungent aroma of the foot may be distasteful in later life, in childhood the strong smell is fascinating. There we all were once upon a time, at her considerable feet, crawling at the base of the center of our universe, Mother. On these bare or shod platforms she approached or left us, bringing or taking away the source of life. When we were very little and they were considerable, their proximity allowed for close inspection. We were imprinted.

I would imagine that the foot/genital connection goes back to the beginning of time. Before there were slippers there were feet, meaning, I suppose, that the symbol of the shoe is once removed. Symbol upon symbol leaves the mind a lot of room in which to fantasize. Barbara Stanwyck, in the movie *The Lady Eve*, entraps Henry Fonda on board a cruise ship by tripping him and, in the process, breaking the heel of her shoe. She leads him seductively to her cabin, wherein there is a trunkful of shoes.

"See anything you like?" she purrs, allowing him to choose. She dangles her naked foot before him as he sweats, he gulps, he slips the shoe on her foot and buckles the ankle strap, overcome. He's been up the Amazon for two years, he explains, studying snakes: "My life is snakes." Now his life is hers, for in slipping the shoe on her naked foot, as the Prince did with Cinderella, in our voyeuristic minds, his penis fits her vagina, perfectly. They are mated.

"Originally, the feet were just like the hands," says Helen Fisher, "so they have tremendous nerve endings in the brain. Much of the brain is taken up with just receiving sensory impulses from the feet and the hands. You receive powerful stimuli from doing things with the feet. Evolutionarily speaking, feet are a very sensuous part of the body. There is a tremendous response in the brain if you suck somebody's feet."

In his book *The Sex Life of the Foot and Shoe*, W. A. Rossi writes that foot and shoe eroticism comes from this sensitivity as well as from the phallic symbolism of the foot, the erotic appeal of which inspired the decoration of the foot. As *Esquire* reported it: "Of all fetish objects, sexy shoes are among the oldest and probably the most common. . . . They taper the toes. They arch the instep. They lift the calves. They tilt the fanny and bow the back and oil the hips and sashay the gait. Their leathery, animal scents and textures evoke the jungle blood sports braided in our genes. They make the foot look shorter and more precious and yet add the formidableness of extra height and often a sort of stiletto menace. A sexy shoe is a masterpiece of concealment and disclosure and so defines the dynamic of lust itself."

We think of men as focused on women's feet when, in fact, there was a time when men were equally focused on their own. Even before clothing lost its formless shape in the early fourteenth century and began to suggest the human form beneath, there was among men a highly suggestive use of the shoe as a tantalizing hint at what lay beneath all that shapeless cloth.

"The emphasis on parts of the body associated with sexuality began in the late eleventh century, with the adoption of elongated, pointed shoe styles," writes Lois Banner. "It spread to the fourteenth century, when short jackets, long legs, and the exposure of the shape of the genitals became the vogue. By the late fifteenth century the preferred body type for men became more massive, while broad and blunted shoes replaced the long pointed ones. The codpiece, a sheath which enclosed the penis, was also developed in this time period."

For several centuries men's elongated shoes were the erotic symbols, a titillating hint of the mystery that lay beneath their clothing. These artistically pointed shoes were called *poulaines* and were probably invented by the Norman knights to better fit in their stirrups (as depicted in tapestries of the Norman Conquest). Another reason the long shoes were probably popular, says Banner, is because of perceptions of aristocratic feet as long and slender and peasant feet as broad and clumsy.

"European folk belief categorized feet, like noses, as related to the penis, the size of one reflective of the size of the other," writes Banner. "Thus at one point the fashion was that the extensions of the *poulaines* should be filled with sawdust so that they would stand upright. And it was not unknown that some wearers of these shoes would shape and color the extension to resemble a penis."

Imagine! Men walked around "flashing" images of their privates painted on the tops of their falsely elongated shoes. What springs to my mind are today's padded, push-up bras, breast augmentations, men's penile implants as well as men's padded underwear. Everything old is new again. Eventually, in 1367, Charles V of France outlawed the wearing of penis-shaped *poulaines*.

Because fact flies faster than fiction as regards feet and sex these days, let me add that on my recent trip to Los Angeles—when I was halfway through this chapter—I was presented with a pair of "penis shoes." On entering my favorite store in Los Angeles, Maxfield's, the manager came forward to show me a pair of men's shoes designed by Yohji Yamamoto, and there they were, nestled in what looked like, smelled like, a standard shoe box. Ah, but these were no ordinary shoes! I urged my husband to slip them on. "Wow!" he exclaimed. "They fit!" Cinderella. And so we bought them, beautifully constructed men's black shoes, except for the fleshy pink penis painted on each, attended on either side by a large fuzzy black ball, each one as big as a golf ball.

This ageless puzzle of feet and shoes, vaginas and penises turns up nowadays in news stories as well as on the fashion pages. One day Marla Maples's public relations man is arrested for, over the years, stealing her shoes. "I wondered where those shoes had gone," mused Ms. Maples (wife of Donald Trump).

In another newspaper article, a man offers a seventeen-year-old one hundred and fifty dollars if she would go to a hotel room with him and let him kiss her bare feet. The police duly arrest a happily married forty-four-year-old assistant district attorney. "He said he had a fetish," the woman adds, "and that he wanted me to go to a hotel with him, put on a skirt and a pair of pumps so he could worship me while he satisfied himself. . . . He told me he could not wait to see those 'beautiful feet' of mine. He has this thing about toes, I think."

Is there indeed a heightened foot and shoe eroticism in the land, or have these difficult days of changing sex roles made us all more aware of what was always there, alerting reporters' and editors' eyes to fasten on a foot and shoe event that might have slipped right past them twenty years ago? My own opinion is that the seismic shifts in reaction to feminism, technology, and reproductive biology have rearoused our interest in sexual symbolism.

For instance, just thinking about Bettelheim's image of Cinderella's tiny slipper as a virginal vagina, meaning a nice, snug fit for the penis of a prospective bridegroom, I am reminded that women today don't look or act like Cinderella, being neither in economic need of a prince, nor virginal, nor do women even require a Prince's penis, given the local sperm bank. When you also factor in the ever earlier onset of menstruation, meaning that adolescent girls are larger of body, it should be noted that they also walk on larger feet.

The American Orthopaedic Foot and Ankle Society estimates that women's feet are on average a size 8 wide today. But the best-selling women's shoe size is 7½ medium, suggesting that the average woman with a size 8 wide is hobbling around in shoes that are both too short and too narrow. In fact, that's just what a 1991 study put out by the AOFAS reports: that 88 percent of those women surveyed were wearing shoes that were too small, and that 80 percent had foot problems. Do we women do this for the man's sake or for our own? Are we squeezing our feet into shoes that are too small so that men see our feet as dainty and therefore a snug match for their penises, or do we do it so that when we look down at our feet our unconscious is reassured that we are as womanly as Cinderella, just a helpless little creature, regardless of our high-paying jobs? Meanwhile, women's feet grow larger and larger, an estimated six million women today requiring a size 10 or larger shoe.

Surely we would work more profitably in shoes that fit; women account for 90 percent of the surgeries for common foot ailments in this nation, which cost us $3.5 billion for surgery and 15 million lost workdays. Add to this madness the return of the six-inch stiletto heel, which my friend Jane wears religiously; when she returns home from work, her calf muscles are so distended that she cannot stand barefoot and must fall from her shoes onto the bed, where she lies until the leg muscles relax and she can walk without pain. How reminiscent of Cinderella's ugly stepsisters, who tried to squeeze their feet into the glass slipper only to rub them until they were raw and bleeding. Cinderella's foot fit the slipper perfectly.

Sooner or later, the shoe, the vagina, and the penis are going to have to sit down together and have it out: What does it all mean? Sometimes a cigar is just a cigar, but how far will our technologically advanced world carry this unconscious pressure of fairy-tale wisdom that encourages working women to squeeze their feet into shoes that hurt? Now that high-heeled boots are back, is the pleasure women feel when they wear them equal to the discomfort? "In the dress code of sadomasochism, boots, of course, are very important as power symbols and very exciting to men," says psychiatrist Avodah Offit. "The current passion for boots seems to me distinctly masculine in derivation. Women wearing [them] tend to imitate or adopt the strength and dominance of men."

Feet tend to swell even more in boots than in shoes, meaning that the feel of sexual power must be very sweet indeed. Men don't force us to buy these objects that restrict our movements, deform our feet, and cripple our backs. We do it for the image in the mirror, the reflection of ourselves as hot and in charge, an extraordinarily satisfying goal that we can live with more happily than with a man; who needs him?

There is no parallel in women's sexual fantasies to those of men who take a woman's shoe to bed. Sex therapists and psychiatrists offer various explanations of foot fetishism. The least persuasive is, "The foot is the farthest from the heart, meaning the farthest from intimacy, which allows the man to have pure sex without entanglements." For me, there is a certain rightness to the early childhood experience of the shoe/foot being that part of mother that is familiarly close to the touch, sight, and smell of the tiny person crawling around her all-powerful feet on the kitchen floor. But let me quote Valerie Steele, who has written extensively and well on fetishism:

"Freud argued that 'The fetish is a substitute for the woman's (the mother's) penis that the little boy once believed in and ... does not want to give up ... for if a woman had been castrated, then his own possession of a penis was in danger.' The fetish represented an unconscious 'compromise' between the 'unwelcome perception' that the mother has no penis and the wish and earlier belief that she does. The ego defends itself by disavowing or repressing an unpleasant perception. 'Yes, in *his* mind the woman has got a penis ... but this penis is no longer the same.... Something else has taken its place.' The fetish thus serves to assuage his fear of castration, at the same time 'transfer[ring] the importance of the penis to another part of the female body' or to some article of clothing."

Steele continues: "The objects chosen as 'substitutes for the absent female phallus' were not necessarily those that appeared elsewhere as symbols of the penis; but they were perhaps related to 'the last moment in which the woman could still be regarded as phallic.' Thus, for example, 'pieces of underclothing, which are so often chosen as a fetish, crystallize the moment of undressing.' Fur or velvet was associated with the pubic hair that should have revealed a penis. The appeal of shoes is related to the association of the foot and penis: 'The foot represents a woman's penis, the absence of which is deeply felt.'"

When men get more deeply into the nursery and children grow up alongside father's heavy cordovans, their reassuring presence on the kitchen floor, their disappearance into the next room arousing alarm, will we all grow fonder of men's shoes and feet? We are used to pictures of little girls climbing into mother's high heels, but sometimes, so do little boys. "One day when I was maybe three or four, I was alone in my mother's bedroom and went into her closet," a captain of industry tells me. "I saw her shoes and was clumping around the room in her high heels when she walked in and gave me hell. She was so upset, I never did it again."

But some men put on women's shoes, dream of sex with a naked woman who is wearing only her Bass wedgies, or they take a woman's stiletto-heeled shoe to bed and masturbate. "The feet are symbols of both humiliation and power," says Offit. "The high heel is a weapon . . . and also a phallic symbol. And at the same time that it cripples a woman, it makes her seem powerful. In heels, the woman can be evilly subdued—she can't run very fast, she's off balance, her feet probably hurt—but she's also taller, wearing a spiked thing that could be driven into a man's body: It's called a stiletto, after all."

The absence of absolutism as regards this business of shoes and feet lends to it a quality of human frailty, our inability to *solve* the issue, which is exciting and ongoing. While fetishism may be an exclusively male phenomenon, as Kinsey said, women's inability to travel with fewer than ten pairs of shoes implicates us too, maybe not as fetishists, yet, but certainly as participants. Being attracted to shoes, it should be remembered, doesn't make one a fetishist; it is wanting the shoe instead of the human that makes one a fetishist.

"Of all forms of erotic symbolism the most frequent is that which idealizes the foot and the shoe," wrote Havelock Ellis. For instance, the "lotus" foot in Chinese pornography is prevalent: "When a Celestial takes into his hand a woman's foot, especially if it is very small, the effect upon him is precisely the same as is provoked in a European by the palpation of a young and firm bosom." Because the foot is so readily associated with sexual attraction, Ellis suggests that "some degree of foot-fetichism [is] a normal phenomenon." According to Freud, the foot/shoe preoccupation "only becomes pathological when the longing for the fetish . . . actually *takes the place* of the normal aim, and . . . becomes the *sole* sexual object."

Prostitute Norma Jean Almodovar offers a more pragmatic perspective: "You're not talking about having intercourse with foot fetishists. They want to fixate on the physical object while you're present. Basically their fantasies are about groveling on the floor, licking the heels of the shoe, which is on your foot, licking the toes of the shoe, maybe having you put the shoe on their genitals. You don't have to step on it hard, just so they can feel the shoe, the heel on their penis. After that, I take off the shoe and they go through the same routine with my bare or stockinged foot, my toes, after which they masturbate and come on my foot."

For more than nine centuries, curled toes have been a stylized symbol of erotic response in Japanese art. Learning this reminds me of a former lover who would cry out in midorgasm, "Oh, my God, my toes have gone into spasm!" His was a "normal" response, according to Kinsey, who wrote that during sex the toe and foot muscles can react this way.

"The popularly accepted idea of cultural quasi-fetishism," Steele points out, "involves the conflation of the distinctions between individual perversions (such as foot and shoe fetishism) and widespread erotic interest in, say, feet and shoes. Thus, many fashion historians argue that the long skirts of the nineteenth century contributed to the development of a cultural obsession with female feet, since concealment theoretically invested these appendages with greater erotic appeal. These historians then jump to the conclusion that this indicated that the incidence of foot and shoe fetishism was significantly higher in the nineteenth century than in earlier or later periods—an hypothesis that the available evidence does not necessarily support."

In Turgenev's *First Love*, an adolescent boy falls in love with a young woman who works on his father's estate: "I gazed at her . . . it seemed to me that I had known her for a long time, and that before her I had known nothing and had not lived. . . . She was wearing a dark rather worn dress with an apron. The tips of her shoes looked out from under her skirt. I could have knelt in adoration of those shoes."

There is nothing like the forbidden to excite fantasy; forbid a child to touch his or her genitals, and the forbidden becomes so loaded with emotion that the idea of breaking the rules, defying the all-powerful mother, becomes the erotic fantasy. The history of our erotic dreams lies in childhood, its roots entangled in naysaying, finger-wagging, promises of hell and damnation. Irresistible.

As today's women step eagerly back into their six-inch stiletto heels, the sex boutique Eve's Garden, in answer to popular demand, adds a new dildo to its fall line, which is wider, making it one and five-eighths inches, to be exact. Can men, with or without penile augmentations, measure up? We take their jobs, we satisfy ourselves sexually with plastic imitations of their penises, and we wear their suits. As we appropriate men's total ensemble, and Patriarchy's definition of masculinity blurs, men dip into our closets. Cross-dressing by heterosexual men has become a popular theme in films on the big screen; in real life, there are now annual conventions for cross-dressers and their wives. As for the raging popularity of drag queens, men like RuPaul, who favor outlandishly feminine female clothing, have become beloved icons. One can't help wondering how far men will carry their appropriation of women's looks. We underestimate men's historical inventiveness in the mirror.

The Codpiece

For instance, in 1367, when Charles V prohibited men from continuing to wear penis-shaped *poulaines*, the elongated shoes, men simply made the codpiece a fashion statement. "In other words," writes Banner, "one might argue that the sexualization of the foot was transferred to the more obvious sexual organ." Evolution. The codpiece, already popular in the gay world, may soon enjoy a broader revival, given Val Kilmer in *Batman Forever* and the look of Calvin Klein's fashion photos, presumably selling underwear. Who can avoid that tantalizing bulge, teasing the eye to explore?

What a fascinating mental picture, a world in which men walked about with their penises proudly emphasized, decorated, embellished in such ways that women's eyes—and other men's—were drawn to them, much as we can't help staring at women's furs, jewels, breasts, ass-clinging satin skirts, and bewitchingly heeled feet. What was it like for men in earlier days to compete with one another in the beauty of their individual codpieces? Did it feel good to be the center of attention? Not for ages have men enjoyed the feel of eyes actually focused on their person. Did it make men less voyeuristic, less abusive of women when they were able to share the limelight with us? The only modern version of the man-with-codpiece that comes to mind is the cowboy in his leather chaps, and there, between his thighs, bull's-eye: the crotch, the denim-covered "basket," unavoidable and unashamed.

Remember The Village People, the gay men's singing group from the seventies and their fondness for cowboys' chaps and sailors' suits? Ah, those tight white navy bell-bottoms, all over town when I was growing up, Charleston being a seaport. How unhesitatingly my youthful, preadolescent eye was pulled to the crotches walking toward me on the sidewalks between movie theater and home. My good friend Bob tells me that when he was in the navy, the first thing a guy did with his new whites was to get them tailored, tops and bottoms so tight that the body became a beacon, not only the "basket" but the deliciously rounded buttocks. Having just emerged from boot camp, the young sailor was aware that his body had never before been so well tuned, the stomach so flat, the muscles pumped; some sailors had their uniforms fitted so tightly that small zippers had to be sewn in around the waist.

The codpiece has its unforgettable place in history. Surely, as men's designers cast about for reinventions—fashion being a merry-go-round—the codpiece, with its variety of decorative appeals, will return; I would welcome it heartily, seeing in its erotic display some respite from cranky feminists' complaints of male voyeurism; let men strut and compete for the common eye.

Describing the grandeur and opulence of court life in the Renaissance, Ackerman writes that clothing, "did not conceal the body, but clung in just the right places to accentuate gender. One of the most curious, perhaps, was the codpiece, worn by European men between the fourteenth and sixteenth centuries. Somewhat like a tribal penis sheath or a jockstrap, its purpose was to protect the penis, but men exaggerated its size and shape—sometimes even decorating it with a gargoyle-like head—to draw attention to the penis and make it appear to be constantly large and erect."

During all this, writes Hollander, women stayed in pretty shapeless clothing as their men donned the new "perfectly fitted tights and tight-fitting doublets . . . laced together around the waist for smooth overall fit. . . . The separate hose were sewn together to become tights, and drawn up firmly to hide the underpants; and once legs showed all the way up, the codpiece was invented, and padded."

Whatever the origin of the codpiece, its ability to demand the eye, to arouse sexual feeling, can't be diminished. Banner suggests that the inspiration for the codpiece may have been to protect the penis during battle. "Yet one recent scholar has argued that the codpiece was in fact devised as a protective device to prevent the staining of expensive fabrics by the oily, mercury-based cream applied to the penis and used as a treatment for syphilis, suddenly epidemic in Europe in the 1490s." Banner concedes, however, that "it was also a sexualized garment, for it riveted attention to the male sexual organ. The conservative parson in *The Canterbury Tales* thundered against the short jacket's exposure of the shape of the genitals. In fourteenth-century mystery and miracle plays, devils as characters often wore large false penises."

Men gave their codpieces various shapes and forms, painted them inventively, all the better to catch the eye. "One might glance at an especially fashionable Elizabethan young man and discover an upturned, mightily erect leather codpiece with a gargoyle face staring back," writes Ackerman. "Somewhere underneath, a normal member was hanging with the homeboys. This is like being cowed by the big booming voice of the Wizard of Oz only to discover a modest-sized man with a megaphone hiding inside the wizard's costume."

Is Ackerman teasing men for cheating via their padded codpieces? What hides inside the Wonderbra? As often as not a little girl of a woman doesn't know whether she wants to have sex with a man or sleep with women; she puts on the sexual signal, as is her right, but when the man responds, she doesn't protect herself contraceptively. What began in the sixties as exciting exhibitionism, which we called freedom, has come to this, a fashion dead end, a sexual display with nothing inside, no sense of power or responsibility.

Lacking our blessing, men are reclaiming the mirror anyway. When Calvin Klein's Marky Mark underwear ads appeared on giant billboards across the country at the end of 1992, there wasn't a whisper from feminist headquarters. "Wearing only a pair of lycra boxer shorts that hugged his muscular thighs and bulged provocatively at the crotch, he stood laughing directly out at us," writes a male journalist. "An article of clothing that we have either emasculated or kept out of sight entirely has now broken out of its sartorial prison and emerged into public view as the object of nothing less than a mass cult, a collective act of fetishization."

Advertisements for "The New Men's Underwear" sound very

much like the hype for the Wonderbra: The exotic briefs and boxer shorts don't simply fit, protect, cover, and support, they "sculpt," "mold," "contour," "chisel," "transform," "embrace," "accentuate," and even, in the case of the form-fitting "Body Brief," ... "kiss your every contour."

The journalist quoted above continues his review of men's new undies thus: "Often needlessly complicated with laces, zippers, and snaps, flies are no longer simply convenient openings but full-fledged codpieces, distended pouches that protrude from the crotch of the brief."

I cheer men forward in their inventive sexual display as we women slowly but surely boost our earning power, requiring male providership less and less. Maybe men's stealing our thunder will incite women to abandon our foolish denials regarding how we compete with one another. Given the pitch of our infighting, the weight of the economic prizes, and the girlish denials we use to conceal what we do, we call our elimination of opponents, male and female, any word but what it really is: competition.

Will our new independence nudge women past the anti-voyeurism rules that have kept our eyes lowered for centuries? Imagine, women as voyeurs! That would be a first, liberty for both men and women. There is no joy in the parade if no one watches.

9

Changing the Double Standard of Aging

═══════

Adultery: Scarlet Letter or Red Cross?

In January 1980, when my house burned down, everything went up in smoke, including my former marriage. It has required the intervening years, in particular the writing of this book, for me to give that fire due credit for ending a chapter in my life I had outgrown years earlier, a fact I was unable to admit as a child might be unable to acknowledge reluctance to leave her parents' home.

Mine was certainly not a typical marriage, but it was a product of that time when sex, economics, beauty, and feminism were a fireball: It bore the seeds of the new deal between the sexes now being negotiated as well as the evolution of our double standard of aging. During that marriage I wrote my first books, and out of that writing came the beginning of self-knowledge. I had the good luck and timing to tackle the issues of women's sexual fantasies and the mother/daughter relationship during modern feminism's most energetic era. Back then, the air was drenched with intoxicating permission to say and think formerly inadmissible ideas.

Many of those doors have already shut again, but that first heart-felt permission of the sixties and seventies aroused my exhibitionistic heart, along with the slumbering intellect that had been put to bed in adolescence when The Nice Girl Rules demanded silence and passivity. Don't listen to the naysayers who would have you believe the seventies were the cause of today's ills; there were excesses, yes, but over-reach was inevitable in the struggle against the moral quicksand of McCarthyism and the bullyboy self-righteousness behind our involvement in Vietnam. Today's feminism may be a semantic jungle, but in the seventies, the proud word stood absolutely for women's freedom to think, speak, act, write. If you weren't there, you cannot appreciate the drama of learning to trust our opinions, use our voices, and the dawning realization that there were chapters of a woman's extended life waiting to be lived.

Writing would be my salvation, a passage through the walls of memory into the unconscious, where I had stored my best self. Permission to think of myself as an initiator reminded me of the girl I'd buried at the onset of adolescence, she who dared to think and do anything. The sexually exhibitionistic fashions of the seventies had meaning, spoke of identity, an experimental effort on our part to find out who we were, including our sexuality. They look foolish today because they are vacuous imitations, a style without content.

Back then, we were not Empty Packages. We had plans, we had a dream, as Martin Luther King Jr. said, and I do not quote him lightly, for the dream is gone. All we have now are the silly, derivative clothes, which we might well learn from. Remember what Anne Hollander says, that what we wear on our backs tells us where we are going even before we consciously know the destination.

Men and women stand side by side in the mirror, putting on each other's clothes, coming to terms with beauty power prompted by our shifting economics; in time, all these changes will decide the new meaning of femininity and masculinity. My sense of myself as a woman began to change when I became a writer, but, in fact, only my attitude and behavior had altered before the fire. The most important level of change, the unconscious, takes time; sometimes that is speeded up, as when your house burns down.

When all the physical traces of my past had turned to ashes, I questioned everything, including my marriage. It wasn't cognitive; others told me later that they thought I was having a nervous breakdown. In fact, I was sanely, intuitively, going back in time in search of myself. That marriage was the first obstacle, a hard nut to crack. I've said that I chose to marry my former husband because he never took his eyes off me, which is what I'd always wanted, not having had it as a baby. Ironically, when we met, I was at the height of sexual success, men waiting in line to dance with me, all my lifelong dreams-to-the-sound-of-romantic-music come true.

But life plays tricks, and when too many eyes focused on me in my sea-green Pucci dress, and offers of love reversed the rejections of adolescence, up from the unconscious swam infantile grandiosity, the monster nursery emotion that ascends to absolute power on the eve of puberty. I was terrified that the telephone in my apartment would never stop ringing, would bring me so many suitors that I would soar too high and become some grotesque, out-of-control Queen of the Yacht Club Regatta. Then, when all eyes were on me, I would be unable to handle the adoration and would spot my dress, humiliating myself.

And so I ran away from what I'd always wanted. I married my first husband, a handsome, intellectual writer from a loveless, lonely childhood with a neediness I sensed behind his cynical exterior. I seduced him, put fresh peaches in his morning champagne, and presented myself as totally independent, attaching no strings to the sex I offered. I thought I knew what men wanted and could do this act brilliantly, all jealous insecurities concealed. It was not a conscious plot, this seduction, more like the programmed movements of a wound-up toy. I was not in love with him when we married, not in that childlike, captive way I would be once I saw him as Mommy/Daddy.

Just before our marriage, a last-ditch healthy instinct propelled me to Rome, where I suppose I hoped that in the arms of safe Italian lovers, safe because they offered no risk, I might rethink the marriage and avoid it. But he wrote me there, and in that letter was a line the unconscious snatched, kissed, and pressed to its heart: "I will spend my life seeing you. Not watching you."

My God, what an offer! All my life I'd been looking for the golden beam between the eye of the Madonna and Child, that pre-Renaissance motif that the baby watchers would later call The Gaze.

Can you see why my former husband's promise was irresistible, coupled as it was with my own fear of grandiosity? His vow to spend his life "seeing" me, not "watching" me, was as warm and nourishing as mother's milk. And he would never wander. Not for me a man with a wandering eye, a man like my father. I knew this about my husband, that I filled his life as well as his eyes. "The way you look satisfies me," he said, words that put so many demons to sleep, though at the time I merely smiled, so impenetrable were my defenses. I'd not thought it through until this book, though I often wondered why I married him, why I didn't continue my erotic adventures. What did I consciously know of the terror of flying too high, soaring on success after years of envying beauty in others, of being invisible in a house of beautiful women?

The words "I love you" paled besides the promise of "The way you look satisfies me," meaning that he would look no further, would be blind to other women. After marriage I would test his eyes, would flirt with other men who sought me out, for the need to be seen and wanted was still there. Oddly, given the security he offered, my hunger for The Gaze grew. Still, his eye never did wander, and in time I took it in, the all-loving parental eye allowing me to be sexual with other men. Of course I stayed with him too long. I was getting everything I'd longed for and missed in the first years of life.

I slipped into the promise of his fidelity as trustingly as a child curls into mother's arms. My women friends were envious and flirted with him, but to no avail. I fed on his Gaze; fortified, I sat down to write. He treated me like his little wifey, and I looked up to him as the great intellectual who also took care of me, not financially as a Good Provider, but as the adoring mother whose gaze never left me. Except when I abandoned his sight to be with other, forbidden men who had nothing to do with smothering, mothering love.

It was I who had become the Good Provider, a role I enjoyed and was used to, having provided for myself since I'd left home (offers of money, I had noticed, always came with strings attached). Safe in my parent/husband's beam of adoration, and excited by good sex beyond the cocoon, I wrote. When checks arrived from publishers, I endorsed them and gave them to him. It was extremely satisfying, this arrangement, and if I had not eventually grown up, I might still be in it today. Is it really all that different from what men set up in traditional marriages, providing for a good wife who is happy working at home and who chooses not to know about his infidelities, given how well he provides, given that he loves her, which is what she wants more than sex?

My adultery is not something of which I am proud, but it was a product of the marriage; I went elsewhere for sex because there was nothing erotic between us. There was love, attachment, closeness, yes, but for great sex there must be two individuals, the exciting distance of separation for the sexual spark to jump and ignite. He and I were too symbiotically fused, mother and child, mom and dad, two peas in a pod. A part of me was blissfully happy at getting what I'd always wanted, but the more he held me at night as we watched television, the less of a candidate he was for sex. Why should I want to soil this blissful, childlike Doll's House with dirty sex?

We are not tolerant of adultery in women. By "we" I mean both men and women, though I believe no one despises the adulteress more than those women who have abandoned sex altogether. Nonetheless, the statistics on women's adultery climb, spurred by our new economics. There is a sense of entitlement that comes with financial independence; when we were beholden to men for the roofs over our heads, women thought twice before committing adultery. Most women never even considered it, nor were they approached by potential lovers, given that they had extinguished the sexual flame soon after the wedding, more so after motherhood.

The replication of their mothers' lives was often encouraged by the husband, who wanted to find on his return to his castle after a hard day in the immoral, dirty marketplace not a sex goddess but The Good Mother. Up she went onto the pedestal, an idealized re-creation of his own Madonna mother.

If women turned a blind eye to their husband's adultery, it was because the "other woman" provided him with something his wife no longer enjoyed. Those wives who "allowed" their husbands to satisfy their sexual appetites elsewhere often won even greater love from their men; these marriages not only endured but often flourished under the double standard. Though the roles were reversed in my own marriage, I still wanted the world to perceive my husband as the big, powerful paterfamilias; if friends were aware of my secret life, they never let on. Nor did I ever boast of my providership.

"Why don't you enjoy your success more?" friends from my single years would ask. But if I didn't demur, didn't allow him to strut, the golden beam he focused onto me would be weakened. I wanted him as powerful as the maternal mother I'd never had. That he, in turn, "allowed" me my sexual excursions and never gave me reason to believe he knew of them made him all the more essential.

Being a Good Provider had everything in the world to do with my adultery. It wasn't consciously thought through, but surely I knew, as every adulterous man knows, that if the worst happened and I was found out, I would not starve. Nonetheless, I chose a lover carefully. When I returned home and found my husband waiting, smiling, loving, I adored him all the more.

Sometimes he did not greet me with adoration but was instead locked in his room drinking. He was a heavy drinker when we met, but what did I or anyone else know about heavy drinking back then? In those days it seemed that everyone drank. I assumed that on any day he chose, he could stop. Because he loved me, he would stop. But he didn't. I needed the illusion that everything was perfect in our marriage. He was my husband and my mother; I felt I literally couldn't live without him. When he would retreat into his room, drinking by himself, I would weep inconsolably. Eventually he did stop drinking, but even then he often stayed in his room for days at a time. Still, I did pay the rent and, yes, I did play the adulteress.

I pressed my royalty checks into his hand. Please, play the Big Banker, my gesture said, for I am too small and naive to deal with money. When eventually I became the breadwinner, I grew smaller and smaller within the marriage and elevated him to Proustian proportions, as the artist of "real" literature while I scribbled what he called "your little books that keep us alive." Ah, my, the deals we make.

Perhaps you see why I have come to feel some black gratitude for that blaze that burned up everything. "When you have a fire like yours," a psychiatrist friend said to me, "you often lose your memory." I regained mine. I needed that apocalypse that destroyed the past, every shred of it, to make me start over. "Enough playing little girl!" said the ashes swimming in the puddles of water left by the firemen's hoses. "Get to work, woman, put your life in order!" Sitting here today, in a marriage so different from the first, I fear it might never have happened without that need to rebuild.

After the fire, we moved into a hotel while I took charge of the cleanup, the removal of charred furniture, my mother's wedding china, hundreds of sodden books, old manuscripts, and my grandmother's paintings. Contractors, architects, and oh, God, yes, the insurance people filled my days along with my editor, with whom I was planning a promotion tour for my new book. I remember addressing the sales force, whipping up enthusiasm, and the rank smell of smoke and condensation from the dress I was wearing, an old Zoran I'd rescued. A few mornings later I got out of bed and fell to the floor; it had to do with my inner ear, my center of balance. "Try not to be emotional," the doctor said.

Unemotionally, I set a high price for my next book; we needed the money. (Who takes out enough insurance to cover the loss of everything? "It's the worst fire I've ever seen in an apartment," the insurance agent told me, adding that she shows the postfire photos to prospective clients.) But more than anything, a part of me hoped that my publisher wouldn't meet my price. I was very tired. They met the price, which numbed me. The prospect of writing a book about jealousy and envy would, in the best of times, have left me exhilarated, but terrified. These were not the best of times.

I went into high gear like a veteran, revved up by the reemergence of survival talents I'd once owned, long before I'd made myself into a caricature of a child wife stealing sexual solace in the arms of forbidden men. Once upon a time, before adolescence, I'd been all of a piece, the bravest, most dependable girl in town. I needed those tools now, an arsenal of optimism, the emotional equipment to survive. Scientists say we have two memory systems, one for ordinary information and one for emotionally charged information. Maybe the emotional memory system evolved for its survival value, making sure animals remembered the events and circumstances most threatening to them. Mine was certainly a case of fight or flight.

Here is what I remembered when my home burned down: When I was a little girl, I'd made myself into a scholar, an athlete, a singer, a dancer, a wall walker who would take any dare, lead any group, confront the coldest adults and extract whatever love was in them. Now that the fire had eaten up everything and the cupboard was bare, I called on that girl. I began the two-month promotion tour of my just published book, wrote page one of the new book, supervised the rebuilding of my house, signed a two-year contract with NBC, and asked my husband to live in Key West, apart from me.

Susan Cheever wrote that when women work outside the home, a problem for their men can be that when "women are operating in a rational situation professionally . . . that may make them question an irrational situation at home." In a sense, it wasn't his fault; he was still the same person. I was the one who had changed.

I went to no pains to hide my next affair. I didn't flaunt it or deny it, but still, I suppose I expected that sooner or later my husband would have to respond. The man who became my lover was someone I'd admired for months, whose beauty and seriousness about his work had filled my fantasies since he'd begun the carpentry on my new apartment. A carpenter, yes, the top of the list of many women's favorite fantasy lovers. Unplanned, as unexpected for me as it was for him, it simply happened, as sex so often did in those years. I suppose I was acting like a man who, feeling entitled because of good work just accomplished, turns and sees a beautiful woman.

Just returned from a week of cross-country book promotion, I had been talking with the architect, who'd stepped out of the room to make a phone call. I looked up, and there he was, my carpenter, so beautiful, so serious, and I walked across the room, put my arms around him, and kissed him. It was a moment of gratitude, admiration, and, yes, entitlement.

He accompanied me on weekends for the rest of the tour. On our flights to San Francisco, Chicago, and Los Angeles, I thought, watching my lover's pleasure, This is what men feel when they take a woman on a wonderful trip, when they have the power to give a gift and share the riches. This is how it feels to be the pleasure giver.

One Sunday we drove to Cape Cod and lay on the beach listening to the romantic music of the summer of 1980: "She's Out of My Life," "Lost in Love," "You're the Biggest Part of Me." Oh, yes, I remember the music. I remember it more than anything, for it infused that love affair with all the romance of my adolescent summers. But there was an essential difference: This time around, I was the initiator, not drifting mindlessly into a sexual romance, but giving as much pleasure as I took.

It was precarious, nonetheless, for he was younger than I, and his youth, along with the romantic music, pulled me back into the fantasy world of adolescence from which I would have to extricate myself, mindful that I paid his wages, that there must be envy on his part, and that it was my responsibility to be sure we both came out of this idyll intact. What a sinkhole this adolescent business was, this sighing and dying, the eager giving over of the self!

I thought of where the passion for romantic music had begun, the nine-year-old girl on the bicycle pedaling to school, the love ballads sung at the top of my lungs when I didn't know what the lyrics meant, only that they echoed the lonely, unloved feelings inside. I couldn't allow myself to surrender to this man in whose arms I wanted to stay one minute, and the next, to open yet another door for him into a world he'd never entered. Until the fire, until the carpenter, I'd not thought it through, that I might have taken into adolescence both the love of romance and the thrill of the initiative. I might have asked Malcolm to dance. That summer with the carpenter, I was like a ghost returning to the place where I'd died, adolescence.

I didn't choose the carpenter for his youth, but for the unique combination of a look, a sweetness, and an almost abstract devotion to work. A man's wealth and power had never swayed me, never has, never will. We women who are good providers, and our numbers grow by the hour, we don't need an old, hoary millionaire. If I was going to risk rejection, it would be for someone I desired, someone whose look went with the music. Also, I had felt his eyes on me and knew that there would be no rejection.

Life had taught me that women have alternative powers to youthful beauty, that we have more to offer than our wombs, and that our looks last longer than our mothers' generation's had. Youth's monopoly on beauty was drummed into us by a society that wanted to keep women "in our place," meaning keep our value confined to the childbearing years between adolescence and menopause. Well, "our place" was changing; we were going everywhere, doing everything, and our excellence at what we did was altering how we felt about ourselves and how others saw us. I knew that when a man looks at a successful, satisfied woman, he may notice her age, but he feels her energy—life— and he wants some of it for himself, just as women traditionally wanted the economic power men offered.

If only women believed in the extended appeal of our looks and accomplishments, as many men do. Young men, grown up in this feminist age, are especially vulnerable to the awesome spectacle of a woman who excites admiration for her whole self, meaning professional as well as sexual. It is we women more than anyone who prolong this patriarchal view of ourselves as "over the hill." We may not be as wealthy as the little, bald tycoons, but we are rich enough to share in that same allure, but only if we wear our power as they do.

Eventually, the carpenter and I parted, but I have never lost sight of what I discovered that summer. Had the planets not aligned, the fire leaving my house bare, my professional life suddenly on an economic level I'd never before enjoyed, I might have continued living as a girl in a doll's house instead of building a grown woman's new home. Though what I am telling is not a "nice" story in the sense that nice girls don't focus on money as a motivating force, I can assure you that economic recognition pushed me through the glass mirror in which I had been reflected as the wife/child of a man without whom I thought I could not live.

I am not setting up my life as exemplary during the six years between the fire and my divorce from my ex-husband; but I did finish that book on jealousy, paid my own way, as well as provided for my ex-husband. The book completed, I filed for divorce. What rankled was the animosity of former friends, both male and female. "You already have a perfectly good husband," a man scolded on spying me in a restaurant with another man prior to the divorce; that this finger-wagging fellow was himself a well-known philanderer didn't lessen my spontaneous blush of shame. I was furious at myself for reacting like a bad girl. But that is how deep The Nice Girl Rules run. Until enough of us make our own decisions regarding sex and beauty and stand by them as we enter The Third Act of our lives, we will be dictated by the rules of sameness that govern women's world: "No one woman must have any more than any other."

"With words, with nonverbal acuity, with networking and negotiating skills—and also with unleashed testosterone—women will probably become increasingly visible in modern national and international business life," wrote anthropologist Helen Fisher. To which I would add, we will become "increasingly visible" more quickly *if* we celebrate other women who carry beauty and sex, as well as professional skills, into later life as men always have. Our ancient envy of sex and beauty in others will make women hesitate and choose one or the other when they might have it all, as older men have.

I do not mean to minimize the power of the double standard of aging. What I would stress is that this opinion begins in women's world, where we see deterioration, meaning loss of value, before it has even begun. We see wrinkles on flesh that is still flawless and draw our imagined imperfections to others' attention. We are incurably catty about our contemporaries; Three Big Girls Can't Play Together in front of the mirror at the office any more than they could in the sandbox. Men watch us tear one another's beauty apart and learn to use it to their advantage. But to insist today that men only want to be with, live with, and sleep with young women is to say that men are impervious to the glamour of intelligence, sophistication, economic power, and, yes, sexual initiative in the hands of a woman who knows what she owns.

Feminism is far enough along for us to abandon the old marching line, "We will not be like men," and accept that there is much in men worthy of imitation. Insisting that women must learn everything from other women limits our lives. As more girl children are raised from the cradle in the arms of a man, we will see women's imitation of men's qualities found so irresistible as to have to be internalized for life's journey.

Becoming the Girl We Left Behind: To Hell with Other Women's Envy!

Women wait. The clock ticks, and we feel time doing us in. Eventually, the waiting look of anxiety, fear, anger becomes a mask. When we were little, we watched eyes hungrily fasten on beauty, hands reach out to her, invitations being whispered in her ear. We assume that in the eyes of others, our waiting look is filled with rejection; no one wants us. If we were more beautiful, we too would not wait.

I am always punctual, no, I am early, a lifelong habit that I am sure was born out of the fear that if I were late, others would not wait, would leave without me. To this day, I am dressed before my husband, waiting for him. Doesn't anything ever go away?

Fear of time passing and our aging begins so ridiculously young; that fact alone should tell us how irrational it is, how much we are still like our mothers, who waited and waited until one day their husbands didn't come home; or they saw an old woman in the mirror and asked, "Is this all there is?" Why, this waiting picture is totally out of sync with everything we have accomplished in the past twenty years. When we wanted an equal wage, we said, "Men get this amount, therefore I want the same." We don't yet have it, but we've moved the bottom line further in our favor than we've changed the tyranny of beauty, the ticking of the clock.

What good is money in the bank if we are less because we are older? What good is the house, the fur coat, the trip to Europe that we pay for if we think of ourselves in that house, that coat, on that trip as waiting for something to happen? Why don't we also say, "Men are seen, wanted, desired until they die, why not us?" and then pursue the answer as energetically as we pursued getting into the workplace?

The answer is that we are loath to challenge our own, meaning other women. Taking the initiative would get us closer to our goal, but in acting alone we step outside The Group. With more than one lover, with sexual beauty that refuses to die, and with our economic success that surpasses theirs, will they take us back? Would mother? The most enduring strength of the old-line feminists is their ability to foist onto men the responsibility for all that is wrong in women's lives. When a woman, by acting on her own, makes the other women aware that the serpent is within, she is a pariah.

"A woman must continually watch herself. She is almost continually accompanied by her own image of herself," writes art critic John Berger. "Whilst she is walking across a room or whilst she is weeping at the death of her father, she can scarcely avoid envisaging herself walking or weeping. From earliest childhood she has been taught and persuaded to survey herself continually. . . . And so she comes to consider the *surveyor* and the *surveyed* within her as the two constituent yet always distinct elements of her identity as a woman. . . . How she appears to others, and ultimately how she appears to men, is of crucial importance for what is normally thought of as the success of her life. Her own sense of being in herself is supplanted by a sense of being appreciated as herself by another."

Though Berger wrote these words almost twenty-five years ago, their description of the balloon over our heads in which we see ourselves perceived by others is chilling in its relevance to our lives today. It is the energy-sapping distraction of always having to watch ourselves that eats away at life, at what we might otherwise have done with that energy, that life.

Men don't live with this constant image of themselves as being perceived. Men weren't raised to wait but, instead, to take the initiative. That springboard that propels even the shy boy into action keeps his eye focused on a more distant goal than preoccupation with how others see him. In preadolescence, when he left mother's car to run into the birthday party, her hand didn't reach out for one last tug at his clothes, one last brush of his hair; he didn't grow up with that feeling that he was never finished, never good enough. When the dance of adolescence arrived, boys raced to win the beauty for the dance, to carry her off into the night before one of the less motivated had selected her.

What girls learn at the dance is what we learned in the nursery, that the first gaze, the first cookie, smile, and outstretched arms went to the fairest; the girl waits, the boy initiates. Prior to adolescence, we girls had also learned some powers of invention. But only the boy was allowed to carry leadership, speed, humor, and initiative into the sexual dance opposite girls. Behind the boy's privilege to initiate sexual contact is the full backing and encouragement of fellowship. Everything we once owned as girls is now embodied in males, and the gift we have to offer in exchange for his initiating a move toward us is our beauty.

We may want a boy with the wit and strength we once owned, but we must watch and wait as the lovelier girl's beauty pulls the boy of our dreams to her. The face that hides anger and impatience begins to incise these emotions into our youthful countenance. Small wonder that these are the looks we hate most in our reflection and those we want to have removed with surgery.

Men will tell you that women are oblivious to the etiquette of rejection. From where we have sat and waited for the prince since adolescence, when the wrong fellow calls, *we* are the ones who feel rejected. The right fellow can call another female, anyone he chooses, but we must continue to wait. Given the quashing of our bravery and speech, we are impatient with men who bungle their invitations, fumble through sexual advances like clods. *We* would have done it better; the ten- and eleven-year-old version of ourselves was a smooth operator, the very model of an initiator of intimacy. What a waste. We turned ourselves into Sleeping Beauty just when we had perfected the role of prince.

Here, now, at the age of wisdom, it is time to take life in hand and bend it, shape it, make it what we will. We are what? Thirty? Forty? Sixty? Whatever the age, no more waiting for the phone to ring, for a man to call, for things to happen. We have nothing to lose but fear. Don't we reach for a phone to make a business call? But when we invite a man to dinner and he rejects us, it cuts to the fiber of our womanliness. In trying to get more than the other girls, we have broken Women's Rules. In pursuing him instead of waiting, we have flashed the sexual card.

What made the passivity of adolescence bearable were the rules regulating sameness; we cannot remember them being spoken out loud, but they were duly taken in, being the same as mother's warning rules that we not outstrip her. Now our shame is in that image of ourselves being surveyed and having failed. Rejected by the man on the phone, we slump in our executive chair, chagrined, red-faced, punished: "We told you so," the surveyors chorus. We hate the man, but more than the loss of him, what festers is the failure in our effort to act instead of wait, to live beyond the inhibiting boundaries of women's world.

Referring to the catalyst that motivated us twenty-five years ago, Gloria Steinem recently said, "The sisterhood we had in mind was shared experience. . . . Shared themes became the source of political insight." To which I would add that the only shared themes are those allowed by modern feminism; it was difficult enough when we were younger to remain in step with everyone else, to not be too big or seem to have more, so as to avoid competition.

But when a middle-aged woman monitors her share of life so that she doesn't arouse envy by seeming bigger than her sisters, it is as if nothing has changed since adolescence, when "shared themes" ruled the lives of all the girls. The rewards of our New Middle Age—the first such age for us women of the twenty-first century—thus become "an anchor to memory." We have been here before. We are richer, have never looked better, feel more sexual and more sure of ourselves, but the anchor to memory reminds us that if we live life on a bigger stage than the other girls, we will be without friends.

This is precisely what I would encourage you to do: to live life on as big a stage as you choose, to take the risk, open the door, and enter the third act of life as fully as possible, knowing our fear is nothing more than the threat of excommunication from The Group of our adolescence, the fear of losing mother when we couldn't live without her. We are no longer needy in that life-and-death way we once were; more important, there are many women out there who will applaud us.

The theme of "shared experience" is comforting in some instances, but when felt as a negative pull that keeps us mired in the basic common denominator of sameness in women's world, it is a rope around the neck. Only we pioneers in this new last third of life that we have won can change what has always been felt about women aging. We are younger women's model of a new future.

The beauty in her twenties, whose cup is full to overflowing, knows well the feeling of envy and competition, but if she sees women twice her age and more who have moved past youthful beauty into something else, something exciting that only comes with age, she will see a woman's life as an adventure that extends beyond the childbearing years; and so will all the other young women around her, who will envy her less. To believe that women's beauty is neither limited to youth nor to the roles that traditional women lived requires models who are the living, breathing proof. It is no good just promising it in a vacuum, we must live it.

We, the newly middle-aged, are the fastest-growing major market, a culture of moneyed, educated men and women who expect to work, play, and have sex as long as possible. According to today's paper, "not only are Americans living longer, but they are developing less chronic disease and disability. . . . The number of diseases afflicting people over 65 declined by more than 11 percent over the last decade." Such a population has never before existed. Synthetic estrogen, testosterone, amazing beauty creams, revolutionary bodybuilding machinery, cosmetic surgery, none is going to disappear. In fact, they will flourish and multiply. There is already less of the moralistic condemnation of "looking good," even if it involves surgery, and there will be even less tomorrow. Healthy good looks' time has come, and they are not so much about eternal youth as about extended life.

No one will influence women's chance to live happily with those choices except other women, who have always ruled one another. If you feel the criticism of your women friends at your trying for a bigger life, then find a new group of women friends. Don't let the sight of someone older than you, who looks better than you, and whose life is more fulfilled than yours leave you grinding your teeth at night. Try to regain the admiration you felt prior to envy; take her as a model.

"There is no greater power in the world than the zest of a postmenopausal woman," said Margaret Mead. As more women discover this, I choose to think that we will refuse to suffer other women's critical intolerance. We will find resources in ourselves we'd forgotten we had, talents abandoned as young girls so as to fit the stereotype.

In a recent interview Dominique Aury, the eighty-six-year-old French journalist who wrote *The Story of O*, said that she had conceived the idea for the book as a love poem to a man she loved and whom she feared she was losing. She was almost fifty when she called on the memory of her erotic fantasies of early adolescence as inspiration for O. "What could I do?" said the eminent journalist and editor, "I couldn't paint, I couldn't write poetry. What could I do to make him sit up? . . . I wasn't young, I wasn't pretty, it was necessary to find other weapons. The physical side wasn't enough. The weapons, alas, were in the head." When she told her lover of her intentions, he replied, "I'm sure you can't do that sort of thing." "You think not?" she said. "Well, I can try."

The Story of O was first published in 1954 and has never been out of print. But what is most appropriate here is that the then middle-aged Aury discovered her magical ability to keep her lover by returning to the erotic fantasies of adolescence, "those slow musings just before falling asleep . . . in which the purest and wildest love always sanctioned, or rather always demanded, the most frightful surrender, in which childish images of chains and whips added to constraint the symbols of constraint."

One of the blessings of being part of that enormous wave of women moving past age fifty today is that we are more authoritative, assertive, and self-assured than any generation of menopausal women before us. And we have more economic power. There are more than 40 million of us, and that number of better-educated, better-informed, economically powerful women grows steadily.

What did we leave back there on the shores of adolescence? As yet, we had little idea of what mature life held for us, but we had more tools than we would ever have again, and they are still there. Today, whether it is a lover we want to keep, or a piece of work we dream of accomplishing if only we had the nerve, we might find our best resources where we left them years ago.

When I was ten and fast becoming more prince than passive princess, my beanstalk was the towering tree outside my bedroom window, my competitive excellence at school was my duel, my ogre's cave the freight trains down by the waterfront that I entered, trembling, to prove my bravery. These may have been male roles, but they fit me, inspired by the fairy tales read to me a few years previous from that big blue book with its raised lettering—the same book that had once been read to my mother. I was my best self then, the girl of my tenth year.

"The passionate, idealistic, energetic young individual who existed before menstruation can come on earth again if we let her," wrote Germaine Greer in *The Change*, her book on menopause. "We might develop better strategies for the management of the difficult transition if we think of what we are doing not as denial of the change or postponement of the change, but as acceleration of the change, the change back into the self you were before you became a tool of your sexual and reproductive destiny. You were strong then, and well, and happy, until adolescence turned you into something more problematical, and you shall be well and strong and happy again."

Until now, society dumped its vitriol and scorn on older women, the woman living alone, the old maid, the witch, she with spotted hands and lines incised on her upper lip. All the resentment of women's power that goes back to the nursery found an ugly repository in the hag, who recognized well why she was singled out, having felt it herself for older women when she was younger. And so it became a self-fulfilling prophecy, not just men's punishment of women but ours too, we who shortened our own lives by not applauding those of our sex who tried to climb higher, reach for more.

From the beginning of life, nothing arouses competition among females as does beauty, and nothing is more forbidden than open rivalry over it. How long will it take for women to accept what men must, that competitive feelings just happen and that there are rules to make rivalry safe, even pleasurable? I hammer away at rivalry and competition because they are beauty's constant companions. If women are going to carry beauty into middle and older age, though it is late to learn how to compete safely, it must be practiced nonetheless.

Today the other woman may have professional success as well as beauty; with no practice in taking her as a model to imitate, we fall victim to our usual self-destructive handling of envy; when we race to share our venom with other women, telephoning, whispering, conspiring to bring her down, we destroy someone who was taking the beachhead for us. Look at the popular shows on television where young, beautiful career women destroy each other. It is a popular plot device because it appeals so mightily to viewers who find more consolation than disdain in the conspiratorial smiles and wiles that eventually destroy the envied one; though I should add that today women viewers are just as gleeful if the envied one turns into a bitch from hell. This too is satisfying. Models of healthy competition, alas, are at a premium.

The sad truth is that women can't sleep quietly with the notion that other women are out there enjoying benefits that they, the envious, do not have. We knock off our best role models, the heroines of our age. Instead of their exciting images giving us a leg up the ladder, we punish them, give them "the treatment" just as we did in school.

When *Marie Claire* published an article on such successful notables as Barbra Streisand, Mary Matalin, Linda Bloodworth-Thomason, Linda Wachner, and Leslie Abramson, the piece was titled "Ballbusters, Success Secrets of Six Pushy Women." The editors and journalists alike seemed unsure as to whether to portray these wealthy, powerful, highly visible women as heroines or as victims of their own rapacious greed.

Of Streisand they say, "Whether based on sexism, jealousy, or the truth, her reputation casts her as domineering and self-absorbed." Of Wachner, president of Warnaco Group (read Wonderbra), they quote her chiding her male executives, "'You're eunuchs!' she screamed. 'How can your wives stand you? You've got nothing between your legs!'" and later, "'I would really love a child, I wouldn't adopt one, I could adopt a husband, and he could have a child.'" They quote Matalin: "I don't really like, in my work life or my play life, people who aren't aggressive and assertive,'" and of Linda Bloodworth-Thomason, writer/producer of *Designing Women*, they say, "She claimed to be surprised and delighted to be thought of as a tough woman. . . . 'Actually I'm thrilled.'"

It is not as though we have a multitude of women as successful as these, yet the chance to demean them was obviously irresistible. The bitchiness in the delivery of these profiles is palpable. Who would want to emulate such dragons? By all means include their reputations for being rude and overbearing, but put them in perspective opposite their achievements. To get where they are, they had to fend off something worse than Big Bad Men, namely, envious and resentful other women. Young women need to see themselves in living, breathing women with whose success they can identify; that opportunity is deftly eliminated.

I'm sick of women journalists ripping apart Streisand, Jane Fonda, and Hillary Rodham Clinton because of what they wear or choose to have done to their bodies. Look at the whole package, everything they have accomplished, instead of searching out Hillary's ill-fated inaugural suit or Streisand's supposed swelled head for daring to speak at Harvard's Kennedy Center, where only important men pontificate.

A few nights ago they replayed the 1994 Streisand special on television and for the first time I saw the opening in Los Angeles, the crowd's thundering adulation, and when she came onstage and sang "It Feels as If We Never Were Apart," the electricity that went through that auditorium reached out and included me. Several years ago her manager, Marty Erlichman, reminisced about Streisand's early days in New York when she couldn't get a gig, when nobody wanted "that voice." Because she had no money and no place to sleep, she carried a folding bed with her; one person or another would offer her an empty studio or rehearsal hall in which to sleep. More and more it seems to me that "we never are apart" from those days in the sixties when I first heard her, when I was still "waiting for something to happen."

Thirty years later, a woman's magazine cites her for being a "ball-buster," which she may be, but oh, my God, all the other things she is, a whole lifetime that brings people thundering to their feet in appreciation for having given us a living talisman of our own lives in the form of this incredible woman.

If women don't treat our heroines as we have treated our heroes, emulating the good, shrugging off the bad, their bravery and goodness will not live on in us. We will never have the heroic female models we so desperately need. Enviously, resentfully, we disparage the whole person, citing their dark side as the reason when, indeed, what we can't stand about them is their enormous success.

We would rather take to lunch the woman who has been jilted by her husband than celebrate she who manages to juggle a brilliant career and a sensual adventure simultaneously. We may not want the latter's life, but her daring says that she has taken a more powerful step against The Old Deal than have The Matriarchal Sisters.

Is it surprising that few successful women allow themselves to believe in what they have accomplished? They smell other women's envy; they fear that other women will hate them for their success, and so they play it down just as they did when they were adolescents. They continue to work hard, but do not reward themselves for fear of arousing envy. Small wonder we have so few admirable older women to emulate, women who have coupled success at their chosen work with beauty and a vibrant sexuality.

Men can't keep us from assuming the privileges that we have won. Only other women's power over us can deter us from becoming big, bigger than they. One of the privileges of growing older is freedom to say and do and look precisely as we feel. We say that Patriarchy limited our lives, that once youthful beauty was gone, Bad Men relegated us to the ash pile. That so many accomplished women today still say that they feel invisible cannot be blamed on men.

We look at ourselves in our smart clothes, sitting in our offices, people respecting our achievements, and we assume that we are independent. Why then do we wither when women's eyes narrow in critical appraisal, their mean lips witchily conspiring to bring us down, or so we fear? Why can we not brush them off, turn back to our work and laugh at their envy? If we were emotionally independent, this is precisely what we would do. It may feel demeaning to a fifty-year-old woman to be told that she is still too tied to mother/other women in a way that should have been outgrown in the first years of life. But the vast majority of us never did.

We practice separation all our lives; ideally it is completed in the nursery, but if that opportunity was lost then, or lost in adolescence or when we married and set up a symbiotic union with our husband, it is still not too late. If we don't do it now, whatever our age, other women's censure of our still trying to be beautiful and sexual will undermine our taking pleasure in whatever success we achieve. In their eyes or in our own inner eye, we will question our judgment in buying the eye-catching suit; we shouldn't have had the surgical tuck, shouldn't be dating more than one man, or a younger man, any man, not if the other girls don't.

Whether we choose to pursue The Hungry Eye "out there" past forty, or give ourselves instead to the rewards of invisibility, we have a gift our grandparents didn't. In 1995, Americans over fifty represented nearly a quarter of the population, and by the year 2000 there will be more than 75 million of them; many women will live to be eighty, as opposed to forty-seven, the average life span a century ago. By sheer numbers, we will have invented this New Middle Age, and given our energy and independence, we will have the opportunity to recapture whatever we surrendered to fit the stereotype of adolescence.

We have less to lose when we are older. With children grown, we no longer have to play the part of The Good Mother; we can be bad, meaning sexual, meaning laughing out loud, wearing whatever we choose. Why diet, work out at the gym three days a week, and not show off that body?

It is other women who see the witch all women fear becoming, the over-the-top spectacle we fear we were last night when we had a wonderful time, though this morning we worry that we drank too much, danced too late, and made fools of ourselves. Maybe we were too sexually bewitching, that crime witches were burned for. When other women go too far and are sexually witchy, we throw them out of the club, which is a way of burning them.

"Women have been burnt as witches simply because they were beautiful," de Beauvoir wrote, and on some level we understand, having "burned" a few of our friends in the past and restricted our own lives sexually out of fear of our being burned. We never forget the men we didn't fuck, the ones we desired more than any others but ran from out of fear . . . of what? Fear of the censure of mother/other women; obligingly, we keep our lives small so that they will still love us.

Cosmetic companies make billions of dollars on the unseparated woman's fear of becoming the Bad Mother of nursery days. Especially in these later years when mother is old or has died, there is the unconscious desire to keep her alive in ourselves, especially to keep alive The Witch, the scolding, antisex mommy whom we feel guilty for hating. When we awake in the morning from our dream sleep in which she rode around on a broom, we stumble to the mirror to see what havoc was done while we slept.

That cream we religiously put on our face before going to bed used to be called Vanishing Cream; we say we put it on to forestall wrinkles, but the unconscious knows we apply it as a magic ritual against nightmares of the Giantess whom we are becoming. You and I are aging better than our mothers, not because the creams have improved; we look better longer because the kind of lives we lead drum into us the message of our independence.

It is one thing to forsake the mirror—"Thank God, that's through, now I can relax and let my hair go gray!"—but happiness in the decision demands we not live with the *grrrr* of envy when friends continue to parade. We are used to beauty envy among twenty-year-olds, but we are the first generation to extend beauty into middle age. Until now, unless one was a film star or very, very wealthy, there was an unspoken agreement among women of "a certain age" that the beauty contest was over. Great self-righteousness was attached to wearing comfortable shoes and no makeup. Here we are, advancing beauty into a new time period, and we are no more practiced in handling competition with other women than we were in adolescence.

Age is inevitable, but death grows more distant as our longevity grows. We are going to have a lot of postmenopausal time, which could be the best in life if we begin to search out admirable women to emulate. Toss aside what does not appeal. Spit in the eye of envy if these women have more than you; heroines are meant to have more. And watch yourself the next time you see an "older woman" wearing something you think is too young for her, including the man on her arm. She is your future.

Think of her as getting out the kinks so that you will have a better time when you are she. Here you are, only twenty-nine, and you already see your dear mother's witchy anxiety in your face, and you hear her nagging voice when you talk to your children. Well, the way life too often works is we become not the mother we loved, which would be an easy tribute, but the mother we hated.

"The overwhelming evidence in research studies and in my own interviews strongly indicates that, in vital age, women as well as men *become more and more themselves*," writes Betty Friedan in her book on aging, which I admire for its optimism. When I read this I thought, Yes, since my mid-forties I've become keenly aware of myself as I was prior to adolescence. "Can age itself be . . . an adventure?" Friedan asks. "We can set about risking, as we have never been able to before, new adventures, living our own age . . . this third age we're entering now, that lovely, liberating *lightness* may be a serious sign—a signpost for survival, a signpost of evolution."

I like that: evolution.

Conquering Fear of Sex

How ironic that we should gain economic power before having conquered our fear of sex. That we didn't put sex at the top of the list alongside economic parity twenty years ago speaks of our fear at facing female power, our own and other women's. To do so would have demanded that we question our ambivalence, the argument within. And we would have had to question our envy of other women's sexual beauty, which arouses far more rancor than their bettering us economically.

We would rather submit to becoming the witch, the crone with crepey skin, straggly gray hair, and yellow teeth, she who personified evil in our nursery days, where our fear of sex began. It was there in mother's arms that we first learned that our sexual parts stood in opposition to her love; touching ourselves turned our beautiful good mother into an angry, ugly harpy.

Terrified of losing her, we split mother in half, keeping The Good

Mommy away from The Bad Mother. As Bettelheim says, splitting "is not only a means of preserving an integral all-good mother when the real mother is not all-good, but it also permits anger at this bad 'step-mother' without endangering the goodwill of the true mother, who is viewed as a different person." It is our job, as we grow up, to fuse the good and bad mother, in her and in ourselves, and in so doing to conquer our fear of sex. That we fail so miserably, that feminism still refuses to address issues of sexuality, leaves us split, good girl versus bad, a divided self whose exhaustion at keeping the beloved mommy safe from the mother we hate is etched in the lines of our face.

We are born taking pleasure from our bodies and only give it up when it is placed in opposition to the loving gaze of she who sustains life. Adolescent beauty may get its lushness from our reproductive power, but we come into this world sexual and will remain so until we die, if that is what we want. When we were nursery small and saw the drawings of old witches in Grimm, we recognized the Bad Mother who punished us. Watching her, learning from her, we put two and two together and understood that nothing put us in danger of losing her love more than sex; she liked nothing less about our bodies and her own than the sexual parts. When we played doctor with our brother, pulled down our pants and peed with our friends under the porch, we knew it was bad, the height of danger. But we did it anyway, just as we would persevere in adolescence, seeking the forbidden sexual feeling with boys, though we knew the consequences if mother found out.

So internalized was mother's disapproving look, it felt as though her eyes were present in the parked car, and we guiltily half expected her to be standing there, waiting to punish us when we got home. But of course she didn't know, which softened our guilt and made her more dear to us than ever. Just as we had split mother into good and bad to preserve her love, we separate our own bad sex from the rest of us: The good girl is mother's girl, the bad our unacceptable sexual self, the part that Bettelheim says we must heroically rescue by conquering our fear.

So long as we were young, we handed over to boys responsibility for our naughty sex. In a devilish way, holding on to our ties of goodness to mother made the forbidden sex with men more exciting; breaking mother's rules promised a life ahead that would move us forward in time, loving dear mother, but surely being more sexual than she.

Had someone accused us of still being little girls symbiotically tied to mother, we would have haughtily given as evidence of our individual identity our sexual adventures and the display of our erotic wardrobes. We were the new generation, not at all like dear old asexual Mom. We would never end up like that.

But we do. There is no test for autonomy that carries as much fear of losing mother/other women's love as that of conquering fear of sex. Every time we touch ourselves, lie down with a man, wear the erotic dress that pulls eyes to us, the excitement is in challenging mother/women; what cuts the moment short and keeps us from ownership of sex is that in winning sex, we would have lost our ties to women. The Oedipal drama still unresolved, the sexual competition with The Other Girls never challenged and won, we return to the company of women, where sameness rules. Men are exciting; sex with them offers a unique glimpse of autonomy. But men cannot give us the symbiotic oneness we should have outgrown but still crave. Only other unseparated women know what we need, needing it themselves, a breast to lie on. The penis can't hold a candle to the breast.

We grow up expecting men to change our opinion of The Sewer, to make us sexual—"Give me an orgasm!"—and essentially to lead us on the journey that Bettelheim mentions, the one in which we overcome fear of sex. *This is not his job.* Nonetheless, we hate a man for failing. We may also love him—we are used to ambivalence—even marry him, but the rage at him for failing to ignite us sexually, along with our envy of his lack of sexual self-consciousness, finds expression when we turn away from him erotically; we invest our entire selves in the children, excluding him. Or we take a lover out of what we perceive to be sexual independence. But if our adultery is inspired by recapturing the thrill of adolescent sex, forbidden by mother, our infidelity is not so much Bettelheim's heroic quest to conquer fear of sex as a child's desire for erotic thrills on the only terms that make sex exciting: when it reunites us with mother's wagging finger.

Having never slain the dragon, having brought no independent fire to sex in our single days, married sex merely becomes something else the man owns, like the house and the car; giving in to "his" sex, his penis, becomes something we resentfully do for him, not for ourselves.

Having made our husbands into cozy symbiotic partners, we no longer desire sex. We become mother, first slowly, then faster when we become mothers ourselves. Many of the women who fought for sexual freedom twenty years ago changed their minds when they held their tiny babies in their arms: "Now I understand why mother acted that way!" Having abandoned their own sexuality, they take their tiny daughter's hand away from between her legs, thus planting the seed for another generation's double standard of aging.

Owning our sex, rejoicing in it, feels forbidden because we fear that going against mother means she will rise up and smite us; what else is powerful enough to stand between independent women and erotic bliss? Put another way, mother's sexual condemnation is the engine that drives our fantasies. These are the best years of my life for having written *My Mother/My Self*, which was published at the height of feminist joy, before sex became a dirty word again.

Good Witch/Bad Witch

When we are incorrectly taught at adolescence that only now are we sexual, we must assume that when we stop bleeding, we are no longer sexual. The ability to carry a child in adolescence is just that, a stage in the evolution of female sexuality that begins at birth. Menopause marks the end of childbearing years, not the death of sex. There have been times in history when menopausal women were thought to be at the height of their sexuality. The older woman as sexual initiator was a popular theme of literature and poetry in earlier centuries. From the twelfth-century *The Art of Courtly Love:* "As regards that natural instinct of passion, young men are usually more eager to gratify it with older women than with young ones of their own age." In her *In Full Flower: Aging Women, Power, and Sexuality*, Lois Banner quotes a sixteenth-century autobiography: "He that wooeth a widow must not carry 'quick' eels in his codpiece, but show some proof that he is stiff before."

I like the image of the mature woman, who has never forgotten (women never do) what was lacking in her own first lover and can teach that slow build to orgasmic passion, having imagined and rerun more tapes of past and future seductions than any man. Throughout the seventeenth and eighteenth centuries, Banner points out, the sexual appetites of older women were seen as prurient: "Even the presumed ugliness of aging had to it an erotic quality, the quality of being beyond the ordinary . . . of indicating new realms of vice."

Our sexual appetites aren't lost as we age; it is the image of ourselves as sexual that we dutifully abandon to fit the bygone stereotype of Patriarchy that regimented women's sex to accommodate the economic power structure; everything and everyone in that structure was designed to keep men's shoulder to the wheel of commerce and women's prodigious sexual power confined to childbearing.

We don't live that way any longer. While there are those who would like to retain certain rigidities from Patriarchy, seeing constancy and security in going back to "the good old days," what use is our new economic power if it doesn't buy us the privileges of aging that men have always enjoyed? "Most men and more women—young women afraid for themselves—punish older women with derision, punish them with cruelty, when they show inappropriate signs of sexuality," writes Doris Lessing in her novel of a sixty-five-year-old heroine who is "in love to the point of insanity" with a man half her age. Lessing has been a feminist heroine for decades; once again, she is right on the money.

In a stunning example of life imitating art, Michiko Kakutani's *New York Times* review of Lessing's book appears as I am writing these pages. "The story Ms. Lessing has chosen to relate in 'Love, Again' is unbelievable, inadvertently comical and clumsily rendered," Kakutani writes. "Ms. Lessing asks us to believe that a sixty-five-year-old woman not only falls into a state of longing and lust, but that she also becomes the love object of several younger men."

Kakutani's envy of Lessing and the novel's heroine is as obvious as it is outrageous. Coming from the most powerful female book critic in the country, Kakutani's words sound like nothing more than the child's denial of mother's sexuality. Will she, a woman in her early forties, feel the same way when she is sixty-five?

Twenty-five years into feminism, we still accept an older man with a much younger woman, but not the reverse. Think Eastwood and Streep, Redford and Pfeiffer, or, in real life, Senator Alfonse D'Amato with gossip reporter Claudia Cohen. If feminism is about anything, it is seeing the women who break new ground as heroines; clearly, this is true in the world of ideas and commerce, but not in the bedroom. How else to explain Kakutani's conclusion that "in earlier Lessing novels, such inventories of a heroine's self were rendered in meticulous emotional detail, and they were used as a kind of commentary on the society in which that heroine lived. For some reason, this does not happen in 'Love, Again,' and as a result the novel feels perfunctory and contrived, as well as implausible in the extreme."

Rereading a 1972 article by Susan Sontag I can't help but think how her description of an aging woman reminds me of women's lifelong attitudes about our sexual selves, in particular those parts of the body that we are taught from the time we are born are ugly, dirty, smell bad, and, therefore now, in older age, must smell and look all the worse:

"Aging in women is a process of becoming obscene sexually," wrote Sontag, "for the flabby bosom, wrinkled neck, spotted hands, thinning white hair, waistless torso, and veined legs of an old woman are felt to be obscene. In our direst moments of the imagination, this transformation can take place with dismaying speed—as in the end of *Lost Horizon*, when the beautiful young girl is carried by her lover out of Shangri-La and, within minutes, turns into a withered, repulsive crone.... One of the attitudes that punish women most severely is the visceral horror felt at aging female flesh.... That old women are repulsive is one of the most profound esthetic and erotic feelings in our culture."

I don't know what comes to mind first, the witch or the vagina, but as Sontag makes clear in her last sentence, they are intermingled. Women's sex is either "bewitching," as in young and beautiful, or ugly, as in the warts on a crone's nose. Between 1500 and 1800, as many as nine million women were killed for being witches. The Church saw women's sexuality as the root of all evil and women as the obstacle to men's holiness. The handbook regarding the persecution of witches, *Malleus Maleficarum*, commissioned by Pope Innocent VIII in 1486, stated that "all witchcraft comes from carnal lust, which in women is insatiable." The *Malleus* made clear that women, by virtue of their sex, whether they be beautiful beyond dreams or blindingly ugly, had terrible power over men.

We mistakenly think that all witches were crones, but the bewitchingly beautiful woman was as likely to be thought a witch as was the old hag; the effects of the beautiful one's sexual power—the man's erection, wet dreams, as well as his impotence at a time when these reactions weren't understood—all gave reason to the belief that she had consorted with the devil. Women were seen as more susceptible to the devil's seduction because they were irrational and more sex driven. And no woman was more susceptible to the devil's wiles than the aging one.

"As sexualized beings, aging women were malevolent creatures," comments Lois Banner, "the devil's 'go-betweens' to the human world. . . . 'Where the Devil cannot go, he sends an old woman.' These women themselves were supposedly engaged in a vast conspiracy of secret prostitution, as they controlled those young female devils (the succubi) and the young male devils (the incubi) whom they sent to seduce others and to enlist them in their satanic worship."

If you look at illustrations of witches you will see that they wear *poulaines*, the same long, pointy shoes that men enjoyed wearing in the eleventh to fourteenth centuries, before the king and the Church forbade them. While men wore *poulaines* to celebrate their mighty penis, the witch wore them, perhaps mockingly, to celebrate women's sexual power over men.

Raised from the cradle not to touch our genitals or think well of them, we understand why menstruation is called The Curse, the power that only witches own. Is it so unusual that when we look in the mirror at age forty or fifty and see loose skin, loss of beauty, that it is painted in the hues of the ugliness of vagina/witch? I sometimes think women rush into asexual old age.

Here we are, wiser, richer, and more accomplished, and it is as if none of our victories have altered the sexual image of the older woman. When we look in the mirror, we see little traces of the witch sneaking up on us, and a frost passes over our hearts. Refusing to believe that a man still wants us, we ask him to turn off the light before we crawl into his bed. When he says he doesn't see the wrinkles, we hate him for lying. By the time the wrinkles do appear, there is triumph in our words, "See, I told you so! Go away, sex, get thee gone, for I never was at peace with you. Now, finally, done with beauty and sex—though I am only forty, fifty, whatever—I can rest on mother's bosom, I can be mother. I am at peace. Age, take me!"

Many women prefer to see menopause as the end of their sexual lives even when scientific proof is offered that their libido decline is not as precipitous as men's. To women who would prefer to close the book on sex, such breakthrough news arrives on an ill wind.

The older mother grows, the more her flesh sags on her bones, the more the unseparated daughter tries to hold on to her internally by becoming not the good but the bad mother. It is not conscious; when friends tell the daughter, after mother's death, that her voice on the phone sounds just like her mother's, the woman shivers, knowing how she hated that voice. Now when she looks at the graying pubic hairs, the hard line of her lips, she sees horror beyond aging; in her preconscious she recognizes not the mother she loved, but The Witch.

"The witch—more than the other creations of our imagination which we have invested with magic powers, the fairy and the sorcerer—in her opposite aspects is a reincarnation of the all-good mother of infancy and the all-bad mother of the oedipal crisis," writes Bettelheim. "But she is no longer seen halfway realistically, as a mother who is lovingly all-giving and an opposite stepmother who is rejectingly demanding, but entirely unrealistically, as either superhumanly rewarding or inhumanly destructive."

I prefer the wisdom of fairy tales to strict psychoanalytic literature, especially as regards fear of sex; the former has a credibility given their lasting power over the centuries and in our own memories as well. Fairy tales are beloved because they mirror our deepest feelings, good and bad. They belong as much in this final chapter as in earlier ones because in the third act of life most of us are no closer to conquering our fear of sex than we were when Mommy read the stories to us.

The fact that we may have raised children of our own has nothing to do with fear of sex; the act of intercourse is merely that, an act, until we challenge and defeat the ancient fear of loss of love should we go against parental antisex rules. "One becomes a complete human being who has achieved all his potentialities," writes Bettelheim, "only if, in addition to being oneself, one is at the same time able and happy to be oneself with another."

There are two stages in becoming a complete human being; tales such as "Snow White" and "Cinderella," wherein the hero and heroine must undergo a series of trials, are about gaining selfhood. The purpose is to bring the central character to the point of revelation that he or she is "worthy of being loved." But there is no mention of Cinderella's or Snow White's feelings for the Prince, just a vague assurance of happily ever after. A sense of incompleteness exists. "These stories, while they take the heroine up to the threshold of true love," writes Bettelheim, "do not tell what personal growth is required for union with the beloved other." One more test is required: The hero/heroine must conquer fear of sex. For this, the Animal Groom Cycle of fairy tales picks up where the Sleeping Princess leaves off.

"Fairy tales suggest that eventually there comes a time when we must learn what we have not known before—or, to put it psychoanalytically, to undo the repression of sex," says Bettelheim. Why do women want sex in the dark? What is so loathsome about the investigation of a man's body? Initially, we were curious, even excited, to look, but as we mix our love of him with sex, the former destroys the latter, making it love *or* sex. If that is so, then the quality of our love must be questioned. As Bettelheim writes: "What we had experienced as dangerous, loathsome, something to be shunned, must change its appearance so that it is truly beautiful. It is love which permits this to happen."

Think of the tale of "Beauty and the Beast," which belongs to The Animal Groom Cycle. In the tale, the heroine faces her fear and the beast becomes beautiful because of her love. Children are assured by these stories that they aren't the only ones to fear sex but that others share their anxiety. "As the story characters discover that despite such anxiety their sexual partner is not an ugly creature but a lovely person, so will the child."

The Romanian fairy tale "The Enchanted Pig" is less well known but is rich in modern-day female heroism; in it, the heroine is made to marry a pig, who at night turns into a man; come morning, he is once again a pig. She follows a witch's advice and ties a string around the man's leg to keep him from changing back into a pig—but because she has tried to hurry things, she earns the pig/husband's displeasure. She is told she will not see him again until she has "worn out three pairs of iron shoes and blunted a steel staff" looking for him.

Bettelheim describes her search: "He disappears, and her endless wanderings in search of him take her to the moon, the sun, and the wind. In each of these places she is given a chicken to eat and warned to save its bones. . . . Finally . . . she comes to a place high up, where she is told her husband dwells." To reach him, she assembles a ladder out of the bones of all the chickens she has eaten on her journey, and even cuts off her little finger to provide the final rung she needs. When she reaches him, the spell is lifted from him. As Prince and Princess, they inherit her father's kingdom and "ruled as only kings rule who have suffered many things."

In fairy tales it is usually an older woman, a stepmother, who casts a spell, or a witch, who turns the man/Prince into an ugly animal, suggesting none too subtly "that girls' sexual anxieties are the result not of their own experiences, but of what others have told them." Or, what other women have *not* told us. We can argue indefinitely about who plants the antisex message in women but there is little argument as to whether or not feminism has educated women to embrace the beauty of our own sexual selves, to embrace men and thus become complete human beings. Feminism has left us nonheroines in our own modern fairy tale.

We must begin by bringing sex into the journey of modern feminism. We stand today at the entrance to the beast's cave, heels dug in, cowardly refusing to complete our task as human beings. Women play a fool's game thinking that by eliminating men from our lives we don't have to conquer fear of sex, when, in fact, the fear was in us long before the opposite sex came to call. Before this moment in history, we were too dependent to go on such a journey. Now we have the tools but have found another reason to postpone the quest: our war against men.

But even the scapegoat of men's brutality doesn't protect us from our fear of aging, which has become worse; when we look in our mirrors, we don't see women aging better than any generation before us, but instead see The Witch, the Bad Mother of fairy tales who didn't like it/us when we touched ourselves. Until The Sewer is found to be lovely—like the pig who was found to be handsome—we will perceive age as ugly. Most grim of all, until we change what was loathsome into something beautiful, which, in essence, is human sexuality, our children will grow up vulnerable to all the deadly plagues associated with irresponsible sex.

Reading the recent literature on aging women written by such feminist heroines as Steinem and Greer can be grim, yes, as in Grimm's fairy tales, for each of these heroines was a young, sexual beauty when feminism began. And brave, oh, my, were they brave! But alas, they bring none of the passion of earlier years to the subject of aging.

When economic and political equality were the goals, these women were the mothers of invention; there was nothing we could not change, they told us, could not accomplish if enough of us wanted it. They were right. Our objectives were extraordinary, some said not doable, but we did it. Because they believed in their vision, we believed in ourselves leading lives our mothers never imagined.

What could be harder to alter than the image of women/mother as caretaker, reconstituted as man's equal in the workplace? Clearly, it is the image of women retaining sexual beauty as we age. By eliminating sex and beauty from the feminist agenda, The Sisterhood removed the major sources of dissension among women. But let us be clear regarding our deepest feelings: We did not pick an ugly woman to represent feminism. We picked a great beauty whose sexual liaisons with powerful men were well known. Steinem was, and remains, feminism's legendary queen, though no fairy-tale heroine who conquers sex.

Here, in an interview with Gail Sheehy, is Steinem's pronouncement on sex: "Sex and sensuality—going to bed for two entire days and sending out for Chinese food—was such an important part of my life, and it just isn't anymore. . . . I don't know how much of it is hormonal and how much is outgrowing it."

It is a perplexing message. Knowing the weight her words carry as the most quoted feminist alive and realizing her place in history, Steinem nonetheless goes further, holding out her success at getting past sex as a goal for other women, to ". . . have faith that it may be true for them, too." What does that mean? Losing interest in sex in the last third of our lives is a godsend, something to which we can look forward?

Let me return to the beginning of the tale, for no feminist was more witchily successful at everything she touched than the young and beautiful Gloria Steinem. "When she had become a spokeswoman for feminism, the reassurance her appearance offered to women that, contrary to the impression given by the media, not all feminists resembled male truck drivers in boots and fatigues, was profound," wrote Steinem's biographer Carolyn Heilbrun.

I would go further than Heilbrun; Steinem's beauty wasn't just "reassurance" to women; in choosing her as feminism's figurehead, all feminists, ugly or beautiful, agreed, consciously or not, that women's sexual beauty was important. We may have turned away from beauty in the seventies in order to make a political point, but in selecting Steinem, we silently held on to our claim to beauty's power. When we eventually reclaimed it with a vengeance in the eighties, Naomi Wolf's *The Beauty Myth* attempted to pin beauty's renewed tyranny on Bad Men. But it didn't stick. How could it? Was not one of the most beautiful women in the world the leader of feminism? Was she not chosen by other women, and isn't the continuation of her beauty to this day also of her choosing?

No one is in a better position to talk straight to the troops than Gloria. She is a woman of bona fide accomplishments who has extraordinary access to airtime. It doesn't require much research for her to know how crucial the issues of aging, sex, and beauty are to women. By all means, let her go her own way personally but, like a good general, she owes it to all of us to explain clearly, unambiguously, her desire for disenfranchising herself. She is noticeably one of those fortunate people who remains lovely and sexual well into the last third of her life, a power that could continue until . . . well, who knows?

For Gloria to say that she is through with sexual beauty is confusing. Especially since shortly after the Sheehy interview a beautiful Steinem, age sixty-one, sat for her portrait, which appeared in *People* magazine's annual issue, read by twenty million women, chronicling the world's fifty most beautiful people. It is not the swan song of a heroine but the asexual promise of a powerful mother who leaves her children believing that sex will always be in opposition to mother's love. Never having managed to publicly consolidate sex with her feminism, Steinem's legacy is of a heroine who never conquered what Bettelheim called the "fear of sex as something dangerous and beastly."

As the first wave of feminist scientists takes on the subject of women's health, the research shows that we are living longer and better than any generation before us. It is nothing less than breathtaking.

More than 43 million women had reached menopause by 1992, and the numbers could increase by another 6 million by 2002. These women are economically independent and look and act younger than our mothers, raising the question: How should we think about ourselves as sexual people?

"From their mid-forties to their sixties," writes Gail Sheehy in *The Silent Passage*, "women tend to become more aggressive and goal-oriented, while men show a tender and vulnerable side that may have been formerly suppressed. Women whose ovaries have stopped putting out the female sex hormone estrogen still produce in the cortex of their ovaries a small but consistent amount of the male hormone, testosterone. The relatively high level of testosterone in about 50 percent of postmenopausal females could partially explain the take-charge behavior so often exhibited by middle-aged women. Meanwhile, men's testosterone levels are gradually decreasing with age."

"Sexuality, before and after menopause, is complex and individual, having far less to do with estrogen levels than with the way each woman feels about herself and her circumstances," emphasizes Bernadine Healy, former director of the National Institutes of Health. "Biologically, while estrogen has a clear effect on the functioning of a woman's vaginal

secretions and sexual organs and may play a role in ardor, it's testosterone that pretty much dominates the libido. So, if anything, as the ratio of testosterone to estrogen rises during and after menopause, a woman's sex drive could increase. . . . What is perfectly clear to me as a doctor and as a woman is that sexuality—especially at menopause—is an intricate mix of mind, body, and circumstances."

This research flies in the face of Steinem's belief that "turning 50 was the end of an era, the era in which a woman is still a sexual, reproductive commodity. . . ." It isn't even true. Freedom from reproductive worries doesn't mean we cease to be sexual at fifty or sixty or beyond. It could mean the beginning of sexual adventure, a new state of mind, which is exactly where good sex begins, between the ears.

It would seem we are independent in doing everything but bringing the image of our sexuality into the twenty-first century. Because beauty is so enmeshed with sex, women in their twenties and thirties hear Gloria's message and see their own beauty already slipping away; if feminism's beautiful leader could not slay the dragon or instruct them in how they might, what chance have they? In time, there will be enough middle-aged women who will become ongoing models of sexual beauty. But a great opportunity will have been lost.

"I couldn't care less. And that is so wonderful," Steinem answered an interviewer who asked her on her sixtieth birthday, "What about sex?" And when that interviewer responded to her answer, "Our readers will be disappointed," Steinem replied, "but they shouldn't be. You're free. Your brain is free to think about other things. You're free from jealousy or competitiveness."

It is interesting that as Steinem withdraws from the sexual arena, she has taken on with a new vigor the subject of competition. With her announcement that she has outgrown sex, she signals to her troops that other women need no longer envy her or feel rivalrous with those men who once carried her off into the night. But how is Steinem herself going to feel when other women—especially those her age—continue to pursue sex, to smile bewitchingly into the mirror and lie down with men? Nothing arouses competition between women like sexual beauty. And Steinem is not without her own spontaneous bursts of rivalry when such brilliant and, yes, sexual people as Paglia speak a feminism that does not agree with hers.

Such acolytes as Susan Faludi keep Steinem's flame alive by writing disparagingly—and very competitively—of the new, young feminists such as Katie Roiphe and Christina Hoff Sommers, who have a sharp sexual edge. Their goals, Faludi claims, are their own fame, not social change. Bad girls! "Theirs will always be a stillborn form of feminism," she resentfully writes, "because it is an ideology that will not and does not want to generate political, social, or economic change. . . . [They] do not look forward to creating a better future, only inward to the further adulation of self." Her envy of their brand of feminism, especially as it embraces sex and puts it on the new feminist agenda, fairly burns up the page.

Nothing, but nothing, infuriates women more than other women enjoying sex. Ironically, the sight and smell of it make Steinem and Faludi's other archenemies—Right Wing Patriarchs—equally furious, thus bringing their two armies uncomfortably close together. Sex, fear of it, creates strange bedfellows.

Twenty-five years ago that other glamorous feminist, Germaine Greer, wrote: "Revolutionary woman may join Women's Liberation Groups and curse and scream and fight the cops, but did you ever hear of one of them marching the public street with her skirt high, crying 'Can you dig it? Cunt is beautiful!' The walled garden of Eden was CUNT. The mandorla of the beautiful saints was CUNT. The mystical rose is CUNT. The Ark of Gold, the Gate of Heaven. Cunt is a channel drawing all towards it. Cunt is knowledge. Knowledge is receptivity, which is activity. Cunt is the symbol of erotic science. . . . It is time to dig CUNT and women must dig it first."

Greer was in her twenties when she wrote this. She was a glorious sight to behold and to hear, an exhibitionistic celebrity. Her sexual vitality gave heart to all of us. Along with the unflinching speaking voice, Greer clearly enjoyed using all her ammunition, by which I mean that the beautiful long hair was tossed, the breasts thrust forward, the ass twitched, and the long legs flashed. She was, and still is, sensational, though this is not always how she presents herself in her book on menopause, *The Change*, where she is decidedly ambivalent.

> The change hurts. Like a person newly released from leg-irons, the freed woman staggers at first. Though her excessive visibility was anguish, her present invisibility is disorienting. She had not realized how much she depended upon her physical presence, at shop counters, at the garage, on the bus. For the first time in her life she finds that she has to raise her voice or wait endlessly while other people push in front of her.

She describes a scene in a restaurant in France where a woman friend rails that the two of them dine alone and invisible while at an adjoining table two men their age ogle young women half their age.

Yes, that can happen, but youthful beauty was never something we allowed ourselves to enjoy; we often felt too conspicuous and accused ogling men of objectifying us. We hadn't yet grown into our full identity, which is interior, a state of mind, value, self-acceptance, worth, courage . . . all of it invisible. Ours is a riper sexuality, if we believe it, feel it. As Greer herself said in that article on Cunt twenty-five years earlier, "Women must dig it first."

When *The Change* was published, *Harper's Bazaar* ran an article on Greer along with a photo of her sitting naked, slouched, long, graying hair half covering her face, droopy-breasted and holding her cat, yes, very witchy. It was confounding, for in her book she doesn't so much celebrate the sexual power of the witch as the witch's aggressiveness that inhibits men. For a woman who had once advertised in her look a bewitching come-hither to men, her book held a disquieting embrace of a witchiness that leaves out men, leaves out the heightened mature beauty and power that women might grow into if we believed it were possible, saw it in ourselves or in a heroine such as Greer, who appeared quite beautiful and vibrant when she signed copies of *The Change* in my local bookstore.

Her rhetoric that day was totally at odds with the way she looked; she spoke as The Bad Witch, powerful, angry, an almost whining note in her voice. I wanted to shake her, hold up the mirror before her, and ask, Why? Is it not good enough, this older beauty? Does she turn against men because they do not look at her with the same instantaneous voyeuristic desire they once showed her? Once you've been an exhibitionistic celebrity in many areas, including intellect and youthful, erotic beauty, it's not good enough being "just" brilliant.

Maybe I have Greer all wrong, but I won't give up on her. She is too important. When my assistant read her book, she groaned, "Oh, God, now they've found something new to whine about." By "they" she means those who started this business years ago, who have achieved so much, who are heroines, but who paint their present years as Grimm. "Greer looked fantastic," said my friend Moira, who has just turned forty-five and was at the book signing with me, "but I was furious at what she had to say. How can someone who has accomplished so much talk such drivel? I just hope to God I don't feel as she does in seven years."

If we are not more trustworthy models, younger women will look at our tired, angry faces, and plunge themselves deeper into the pursuit of youthful beauty, denying that they will ever be like us. Here are the heroines, lamenting the fact that no one looks at them and salivates as they once did. Well, not all heroines. Consider Faye Wattleton, the fifty-two-year-old former head of Planned Parenthood. I videotaped an interview with her ten years ago, in which she said she had been raised by the women in her family to respect and prolong beauty's power. When I mention her name to women, whether they know her personally or not, they voice admiration of her beauty, her professional success, and her commitment to feminism, *all* of which she preserves as might a person who has inherited great wealth.

I wish Greer would read again her own paragraph from *The Female Eunuch*: "Sex must be rescued from the traffic between powerful and powerless, masterful and mastered, sexual and neutral, to become a form of communication between potent, gentle, tender people, which cannot be accomplished by denial of heterosexual contact."

I want the freedom that comes with ripe age, the chance to be fully myself that Greer celebrates, but I refuse to accept that this freedom only arrives when we are supposedly of no sexual interest to men. If feminism isn't sexually open to men, not just the penis in the vagina but warm, embracing, erotic in that deep, hot, unconsummated way that is often the most searing sex, then we will have failed. I do not consider Matriarchy a sign of feminism's success. Drooping breasts and gray hair will come to all of us, but I do not want to shove them in men's craws as does that witchily ugly picture of the naked Greer with her cat.

What a Difference a Father Would Have Made in This Third Act Had He Been a Lead Character in the First

I see two major social changes occurring in tandem: our view of the man as a caretaker and our view of the post-fifty woman as powerful.

Without a man involved in the earliest modeling of our lives, when the clay was still damp, we grow up expecting men to change our minds about beauty, sex, everything. How can they? Who can alter the course of the wind, moon, and stars, the celestial road map laid down in a nursery controlled by an angel who was also The Witch? The Prince was expected to be the payoff. We knew little about The Prince, given he was male, which made for much dreaming and idealization beyond anything a mere male mortal could deliver.

Father may be male, but he entered late, not having been in the nursery. The Oedipal years arrive after years of concession, loss, and surrender, by which I mean women seldom get back what was sacrificed to keep mother love when we were dependent and she our only source of life. How could father have any idea of the quantity of approval and encouragement his daughter requires to undo mother's omnipotent judgments, especially where sex and beauty are concerned?

And so the job is passed on to The Prince, who is no better at making women feel beautiful and sexual. We never forgive men. When we get to age forty-five or fifty and still have never believed a man's opinion of our sexual beauty, we concede to mother: We see the Witch creeping up on big cat's paws and we say, "I'm old," before we are. What a waste.

Imagine how our extended lives might evolve if father had raised us from the start, either alongside mother or on his own, had she chosen to work outside the home. It is imagery worth pursuing given its inevitability unless, of course, the Feminist Matriarchy takes over. (Goddess forbid.) One of the reasons we are looking better these days is that we already "act like men," meaning that we are good providers with strong voices. When a woman was accused of "acting like a man" in the olden days, you can be sure it wasn't meant as a compliment; nor did you expect that woman to be beautiful.

Today we look better than our mothers at our age precisely because the way we live animates our features, stirs the blood, and relieves the anxiety, depression, and anger that aged our mothers before their time. If having entered men's world and acquired some of their privileges has done this, why don't we put an expert at life enhancement in the nursery, where our children can literally take in fine "male" qualities, if not with father's milk then from his strong arms, tender hands, his different kind of love, and his far less critical eyes that beam a man's approval and encouragement? Men aren't angels, but they tend to be more independent, assertive, and sexual than women.

Might it not follow that as more women gain economic power,

men would not have to measure their manliness by how much money they made? They would be open to alternative definitions of masculinity, just as we women have extended the meaning of who and what a woman is. Loving children as he does, he might relish an equal role in the nursery, perhaps take it on as his full-time work.

What I count on is that when the man in the nursery does his job as well as the woman in the workplace does hers, we will eventually see the "naturalness" of the deal. It comes down to a bargain: If women are to prolong sexual beauty, we must cede men a power of comparable value. These bargains between the sexes aren't written down at summit meetings, but if men felt that we were on their side, then they would be on ours. As it stands, girls raised solely by women in the Matriarchal Nursery grow up afraid to enjoy sexual beauty because it would lose them the only source of love they were raised to trust. Had father also been a caretaker, this fear of exclusion from women's world would be lessened. Should women turn against us, we would always believe in another source of love.

Without our unhealthy symbiotic attachment to mother, we would be less likely to split her into Good and Bad Witch so as to keep her love intact. We would see mother whole; we would not question men's love so quickly; we would accept our sexual beauty, feeling no threat of loss.

All the money in the world cannot buy sufficient surgery to keep aging women from questioning our mirrors and despising ourselves for trying to look younger when the inner voice says, "Your time is past." That inner voice is the double standard of aging: so long as a man maintains the power to provide, his visual worth doesn't diminish with age.

When people do not look at a man, he is not threatened by invisibility; he knows he exists irrespective of others' eyes on him because this is how he grew up. A man begins life needing mother's eye, feeling lost without it, but he moves away with less fear and more approval; he gains his own internal eye. A man enjoys being looked at but doesn't, as Berger writes, walk around with a balloon constantly over his head in which he imagines how others are seeing him.

When a man arrives at age fifty, sixty, eighty, his skin may be wrinkled, his hair gone, but he doesn't feel less a man because of it. His concerns come primarily from economic success. Should a woman desire him for his money or his seed, he would not question why she sees him as a Prince. But even financially independent women who have no desire for a man question their value as they age. What is so different in women that we cannot walk past the hall of mirrors as convincingly as men?

My answer would be that mother doesn't see herself in her son; men grow up with a physical difference that boosts their separation from her. His penis reinforces society's pressure on her to let him go his own way. Its erections and secretions will not obey her. His identity will be very much influenced by mother's opinion of his maleness, but in the end it usually remains his.

Is it any wonder that without a man in the nursery, the power of the penis is exaggerated, sometimes even used as a weapon against women? Maybe the boy/man couldn't stand up to the Giantess of the Nursery, couldn't defend himself emotionally, verbally, and wouldn't strike out at her. But he could and does at other women who often bear the brunt of the rage that began back then.

Maybe father in the nursery wouldn't eliminate men's later brutality against women, but with a strong male image from the day he was born, a man who held, fed, and disciplined him, a boy would grow to manhood with a much richer picture of how to be a man. Just as women's beauty is built into mother's earliest role, father's would be too, meaning both girls and boys would grow up seeing a male as well as a female beauty ideal. For this to happen, women must first acknowledge that caretaking is not just sacrifice but also the most powerful role in life. And they must be willing to share it.

As it is, men never get over their fear of women's power, which they believe in far more than we. They didn't let us in the workplace out of a sense of fairness and rightness. They knew we could beat them. The money that had made them powerful was a Band-Aid on the emotional wounds inflicted by the Giantess of the Nursery; when massed female power reappeared in the form of angry feminism, men knuckled under enough for us to enter. Once The Witch gets her toe in the door, she is in.

Despite everything we have won, women refuse to see ourselves as owning mother's witchy power, preferring instead the very effective image of little, mistreated people at the mercy of the big, bad wolf. We blame the double standard of aging on men: Given a lineup of women they don't know, most men would pick the young beauty. *But so would we.* When a man loves a fifty- or seventy-year-old woman, however, and desires her sexually, it isn't he who turns away. We women take ourselves out of the running; even when our bodies were lush, we hated them. Now that the visible signs of the crepey-skinned witch are upon us, we turn from sex with self-disgust, seeing in men's eyes our own revulsion.

There is absolutely nothing we women could not accomplish—including the abolition of this double standard of aging—if we could get the deadwood out of our houses and encourage one another to take in the power of our sexual beauty, which lives beyond menopause, and which is not restricted to and defined by youth. Not to sound witchy, but we only have to believe it to make it so; men already do.

Men in the nursery would turn around women's view of sex and beauty as defined by youth like nothing else could. It is evolution at its best, men picking up the slack now that women have left the nursery door ajar so as to enter the workplace. When a loved man's voice reads to his daughter the fairy tales from the Animal Groom Cycle, wherein the heroine conquers her fear of sex and thus becomes a whole person, his image and his words will be taken in by his daughter as a promise to grow on, an alternative opinion to mother's. You and I are too old to receive this from Daddy, but we could give it to the next generation, a truly magnificent gift from good feminists to our children.

Wearing Our Power Beautifully

Under Patriarchy, a woman's worth lessened as she aged, but while we may no longer be capable of reproduction, we are becoming better and better providers; this is how we must begin to weigh our value. In a culture in which success is god, we are free to be advertisements for ourselves. It is quite a coup, wearing our beauty on our own arm, so to speak.

We are attracted to successful people and want to warm ourselves in their glow. If the successful one is also good-looking, the attraction is multiplied. When you put a woman's beauty together with her accomplishment, you have a very attractive package indeed, inside and out. Women have only to wear their success self-confidently, and we will not be without friends and lovers, if that is what we desire. In the words of a male colleague of then fifty-year-old psychologist Judith Rodin, president of the University of Pennsylvania, "She's the kind of person who became more glamorous and more charismatic as she got larger grants and more fame." Rodin is stunning, a mother, and has been married three times. I like her colleague's quote because it speaks of how beauty and achievement mesh, the one feeding the other, if that is what we choose.

As we reap the rewards of modern feminism, we carry into our extended years everything won for women when we were younger. It is a moment to celebrate, not to lie down and die. Our new economics have won us a realignment of the sexes, ours to design and live. What comes to mind are the Olympic Games, a beautiful athlete running across the World, lighting the torches: Let the games begin! This beautiful running person is you and I, who in middle age have never looked better or worked so hard to win the privilege of being the first generation to break Patriarchal World's double standard of aging.

What is the point of owning economic power if it doesn't buy us the privileges of aging that men have always enjoyed? Men cannot give us this; when we were twenty, we didn't believe in their protestations of love or their adoration of our beauty. Now that we are forty-five or seventy we certainly wouldn't believe them; all along, what was missing was our own admirable self-image. To evolve fully, women must reinforce one another, cease devaluing the other woman, and instead take her achievement as the new benchmark.

We see men as through a lens called Daddy/wealth/money/power; even if he simply makes ends meet, we still give him the right to choose us, which power determines how we see ourselves. Our economics have given us the right to alter the Patriarchal Deal, meaning to the richest man went the most beautiful *young* woman. Men can still extract this prize, but we need no longer rely on his money or his evaluation of us. Let him choose youth; we have a new power; bewitchment lies not in the eye of the beholder but of she who owns it and believes in sexual beauty until she dies.

Older women were once seen as witches because of their power; it was the older woman's embodiment of sexual energy, not her dried-up old sex that frightened men and other women too, who were not so emboldened. Riding on a broomstick, indeed. Is not the broom handle the penis? According to Lois Banner, "the two derogatory names most commonly used by women against women in the medieval period were 'whore' and 'witch.' All women could be whores; all women could be witches."

The model we present from here on, the way we look, carry our-selves, see, and think of ourselves, will be remembered as the first wave of modern feminist power, an evolutionary change. Seeing us, young women will no longer fear that life ends with youth. If, how-ever, we continue lamenting that eyes no longer fasten on us as they did when we were young, everything we have accomplished will be as dust. It is no good that older feminists today say beauty is not impor-tant; it is always important. It is the measure of beauty that changes. If youth's monopoly is to alter, the Good Witch must be seen as she was originally drawn—creative, wise, going about her powerful business, and beautiful beyond the telling of it.

Bemoaning the invisibility of older women makes a farce of the past twenty years; it says that sex objects are all we ever were and have remained. Today's return to the tyranny of youthful beauty compli-cates our work; adolescent fashions from our own youth in the sixties and seventies mimic our inability to invent an image of lush, mature beauty.

Who are we? It is not so much the clothes we wear but the way we carry, think of, and see ourselves. We need a look that celebrates Women's New Middle Age. Enough of this business of squeezing into the hip huggers and shrunken T-shirts we wore twenty years ago; it says we are afraid of becoming big and beautiful. We are not our mother's generation. The sooner we outgrow the fear of surpassing her, the closer we will be to achieving our new look.

So far, the hungry eye is only used to one limited dish: youth. It will not taste this new, richer offering if we who live it do not believe in it. The eye's search for youthful beauty is automatic and eternal, irrespective of the contents of the lush package. Reproduction is on the mind of the biological eye. But we are more than breeders, you and I. We are women of content, and it is our vision of ourselves as more exciting and appealing as we age that makes it so; when other women see us, they will take our look to their own mirrors; we will be a lens through which they see themselves anew. It is all a matter of the eye getting used to seeing an older woman as admirable, once the mind has altered its opinion and informed the eye.

Our ease will draw people to us, which will make us less depen-dent on youthful beauty. People today, more than ever, are drawn to those who have a certain serenity. Young beauty attracts a crowd, but there is seldom serenity; picked like a flower at its height of perfection by a man, the beauty can only borrow ease from him. Knowing her value is dictated by time, she fears the clock ticking.

When you and I, twenty, thirty, forty years older than she, give ourselves over to envy of her youth, we are forgetting how perilous life felt back then. This is what nasty resentment does. As we believe in our new power, other women and men want to be around us; men always follow strong women who love them.

Competing for the eye with a nineteen-year-old is doomed to failure. Measuring our success in visibility at age fifty with what it was when we were thirty is the action of a fool. We are no longer in the gene pool, competing with other females looking for a mate with whom to reproduce their line. We are older and wiser and do not want the indiscriminate eye; in fact, we do not want to be chosen, but to do the selecting ourselves. This is not dancing class. These are the years in which we may make the first move.

The "old wives' tales" regarding the loss of sexual desire with age are just that, tales told by old women to keep other women in their place, meaning that no one should get more of the pie than any other. "The woman's capacity for orgasm is not impaired in any way by aging," wrote Masters and Johnson in 1994. "In one study, the frequency of orgasm for sexually active women was actually found to increase in each decade of life, through the eighties."

When you read this quote, does something inside squirm at the thought of aging female flesh in the throes of ecstasy, witchlike? Remember that women in their thirties already see "old female flesh" and are convinced that men will see them as they see themselves. Our invisibility is a self-fulfilling prophecy.

Most of my women friends are past the age of fifty, and they look as good as women in their thirties; not as *young*, but then, youth isn't what they have to offer. The middle-aged woman isn't what she used to be. Norma Desmond, heroine of the film and Broadway musical *Sunset Boulevard*, was originally written to be age fifty, a hag, an over-the-hill film star who could no longer show her face. That movie was produced in 1950. Today, we laugh at fifty as old; is it our eye that has changed, or women? I would say both, with heavy emphasis on the latter.

Andrew Lloyd Webber, who composed the music for the stage version, quoted some Hollywood wives who chorused, "We're all fifty, and we're all beautiful!" Remember Swanson in the part, how old she looked? Or was it how young I was? And so I watched it again a few nights ago. She does look old. Supposedly, William Holden felt it was demeaning to play opposite such an old woman and had to be coerced into playing his role, ironically one of his best. "Today, fifty is nothing," says Lloyd Webber, "but in those days, when they made the film, it was shocking." Who made fifty an obsolete definition of old? You and I.

A man of forty-five looks distinguished, but a woman of the same age is over the hill, Debby Then, a scholar at The Center for the Study of Women at UCLA, is reported as saying. As a woman who looks at men, I would answer that to me very few men look distinguished at forty-five until, perhaps, I learn who they are, what they have done, and read their accomplishment into their faces. "Women in their forties are feeling better than ever about themselves," Debby Then continues, "but unfortunately, that's when they become invisible to society."

I prefer Carolyn Heilbrun's approach to women, beauty, and age. "It is perhaps only in old age, certainly past fifty, that women can stop being female impersonators, can grasp the opportunity to reverse their most cherished principles of femininity." As an admirable model of an older woman, Heilbrun chose Margaret Mead. "I remember having lunch with my aunt," she says, "who was asking me, 'Why don't you do something with yourself?' I looked over at Margaret Mead, who . . . was about 5 feet tall and weighed 180 pounds . . . and was surrounded by people, including young men. I figured I'd settle for that."

Mead is often cited by other women as a grand example of the older woman spitting in the eye of invisibility. In her autobiography, from which I've briefly quoted, Mead celebrates the menopausal years, the freedom from childbearing, as a time in life when something "very special" is available to women: "Suddenly, their whole creativity is released—they paint or write as never before or they throw themselves into academic work with enthusiasm." As for her looks and sexuality, Mead's daughter wrote of her that "she seemed to become prettier, she bought a couple of designer dresses for the first time, from Fabiani, and I think she started a new romantic relationship. Without question, she went through a complete professional renaissance."

"When I look at the advertisements that are coming out of the beauty industry, I'm struck by how very much the woman is suggested to be making herself beautiful for others," said psychologist Georgia Witkin, who participated in my 1989 Power of Beauty Symposium. "I spoke to 1,500 women for a book I wrote called *The Female Stress Syn-*

drome, and I found out that we look at ourselves in a reflection or a mirror on the average of seventeen times a day. That's everything from storefront reflections to makeups and makeovers. During those seventeen times, what women told me they were looking for was not how they looked to others but to themselves. And if they seemed to have pink cheeks and if their lips seemed red and their eyes bright, they said to themselves, 'Well, then, I must be feeling well. I must be young, I look it.' We want beauty not just for others; we want to look the way we feel, which is quite young, quite strong, and quite beautiful, although we are maturing."

At that same symposium, where television journalist Nancy Collins asked a roomful of mostly male executives from a major cosmetic house why they still used twenty-year-old women to advertise their antiaging creams, the answer was that it was what consumers wanted. Since that symposium, the number of beautiful models over the age of forty in advertisements of women's beauty products has multiplied; models such as Lauren Hutton, Patti Hansen, Carmen, and Isabella Rossellini are the vanguard. Men who run large cosmetics houses are out to earn bigger bucks; if older women can be proven to sell antiaging cream better than younger women, they will go with the former. But the decision as to how much and for how long we want to draw the sight lines to ourselves is ours.

We say we hate being beauty objects when what we really hate is being invisible and without power. Menopause might be a pleasant respite for those who hate the stares. When a generation of women grow up taking into adolescence their big, brave eyes with which they looked at the world, along with all the other talents prized prior to their first bleeding, then when that bleeding is done, they would have inside them all the skills and abilities practiced since birth.

Invisibility would not be so feared because our value would be internalized. We would remember the benefits from our years prior to adolescent sexual beauty when people responded more to our voices, charm, athletic and scholastic ability. Not being on stage all the time meant freedom then. I realize that this is what my dreams of lost suitcases and clothes closets are about, and why I began this book unsure of whether I wanted to continue being seen or not.

I never expected to be seen as lovely prior to adolescence, but to be loved by others simply because I'd walked in the door, bringing a breath of life to the people who wanted to be around someone so easy in her skin. Our generation won't change the double standard of aging in our lifetime, but we've begun to acquire power we once thought became women's only when we married. It never did. Nor did a man have access to our power. Now we each have a portion of what once belonged exclusively to the opposite sex, and we can share it with one another or we can live alone.

We will be more actively involved in becoming the kind of people we want to be. This is what people will read into our faces, no longer young as they were but no more creased than the faces of men: youthful beauty fades, but intellect, energy, leadership, all the lifelong qualities that men have, including sexual energy, these will be women's characteristics too.

I do not approach old age with glee, but I hate waste. I choose to believe that young women are now growing up taking admirable women as models; as young girls they see respect paid to women of all ages, as it is to men; economic success will always be admired because our god is economics. But so will achievement in other fields. As children see their parents genuflecting in front of seventy-year-old women like Pamela Harriman, our wealthy ambassador to France, they will note that it is not because of a pretty face. And they will see gifted women such as Maya Angelou, Elizabeth Dole, Sandra Day O'Connor receiving deference, as well as thousands of other admirable women now in the making.

In ten years, you will still hear women complaining about invisibility, but hopefully there will be less desperation and more humor in their voices, for they will have taken in their full value. Who wants to lose one's looks? Not I. Not men either. But what sustains me is a belief that these will be the best years.

What Should the Good Witch Wear?

Today's tailors have their work cut out for them; every year millions of women are passing age fifty, and we have never looked better. We are also richer than our age group has ever been, and our wealth is not inherited from dead husbands whom we've outlived. Having made our own money, we feel freer to spend it on ourselves. We want to look the way we feel: vital, sexual, more in charge of our lives than ever.

We are the new Good Witches who do not want to be invisible, nor do we want to look grotesque, as older women do when wearing the clothes of an adolescent. Anne Hollander is the prophet come to tell us that clothes have a language and speak for us. Women always knew this, but it was the good woman's role to say, "It's not how you look, dear, or what you wear, but who you are inside." Well, yes, being good is important, but it is possible to be "good" and also be sexual and beautiful.

"We're tired of being good all the time," says novelist Margaret Atwood, a seasoned voice of honesty. "When you deprive women of any notion of threat, it pretty much puts them back in the Victorian age. All innocent, and without power, except the power of being good."

The fashion designers don't know how to see us, so revolutionary is this new category of women's extended life. Mature women were never thought of as deserving a special image. They weren't working en masse in offices, holding high positions in government, wielding financial portfolios. When I was young, the mothers of my friends never arrived at mature sexual beauty; they had reached their beauty peak in adolescence, saved virginity for marriage, and gone quickly from Prom Queen to motherhood, the latter look devoid of sexuality. As a new generation of young women grew into the fashion spotlight, their mothers visually disappeared into the landscape. Only the great movie queens with fashion designers like Edith Head and Adrian had the mature erotic beauty thing down pat; these stars had extraordinary lighting to accentuate the mesmerizing quality of sexual ease they were trained to draw up from deep down inside. That is why we called the movies "make-believe." We never saw women like that in the flesh.

But you and I do not age as our mothers did; many of us work outside the home and have good money to spend: Women ages fifty-five to sixty-four earn 41 percent more than that age group did thirty years ago; women over sixty-five make more than twice as much. I emphasize the money because you would think cash, if nothing else, would make the fashion designers scramble. But we cannot blame the tailors, whose job isn't psychiatry. "What do women want?" has taken on new meaning; an army of us has evolved with neither a psychological nor nor a visual model of a mature sexual beauty. We have nothing to wear!

Fashion critic Holly Brubach wrote of the seventies, "There's something especially alarming about the recycling of that decade, as if all history were turning into a hall of mirrors. . . . It seems to me easier to take shelter in the style of another decade than to invent a style for one's own time and refurbish the world in it. Either way, it's a cop-out, a means of abdicating the life that we've been dealt."

Most of the tailors who resurrect the fashions we wore when we changed the world in the sixties and seventies weren't even around then. Do they play our old music and reinvent the clothes in the hope that the "look" might recapture the old momentum and get us out of this rut we're in? Fashion designers can only invent clothes when people are ready to wear them, because the look fits the times. We aren't there yet, therefore they can't dress us.

"The silence of being unseen can be devastating after a lifetime of listening for the compliment or searching for the approving glance that confirms one's ability to please," wrote psychologist Rita Freedman in 1986. But the devastation felt by young women today comes after a "lifetime" of only twenty-five years. They are caught between an impoverished self in the nursery and the fear of growing older, there being so few images of admirable older women out there.

Women's magazines reinforce their anxiety that life only exists in this moment. Get yourself looked at now, for only obscurity lies ahead. I remember well the fashion bibles I grew up seeing on coffee tables, mother's magazines like *Vogue* and *Harper's Bazaar* with their mesmerizing images of beautiful adult women who promised mystery, an exciting future owned by grown-ups. At sixteen we didn't want to look that way, not yet, but these exotic women, like the movie queens on the big screen at The Gloria, offered an alternative future of sexual beauty to that of dear old mom.

In the sixties and seventies, when the baby boomers, by sheer numbers, conquered the media—"The Youthquakers" was what Diana Vreeland called them—images of Jean Shrimpton, Penelope Tree, and Twiggy took over the fashion pages. The rush of music, art, and writing provided content to The Look. These books and songs and paintings were the message heard round the world. The voices of early Feminism played to the backdrop of Warhol's paintings, The Stones' music, and the shrunken T-shirts and long hair of The Youthquakers. Everything interesting and important was in sync with the Civil Rights Movement, abortion rights, the protest against the Vietnam War.

That said, there are things worth preserving from the past that got

lost in the revolutions. We who lived through them are the last generation to have been born into a world of tradition and manners. If we
don't incorporate that civility and live it so that our parents' look that
we loved is in us, then it will become extinct. There are reasons we run
the old movies again and again and reinvent the old clothes; Frank
Sinatra and Tony Bennett sound as sweet as the summers of youth in
our parched world, even to people who didn't hear them the last time
around. Everyone is hungry.

We must find a look for The Good Witch. Are women uncomfortable looking powerful, associating strength with age, meaning mother?
We bring to the sight of a beautiful fifty-year-old woman a different
memory than we bring to a man. Should we just glimpse her, not
know her, we would be drawn to her beauty. But then someone tells us
her age and we see her differently. The image of the first woman in our
lives shades how we see ourselves aging and, by extension, how we
see other aging women; part of the pleasure in destroying older
women is getting back at the witch in the nursery, not the good one,
the bad.

When we see ourselves in the mirror, age fifty or sixty, we are
reluctant to rely on our looks. Only the emotionally separated, individuated woman arrives at a stage where she can see the internalized
mother whole, thereby seeing herself as whole too. Those of us who
never did are left with the Good Witch and Bad Witch of fairy tales,
with the split of the most powerful woman in the world into the loved
and the hated mother. Of course we don't want to look powerful.

The Brothers Grimm, in the "Snow White" and "Hansel and Gretel" tales they collected, were so disturbed to find mothers at the center
of the stories about murder, jealousy, abandonment—which had been
passed on orally from one generation of old women to the next—that
they changed the character into a stepmother for the collection's third
edition, published in 1819. "For them, the bad mother had to disappear in order for the ideal to survive and allow Mother to flourish as
symbol of the eternal feminine, the motherland, and the family itself as
the highest social desideratum." It is too bad. Children need to hear
reality spoken; they can take it. So can we. Otherwise, when we look at
a powerful older woman, ourselves or another, what we see and fear is
The Bad Witch.

My own ambivalence regarding my need to be seen, as against
emptying the crowded closets and traveling with one small suitcase, is

in this puzzle somewhere; exhibitionism, putting oneself out there in a dazzling dress, carries with it the threat of loss of control, as when flying. For instance, when I board a plane I instinctively reach for fashion magazines; nothing diverts me from fear of loss of control in flight like judging beauty. I turn the pages of *Vogue* with languid anticipation, alternately relieved—a rush of superiority—that nothing is good enough to catch my eye, and then an Aha! of adrenaline when I spy something that would make an entire restaurant turn to gaze.

Imagining myself in beautiful clothes has got me through a lot of bumpy flights. Nowadays, when the airplane lands safely, and I cheat death again, I see that I have turned down the corners of fewer and fewer fashion pages. I am an addict in remission, sympathetic to why women are buying less: we, the best-looking, moneyed generation ever of women our age, are different from our mothers and nothing represents us. When the eye focuses on middle-aged women, it can't take us in. Even so-called adult women's magazines are unable to move beyond adolescent beauty, are at a cultural impasse.

Flying down to Key West yesterday I read an article in *Harper's Bazaar* about the "invention" of a hot new model. "Agents call it inventing the girl," said the writer, "you pick and choose their work. . . . You position them. You decide how they're going to be seen . . . to satisfy our culture's hungry eye . . . hers is a loveliness that seems to compose itself and draw you in the longer you look."

But this is no Garbo face, as the last line above might suggest, it is a pretty face of the latest eighteen-year-old, chain-smoking icon in jeans and tank top. All of her pet peeves and philosophy are duly noted in the text. The median age of the female reader of *Vogue* is an adult 32.4. Is it true that "youth is the only thing worth having," as Dorian Gray said? Our own preoccupation with it goes beyond fear of age itself, as if the beautiful new turn-of-the-century woman that our revolution has given us is, as men used to say, "too much woman for me."

Why don't the editors, stylists, and photographers who create these fashion magazines devise a look for the eye and wallet of the majority of their readers? Just before Alexander Liberman retired as creative director of Condé Nast—which owns *Vogue*—where he had been for more than fifty years, I met him briefly in his office. Respectful, even intimidated, aware of the reverence in which he was held, I asked why these adult magazines didn't have a more sophisticated look, as did the issues he designed thirty and forty years ago, which chronicled women of the world who belonged to a fashionable pantheon of supreme beauties like Lisa Fonssagrives-Penn, Babe Paley, Liz Whitney, and Slim Keith. I've always remembered Avedon's miraculous shot of Dovina with the elephants, Horst's mesmerizing black-and-white photo of Coco Chanel, and Liberman's own of Marlene Dietrich. Posed in a style that said chic, soignée, cosmopolitan, these women, I said to Liberman, were a mystery I didn't understand when young but which impressed me as my future.

"You can't sell a magazine that appeals to matrons," he advised me with disdain. And then, "You are living in the past." I was so taken aback, I stood up, speechless. The interview was over.

I like to think that it is not just the mediocrity of fashion that accounts for the dearth of pages in *Vogue* that interest me but that I also have a better opinion of myself these days and am therefore less in need of fancy wrappings. Not a great opinion, but better, and very much a product of twenty-five years of writing, which has taught me that I was happiest in my skin when I was ten. It was precisely that ease, more than anything, that I would like to recapture. I never looked in mirrors then. I believed in the bright, articulate, athletic girl I was, and brave, oh, how brave! How did I lose her?

When I was in the eighth grade, my grandfather sent my mother a silver evening bag for Christmas; inside was a gold tube of lipstick embossed with the figure of an elegant stork. Sherman Billingsley, the colorful owner of the Stork Club in New York, was famous for handing out such favors. The lipstick itself was a color I'd never before seen, a hot, shocking pink, which captivated me as in a fairy tale: "Take me," it said, and I did.

We girls were just beginning our beauty rituals—one starts early in the South—and when I put on my shocking-pink lipstick, everybody gazed. I was accustomed to people admiring my splendid report cards, my athletic prowess, my death-defying leaps through space from tree to tree, but now they looked at my mouth, my face. It was an altogether different feeling, having a part of my body admired.

Maybe forty years later, on a summer day calling for the hot-pink lipstick I'd continued to keep as a part of my wardrobe, my husband and I drove down the road to visit our friends Charles and Belinda. We had taken separate houses in Malibu for the month of August, and it was a perfect day for drinking Bellinis. We sat in their garden and laughed a lot, champagne and peach nectar being an ebullient high. Eventually we ambled indoors to view a painting of a Rousseau jungle of animals that Belinda had just completed, she being a fancier of wildlife and parrots in particular, two of which she and Charles owned. He asked if I would like to have his parrot sit on my shoulder and, as I knew the bird to be the far tamer of the two, I agreed.

Standing there very still, smiling my hot-pink smile, I didn't see Belinda quietly circling behind me and without warning placing her irascible bird on my other shoulder, causing my head to turn abruptly. The bird squawked and sunk its beak into my face. I could feel the warm blood running down my cheek and hear Belinda's laughter as she tipsily led me to her dressing table and applied astringent. Seeing the torn, bloody skin just below my eye, I began shaking so visibly that my husband had to take me home.

When I stood at my own mirror and saw the crater in my cheek, and realized how close it was to my one good eye, I began to cry big tears, which is not at all like me. It wasn't the pain, but something else so deep and sad that I couldn't name it for days. Why had she put that bad-tempered bird so close to my face without even a word of warning?

"It was your flamboyant look, that hot-pink lipstick," she said when she telephoned to tell me what her "bird expert" had said regarding the incident. "The lipstick and that blond hair. You're so flashy. It made my darling Petrov angry."

She was more amused than concerned, having been bitten several times by her birds and feeling something else too. "You should have seen my friend Jane," she went on, "when tiny Petrov chased her up the stairs. All that red hair of hers got to him. She was screaming, but it was hilarious, little Petrov hopping up the stairs after that big, gorgeous woman."

She is a beautiful woman herself, Belinda, though she goes out of her way to let the great bones, the hair, the skin, the whole masterpiece crumble through neglect. The demolition is so intentional. Still, it refuses to die. On her coffee table is an old issue of *Vogue* magazine with her on the cover as the most beautiful debutante of the year. What kind of unhappiness provokes her to put on display her youthful beauty even as she destroys what remains of it?

Clearly, what beauty won her was not good enough. Better to thumb her nose at us for still worshiping what she now hates, the remains of what once promised so much. The magazine lies on the table, where she can walk by it, intentionally wearing something dowdy. Once Galanos, Halston, and Saint-Laurent begged her to wear their designs so that others might worship her in them, hence them on her. I study her closely, for I don't want to become angry, envious of other women who refuse to imitate her bitter capitulation to age.

In a version of the Cinderella fairy tale, after the two evil and envious stepsisters have been bested by the beautiful Cinderella in the competition for the King's son, they try to get back into her good graces so as to share in her fine fortune. On the way to the church where the wedding will take place, two birds come and peck out one eye from each of the bad sisters; after the ceremony, the birds appear again and peck out the other eye from each. "And thus, for their wickedness and falsehood, they were punished with blindness all their days."

Bruno Bettelheim's comment on the birds' blinding the sisters is that it is a symbol of their insensitivity, "but also the logical consequence of [their] having failed to develop a personality of their own. . . . [They did not] develop a separate self . . . discover the difference between good and evil, develop initiative and self-determination . . . they remain empty shells."

So much of life spent trying to be seen. With all my talk of emptying closets, I do not want to end up like Belinda with her evil birds. To decide to stop pulling the eye to oneself is a fine decision but must be made in full consciousness of what is being given up. Slaughtering what remains of beauty without acceptance of how you will feel when other women star in what was once your role, well, it can lead to a lot of birds being sent to assuage your envy, peck out the eyes of the "flashy" ladies who have dared to make you mindful of what you once owned.

Somehow, perhaps in the writing of this book, I want to come to terms with my need to be seen so that when the time for flashy clothes is done—I don't see hot-pink lips when I'm on a walker—I will have internalized the belief that I am lovable for other, invisible qualities. That business of separation and individuation of which Bettelheim and Mahler speak begins in the nursery and, though it should ideally end around age two, wiser men and women know we work on it all our lives.

"Behind every terror lies a wish," Freud said, and no doubt when the breeze in Key West blows the sheer Zoran top against my breasts, I am split: Part of me wishes to be seen, the other half fears that I will be. Psychiatrist Eric Berne wrote about this in his book *Games People Play*, where he explains that instead of being a healthy adult who only does what he himself approves of, some of us play the game of being both critical parent and naughty child. If, indeed, I am still stuck at that stage of rebelling against my very critical mother who wouldn't see me, I am resigned to it. It is my way of remaining tied to her, of still trying to get from her what I couldn't as a tiny child. Do I write my books against her, did Freud, does Paglia; and does Madonna, like Marilyn Monroe and Gypsy Rose Lee, take off her clothes to get back at her/them? Or do we ever reach a point where we do it for ourselves?

If the occasional bird gouges flesh from my face for my "flashiness," the occasional friend telephones to remind me not to miss the latest evil review of a book I have written, I remind myself of the rewards of my exhibitionism, that this is what won my husband's love more than anything.

When I first began to interview gurus in the behavioral world, I was repeatedly corrected for using the word *voyeur* when referring to how we women looked at men in their tight jeans in the seventies, our eyes drawn to their creatively arranged crotches. "Men, not women, are the voyeurs," I was corrected. And when I spoke of myself as an exhibitionist, I was also informed that the word *exhibitionist* referred to a male flasher who unzipped his fly in the park.

In her book *Female Perversions*, psychiatrist Louise Kaplan offers such a fascinating, contemporary explanation of why some of us need to exhibit our selves. Let me quote her at length, for in these days of insufficient parenting, more and more young women are growing up without The Gaze and thus seek reassurance that they exist through exhibitionism. Here is Kaplan on "homeovestism," a term coined by the Canadian psychoanalyst George Savitzianos. She begins by describing a fictional character:

> Emma Bovary, who acts or dresses exactly like some stereotyped notion of a woman, may be a female homeovestite, a woman who is unsure of her femininity, a woman who is afraid to openly acknowledge her masculine strivings. . . . The concept of homeovestism, with its implication of gender impersonation, may also be more faithful to what is going on when a woman dresses up to exhibit herself as a valuable sexual commodity than the term exhibitionism. . . . In an offhand way, the psychiatric profession and the public alike often speak of stripteasers and women who

act in porn movies or who pose for pornographic magazines as exhibitionists. While the basic gratifications of exhibitionism ... play some part in attracting women to these callings, ultimately the countless women who dress up in women's underwear, veils, or other semi-exposing female garments to pose in sexually explicit or sexually suggestive postures do so to reassure themselves that they will not be abandoned or annihilated. Their very existence is at stake. The fetishized body of the porno actress is all that is left of a little girl who could never make any sense at all of why love had been taken away from her. ... Women like ... culture heroine Marilyn Monroe are prisoners in bodies that cannot come to life except through impersonations of femininity. These female female impersonators are as dominated by their rigid sexual scenarios as are the men they capture, captivate, and serve.

What I like about Kaplan's broader definition of exhibitionism is that it explains our grown-up need to be looked at in terms of The Gaze of earliest life. How much longer will it take us to understand that what happens in the nursery goes beyond feeding and caretaking, that the pattern of a lifetime is being laid down? Until we accept this, we will have young men and women hungrily roaming the streets of the world, greedy for the sight of themselves in the eyes of others, and furious unto violence when no one sees them. The small child's fear of being "abandoned or annihilated," of never making "any sense at all of why love has been taken away," as Kaplan writes, has produced children from empty nurseries grown into young people whose exhibitionistic dress and talk have become not just a fashion trademark but a way of life: "Look at me! Look at me, damn it, or I'll kill you!"

In writing I came to see that The Nice Girl I'd so far presented to the world was very angry indeed and, yes, very much in need of being seen. It had everything to do with the absence of my father, not just his not being there to take up the slack in my mother's visual regard and see me as The Adorable One, but also with his being such a damn mystery. Now, looking back, I can see why writing about forbidden subjects like sex and dressing to catch the eye had such a life-and-death urgency. I would like to say that being labeled a dirty writer by The Ladies of the media hurts less with time, but a Nice Girl never really gets over it. Nonetheless, I could no more stop writing about sex than a child could turn away from the spotlight of mother's eyes.

In her autobiography *Fear of Fifty*, Erica Jong painfully recalls, "It is hard even now to remember the hatred that came on the heels of *Fear of Flying*. Women journalists who confessed deep identification in private would attack in public, often using the very confidences they had extracted from me, citing their feminine identification. The sense of betrayal was extreme. I felt more silenced by these bitter personal attacks than I ever did by male critics."

Erica and I have known each other since our books on women's sexuality, hers fiction, mine nonfiction, were published in the early seventies; I identify all too well with what she says. One of the rewards of growing older is that you care less about what others think: "What will the neighbors say?" I may not wear the scanty clothes in which I once showed off my body, but my mind is certainly less inhibited. When I was in my twenties and younger, the desire to show off and be sexual was at war with the fear of what the other girls would say. Like Erica, I was stunned by the reaction of women friends to *My Secret Garden*; women who were strangers were very much on my side. It was in spite of my friends' disdain that I continued to write about sex.

Writers are high on the charts when it comes to suicide, nervous breakdowns, pathological depression, and stomach ulcers. Years ago, I read a list of Nobel Prize–winning authors who died of alcoholism. Uncovering emotion so that the reader resonates demands a lot of digging on a writer's part, the removal of memory blocks inscribed "Do Not Remove." That so many of us stick with the solitary life, the unwrapping of insight that turns out to be fury, says to me that what we do is worth it. "I was afraid that if I let out my rage I would somehow destroy the world," wrote Richard Rhodes, referring to his writer's block. And from Virginia Woolf, "I feel certain that I am going mad." Byron, Shelley, Melville, and Coleridge all suffered from various forms of manic depression and mood depression. Teutonic rage is usually that of an infant, which is why we call it infantile omnipotence. A wise person once told me that writer's block was mother sitting in the unconscious with a blue pencil. I'll buy that.

Anger is expressed on the face by "the angry frown": knit brows, a hard stare, and tight lips to cover the teeth, says Carl Izard, who studies nonverbal communication. When anger is repressed, he says, there is a "covering expression" that masks the face, a look I remember as that Nice Woman mask that women of my mother's generation wore, a communal wall of repressed emotion that made them look old before their time. Women hate the ever-narrowing lips. Today we inject them with collagen, and New World dentistry replaces the teeth we angrily grind down at night. But the people most eager for collagen injections are in their twenties.

The desperation to be seen is no longer confined to any generation. Beauty's rewards have lost much of the old moralistic preachiness attached to "scientifically" improving one's appearance. "The appeal of the straightforward, clean-scrubbed look, unfalsified by 'paint,' is essentially moral," writes Holly Brubach. "We admire a woman for the courage to show herself to the world as she is, and in the end it's the courage we find attractive." Certainly that idea is still with us, built into the backbone of our Protestant ethic. But as we extend youthful beauty with exercise, surgery, better health, and self-chosen work, my own vote for courage goes to the risk taker who flaunts the rules of morality and dares to wear paint, show leg, cleavage, and flesh, who goes for surgery so long as she carries it off with confidence.

We admire Joan Collins's looks because she has performed her exhibitionistic role with great aplomb; by putting us at ease, she allows us to take her in. I think the ease is what I admire most of all, since it flies against envy. I am suspicious of those who raise themselves to sainthood for eschewing cosmetic surgery even as they denigrate those who vote for it. Sneering at the woman who looks great after having her eyes done gives the envious have-nots a shot of moral superiority, when indeed they are no different from the busybodies who tattletaled about the first women who smoked in public.

Barbara Bush, with her white hair and fake pearls, didn't convince me that she was happy in her choice. She always struck me as an angry, envious woman. When the beauty industry today actually uses envy in their advertising, I rejoice; get it out there, tell it like it is. When it encapsulates the culture's hidden agendas, advertising rises to an art form: "They say men get character lines as they get older and women just get wrinkles . . . oh, really?" says the woman in the Oil of Olay commercial. "I don't plan to grow old gracefully, I intend to fight it every inch of the way."

What we want is to look better as we age and still be "good people" like our mothers. This is what the have-nots prey upon, the immorality of our daring to improve appearance beyond what is "natural." The anxiety of the fifty-year-old woman who has surgically made herself beautiful is the fear of the adolescent girl whose sexual beauty won her the love of more than her share of boys: Afraid that the other girls will love her less, she lowers her erotic flame. We might choose to have liposuction and painted auburn hair if only we didn't have to forfeit goodness, kindness, and the approval of others. What a ridiculous dilemma. Why do we give to others the verdict on our morality? Some resentment of beauty will never go away, especially when carried past youth into those years when women are expected to go quietly into invisible oblivion.

We in The Third Act of our lives are the last generation to remember the inevitability of women growing into grandmothers with white hair and soft, big bosoms on which to pillow our heads, grandmothers notoriously bereft of envy, who once filled in for mothers who had no talent for seeing small children. The sadness on the streets speaks of how much we miss the look of people who looked at peace with themselves, meaning that we could relax with them and not try so hard, there being no competition. Grandmothers who smelled of lavender and had soft, wrinkled skin gave us that deep, loving gaze that said, "Go, my darling, discover your world, for I have seen you and I love what I see." But there is a shortage of grandmothers, white hair and fat underarms being very much out of style.

Other cultures seem to have less trouble than we do combining beauty with serious intent. They don't see the pursuit of beauty, at whatever age, as the work of a fool. On the contrary, beauty's role seems to be part of their culture; is it perhaps because they are also older than we? During World War II, when there were no pretty clothes available in Paris, only breadlines, the same woman who fought in the Resistance invented whatever style she could. Parisian women made hats out of old newspapers and chicken feathers, a wedding dress out of found parachute silk. Far from making others think less of them, their originality in serving beauty was esteemed.

There is a famous photo from those war years, when electricity was rationed, of Frenchwomen sitting under hair dryers powered by several men on bicycles, visible in the room below. This was not vanity run amok but a symbol of survival, women's beauty being as unquestionably worth fighting for as the Louvre or Chartres Cathedral.

In the end, the deals we make between ourselves, which allow us to see one another as powerful and bewitching, or not, are solely women's vision. Every attempt a woman makes to own sex and beauty is in opposition to attaining the love and acceptance of women's world. Until the reassuring image of a new generation of women has made the journey into a world of sexual beauty, younger women will watch us cautiously, enviously, until the turf is truly won. Then there will be a stampede, not into old age, but into life ongoing. It is modern women's journey, and the enemy is within.

Solving the Riddle of Love and Money

Money enables every woman I know to make the choices she does, to live alone or not, to continue working or not, to be as demanding and giving as she chooses. It allows her to make a love relationship with a man that doesn't hinge on his promise of providership. Feminism has always pushed for economic parity, but we still don't teach the relationship between economics and emotional independence, not just paying our bills but making our money work for us on the deepest, unconscious level, where autonomy lives, where in its own unique way it oils separation.

Even with six-figure incomes women can pass as independent, but in the way they handle money, they show themselves to be as tied to Mommy as an adolescent. That is why money is so tricky; little girls pass as powerful adults just by being big spenders. They even fool themselves. Money can't make us emotionally independent, but it can pave the way, freeing us from Mommy's promise that if we stayed close, she would always love us. Today mother would deny she ever said it, as strongly as we would deny that we still live by her rules, but when we have the funds to pay for an apartment and a diaphragm but leave the door to the former unlocked and the latter unused, whose little dependent girl are we?

Women didn't discuss money when I was growing up. It simply wasn't done. I celebrate wholeheartedly women's economic independence, appreciating that it buys responsibility. This is why I cheered former governor of Texas Ann Richards when she spoke at Texas Girls High School, a speech that may have contributed to her not gaining reelection. Her opponent, George W. Bush Jr., recognized ammunition when he heard it, accusing her of being un-American for urging young women to learn to take care of themselves economically.

"The important question you have to ask yourself," said Richards, "is not 'What do I want to be when I grow up?' It is 'Who am I?' and 'What do I want to do with my life?' And you cannot count on Prince

Charming to make you feel better about yourself and take care of you. . . . In the real world, half of all marriages end in divorce. And over 70 percent of divorced women find themselves slipping toward poverty. . . . The only person you can count on to be there when you need help is you. And almost everything worth having requires a great deal of work, work that does not always pay off right away. . . . If there is one single thing that holds [women] back . . . *it is our reluctance to face the reality of money.* . . . You've got to be willing to take charge of your life and responsibility for yourself." (The emphasis is mine.)

"This is not the message Texans want their leaders to give our daughters or sons," George Bush roundly countered, accusing Richards of being antifamily. "Our leaders should be building up the family, not tearing it down." The heart sinks when such a twisted opinion can win a man an election. But Bush knew that he was playing into a deep longing that we all have, a security we dreamed we had as children; maybe some of us did have it, but if you hold it out to schoolgirls today, it is a lie. We won't bring back the family as we dream of it by raising girls to be as totally dependent on a man as a baby is on a mother.

I recognized my mother's economic dependence and took it as the model of how I did not want to be when I grew up. I am deeply grateful that I can provide for myself today, but I would not wish my earliest lessons in getting here on to another child. Instead, I would have mothers and fathers go out of their way to teach daughters to respect what self-sufficiency gives an individual. The Bushes of the world play on a nostalgia for a world that never really existed, and I would imagine that George Bush Jr. is also opposed to our best hope for the future, which is fathers as caretakers alongside mothers who share in the work of providing.

It is possible to be a feminist and have others pay for your food and clothing. But it is harder, much harder than when you are able to care for yourself economically. Money comes with strings attached, even when given with love, perhaps more so. Economic dependency on others gives them the right to critique us, or so they may think. When we are dependent on others for the roof over our head, behind conscious thought is the fear, What if they take it all away tomorrow?

A woman in a traditional marriage would vehemently deny that she resents her husband's power over her; at the root of her faith in their marriage deal—wherein he provides economically and she is the caretaker—is her training at mother's knee: If she was good and obeyed The Rules (meaning, didn't separate from mother), she would be rewarded by a Prince. For fifteen, twenty years, the daughter held to the bargain; she sacrificed independence, initiative, powers of speech, the urge to lead instead of being led until one day faith paid off in the form of The Prince. For her even to consider the possibility of losing her identity, which is invested in him, is unthinkable, even when she finds the bill from a local hotel in his coat pocket.

This is a picture of traditional woman, someone who believes in our mothers' and grandmothers' way of life, much of which I miss sorely; but that is what happens in revolutions: In the upheaval, more is destroyed than was intended. Giving women the opportunity to choose to pay their own way and be economically independent is a great achievement. The operative word is choice; feminism's denigration of the role of women who choose to work at home is a disgrace.

My friends who also went through the sixties and seventies agree with me that these years today are the best in our lives. Being able to pay the rent has a lot to do with it. More than chronological age, emotional gravity made our mothers old before their time. When husbands wandered, other wives gathered round as at a death, and the dirge began: "This is how men are." Their faces were shaped by resignation, the lines at the corners of their mouths grew longer, deeper; submission to the inevitable tightened their communal biting of the bullet. Inside, each woman gathered her rage into a knot that tightened until the migraines began, the alcohol was drunk, the cancer cells multiplied, and the symbolic death loomed, literal.

As successive generations of women enter the workplace—and they will—and the average wage for women rises—as it will—I see the double standard of aging continuing to level out. As women take more security in knowing that we can provide for ourselves, hopefully, we will be less critical of the mirror, less inclined to see our value decreasing with age. With a better economic cushion, we should begin to take on a sense of ease in our skins that men have enjoyed, an ease that will be terribly attractive to men, especially younger men who have grown up in a world where they are accustomed to women economically as well as maternally powerful.

Men begin life taking in the beauty of woman power; add economic power to the never forgotten radiance of she who runs the nursery and you make the double standard of aging obsolete, or at least optional. All that remains is for the woman to believe it, to see her self as men see her, to look at her image, not the imperceptible tiny lines at the corners of the mouth, but the whole image that extends beyond the mirror, beyond the house, to include everything she does and is.

The more economic power a man has, the more readily he approaches a woman. He will be hurt if she rejects him, but it will not deter him from making another call. Money in the bank is meaningful to a man; he has grown up watching men use this power and seeing women react to it. But we women haven't yet experienced decades of parlaying our own money into personal conquest. The only commodity we have seen women trade in is beauty.

Though it is a fleeting, unstable commodity, being in the eyes of one beholder and not the next, we trust beauty more than money, and we grieve at its loss, ironically, today more than ever. In a recent survey, nearly 50 percent of American women ages eighteen to seventy said that they were dissatisfied with how they looked, compared to 30 percent who felt that way ten years ago. Our problem is that we gained some economic wherewithal before we got emotional separation, sort of the cart before the horse. Very well, we must work with what we've got, consciously investing money, spending it to further individuation.

Even as we pressed for an equal wage twenty years ago, the feeling in the air was that in achieving economic freedom we would be different from men, that we would undergo some spiritual rebirth from which we would emerge autonomous, without having soiled ourselves with filthy lucre. Why do these Matriarchal Feminists think that when we are as economically and politically powerful as men, we will be better, kinder, more generous, and holier than they? We are people who happen to be of the female gender, and as regards goodness and kindness, no different from men, some of whom are kind and some not.

"A girl should learn to type because you never know when it might come in handy" was as much encouragement toward economic independence as women used to receive growing up. Given the promise of a Prince who was going to make up for everything they had sacrificed—bravery, speech, initiative, their whole identity—the fallback position of a typing skill made no sense. Of course, no one learned to type. After all, there was a Prince coming!

Dependency is sweet, but swallowed anger at having no anchor of one's own destroys beauty; as children grew up and youthful good looks disappeared, our mothers knew the value of their half of the deal with their husbands was lessening. They couldn't afford to know it consciously, but these truths were the stuff of novels, films, and as the smiling woman closed the book, left the movie theater, content in her good fortune that it could never happen to her, in her dreams at night it happened. It wasn't just that our mothers didn't go to a gym or diet that made them age less well than we; it was the unthinkable prospect of abandonment.

Men didn't set out to dupe their wives; they too had meant to love until death. But things happen. No amount of "I love yous" could assuage what women felt when their husbands looked at other women; the wife didn't look at other men and no man had looked at her in that way for years. She denied its meaningfulness, but denial sucks up energy over time. So does protracted loss of identity as children grow up and leave.

Divorce lawyers had, and still have, a hard time convincing the jilted wife that if she doesn't take certain measures, the disappearing husband will leave her penniless. "Oh, no, he will still take care of me," she tearfully insists; that is how totally she had believed in the Prince years ago when she abandoned all the life-enhancing talents she'd once possessed in order to be the pliant, submissive, dependent Princess. Money isn't everything, but it isn't without meaning. Knowing where your next meal is coming from, having money in your own name, does a lot for circulation, digestion, and a good night's sleep.

Since I was raised never to discuss money, I obeyed the feminine vow of silence regarding it and, telling no one, quietly saved my small change in the glass bank shaped like the world. The determination to leave home for a life of my own had at its heart the vow never again to feel left out or afraid. The full meaning of dependency wasn't yet understood, but I certainly felt its emotional weight, my mother's and my own, and the role of money was not lost on me. The freedom my grandfather enjoyed, the respect he engendered opposite the anxiety of women, educated me.

Children absorb far more than parents imagine; I understood that she who could not pay her own way would have my mother's anxious look, those deep sighs for which I felt responsible, wrongly so, but felt it nevertheless. Watching my grandfather come and go in our little world, always arriving from distant ports with beautiful gifts for my mother and aunt—silk scarves painted by Picasso from Paris, white leather luggage lined in red satin from Madrid—how could I not want to be him instead of these frightened women? It was his aura I wanted, his almost tangible sureness of self. That he was a man didn't in the least complicate my preadolescent plan.

My mother smiled quizzically at the glass bank on the bookcase next to my bed, and while it irked her that my sister often lost or misplaced her allowance, it bound the two of them more closely. Put another way, failing at independence was how women were.

When I became a sexual woman, the riddle of love and money took a more sophisticated turn; the little girl bravado turned to a look of sexual independence. I wore it with the full knowledge that it attracted all kinds of men, and no man appealed less than one with money. What I didn't like about them was that they saw their portraits in their bank accounts, meaning they never let a woman in, never let anyone in. Protected behind money's padded walls was that very part of them I wanted to reach with my sex, my promise that there was nothing from their early emotional self that they could show me that I would not accept. I wanted a man I could awaken, as The Prince had awakened Sleeping Beauty, a man whose defenses had not been made impenetrable by the security of money, a false freedom anyway, given that it leaves that kind of man brain-dead, emotionally cut off, invisible to himself and useless to me.

I didn't want a lot of money, still don't, just enough independence not to need men so desperately that I couldn't see myself in them, them in me. It is exciting when a man borrows emotionally from me, when he takes courage, or extends his freedom, or plays with beauty's power. These exchanges between a man and a woman are as thrilling as sex—well, they are sex. Eventually I would write about the extended influence of the first years of life, but when I was twenty-two I knew in a nonintellectual, sensory way that if I could awaken a man to believe that what I loved in him was not money but the core of him, what came before society's kiss of wealth-as-character, he would know that I was not easily replaceable. It was love eternal, not a good provider, I was after. I was a good provider.

I remember a panel discussion in the mid-seventies wherein four married couples, including my then husband and I, were asked to discuss something like "Marriage and Feminism." When I suggested how earning my own way had served me as a feminist, there was an angry reaction from the audience. "Money is not what feminism is about!" someone shouted. But when women walked out of marriages wholesale in the seventies, leaving home and family behind in order "to find themselves," they were responding to an inner conviction that they didn't feel free even to think their own thoughts, much less act the way they wanted to within a structure—the married home—that was based on the same premise and run by the same rules as their parents' home. There were some mistakes made in women's revolutionary exodus from home and responsibility in those years, but the intuitive rush out the door was the hunger to get something back that hadn't been delivered under Patriarchy's Deal.

If others take care of you economically, doling out funds from an account that is in their name alone, generous as they may be, you are in the role of the good child who does her work and gets an allowance. Money arguments are at the top of the list of where trouble starts within a marriage. What makes the reality of economic dependency painfully difficult to explain is that it feels good to many a woman. This kind of woman doesn't want her own bank account, because to her it would be saying to her husband, "I don't need you." In her preconscious thinking it would be an inducement for him to leave her. The Governor Bushes of this world promote women's dependency as family values.

It is a kind of Patriarchy that blindly refuses to accept the *value* of what has been accomplished in the past two decades, a level of independence for women that would evolve into a new and more real form of family values that is more than words, meaning a choice is made every day to remain together as a loving family because both husband and wife—not just the man—have the wherewithal to be independent. Instead, they choose to stay together, even after bitter arguments, because what would be lost is known absolutely, having often been reviewed and found too precious ever to lose.

Because women who work at home provide a role as important as their husband's salaried job, they too should be paid a salary, a portion of his. Deposited in an account in her name, it would automatically substantiate her separate self; the rewards might not be conscious, but the repeated transactions of paying for goods and services with one's own funds, which have been earned, tells her, whether or not she wants to hear it, that she exists unto herself and that, lo and behold, people don't love her less for having an identity of her own. On the contrary, they are more drawn to her given that the weight of dependency has been removed and that independence provides an attractive spark.

Her children would grow up with a model of a woman who was both loving and independent within a caring marriage, giving her daughters a memory of the most important woman in their lives as someone whose self wasn't lost in neediness, that "I'll die if you leave me!" brand of femininity. And her sons would have a working knowledge of a mate, not just someone whose entire identity was in blindly serving husband and children but who *chose* each day to be a mother and a wife; because of her choice, there would be less burden felt by the son to repay her for giving up her life, and since she literally paid her own way, he would feel free to define manliness as something more than earning as much as possible.

A woman who chooses to work at home may not like the idea of receiving payment that is kept in her own name in a bank, for it wasn't how her own mother lived within marriage. Taking money from her husband somehow feels like it gives him license to leave her, that she is a form of hired help rather than his little wifey. That sounds ridiculous, yes, but I've been there, and while in my own life I was the breadwinner, I didn't want to feel like the provider and eagerly, gratefully handed the money over to him, as if to say, "You are big and I am just a little girl." Men too try to find with wives what they had with Mommy, but they don't usually use money as the conduit; women's confusion of love and money says, "If I earn a lot of money, then who will take care of me?" Money is the enemy of symbiosis—unless you disown it, give it away as I did.

The money riddle is so much more complicated than any of us are ready to admit. Rewarding as it is to buy our own food, pay our rent, not enough time has yet gone by for women to take in what we have won. Our mothers' bargains, under which we grew up, still haunt us, perhaps only in dreams at night, but it would be unnatural if they did not. It doesn't help that feminism refuses to spell out the realities of cold, hard money in the bank; it would mean that those who had more money than the other girls would arouse the dreaded monster, competition.

Because many women work outside the home today doesn't automatically mean they are separate and independent. But without money with which to buy food and pay the rent, we are obviously tied, tied to mother/father, to husband, to welfare, to a more comfortable definition of a woman than the one we are now fashioning, sometimes, I think, against our will. In women's world we still refuse to give "dirty money" its full credit; like sex, to which it is very much allied, there is that niggling, uncomfortable feeling that money somehow isn't feminine, womanly. Lest my message get twisted in the feminist translation, let me repeat that it is not a question of how much money we make; the big earner isn't automatically more separate. It is the emotional and psychological awareness of what our economic independence buys us that must be internalized.

A good exercise in learning the liberating influence of money is to use it on a man, buy him dinner, give him pleasure, enjoy how good it feels to be the initiator. It is good practice to pick up the check; you've done something your mother never did. He will thank you for dinner, not a world-shaking event, but a rewarding step toward bursting that balloon over our heads in which we see ourselves being constantly observed by others.

A long-ago lover used to enjoy drinking at bars, as did I. I would sit and he would stand beside me, elbow on the bar, and we would talk for hours in that special way lovers do in saloons. He would toss some bills on the bar when we arrived, and as we drank, the bartender would simply take cash out of the bills and make change; he never interrupted us, and my lover never looked at the money, nor did he count it when we left. "A fool with his money . . ." you might say, but I took it quite differently, admiring his and the bartender's ease. Ease, as you may have noticed, is very big with me; I want to be easier.

Women are not at ease, and few things make a group of us more unattractively uneasy than settling the check at lunch. Me, I would like to stand at the bar and put a big bill out there and talk to my man without thinking about money.

Twenty-five years ago, we said we didn't want men paying for our dinners, opening doors for us, lighting our cigarettes. Doing everything ourselves was one of the ways in which we were "demolishing forever the myth of male superiority." Frankly, I like having my chair pulled out for me, but I also like paying for a man's meal and taking his hand in mine, nor do I mind picking up his dry cleaning or cooking his dinner, which is satisfying when *chosen* to be performed.

Wasn't this the reasoning behind opening our own doors back then, to eventually turn the tables and earn the right to initiate, make the first move, as men always had? Did we snarl at men who flicked their Bic when we took cigarette in hand, just to be mean, just for the pleasure of being sufficiently free to beat up on them? What a dead end.

Good feminism, as I see it, isn't just about an equal wage, but about the equal opportunity to reinvent our self-image, to somehow let our economic independence seep into our pores so that we wear it comfortably, thus allowing it to massage the tensions that our mothers had, constantly seeing themselves being observed in that balloon. That exercise is what ages us. When we take the initiative that our new economics offer, we are less preoccupied with the balloon.

When a woman pays for a man's dinner, does it upset the Darwinian applecart? Should they then go to his apartment, is she expected to make the first move, or if he does, without her spoken agreement, can she accuse him of date rape? I can remember various attendant emotions in paying for men's meals in restaurants and, according to anthropologist Helen Fisher, the rite of feeding within courtship is not without significance. While she notes that some female mammals do feed their lovers, courting women feed men with nowhere near the regularity that men feed women: "'Courtship feeding,' as this custom is called," she says, "probably predates the dinosaurs, because it has an important reproductive function. By providing food to females, males show their abilities as hunters, providers, and worthy procreative partners."

As more women become good providers, thus throwing all attendant roles into play, doesn't it require that we women alter our self-image? The person who pays the bill isn't expected to have a passive, demure, irresponsible look or feel about her. She is saying something in her economic provider role, perhaps not that she wants to have sex after dinner, but if she does follow the man to his apartment, how is the man to read her actions? Does he wait for her to make the first move, as she did for the bill at dinner? Certainly, going to his apartment after having paid for his dinner says she is an active participant in the evening. What happens next is *in part* her responsibility. Rape is a crime, but the fuzziness of "date rape" at a time when women pay for themselves, pay for the man, hold down responsible jobs, and wear near-naked clothes puts into question what the roles of economics and beauty are, how they interact and influence all relationships.

Fifteen years ago on NBC's *The Tomorrow Show*, Tom Snyder used to interrupt me with, "Yeah, yeah, Nancy, but why do we guys always have to take you women to dinner first? Why can't we just have sex?" Maybe Helen Fisher's explanation of the "courtship ritual" wouldn't mollify Tom, being a male keenly aware that women were earning amounts increasingly close to what he made. That was 1981, and while feminists were demanding to pay their own way, still others were hanging on to their traditional privilege of being fed by a man, thus making sure he would provide not just for tonight's meal but for the nine months of her pregnancy too.

Our new economics gives us the chance to offer the world more than beauty, in fact, to offer ourselves something other than good looks by which to know our value. When we approach a man and take responsibility for his happiness, if only for an evening, we learn something we have always envied in men: Instead of waiting and relying on beauty to reward us, by telephoning him, paying for his dinner, and initiating whatever else we may want out of the evening, we have actively gambled with rejection and not died.

Money isn't everything, but it takes the killer edge off survival, physical and emotional. In this knowledge is born the relaxed way a man stands, his big laugh, the freedom to say whatever comes into his head, as stupid as it may be. Why, he doesn't even realize that the hem is coming out of his jacket, that his hair needs combing! But that is exactly what appeals: that he doesn't give that big a damn what the mirror projects. In the end, men's ease has always been theirs because the anxiety over appearance was ours.

The Prince, the Minstrel, the Tailor, the Wedding: A Musical! Produced by the Girl I Left Behind

Two years after the fire, I met the man I would marry and with whom I've been spending the best third of my life. Had the fire not burned up everything, our meeting and marriage would not have happened. I get a chill thinking what might not have been. I would never have recognized The Prince, so cleverly disguised that night I opened the door, would certainly never have seduced him had the fire not awakened me to the girl I'd left behind, my best self.

He telephoned on a late afternoon in August, catching me walking past the phone, usually answered by machine; I'd been having a bad day with envy, trying to capture the killer feel of it on paper, therefore grinding my teeth a lot. And so the ringing phone was a momentary respite and I picked it up. A man's gentle voice tentatively reminded me that we had met several months earlier at a dinner party in honor of a mutual friend's film, and then, hearing no response, he asked me how I was. "I'm battling with siblings," I grumbled by way of hello. Would I like to have a drink? I had planned to stay home that night. But it was past four o'clock and I was already restless. Later he would tell me, "I figured if you turned me down I could always rationalize it was because it was so late in the day." The intrepid newspaper editor feared rejection. It touched my heart, which had a weakness for sheep in wolves' clothing.

He came for drinks and never left is how we tell it now. In fact, when the doorbell rang I had no expectations, no memory of his physical self. And there he was, instantly dear, black curls, head slightly lowered like a bashful fellow on a date. We sat out on the terrace, he with a beer talking about some balanced or unbalanced budget in Mexico while I watched the late afternoon August sun work its magic on Fifth Avenue windows across the park; floor by floor the little squares blazed into vermilion as the sun hunkered down behind the horizon on the far shore of the Hudson. The air was so sweet and heavy you might have parachuted on it down the seventeen floors to the sidewalk.

"Who's playing the piano?" he asked. I told him it was Peter Allen, and we stopped to listen as Pete's voice rose, stopped, and started again. "He's writing a musical," I said. The song he sang was called "Come Save Me." We wouldn't be able to save Pete, though I didn't know it then.

When it was dark, we taxied to an East Side restaurant where, over dinner, we continued our impersonal chat, so unlike everything since. Afterward we walked out onto Madison Avenue and he took my hand. It was just a handhold. He might as well have scooped me up in his arms, leapt on his horse, and ridden off into the night. It was a most remarkable handhold, so much so that I blanked on the names of two good friends walking by. I was that sure of what was about to happen.

What followed was a scene I'd been genetically programmed to play all my life. We returned to my apartment, I poured him a drink, put on Roberta Flack—who just happened to be singing "I'm the

One"—and leaned across and kissed him, he in midsentence. I'd had no fear since the fire. It had burned away the Nice Girl crust. Risking rejection, taking chances, making the first move had once again become my nature. My Prince responded as in a fairy tale, awakening. He came alive.

Do you know that being seduced is one of men's favorite sexual fantasies? Men close their eyes and become hard at the thought of a woman taking the lead, allowing them to drop the in-charge demeanor that they feel women demand and that they demand of themselves should they be rejected. No sweat, honey; easy come, easy go. That night I took him by the hand and led him downstairs to my bedroom, all freshly painted, carpeted, everything a lovely hue of nude.

During the next three days he managed to say good-bye and farewell to the several women he'd been seeing, and when a week later he left for Europe to create a newspaper, we vowed to speak every day by phone and to meet, his country or mine, every two or three weeks. Three years later I completed *Jealousy*, two years after that got my divorce, and we married. Oh, how we married!

Peter Allen determined the staging of our wedding when, one night after dinner, as we parted at our respective doors he said, "You two get married, I'll sing and dance at your wedding!" It was an offer we could not refuse. Marriage was on our minds, but now we needed a set appropriate for mounting not just a wedding, but a musical.

Two weeks later Norman put an engagement ring on my finger; we were having dinner in The Rainbow Room atop Rockefeller Center. "There," I said, pointing to the little stage high above the orchestra, "there is where we should be married." Norman tilted his head and looked up. "There?" he asked, certain that I was joking, but not altogether sure. We had been through many trials and tests, as Bettelheim would say, not the least of which was Norman's pained sense of invisibility during the low-profile years of our love affair prior to the grim divorce. "I want to hire an airplane," he used to lament, "and write Norm loves Nancy across the sky!" Well, here is a platform in the sky, I said to him. He squeezed my hand, on which he'd just placed the ring, looked back up at the platform and then at me and said, "I trust you."

It would be a fairy-tale wedding in all ways, including the last trial/test, which was the misadventure of my dress; it didn't materialize, literally, meaning the fabric and the tailor disappeared, *whooosh!* Today, eight years later, a panicked bride might readily find another wedding dress; even Armani is designing a bridal collection, but in 1988, dressed-up weddings hadn't yet recycled out of feminism. Even the bridal departments at Saks and Bergdorf's were dusty alcoves with gowns of little imagination; wedding announcements didn't fill a page in the *New York Times*. What was the heroine in the wedding musical to wear?

Enter the master of threads, whose name I'd known since the late sixties when I'd watched Barbra Streisand sing and dance in his creations. The first "Important" dress I bought was designed by Donald Brooks. When a mutual friend contacted him, he declined, saying he was too busy designing costumes for a film to invent a wedding dress for a stranger. But I didn't stay one for long; I auditioned for him at The Russian Tea Room over vodka and blinis, and before we'd downed the last, he'd drawn on a paper napkin a gown fit for Marlene Dietrich, complete with a lace hood.

It was July, however, and most of the fabric showrooms were closed. But Donald, being a wizard, found bits and pieces of white lace sufficient for a gown to be stitched by a Spanish seamstress who spoke no English. When he arrived for the last fitting, two days before the wedding, I greeted him wearing his dress from twenty years prior, a long, one-shoulder sinuous wool jersey column of wide navy-and-white stripes. He and I had come full circle.

And so Norman and I were married in the world's most beautiful nightclub, on a stage high above the revolving dance floor where performing artists in the 1930s used to make their Ta-Da! entrance before descending the curved Art Deco staircases that embrace the orchestra below.

It was a night out of a finale in one of my childhood movie musicals at The Gloria—a once-in-a-lifetime celebration and a deliberate contrast to the preference for privacy that we've had before and after the wedding. As we were pronounced husband and wife, Peter Duchin's orchestra began to play, the golden curtains around the room rose to reveal all of Manhattan, and the dance floor began to spin. Round and round it went, out came the banquet, up sprang the dancers, in rolled the wedding cake, and then, just when you thought you couldn't take any more pleasure, Peter Allen offered his gift to us, his band, his backup girl singers and Pete playing his piano, dancing, his dinner jacket thrown to the wind, the crowd calling for another chorus of "Rio." No one could make you happier than Peter Allen.

The day after the wedding, Norman and I went to our home in Connecticut where, during those perfect July days, I would ask him to tell me again and again, in detail, what our wedding had been like. When you produce your own wedding, it is hard suddenly to become the bride; I was there, but I had big memory blocks. For instance, I scolded him for not dancing with me. "But I danced half the night with you!" he protested.

What I remembered was that it had been glorious, and something else too, something that kept me getting up from where we lay around the pool and retreating into the house to write, something that demanded to be told: "Let me out!" By the end of the week, I had written a short story about a young girl growing up in a small Southern town, a story that began on a high brick wall in the shadows of St. Phillip's and St. Michael's churches, which bordered my old neighborhood. When I finished, I took it out to Norman, who read it, smiled, and thanked me.

"For what?" I asked.

"Isn't your story in answer to my toast to you at our wedding?"

"You made a toast?"

Here is my husband's wedding toast, which I offer to all once brave ten-year-olds:

When Nancy was a little girl growing up in Charleston, she was ever the adventurous leader of the pack. With friends in tow, she would run along the highest walls in town yelling, "Farther! Faster!" challenging her friends to keep up. There was no dare she wouldn't take, no thrill she wouldn't seek, no challenge she wouldn't happily embrace.

Tonight, standing at the top of the Rainbow Room's fabled staircase, looking out at all of you and all of New York, I understand the effect young Nancy must have had on her friends. Taking her hand, following her lead, is what makes me braver than I've ever been, more willing to live life at its fullest. Dearest, darling Nancy. Meeting you, marrying you, is the thrill of my life, the adventure I want to pursue. I look forward to the good times ahead, with no dread and no regrets. Here is to our marriage and our life together and to the many high walls we'll climb, living life to its fullest.

I understand now why I'd not been able to hear those words when first spoken; even now it is difficult to take them in. It hadn't been just the excitement of the wedding, but the content of what he said, so close to the bone, so much what I had always wanted to hear. Was it too painful or too wonderful? Maybe Nancy the woman couldn't hear the gift, but the girl heard, which is why I'd had to go inside and write the story. She has been speaking to me all my life, demanding her presence in every book I have written.

That autumn after our wedding, I was reluctant to return to the loneliness of the writing room. It had been years since I'd had time on my hands. I read, walked, leafed through magazines, enjoyed my first lunches with friends in years. But the worker in me was growing restless. I couldn't resist getting into the research that eventually led to the outline for this book.

A book is a journey, and while we may begin with an outline, it is not a map, by which I mean our subject hopefully takes us over, grabs us, and leads us into unimagined territory. We follow, trusting that the subject knows the way better than conscious intellect. Isn't this why we chose the subject in the first place? Once upon a time we buried an idea that was too hot to handle, something we weren't yet ready for, but which we couldn't forget; eventually we are reminded, perhaps by a dream, that we must dig up that idea that very much wants to be consciously addressed. The time is right. Instinctively, we go to the spot and dig up the bone.

Isaac Bashevis Singer did his best writing in bed, immediately upon waking, when he was just coming out of dream sleep. Where did I read that long ago? Oh yes, I nodded, understanding totally. What I love about the unconscious is its dogged determination to remind me while I sleep of what I refused to face during the day. For instance, my sleep patterns changed totally when I married that first time around.

I'd never had trouble sleeping until then. No matter what anxieties beset me by day, I would lay myself down to sleep and do just that. But when I married the wrong man, insomnia took me over. I tried hypnosis, sleeping pills, but nothing worked. Then one day during a talk with my old friend and mentor Robertiello, I mentioned my sleep problem, and he said, matter-of-factly, "You and your husband are so symbiotic you're afraid that if you fall into a deep sleep you will lose your identity. You fight sleep to hang on to your self." I was never so distant from the girl of my tenth year as I was in that marriage.

In this marriage to Norman I have been my most content; it is why this idea of emptying the closets and traveling with one small suitcase arose. What do I need of fancy wrappings? The girl of my tenth year, she who my husband saw and loves most, didn't give a damn about beauty. I sometimes fear he sees her more clearly than I, which is when I slip into inauthenticity by day, and lose my way in bad dreams at night. Last night, for instance, I was on the road again, and there were the suitcases. To my horror, they were empty. All the fine clothes I'd packed to wear to the wedding to which Norman and I were driving had disappeared.

We were in some honky-tonk town, a garishly lit main drag that resembled Key West's stretch of T-shirt shops. Realizing I would never find anything "good enough" in this place and that I couldn't possibly attend a wedding in anything less than "perfect," Norman offered to drive me back home. But that would require an eight-hour trip. We would miss the wedding because of my stupidity, craziness, weakness. I stood in the street with the suitcases open, empty, revelers all around perfectly happy in whatever they were wearing. Why couldn't I be like that, "letting my goodness shine through" as my Sunday school teacher would have said? Obviously, I fear that inside there is only badness, which only exhibitionistic dress can conceal.

"Luggage that one travels with is a load of sin . . . that weighs one down," wrote Freud. Oh, yes, Dr. Freud, I'll buy that! "But precisely luggage often turns out to be an unmistakable symbol of the dreamer's own genitals," the master adds. Humiliation. Loss of control. Soiling myself. The other perennial nightmare my unconscious refuses to give up. Me and all the other women for whom the feminine hygiene commercials are created.

Where did Freud get these ideas? I imagine the great man on a morning in turn-of-the-century Vienna sitting up in bed, he fresh out of dream sleep, writing down the last frames from the unconscious. "Lost luggage," he writes, "is a symbol of losing one's identity." Ah yes, right again, whether in dreams or in reality, my own fear of lost luggage is that without my sensational wardrobe, I would either be unacceptable or invisible.

Maybe traveling with one small suitcase isn't the definition of goodness; maybe it doesn't have to be that black-and-white, meaning living on a farm with just two pairs of jeans, some cows in the barn, and Bongo's grandpuppies. Maybe what is wanted is giving up the boo-hooing that Mommy didn't love me and made me wear my sister's old evening dress to the Yacht Club dance where no one saw me. And then it hits me that if I *had* enjoyed The Gaze, I wouldn't be in this life with my husband who sees me and loves the exhibitionistic writer of naughty books. How can you cling to the past with a man like this?

I lug my suitcases through my dreams as through life, always anxious lest the airline lose my identity. Even in adolescence—especially then, which is when it began—I overpacked. When I began this book, faced the empty page, I had no idea of how to begin. Just to put something down, and with every intention of crossing it out later, I wrote, "I am a woman who needs to be seen. I need it in a basic way, as in to breathe, to eat. Or not to be seen, that is the other increasingly attractive option." No sooner were the words on paper than I began to empty my closets, some days getting up from my work to go upstairs and fill another box with barely worn clothes to be sent to relatives and friends. I will finish this book with far more than two inches of space between coat hangers. But am I a better person?

The truth is that the woman Norman loves is the girl he toasted at our wedding. It is I who don't accept her fully. That girl thrived on being seen for who she was inside, not for what she wore on her back. Her survival plan was far better than anything I've come up with since. Getting attention, winning love, was accomplished with kindness, humor, inventiveness, a good story well told. Why, love was the easiest thing in the world to win when I was ten.

I believe we make our most important survival decisions so early in life that we cannot remember them. If enough time goes by, however, and we are alert to life's repetitions, a sense of déjà vu strikes again and again. We get wise. We have lasted, and it isn't just by chance. The repetitious chords tell us that we influence what happens to us next. We aren't this powerless person to whom things happen randomly, who has good luck or bad. There it goes again, the familiar chord, reminding us that we've been here before, giving us another chance to knit together the shirttails of life. We are of a piece.

I am not some made-up person who unravels when she looks in the mirror; I have a passport photo that has gotten me through life again and again, and it is inside me. My husband's words at our wedding opened a window onto the next chapter, allowing me to see the girl I'd once been and, in his words, still am. She was that chord striking again and again, that déjà vu whenever I survived the unsurvivable.

She is waiting in the Lost and Found where I left her, all legs, old jeans, flannel shirt, pigtails, and bangs. No one would look at her twice. She is invisible, until she smiles, seeing me, catching my eye. She comes to life, talking, filled with animation, walking toward me, telling me a story, reaching for my hand, totally convinced that I will love her. I cannot take my eyes off her. And she is not pretty.

"I'll walk you home," she says, and we start down King Street, past The Gloria Theatre, she already close to my height. The musical *Easter Parade* is playing, which she tells me she has seen twice. Across the street is the bakery where we used to fill brown paper bags with jelly doughnuts and éclairs, perfect food for a musical. When we pass Belk's Department Store, scene of my shoplifting, I look to her sheepishly, but she is ahead of me, standing outside the house where Amorous lived. The *Charleston News and Courier* had given him that name, this Don Juan who'd disrupted the town, entering houses in the middle of the night, crawling into women's beds, holding them close, and then, with a kiss, departing as silently as he'd arrived. Amorous only went to the best houses, where he had an uncanny sense of direction, as though he had been there before.

"Remember the siren mother got in case Amorous visited her?" my companion asks. How could I forget the day the electricians installed the switch beside my mother's bed, the electrical cord running out through the window to a siren big enough to awaken the entire town? How often I had sat on her bed, my finger on that switch, itching to turn it on. Eventually poor Amorous was caught, though his identity was never divulged, he being the slightly demented son of one of Charleston's finest old families. Of course he knew his way around those houses he entered in the dark of night; he'd been to all of them as a guest.

But I see what is ahead of us, Schwettman's apothecary mortar and pestle sign hanging out over the sidewalk, and under it, leaning against the big plate-glass window, Malcolm, Jimmy, Billy, and Tommy. My protective hand reaches out, the words already in my mouth that Aunt Pat used to say to me by way of encouragement: "Stand up straight, shoulders back, remember that the Goldwyn Girls are the most beautiful girls in the world!" Then it strikes me that my companion is only ten, still this side of adolescence. Oblivious to the boys who don't even give her a glance, she swings past the screen door, beckoning me to follow. But I wait outside, watching her through the window as she hangs over the counter ordering two chocolate nut sundaes, the kind with the walnuts in syrup, our favorite.

How young the boys look, as open and ill-prepared as I would be for adolescence, just around the corner. In a couple of years, because no one had given her one, that lovable girl would buy herself an ID bracelet—we called them slave bracelets—with Malcolm's name on one side and Tommy's on the other; she will, of course, not be able to wear it.

Our sundaes in hand, we walk the remaining block to Broad Street, turn left, past the lovely antebellum mansion where the dentist on the second floor had recently fitted her with braces; in a couple of years she will have self-consciously learned to smile with her upper lip curved over the hated steel. A few buildings down we stop at the window of the tiny shop where I used to buy and trade stamps; I want to tell her that eventually she will travel to many of the countries on those beautiful little squares and rectangles, but she is already optimistic, which is what will get her there, on and off all those ships and planes.

At the corner of Broad and Meeting we turn right at the post office, pass the Hibernian Hall where she will soon attend Madame Larka's heart-in-mouth dance classes, and then at the corner of Tradd Street we turn and walk until we reach the tall pink house with the blue shutters, the wrought-iron balcony on the second floor just off the music room, the piano that I would never learn to play because "they" played. Would that I could convince her not to be so foolish, not to limit her life out of anger at mother for not seeing her, envy of her sister for being seen.

I turn, but she is gone. No, wait, I want to call, Don't go, not yet! And then I hear her, "Nancy, Nancy!" I know the way: through the big wrought-iron gate, past the little guest house, and up into the branches of the fig tree, and from there to the adjoining wall. I watch her swing into a taller tree and then with one enormous *swooosh!* she is atop the three-story retaining wall, all that is left of an old mansion. Dust and dislodged bricks fly from under her feet as she runs half the wall's length, her passing catching the eye of the old, gray-haired matriarch who is yelling at her from a high verandah on the East Bay side of the wall, not far from Aunt Pat's studio, where I learned to paint and wrote my first story. That old woman used to get so angry at me, sending her Dobermans out to race three stories below, back and forth in the thick underbrush.

From atop that old wall she can see our house where my mother and sister and I lived when I was little and the glass bank of the world only half filled. How to warn her of adolescence, the power of beauty that won't be hers and what she will forfeit just to be an also-ran. Don't do it, I call out, but of course it's no use. It will all have to be gone through. It is how she will get here. In the end, it will be she who saves me:

"Top o' the wall, Mom!"

Notes

===

CHAPTER 1

3   "Soon after we can see . . . ": John Berger, *Ways of Seeing* (London: BBC/Penguin, 1977 [1972]), p. 9.

5   "he saw me": Doris Lessing, *The Golden Notebook* (New York: Bantam, 1981 [1962]), p. 591.

8   The number of children: Steven A. Holmes, "Out-of-Wedlock Births Up Since '83, Report Indicates," *New York Times*, July 20, 1994, pp. A1ff.

12   "Battering has long been . . .": Achy Obejas, "Women Who Batter Women," *Ms.*, September/October 1994, p. 53.

    "I one my mother . . . ": Iona and Peter Opie, *I Saw Esau: The Schoolchild's Pocket Book* (London: Walker, 1992 [1947]), p. 75.

13   "were clearly not rhymes . . . ": Ibid., pp. 11–12.

15   "Today it's the preference for gender . . . ": Nora Frenkiel, "'Family Planning': Baby Boy or Girl?" *New York Times*, November 11, 1993, p. C6.

17   "Although it may be unconscious . . . ": Ibid., p. C6.

    ". . . a greater than twofold . . . ": Muhammad N. Bustan and Ann L. Coker, "Maternal Attitude Toward Pregnancy and the Risk of Neonatal Death, *American Journal of Public Health* 84, no. 3 (1994): 411–414.

18   "transfer many different emotional investments . . . ": Ethel S. Person, *By Force of Fantasy: How We Make Our Lives* (New York: Basic, 1995), pp. 111–112.

20 fathers' expected degree of responsibility . . . : Judith H. Langlois and Cookie White Stephan, "Beauty and the Beast: The Role of Physical Attractiveness in the Development of Peer Relations and Social Behavior," in *Developmental Social Psychology: Theory and Research,* Sharon S. Brehm et al. (New York: Oxford University Press, 1981), p. 160, citing R. D. Parke et al., "Fathers and Risk: A Hospital Based Model of Intervention," in *Exceptional Infant IV: Psychosocial Risks in Infant-Environmental Transactions,* D. B. Sawin et al.(New York: Brunner/Mazel, 1980).

"The less attractive the baby . . . ": Judith Langlois and Rita Casey, "Baby Beautiful: The Relationship Between Infant Physical Attractiveness and Maternal Behavior" (paper presented at the fourth biennial International Conference on Infant Studies, New York, 1984).

line drawings of infant faces . . . : Katherine A. Hildebrandt and Hiram E. Fitzgerald, "Facial Feature Determinants of Perceived Infant Attractiveness," *Infant Behavior and Development* 2 (1979): 329–339.

21 babies look longer at attractive faces . . . : Judith H. Langlois et al., "Facial Diversity and Infant Preferences for Attractive Faces," *Developmental Psychology* 27, no. 1 (1991): 79–84.

Nor does it matter . . . : Judith H. Langlois et al., "Infants' Differential Social Responses to Attractive and Unattractive Faces," *Developmental Psychology* 26, no. 1 (1990): 153–159.

photos of newborn infants were rated . . . : Katherine Hildebrandt Karraker et al., "Responses of Students and Pregnant Women to Newborn Physical Attractiveness" (paper presented at the meetings of the American Psychological Association, New York, August 1987), p. 2.

"for infants . . . what is beautiful . . . ": Katherine Hildebrandt Karraker and Marilyn Stern, "Infant Physical Attractiveness and Facial Expression: Effects of Adult Perceptions," *Basic and Applied Social Psychology* 11, no. 4 (1990): 381.

"presumably to compensate . . . ": Katherine Hildebrandt and Teresa Cannan, "The Distribution of Caregiver Attention in a Group Program for Young Children," *Child Study Journal* 15, no. 1 (1985): 51–52.

25 "I enter the world of her face . . . ": Daniel Stern, *Diary of a Baby* (New York: Basic, 1990), pp. 58–59.

"Babies act as if the eyes . . . ": Ibid., p. 49.

26 "you ask her, 'Can I see you?' . . . ": Ibid., p. 50.

"Sawubona": Bill Keller, "What's 'Shock' in Zulu? Whites Visiting to Say Hi," *New York Times,* May 31, 1994, p. A4.

"pulled to her eyes . . . ": Stern, *Diary of a Baby,* p. 63.

children of this age did figure drawings . . . : T. Shapiro and J. Stine, "The Figure Drawings of 3-Year-Old Children," *Psychoanalytic Study of the Child* 20 (1965): 298–309.

"looking into eyes . . . ": Stern, *Diary of a Baby,* p. 63.

27   When two animals lock . . . : Ibid., p. 50.
     "Perhaps it is the eye . . . ": Helen Fisher, *Anatomy of Love: The Natural History of Monogamy, Adultery, and Divorce* (New York: Norton, 1992), p. 23.
     ". . . it is mainly in the face . . . ": Stern, *Diary of a Baby*, p. 48.

28   *"The world is howling . . . "*: Ibid., p. 32.

29   "And his new animation . . . ": Ibid., pp. 43, 64–65.
     ". . . the stuff of being-with-another-person . . . ": Ibid., p. 67.
     Around the sixth week of life . . . really looking at her: Kenneth S. Robson, "The Role of Eye-to-Eye Contact in Maternal-Infant Attachment," *Journal of Child Psychology and Psychiatry* 8 (1967): 16.

30   the quality of her attachment . . . : Ibid., p. 22.

33   crucial to the development of self-esteem: Richard Robertiello, *Your Own True Love* (New York: Richard Marek, 1978), p. 120.
     Margaret Mahler's theories: For more on Mahler, see Margaret S. Mahler, *On Human Symbiosis and the Vicissitudes of Individuation*, vol. 1 of *Infantile Psychosis* (New York: International University Press, 1968); Margaret S. Mahler, *The Psychological Development of the Human Infant* (New York: Basic Books, 1976); Richard Robertiello, *Hold Them Very Close, Then Let Them Go: How to Be an Authentic Parent* (New York: Dial, 1975); Nancy Friday, *My Mother/My Self* (New York: Delacorte, 1977).

40   "Patriarchy thrives . . . ": Elizabeth Debold et al., *Mother Daughter Revolution: From Betrayal to Power* (New York: Addison-Wesley, 1993), p. 17.

42   "As soon as I saw my daughter . . . ": Ibid., p. 5.
     "The relationship most essential to disrupt . . . ": Shere Hite, *The Hite Report on the Family* (New York: Grove/Atlantic, 1995), p. 350.

48   common practice in ancient Rome . . . : John Noble Wilford, "Children's Cemetery a Clue to Malaria as Rome Declined," *New York Times*, July 26, 1994, p. C9.
     "Of all the characteristics . . . ": Barbara Tuchman, *A Distant Mirror: The Calamitous 14th Century* (New York: Ballantine, 1979 [1978]), p. 49.
     Children in medieval artworks . . . : Philippe Ariès, *Centuries of Childhood: A Social History of Family Life*, trans. Robert Baldick (New York: Vintage, 1962 [1960]), pp. 33, 411.
     moralization of society . . . "modern concept of the family": Ibid., pp. 412–413.
     "gave us our selves . . . ": Neil Postman, *The Disappearance of Childhood* (New York: Delacorte, 1982), p. 28.

50   the candidate for governor of Minnesota . . . : Richard L. Berke, "Religious Right Gains Influence and Spreads Discord in G.O.P.," *New York Times*, July 3, 1994, pp. A1ff.
     "Be it subtly . . . ": Mark Leyner, "Samurai Father," *Esquire Gentleman*, Spring 1994, p. 81.

53   "I think women should be more violent . . .": John Lahr, "Dealing with Roseanne," *New Yorker*, February 17, 1995, p. 58.

53   "Babies and young children . . .": Penelope Leach, *Children First: What Our Society Must Do—and Is Not Doing—for Our Children Today* (New York: Knopf, 1994), p. 19.

55   "woman dresses . . .": Simone de Beauvoir, *The Second Sex* (New York: Vintage, 1989 [1952]), p. 538.
     "fathers . . . get gooseflesh . . .": Nancy R. Gibbs, "Bringing Up Father," *Time*, June 28, 1993, p. 58.

56   We *know* from scientific studies . . . lowered-pitched: Kyle D. Pruett, "Father's Influence in the Development of Infant's Relationships," *Acta Paediatrica Scandinavica* 77, supplementum no. 344 (1988): 43–53. R. Parke, *Fathers* (Cambridge, Mass.: Harvard University Press, 1981), p. 35 (cited by Pruett). Martin Greenberg and N. Norris, "Engrossment: The Newborn's Impact upon the Father," *American Journal of Orthopsychiatry* 44, no. 4 (1974): 520–531.
     "Contrary to the notion . . .": Michael Lamb, "The Changing Roles of Fathers," in *The Father's Role: Applied Perspectives*, ed. M. E. Lamb (New York: Wiley, 1986), p. 11.

57   "Society sends men two messages . . .": Gibbs, "Bringing Up Father," pp. 53–54.

58   27 percent of all children . . . : U.S. Census, "Marital Status and Living Arrangements," March 1994, p. ix.
     "nearly one-fourth of all American infants . . .": Susan Chira, "Study Confirms Some Fears on U.S. Children," *New York Times*, April 12, 1994, pp. 1, 13.

59   "What [fathers] are hearing . . .": Gibbs, "Bringing Up Father," p. 53.
     between 60 and 80 percent . . . : J. H. Pleck et al., *Husbands' and Wives' Paid Work, Family Work, and Adjustment* (Wellesley, Mass.: Wellesley College Center for Research on Women, 1982); and R. P. Quinn and G. L. Staines, *The 1977 Quality of Employment Survey* (Ann Arbor, Mich.: Survey Research Center, 1979). Cited in Michael E. Lamb, "The Changing Roles of Fathers," p. 21.
     "[My husband] and I have a balance . . .": Patrice Duggan Samuels, "Dads to the Rescue for the Child-Care Needs," *New York Times*, February 12, 1995, p. F23.

61   "Today, pregnant teenagers . . .": Lena Williams, "Pregnant Teenagers Are Outcasts No Longer," *New York Times*, December 2, 1993 p. C1.

63   fathers do not hover . . . : Henry Biller and D. Meredith, *Father Power* (New York: David McKay, 1974).

67   "One of the most dramatic findings . . .": Kyle D. Pruett, *The Nurturing Father: Journey Toward the Complete Man* (New York: Warner, 1987), p. 48,

citing Seymour and Hilda Parker, "Cultural Rules, Rituals and Behavior Regulation," *American Anthropologist* 86 (1984): 584–600.

CHAPTER 2

70 "saw that the tree was good . . . ": Genesis 3:6–7.

71 "did ever anybody . . . ": Herman Melville, *Billy Budd* (London: John Lehmann, 1946), p. 58.

72 "Envy is the sin . . . ": A. S. Byatt, "The Seven Deadly Sins/Envy: The Sin of Families and Nations," *New York Times Book Review*, July 18, 1993, p. 3.

73 "If good exists . . . ": George Foster, "Cultural Responses to Expressions of Envy in Tzintzutzan," *Southwestern Journal of Anthropology* 21, no. 1 (Spring 1965): 26.

74 "Envy is the angry feeling . . . ": Melanie Klein, *Envy and Gratitude and Other Works 1946–1963* (New York: Delacorte, 1977), p. 181.
   "I consider that envy . . . ": Ibid., p. 176.

75 "In a house where envy . . . ": Leslie H. Farber, *Lying, Despair, Jealousy, Envy, Sex, Suicide, Drugs and the Good Life* (New York: Harper Colophon, 1978), p. 44.

76 "Envy's face was sickly pale . . . ": Ovid, *Metamorphoses* (New York: Penguin, 1955), pp. 70–71.

77 "Allegory and fairy tales . . . ": Byatt, "The Seven Deadly Sins/Envy: The Sin of Families and Nations," p. 25.

80 "How remarkable it is . . . ": George M. Foster, "The Anatomy of Envy: A Study in Symbolic Behavior," *Current Anthropology* 13, no. 2 (April 1972): 184.

86 "The fact that in our paranoid society . . . ": Willard Gaylin, *Feelings* (New York: Ballantine, 1980 [1979]), pp. 131, 129–130.

87 ". . . that object of every necrophiliac's lust . . . ": Andrea Dworkin, *Woman-Hating: A Radical Look at Sexuality* (New York: E. P. Dutton, 1974), p. 33.

88 "While some literal-minded parents . . . ": Bruno Bettelheim, *The Uses of Enchantment* (New York: Knopf, 1976), p. 226.

91 "Because he wants others . . . ": Ibid., p. 240.

92 Preschoolers will tell you . . . : Karen K. Dion, "Young Children's Stereotyping of Facial Attractiveness," *Developmental Psychology* 9, no. 2 (1973): 183–188.
   "One sibling is always more prominent . . . ": Stephen Bank and Michael D. Kahn, *The Sibling Bond* (New York: Basic, 1982), p. 51.

94 "reworked and kept alive": Stern, *Diary of a Baby*, p. 136.

95 "Since [the child] cannot comprehend . . . ": Bettelheim, *The Uses of Enchantment*, p. 74.

97   "It is, in the final analysis, love . . . ": Ibid., p. 110.

102   a study was done on fifth-grade girls . . . : Norman Cavior, "Physical Attractiveness, Perceived Attitude Similarity, and Interpersonal Attraction Among Fifth and Eleventh Grade Boys and Girls" (doctoral dissertation, University of Houston, August 1970).

105   "I went to my father's garden . . . ": Opie, *I Saw Esau*, p. 72.

109   "pee into the bowl like a big man . . . destiny is being shaped": Philip Roth, *Portnoy's Complaint* (New York: Random House, 1969 [1967]), pp. 132–133.

113   . . . received accurate words for their genitals . . . : M. Cecile Fraley et al., "Early Genital Naming," *Developmental and Behavioral Pediatrics* 12, no. 2 (October 1991): 303.

114   "Over the years . . . ": Christiane Northrup, *Women's Bodies, Women's Wisdom* (New York: Bantam, 1994), pp. 241–242.

115   Joycelyn Elders on masturbation: Michael K. Frisby, "Clinton Fires Surgeon General Elders Citing Differences in Opinions, Policy," *Wall Street Journal*, December 12, 1994, p. A16.

119   "Advertisers are so afraid . . . ": Susan Chira, "No Cookie-Cutter Mothers in 90's," *New York Times*, May 8, 1994, sec. 1, p. 26.
      ". . . to wash her little cleft . . . ": Saul Bellow, *Herzog* (New York: Penguin, 1985 [1964]), p. 257.

120   51 percent of the husbands . . . : Robert P. Quinn and Graham L. Staines, *The 1977 Quality of Employment Survey: Descriptive Statistics, with Comparison Data from the 1969–1970 and the 1972–1973 Surveys* (Ann Arbor: University of Michigan Survey Research Center, 1977), table 15.32.
      The *Los Angeles Times* . . . "fast-track job": Gibbs, "Bringing Up Father," p. 56.
      "is one of the scarcest commodities . . . ": Leach, *Children First*, pp. 121, 120.

CHAPTER 3

125   "This world of childhood memories . . . ": Stacy Schiff, *Saint-Exupéry: A Biography* (New York: Knopf, 1993), p. 43.

137   "Dear *American Girl* . . . ": *American Girl*, July/August 1994, p. 48.

139   "Within the first years of life . . . ": Paul Ekman, *Telling Lies: Clues to Deceit in the Marketplace, Politics, and Marriage* (New York: Norton, 1985), p. 125.
      "I believe that those habits . . . ": Ibid., p. 125.

141   Girls and boys bully their peers . . . : Heather Welford, "Best Friends and Bully Girls," *The Guardian*, November 23, 1993, p. T16.
      "I worry about what I've said today . . . ": Margaret Atwood, *Cat's Eye* (New York: Doubleday, 1989), pp. 124–126.
      ". . . there will be no end to imperfection . . . ": Ibid., p. 148.

143 "because of the girl factor . . . ": Laura Shapiro with Yahlin Chang, "The Girls of Summer," *Newsweek*, May 22, 1995, p. 56.

144 "The child begins to feel . . . ": Bettelheim, *The Uses of Enchantment*, pp. 219–220.

145 "When the father first emerges . . . ": Dorothy Dinnerstein, *The Mermaid and the Minotaur* (New York: Harper Colophon, 1971 [1963]), pp. 51–52.

155 ". . . responsibility, equality, sensitivity . . . ": Sheila Benson, "True or False: Thelma and Louise Just Good Ol' Boys?" *Los Angeles Times*, May 31, 1991, p. F1.

156 "Shortchanging Girls, Shortchanging America . . . ": American Association of University Women, "Shortchanging Girls, Shortchanging America," January 1991; see also Christina Hoff Sommers, "The Myth of Schoolgirls' Low Self-Esteem," *Wall Street Journal*, October 3, 1994, p. A20; Christina Hoff Sommers, *Who Stole Feminism?: How Women Have Betrayed Women* (New York: Simon and Schuster, 1994), pp. 137–152.

157 "There they are, together, *stuck together* . . . ": Doris Lessing, *Under My Skin: Volume One of My Autobiography, to 1949* (New York: HarperCollins, 1994), p. 120.

161 "those who were best able to resolve conflicts . . . ": Michael Segell, "The Pater Principle," *Esquire*, March 1995, p. 122.
John and his sister Fanny . . . : John Irving, *The Hotel New Hampshire* (New York: Ballantine, 1995 [1981]), pp. 50–51.

163 "watches wistfully as they . . . ": Joyce Johnson, *Minor Characters* (New York: Houghton Mifflin, 1983), p. 84.

CHAPTER 4

180 G. Stanley Hall: For a discussion of Hall's, Locke's, and Rousseau's contributions to the study of adolescence, see Louise J. Kaplan, *Adolescence: The Farewell to Childhood* (New York: Simon and Schuster, 1984).

181 "There is a progressive awareness . . . ": B. Inhelder and J. Piaget, *The Growth of Logical Thinking* (New York: Basic, 1958), quoted in Peter Blos, *On Adolescence: A Psychoanalytic Interpretation* (New York: Free Press, 1966 [1962]), p. 124.
"Western democratic, capitalistic society . . . ": Blos, *On Adolescence*, pp. 203–204.

182 "physically mature beasts . . . ": Virginia Rutter, "Adolescence: Whose Hell Is It?" *Psychology Today*, January/February 1995, p. 68.
"Because the school was designed . . . ": Neil Postman, *The Disappearance of Childhood* (New York: Delacorte, 1982), p. 41.
"Only a few years ago . . . ": Laurence Steinberg, *Adolescence* (New York: Knopf, 1985), p. v.

183   nearly $100 billion a year in 1994: Peter Zollo, "Talking to Teens," *American Demographics*, November 1995, p. 24.

188   close to 30 percent . . . : Alan Guttmacher Institute, "Teenage Reproductive Health in the United States," 1994.

"and the economy was such . . .": Sue Woodman, "How Teen Pregnancy Has Become a Political Football," *Ms.*, January/February 1995, p. 92.

"It also hints at the negative feelings . . . ": Rutter, "Adolescence: Whose Hell Is It?" p. 68.

"Almost always . . . ": Louise J. Kaplan, *Female Perversions: The Temptations of Emma Bovary* (New York: Doubleday, 1991), p. 248.

More than 1.6 million young people: U.S. Census, "Who's Minding the Kids?" 1994.

191   the hipline of a size 10 dress . . . : Sam Roberts, *Who We Are: A Portrait of America Based on the Latest U.S. Census* (New York: Times Books, 1994), p. 252.

192   "*Are you there God? . . .* ": Judy Blume, *Are You There, God? It's Me, Margaret* (New York: Dell, 1991 [1970]), p. 100.

193   "Primitive menstrual taboos . . . ": Susan Brownmiller, *Femininity* (New York: Linden, 1984), pp. 193–195.

"The sex organ of a man . . . ": de Beauvoir, *The Second Sex*, p. 386.

195   in 1986, $23,974,600 was spent . . . : Mediawatch Multi-Media Service, "Product versus Media Report," 1995.

197   From Aristotle's time . . . spread with it: Barbara G. Walker, *The Women's Encyclopedia of Myths and Secrets* (San Francisco: HarperCollins, 1983), p. 635.

200   "It is not easy to play the idol . . . ": de Beauvoir, *The Second Sex*, p. 357.

According to an article . . . as menstruation: Susan C. Roberts, "Blood Sisters," *New Age Journal*, May/June 1994, p. 137.

Gilligan wanted to avoid flak . . . : Ibid.

201   boys and girls have roughly equivalent self-images . . . : Roberta G. Simmons and Florence Rosenberg, "Sex, Sex Roles, and Self-Image," *Journal of Youth and Adolescence* 4, no. 3 (1975): 229–258.

Asked "How good-looking . . ." the worse their self-consciousness: Roberta G. Simmons et al., "Disturbance in the Self-Image at Adolescence," *American Sociology Review* 38 (1973): 553–568.

"not to distinguish . . . ": David Elkind, "Egocentrism in Adolescence," *Child Development* 38 (1967): 1029–1030.

202   Twelve percent of all fifteen- to nineteen-year-old girls . . . : Alan Guttmacher Institute, "Teenage Reproductive Health in the United States," 1994.

211   "My mother is always in my room . . . ": *Seventeen*, September 1995, p. 98.

214   "In either case, the children . . . ": Rutter, "Adolescence: Whose Hell Is It?" pp. 58–59.

215   "share all their secrets with Mother . . . ": Kaplan, *Adolescence*, p. 170.

216 "How do you see your generation?" . . . : "My Generation: The *Seventeen* Survey," October 1989, p. 101.

217 girls with "traditional values" . . . : Vangie Foshee and Karl Bauman, "Gender Stereotyping and Adolescent Sexual Behavior: A Test of Temporal Order," *Journal of Applied Social Psychology* 22, no. 20 (1992): 1574–1575.

220 "the designer insisted that fashion . . . ": Bernadine Morris, "From DKNY, Eclecticism for Mothers, Daughters," *New York Times*, April 7, 1994, p. C10.

222 "It is an odd fact . . . ": Kaplan, *Adolescence*, p. 14.

223 "Starting in the third grade . . . ": Susan Harter, "Causes and Consequences of Low Self-Esteem in Children and Adolescents," in *Self-Esteem: The Puzzle of Low Self-Regard*, ed. R. F. Baumeister (New York: Plenum, 1993), pp. 95–96.

224 "the classroom teachers of the early adolescents . . . ": K. Lenerz et al., "Early Adolescents' Organismic Physical Characteristics and Psychosocial Functioning: Findings from the Pennsylvania Early Adolescent Transitions Study (PEATS)," in *Biological-Psychosocial Interaction in Early Adolescence: A Life-Span Perspective*, ed. Richard M. Lerner and T. T. Fochs (Hillsdale, N.J.: Erlbaum, 1987), pp. 225–247. Cited in *Body Images*, ed. Thomas F. Cash and Thomas Pruzinsky (New York: Guilford, 1990), pp. 118–119.

225 "There's nothing wrong . . . ": "My Generation: The *Seventeen* Survey," p. 103.

227 "I lost my virginity last year . . . ": *Seventeen*, June 1995, p. 58.

228 "Eula Varner was not quite thirteen . . . ": William Faulkner, *The Hamlet* (New York: Vintage, 1991 [1931]), pp. 105–106, 141–142.

238 In the study ". . . relating to males": E. Mavis Hetherington, "Effects of Father Absence on Personality Development in Adolescent Daughters," *Developmental Psychology* 7, no. 3 (1972): 313–326.
    "The women from intact families . . . ": Reported in Henry B. Biller and Robert J. Trotter, *The Father Factor: What You Need to Know to Make a Difference* (New York: Pocket, 1994), p. 186.

242 more than one million of the United States' nine million girls . . . : Guttmacher, "Teenage Reproductive Health in the United States."
    who grow up without their fathers . . . : Hetherington, "Effects of Father Absence."

243 His most famous daughter, Anna . . . : Adam Phillips, *On Flirtation* (Cambridge, Mass.: Harvard University, 1994), pp. 90–93.

CHAPTER 5

250 "For the first time in her life . . . ": Isabel Allende, *The House of the Spirits* (New York: Knopf, 1985), p. 281.

254 More than one million incidents of domestic violence . . . : Ronet Bach-

man and Linda Saltzman, "Bureau of Justice Statistics Special Report: National Crime Victimization Report," August 1995, p. 3.

255 "... many men fix on their object of desire ... ": Paul Theroux, "The Roots of Desire," *Vogue*, October 1995, p. 250.

"cone bra like an icon ... ": Ibid., pp. 248–250.

257 73 percent of boys from twelve to nineteen ... Teen Research Unlimited, unpublished figures, 1995.

261 "i am a big man ... ": Nine Inch Nails, "big man with a gun," *the downward spiral*, TVT-Interscope Records, 1994.

267 In Hunt's study on sex ... : Morton Hunt, *Sexual Behavior in the 1970s* (Chicago: Playboy Press, 1974), p. 77.

268 "Obviously . . . masturbation . . . ": Harold Leitenberg et al., "Gender Differences in Masturbation and the Relation of Masturbation Experience in Preadolescence and/or Early Adolescence to Sexual Behavior and Sexual Adjustment in Young Adulthood," *Archives of Sexual Behavior* 22, no. 2 (1993): 96.

"after puberty, a boy must find constructive goals ... ": Bettelheim, *The Uses of Enchantment*, p. 186.

270 "High school girls are less comfortable ... ": Tamar Lewin, "Boys Are More Comfortable with Sex Than Girls Are," *New York Times*, May 18, 1994, p. 20.

271 Paul Newman mentioned ... : Paul Newman, interview by James Lipton, *Inside the Actor's Studio*, Bravo, April 26, 1995.

272 "Cultural factors ... ": Clara Thompson, "Penis Envy in Women," *Psychiatry* 6 (1943): 123–124.

275 average age of marriage ... : U.S. Census Bureau, "Marital Status and Living Arrangements," March 1994.

276 "The parts of the body do not all grow ... ": Steinberg, *Adolescence*, pp. 31–32.

277 Between 1960 and 1992, suicide rates for white males ... : National Center for Health Statistics, Division of Vital Statistics, published and unpublished data.

280 "Look, the way I figure it ... ": Wendy Bounds, "Dating Game Today Breaks Traditional Gender Rules," *Wall Street Journal*, April 26, 1995, p. B4.

"Your son's relationship with girls ... ": Biller and Trotter, *The Father Factor*, p. 183.

281 "the absence of fathers is linked ... ": Joseph P. Shapiro et al., "Honor Thy Children," *U.S. News & World Report*, February 27, 1995, p. 39.

the annual rate at which fifteen- to nineteen ... : Fox Butterfield, "Teenage Homicide Rate Has Soared," *New York Times*, October 14, 1994, p. A22.

282 the Oedipus myth "holds less meaning ... ": Walter Goodman, "Writers

Discuss Theme of Myths in Modern Life," *New York Times*, October 13, 1984, p. A13.

"Safety for Women? . . . ": Ellen Goodman, "Safety for Women? Try Removing Men," *Santa Barbara News-Press*, January 9, 1990, cited in Warren Farrell, *The Myth of Male Power: Why Men Are the Disposable Sex* (New York: Simon and Schuster, 1993), p. 220.

283   "girls are likely to choose boyfriends . . . ": Frank Pittman, *Man Enough: Fathers, Sons, and the Search for Masculinity* (New York: G.P. Putnam, 1993), quoted in Lee Smith, "The New Wave of Illegitimacy," *Fortune*, April 18, 1994, p. 94.

"It seems to me that Bly has framed his cure . . . ": Marina Warner, *Six Myths of Our Time* (New York: Vintage, 1995 [1994]), p. 41.

284   "Fear of men has grown . . . ": Ibid., pp. 32–33, 36–37.

Studies tell us . . . : U.S. Justice Department, "The Survey of State Prison Inmates," 1991.

The Glueck study . . . : John Snarey, *How Fathers Care for the Next Generation* (Cambridge, Mass.: Harvard University, 1994), pp. 149–191, 349–356.

285   "boys and girls express emotions equally . . . ": Farrell, *The Myth of Male Power*, p. 165.

"Fathers who provided high levels . . . ": Snarey, *How Fathers Care for the Next Generation*, p. 173.

286   "There is a time in the life of every boy . . . ": Sherwood Anderson, *Winesburg, Ohio* (New York: Bantam, 1995 [1919]), pp. 219–220.

287   "the limitless future of childhood . . . ": Blos, *On Adolescence*, p. 14.

CHAPTER 6

292   "Before the Brat Pack . . . ": "The Beautiful People," *W*, January 1995, p. 86.

297   "Bras were never burned . . . ": Robin Morgan, *Sisterhood Is Powerful* (New York: Random House, 1970), p. 521n.

"I can think of two material items . . . ": Tom Robbins, "The Mini, a Natural High," *New York Times*, April 6, 1995, p. C1.

300   . . . want a virgin bride . . . : A New *Glamour* Survey, Hearts and Minds What Do College Men and Women Really Mean to Each Other?" *Glamour*, August 1981, p. 328; "My Generation: The *Seventeen* Survey," p. 4; "Love and Sex in the 90s: The *Seventeen* Survey," 1991, p. 60.

301   "Why can't men be glamourous . . . promoting so brazenly": Amy M. Spindler, "In Milan, Brazen Men Parading," *New York Times*, January 19, 1995, p. C13.

301   "A full bosom . . . ": Germaine Greer, *The Female Eunuch* (London: MacGibbon & Kee, 1970), p. 34.

"the Wonderbra, for its contribution to fashion": Nadine Brozan, "Fashion Award Winners," *New York Times*, November 18, 1994, p. B8.

302 "No penetration . . . ": Sally Belfrage, *Un-American Activities* (New York: HarperPerennial, 1995 [1994]), p. 199.

305 "Please, God, let him telephone me now . . . ": Dorothy Parker, "A Telephone Call," *Complete Stories* (New York: Penguin, 1995), p. 81. Originally published in *The Bookman*, January 1928.

311 "our clothing is an extension of our skin . . . ": Karen De Witt, "So, What Is That Leather Bustier Saying?" *New York Times*, January 1, 1995, sec. 4, p. 2.
"The esthetic running through Warhol's films . . . ": Stephen Holden, "For Warhol, to Be Was to Be on Screen," *New York Times*, January 27, 1995, p. C28.

313 "The essence of the 60's . . . ": Laurel Graeber, "So Where Is That Lava Lamp Now?" *New York Times*, April 6, 1995, p. C6.
"Fresh and frank . . . ": Clive Barnes, "'Hair'—It's Fresh and Frank," *New York Times*, April 30, 1968, p. 40.

314 "The happiness of being envied . . . ": Berger, *Ways of Seeing*, pp. 132–133.

315 "The 60's spawned . . . ": "In Praise of the Counterculture," *New York Times*, December 11, 1994, p. 14.

319 "Anybody who could write . . . ": Barbara Grizzuti Harrison, "Talking Dirty," *Ms.*, October 1973, p. 41.

320 "feminist leaders who find . . . ": William Raspberry, "An Interest in Failure," *Washington Post*, November 5, 1993, p. A27.

321 "It is often falsely assumed . . . ": Greer, *The Female Eunuch*, p. 67.
"The Sexual Revolution and The Women's Movement . . . ": Anselma Dell' Olio, "The Sexual Revolution Wasn't Our War," *Ms.*, Spring 1972, p. 104.

322 "Why have the sixties . . . ": Jennifer Egan, *The Invisible Circus* (New York: Talese-Doubleday, 1995), jacket flap.

324 *Time*/CNN poll: Nancy Gibbs, "The War Against Feminism," *Time*, March 9, 1992, p. 54.
editors of the top women's magazines . . . : Wendy Kaminer, "Feminism's Identity Crisis," *Atlantic Monthly*, October 1993, p. 53.

325 average age of marriage in 1960: U.S. Census, "Marital Status," p. vii.

327 "The problem that has no name . . . ": Betty Friedan, *The Feminine Mystique* (New York: Dell Laurel, 1983 [1963]), p. 364.
"sweeping generalities . . . ": Lucy Freeman, "The Feminine Mystique," *New York Times Book Review*, April 7, 1963, p. 46.

328 "overnight bestseller . . . ": "Angry Battler for Her Sex," *Life*, November 1, 1963, p. 84.
"the seduction of women's talk . . . ": Marina Warner, *From the Beast to the Blonde: On Fairy Tales and their Tellers* (New York: Farrar, Straus, and Giroux, 1995), p. 31.
"I wrote the word 'NOW' . . . ": Friedan, *The Feminine Mystique*, p. 384.

329 "I couldn't define 'liberation' for women . . .": Ibid., p. 386.

330 "Except that I like this book . . .": Gloria Steinem, *The Beach Book* (New York: Viking, 1963), p. ix.

331 "Personification of womanpower ": "Thinking Man's Shrimpton," *Time*, January 3, 1969, p. 38.

    raising "money and consciousness . . .": "Gloria Steinem: A Liberated Woman Despite Beauty, Chic and Success," *Newsweek*, August 16, 1971, p. 51.

    "By speaking together . . .": Gloria Steinem, *Outrageous Acts and Everyday Rebellions* (New York: Signet, 1986 [1983]), p. 5.

    "white, well-educated, suburban women": *Signature: Gloria Steinem*, CBS Cable, November 4, 1981. Interviewed by Patrick Watson.

    "One could argue . . . revolutionary changes": Flora Davis, *Moving the Mountain: The Women's Movement in America Since 1960* (New York: Simon and Schuster, 1991), pp. 70, 69.

332 "We tangled a lot . . .": "Playboy Interview: Betty Friedan," *Playboy*, September 1992, p. 62.

    "a glossy magazine . . .": Davis, *Moving the Mountain*, p. 117.

333 "As they began to treat the movement . . .": Ibid., pp. 118–119.

    "Steinem's expressed attitude . . .": "Gloria Steinem: A Liberated Woman," p. 52.

334 "Am I a feminist? . . .": *Cosmopolitan* marketing, 1995.

335 "It isn't that women are attracted to pornography . . .": Steinem, *Outrageous Acts*, p. 258.

    "So women who 'ooh' and 'ah' . . .": Liz Smith, "Gloria Steinem, Writer and Social Critic, Talks about Sex, Politics and Marriage," *Redbook*, January 1972, p. 76.

336 "A lot of the failures of the movement . . .": Jay Cocks, "How Long Till Equality?" *Time*, July 12, 1982, p. 22.

    "I'm not going to lie . . .": "Playboy Interview," p. 149.

337 "stomping on a movement . . .": Susan Faludi, *Backlash* (New York: Crown, 1991), p. 322.

    "What's important is that we . . .": Molly O'Neill, "Decades as Icon; Now, Freedom," *New York Times*, February 9, 1995, p. C10.

338 "Kohn is describing competition . . .": Andrew Bard Schmookler, "No Contest: The Case Against Competition," *Los Angeles Times/The Book Review*, September 28, 1986, p. 11.

    "I hate victimology . . .": "Camille," *60 Minutes*, CBS, November 1, 1992. Interview by Steve Kroft.

    "No, you're not going to ask . . .": Ibid.

339 "the Paglia cigarette boat . . .": Ibid.

341 "Gone are the appealing men . . .": Margaret Carlson, "Batteries Not Included," *Time*, December 2, 1991, pp. 78–79.

"These [feminine hygiene] products . . . ": Nora Ephron, "Dealing with the, Uh, Problem," *Esquire*, March 1973, p. 184.

343   Among thirty- to thirty-four-year-olds . . . : Alan Guttmacher Institute, "Preventing Pregnancy, Protecting Health: A New Look at Birth Control Choices in the United States," 1991.

345   "She say, Here, take this mirror . . . ": Alice Walker, *The Color Purple* (New York: Washington Square, 1983 [1982]), pp. 79–80.

"I'm very much a feminist . . . ": Laura Blumenfeld, "Feminists Hit a Bump and Grind at Lesbian Club," *Washington Post*, July 25, 1991, p. D2.

347   "the Mao Tse-tung of Women's Liberation": "Who's Come a Long Way, Baby?" *Time*, August 31, 1970, p. 16.

"Patriarchy has God on its side . . . ": Kate Millett, *Sexual Politics* (Garden City, N.Y.: Doubleday, 1970), pp. 51–52.

348   "See, I'm single . . . ": *Saturday Night Live*, February 19, 1994.

349   A recent Diet Sprite . . . : Maureen Dowd, "Our True Lies," *New York Times*, August 20, 1995, p. A13.

"underground comic universe . . . ": Roberta Smith, "A Parallel Art World, Vast and Unruly," *New York Times*, November 20, 1994, sec. 1, pp. 1, 42–43.

350   "Traditionally, women who make people laugh . . . ": Susie Linfield, "Women Comics Stand and Deliver," *New York Times*, July 12, 1992, p. 11. When male comics finish their acts . . . : *Wisecracks*, 1992. 93 minutes. A Zinger Films production in co-production with Studio D of the National Film Board of Canada.

351   "With Kotex towels . . . ": Ibid.

"There is a male comedian working today . . . ": Ibid.

352   "The great annual festival of Aphrodite . . . ": Walker, *The Women's Encyclopedia*, pp. 1091–1092.

353   as Lily Tomlin put it . . . : Maureen Dowd, "Fashion Week Fabrics," *New York Times*, April 7, 1995, p. A34.

355   "But the fashion industry trammeled . . . ": Naomi Wolf, *The Beauty Myth* (New York: Morrow, 1991), p. 45.

358   "Nail polish or false eyelashes isn't politics . . . ": Trucia Kushner, "Finding a Personal Style," *Ms.*, February 1974, p. 83n.

361   "I would grind my teeth . . . ": Virginia Kelley and James Morgan, *Leading with My Heart* (New York: Simon and Schuster, 1995 [1994]), p. 212.

363   "In the modern workplace, men are drones . . . ": Camille Paglia, *Vamps and Tramps* (New York: Vintage, 1994), p. 52.

365   "Lying, of course, is a way of gaining power . . . ": "Sissela Bok," *Bill Moyers' World of Ideas*, WNET and WTTW, October 3, 1988.

366   "Whether by virtue of full breasts . . . ": Letty Cottin Pogrebin, "Competing With Women," *Ms.*, July 1972, pp. 78, 132.

368 being good-looking was a plus for men . . . timidity, etc.: Madeline E. Heilman and Lois R. Saruwatari, "When Beauty Is Beastly: The Effects of Appearance and Sex on Evaluations of Job Applicants for Managerial and Nonmanagerial Jobs," *Organizational Behavior and Human Performance* 23 (1979): 360–372.

each additional attractiveness point . . . : Irene Hanson Frieze et al., "Attractiveness and Business Success: Is It More Important for Women or Men?" (paper prepared for the 1989 Academy of Management Meetings, Washington, D.C., August 1989); Irene Hanson Frieze et al., "Perceived and Actual Discrimination in the Salaries of Male and Female Managers" (paper presented at the 1986 Academy of Management Meetings, Chicago).

By 1993, people perceived as good-looking . . . ": Daniel S. Hamermesh and Jeff E. Biddle, "Beauty and the Labor Market," National Bureau of Economic Research, November 1993.

"most people judge you . . . ": *McCall's*/Yankelovich Confidence Study: Health and Appearance, 1993.

"We American women . . . ": Holly Brubach, "Landscapes with Figures," *The New Yorker*, April 30, 1990, p. 106.

370 "letting us know . . . seductress underneath": Anne Taylor Fleming, "Peekaboo Power Suits," *New York Times*, January 28, 1993, p. 21.

"No. Women dress for other women . . . ": "A Doctor Is No Better Than His Patient: An Interview with Norman Mailer," *Cosmopolitan*, May 1990, p. 404.

371 "Rather than finding a source in competition . . . ": Steinem, *Revolution*, p. 189.

"superior performance . . . ": Ibid., p. 189.

372 "progress becomes . . . connectedness": Ibid., p. 189.

373 "How does a daughter deal . . . ": P. J. Caplan, *Between Women: Lowering the Barriers* (Toronto: Personal Library, 1981), p. 120. Quoted in Robert W. Firestone et al., "The Mother-Daughter Bond," The Glendon Association.

CHAPTER 7

383 "Men seek attractive women as mates . . . ": David M. Buss, *The Evolution of Desire* (New York: Basic, 1994), p. 59.

"people suspect that a homely man . . . ": Ibid.

387 "When a man looks into a mirror . . . ": Stephen Brewer, "Put Your Face Here," *Esquire*, August 1990, p. 34.

388 "Their beauty, for Brontë . . . ": Millett, *Sexual Politics*, p. 140.

392 1994 University of Chicago Study . . . : Robert T. Michael et al., *Sex in America: A Definitive Survey* (New York: Little, Brown, 1994), pp. 146–147.

393 Forty-six percent of the entire mass market . . . : Dana Wechsler Linden and Matt Rees, "I'm Hungry. But Not for Food," *Forbes*, July 6, 1992, p. 70.

394 "We may have some sexual tastes . . . ": Helen Fisher, *Anatomy of Love* (New York: Norton, 1992), p. 205.

399 "To the late nineteenth-century male . . . ": Bram Dijkstra, *Idols of Perversity* (New York: Oxford University Press, 1986), p. 87.
"Out of the upper-right corner . . . ": Ibid., p. 81.

401 "fashion tends to show us . . . ": De Witt, "So, What Is That Leather Bustier Saying?" p. 2.

402 "The gaze is probably . . . ": Fisher, *Anatomy of Love*, pp. 21–23.

403 "Look at her. All over . . .": Susie Bright, "How to Make Love to a Woman: Hands-on Advice from a Woman Who Does," *Esquire*, February 1994, p. 108.

404 the women whom Lawrence treats . . . : Brenda Maddox, *D. H. Lawrence: The Story of a Marriage* (New York: Simon and Schuster, 1994), described in Christopher Lehmann-Haupt, "D. H. Lawrence Seen in One Intense Lens," *New York Times*, November 14, 1994, p. C18.

405 "He was dizzy with the spectacle . . . ": Carol De Chellis Hill, *Henry James' Midnight Song* (New York: Poseidon, 1993), pp. 206–207.
in North Carolina and Mississippi . . . : Robert Wayne Pelton, *Loony Sex Laws That You Never Knew You Were Breaking* (New York: Walker, 1992), pp. 6, 157.

412 "What if you want to get out of the box . . . ": Quoted in Christina Hoff Sommers, "A Holiday Based on Ms. Information," *Wall Street Journal*, April 10, 1995, p. A20.

413 "There is often ambivalence . . . ": Susan Edmiston, "Reconcilable Differences," *Mirabella*, March 1990, p. 112.
"True, there are still far fewer women . . . ": Laura A. Ingraham, "Enter, Women," *New York Times*, April 19, 1995, p. A23.

414 "In the latter part of the twentieth century . . . ": Andrew G. Kadar, "The Sex-Bias Myth in Medicine," *Atlantic Monthly*, August 1994, p. 70.

415 "If women ever take over everything . . . ": Norman Mailer, "Norman Mailer on Madonna: Like a Lady," *Esquire*, August 1994, p. 50.

416 "With women as half . . . ": Gloria Steinem, "What It Would Be Like to Win," *Time*, August 31, 1970, p. 22.
"Women with normal work identities . . . ": Ibid., p. 22.

417 "When you control the resources . . . ": Jerry Adler et al., "You're So Vain," *Newsweek*, April 14, 1986, p. 55.
Atlanta . . . "'best foot forward'": Ibid., p. 51.
"The Right Suit . . . the real me": Ibid., p. 52.

418 "The erotic clothing men wore . . . ": Lois W. Banner, *In Full Flower:*

Aging Women, Power, and Sexuality (New York: Vintage, 1993 [1992]), p. 212.

420 Hillary Rodham Clinton's "enforcer" . . . : Jill Abramson and Ellen Joan Pollock, "'Hillary's Enforcer': How Susan Thomases, Top Clinton Adviser, Fell Hard from Grace," *Wall Street Journal*, April 8, 1996, p. A1.

421 "Men never admit . . . ": Skip Hollandsworth, "Why I Hate Hunks," *Mademoiselle*, October 1990, p. 86.

425 "Women's Liberation has to be terribly conscious . . . ": "Who's Come a Long Way, Baby?" p. 20.

426 in modern myths . . . : Warner, *Six Myths of Our Time*, p. 36.
"Men are expensive . . . ": June Stephenson, *Men Are Not Cost Effective: Male Crime in America* (New York: HarperPerennial, 1995), pp. 450–452.

427 "I don't see how society . . . ": Donna Minkowitz, "In the Name of the Father," *Ms.*, November/December 1995, pp. 71, 64.

428 "If you take the breeding power . . . ": Camille Paglia, "When Camille Met Tim," *Esquire*, February 1995, p. 70.
"The birth of a child . . . ": Ibid., p. 71.

431 "Evidence from dozens of studies . . . ": Buss, *The Evolution of Desire*, pp. 23–24.

432 "women across all continents . . . ": Ibid., p. 25.
educated women "express an even stronger . . . ": Ibid., p. 46.

434 "Intimate Terrorism": Michael Vincent Miller, *Intimate Terrorism: The Deterioration of Erotic Life* (New York: Norton, 1995).
"New marriages where the wife is ambitious . . . ": Philip Blumstein and Pepper Schwartz, *American Couples* (New York: Morrow, 1983), p. 312.

435 "Clothes of such brilliant luxury . . . ": Julie Baumgold, "Dancing on the Lip of the Volcano: Christian Lacroix's Crash Chic," *New York*, November 30, 1987, p. 36.
"the man who makes clothes . . . ": Ibid., p. 38.

437 "Nationally, the procedures most often performed on men . . . ": Jacqueline Stenson, "With Cosmetic Surgery, Men Can Change Everything from Pecs to Private Parts," *The Washingtonian*, May 1993, p. 92.

442 "First, beauty is power . . . ": Judith Thurman, "What If He's Cuter Than You?" *Mademoiselle*, April 1985, p. 120.

443 "Women tend to like what they've got . . . ": Jill Neimark, "How Men Measure Up," *Psychology Today*, November/December 1994, pp. 35, 38.

444 "I'm seeing more and more males . . . ": Ibid., p. 70.
Since 1987, the number of men exercising . . . : American Sports Data, a research firm, reports that the number of men exercising 100 or more times per year has grown from 17.2 million in 1987 to 22.6 million in 1994. In a 1994 survey, 6,000 men . . . : *GQ*, "Men in the Nineties: The Quiet Revolution," 1994, pp. 20, 21, 27.

445 55 percent of women . . . : Families and Work Institute, "Women: The New Providers," May 1995, p. 33.

Women still average . . . 114 percent: U.S. Bureau of Labor Statistics figures, reported in Donna D. H. Walters, "Working Women Play Key Role at Home, Study Finds," *Los Angeles Times*, May 11, 1995, p. A22.

48 percent of the women . . . : Families and Work Institute, "Women the New Providers," p. 29.

446 When French seamstresses . . . : Anne Hollander, *Sex and Suits: The Evolution of Modern Dress* (New York: Knopf, 1994), pp. 65, 72.

. . . the Neo-classic movement . . . : Ibid., pp. 83–97.

"The modern business suit [as we know it] . . .": Martin and Koda, *Jocks & Verds*, p. 151.

447 With the invention . . . indistinguishable from the next: Ink Mendelsohn, "We Were What We Wore," *American Heritage*, December 1988, pp. 42–43.

". . . the fastest and sexiest advances . . .": Hollander, *Sex and Suits*, p. 182.

448 ". . . women finally took over the total male scheme of dress . . .": Ibid., p. 182.

"Just as women are expected . . .": Amy M. Spindler, "How Much Glamour Can a Man Take?" *New York Times*, June 30, 1994, p. C11.

449 "Both sexes play changing games . . .": Hollander, *Sex and Suits*, p. 181.

CHAPTER 8

452 "Violence is the male . . .": Andrea Dworkin, *Pornography: Men Possessing Women* (New York: Perigee, 1981 [1979]), p. 55.

454 "The penis is conceived as a weapon . . .": Greer, *The Female Eunuch*, p. 317.

"JOHNNY: Open your robe . . .": Terrence McNally, "Frankie and Johnny in the Clair de Lune," *Three Plays by Terrence McNally* (New York: Plume, 1990 [1986]), p. 105.

458 "Impotence is a big problem . . .": Beverly Beyette, "Kinsey Institute's Reinisch Wants to Renew, Expand Sexual Studies; American Sex Habits Changed Since 1948—But Not That Much," *Los Angeles Times*, May 18, 1986, p. 1.

F. Scott Fitzgerald tells Hemingway . . . : Ernest Hemingway, *A Moveable Feast* (New York: Collier, 1987 [1964]), p. 190.

459 "My father would take . . .": "When Camille Met Tim," p. 72.

460 "between 1990 . . . competitive about that": Kevin Cook, "Is Bigger Better?" *Vogue*, April 1995, p. 266.

"Women who rated themselves as more attractive . . .": Neimark, "How Men Measure Up," p. 72.

would rather be (A) 5 feet 2 inches tall . . . : "Have You Ever Measured Your Penis?" *Glamour*, January 1995, p. 136.

461 "[The models] were mounted in . . . ": Chip Brown, "Heel, Boy!" *Esquire*, November 1995, p. 107.

"A tiny receptacle . . . ": Bettelheim, *The Uses of Enchantment*, pp. 265.

"Since for over two thousand years . . . ": Ibid., p. 269.

463 "Of all fetish objects . . . ": Brown, "Heel, Boy!" p. 103.

"The emphasis on parts of the body . . . ": Banner, *In Full Flower*, p. 203.

"European folk belief . . . ": Ibid., p. 207.

464 a man offers a seventeen-year-old . . . : Susan Forrest, "DA Booted," *Newsday*, November 5, 1993.

465 "88 percent of those women . . . ": Carol Frey et al., "American Orthopaedic Foot and Ankle Society Women's Shoe Survey," *Foot and Ankle*, 1993, p. 79.

six million women . . . : John Pierson, "Man Walked on the Moon, Why Can't Man Make a Woman's Dress Shoe That Doesn't Hurt?" *Wall Street Journal*, January 10, 1996, p. B1.

women account for 90 percent . . . : American Orthopaedic Foot and Ankle Society, "Position Statement on Women's Shoewear and Foot Problems," 1991.

466 "In the dress code of sadomasochism . . . ": Sherry Magnus, "Feet, Sex and Power . . . The Last Erogenous Zone," *Vogue*, April 1982, p. 384.

"Freud argued that . . . is deeply felt": Valerie Steele, *Fashion and Eroticism* (New York: Oxford University Press, 1985), pp. 32–33.

467 "The feet are symbols . . . ": Magnus, "Feet, Sex and Power," p. 384.

"Of all forms of erotic symbolism . . . ": Havelock Ellis, *Studies in the Psychology of Sex*, vol. 2 (New York: Random House, 1937), p. 15.

"When a Celestial . . . ": Ibid., p. 22, quoting Dr. J. Matignon, "A propos d'un Pied de Chinoise," *Archives d'Anthropologie Criminelle*, 1898.

"some degree of foot-fetichism . . . ": Ellis, *Studies in the Psychology of Sex*, p. 21.

468 "when the longing for the fetish . . . ": Sigmund Freud, *Three Essays on Sexuality*, vol. 7 of *The Standard Edition of the Complete Psychological Works of Sigmund Freud* (London: Hogarth Press and the Institute of Psycho-Analysis, 1986 [1953]), p. 154.

"The popularly accepted idea of cultural quasi-fetishism . . . ": Steele, *Fashion and Eroticism*, p. 30.

"I gazed at her . . . ": Ivan Turgenev, *First Love* (New York: Penguin, 1978 [1950]), p. 33.

469 ". . . to the more obvious sexual organ": Banner, *In Full Flower*, p. 207.

470 "did not conceal the body, but clung . . . ": Diane Ackerman, *A Natural History of Love* (New York: Vintage, 1995 [1994]), pp. 74–75n.

"perfectly fitted tights . . . ": Hollander, *Sex and Suits*, pp. 43–44.

471   "Yet one recent scholar . . . large false penises": Banner, *In Full Flower*, pp. 205, 207.

"One might glance . . . ": Ackerman, *A Natural History of Love*, p. 248.

"Wearing only a pair . . . ": Daniel Harris, "The Current Crisis in Men's Lingerie: Notes on the Belated Commercialization of a Noncommercial Product," *Salmagundi*, Fall 1993, pp. 130, 131.

472   "sculpt," "mold," "contour" . . . : Ibid, p. 132.

"Often needlessly complicated . . . ": Ibid., p. 136.

CHAPTER 9

479   when women work outside the home . . . : Susan Cheever, *A Woman's Life: The Story of an Ordinary American and Her Extraordinary Generation* (New York: Morrow, 1994), p. 120.

482   "With words, with nonverbal acuity . . . ": Fisher, *Anatomy of Love*, pp. 308–309.

484   "A woman must continually watch herself . . . ": Berger, *Ways of Seeing*, p. 46.

486   "The sisterhood we had in mind . . . ": Sue Halpern, "Soul Sisters," *Harper's Bazaar*, July 1994, p. 48.

487   "not only are Americans living longer . . . ": Gina Kolata, "News of Robust Elderly Belies Fears of Scientists," *New York Times*, February 27, 1996, p. C3.

"What could I do? . . . symbols of constraint.": John De St. Jorre, "The Unmasking of O," *New Yorker*, August 1, 1994, pp. 43, 45.

488   "The passionate, idealistic . . . ": Germaine Greer, *The Change* (New York: Knopf, 1992), pp. 53–55.

490   "Whether based on sexism . . . ": Aimee Lee Ball, "Ballbusters: Success Secrets of 6 Pushy Women," *Marie Claire*, September/October 1994, p. 58.

492   In 1995, Americans over fifty . . . : U.S. Census Bureau, "Projection of the Population, by Age, Sex, Race, and Hispanic Origin."

493   "Women have been burnt . . . ": de Beauvoir, *Second Sex*, p. 191.

494   "The overwhelming evidence . . . ": Betty Friedan, *The Fountain of Age* (New York: Simon and Schuster, 1993), pp. 483, 568, 597.

495   "is not only a means of preserving . . . ": Bettelheim, *The Uses of Enchantment*, p. 69.

497   *The Art of Courtly Love:* Banner, *In Full Flower*, p. 172.

"He that wooeth a widow . . . ": Ibid.

"Even the presumed ugliness of aging . . . ": Ibid., p. 174.

498   "Most men and more women . . . ": Doris Lessing, *Love, Again* (New York: HarperCollins, 1996), p. 133.

"The story Ms. Lessing has chosen . . . ": Michiko Kakutani, "Who Exactly Is This Sexagenarian Sex Kitten?" *New York Times*, March 15, 1996, p. C30.

"in earlier Lessing novels . . . ": Ibid.

499 "Aging in women is a process . . . ": Susan Sontag, "The Double Standard of Aging," *Saturday Review*, September 23, 1972, p. 37.

"all witchcraft comes from carnal lust . . . ": Heinrich Krämer and Jacob Sprenger, *The Malleus Maleficarum*, trans. Montague Summers (New York: Dover, 1971), p. 47, quoted in Banner, *In Full Flower*, p. 191.

500 "As sexualized beings . . . ": Banner, *In Full Flower*, p. 193.

501 "The witch—more than the other creations . . . ": Bettelheim, *The Uses of Enchantment*, p. 94.

"One becomes a complete human being . . . ": Ibid., p. 279.

"These stories, while they take . . . ": Ibid., p. 278.

"Fairy tales suggest . . . permits this to happen.": Ibid., p. 279.

502 "What we had experienced as dangerous . . . ": Ibid., p. 278.

"As the story characters discover . . . ": Ibid., p. 298.

"The Enchanted Pig . . . suffered many things": Ibid., p. 296.

"that girls' sexual anxieties . . . ": Ibid., p. 297.

504 "Sex and sensuality—going to bed for two entire days . . . ": Gail Sheehy, *The Silent Passage* (New York: Random House, 1991), p. 89.

"When she had become a spokeswoman . . . ": Carolyn Heilbrun, *Gloria Steinem: The Education of a Woman* (New York: Dial, 1995), p. 122.

505 *People* magazine's annual issue . . . : "The 50 Most Beautiful People in the World," *People*, May 8, 1995, p. 91.

More than 43 million women . . . : Gail Sheehy, *The Silent Passage*, p. 7.

"From their mid-forties to their sixties . . . ": Ibid., p. 147.

"*Sexuality, before and after menopause* . . . ": Bernadine Healy, *A New Prescription for Women's Health: Getting the Best Medical Care in a Man's World* (New York: Viking, 1995), p. 183.

506 "turning 50 was the end of an era . . . ": O'Neill, "Decades as an Icon," p. C10.

"I couldn't care less . . . ": "Feminist Fatale," *Longevity*, July 1994, p. 16.

507 "Theirs will always be a stillborn form of feminism . . . ": Susan Faludi, "I'm Not a Feminist but I Play One on TV," *Ms.*, March/April 1995, p. 39.

"Revolutionary woman may join . . . ": Germaine Greer, *The Madwoman's Underclothes* (New York: Atlantic Monthly Press, 1987 [1986]), pp. 37–38.

"The change hurts . . . ": Greer, *The Change*, p. 53.

509 "Sex must be rescued . . . ": Greer, *The Female Eunuch*, p. 18.

513 "She's the kind of person . . . ": Molly O'Neill, "In an Ivy League of Her Own," *New York Times*, October 20, 1994, p. C1.

514 "the two derogatory names . . . ": Banner, *In Full Flower*, p. 194.

516 "the woman's capacity for orgasm . . . ": William H. Masters et al., *Heterosexuality* (New York: HarperCollins, 1994), p. 470, citing B. D. Starr, and M. B. Weiner, *The Starr-Weiner Report on Sex and Sexuality in the Mature Years* (Stein and Day, 1981).

517 "Today, fifty is nothing . . . ": Bernard Weinraub, "Hollywood Braces for Look into Mirror of 'Sunset Boulevard,'" *New York Times*, December 9, 1993, p. C17.

A man of forty-five looks distinguished . . . : Lynn Darling, "Age, Beauty and Truth," *New York Times*, January 23, 1994, sec. 9, p. 5.

"It is perhaps only in old age . . . ": Carolyn Heilbrun, *Writing a Woman's Life* (New York: Ballantine, 1989 [1988]), p. 126.

"I remember having lunch . . . ": Darling, "Age, Beauty and Truth," p. 5.

"Suddenly, their whole creativity is released . . . ": Margaret Mead, *Blackberry Winter: My Earlier Years* (New York: Morrow, 1972), pp. 246–247.

"she seemed to become prettier . . . ": Sheehy, *The Silent Passage*, p. 145.

520 "We're tired of being good all the time . . . ": Laurel Graeber, "Zenia Is Sort of Like Madonna," *New York Times*, October 31, 1993, p. 22.

Women ages fifty-five to sixty-four earn 41 percent more . . . : U.S. Census, "Current Population Reports," Series P-60. Figures adjusted to reflect constant 1993 dollars.

"there's something especially alarming . . . ": Holly Brubach, "Retroactivity," *New Yorker*, December 31, 1990, p. 76.

521 "The silence of being unseen . . . ": Rita Freedman, *Beauty Bound* (Lexington, Mass.: Lexington, 1986), p. 204.

522 "For them, the bad mother had to disappear . . . ": Marina Warner, *From the Beast to the Blonde: On Fairy Tales and Their Tellers* (New York: Farrar, Straus and Giroux, 1995 [1994]), pp. 211–212.

523 "Agents call it inventing the girl . . . ": Guy Trebay, "Inventing Kirsty," *Harper's Bazaar*, July 1994, p. 127.

"youth is the only thing worth having": Oscar Wilde, *The Picture of Dorian Gray* (London: Penguin, 1985 [1891]), p. 50.

526 "but also the logical consequence . . . ": Bettelheim, *The Uses of Enchantment*, pp. 274–275.

Games People Play: Eric Berne, *Games People Play* (New York: Ballantine, 1985).

527 "Emma Bovary . . . capture, captivate, and serve": Kaplan, *Female Perversions*, pp. 251, 257–258, 261.

529 "It is hard even now to remember . . . ": Erica Jong, *Fear of Fifty: A Midlife Memoir* (New York: HarperCollins, 1995 [1994]), p. 332.

"I was afraid that if I let out my rage . . . ": Richard Rhodes, *How to Write: Advice and Reflections* (New York: Henry Holt, 1995), p. 4.

530 "The appeal of the straightforward . . . ": Brubach, "Landscapes with Figures," p. 107.

531 During World War II ...: Holly Brubach, "Survivors," *New Yorker*, August 27, 1990, pp. 74–75.

532 "The important question ...": Ann W. Richards, "Girls, Pull Your Freight," *New York Times*, June 25, 1994, p. 23.

533 "This is not the message ...": Sam Howe Verhovek, "Family Becomes Issue in the Texas Governor's Race, *New York Times*, June 22, 1994, p. A16.

535 nearly 50 percent of American women ...: Thomas F. Cash and Patricia E. Henry, "Women's Body Images: The Results of a National Survey in the U.S.A.," *Sex Roles* 33, nos. 1/2 (1995): 19–28.

541 " 'Courtship feeding' ... ": Fisher, *Anatomy of Love*, p. 35.

548 "Luggage that one travels with ... ": Sigmund Freud, *The Interpretation of Dreams* (New York: Basic, 1965 [1914]), p. 393.

Bibliography

Abramson, Jill, and Pollock, Ellen Joan. "'Hillary's Enforcer': How Susan Thomases, Top Clinton Adviser, Fell Hard from Grace." *Wall Street Journal*, April 8, 1996, pp. A1ff.

Ackerman, Diane. *A Natural History of Love*. New York: Vintage, 1995 (1994).

Adler, Jerry, with Michael, Renee; Greenberg, Nikki Finke. "You're So Vain." *Newsweek*, April 14, 1986, pp. 48–55.

Alan Guttmacher Institute. "Preventing Pregnancy, Protecting Health: A New Look at Birth Control Choices in the United States." 1991.

———. "Teenage Reproductive Health in the United States." 1994.

Allende, Isabel. *The House of the Spirits*. New York: Knopf, 1985.

American Association of University Women. "Shortchanging Girls, Shortchanging America." January 1991.

American Girl. July/August 1994, p. 48.

American Orthopaedic Foot and Ankle Society. "Position Statement on Women's Shoewear and Foot Problems." 1991.

Anderson, Sherwood. *Winesburg, Ohio*. New York: Bantam, 1995 (1919).

"Angry Battler for Her Sex." *Life*, November 1, 1963, pp. 84–85.

Ariès, Philippe. *Centuries of Childhood: A Social History of Family Life*. Translated by Robert Baldick. New York: Vintage, 1962 (1960).

Atwood, Margaret. *Cat's Eye*. New York: Doubleday, 1989.

Bachman, Ronet, and Saltzman, Linda. "Bureau of Justice Statistics Special Report: National Crime Victimization Report." August 1995.

Ball, Aimee Lee. "Ballbusters: Success Secrets of 6 Pushy Women." *Marie Claire*, September/October 1994, pp. 58–68.

Bank, Stephen, and Kahn, Michael D. *The Sibling Bond*. New York: Basic, 1982.

Banner, Lois W. *In Full Flower: Aging Women, Power, and Sexuality*. New York: Vintage, 1993 (1992).

Barnes, Clive. "'Hair'—It's Fresh and Frank." *New York Times*, April 30, 1968, p. 40.

Baumgold, Julie. "Dancing on the Lip of the Volcano: Christian Lacroix's Crash Chic." *New York*, November 30, 1987, pp. 36–49.

"Beautiful People, The." *W*, January 1995, pp. 86–94.

Beauvoir, Simone de. *The Second Sex*. New York: Vintage, 1989 (1952).

Belfrage, Sally. *Un-American Activities*. New York: HarperPerennial, 1995 (1994).

Bellow, Saul. *Herzog*. New York: Penguin, 1985 (1964).

Benson, Sheila. "True or False: Thelma and Louise Just Good Ol' Boys?" *Los Angeles Times*, May 31, 1991, p. F1.

Berger, John. *Ways of Seeing*. London: BBC/Penguin, 1977 (1972).

Berke, Richard L. "Religious Right Gains Influence and Spreads Discord in G.O.P." *New York Times*, July 3, 1994, pp. A1ff.

Berne, Eric. *Games People Play*. New York: Ballantine, 1985.

Bettelheim, Bruno. *The Uses of Enchantment*. New York: Knopf, 1976.

Beyette, Beverly. "Kinsey Institute's Reinisch Wants to Renew, Expand Sexual Studies; American Sex Habits Changed Since 1948—But Not That Much." *Los Angeles Times*, May 18, 1986, p. 1.

Biller, Henry B., and Trotter, Robert J. *The Father Factor: What You Need to Know to Make a Difference*. New York: Pocket, 1994.

Blos, Peter. *On Adolescence: A Psychoanalytic Interpretation*. New York: Free Press, 1966 (1962).

Blume, Judy. *Are You There, God? It's Me, Margaret*. New York: Dell, 1991 (1970).

Blumenfeld, Laura. "Feminists Hit a Bump and Grind at Lesbian Club." *Washington Post*, July 25, 1991, pp. D1–2.

Blumstein, Philip, and Schwartz, Pepper. *American Couples*. New York: Morrow, 1983.

Bounds, Wendy. "Dating Game Today Breaks Traditional Gender Rules." *Wall Street Journal*, April 26, 1995, pp. B1ff.

Brewer, Stephen. "Put Your Face Here." *Esquire*, August 1990, p. 34.

Bright, Susie. "How to Make Love to a Woman: Hands-on Advice from a Woman Who Does." *Esquire*, February 1994, p. 108.

Brown, Chip. "Heel, Boy!" *Esquire*, November 1995, p. 102–107.

Brownmiller, Susan. *Femininity*. New York: Linden, 1984.

Brozan, Nadine. "Fashion Award Winners." *New York Times*, November 18, 1994, p. B8.

Brubach, Holly. "Landscapes with Figures." *New Yorker*, April 30, 1990, pp. 103–107.

———. "Retroactivity." *New Yorker*, December 31, 1990, pp. 74–81.

———. "Survivors." *New Yorker*, August 27, 1990, pp. 72–77.

Buss, David M. *The Evolution of Desire*. New York: Basic, 1994.

Bustan, Muhammad N., and Coker, Ann L. "Maternal Attitude Toward Pregnancy and the Risk of Neonatal Death." *American Journal of Public Health* 84, no. 3 (1994): 411–414.

Butterfield, Fox. "Teenage Homicide Rate Has Soared." *New York Times*, October 14, 1994, p. A22.

Byatt, A. S. "The Seven Deadly Sins/Envy: The Sin of Families and Nations." *New York Times Book Review*, July 18, 1993, pp. 3ff.

Caplan, P. J. *Between Women: Lowering the Barriers*. Toronto: Personal Library, 1981, p. 120. Quoted in Robert W. Firestone et al., "The Mother-Daughter Bond." The Glendon Association.

Carlson, Margaret. "Batteries Not Included." *Time*, December 2, 1991, pp. 78–79.

Cash, Thomas F,. and Henry, Patricia E. "Women's Body Images: The Results of a National Survey in the U.S.A." *Sex Roles* 33, nos. 1/2 (1995): 19–28.

Cash, Thomas F., and Pruzinsky, Thomas, eds. *Body Images*. New York: Guilford, 1990.

Cavior, Norman. "Physical Attractiveness, Perceived Attitude Similarity, and Interpersonal Attraction Among Fifth and Eleventh Grade Boys and Girls." Doctoral dissertation, University of Houston, August 1970.

Cheever, Susan. *A Woman's Life: The Story of an Ordinary American and Her Extraordinary Generation*. New York: Morrow, 1994.

Chira, Susan. "No Cookie-Cutter Mothers in 90's." *New York Times*, May 8, 1994, sec. 1, p. 26.

———. "Study Confirms Some Fears on U.S. Children." *New York Times*, April 12, 1994, pp. A1ff.

Cocks, Jay. "How Long Till Equality?" *Time*, July 12, 1982, pp. 20–29.

Cook, Kevin. "Is Bigger Better?" *Vogue*, April 1995, pp. 266–268.

Cosmopolitan magazine, marketing material, 1995.

Darling, Lynn. "Age, Beauty and Truth." *New York Times*, January 23, 1994, sec. 9, pp. 1ff.

Davis, Flora. *Moving the Mountain: The Women's Movement in America Since 1960*. New York: Simon and Schuster, 1991.

De St. Jorre, John. "The Unmasking of O." *New Yorker*, August 1, 1994, pp. 42–50.

De Witt, Karen. "So, What Is That Leather Bustier Saying?" *New York Times*, January 1, 1995, sec. 4, p. 2.

Debold, Elizabeth; Wilson, Marie; Malave, Idelisse. *Mother Daughter Revolution: From Betrayal to Power*. New York: Addison-Wesley, 1993.

Dell' Olio, Anselma. "The Sexual Revolution Wasn't Our War." *Ms.*, Spring 1972, pp. 104–109.

Dijkstra, Bram. *Idols of Perversity*. New York: Oxford University Press, 1986.

Dinnerstein, Dorothy. *The Mermaid and the Minotaur*. New York: Harper Colophon, 1971 (1963).

Dion, Karen K. "Young Children's Stereotyping of Facial Attractiveness." *Developmental Psychology* 9, no. 2 (1973): 183–188.

"A Doctor Is No Better Than His Patient: An Interview with Norman Mailer." *Cosmopolitan*, May 1990, pp. 332–333ff.

Dowd, Maureen. "Fashion Week Fabrics." *New York Times*, April 7, 1995, p. A34.

———. "Our True Lies." *New York Times*, August 20, 1995, p. A13.

Dworkin, Andrea. *Pornography: Men Possessing Women*. New York, Perigee, 1981 (1979).

———. *Woman-Hating: A Radical Look at Sexuality*. New York, E. P. Dutton, 1974.

Edmiston, Susan. "Reconcilable Differences." *Mirabella*, March 1990, pp. 110–112.

Egan, Jennifer. *The Invisible Circus*. New York: Talese-Doubleday, 1995.

Ekman, Paul. *Telling Lies: Clues to Deceit in the Marketplace, Politics, and Marriage*. New York: Norton, 1985.

Elkind, David. "Egocentrism in Adolescence." *Child Development* 38 (1967): 1025–1034.

Ellis, Havelock. *Studies in the Psychology of Sex*. Vol. 2 New York: Random House, 1937.

Ephron, Nora. "Dealing with the, Uh, Problem." *Esquire*, March 1973, pp. 90–93ff.

Faludi, Susan. "I'm Not a Feminist but I Play One on TV." *Ms.*, March/April 1995, p. 30–39.

———. *Backlash*. New York: Crown, 1991.

Families and Work Institute. "Women: The New Providers." May 1995.

Farber, Leslie H. *Lying, Despair, Jealousy, Envy, Sex, Suicide, Drugs and the Good Life*. New York: Harper Colophon, 1978.

Faulkner, William. *The Hamlet*. New York: Vintage, 1991 (1931).

"Feminist Fatale." *Longevity*. July 1994, p.16.

"50 Most Beautiful People in the World, The." *People*, May 8, 1995, pp. 66–183.

Fisher, Helen. *Anatomy of Love: The Natural History of Monogamy, Adultery, and Divorce*. New York: Norton, 1992.

Fleming, Anne Taylor. "Peekaboo Power Suits." *New York Times*, January 28, 1993, p. A21.

Forrest, Susan. "DA Booted." *Newsday*, November 5, 1993.

Foshee, Vangie, and Bauman, Karl. "Gender Stereotyping and Adolescent Sexual Behavior: A Test of Temporal Order." *Journal of Applied Social Psychology* 22, no. 20 (1992): 1561–1579.

Foster, George M. "The Anatomy of Envy: A Study in Symbolic Behavior." *Current Anthropology* 13, no. 2 (April 1972): 165–202.

———. "Cultural Responses to Expressions of Envy in Tzintzutzan." *Southwestern Journal of Anthropology* 21, no. 1 (Spring 1965): 24–35.

Fraley, M. Cecile; Nelson, Edward C.; Wolf, Abraham W.; Lozoff, Betsy. "Early Genital Naming." *Developmental and Behavioral Pediatrics* 12, no. 2 (October 1991): 301–304.

Freedman, Rita. *Beauty Bound*. Lexington, Mass.: Lexington, 1986.

Freeman, Lucy. "The Feminine Mystique." *New York Times Book Review*, April 7, 1963, p. 46.

Frenkiel, Nora. "'Family Planning': Baby Boy or Girl?" *New York Times*, November 11, 1993, p. C6.

Freud, Sigmund. *The Interpretation of Dreams*. New York: Basic, 1965 (1914).

———. *Three Essays on Sexuality*, Vol 7. of *The Standard Edition of the Complete Psychological Works of Sigmund Freud*. (London: Hogarth Press and The Institute of Psycho-Analysis, 1986 (1953).

Frey, Carol; Thompson, Francesca; Smith, Judith; Sanders, Melanie; Horstman, Helen. "American Orthopaedic Foot and Ankle Society Women's Shoe Survey." *Foot and Ankle*, 1993, pp. 78–81.

Friday, Nancy. *Jealousy*. New York: Perigord, 1985.

———. *My Mother/My Self*. New York: Delacorte, 1977.

Friedan, Betty. *The Feminine Mystique*. New York: Dell Laurel, 1983 (1963).

———. *The Fountain of Age*. New York: Simon and Schuster, 1993.

Frieze, Irene Hanson; Olson, Josephine E.; Good, Deborah Cain. "Perceived and Actual Discrimination in the Salaries of Male and Female Managers." Paper presented at the 1986 Academy of Management Meetings, Chicago.

Frieze, Irene Hanson; Olson, Josephine E.; Russell, June. "Attractiveness and Business Success: Is It More Important for Women or Men?" Paper prepared for the 1989 Academy of Management Meetings in Washington, D.C., August 1989.

Frisby, Michael K. "Clinton Fires Surgeon General Elders Citing Differences in Opinions, Policy." *Wall Street Journal*, December 12, 1994, p. A16.

Gaylin, Willard. *Feelings*. New York: Ballantine, 1980 (1979).

Gibbs, Nancy R. "Bringing Up Father." *Time*, June 28, 1993, pp. 52–61.

———. "The War Against Feminism." *Time*, March 9, 1992, pp. 50–57.

"Gloria Steinem: A Liberated Woman Despite Beauty, Chic and Success." *Newsweek*, August 16, 1971, pp. 51–55.

Goodman, Walter. "Writers Discuss Theme of Myths in Modern Life." *New York Times*, October 13, 1984, p. A13.

GQ. "Men in the Nineties" Survey. 1994.

Graeber, Laurel. "So Where Is That Lava Lamp Now?" *New York Times*, April 6, 1995, p. C6.

——. "Zenia Is Sort of Like Madonna." *New York Times*, October 31, 1993, p. 22.

Greenberg, Martin, and Norris, N. "Engrossment: The Newborn's Impact upon the Father." *American Journal of Orthopsychiatry* 44, no. 4 (1974): 520–531.

Greer, Germaine. *The Change*. New York: Knopf, 1992.

——. *The Female Eunuch*. London: MacGibbon & Kee, 1970.

——. *The Madwoman's Underclothes*. New York: Atlantic Monthly Press, 1987 (1986).

Halpern, Sue. "Soul Sisters." *Harper's Bazaar*, July 1994, p. 48.

Hamermesh, Daniel S., and Biddle, Jeff E. "Beauty and the Labour Market." National Bureau of Economic Research, November 1993.

Harris, Daniel. "The Current Crisis in Men's Lingerie: Notes on the Belated Commercialization of a Noncommercial Product." *Salmagundi*, Fall 1993, pp. 130–139.

Harrison, Barbara Grizzuti. "Talking Dirty." *Ms.*, October 1973, pp. 40–44.

Harter, Susan. "Causes and Consequences of Low Self-Esteem in Children and Adolescents." *Self-Esteem: The Puzzle of Low Self-Regard*, ed. R. F. Baumeister. New York: Plenum, 1993, pp. 87–116.

"Have You Ever Measured Your Penis?" *Glamour*, January 1995, pp. 136–139.

Healy, Bernadine. *A New Prescription for Women's Health: Getting the Best Medical Care in a Man's World*. New York: Viking, 1995.

Heilbrun, Carolyn. *Gloria Steinem: The Education of a Woman*. New York: Dial, 1995.

——. *Writing a Woman's Life*. New York: Ballantine, 1989 (1988).

Heilman, Madeline E., and Saruwatari, Lois R. "When Beauty Is Beastly: The Effects of Appearance and Sex on Evaluations of Job Applicants for Managerial and Nonmanagerial Jobs." *Organizational Behavior and Human Performance* 23 (1979): 360–372.

Hemingway, Ernest. *A Moveable Feast*. New York: Collier, 1987 (1964).

Hetherington, E. Mavis. "Effects of Father Absence on Personality Development in Adolescent Daughters." *Developmental Psychology* 7, no. 3 (1972): 313–326.

Hildebrandt, Katherine, and Cannan, Teresa. "The Distribution of Caregiver Attention in a Group Program for Young Children." *Child Study Journal* 15, no. 1 (1985): 43–54.

Hildebrandt, Katherine A., and Fitzgerald, Hiram E. "Facial Feature Determinants of Perceived Infant Attractiveness." *Infant Behavior and Development* 2 (1979): 329–339.

Hill, Carol De Chellis. *Henry James' Midnight Song*. New York: Poseidon, 1993.

Hite, Shere. *The Hite Report on the Family*. New York: Grove/Atlantic, 1995.

Holden, Stephen. "For Warhol, to Be Was to Be on Screen." *New York Times*, January 27, 1995, p. C28.

Hollander, Anne. *Sex and Suits: The Evolution of Modern Dress*. New York: Knopf, 1994.

Hollandsworth, Skip. "Why I Hate Hunks." *Mademoiselle*, October 1990, p. 86.

Holmes, Steven A. "Out-of-Wedlock Births Up Since '83, Report Indicates." *New York Times*, July 20, 1994, pp. A1ff.

Hunt, Morton. *Sexual Behavior in the 1970s*. Chicago: Playboy Press, 1974.

"In Praise of the Counterculture." *New York Times*, December 11, 1994, p. 14.

Ingraham, Laura A. "Enter, Women." *New York Times*, April 19, 1995, p. A23.

Irving, John. *The Hotel New Hampshire*. New York: Ballantine (1981).

Johnson, Joyce. *Minor Characters*. New York: Houghton Mifflin, 1983.

Jong, Erica. *Fear of Fifty: A Midlife Memoir*. New York: HarperCollins, 1995 (1994).

Kadar, Andrew G. "The Sex-Bias Myth in Medicine." *Atlantic Monthly*, August 1994, pp. 66–70.

Kakutani, Michiko. "Who Exactly Is This Sexagenarian Sex Kitten?" *New York Times*, March 15, 1996, p. C30.

Kaminer, Wendy. "Feminism's Identity Crisis." *Atlantic Monthly*, October 1993, pp. 51–68.

Kaplan, Louise J. *Adolescence: The Farewell to Childhood*. New York: Simon and Schuster, 1984.

———. *Female Perversions: The Temptations of Emma Bovary*. New York: Doubleday, 1991.

———. *Oneness and Separateness: From Infant to Individual*. New York: Simon and Schuster, 1978.

Karraker, Katherine Hildebrandt, and Stern, Marilyn. "Infant Physical Attractiveness and Facial Expression: Effects of Adult Perceptions." *Basic and Applied Social Psychology* 11, no. 4 (1990): 371–385.

Karraker, Katherine Hildebrandt; Vogel, Dena Ann; Evans, Suzanne. "Responses of Students and Pregnant Women to Newborn Physical Attractiveness." Paper presented at the meetings of the American Psychological Association, New York, August 1987.

Keller, Bill. "What's 'Shock' in Zulu? Whites Visiting to Say Hi." *New York Times*, May 31, 1994, p. A4.

Kelley, Virginia, and Morgan, James. *Leading with My Heart*. New York: Pocket (1995).

Kinsey, Alfred; Pomeroy, Wardell B.; Martin, Clyde E. *Sexual Behavior in the Human Male*. Philadelphia: W. B. Saunders, 1948.

Klein, Melanie. *Envy and Gratitude and Other Works 1946–1963*. New York: Delacorte, 1977.

Kolata, Gina. "News of Robust Elderly Belies Fears of Scientists." *New York Times*, February 27, 1996, pp. A1ff.

Kushner, Trucia. "Finding a Personal Style." *Ms.*, February 1974, pp. 45–51ff.

Lahr, John. "Dealing with Roseanne." *New Yorker*, February 17, 1995, pp. 42–60.

Lamb, Michael E., "The Changing Roles of Fathers." In *The Father's Role: Applied Perspectives*. New York: Wiley, 1986, pp. 3–27.

Langlois, Judith, and Casey, Rita. "Baby Beautiful: The Relationship Between Infant Physical Attractiveness and Maternal Behavior." Paper presented at the fourth biennial International Conference on Infant Studies, New York, 1984.

Langlois, Judith H.; Ritter, Jean M.; Roggman, Lori A.; Vaughn, Lesley S. "Facial Diversity and Infant Preferences for Attractive Faces." *Developmental Psychology* 27, no. 1 (1991): 79–84.

Langlois, Judith H.; Roggman, Lori A.; Reiser-Danner, Loretta A. "Infants' Differential Social Responses to Attractive and Unattractive Faces." *Developmental Psychology* 26, no. 1 (1990): 153–159.

Langlois, Judith H., and Stephan, Cookie White. "Beauty and the Beast: The Role of Physical Attractiveness in the Development of Peer Relations and Social Behavior." In Brehm, Sharon S., et al. *Developmental Social Psychology: Theory and Research*. New York: Oxford University Press, 1981.

Leach, Penelope. *Children First: What Our Society Must Do—and Is Not Doing—for Our Children Today*. New York: Knopf, 1994.

Leitenberg, Harold; Detzer, Mark J.; Srebnik, Debra. "Gender Differences in Masturbation and the Relation of Masturbation Experience in Preadolescence and/or Early Adolescence to Sexual Behavior and Sexual Adjustment in Young Adulthood." *Archives of Sexual Behavior* 22, no. 2, (1993): 87–98.

Lessing, Doris. *The Golden Notebook*. New York: Bantam, 1981 (1962).

———. *Love, Again*. New York: HarperCollins, 1996.

———. *Under My Skin: Volume One of My Autobiography, to 1949*. New York: HarperCollins, 1994.

Lewin, Tamar. "Boys Are More Comfortable with Sex Than Girls Are." *New York Times*, May 18, 1994, p. A20.

Leyner, Mark. "Samurai Father." *Esquire Gentleman*, Spring 1994, pp. 81–86.

Linden, Dana Wechsler, and Rees, Matt. "I'm Hungry. But Not for Food." *Forbes*, July 6, 1992, pp. 70ff.

Linfield, Susie. "Women Comics Stand and Deliver." *New York Times*, July 12, 1992, sec. 2, p. 11.

"Love and Sex in the 90s Survey." Seventeen, March 1991.

Maddox, Brenda. *D. H. Lawrence: The Story of a Marriage*. New York: Simon and Schuster, 1994. Reviewed in Christopher Lehmann-Haupt, "D. H. Lawrence Seen in One Intense Lens," *New York Times*, November 14, 1994, p. C18.

Magnus, Sherry. "Feet, Sex and Power . . . The Last Erogenous Zone." *Vogue*, April 1982, pp. 284–285ff.

Mahler, Margaret S. *On Human Symbiosis and the Vicissitudes of Individuation.*

Vol. 1, *Infantile Psychosis*. New York: International University Press, 1968.
————. *The Psychological Development of the Human Infant*. New York: Basic Books, 1976.

Mailer, Norman. "Norman Mailer on Madonna: Like a Lady." *Esquire*, August 1994, pp. 41–56.

Martin, Richard, and Koda, Harold. *Jocks & Nerds: Men's Style in the 20th Century*. New York: Rizzoli, 1989.

Masters, William H.; Johnson, Virginia E.; Kolodny, Robert C. *Heterosexuality*. New York: HarperCollins, 1994.

McCall's/Yankelovich. Confidence Study: Health and Appearance, 1993.

McNally, Terrence. "Frankie and Johnny in the Clair de Lune." *Three Plays by Terrence McNally*. New York: Plume, 1990 (1986).

Mead, Margaret. *Blackberry Winter: My Earlier Years*. New York: Morrow, 1972.

Mediawatch Multi-Media Service. "Product versus Media Report." 1995.

Melville, Herman. *Billy Budd*. London: John Lehmann, 1946.

Mendelsohn, Ink. "We Were What We Wore." *American Heritage*, December 1988, pp. 37–45.

Michael, Robert T.; Gagnon, John H.; Laumann, Edward O.; Kolata, Gina. *Sex in America: A Definitive Survey*. New York: Little, Brown, 1994.

Miller, Michael Vincent. *Intimate Terrorism: The Deterioration of Erotic Life*. New York: Norton, 1995.

Millett, Kate. *Sexual Politics*. Garden City, N.Y.: Doubleday, 1970.

Minkowitz, Donna. "In the Name of the Father." *Ms.*, November/December 1995, pp. 64–71.

Morgan, Robin. *Sisterhood Is Powerful*. New York: Random House, 1970.

Morris, Bernadine. "From DKNY, Eclecticism for Mothers, Daughters." *New York Times*, April 7, 1994, p. C10.

Moyers, Bill. "Sissela Bok." *Bill Moyers' World of Ideas*, WNET and WTTW, October 3, 1988.

"My Generation: The *Seventeen* Survey." Seventeen, October 1989.

National Center for Health Statistics—Division of Vital Statistics, published and unpublished data.

Neimark, Jill. "How Men Measure Up." *Psychology Today*, November/December 1994, pp. 32–39ff.

"New *Glamour* Survey, Hearts and Minds: What Do College Men and Women Really Mean to Each Other, A." *Glamour*, August 1981, pp. 230–231ff.

Newman, Paul. Interview by James Lipton. *Inside the Actor's Studio*. Bravo, April 26, 1995.

Northrup, Christiane. *Women's Bodies, Women's Wisdom*. New York: Bantam, 1994.

O'Neill, Molly. "Decades as Icon; Now, Freedom." *New York Times*, February 9, 1995, pp. C1ff.

———. "In an Ivy League of Her Own." *New York Times*, October 20, 1994, pp. C1ff.

Obejas, Achy. "Women Who Batter Women." *Ms.*, September/October 1994, p. 53.

Opie, Iona, and Peter Opie. *I Saw Esau: The Schoolchild's Pocket Book*. London: Walker, 1992 (1947).

Ovid. *Metamorphoses*. New York: Penguin, 1955.

Paglia, Camille. "When Camille Met Tim." *Esquire*, February 1995, pp. 68–73.

———. *Vamps and Tramps*. New York: Vintage, 1994.

Parker, Dorothy. "A Telephone Call." *Complete Stories*. New York: Penguin, 1995. Originally published in *The Bookman*, January 1928.

Pelton, Robert Wayne. *Loony Sex Laws That You Never Knew You Were Breaking*. New York: Walker, 1992.

Person, Ethel S. *By Force of Fantasy: How We Make Our Lives*. New York: Basic, 1995.

Pierson, John. "Man Walked on the Moon, Why Can't Man Make a Woman's Dress Shoe That Doesn't Hurt?" *Wall Street Journal*, January 10, 1996, p. B1.

Phillips, Adam. *On Flirtation: Psychoanalytic Essays on the Uncommitted Life*. Cambridge, Mass.: Harvard University, 1994.

"Playboy Interview: Betty Friedan." *Playboy*, September 1992, pp. 51–62ff.

Pogrebin, Letty Cottin. "Competing With Women." *Ms.*, July 1972, pp. 78–81ff.

Postman, Neil. *The Disappearance of Childhood*. New York: Delacorte, 1982.

Pruett, Kyle D. "Father's Influence in the Development of Infant's Relationships." *Acta Paediatrica Scandinavica* 77, supplementum no. 344 (1988): 43–53.

———. *The Nurturing Father: Journey Toward the Complete Man*. New York: Warner, 1987.

Quinn, Robert P., and Staines, Graham L. *The 1977 Quality of Employment Survey: Descriptive Statistics, with Comparison Data from the 1969–1970 and the 1972–1973 Surveys*. Ann Arbor, Mich.: University of Michigan Survey Research Center, 1977.

Raspberry, William. "An Interest in Failure." *Washington Post*, November 5, 1993, p. A27.

Rhodes, Richard. *How to Write: Advice and Reflections*. New York: Henry Holt, 1995.

Richards, Ann W. "Girls, Pull Your Freight." *New York Times*, June 25, 1994, p. 23.

Robbins, Tom. "The Mini, a Natural High." *New York Times*, April 6, 1995, p. C1.

Robertiello, Richard. *Hold Them Very Close, Then Let Them Go: How to Be an Authentic Parent*. New York: Dial, 1975.

———. *Your Own True Love*. New York: Richard Marek, 1978.

Roberts, Sam. *Who We Are: A Portrait of America Based on the Latest U.S. Census*. New York: Times Books, 1994.

Roberts, Susan C. "Blood Sisters." *New Age Journal*, May/June 1994, pp. 86–89ff.

Robson, Kenneth S. "The Role of Eye-to-Eye Contact in Maternal-Infant Attachment." *Journal of Child Psychology and Psychiatry* 8 (1967): 13–25.

Roth, Philip. *Portnoy's Complaint*. New York: Random House, 1969 (1967).

Rutter, Virginia. "Adolescence: Whose Hell Is It?" *Psychology Today*, January/February 1995, pp. 54–68.

Samuels, Patrice Duggan. "Dads to the Rescue for the Child-Care Needs." *New York Times*, February 12, 1995, p. F23.

Saturday Night Live. NBC, February 19, 1994.

Schiff, Stacy. *Saint-Exupéry: A Biography*. New York: Knopf, 1993.

Schmookler, Andrew Bard. "No Contest: The Case Against Competition." *Los Angeles Times, The Book Review*, September 28, 1986, p. 11.

Segell, Michael. "The Pater Principle." *Esquire*, March 1995, pp. 121–127.

Seventeen, June 1995, p. 58.

Seventeen, September 1995, p. 98.

Shapiro, Joseph P., and Schrof, Joannie M., with Tharp, Mike. "Honor Thy Children." *U.S. News & World Report*, February 27, 1995, pp. 38–49.

Shapiro, Laura, with Chang, Yahlin. "The Girls of Summer." *Newsweek*, May 22, 1995, p. 56.

Shapiro, Theodore, and Stine, John. "The Figure Drawings of Three-Year-Old Children: A Contribution to the Early Development of Body Image." *Psychoanalytic Study of the Child* 20, (1965): 298–309.

Sheehy, Gail. *The Silent Passage*. New York: Random House, 1991.

Signature: Gloria Steinem. Interviewed by Patrick Watson. CBS Cable, November 4, 1981.

Simmons, Roberta G., and Rosenberg, Florence. "Sex, Sex Roles, and Self-Image." *Journal of Youth and Adolescence* 4, no. 3 (1975): 229–258.

Simmons, Roberta G.; Rosenberg, F.; Rosenberg, M. "Disturbance in the Self-Image at Adolescence," *American Sociology Review* 38 (1973): 553–568.

60 Minutes. "Camille." CBS, November 1, 1992. Interview by Steve Kroft.

Smith, Lee. "The New Wave of Illegitimacy." *Fortune*, April 18, 1994, pp. 81–94.

Smith, Liz. "Gloria Steinem, Writer and Social Critic, Talks about Sex, Politics and Marriage." *Redbook*, January 1972, pp. 69–76.

Smith, Roberta. "A Parallel Art World, Vast and Unruly." *New York Times*, November 20, 1994, sec. 1, pp. 1ff.

Snarey, John. *How Fathers Care for the Next Generation*. Cambridge, Mass.: Harvard University, 1994.

Sommers, Christina Hoff. "A Holiday Based on Ms. Information." *Wall Street Journal*, April 10, 1995, p. A20.

———. "The Myth of Schoolgirls' Low Self-Esteem." *Wall Street Journal*, October 3, 1994.

———. *Who Stole Feminism?: How Women Have Betrayed Women*. New York: Simon and Schuster, 1994.

Sontag, Susan. "The Double Standard of Aging." *Saturday Review*, September 23, 1972, pp. 29–38.

Spindler, Amy M. "How Much Glamour Can a Man Take?" *New York Times*, June 30, 1994, p. C11.

———. "In Milan, Brazen Men Parading." *New York Times*, January 19, 1995, p. C13.

Steele, Valerie. *Fashion and Eroticism*. New York: Oxford University Press, 1985.

Steinberg, Laurence, with Steinberg, Wendy. *Crossing Paths: How Your Child's Adolescence Triggers Your Own Crisis*. New York: Simon and Schuster, 1995 (1994).

Steinberg, Laurence. *Adolescence*. New York: Knopf, 1985.

Steinem, Gloria. *The Beach Book*. New York: Viking, 1963.

———. "What It Would Be Like If Women Win." *Time*, August 31, 1970, p. 22.

———. *Outrageous Acts and Everyday Rebellions*. New York: Signet, 1986 (1983).

———. *Revolution from Within: A Book of Self-Esteem*. Boston: Little, Brown, 1993 (1991).

Stenson, Jacqueline. "With Cosmetic Surgery, Men Can Change Everything from Pecs to Private Parts." *The Washingtonian*, May 1993, p. 92.

Stephenson, June. *Men Are Not Cost Effective: Male Crime in America*. New York: HarperPerennial, 1995 (1991).

Stern, Daniel. *Diary of a Baby*. New York: Basic, 1990.

Teen Research Unlimited. Published and unpublished data, 1995.

Theroux, Paul. "The Roots of Desire." *Vogue*, October 1995, pp. 248–250.

"Thinking Man's Shrimpton." *Time*, January 3, 1969, p. 38.

Thompson, Clara. "Penis Envy in Women." *Psychiatry* 6, (1943): 123–125.

Thurman, Judith. "What If He's Cuter Than You?" *Mademoiselle*, April 1985, p. 120.

Trebay, Guy. "Inventing Kirsty." *Harper's Bazaar*, July 1994, pp. 127ff.

Tuchman, Barbara. *A Distant Mirror: The Calamitous 14th Century*. New York, Ballantine, 1979 (1978).

Turgenev, Ivan. *First Love*. New York: Penguin, 1978 (1950).

U.S. Census. "Current Population Reports." Series P-60.

U.S. Census. "Marital Status and Living Arrangements." March 1994.

U.S. Census. "Projection of the Population, by Age, Sex, Race, and Hispanic Origin."

U.S. Census. "Who's Minding the Kids?" 1994.

U.S. Justice Department. "The Survey of State Prison Inmates," 1991.

Verhovek, Sam Howe. "Family Becomes Issue in the Texas Governor's Race." *New York Times*, June 22, 1994, p. A16.

Walker, Alice. *The Color Purple*. New York: Washington Square, 1983 (1982).

Walker, Barbara G. *The Women's Encyclopedia of Myths and Secrets*. San Francisco: HarperCollins, 1983.

Walters, Donna D. H. "Working Women Play Key Role at Home, Study Finds." *Los Angeles Times*, May 11, 1995, p. A22.

Warner, Marina. *From the Beast to the Blonde: On Fairy Tales and Their Tellers*. New York: Farrar, Straus and Giroux, 1995 (1994).

———. *Six Myths of Our Time*. New York: Vintage, 1995 (1994).

Weinraub, Bernard. "Hollywood Braces for Look into Mirror of 'Sunset Boulevard.'" *New York Times*, December 9, 1993, pp. C13ff.

Welford, Heather. "Best Friends and Bully Girls." *The Guardian*, November 23, 1993, pp. T16–21.

"Who's Come a Long Way, Baby?" *Time*, August 31, 1970, pp. 16–21.

Wilde, Oscar. *The Picture of Dorian Gray*. London: Penguin, 1985 (1891).

Wilford, John Noble. "Children's Cemetery a Clue to Malaria as Rome Declined." *New York Times*, July 26, 1994, pp. C1ff.

Williams, Lena. "Pregnant Teenagers Are Outcasts No Longer." *New York Times*, December 2, 1993, pp. C1.

Wisecracks, 1992. 93 minutes. A Zinger Films production in co-production with Studio D of the National Film Board of Canada.

Wolf, Naomi. *The Beauty Myth*. New York: Morrow, 1991.

Woodman, Sue. "How Teen Pregnancy Has Become a Political Football." *Ms.*, January/February 1995, pp. 90–92.

Zollo, Peter. "Talking to Teens." *American Demographics*, November 1995, p. 24.